DEVIANCE

THE INTERACTIONIST PERSPECTIVE

TENTH EDITION

EARL RUBINGTON

Northeastern University

MARTIN S. WEINBERG

Indiana University

PEARSON

Boston New York San Francisco
Mexico City Montreal Toronto London Madrid Munich Paris
Hong Kong Singapore Tokyo Cape Town Sydney

9/11

#128237494

Senior Acquisitions Editor: Dave Repetto
Series Editorial Assistant: Jack Cashman
Senior Marketing Manager: Kelly May
Production Editor: Pat Torelli
Editorial Production Service: GGS Book Services
Composition Buyer: Linda Cox
Manufacturing Buyer: Debbie Rossi
Electronic Composition: GGS Book Services
Cover Administrator: Kristina Mose-Libon
Cover Designer: Eva Ruutopold

For related titles and support materials, visit our online catalog at www.ablongman.com.

Between the time website information is gathered and then published, it is not unusual for some sites to have closed. Also, the transcription of URLs can result in typographical errors. The publisher would appreciate notification where these errors occur so that they may be corrected in subsequent editions.

Library of Congress Cataloging-in-Publication Data

Deviance : the interactionist perspective / [compiled by] Earl Rubington, Martin S. Weinberg.—10th ed.
      p. cm.
  Includes bibliographical references.
  ISBN-13: 978-0-205-50371-1
  ISBN-10: 0-205-50371-3
1. Deviant behavior. 2. Social interaction. I. Rubington, Earl. II. Weinberg, Martin S.
  HM811.D535 2007
  302.5′42—dc22

                                   2007019678

Printed in the United States of America

10 9 8 7 6 5 4 3 V036 11 10

To
Sara and Alex,
Barbara, Ellana, Marion, Caitlin,
Charles, Lilly, Julia, Reilly,
and Jonathan

Contents

PREFACE

The purpose of this book has been to present students with recent and important work in the sociology of deviance. We have, however, limited ourselves to one particular approach to this study. We call this approach the interactionist perspective.

The interactionist approach to the study of deviance is by no means new. But until the appearance of the first edition of *Deviance: The Interactionist Perspective*, students had to search for statements of the approach as well as for studies that exemplified it. The purpose of the first edition, then, was to present the interactionist approach to the study of deviance and to make readily available the excellent studies that set forth or illustrate it. In the succeeding editions, we have updated the readings and made special efforts to make our own text more readable.

We see this book as having two major uses. As a statement on the interactionist perspective on deviance and a collection of readings employing that approach, the book can be used in deviance courses that are taught from the interactionist point of view. The second use is that of adjunct to deviance courses that are organized around other points of view. Most of the papers presented in this book can easily stand on their own merits, and even if the book does nothing more than familiarize readers with these works, it will have served its purpose.

In this edition we have incorporated nine new readings and modified the book's text. In this way, we have continued to update *Deviance: The Interactionist Perspective*.

E. R.
M. S. W.

General Introduction

This book examines deviance as a social phenomenon. Central to this approach is the notion that deviance is, above all, a matter of social definition. That is, an alleged behavior or condition is "deviant" if people say it is. The social aspect of deviance becomes clear when someone perceives another person as departing from accepted norms, interprets the person to be some kind of deviant, and influences others also to regard the person as deviant and to act on the basis of that interpretation. As a *social* phenomenon, then, deviance consists of a set of interpretations and social reactions.

When people are constructed as being deviant, they are usually regarded as being a particular *type* of deviant. These types may be general (for example, ex-convict, mentally ill, sexually "loose," retarded), or they may be more specific (for example, car thief, paranoid schizophrenic, call girl, a person with Down syndrome). Whether these labels are general or specific, they usually suggest what one can expect of the so-called deviant and how one should act toward him or her (for example, with suspicion, avoidance, vigilance, vengeance). And in coming to terms with such labeling, the "deviants" may revise their self-concepts and their actions in accordance with the way they have been labeled. For example, a child who has been typed by school authorities as having a speech problem may become self-conscious and shy, with a concomitant loss of self-esteem, because the child has been told that he or she doesn't talk properly.

At the same time, social typing does allow people to relate to one another in an organized manner. Imagine how much more complicated it would be for police officers, for example, to do their jobs if they did not have a set of categories in which to place people ("She's a hooker"; "He's a junkie"; "He looks like he might be casing that store"; "She's a teenage runaway"; "He's a derelict with no place to go").

The interactionist perspective focuses on just such issues as these—how people label one another, how they relate to one another on the basis of these labels, and the consequences of these social processes. As such, the interactionist perspective helps immensely in our understanding not only of the sociology of deviance but also of social process in general.

THE PLAN OF THE BOOK

The selections that follow spell out the interactionist perspective in greater detail. The first half of the book, which consists of Parts One and Two, deals with how people define some persons as deviant and act on the basis of these definitions. Part One shows how deviance is dealt with in informal relations and how a person is singled out and assigned a deviant status. Part Two deals with these processes in the formal regulation of deviance. For example, it considers how agents of social control, such as the police, define persons as deviants, how they act on these definitions, and what some of the consequences of formal sanctions are.

The second half of the book (Parts Three and Four) discusses deviants themselves: how they respond to being typed by others, how they type themselves, and how they relate to other deviants. Part Three examines the social organization of deviance and how people get into a deviant group and learn its norms. Finally, this section examines the social diversity that can exist in what many people assume is a homogenous group. Part Four shows how persons may take on deviant identities through self-typing, how they manage deviant identities, and how they may eventually regain "respectability."

This book, then, focuses not on people's motivations for doing things that are regarded as deviant but rather on the *sociology* of deviance—the processes that divide society into different types of people and the social effects of these processes.

PART ONE

THE SOCIAL DEVIANT

Sociology is the study of social relations. Sociologists study how people arrive at common constructions of their situation; how they form groups based on such constructions; and how they go on to set down rules of conduct, assign social roles to each other, and enforce their rules. Sociologists examine these questions as part of the larger question: How do people attempt to produce and sustain social order?

Deviance implies an alleged breach of a social norm. By looking at deviance we can come to a better understanding of social interaction. At the same time, the study of deviance also sheds light on the way "deviant" patterns and lifestyles are organized.

There are at least two ways of studying deviance as a social phenomenon. The first is to approach deviance as objectively given; the second, as subjectively problematic.

DEVIANCE AS OBJECTIVELY GIVEN

Sociologists who treat deviance as objectively given delineate the norms of the society under study and regard any deviation from these norms as "deviant." These sociologists generally make three assumptions. First, they assume that there is widespread consensus in the society in the realm of norms; this widespread agreement, they believe, makes it relatively easy to identify deviance. Second, they assume that deviance typically evokes negative sanctions such as gossip or legal action. Third, they assume that the punishment meted out to the deviant reaffirms for the group that it is bound by a set of common norms. The major questions raised by this approach are the following: What sociocultural conditions are most likely to produce deviance? Why do people continue to deviate despite the negative sanctions that are brought to bear on them? How can deviance best be minimized or controlled?

From these assumptions and questions, certain procedures have evolved for studying deviants. First list the "dos" and "don'ts" of the society or group. Then study the official records kept on persons who violate these rules. Interview persons appearing in these records, and consult agents of social control such as police and judges. Try to discover the ways in which deviants differ from nondeviants (e.g., are deviants more likely than nondeviants to come from broken homes?) in order to discern the kinds of social and cultural conditions that seem to make deviant behavior more likely. Try to derive a theory to "explain" deviance, and then apply the theory for the correction and prevention of deviance.

The strength of this approach is the sharpness and simplicity with which it phrases questions. The weak points of this approach follow from its key assumptions. The United States has so many different groups and ways of thinking that people often do not agree on norms. Because of this lack of agreement, and also because of the fact that some people get caught whereas others avoid discovery, it is often very difficult to identify who is deviant and who is not. Also, most social control agencies operate with selective enforcement, so that certain categories of people are more likely than others to be punished for their deviance. Thus, the nature, causes, and consequences of deviance are neither simple nor uniform.

DEVIANCE AS SUBJECTIVELY PROBLEMATIC

Sociologists who focus on the social differentiation of deviants generally make another set of assumptions. First, they assume that when people and groups interact they communicate with one another by means of shared symbols (verbal and body language, style of dress, etc.). Through such symbolic communication, it is assumed, people are able to type one another and formulate their actions accordingly. Second, they assume that deviance can best be understood in terms of this process, that deviant labels are symbols that differentiate and stigmatize the people to whom they are applied. Finally, sociologists using this approach assume that people act on the basis of such constructions. Thus, people treat the alleged deviant differently from other people. The alleged deviant, in turn, may also react to this definition. On the basis of these assumptions, sociologists using this perspective focus on social definitions and on how these influence social interaction. On the one hand, they focus on the perspective and actions of those who define a person as being deviant. They look at the circumstances under which a person is most likely to get set apart as deviant, how a person is cast into a deviant role, what actions others take on the basis of that construction of a person, and the consequences of these actions. On the other hand, these sociologists also focus on the perspective and reactions of the person adjudged to be deviant. They consider how a person reacts to being so adjudged, how a person adopts a deviant role, what changes in group memberships result, and what changes occur in the alleged deviant's self-concept.

Whereas the objectively given approach focuses primarily on the characteristics of the deviant or the conditions that give rise to deviant acts, the subjectively problematic approach focuses on the constructions and actions both of the deviants themselves and of the people who label them deviant, and on the social interaction between the two. Thus, we call the latter approach the interactionist perspective.

This book adopts the interactionist perspective, approaching deviance as subjectively problematic rather than as objectively given. In this book, then, deviants are considered simply as people who are socially typed in a certain way. Such typing usually involves an attempt to make sense of seemingly aberrant acts. As people seek to make sense of such acts, they generally employ stereotypical interpretations that define the actor as a particular kind of person (a kook, a drunk, a sociopath, etc.), that include a judgment about the moral quality of the deviant or his or her motives, and that suggest how a person should act toward the deviant. The social constructions of deviance, then, consist of a *description*, an *evaluation*, and a *prescription*. For example, a "kook" is a person who is mildly eccentric (description). The term connotes that "kooks" are odd but not particularly evil or dangerous (evaluation). Thus, one may display dislike or friendly disrespect toward them (prescription). A person who comes to be defined as a "sociopath," on the other hand, is considered to be both odd and severely unpredictable (description). The sociopath is often regarded as self-centered, evil, and dangerous (evaluation), and the sociopath is to be taken seriously at all times; a person who shows dislike or disrespect toward a "sociopath" does so at great personal risk (prescription). Thus, the construction of a person as a particular type of deviant organizes people's responses to that person, and the more people who share the definition that a person is a particular type of deviant, the greater the social consequences.

Taking the subjective approach to deviance, Part One of this book examines such phenomena more specifically. The topics treated in this part of the book include how people type, or label, others as deviants, the cultural context of typing, the accommodations people make to the so-called deviance, and how people may collaborate to exclude deviants from their midst.

THE PROCESS OF SOCIAL TYPING

Sociologically, deviance is approached here in terms of social differentiation. This differentiation arises from the perception that something is amiss. If a potential typer, or labeler, ignores or excuses the alleged aberrant quality of a person or event, it goes unlabeled as deviant. For instance, a person who works hard is expected sometimes to be tired and cranky, and in such situations people may not attach any particular importance to this behavior. Once an act or a person is typed as "deviant," however, a variety of social phenomena may come into play. These phenomena include who types whom, on what grounds, in what ways, before or after what acts (real or imputed), in front of what audience, and with what effects.

Let us for a moment consider the conditions that seem to make typing more effective. First, typing generally has the most effect when the typer, the person typed as deviant, and other people all share and understand the deviant definition in their social relationships. The typer and others act toward the "deviant" in accord with their shared understanding of the situation. Aware of having been so typed, the deviant, in turn, takes that shared understanding into account in relating to people. Thus, willingly or otherwise, all parties may subscribe to the definition. When all agree in this way, the construction of the person as a particular type of deviant is most socially effective, or confirmed. As an example, Frank Tannenbaum, one of the fathers of the interactionist perspective on deviance, has said: "The process of making the criminal . . . is a process of tagging, defining, identifying, segregating, describing, emphasizing, and evoking the very traits that are complained of. . . . The person becomes the thing he is described as being." Tannenbaum says that "the community cannot deal with people whom it cannot define" and that "the young delinquent becomes bad because he is defined as bad and because he is not believed if he is good."[1] In contrast, people with physical disabilities (such as individuals in wheelchairs) and other people with whom they come in contact do not always share the same definition of the deviance or understanding of the situation. This can lead to misunderstandings about how to relate to one another in certain circumstances (e.g., in stores and restaurants).

Second, social types are generally more apt to be accepted by other people if a high-ranking person does the typing. Effective social typing usually flows down rather than up the social structure. For example, an honor bestowed by the president of the United States is more likely to be consequential than an honor bestowed by a low-ranking official. Conversely, a denunciation by a high-ranking person such as the CEO of a company will usually carry more weight, and be confirmed by more people, than a denunciation by a low-ranking person such as one of the company's janitors.

Third, deviant typing is also more apt to be effective if there is a sense that the alleged deviant is violating important norms and that the violations are extreme. For instance, if factory workers are tacitly expected to turn out only a limited amount of work, a worker who produces much more than the norm may be singled out and ostracized as a "rate-buster." On the other hand, a person who jaywalks is unlikely to be typed and treated as a deviant. Likewise, people who are redheads (a characteristic that is not an extreme violation of an important norm) often feel stigmatization when they are children and adolescents, but in adulthood relinquish the effects of negative typing.

Fourth, it also seems that negative social typing is more readily accepted than positive typing. For one thing, "misery loves company"; people find comfort in learning about the frailties of others. In addition, norms seem to be highlighted more by infraction than by conformity. Also, negative typing is seen as a valuable safeguard if the type indicates an aberrant pattern that will probably continue and that has major consequences. Some police officers, for instance, expect upper-class adolescents to misbehave in their youth but later to become influential and respected citizens, while they expect slum adolescents who are vandals, troublemakers, or delinquents to become hardened criminals in adulthood; thus, such police officers are more likely to negatively type slum youths than upper-class youths who break the same laws.

Fifth, typing will be accepted more readily if the audience stands to gain from the labeling. Endorsing attention to another person's deviant behavior, for example, may divert attention from one's own. It may also sustain a status difference between oneself and the so-called deviant.

When social typing is effective, three kinds of consequences most often follow: self-fulfilling prophecy, typecasting, and recasting. In the self-fulfilling prophecy, typing is based on false beliefs about the alleged deviant, but the actions other people take on the basis of these false beliefs eventually make them become a reality. For example, both black and white police officers believe that it is more difficult to arrest blacks than whites. As a result, they tend to use more force in arresting blacks, and in turn they experience more resistance from blacks. In typecasting, the deviant stereotype is so widely accepted that confirmation of the typing proceeds rapidly, and typer, audience, and the person typed relate to each other in an automatic manner. For instance, if one person types another as a thief, any audience can generally predict and understand the typer's attitudes and actions. In recasting, the most complex of the three consequences, the deviant is expected to behave conventionally and is encouraged to disprove the deviant typing (e.g., to reform). Probation officers, for example, may encourage conventionality by restricting the opportunities of their probationers to continue their deviant ways. In the first two consequences of typing, the typer and audience restrict the deviant's opportunities to disprove the deviant typing. In recasting, the typer and the audience restrict the deviant's opportunities to confirm the deviant typing.

THE CULTURAL CONTEXT

The process of social typing occurs within a cultural context. Each culture, for example, has its own assortment and corresponding vocabulary of types. Thus, in our own culture we no longer talk about "witches"; consequently, no one is so typed. Similarly, if we had no word for or concept of "sociopath," no one would be so typed. The culture's repertoire of deviant types and stereotypes is ordinarily created, defined, sustained, and controlled by highly valued realms of the culture (e.g., psychiatry, law, religion). It should also be noted that different categories are used in different subcultures. "Sinners," for example, are typed only in the religious sector. Similarly, the term "crack-baby," when originally applied in the delivery room subculture, signified the moral judgments those within that subculture placed on the baby's mother. This pejorative construction has now entered into the dominant culture.

Different groups and cultures have different ideas about deviance. This difference in cultural contexts leads lower-class families more than middle-class families to accept their children who are labeled as intellectually disabled. Another example is how the cultural context of some work settings shapes viewing certain behaviors as "sexual harassment" while in other work settings similar behaviors may be perceived only as joking or harmless flirting. A final example is how the dominant culture privileges some social categories over others. Thus, because of the more negative cultural interpretations that are applied to women's bodily functions than men's, heterosexual women are more likely than heterosexual men to experience great concern when there is an audience to their private toilet behavior.

Also, typing often has an ethnocentric bias. People in one culture or subculture may be quick to type an outsider as deviant, for instance, simply because the outsider's lifestyle is so different from their own. Among persons within the same culture or subculture, on the other hand, the risks of being typed deviant are usually smaller.

Once a person has been labeled, the question of how to relate to the deviant is more easily resolved when cultural prescriptions exist. These include the prescriptions, for example, that sick people should be treated and evil people punished. In sum, typing is easier to act on when cultural guidelines exist.

ACCOMMODATION TO DEVIANCE

As noted previously, sociologically, deviants are persons who have been effectively labeled as deviant, and *effectively* means simply that the label does affect social relations. The person who has been typed as a deviant, for example, acquires a special status that carries a set of new rights and duties or changes in old ones and a new set of expectations about future conduct. Thus, when people type a certain person as deviant, they imply, "We now expect you to engage in deviant actions." In some cases, this expectation amounts to a license to deviate, as when a group may not only tolerate but actually shelter a deviant in its midst. More often, however, the expectation of deviant conduct gives other people license to treat the deviant in a demeaning way. Even people who suffer from victimization by deviants (e.g., families of homicide victims) can be labeled deviant if they fail to follow the expectations that surround accommodations to them.

The pace of events in labeling is one of the critical factors in this entire process. If aberrant conduct occurs only gradually and irregularly within a small, intimate group, deviant typing may not take place at all. Even if the events place some immediate strain on relationships, members of the group may adjust to the strain without perceiving the person any differently. Eventually, though, some critical point may be reached at which the group becomes aware that things are not what they used to be. Sometimes the members of the group have long entertained suspicions of deviance, and their accommodation represents an acknowledgement that the deviation is here to stay. In other instances, though, even as they type the person as deviant, group members may be optimistic that the deviance is only temporary. In any case, the group's accommodation to the so-called deviance has usually been going on for some time before labeling actually occurs.

THE ROLE OF THIRD PARTIES

As already noted, in intimate groups, people are usually slower to type one of their members as deviant than are outsiders. Such in-group labeling does happen at times, however, particularly if the deviant's aberrant behavior has begun to cause considerable strain for the rest of the group. When such strain exists, the typing of the person as deviant is often facilitated or precipitated by some outsider or outside agency—in short, by some third party.

In some cases the third party may act without solicitation. A wife, for example, may fail to recognize that her husband is involved with another woman until the community gossip (the third party) informs her; she may then type her husband as a philanderer and may, through separation or divorce, exclude him from the family.

In other cases a member of a primary group may seek out a third party in order to validate such typing or to exclude the deviant from the group. If a man's wife is emotionally disturbed, for example, he may turn to third parties outside the family (a psychiatrist, the courts, the sheriff, etc.) in order to remove his wife from the home, officially labeling her as mentally disturbed and seeking treatment for her. Another example is that, after a stay in a battered women's shelter, some women can end their relationship with abusive husbands. Severance becomes more likely if they come to see themselves through the eyes of shelter staff counselors. Counselors help them to redefine themselves as victims of unjust abuse, their husbands as the deviant persons.

Thus, we have seen some of the ways in which the social definition of deviants proceeds. A real or imputed violation of norms can activate the process of social typing, and a variety of social factors affect its success. The nature and likelihood of this typing are influenced by the cultural context. People may at first attempt to accommodate these alleged violations. Over the course of time, however, the deviant may no longer be protected. Third parties may intervene, and at that point exclusion of the deviant may take place.

NOTE

1. Frank Tannenbaum, *Crime and the Community* (New York: Columbia University Press, 1938), pp. 19–20.

CHAPTER 1

THE PROCESS OF SOCIAL TYPING

Outsiders

HOWARD S. BECKER

When people hear that a person has broken a rule, they are likely to ask, "What kind of person would do a thing like that?" What they have heard other people say in the past about deviants leads them to designate the alleged rule breaker as a certain kind of deviant social type. When researchers study the records of people who have committed crimes or who are patients in mental hospitals, they also classify the offenders or the patients into certain categories. In both instances, whether talking about or studying those thought to have broken the rules, a construction of the "kinds of people" who violate rules is supported, shared, and transmitted for use in future communication about similar actors. The result is a cultural catalog of deviant social types.

Howard S. Becker, in the following excerpt from his classic book *Outsiders: Studies in the Sociology of Deviance*, points out that the only thing all people so categorized have in common is the fact that they have been labeled deviant. Thus, his definition: Deviant behavior is behavior that people label deviant, and for labeling to take place there have to be responses of other people who may apply negative sanctions of one kind or another. He goes on to point out the variety of conditions under which labeling takes place along with the consequences of such labeling.

On the one hand, many people break rules and are never labeled. On the other hand, some are falsely accused. Time, place, the status of the rule, the person being considered, and the rule enforcer are all contingencies. For some who have come to official attention, a deviant career can be their fate.

[One sociological view] . . . defines deviance as the infraction of some agreed-upon rule. It then goes on to ask who breaks rules, and to search for the

factors in their personalities and life situations that might account for the infractions. This assumes that those who have broken a rule constitute a homogeneous category, because they have committed the same deviant act.

Such an assumption seems to me to ignore the central fact about deviance: it is created by society. I do not mean this in the way it is ordinarily understood, in which the causes of deviance are located in the social situation of the deviant or in "social factors" which prompt his action. I mean, rather, that *social groups create deviance by making the rules whose infraction constitutes deviance,* and by applying those rules to particular people and labeling them as outsiders. From this point of view, deviance is *not* a quality of the act the person commits, but rather a consequence of the application by others of rules and sanctions to an "offender." The deviant is one to whom that label has successfully been applied; deviant behavior is behavior that people so label.[1]

Since deviance is, among other things, a consequence of the responses of others to a person's act, students of deviance cannot assume that they are dealing with a homogeneous category when they study people who have been labeled deviant. That is, they cannot assume that those people have actually committed a deviant act or broken some rule, because the process of labeling may not be infallible; some people may be labeled deviant who in fact have not broken a rule. Furthermore, they cannot assume that the category of those labeled deviant will contain all those who actually have broken a rule, for many offenders may escape apprehension and thus fail to be included in the population of "deviants" they study. Insofar as the category lacks homogeneity and fails to include all the cases that belong in it, one cannot reasonably expect to find common factors of personality or life situation that will account for the supposed deviance.

What, then, do people who have been labeled deviant have in common? At the least, they share the label and the experience of being labeled as outsiders. I will begin my analysis with this basic similarity and view deviance as the product of a transaction that takes place between some social group and one who is viewed by that group as a rule-breaker. I will be less concerned with the personal and social characteristics of deviants than with the process by which they come to be thought of as outsiders and their reactions to that judgment. . . .

In any case, being branded as deviant has important consequences for one's further social participation and self-image. The most important consequence is a drastic change in the individual's public identity. Committing the improper act and being publicly caught at it places him in a new status. He has been revealed as a different kind of person from the kind he was supposed to be. He is labeled a "fairy," "dope fiend," "nut" or "lunatic," and treated accordingly.

In analyzing the consequences of assuming a deviant identity let us make use of Hughes' distinction between master and auxiliary status traits.[2] Hughes notes that most statuses have one key trait which serves to distinguish those who belong from those who do not. Thus the doctor, whatever else he may be, is a person who has a certificate stating that he has fulfilled certain requirements and is licensed to practice medicine; this is the master trait. As Hughes points out, in our society a doctor is also informally expected to have a number of auxiliary traits: most people expect him to be upper middle class, white, male, and Protestant. When he is not there is a sense that he has in some way failed to fill the bill. Similarly, though skin color is the master status trait determining who is . . . [Black] and who is white, . . . [Blacks] are informally expected to have certain status traits and not to have others; people are surprised and find it anomalous if a . . . [Black] turns out to be a doctor or a college professor. People often have the master status trait but lack some of the auxiliary, informally expected characteristics; for example, one may be a doctor but be female or . . . [Black].

Hughes deals with this phenomenon in regard to statuses that are well thought of, desired and desirable (noting that one may have the formal qualifications for entry into a status but be denied full entry because of lack of the proper auxiliary traits), but the same process occurs in the case of deviant statuses. Possession of one deviant trait may have a generalized symbolic value, so that people automatically assume that its bearer possesses other undesirable traits allegedly associated with it.

There is one other element in Hughes' analysis we can borrow with profit: the distinction between master and subordinate statuses.[3] Some statuses, in our society as in others, override all other statuses and have a certain priority. Race is one of these. . . . [Being Black] will override most other status considerations in most other situations; the fact that one is a physician or middle-class or female will not protect one from being treated as . . . [Black] first and any of these other things second. The status of deviant (depending on the kind of deviance) is this kind of master status. One receives the status as a result of breaking a rule, and the identification proves to be more important than most others. One will be identified as a deviant first, before other identifications are made. . . .

NOTES

1. The most important earlier statements of this view can be found in Frank Tannenbaum, *Crime and the Community* (New York: Columbia University Press, 1938), and E. M. Lemert, *Social Pathology* (New York: McGraw–Hill, 1951). An article stating a position very similar to mine is John Kitsuse, "Societal Reaction to Deviance: Problems of Theory and Method," *Social Problems* 9 (Winter 1962), 247–256.

2. Everett C. Hughes, "Dilemmas and Contradictions of Status," *American Journal of Sociology* L (March 1945), 353–359.

3. *Ibid.*

Redheads as Deviant Types

DRUANN MARIA HECKERT and AMY BEST

Crimes against persons (assault, murder, rape, robbery) all use force and are examples of voluntary deviance. Persons who freely choose to perform these acts arouse moral indignation as well as criminal sanctions. On the other hand, involuntary deviance is more apt to evoke negative social sanctions than criminal sanctions. Nevertheless, involuntary deviants through their actions or their appearance violate the taken-for-granted expectations of everyday life (schizophrenics may not talk sensibly, disabled people may disrupt pedestrian traffic). A construction of being socially deviant, although involuntarily so, still produces many of the consequences that labeling theory predicts. Once assigned to a deviant social category, involuntary deviants can be redefined, their character disparaged, their status diminished, their self deflated. Expectations of incompetence, unreliability, and unpredictability may replace expectations of conformity to general social norms.

Druann Maria Heckert and Amy Best (redheads themselves) interviewed people with red hair. They found that being born with red hair produced the negative consequences that labeling theory suggests. Red-haired youths, when interacting with peers who acted on their stereotyped beliefs about people with red hair, found their character, competence, and confidence called into question. Their red hair caused them to become the center of negative attention for a considerable period of time. The authors show, however, how an interesting turn of events changed the redheads' social situation, leading them to see themselves in a more positive light. Through the passage of time, they once again experienced self-redefinition.

Hair is an important aspect of how people define themselves and how other people define them. Red hair, besides being statistically very rare, presents an interesting case because it has been stigmatized. As such, labeling theory, which has offered much insight into deviance in general, will be utilized to examine the stigmatization of redheads.

We analyze the relative nature of deviance and the importance of attractiveness within the context of red hair, including the ways in which redheads perceive their stigmatization. We describe various stereotypes (as redheads understand them) that form the content of societal labeling. In addition, we discuss the negative impact that this labeling has on redheads, especially as children, in relation to a lowered sense of self-esteem, a feeling of differentness, and a perception of being forced into the role of the center of attention. Finally, we assess the transformation of self, from red hair being viewed as a negative aspect of self among children and adolescents to being viewed as a positive aspect of self among adults.

METHODS

Qualitative methods served as the basis for this study, and 20 redheads were interviewed. . . . The interviews were structured, but open-ended questions were emphasized (Nachmias and Nachmias 1996, pp. 232–254). It is interesting to note our perception that the fact that we are both redheads—each conducting 10 interviews—made for the easy establishment of rapport (since apprehension was minimized) and thus ultimately facilitated our solicitation and acquisition of personal information (Spradley 1979, pp. 78–83).

The only limitation we placed on the individuals to be interviewed was that they were natural redheads. In other words, we wanted to focus on individuals who had been socialized as redheads.

According to a popular maxim, a person can have red hair (i.e., dyed red hair), but still not be a redhead (i.e., not have experienced the socialization of a person born with red hair). The respondents were almost equally divided between males and females (i.e., 9 males and 11 females). All of the persons interviewed were white. . . . The people in our sample were fairly young, ranging in age from 11 to 37. This narrow range was partially rooted in the fact that redheads who had become gray were not obvious as redheads. Since red hair is a crucial aspect of identity for those who have it, research on redheads who have turned gray would make for an interesting study of socialization and identity. With the exception of one respondent, who resides in the South, all of our subjects were located in the Northeast region. Finally, the sample was drawn primarily from what appears to be the middle class or the middle class-to-be (i.e., college students). . . .

THE RELATIVE NATURE OF DEVIANCE AND REDHEADS AS DEVIANTS

Labeling theory, or societal reaction theory, is an approach to the understanding of deviance which is grounded in symbolic interactionism. While not necessarily focusing on the same matters as other theories of deviance, such as etiological issues or the causes of primary deviance, labeling theory has certainly enhanced our understanding of the nature of deviance by raising issues that are not addressed by other theoretical approaches. Labeling theory has advanced our understanding of deviance by assessing the relative nature of deviance, analyzing how the societal reaction can create deviance, and conceptualizing the ways in which labeling has an impact on those groups and individuals subjected to that societal reaction.

Labeling theory offers a relativistic stance towards deviance. By definition, deviance has been conceptualized as that which has been labeled or stigmatized by society (cf. Becker 1963, p. 9; Erikson 1964, p. 10; Lemert 1972, p. 22). Labeling theory begins with the understanding that constructions of deviance vary across time and place and group. Becker (1963, p. 9) perhaps best summarized this approach to deviance by hypothesizing that, while initiated by moral entrepreneurs and mediated by power relationships, deviance is a societal construction: "Social groups constitute deviance by making rules whose infraction constitutes deviance, and by applying those rules to particular people and labeling them as outsiders." Clearly, red hair can be conceptualized as a form of deviance in that it has been stigmatized in various historical and cultural contexts. Moreover, it is currently stigmatized in American society.

Goffman (1963, p. 3) defined stigma as "an attribute that is deeply discrediting" to the individual, based on the connections between such attributes and the stereotypes that accompany those attributes. In addition, he (1963, p. 4) outlined three major types of stigma: bodily disfigurements, "blemishes of individual character" (including concrete examples such as addiction or mental disorder), and group affiliation (including racial, national, and religious origin). While red hair does not fit into this typology, red hair does correspond with an extension of this formulation that was advanced by Kitsuse (1980). Noting the omnipresent difficulties in defining deviance—simultaneously "too inclusive and too exclusive"—Kitsuse (1980, p. 2) expands the notion of stigma to "genetic stigmata" to incorporate other marginalized people. According to Kitsuse (1980, p. 2).

If, as a technical matter, women do not qualify as bearers of tribal stigmas, perhaps we can add "genetic stigma" to Goffman's three types of stigma, to provide not only for genetic determination of sex characteristics, but also of body type, eye and hair-color, left-handedness, and other characteristics that in other times and places have been and in some future place and time may be burdened with stigma.

While perhaps this broadens the list of potential deviance too greatly, there can be no doubt that red hair is currently subject to considerable stigmatization. However, blonde women do bear the brunt of a cultural attribution of stupidity.

APPEARANCE NORMS

In the first place, as Schur (1983, pp. 66–70) has noted, appearance norms (or norms governing physical appearance) do exist, and violations of these norms do constitute deviance. What is physical attractiveness? Who are the physically attractive? Perhaps, as in the case of art (Gillespie and Perry 1973, p. 49), the crucial aspect of these questions is the meaning a public attaches to the definition of attractiveness since there can be no conclusive or satisfactory response. Nevertheless, cultural standards do seem to exist—albeit cross-culturally and historically relative—as according to Morse, Reis, Gruzen, and Wolff (1974, p. 529), "there are general standards of attractiveness within American society to which both males and females from the same cultural background will subscribe." Berscheid and Walster (1974, p. 181) add the following observation:

Despite the frequently heard assertion that individual differences in criteria for physical attractiveness are impossibly vast, and beauty is entirely in the eye of the beholder, people typically show a great deal of agreement in their evaluations of others. There exists no compendium of physical characteristics, which people find attractive in others, even within a single society. It appears, however, that the culture transmits effectively, and fairly uniformly, criteria for labeling others as physically "attractive" and "unattractive."

Clearly, notions of attractiveness are social constructions, and the relative nature of the definitions of attractiveness are immense. As Hatfield and Sprecher (1986, pp. 17–18) note, beauty standards are quite malleable across time and across cultures; there simply are no "universal beauties."

So strongly do these appearance norms operate in society that, overall, the physically attractive are, for the most part, preferentially treated in many important aspects of life (cf. Dion 1972; Byrne 1971; Reis, Wheeler, and Nezlik 1980; Reis, Wheeler, Spiegel, Kerns, Nezlik, and Perry 1982; Krebs and Adinolfi 1975; Benson, Karabenick, and Lerner 1976; Landy and Sigall

1974). According to Dion, Berscheid, and Walster (1972, p. 289) "what is beautiful is good"; conversely, the existing literature suggests that "what is not beautiful is not good."

THE SYMBOLIC IMPORTANCE OF HAIR
AND THE STIGMATIZATION OF RED HAIR

One crucial part of the definition of attractiveness (and thus adherence to appearance norms) is hair (cf. Alexander and Schouten 1989; Cahill 1989; Cooper 1971; Synnot 1987). As noted by Synnot (1987, p. 381), "Hair is perhaps our most powerful symbol of individual and group identity—powerful first because it is physical and therefore extremely personal, and second because, although personal, it is also public rather than private." Regarding red hair, Cooper (1971, pp. 72–77) argues that unlike the consistent Western appeal of blonde hair and lack of any historically distinctive pattern toward brunettes, red hair has "blazed an erratic trail." On the one hand, Italy and Greece are examples of societies where culture has favored redheads, who were, for example, glorified by Titian. On the other hand, Cooper (1971, p. 75) notes that red hair has often been stigmatized:

> But at times in England, France, Germany, Spain, and America, red hair has been unpopular and distrusted. At the height of Europe's witch hunts in the 16th and 17th centuries, many women suffered the shame and pain of being stripped, shaved, and "pricked" by a witch hunter, endured torture, and were put to death, simply because they were redheads—and preferably, young and attractive. The fear of red hair may have stemmed from the belief that Judas, who betrayed Christ, was red-haired. . . . In Germany, barbers advertised all sorts of concoctions for altering the red shade of hair, and in America, a newspaper was once driven to explain that twenty-one men in Cincinnati, who had married red-haired women, were color-blind and had mistaken red for black.

Red hair has been the basis for a clear and historical pattern of stigmatization.

While Cooper (1971, p. 75) notes that this century has been kinder to red hair, empirical evidence indicates a persistent stigmatization. Feinman and Gill (1978, p. 47) examined the preferences for opposite-sex coloration of 482 female and 549 male white college students: 82% of the males expressed a dislike and 7% expressed a like for red hair on females; 84% of the females claimed a dislike and 2% claimed a like of red hair on males. The next closest number in terms of disliking a hair color was that of black hair, which 14% of men did not like on women. These figures are consistent with Feinman and Gill's (1978, p. 49) observation that our society molds a male preference for fair females and a female preference for dark males (i.e., tall, dark, and handsome). Furthermore, the skin color (i.e., very light that freckles) of most redheads was also the most disliked of the eight skin colors which they examined. The other skin colors were black, brown, red brown, dark white, medium white that tans to gold, medium white that tans to red brown, and very light that does not freckle. Interestingly, so strong was the dislike for red hair that Feinman and Gill (1978, p. 49) called it their most striking finding and wondered, "Why is there such a tremendous aversion to redheads?" Red hair continues to be a source of stigmatization.

THE PERCEPTION OF REDHEADS

Red hair is stigmatized, and it is a form of deviance—albeit minor. Redheads seem to be very aware of their stigmatization in society, and our subjects expressed a variety of reactions to that stigma. As a 21-year-old male stated, "It varies from person to person. Some people just don't like red hair. You know the thing that redheads are either good looking or not. Some people just think everyone should have brown hair." Another male respondent hypothesized that blondes are "always popular" and brunettes are "constant." On the other hand, he noted, "Red hair is more like wide and narrow ties. It waxes and wanes like other fashions. Mostly it is not popular."

One pertinent indicator of stigmatization is just how profoundly redheads have internalized the reigning cultural definitions. Goffman (1963, pp. 106–107) described this type of ambivalence that the stigmatized feel toward their own category as follows:

> Given that the stigmatized individual in our society acquires identity standards which he applies to himself in spite of failing to conform to them, it is inevitable that he will feel some ambivalence about his own self. . . . The stigmatized individual exhibits a tendency to stratify his "own" according to the degree to which their stigma is apparent and obtrusive. He can then take up in regard to those who are more evidently stigmatized then himself the attitudes the normals take to him.

A fairly common response to the respondents in this study was to suggest that, unlike other hair colorings, redheads could be dichotomized into the extraordinarily ugly and the extraordinarily attractive. Perhaps this second category is an expression of profound ambivalence and a way that redheads are able to save face by seeing themselves as the exception, while still adhering to the reigning cultural definition of their category. For example, a young female offered the opinion that red hair is a double-edged sword: "When red hair is beautiful it's amazing, so much more amazing than any other color, but the rest are ugly." Another young female noted, "I'm a kind of mild redhead. There's nice red hair and there's doggy red hair. . . . It's funny, redheads go in one of a few directions. Horrible red hair, or striking red hair, or kooky red hair." A young male observed that redheads are gorgeous or very ugly, and while a redhead might have the talent to play a leading role (rather than a comical or secondary role) in the mass media, society simply does not demand it. Another young male stated, "When I see an ugly redhead I think it's the most atrocious thing in the world. Society of appearances. Some people with red hair just don't look good, and some look great." One respondent, whose hair was a muted red, raised the issue of passing: "I'm getting a free ride on the redhead train; I can jump off and be on the brown head train." He observed that his particular experiences

have been easier, but clearly he has stratified himself as "a less apparent and obtrusive" redhead as observed by Goffman (1963, p. 107). Indeed, we noted that the more an individual resembled the stereotypical image of a redhead (i.e., bolder hair color, fairer skin, and more overt freckles), the greater was the perception of stigmatization. Conversely, the more they deviated from that stereotypical image (i.e., a more muted shade of hair color, darker skin, and the absence or near-absence of freckles), the lesser was the perception of stigmatization.

Many of those interviewed also rendered strong opinions about the attractiveness of redheads in relationship to gender. A 36-year-old male noted that he had always shunned redheaded women. However, as he matured, he found it attractive, but only attractive on beautiful women (e.g., women who resemble Julia Roberts). On the other hand, he felt that red hair was simply "less egregious" on males than on females. Nevertheless, more commonly, those interviewed presented the view that red hair was more egregious on males than on females. A young female announced that redheaded women are either "extremely attractive" or "fairly ugly," which she believed to be more common. On the other hand, she stated that all redheaded men are unattractive. Another female suggested that society defines red hair as attractive on women, but on men, "not at all." As a young female stated, "I don't find myself being attracted to men with red hair. I've never met a woman that finds red-haired men to be sexy." Another young female respondent proclaimed that redheaded men are unappealing, especially in comparison to redheaded women. She added, "redheaded men aren't sexy. . . . I would want a girl with red hair but not a boy . . . they just don't look the same." A young male admitted that redheaded women are "something to see" or exotic; nevertheless, his experience was that redheaded men are defined as not at all attractive since women generally preferred, "dark hair, the Italian look, darker skin." Finally, one male respondent stated that he did not find most redheaded females to be attractive. However, he conceded that if a redheaded female did happen to be attractive, she would indeed be a "rare beauty"; nevertheless, he noted that a man with bright red hair is just "not as handsome as men with other hair colors" and that men with any shade of red hair are never perceived to be "stud, sexy" types.

Clearly, redheads are quite aware of their societal stigmatization. In fact, more than simply being aware of their stigmatization, they are active participants in the cultural definitions of attractiveness into which they have been socialized.

THE LABELING OF RED HAIR

The symbolic interactionist approach to deviance involves describing the process through which the labeling of individuals proceeds. Schur (1971, pp. 41–60) hypothesized that the labeling process includes the following elements: stereotyping, or the imputation of traits such as differentness to the individual or the behavior of the individual; retrospective interpretation, or the reevaluation of the past behavior of the individual; and negotiation, or the bargaining that takes place which involves the discretionary power of the control agents of society. In the case of hair color, stereotyping is the most important of the labeling processes. The stereotyping of hair colors appears to permeate cultural beliefs, as is evidenced by the recent popularity of "dumb blonde" jokes. Synnot (1992, p. 386) cites further evidence:

> According to a survey in the United States, males described redheaded females as "the active executive types, no-nonsense and physically rather unattractive," blondes as "beautiful, rich, and extremely feminine," and dark-haired women as "good, intelligent, and familiar.". . . Females, on the other hand, described male redheads as "good, but effeminate, timid and weak," blondes as "attractive, successful and happy," and dark-haired men were seen as "average."

Hair color, seemingly a most innocuous variable, actually served as the basis for much cultural stereotyping.

CULTURAL STEREOTYPES AS PERCEIVED BY REDHEADS

Redheads are very aware of the stereotypes that exist in society. Indeed, they have internalized them as a result of personal experiences. Many stereotypes were mentioned by our respondents, including those that applied to all redheads and those that were gender specific. These stereotypes went way beyond any relationship to hair color and extended to personality characteristics and even to ethnicity.

The Flaring Temper

The most frequently mentioned stereotype revolved around anger or a hot temper. Virtually every respondent brought up this stereotype. One referred to this stereotype as the "feisty tempered will." Another referred to it as the "vicious temper," while a young female stated that "guys always say, gee her temper is really flaring." One female noted that when she is asked if she has a temper, she simply says yes and walks away. Another female recounted that her redheaded sister was in labor for 44 hours prior to giving birth, and even though the child turned out to be a brunette female, "When she pushed the doctor was like, my goodness, this one is giving us a hard time, he is a little boy with fiery red hair." A hot temper is perhaps the most ubiquitous stereotype of redheads.

The Clown

Another very common stereotype, as perceived by redheads, is that of being a clown. Considering that many symbolic representations of clowns (e.g., Ronald McDonald and Bozo) do have red hair, the culture clearly reinforces this imagery. A 25-year-old female expressed this stereotype in the following way: "Lucille Ball, she's wacky, not stupid but a nut case. Redheads are kind of wacky. They're zany except Richie Cunningham types; they're more like goobers." A young female noted, "It is definitely not a good way to portray us as clowns." As she mentioned, clowns would never have brown hair, as clowns are supposed to be funny looking, and they get that way by giving them red hair. A young male made the following observation:

> I have a sense of humor and that stems from my hair. If you have red hair and you don't have a sense of humor, you are going to get ranked on and you are not going to be able to laugh at yourself. Maybe I did think I looked silly, too, when I looked in the mirror. It's red hair, it's bright. I think red hair is symbolic of people who want to have fun and not care about what other people think. So, apparently that's how we are supposed to act, too. I guess redheads aren't to be taken seriously. I mean we may act a little crazy.

A 36-year-old male stated, "We're goofy." He acknowledged that he often makes self-deprecating remarks, such as "I look like Ronald McDonald" or "I look like Bozo," as a way of deflecting an anticipated response. As a young male noted, redheads are associated with the comical, with clowns, and they are supposed to be funny. He admitted that, in part, it is probably a self-fulfilling prophecy, but he defines himself as funny. Another male suggested that the clown imagery "marginalized us" in that redheads are not seen as "a significant part of our culture . . . it is a demeaning way of fitting us in the culture." Obviously, redheads feel that a major stereotype enforced upon them is that of the clown.

Birenbaum and Sagarin (1976, p. 108) have argued that while humor is utilized by nondeviants to express the stereotypes of deviants, deviants also can take advantage of humor:

> Humor is a two-sided weapon; it can be used not only to subject people to ridicule but also to disarm those who are likely to be uncomfortable in the presence of a deviant. It makes light of tragedy, brings the unmentionable into the forefront of conversation, and, in short, permits the heavy air of embarrassment to be lifted.

Interestingly, a "minstrelization" or the "role of the clown" are potentially available to deviants

as a coping mechanism. The case of redheads is somewhat unique in that the "clown role" is one of the major stereotypes already attributed to them; no great leap is required to utilize humor or to confirm the expectations of clownishness.

The Weird Redhead

Another stereotype that was mentioned frequently was that redheads are viewed as weird. As a 22-year-old male suggested, "People think redheads are a little weirder, which perhaps we are. The redheaded people I know are pretty different. It's like this brotherhood and sisterhood. I look forward to seeing people with red hair. It is something that we share." One respondent noted that "the freakouts" in movies all have red hair, and he pointed to the portrayal of the redheaded character, Malachai, in the movie, *The Children of the Corn*, which focused on marauding adolescent murderers in the Midwest. In addition, a young male recalled that, in high school, he and another tall redheaded male were called the "freak brothers," and he feels that the root cause of this label was hair color. Similarly, one young female suggested that all of her friends assume that she has "a couple of screws loose"—albeit in a nice way. She stated that she does a lot to entertain them, but they think that she is illogical, that she is especially likely to say crazy things, and that her "brain is on slow-mo" (i.e., it does not process things quickly). As redheads perceive the situation, weirdness is often attributed to them.

The Redhead as Irish

Apart from any personality characteristics, many redheads noted that Irish ethnicity is often attributed to them, sometimes correctly and sometimes incorrectly. According to Meyerowitz (1991, p. 12), Scotland has the highest percentage of redheads of any nation at 11%, greatly exceeding the 2 or 3% of redheads in the world population. Nevertheless, in the United States, many of the respondents felt that red hair is often interpreted as an almost exclusively Irish characteristic. As a male respondent expressed it, the stereotype is simply "the Irish thing." Another noted, "People assume you are Irish." Furthermore, stereotypes about the Irish (e.g., overindulgence in alcohol) are also applied to redheads. A nonIrish redhead recalled that, in addition to getting free drinks on St. Patrick's Day, there have been many times when she has informed inquiring minds that she is definitely of Eastern European descent, only to have them retort that she needed to investigate her lineage more closely.

For those respondents who were of total or partial Irish descent, many felt that red hair has had an impact on their feelings of ethnicity. A 21-year-old female stated that, since she is half-Irish, she loves St. Patrick's Day, as people will assume that her hair color is related to her Irish heritage. For her, the hair and the ethnicity are "inextricably connected." While having ambivalent feelings about the relationship, a 37-year-old male (with a strawberry blonde mother, a redheaded father with nine redheaded siblings, and four redheaded siblings of his own) explained that while his ethnic background included five different groups, his family felt profound ties with Irish Catholicism in a belief that, because of the hair color, they were "special in the eyes of God." Hair color and ethnic-religious status easily coalesced. This aspect of the stereotyping is a fascinating phenomenon in that more than personality characteristics are enforced on redheads; even ethnicity (often falsely) is thrust upon them. Red hair can become a master status.

The Redhead as Sun Challenged

One stereotype that many redheads confirmed was that they must avoid over-exposure to the sun. As a young female noted, all redheads are assumed to have fair skin, to burn in the sun, and to be incapable of tanning. Another young female observed that, in a culture which adores sun worshippers, during the summer, she "looks like a ghost, out of

place." A 22-year-old female elaborated on this problem:

> Summertime, I hate it. I'm very fair. I can't go in the sun. I burn, white, white legs. I totally feel uncomfortable in the sun. I think redheads are more sensitive to heat. I don't do well in the heat, maybe something chemical. How many redheads do you see on the beach and when you look over at them you say, I hope she's wearing her sunblock.

Clearly, our respondents acknowledge that, in most cases, redheads and the sun simply do not belong together.

Redheaded Women as Wild and Redheaded Men as Wimps

Ironically, one set of stereotypes regarding redheads is diametricaly opposed and gender specific. Redheaded females tend to be deemed wild and sexy; at the same time, however, redheaded males are desexualized in that they are stereotyped as wimps in a culture which portrays machismo and stud imagery as desirable for males. Among our respondents, redheaded females and males concurred that redheaded females are stereotyped as sexy. As one female put it, redheaded females are seen as "spitfires . . . a little wild, self-assured, sexy." A 36-year-old male added that a redheaded female is stereotyped as having a "fierce, fiery personality, like an untamed heroine in a romance novel." One female suggested that the cultural imagery is "fiery, wild, and loose," and that there is "a mystique behind red hair, it's intriguing." She feels that the high number of sexual jokes of which she is the recipient are rooted in her hair color. Another young female claimed, "You know what they say about redheads. Well, that we're good in bed." A young male said, "someone told me that in a sex scale if you have sex with a redhead it counts for more points." Another young male stated the stereotype most succinctly when he reported that he had a friend who simply would not date redheaded women because he was afraid of them. Almost unanimously, redheads feel that redheaded women are stereotyped as oversexed beings.

At the same time, quite curiously, the exact opposite is attributed to redheaded men. Both redheaded women and men reported that redheaded men are stereotyped as wimps, or as desexualized beings. Many redheaded women specifically mentioned that they did not find redheaded men sexually desirable and did not want to date them. Two of our respondents even went so far as to express a wish not to have redheaded sons. This attribute is evident in the following statement by one young female: "Male redheads are goobers, they are Richie Cunninghams . . . a good little boy, momma's boys . . . wimp, boring, and dopey." The internalization of this cultural stereotype was quite pronounced among our redheaded women. Redheaded men were also quite aware of this cultural imagery and obviously much affected by it. A young male admitted, "A lot of men don't want red hair. They may think it's wimpy or something." Likewise, a 26-year-old male (who felt that his almost paralyzing shyness and lack of self-esteem as an adolescent was rooted in his hair color) noted that, as a child, adults would always say, "He's cute . . . the cute, little redheaded all-American, freckle-faced boy." He defined this "freckle-faced, all-American, Richie Cunningham thing" as a stigma that had always burdened him with "the nice guy thing" in a culture where women are often socialized not to find that quality sexy or even attractive in males. Asked to name role models for redheads, one 21-year-old male responded that there was Opie and Richie Cunningham—period (two characters portrayed by Ron Howard). Thus, both redheaded males and redheaded females felt that redheaded males are perceived in our culture as wimps or nice guys—in either case, not sexually desirable.

Perhaps in an effort to wage a campaign against the image that society offers him, one male redhead proudly pronounced that redheaded role models are always big bullies. To support his argument, he cited characters in a Christmas story as well as an obscure painting by Norman Rockwell. In addition, he passionately proclaimed that redheaded men are jerks. This personally drawn portrait was singular, and it may have been an act of rebellion against a stifling societal portrait; in any event, no other redhead concurred.

The Redhead as Intellectually Superior

One final stereotype was mentioned by only a few respondents, and it was perhaps another way of presenting a positive stereotype to resist many negative ones. Redheads were described as superior intellectual beings. As a young male respondent suggested, his stereotype was that redheads share great intelligence. He stated that he and his other redheaded friends always make overt references and jokes about this alleged superiority, and, if there is a problem, they always state, "We're redheads . . . we will solve the problem." He also provided a litany of historical examples to offer evidence in support of his claims. Another male argued that the superior intelligence of redheads is causally connected to the fact that, as there is only a 3% genetic probability, "redheaded sperm" are intrinsically superior to other sperm. While these statements may have been offered in jest, positive in-group stereotyping can serve to deflect negative ones.

Appellations Supportive of Stereotypes

In conjunction with stereotyping processes, virtually all of the respondents had either been referred to by a nickname or called a name that was related to their hair color. Clearly, these appellations serve to provide visual imagery for the verbal assertions of stereotyping. These names were applied to redheads by both strangers and primary group members. Some of these names were abhorred; others were accepted. "Red" and "Carrot top" are almost ubiquitous, and they were frequently mentioned. Other names that were found in this sample include the following: red rooster, torch, torchhead, Barbarossa (i.e., red beard), red q-tip, fire crotch, Danny Partridge, copper top, copper head, penny, Little Orphan Annie, Annie, rosey red, fireball, Howdy Doody, and hydrant (as in fire hydrant). These names reinforce certain stereotypes, and they emphasize the difference of red hair.

In summary, stereotypes about redheads are extensive and inconsistent. At times, they take the form of master statuses in that characteristics attributed to redheads often refer to phenomena that have nothing to do with appearance. Redheads are assumed to have many personality characteristics and even ethnicity on the basis of nothing other than the color of their hair.

THE IMPACT OF LABELING ON THE LABELED

Labeling theory suggests that the labeling of individuals has an impact on their lives, most often in a negative fashion. Tannenbaum (1980, pp. 244–247) observed that there is a dramatization of evil, Erikson (1964, p. 167) noted that there can be a self-fulfilling prophecy, and Lemert (1972, pp. 48–63) examined the transformation from primary to secondary deviation. The career of the deviant, as shaped by societal reaction, is a primary focus of labeling theorists.

Redheads acknowledge that many cultural stereotypes exist about them. While these stereotypes are obviously not as pernicious as those that concern various racial and ethnic groups, the stereotypes that are applied to redheads definitely affect their lives. Thus, the impact of labeling on the labeled is a very pertinent issue.

NEGATIVE TREATMENT AS CHILDREN

A fairly common pattern among redheads is that, as children, they receive much negative treatment from their peers. At the same time, they tend to receive many positive comments from adults, especially from elderly women. As a male stated, "Adults say how beautiful your hair is, and kids make fun of you." He often wore hats in an effort to avoid being noticed. One 21-year-old female reported that she attempted to straighten her hair to make it appear less overtly red and attempted to

dye it brown, only to have it turn out pink. This was her response to the fact that while her family and older people gave her positive reinforcement about her hair, the kids were cruel, taunted her, and assumed that she was strange. Another young woman described this bifurcated treatment in the following way: "Well, I guess it's a positive and negative thing. Children teased me about my red hair and adults loved it. I used to be called things like 'carrot top' and 'Annie' or people would think I'd be ill-tempered. Adults would say, 'Oh you have beautiful red hair.' " As redheads perceived their childhoods, older women seemed especially prone to appreciating their much maligned hair. One young woman said, "Blue-haired old ladies think it's the ideal." An 11-year-old female asked about their admiration: "Just seems to be old ladies, not old men, not young men, not young women, not children, just old ladies. Why is that?" The 11-year-old girl added that their comments include, "Oh, how much they love the hair, how wonderful . . . how nice your hair is, old lady things."

This pattern creates a strange dichotomy. Red hair is the source of much positive attention, but the positive attention from adults is not as crucial to the shaping of a sense of self as is the negative attention that comes from peers. While one male reported that he preferred to believe the comments of his grandmother's friends, since they offered some validation, virtually all respondents noted that the positive attention from adults was less important to them than was the negative attention from peers.

It is apparent that the labeling of redheads does have an impact on redheads, especially as children and adolescents. The common forms of this impact included a lowered level of self-confidence, a sense of being different, and a sense of being the center of attention. A few of our respondents would initially offer their opinion that red hair had not had an impact on their sense of self; nevertheless, virtually all of them referred to some of these effects.

Even though, in some ways, the stereotypes of redheaded males would appear to be more threatening to their conceptualization of self, males were more likely to suggest overtly that being redheaded had not shaped them and then proceed to explicitly and implicitly offer considerable evidence that it had indeed shaped their sense of self. This ambiguity was expressed by a 20-year-old male:

> When I was young, a lot of kids would tease me and might have referred to my hair once or twice, but I don't remember my hair being an issue. I got a lot of compliments from adults. . . . I was self-conscious about my hair because I think I noticed that not many people had red hair. I guess I was a little embarrassed about it. . . . I am proud to be a redhead even though I'm still unsure what it means to some people . . . the freakishness and uniqueness.

Perhaps this tendency is rooted in the fact that males are simply less likely to define themselves and to be defined by others in terms of their appearance than are females. Thus, all of the redheaded women in this sample, even though subject to perhaps more benign cultural designations, immediately pinpointed hair color as the source of their negative experiences and more easily discussed the topic. For example, as a 20-year-old female put it, "I thought everybody hated me because I had red hair. If there is any reason they disliked me, it was the red hair." She then quickly identified red hair as the source of her childhood and adolescent angst (i.e., in her case, insecurity and total lack of self-confidence). In short, while both redheaded males and females appear to be molded by hair, females were more willing to identify hair as the causal variable.

LOWERED SELF-ESTEEM

Cooley (1902) proposed that our notions of self are grounded in our imagination of our appearance in the eyes of others, our imagination of their judgment of that appearance, and the self-feelings that result. Kaplan (1975, p. 37) explains the relationship between self-esteem and deviance as follows:

> The relevant literature is in general agreement with the propositions that an individual will tend to develop negative self-attitudes if he has, in

balance, a history of perceiving and interpreting the behavior of highly valued others toward him as expressive of negative attitudes toward him in general or toward personally valued aspects of him.

Negative treatment does not exist in a vacuum; clearly, the perception of self is shaped by such treatment. One common experience that redheads reported was that of a lowered sense of self-esteem. As children and as adolescents, the redheads in this sample typically experienced heightened insecurity and lack of confidence. Consider the following statement by one of the young men in our sample:

> It's a bad thing to have red hair when you are a little kid. It definitely affected the way I wanted to be seeing myself because I wanted to make it known that I didn't care what people thought about my red hair. . . . My mom also has red hair. She would say, "Oh, it's the most beautiful thing in the world. You should be so thankful that you have what no one else has," and I would say, "But I don't like it because everyone makes fun of me." It definitely made me feel self-conscious to have red hair.

As a young female put it, regarding her own sense of self, "When my friends called me 'carrot top,' I always felt really inferior to them. Like they were looking down on me. I never thought I could be equal to them." When discussing her lowered sense of self-esteem, another female analyzed the situation as follows:

> I feel dorky, especially next to a blonde. Going back to the beach thing, you feel not so feminine. You feel so ugly, and that goes along with TV commercials. It's totally defaming to redheaded women, the boobs, the tan, the blonde hair, the bikinis. You don't feel normal. If you are a redhead, you don't like to put a bathing suit on. That's because of our society. It's unfortunate. How many times have I been told you're pasty white or on the beach and a guy says look at that redhead. Not once. You hear derogatory comments. It's horrible.

The self-esteem problems were severe. Commenting on the attractiveness of his lower face, and comparing his face to John F. Kennedy, Jr., a red-headed male stated, "It's amazing how red hair and beady eyes can destroy things." A 26-year-old male admitted that, as a child and as an adolescent, he felt different from the blondes and brunettes, and, in fact, he felt singled out. Reflecting on his youth, he remembers that he had extraordinarily low self-confidence and was constantly upset about his hair. He felt that these problems resulted from the comments of his peers—comments that badly hurt his feelings. For example, he remembers a kid who taunted him by saying that all redheaded people were ugly. He realizes that the children and adolescents who made his life difficult did not mean any harm, but it was still a very serious issue for him as an adult. A 36-year-old female reported that her hair definitely contributed to her lack of self-confidence; in fact, she feels that her insecurity was primarily attributable to her hair color. So much did her color distort her perceptions, that she felt very upset when her daughter was born with red hair, as she wanted to shield her daughter from what she had experienced. Indeed, she recalls trying to persuade her daughter to wear make-up (i.e., to lessen the impact of red hair on the presentation of self) at an early age when many parents are still trying to prevent their daughters from wearing make-up. This is an example of what Goffman (1963, p. 44) called a disidentifier: "a sign that tends—in fact or hope—to break up an otherwise coherent picture but in this case in a positive direction desired by the actor, not so much establishing a new claim as throwing severe doubt on the validity of the virtual one." All in all, the general feeling among our redheads was perhaps best summarized by a young male when he stated, "You live for so long with being unique and freakish. You're a little outside of social norms. You're forced to be independent. I was self-conscious about my hair. I felt insecure in social situations." Thus, a lack of self-confidence and greater insecurity seems to be a fairly typical pattern among the redheads interviewed in this sample.

Feelings of Differentness

Another way in which the redheads in this sample seemed to be affected by their hair color is a profound sense of being different from other people. This sense of difference was quite significant in that it permeated their sense of self. A young male reported, "It probably made me feel a little outcasted." A young female added, "The positive responses made me feel good but the negative ones hurt me and made me feel different. The negative ones were worse because they came from my peers." Describing this sense of differentness, a 20-year-old female assessed the situation in the following manner:

> I definitely felt different. Not a blonde or brunette, not the average; awkward, kind of pale, no eyelashes, maybe even a little albino. . . . No, I always hated it. I just wanted blonde hair or brown hair. I always thought redheads were kind of feeble. . . . Adults seemed to appreciate the color. My peers made me feel different. I didn't like it. If you're not comfortable with something and you feel a little different, someone takes notice of you; as a child you feel as though you're different. As far as appearances go, that's pretty crucial. As a child you believe your peers more. Negative feelings tend to mean more than positive feelings.

A 21-year-old female suggested that, as a child and adolescent, she had a strong sense of being different, but, as an adult, she just has a feeling that she doesn't blend in with other adults. Another female stated the issue precisely: "It's a different experience." A 21-year-old female with an identical twin sister observed that she always stood out and people would always look at them. Besides producing a childhood desire to have blonde or brown hair, she felt that other children made her feel different. During the previous year, when her sister visited her and they went out for an evening's entertainment, she remembered "standing out like a sore thumb . . . feeling like a freak show. I stand out. I always have."

According to a young male, "Redheads know that they are unusual, so if you see another redhead, you know they are not run of the mill . . . not like everyone else, but exotic." One female reported that this sense of differentness causes her to shun other redheads (aside from family members). Her desire to avoid other redheads is caused by the perception that she can feel more "normal" or less different if she is with the normatively hair-colored people in society. As a male respondent put it, "Red hair is a quality that makes them different—albeit in a relatively innocuous way." The treatment of redheads by others is "conspicuously condescending," and normal people speak to redheads as "something other." In essence, redheads face life feeling that we are "singled out, even when we are not. Being aware of your difference—a different experience. . . . Is Hamlet more human due to his hyper-self-consciousness, or is he a jerk?" In some respects, this sense of difference can even become a self-fulfilling prophecy in that some redheads eventually aspire to be different in other ways. As a young male noted,

> It makes you different, but I pride myself on being different. . . . I stood out so they always noticed me. I like to keep people on their toes. I'll wear a skirt to class. I like to see people's reactions. I enjoy the attention for the recognition of being a big obnoxious guy. I don't know why.

One female respondent admitted that red hair makes her feel different; she is aware that she is "just not like everyone else." Consequently, she often wants to be different in other ways, and this tendency manifests itself in her proclivity to argue the opposite point of view when she is having a discussion with someone, even if it is not what she believes to be the case. This tendency to "jump on the other side, always," results from her sense of being different than other people. A sense of differentness dominates the lives of redheads.

Redheads as the Center of Attention

Goffman (1963, p. 16) commented on the obtrusive quality of stigma among those whose deviance is obvious:

> When the stigmatized person's failing can be perceived by our merely directing attention (typically, visual) to him—when, in short, he is a discredited, not discreditable, person—he is likely to feel that to be present among normals nakedly exposes him to invasions of privacy, experienced most pointedly perhaps when children simply stare at him.

One way in which redheads typically feel shaped by hair color is a sense of being the undisputed center of attention, even if that is not desired. The obtrusive quality of their hair is quite evident; redheads perceive that others unduly place them in the spotlight. As an 11-year-old female stated, "I don't like red hair. It's too bright and sticks out." Because it sticks out, redheads feel that they receive too much attention. A 22-year-old female described the experience in the following manner:

> Attention I've received has been both negative and positive. It definitely brings you attention. Maybe that's what I don't like. I don't really like people to notice me. I think redheads stand out. People always refer to me as the girl with the red hair. I think you are self-conscious because you are different.

One female college student expressed ambivalent feelings about her perception that professors directed far more attention to her. She is convinced that this attention stems from her hair color. While some disliked this attention, others seemed to gravitate toward it, and they attempted to turn this focus into a positive aspect of life. As a female stated, "People like my hair, and I like the attention." Another female noted that the attention became so important to her that she did not like to share it. She said, "We like to be in the spotlight. I like to be the center of attention. I like to be the only redhead." Elaborating on this experience, a young male added:

> *I've received a lot of attention because of my hair and that's another aspect of my personality. I crave attention and if you have red hair you can't get around it. . . . I dyed my hair black—I looked for green and purple. I wanted something that was going to be really offensive. I dyed half of it. I enjoyed not having red hair for a couple of months, but when I got my red hair back, I felt a lot more like myself.*

Unavoidably, red hair provides the individual with a great deal of attention. While some disliked the focus, others liked it. Either way, the attention thrust upon them shaped their sense of self.

THE TRANSFORMATION OF SELF

Another important experience that seemed fairly common among redheads was the transformation of a profoundly negative situation as a child and adolescent into a far more positive situation as an adult. For some of our respondents, this transition occurred during late adolescence; for most of our respondents, it transpired during adulthood. In any event, this process is paradoxical. That characteristic which made them subject to negative treatment early in life comes to be appreciated, to be an essential part of the identity of a typical redhead, and a source of some of their positive feelings about themselves. Kitsuse (1980) advanced the notion that, in addition to the deviant career trajectory of the "oversocialized" primary deviant turning into the secondary deviant, tertiary deviance is another potential outcome. As Kitsuse (1980, p. 9) put it, tertiary deviance refers to "the deviant's confrontation, assessment, and rejection of the negative identity imbedded in secondary deviance, and the transformation of that identity into a positive and viable self-conception." While activism defines this particular response, adult redheads (usually secondary deviants in their younger years due to the reaction of their peers) transform the negative into the positive, thereby realizing at least the underlying notion of tertiary deviance.

A 36-year-old female eptomizes this fairly typical transition. She observed that her childhood and adolescence were painful due to her red hair, but, as an adult, she is far more comfortable with her hair and even likes it. For her, there is irony in the fact that while many in our society define red hair as unattractive, in a "strange way," she views it as attractive, and there is even a certain glamour attached to it, which is embodied in such famous movie stars as Rita Hayworth and Ann Margaret. When she was young, she always wished that, "some day, she would go from ugly duckling to swan."

This metaphor is perhaps the best description of the trajectory for many redheads. The redheads in our sample did not explicitly define what produces this metamorphosis; nevertheless, the experience was typical. Perhaps, it can be explained by the fact that children are more concerned with conformity while adults are more concerned with individuality. A young male stated, "I guess as I got older, I really enjoyed it more, while you are vulnerable as a child." A young female added, "It was really a dramatic change. . . . Now that I'm older things are even more positive." A 22-year-old female concurs:

> *When I got to college, I really liked having red hair. I finally learned how to take a compliment. Now I definitely have more confidence. Before, I would walk with my head down, and now I'm almost proud of the fact that I have red hair— because we are so different. I've learned to accept it and be proud of it.*

Suggesting that this transformation occurred in high school, a 20-year-old male noted, "It's something I can take great pride in. I guess that's all I can say. I wouldn't want my hair to be any other color. When I was ten, I would have given any amount to have brown hair." Another male, who described a painful childhood and adolescence, realizes that he is now comfortable with his hair, as it is a part of himself and a part of his identity. In fact, he surprised himself when, upon hearing of the birth of a redheaded baby, he said, "The baby is blessed with red hair." He never thought the day would come when he would perceive red hair to be a blessing. Thus, red hair typically comes to be defined as an asset—a transition that is rarely expected during one's youth.

To summarize, in the early part of their lives, redheads are often subject to positive treatment from adults but negative treatment from their peers. This bifurcated treatment makes for a lowered self-esteem, a pronounced sense of being different, and a feeling of being the center of attention. As adults, however, redheads come to accept their hair color and even appreciate how it has shaped them.

CONCLUSION

In this paper, we have shown how labeling theory can account for the treatment of red hair and redheads. What is more, the study of red hair helps us to understand deviance and construction of self-identity. The redheads we interviewed were aware of their stigmatization in society, were perceptive concerning what they believed to be societal stereotypes, and were quite conversant with the labeling of red hair. The stereotypes of redheads (which they often internalize) include a flaring temper, clownishness, weirdness, Irish ethnicity, a need to avoid the sun, sexy women, wimpy men, and intellectual superiority. Labeling theory also helps us to examine the impact of labeling on those who are labeled. The redheads we interviewed were aware that the labeling process had shaped their identity in various ways. Redheads tend to receive negative treatment, especially from their peers during their youth. Consequently, they experienced lowered self-esteem, feelings of differentness, and the sense that they were a constant center of attention. As adults, the redheads we interviewed transformed their sense of self by developing an appreciation for their red hair, especially for the way it contributes to their individuality.

Future research could expand on this study by examining the labeling that is applied to other hair colors. For example, how do the stereotypes of blondes—which according to Cooper (1971,

pp. 75–77) have included innocence, sexiness, and stupidity—affect blonde women? How are individuals who purposefully dye their hair flamboyant colors (such as purple, green, or for that matter, *red*) expressing their sense of identity, and how does societal reaction to such hair colors affect those who choose them? In a society that defines youth as a standard aspect of beauty, how are individuals whose hair has turned gray affected by their hair? Further research could also examine other factors related to hair. For example, how do bald (and balding) men deal with the presentation of self in a society that obviously values a full head of hair? With regard to hair texture, how are African-American women affected by their hair when dominant definitions of attractiveness promote racially exclusive definitions of attractive hair? These questions suggest that hair is an important part of the relationship between "appearance and the self" (Stone 1962).

REFERENCES

Alexander, James M., and John W. Schouten. 1989. "Hair Style Changes and Transition Markers." *Sociology and Social Research* 74:58–62.

Becker, Howard. 1963. *Outsiders*. New York: The Free Press of Glencoe.

Benson, Peter L., Stuart A. Karabenick, and Richard M. Lerner. 1976. "Pretty Pleases: The Effects of Physical Attractiveness, Race, and Sex on Receiving Help." *Journal of Experimental Social Psychology* 12:408–416.

Berscheid, Ellen, and Elaine Walster. 1974. "Physical Attractiveness." Pp. 157–215 in L. Berkowitz (ed.), *Advances in Experimental Social Psychology VII*. New York: Academic Press.

Birenbaum, Arnold, and Edward Sagarin. 1976. *Norms and Human Behavior*. New York: Praeger.

Byrne, Donn. 1971. *The Attraction Paradigm*. New York: Academic Press.

Cahill, Spencer E. 1989. "Fashioning Males and Females: Appearance Management and the Social Reproduction of Gender." *Symbolic Interaction* 12:281–298.

Cooley, Charles Horton. 1902. *Human Nature and the Social Order*. New York: Charles Scribner's Sons.

Cooper, Wendy. 1971. *Hair: Sex, Society, and Symbolism.* New York: Stein and Day.

Dion, Karen K. 1972. "Physical Attractiveness and Evaluation of Children's Transgressions." *Journal of Personality and Social Psychology* 24:207–213.

Dion, Karen, Ellen Berscheid, and Elaine Walster. 1972. "What Is Beautiful Is Good." *Journal of Personality and Social Psychology* 24:285–290.

Erikson, Kai T. 1964. "Notes on the Sociology of Deviance." Pp. 9–20 in H. Becker (ed.), *The Other Side.* New York: The Free Press.

Feinman, Saul, and George W. Gill. 1978. "Sex Differences in Physical Attractiveness Preferences." *The Journal of Social Psychology* 105:43–52.

Gillespie, David F., and Ronald W. Perry. 1973. "Research Strategies for Studying the Acceptance of Artistic Creativity." *Sociology and Social Research* 58:48–52.

Goffman, Erving. 1963. *Stigma: Notes on the Management of Spoiled Identity.* Upper Saddle River, NJ: Prentice Hall.

Hatfield, Elaine, and Susan Sprecher. 1986. *Mirror, Mirror . . . The Importance of Looks in Everyday Life.* Albany: State University of New York Press.

Kaplan, Howard B. 1975. *Self Attitudes and Deviant Behavior.* Pacific Palisades, CA: Goodyear Publishing.

Kitsuse, John. 1980. "Coming Out All Over: Deviants and the Politics of Social Problems." *Social Problems* 28:1–13.

Krebs, Dennis, and Allen A. Adinolfi. 1975. "Physical Attractiveness, Social Relations, and Personality Style." *Journal of Personality and Social Psychology* 9:247–256.

Landy, David, and Harold Sigall. 1974. "Beauty as Talent: Task Evaluation as a Function of the Performer's Physical Attractiveness." *Journal of Personality and Social Psychology* 31:245–253.

Lemert, Edwin M. 1972. *Human Deviance, Social Problems, and Social Control.* Englewood Cliffs, NJ: Prentice-Hall.

Meyerowitz, Joel. 1991. *Redheads.* New York: Rizzoli International Publications.

Morse, Stanley T., Harry T. Reis, Joan Gruzen, and Ellen Wolff. 1974. "The Eye of the Beholder: Determinants of Physical Attractiveness Judgments in the United States and South Africa." *Journal of Personality* 42:528–541.

Nachmias, Chava-Frankfort, and David Nachmias. 1996. *Research Methods in the Social Sciences,* 5th ed. New York: St. Martin's Press.

Reis, Harry T., Ladd Wheeler, and John Nezlik. 1980. "Physical Attractiveness in Social Interaction." *Journal of Personality and Social Psychology* 38:604–617.

Reis, Harry T., Ladd Wheeler, Nancy Spiegel, Michael H. Kerns, John Nezlik, and Michael Perry. 1982. "Physical Attractiveness in Social Interaction II: Why Does Appearance Affect Social Experiences?" *Journal of Personality and Social Psychology* 43:979–996.

Schur, Edwin M. 1971. *Labeling Deviant Behavior.* New York: Harper and Row.

Schur, Edwin M. 1983. *Labeling Women Deviant.* Philadelphia: Temple University Press.

Spradley, James P. 1979. *The Ethnographic Interview.* New York: Holt, Rinehart and Winston.

Stone, Gregory P. 1962. "Appearance and the Self." Pp. 86–118 in A. M. Rose (ed.), *Human Behavior and Social Process.* Boston: Houghton Mifflin.

Synnot, Anthony. 1987. "Shame and Glory: A Sociology of Hair." *The British Journal of Sociology* 38: 381–413.

Tannenbaum, Frank. 1980. "The Dramatization of Evil." Pp. 244–248 in H. Traub and C. B. Little (eds.), *Theories of Deviance.* Itasca, IL. F. E. Peacock.

Wheelchair Users

SPENCER E. CAHILL and ROBIN EGGLESTON

Social interaction always takes place in specific social situations. Culture offers answers to questions on what to think and feel and what to say and do. People acquire definitions of these situations through the process of social learning. Through coaching, observation, and experience, they learn how to act with specific others. Included in the culture's collective definitions of situations are social constructions of deviant social types. These constructions make distinctions between people who violate legal, moral, or social norms. In general, the severity of sanctions, formal as well as informal, vary in accordance with the perceived seriousness and frequency of the offenses.

Unless people work in the institutions of social control, such as religion, law, or medicine, they are not likely to have had any personal contact with the more serious social deviants such as criminals or psychotics. Thus, any ideas they have about flagrant violators of legal or moral norms have come to them through conversations with friends or family, or from the major communications media. Depictions of deviant social types from these sources may consist of negative stereotypes. By contrast, one's chances of coming into contact with the everyday variety of deviants are much greater. Therefore the chances of interacting with people who regularly violate social norms about dress, adornment, beliefs, and appearances are much greater.

Spencer E. Cahill and Robin Eggleston's study of what happens when people in wheelchairs meet "walkers" in public places demonstrates the subjectively problematic character of the deviance process. Some define wheelchair users as burdens, nuisances, or people to be avoided. Others, including service workers, define them as people who need help. If some wheelchair users seek help, others seek to avoid the appearance of helplessness. Clearly, conflicts can exist between the parties to the interaction. As this article shows, under these conditions, trouble is to be expected when the hale and hearty meet the disabled.

Some years ago, Erving Goffman (1963b) introduced the concept of stigma into the study of social life. It has been our standard appellation for physical disabilities ever since—until, recently, that is. Students of social life can no longer casually describe persons with disabilities as stigmatized without fear of argument. The possible objections are varied.

Reprinted from Spencer Cahill and Robin Eggleston, "Reconsidering the Stigma of Physical Disability: Wheelchair Use and Public Kindness," *The Sociological Quarterly*, Vol. 36, No. 4, Fall 1995, pp. 681–698. Copyright © 1995 by The Midwest Sociological Society. Reprinted by permission of Blackwell Publishing.

First, it is arguable and has been argued (e.g., Murphy, Scheer, Murphy, and Mack 1988) that the concept of stigma is so inclusive as to be uninformative. Not only does Goffman (1963b, p. 4) lump individuals with all variety of physical disabilities, "blemishes of personal character," and despised tribal identities under the conceptual heading of the stigmatized. He also suggests that the only "unblushing American" is a "young, married, white, urban, northern, heterosexual Protestant father of college education, fully employed, of good complexion, weight and height, and a recent record in sports" (Goffman

1963b, p. 128). In comparison, Goffman implies that everyone else is at least periodically stigmatized. Analogies among the treatment of the widely disparate categories of people who fall short of that identificatory ideal may be instructive for some purposes, but they can also be misleading. There are undoubtedly revealing parallels between the treatment of persons with various disabilities, homosexuals, African Americans, women, lower-class white males, and others, but there are just as undoubtedly empirically and theoretically significant differences. The broadly inclusive concept of stigma can easily obscure those differences and blind students of social life to their significance.

Second, as Robert Bogdan and Steven Taylor (1989) argue, unquestioned acceptance of the stigmatization of people with disabilities draws attention to their social rejection and away from possible instances of social acceptance. Bogdan and Taylor readily concede that countless examples of social rejection are easily found. Yet, as they demonstrate, examples of the social acceptance of people with disabilities might also be found if students of social life would look for and seriously consider them rather than ignore and explain them away. Mixed contacts between so-called normals and individuals with disabilities may be far more varied and complex than our often lazy reliance on the concept of stigma implies. Goffman arguably bears at least some responsibility for such negligence. Although he (Goffman 1963b, p. 139) argues that "normal" and "stigmatized" refer to situated identities rather than categories of individuals, he quickly adds that lifelong attributes may cause an individual "to be type-cast . . . making it natural to refer to him, as I have done, as a stigmatized person." However natural it may be, referring to people with disabilities as stigmatized persons invites neglect of the situated complexity and variability of identity construction, preservation, spoilage, and restoration.

Finally, as Goffman (1963b, p. 137) suggests, an attribute can historically lose "much of its force as a stigma." That is arguably the case with some physical disabilities in recent American history. When Goffman first published *Stigma* in 1963, so-called "ugly laws" in American cities such as Chicago banned the "diseased, maimed, mutilated or in any way deformed" from public places (Kleinfield 1977, p. 35). Today, the widely publicized *Americans with Disabilities Act of 1990* requires that "public accommodations and commercial facilities" be "readily accessible to and usable by individuals with disabilities." Despite its many exemptions, vague language, and questionable provisions for enforcement, this federal statute arguably "symbolizes a change in cultural values toward" people with disabilities (Albrecht 1992, p. 95). So too may the recent inclusion of such people in commercial advertisements (Roberts and Miller 1992) and research indicating that high school and college students are now more likely to laud than demean persons with certain disabilities when responding to questionnaires (Schwartz 1988). There are clearly good reasons for students of social life to reconsider how we conceptually label and think about the social consequences of physical disability.

We undertake that reconsideration in this article using the empirical example of public wheelchair use. Our specific focus is "mixed contacts" in public places between individuals whose principle mode of mobility is a wheelchair and those whom they often call "walkers." Although Bogdan and Taylor (1987, p. 36) suggest that students of social life have "concentrated on rejection and stigma" because they have "mainly studied casual and impersonal interaction" between typical and atypical people, there are good theoretical reasons for such a focus. Sustained relations between typical and atypical people may be more varied and complex, as Bogdan and Taylor argue, but they tell us little about the more general place of people with disabilities in contemporary social life. In contrast, our various categories of individuals, now including wheelchair users, routinely intermingle in public places, expressing and reaffirming collective ideas and sentiments concerning one another (Cahill 1994). It is there that our collective rejection, acceptance, or, perhaps more ambivalent views of wheelchair users would most clearly tell.

Our approach to the study of wheelchair users' public contacts with walkers was suggested by Goffman (1971, p. 342 n. 5). As he advises, we undertake "the serious ethnographic task of assembling the various ways in which" wheelchair users are treated by and treat others "and deducing what is implied about" them "through this treatment." After briefly describing the empirical basis for our analysis of wheelchair users' public treatment, we review some previous characterizations of wheelchair users' relations in public. Although those characterizations compellingly capture the crueler side of wheelchair users' public lives, we argue that there is another, often kinder side. We then concentrate on this neglected facet of wheelchair users' public experiences: encounters in which uncommon assistance is required, requested, granted, or offered. We conclude by drawing some general lessons from our analysis of these encounters about the place of wheelchair users in contemporary social life and about the price they pay for social acceptance. Although wheelchair users' public treatment does not directly tell us about their fate in other social settings or about social reactions to persons with other disabilities, it does suggest that relations between typical and atypical people may be far more complex and ambiguous than the concepts "normal" and "stigmatized" suggest.

LEARNING ABOUT AND FROM WHEELCHAIR USERS

The empirical materials on which the following examination of wheelchair users' public experiences is based are varied and of varied evidential status. They include transcripts of twelve conversational interviews of wheelchair users that we collectively conducted and recorded. Although admittedly a convenience sample, we talked with as diverse a group of wheelchair users as possible. These informants included a preadolescent girl, six women, and five men. They ranged from 11 to 62 years of age, had been using a wheelchair in public places for as little as three months and for as long as fifty years, and had a variety of diagnosed medical conditions including cerebral palsy (2), multiple sclerosis (3), muscular dystrophy (1), traumatic brain injury (1), and paraplegia resulting from spinal cord injury (4) and viral infection (1). Our conversations with these informants lasted from one and a half to four hours and yielded 150 single-spaced pages of transcripts.[1]

We also draw upon two other sources of empirical information including field notes recorded during participant observation in public places. Although most of these were recorded by the second author who has used both an electrically powered and manual wheelchair in public places for a number of years, the first author also recorded some field notes while using a wheelchair in public places for the specific purpose of participant observation. This included excursions to shopping malls, forays down sidewalks, and a visit to a restaurant with the second author and another regular wheelchair user. In addition, we draw upon autobiographical accounts authored by wheelchair users. These include books (e.g., Callahan 1989; Murphy 1987), essays (e.g., Brightman 1985; Campling 1981; Dubus 1991), and brief anecdotes included in longer works (e.g., Kleinfield 1977; Maloff and Wood 1988).

We repeatedly reviewed and compared information from these varied empirical materials both during and after their collection in order to identify recurring themes and patterns. Although varied, these empirical materials are admittedly limited to wheelchair users' descriptions of their public experiences. In that sense, the following analysis is written from the perspective of wheelchair users. However, we also deduce what is implied about wheelchair users through how they treat and are treated by others in public. Thus, our analytic focus is not so much wheelchair users' definitions of their public experience but social definitions of wheelchair users. Those definitions reside not in people's minds but in the interactional traffic between wheelchair users and those whom they encounter in public places. Our concern is interactional traffic and its definitional implications.

NONPERSONS AND OPEN PERSONS

The concepts of deviance (Davis 1961), stigma (Goffman 1963b), and, more recently, liminality (Murphy 1987; Murphy et al. 1988) have guided previous examinations of wheelchair users' relations in public. These guiding concepts have drawn attention to the darker side of wheelchair users' public treatment. Two general types of experiences have drawn the most attention: nonperson treatment and infringements of privacy rights.

In its more benign form, nonperson treatment involves acting as if another were not there at all, "an object not worthy of a glance" (Goffman 1963a, p. 83). Robert Murphy and his colleagues (1988, p. 239) suggest that this is a common experience of wheelchair users in public places: "All users of wheelchairs know that when they are in public places, they are commonly noticed by everyone and acknowledged by nobody." One of our informants did report being subjected to such treatment in a department store:

> It was a young kid . . . in the men's department. He saw me coming. He starts vigorously folding shirts that didn't need folding just so he wouldn't have to wait on me. He took a shirt, and he burst it, and he'd fold it up again. . . . So I just sort of stayed in the area, but after a while it was obvious that he didn't want to approach me.

However, this informant also readily admitted that this was an exceptional experience.

Such nonperson treatment was neither our informants' nor our own usual experience when using a wheelchair in public places. Although not unknown, neither were intrusive stares, contrary to Goffman's (1963a, p. 86) earlier claim that "in our own American society . . . we know that one of the great trials of the physically handicapped is that in public places they will be openly stared at." With the notable exception of curious young

children and an occasional gawker of more advanced age, what our informants and we commonly received from strangers was what they commonly give one another: civil inattention. In a sense, the recipient of civil inattention—a glance followed by the immediate withdrawal of visual attention (Goffman 1963a, p. 84)—is noticed but unacknowledged. But this is the usual fate of not only wheelchair users but almost everyone who frequents public places. It is also usually a welcome fate indicating that we are not targets of strangers' special curiosity or design.

A less benign form of nonperson treatment and a reportedly more common experience of wheelchair users in public places is to be "talked past and talked about as though absent" (Goffman 1979, p. 5). Many of our informants complained about being subjected to such treatment by the personnel of commercial establishments:

> You go to a restaurant, and you're with your able-bodied friends, and the waitress says "What will she have?" And like I've gone to a restaurant and they don't know where to put you. They make such a big deal out of it. They even talk right in front of me, about me as if I'm not there. "Well, where are we gonna put her?"
>
> We'll be shopping for food, and Sue will be in front of me. And we'll be getting the food checked out on the register, and I'll have the money. And they'll turn to Sue for the money, and Sue will point to me. I'll give them the money. They'll give her the change.
>
> Salespeople are—if I'm alone—salespeople treat me very well. If there's someone else with me often they'll assume that other person is an attendant, and that they must deal with that person, which I don't like very much.

As these complaints suggest and the final one highlights, wheelchair users are most commonly subjected to such nonperson treatment when in the company of walking companions. We will return to this issue in another context.

Ironically, others not only reportedly treat wheelchair users in public places as though absent but also take conversational advantage of their obvious presence. That is, they treat them as open persons who can be addressed at will (Goffman 1963a, p.126). Common warrants for such uninvited conversational overtures include technical interest in the operation of a wheelchair or some other equipment and financial interest in their cost:

> *Another thing that people tend to ask me about is that they see me out near the van, and they'll stop me when I'm getting in my van and [say] "Well gee, where did you get this?" Or "how much did it cost?" No one would stop you and ask you how much your car cost. But they feel like they can stop me and ask me how much my lift or my chair or whatever cost.*

This woman apparently considered such uninvited inquiries as encroachments on what Goffman (1971, pp. 38–40) terms her conversational and informational preserves. She clearly did not think that she had the same control as the first author, who does not regularly use a wheelchair, over who can summon her into talk or over facts about herself and her expenditures.

Another common warrant for individuals' uninvited and sometimes unwelcome conversational overtures to unacquainted wheelchair users in public is what Carol Brooks Gardner (1992, p. 204) aptly terms "kinship claims." Such claims are a standard means by which strangers "establish their rights to breach silence, establish address rights, and ratify talk with others by means of suggesting affiliation." However, as Gardner (1992, p. 210) and a number of our informants note, others' claimed kinship with wheelchair users is often based on very slim grounds.[2]

> *I've had people who try to relate to you by telling you their mother was in a chair or "my aunt used to use a chair."*
>
> *I've been sitting at a card store and have somebody just come and start talking to me. "Oh gee, my mother uses a chair." "My cousin uses a chair."*

Gardner (1992, pp. 216–222) reports that individuals with disabilities sometimes take advantage of the conversational advantages taken with them to "educate the public." Nonetheless, others' often shaky claims of kinship with wheelchair users clearly abridge their right to be let alone when in public.

There are also occasions when strangers treat wheelchair users' very presence in a wheelchair or in public as remarkable. For example, Cheryl Davis (1987) reports that one morning on the subway a fellow woman passenger unceremoniously informed her that "you're much too pretty to be in a wheelchair." Although apparently intended as a compliment, the implication was that an attractive young woman did not belong "in a wheelchair." At other times, strangers heartily congratulate wheelchair users for simply being in a public place. One of our informants reports that upon passing a woman with whom she was unacquainted on her way to the bathroom in a bar the woman pointed a thumb skyward and remarked: "Hey, more power to you." Similarly, strangers, especially more elderly ones, have boldly announced to the second author: "I think you're wonderful." Their only apparent reason for wonder was her public use of a wheelchair.

Thus, wheelchair users are often treated as incomplete and "in-valid" (Zola 1982) persons in public places. They often are not recipients of the same deference that unacquainted individuals commonly give to one another (Goffman [1956] 1982). Like children (Cahill 1990), they are sometimes treated as though absent and in the next moment as open persons with limited rights to public privacy. That is one side of their public lives, but there is another about which our informants talked at length. Andre Dubus (1991, p. 144), who has used a wheelchair since being injured in a traffic accident, poignantly describes this somewhat brighter side of wheelchair users' public lives: "Again and again, for nearly two years, my body has drawn sudden tenderness from men and women I have seen for only those moments in their lives when they helped me with their hands or their whole bodies or only their eyes and lips and tongues." This is the side of wheelchair users' public lives from which the guiding concepts of deviance, stigma, and liminality divert attention.

OBJECTS OF PUBLIC KINDNESS

Graciously or ungraciously dealing with nonperson treatment and uninvited conversational overtures may be the least of the challenges wheelchair users face when in public places. Neither the natural nor built environment is particularly friendly to the mechanical operation or human piloting of wheelchairs. For the wheelchair user, mud, snow, steps, curbs, and heavy doors are more than minor inconveniences. Merchandise on either high or low shelves is hopelessly out of reach. Then there are the challenges posed by a less than cooperative body. Because of these special challenges, wheelchair users sometimes require and perhaps even more often receive uncommon assistance from others when in public places. That is the focus of what follows: public encounters between wheelchair users and others in which uncommon assistance is requested, granted, or offered. From the perspective of wheelchair users, these encounters may involve three distinct types of people. They may be categorically known, knowing, or unknown (to borrow and do a bit of violence to Lofland's [1973] typology of public actors).

THE CATEGORICALLY KNOWN

Categorically known individuals are those whose situated role is immediately apparent from their clothing or microecological position. Common examples include waiters and waitresses, salesclerks, and security officers. Those who occupy such immediately apparent public roles are expected to assist customers or those in obvious need, but the service sometimes required by wheelchair users goes beyond what is expected. Perhaps that is why the occasional salesclerk will studiously ignore a patiently waiting customer in a wheelchair and why restaurant personnel will sometimes engage in the kind of staging talk (Goffman 1959, pp. 175–176) in the immediate presence of a wheelchair user that is usually conducted beyond the hearing of clientele. They do not know what will be expected of them or did not expect what is. Yet no matter how memorable, such nonperson treatment was neither our informants' nor our own usual experience in public contacts with categorically known others.

A few of our informants even claimed that their use of a wheelchair was an advantage in obtaining fast and courteous service in public places:

> *You can walk into places, and you can't find anybody to help you or find anything. But, it's almost as if you're not going to get caught ignoring someone in a wheelchair. So [salesclerks] have been real nice.*
>
> *[Salesclerks are] usually good. It was like before I got sick they were like icky. Now, they treat me like a person.*

Another sixty-year-old wheelchair user reported that the exceptional service she requires when grocery shopping allows her to obtain exceptional merchandise.

> *And, you know one of my tricks. I go to one of the fellas that are working in produce, and I say, "Would you mind picking me a head of lettuce or a bunch of broccoli?" And they'll look all over, and I'll say, "Be sure it's a good one."*

There are, then, compensations for the occasional nonperson treatment to which categorically known providers of public services sometimes subject wheelchair users.

Although often gladly provided, the unusual public service that wheelchair users sometimes require is just as often provided clumsily. Our experience when patronizing a restaurant with another wheelchair user is one example.

> *As we wheeled into the restaurant, we were cheerfully greeted by the hostess who inquired, "lunch?" I answered in the affirmative and added that "there are three of us, and we're all using chairs." She did not blink. Yet, rather than first going to a*

table and removing the chairs, she motioned for us to follow and immediately led us to a table. While we waited, she noisily removed chairs from around the table drawing the discomforting attention of the surrounding diners. She then informed us that "your waitress will be with you shortly" and walked back to the entrance. As we wheeled to the table, we realized that we were all lined up on one side of this long rectangular table facing the wall. So as to achieve a more conversationally comfortable seating arrangement, we struggled to move the remaining chairs away from the ends of the table and rearrange the place settings, drawing discomforting attention to ourselves once again.

The service that we received was unquestionably courteous but also unquestionably made us the center of embarrassing attention.

One of our informants was the recipient of even more embarrassing attention at another restaurant. Upon arriving with friends at the restaurant that she had been told was accessible to wheelchair users, she found four or five steep steps leading up to the entrance. The apologetic manager immediately recruited five members of the kitchen staff to help him carry her and her heavy, electrically powered wheelchair up the steps and into the restaurant. She was grateful for this exceptional service but embarrassed by all the attention nonetheless. In her words, "I get embarrassed when people make too much of a fuss over me." And categorically known providers of public services often make much more of a fuss over wheelchair users' special needs than necessary.

In addition, their clumsy provision of the special public services that wheelchair users sometimes require can be physically as well as emotionally painful. A thirty-nine-year-old quadriplegic told Sonny Kleinfield (1977, p. 141) of the following incident at a department store where he had gone to shop for a ski jacket.

This salesman tried putting it on me like my arm was made of rubber. So I started yelling, "Hey, what the hell are you doing. That's an arm there, buddy, not a sausage." The man dropped the jacket and broke out into this profuse sweat.

Like this salesman, many categorically known providers of public services kindly offer to assist wheelchair users only to find that they are not capable of delivering what they have implicitly promised, or at least not very well.[3]

Although perhaps not as maddening as wheelchair users' occasional experience of non-person treatment, these more common experiences with the categorically known are no less frustrating. The wheelchair user must sometimes finish what the provider of a service started, give extensive directions, attempt to relieve his or her discomfort, and may still be left in the lurch as was the second author when shopping for athletic shoes.

My friend and I were browsing in the store, and the salesman, who was wearing one of those referee shirts, kept asking if he could help us. While my friend continued to browse, I attempted to try on a pair of shoes. I was struggling quite a bit and for some time before he asked: "Would you like me to help you?" I answered, "Yes, that would be helpful." So he came over and began to unlace the shoes. He had a shoe cradled in his hand, and I was trying to help him put my foot in the shoe when it apparently dawned on him that he had to guide my foot into the shoe because I was not able to do so. As if waking from a sleep, he suddenly said, "I'd rather not do this." I said, "That's okay. You're not hurting me, and if you are I'll tell you." He said, "No, no. That's all right. We'll wait for your friend. I'd feel more comfortable if we waited for your friend."

This introduces the second category of persons upon whom wheelchair users rely for assistance in meeting the challenges of participating in public life. Wheelchair users who frequent public places quickly learn that the kindness of categorically known providers of public services has a price and definite limits. So as to avoid paying that embarrassing and occasionally painful price or testing those limits, wheelchair users often frequent public places in the company of those whom they personally know.

THE KNOWING

Goffman (1963b, p. 28) used the term "wise" to refer to those "who are normal but whose special situation has made them intimately privy to the secret life of the stigmatized individual and sympathetic to it." In a similar vein, we refer to walking friends or family members who are aware of, sympathetic with, and prepared to deal with the needs and public plight of a wheelchair user as the "knowing." As Fred Davis (1961, p. 129) and others have documented (e.g., Fisher and Galler 1988), acquiring such wisdom is often an arduous and interpersonally taxing process for both the student and her or his wheelchair-using instructor. One of our informants volunteered the following example.

> I got into this big argument with Ellen. You know we go shopping together, and she can't resist pushing me. And it pisses me off. . . . I finally had to have this talk with her and say, "Look Ellen, when I need your help believe me I will ask you in a second. But if I don't ask you, please let me do it myself." And she got kind of huffy, but then I said to her, "You know you'd react the same way." And she said, "I know."

Despite such difficulties, once instructed and experienced in providing the wheelchair user the help he or she needs (or does not need), knowing friends and family members can provide a ready fund of assistance upon which the wheelchair user can draw when in public places.

Knowing public companions can therefore insulate wheelchair users from potentially uncomfortable public encounters with both categorically known and unknown strangers. Practiced in the arts of assisting the wheelchair user, they can ease her foot into a shoe or his chair over a curb without comment or embarrassing fanfare. Wheelchair users whose arms or hands are uncooperative especially welcome knowing dinner companions at restaurants. The wheelchair user need not limit her or his choices to dishes with bite-size ingredients or request that his or her order be specially prepared. When ordering a dish that must be cut into bite-size portions, knowing companions will nonchalantly do so without attracting attention, as those of one of our informants and of the second author often do.

For wheelchair users, there is much to recommend participating in public life as part of what Goffman (1971, p. 19) calls a "with" that includes at least one knowing companion. There are also good reasons for not doing so. As previously mentioned, wheelchair users are more likely to be subjected to nonperson treatment when accompanied by walking companions than when alone. Apparently uncertain of what to expect or what is expected of them, categorically known providers of public services tend to turn to those whom they consider of their own kind for advice. For example, at a restaurant one evening, one of our informants and his wife had been waiting some time for a table when the hostess approached and informed him, "Your table is ready." She then turned to his wife and asked, "Will he be getting out of the chair?" If he had been alone, the hostess would have had little choice but to ask him directly.

Knowing companions are also known to exacerbate the public discomfort of wheelchair users by creating more of a fuss over such slights than the wheelchair user would prefer. For example, one of our informant's male companions insisted on making a dramatic exit from a restaurant after some confusion over where "to put her" and being asked, "What would she like?"

> He was so frustrated by the whole thing, and he said, "We're out of here." I said, "Don't make an issue out of it." "The issue's made. We're out of here." Got my purse, got my coat, and we started to leave. We had the manager on our coat tails, "What happened?" And I think that's more embarrassing.

As Goffman (1963b, p. 131) observes, "by always being ready to carry a burden that is not 'really' theirs," the wise, or knowing, "can confront everyone else with too much morality," causing discomfort to everyone present. And, like our informant's male companion, they may thereby add to wheel-chair users' already substantial public burden. When knowing companions' kindness turns into moral outrage, the wheelchair user is as much the center of embarrassing attention as when the less knowing dramatically or clumsily attempt to provide exceptional service.

THE UNKNOWN

Whether accompanied by knowing companions in public places or not, wheelchair users sometimes desire or require and are often willing but sometimes unwilling recipients of assistance from those whom they neither personally nor categorically know. Wheelchair users have little choice but to seek help from total strangers when alone in public and there is no one whose apparent role involves the provision of whatever assistance they may need. Even when accompanied by knowing companions, wheelchair users may occasionally require assistance that their companions cannot adequately provide without help. And strangers often offer their services to wheelchair users when not requested, sometimes when their help is neither desired nor welcomed.

Most of the assistance that wheelchair users require of or receive from strangers in public places qualifies as what Goffman (1963a, p. 127) calls the "satisfaction of free needs." The wheelchair user is in patent need of help, and this "help is of little moment to the putative giver." Perhaps the most common examples of these free needs are help in opening a door, in getting over a curb, and in procuring items that are out of reach. In our society, as Goffman (1963a, p. 130) observes and wheelchair users are apparently aware, "bonds between unacquainted persons are felt to be strong enough to support the satisfying of 'free needs,' even where the person receiving the service is the one who initiates the encounter that makes it possible." Our informants reported regularly initiating such encounters by requesting assistance from strangers.

Some of our informants were more forward than others in requesting assistance from strangers

in public. The approach of a forty-year-old male paraplegic was unique though reportedly effective: "I go, 'Whoa, you with the biceps. I need to go there. Come on, come on. Impress your girlfriend.' Works every time. It's machismo." Other informants reported carefully selecting the particular strangers from whom they requested assistance. In the words of a fifty-five-year-old woman who had used a wheelchair for fifty years, "I certainly do [pick whom I ask]. Someone who just has a pleasant expression." And many reported that they felt compelled to offer apologies and accounts (Goffman 1971) for even minor impositions upon strangers' good will.

> I can't reach the ground from my chair so if I drop something, I have to ask somebody to pick it up or something. "I'm so sorry." Or if I'm in the grocery store and I need something, and I ask someone to get it. "Oh thank you. I'm sorry to bother you."
>
> I find myself making excuses. Saying things like, "Oh, it's just not been my day. I just can't seem to reach anything. It seems everything I want is up."

Yet, as one of our informants remarked, "It's so funny, because people would bend over backwards to help you."

That was both our own and our informants' usual experience. When asked, the overwhelming majority of strangers are more than willing to satisfy wheelchair users' "free needs." The experience of one of our male informants is typical:

> I stopped at a store, and the curb was about that high [holding up his hands about six inches apart]. I could never get across so I just waited outside the door until a muscular gentleman came out, and I asked him whether he would help me over the curb which he did very nicely. So people are invariably very good about helping when requested.

Another of our informants who regularly travels the streets of a small city in her electrically powered wheelchair occasionally has leg spasms that cause one of her feet to slip off the footrest of her wheelchair. When this occurs, she waves to passing motorists to stop and asks for their help in getting her foot back upon the footrest. "And I have had nothing but positive results with people stopping to help."

Indeed, many strangers with whom wheelchair users come into contact in public places are "very good about helping" even when it is not requested. As one of our informants reported, "People often come running from quite some distance to open the door." In addition to opening doors, our informants reported that strangers have volunteered to wait in queues on their behalf, to fold and load their wheelchair into their car or van, and to perform a variety of other services.

Sometimes these voluntary offers of aid are less voluntary than the grantor realizes. Well aware of strangers' kindness, wheelchair users sometimes rely on what Gardner (1986, p. 54) terms "mute petitions" rather than direct requests for desired aid thereby avoiding the varied risks of initiating a conversational encounter with a stranger. One of our male informants told of this example:

> I was going to the mall the other day, and I was having a bad day. I get a pain in this leg, and it was really bothering me. So, I was wheeling up to the mall, and I didn't feel like opening the door— I could, but I didn't feel like hassling with it. And I could see this woman's reflection in the door coming up behind me. So, I slow down so she could catch up to me, and I reach for the door having no intention of opening it, and she says, "Can I help you sir?" And she opens the door.

With such mute petitions or requests, wheelchair users need not apologize for or excuse their needy circumstance but merely thank their benefactor for what he or she believes to be an unsolicited act of public kindness.

As at least some wheelchair users have discovered, the cup of public kindness can be practically bottomless. One of our informants learned this at a restaurant bar one evening:

> I had to go to the bathroom, and I was with three guys. And I had to go bad. It wasn't accessible.

> Usually I can do it if there's something I can hold on to, but not with this one. So, two women helped me I didn't even know. They go, "Well, honey we'll help you." They were drinking. They were about fifty. I was more embarrassed than anything.

And once a wheelchair user finds how full the cup of public kindness can be, he or she may heartily drink from it as did a wheelchair user whom Robert Duke (1988, p. 13) encountered on the streets of New York City. After granting this stranger's request to be pushed a few blocks to a store, Duke agreed to take the man to a nearby public bathroom.

> I pointed him toward the handicapped stall.
> "Not in there," he said. "I can use the urinal."
> "How do we do this?"
> "Take down my pants," he said. He helped me as much as he could to shed his clothes and pull his reluctant body upright. At last we made it into position with his armpits resting on my elbows.

As these two examples illustrate, walking strangers sometimes satisfy and wheelchair users occasionally ask them to satisfy needs that seem anything but "free."

Some bold wheelchair users tax helpful strangers' physical capacities rather than their sense of propriety. For example, one of our male informants honeymooned in Niagara Falls and was able to convince five male strangers to carry him down and back up over one hundred steps so that he could ride the well-known sight-seeing boat that travels near the falls. The depth of public kindness toward strangers in wheelchairs on which this informant drew may not be as rare as previous characterizations of wheelchair users' public treatment would seem to suggest. For example, Ed Long (1985), who uses an electrically powered wheelchair because of muscular dystrophy, writes that he decided to take his female companion to dinner in Greenwich Village after witnessing an acquaintance successfully impose on strangers to carry him and his wheelchair down two flights of stairs leading from a street to the subway station below. Despite the popular image of New Yorkers, Long had little difficulty getting strangers to carry him and his chair up and down stairs leading from street to subway until he and his companion returned to their point of departure. No one was around because of the late hour so he and his companion finally requested help from a security guard who was not pleased about the imposition. He lectured Long (1985, p. 89), "You don't belong down here. I don't ever want to see you down here again." As Long learned, the unknown may be far more willing to help a wheelchair user than those who are categorically known to protect and serve the public.

Yet, strangers who bend over backwards to help wheelchair users in public places sometimes bend wheelchair users over backwards in the process. One of our informants attributed such public manhandling of wheelchair users to a "bizarre mindset that somehow the wheelchair is like a fish tank." He illustrated what he meant by telling us of an incident that occurred at the Los Angeles airport after he and an acquaintance who also uses a wheelchair decided to take an escalator. Although experienced in maneuvering a wheelchair on and off escalators, they wheeled into trouble at the top of this particular one.

> *Larry missed and went sideways, and I broke my stride. And when I tried to go, I hit into the step, and the chair lurched forward, and I went flying out of the wheelchair. I landed right smack on my stomach. So, there was a father and two sons. And without a word, all three of them, one took me underneath, one took me by the middle, and the other took my legs. And they threw me into the chair head first, upside down with my head leaning over the back. And all I could think of was like you kicked over the fish bowl. And your guppies are on the floor, and you fling them back in. And they did it, and they were real proud.*

Categorically known providers of public services are clearly not the only walkers who clumsily attempt to help wheelchair users.

This is only one of wheelchair users' complaints about the kindness shown to them by strangers in public places. Helpful strangers have also been known to bend wheelchairs (as well as those who use them) out of shape.

> *At a car wash, the attendant offered to help me put my wheelchair into the car. The chair is easy to fold if you know how, but she didn't listen to my instructions. She just started pulling parts off the chair, really making mincemeat of it, trying to fit it into the car. It took quite a while for me to put it together again later. (Maloff and Wood 1988, p. 8)*

And, as one of our informants reported, even when helpful strangers do not make mincemeat of a wheelchair while voluntarily loading it into its user's car, they commonly take far longer to do so than its more experienced user would. Similarly, helpful strangers sometimes cost users of wheelchairs and other mobility enhancing devices valuable energy as well as time. One of our informants who uses what is commonly known as a walker rather than his wheelchair when shopping told us of a particularly telling example.

> *I was in the drug store, and I got on my knees. I didn't fall. I was looking at some stuff [on the bottom shelf]. This guy came over and picked me up. He grabbed me and yanked me. I got kinda upset. I said, "I know you're trying to help, but I just got down there."*

It would seem that some animate walkers think the inanimate variety is as much like a fish bowl as a wheelchair.

In any case, the public kindness of strangers can be quite unkind to wheelchair users, especially when unexpected. One of our informants told of just how painful it can be:

> *I mean ask me, "can I help you?" That doesn't bother me. But just don't latch onto the back of the chair. I've been hurt. It jams your—I mean you're pushing it a certain level. You've got your hands on the chair, and they start pushing, and I've jammed my fingers. You know, you end up getting hurt rather than being helped.*

And walking strangers who rush to the aid of wheelchair users in public places without asking or being asked probably end up hurting more feelings than fingers.

In Gardner's (1986, pp. 54–55) terms, such overly helpful strangers respond to the very use of a wheelchair in public as an "implied petition" for aid, and, as Gardner notes, "implied petitioning is rife with opportunities for misjudgment." Solicitous strangers may find that they have judged wheelchair users less competent than those wheelchair users want to be considered or consider themselves. Resentment is the usual result, as it was in the following encounter between one of our informants and a helpful stranger:

> I sometimes drive for my groceries, and there was a fellow who followed me around the store and wanted to help me get things off the shelf. Then, when I went out to the car—I hang my grocery bags on the handles of my wheelchair—and I was taking them off, and at the same time he was trying to help me take the grocery bags off. I told him I didn't want his help, and we were having a kind of wrestling match there trying to see who could get my grocery bags off and load them into the trunk of the car. I told him several times that I really did not need his help—that I liked to do things for myself, but he just would not listen.

It is not just wheelchair users whose feelings get hurt by overly helpful strangers. If the wheelchair user protests, the feelings of their self-appointed benefactor may be injured as well. Instead of feeling the warm glow of having helped a fellow human in need, they may be hit with a hot flash of embarrassment mixed with anger.

THE WAGES OF PUBLIC KINDNESS

Public places and those who populate them seem more accepting of wheelchair users than the more common focus on deviance and stigma suggests. Wheelchair users are unquestionably disregarded and treated disrespectfully in public places, but that is only part of the story of their public lives. Categorically known providers of public services often graciously offer and provide wheelchair users uncommon services. Well-known and knowing companions often smooth the way for wheelchair users' participation in public life and "with" them publicly demonstrate that wheelchair users are worthy of companionship (Goffman 1971, p. 21). Perhaps even more impressive are the solicited and unsolicited acts of public kindness with which total strangers shower wheelchair users. Along with Bogdan and Taylor (1987; 1989), wheelchair users' public experiences argue for a consideration of acceptance as well as rejection in studies of relations between typical and atypical people.

The picture of wheelchair users' public acceptance can be overdrawn, however. Categorically known providers of public services may offer wheelchair users more than they ultimately will or can deliver, at least with ease. Knowing companions may either divert too much attention from or draw too much attention to wheelchair users. And, to a large extent, wheelchair users are at the mercy of others' good will when in public places because of the unfriendliness of the built environment to their mode of mobility. Our public places may now be more accessible to and those who populate them more accepting of wheelchair users than in the recent past, but wheelchair users are still made to feel like visitors who are dependent on the graciousness of their walking hosts. They consequently pay for their public acceptance.

In addition to occasional pain, squandered time, and wasted energy, the price wheelchair users commonly pay for the public kindness on which they must sometimes depend is what Candace Clark (1990, p. 306) calls "place." As she explains, place refers to microlevel positions like follower and leader that are "to everyday interaction what social status is to social structure." We would add that those microlevel positions include the "places" of petitioner, benefactor, and beneficiary of public aid. These are places that are often occupied in public encounters between wheelchair users and those who walk. Every time wheelchair users request assistance, they mark their place as subordinately dependent petitioners. Every time walkers offer or grant a wheelchair user assistance, they mark their place as superordinately capable and gracious benefactors. Every time wheelchair users accept such assistance, they mark their place as subordinately grateful beneficiaries. Like status symbols, these "place markers" (Clark 1990, p. 310) are expressions of relative social rank. So too are the acts of unsolicited and sometimes unwelcome assistance that strangers impose on wheelchair users in public places. They are also what Clark (1990, p. 314) calls "place claims" that put wheelchair users in what their self-appointed benefactors consider their proper place. All these fleeting, little diminishments of place may seem a small price for wheelchair users to pay for public acceptance and kindness, but their total cost can be substantial.

Yet the heavy interactional investment that wheelchair users must make for the return of public kindness and acceptance does not recommend conceptually characterizing wheelchair use as a stigma or the social identity of their users as spoiled. Although public wheelchair use sometimes evokes "negative and punitive responses" (Susman 1994, p. 16), those responses arguably result from uncertainty and thoughtlessness rather than disdain. Perhaps others can be fairly accused of sometimes ineffectually denying or disavowing obvious differences between their own and wheelchair users' mode of mobility and public position (Davis 1961; Goffman 1963b, pp. 121–123) but not on those many occasions when they offer and provide wheelchair users uncommon assistance. By giving assistance, they acknowledge and practically avow the obvious difference between their own and wheelchair users' physical abilities. And that acknowledgement and avowal is not without risk.

Individuals who offer or honor wheelchair users' requests for uncommon assistance hazard their own as well as the wheelchair user's place and face (Goffman [1955] 1982). They implicitly claim that they are capable of providing the offered or requested assistance. Yet, they sometimes find

themselves unable to do so competently and [find] themselves, consequently, both in the "wrong face" (Goffman [1955] 1982, p. 8) and in a suddenly diminished place. Similarly, individuals who implicitly claim the elevated place of benefactor by providing unsolicited assistance to a wheelchair user may find themselves put in the lowly place of an insensitive cad by the intended beneficiary. Thus, walkers may approach public encounters with wheelchair users with trepidation not because they consider the wheelchair users' identity spoiled but because they fear spoiling their own.

BEYOND THE STIGMA OF DISABILITY

The public treatment of wheelchair users clearly illustrates that negative and positive responses to persons with disabilities are not mutually exclusive alternatives, as is sometimes implied (e.g., Susman 1994). Wheelchair users' experiences in public places teach us that social relations are not always easily classified as positive or negative, accepting or rejecting, kind or cruel. Relations between wheelchair users and those whom they encounter in public places are all these and more. Wheelchair users' place in contemporary social life is far more uncertain and unsettled than the designation "stigmatized person" suggests.

The more recent characterization of wheelchair users as liminal seems more fitting but only if carefully circumscribed. Murphy and his colleagues (1988) argue that because wheelchair users are "betwixt and between" the socially defined states of sickness and health they occupy the kind of twilight zone of social indefinition that Arnold van Gennep ([1909] 1960) and Victor Turner ([1964] 1979) term "liminality" Although a case could be made that wheelchair users' shifting place in public life is symptomatic of such social indefinition, we must be more conceptually careful with the expression "liminality" than we have been with the expression "stigma." Like stigma, as Goffman argues but as both he and others largely ignore, liminality is not a characteristic of people but of social situations.

According to Turner (1987, p. 34), liminality is a phase in the recurrent dramas of social life. Although his primary concern is dramatic conflicts between groups and inconsistent cultural principles, he acknowledges the similarity between such collective dramas and the kind of interpersonal dramas of everyday social life on which Goffman focuses attention (Turner 1987, p. 107). The kind of social drama on which Goffman (1963b, p. 2) focuses attention in *Stigma* concerns definitional conflicts between virtual social identities—those we expect individuals in particular social settings to possess—and actual social identities—those that individuals "could in fact be proved to possess." This kind of social drama unquestionably punctuates wheelchair users' public lives.

Like anyone who ventures into public places, a wheelchair user's mere presence in such a setting effectively projects an implicit claim to the virtual social identity of competent public actor—a person who sustains certain standards of conduct and deserves corresponding respect and regard (Cahill 1995, p. 258). Whenever others subject wheelchair users to nonperson treatment, infringements of privacy rights, or unsolicited and unwanted assistance, they place them in an identity that is incompatible with the virtual identity of competent public actor. Wheelchair users consequently find themselves betwixt and between identities in a kind of twilight zone of social indefinition. Yet, such liminality is not permanent. Its resolution depends on what Turner (1987, p. 34) calls the "redressive or remedial procedures" that follow. The wheelchair user may effectively reclaim the identity of competent public actor and perhaps, in the process, place her or his tormentor into the actual social identity of insensitive cad. On the other hand, the wheelchair user may temporarily submit to the stigmatized role into which others have cast him or her.

Liminality is also a consequence of wheelchair users' common requests for uncommon public assistance. Although often necessitated by the unfriendliness of public settings to their mode of mobility, wheelchair users who request such assistance risk their claim to the identity of competently self-sufficient public actor. Yet, those requests are commonly accompanied and followed by ritual interchanges (Goffman 1971, pp. 95–187) of apologies, accounts, gracious provision of assistance, and expressions of gratitude. Such ritual procedures quickly resolve the wheelchair users' momentary liminality or, in Gardner's (1986, p. 65) words, "out-of-role status." Thus, in public life at least, the issue is not so much whether wheelchair users are stigmatized, liminal, or normal but under what circumstances and how. Conceptually evading the situated complexity and variability of identity construction, preservation, spoilage, and restoration will not advance our understanding of wheelchair users' place in contemporary social life or that of persons with other disabilities.

We are not suggesting that wheelchair users' public treatment tells us much about their treatment in other settings or about the social place and definition of people with other disabilities. Rather, we are proposing that students of social life ethnographically study the various ways in which persons with different disabilities treat and are treated by others, deduce what is implied about them through this treatment, and then reconsider just how fitting our comfortably worn concepts are. Perhaps stigma, deviance, and liminality will still have a place in our descriptions of social reactions to and definitions of individuals with physical disabilities, but it may well be a more circumscribed place than in the past. At least the example of wheelchair users' public treatment suggests as much.

NOTES

1. We met our informants through a variety of personal contacts. Two are committed activists in the disability rights movement, two others are more reluctant activists, and the rest are not active in the movement. Seven were unemployed at the time of the interviews including the eleven-year-old girl who attends junior high school, a young woman who hopes to enroll in college in the near future, and another woman who plans on pursuing graduate studies. Three were retired, and one fifty-five-year-old woman had never been employed. Among the

employed were a social worker, state civil servant, college professor, self-employed entrepreneur, and hardware store clerk. Eight had bachelor's degrees and two of these had postgraduate degrees. Six had never been married, two were widowed, and four were currently married, including three of the men and one woman. The mean age of these informants was 39.7 years; the mean length of their public use of wheelchairs was 13.1 years.

2. Two of our male informants who used wheelchairs during the 1970s report that they were often misidentified as Vietnam veterans. This misidentification was often the basis for kinship claims from which they benefited. Veterans and other patriotic walkers regularly offered to buy them drinks and do other favors in recognition of their assumed kinship.

3. The second author recalls a harrowing experience on a New York City bus at the hands of an inept provider of public service. As is usual on city buses equipped for wheelchairs, the driver supposedly fastened the wheels of her chair to the floor of the bus. Yet, when the bus started to move, she and her chair went rolling down the aisle in the opposite direction.

REFERENCES

Albrecht, Gary. 1992. *The Disability Business.* Newbury Park, CA: Sage.

Americans with Disabilities Act of 1990. Public Law 101-336. 101st Congress, 993 sess., July 26, 1990.

Bogdan, Robert, and Steven Taylor. 1987. "Toward a Sociology of Acceptance: The Other Side of the Study of Deviance." *Social Policy* 18 (Fall):34–39.

———. 1989. "Relationships with Severely Disabled People: The Social Construction of Humanness." *Social Problems* 36:135–148.

Brightman, Alan (ed.). 1985. *Ordinary Moments: The Disabled Experience.* Syracuse, NY: Human Policy Press.

Cahill, Spencer. 1990. "Childhood and Public Life: Reaffirming Biographical Divisions." *Social Problems* 37:390–402.

———. 1994. "Following Goffman Following Durkheim into the Public Realm." Pp. 3–17 in S. Cahill and L. Lofland (eds.), *The Community of the Streets.* Greenwich, CT: JAI Press.

———. 1995. "Embarrassability and Public Civility." Pp. 253–271 in M. Flaherty and C. Ellis (eds.), *Social Perspectives on Emotion,* Vol. 3. Greenwich, CT: JAI Press.

Callahan, John. 1989. *Don't Worry, He Won't Get Far on Foot.* New York: Random House.

Campling, Jo (ed.). 1981. *Images of Ourselves: Women with Disabilities Talking.* London: Routledge and Kegan Paul.

Clark, Candace. 1990. "Emotions and Micropolitics in Everyday Life: Some Patterns and Paradoxes of 'Place.' " Pp. 305–333 in T. Kemper (ed.), *Research Agendas in the Sociology of Emotions.* Albany: State University of New York Press.

Davis, Cheryl. 1987. "Day on Wheels." *Progressive* 51 (November): 34.

Davis, Fred. 1961. "Deviance Disavowal: The Management of Strained Interaction by the Visibly Handicapped." *Social Problems* 9:121–132.

Dubus, Andre. 1991. *Broken Vessels.* Boston: Godine.

Duke, Robert. 1988. "Whose Good Deed?" *New York Times Magazine,* July 10, 12–13.

Fisher, Bernice, and Roberta Galler. 1988. "Friendship and Fairness: How Disability Affects Friendships between Women." Pp. 172–194 in M. Fine and A. Asch (eds.), *Women with Disabilities.* Philadelphia: Temple University Press.

Gardner, Carol Brooks. 1986. "Public Aid." *Urban Life* 15:37–69.

———. 1992. "Kinship Claims: Affiliation and the Disclosure of Stigma in Public Places." Pp. 203–228 in J. Holstein and G. Miller (eds.), *Perspectives on Social Problems,* Volume 4. Greenwich, CT: JAI Press.

Gennep, Arnold van. [1909] 1960. *The Rites of Passage.* Chicago: University of Chicago Press.

Goffman, Erving. [1955] 1982. "On Face Work." Pp. 5–45 in *Interaction Ritual.* New York: Random House.

———. [1956] 1982. "The Nature of Deference and Demeanor." Pp. 47–95 in *Interaction Ritual.* New York: Random House.

———. 1959. *The Presentation of Self in Everyday Life.* Garden City, NY: Doubleday.

———. 1963a. *Behavior in Public Places.* New York: Free Press.

———. 1963b. *Stigma.* Upper Saddle River, NJ: Prentice-Hall.

———. 1971. *Relations in Public.* New York: Basic.

———. 1979. *Gender Advertisements.* New York: Harper and Row.

Kleinfield, Sonny. 1977. *The Hidden Minority: America's Handicapped.* Boston: Little, Brown.

Lofland, Lyn. 1973. *A World of Strangers.* New York: Basic.

Long, Ed. 1985. "Riding the Iron Worm." Pp. 79–98 in Alan Brightman (ed.), *Ordinary Moments.* Syracuse, NY: Human Policy Press.

Maloff, Chalda, and Susan Macduff Wood. 1988. *Business and Social Etiquette with Disabled People.* Springfield, IL: Charles Thomas.

Murphy, Robert. 1987. *The Body Silent.* New York: Henry Holt.

Murphy, Robert, Jessica Scheer, Yolanda Murphy, and Robert Mack. 1988. "Physical Disability and Social Liminality: A Study in the Rituals of Adversity." *Social Science and Medicine* 26:235–242.

Roberts, Elizabeth, and Annetta Miller. 1992. "This Ad's for You: Madison Ave. Discovers Disabled Consumers." *Newsweek,* February 24, 40.

Schwartz, Howard. 1988. "Further Thoughts on a 'Sociology of Acceptance' for Disabled People." *Social Policy* 19 (Fall):36–39.

Susman, Joan. 1994. "Disability, Stigma and Deviance." *Social Science and Medicine* 38:15–22.

Turner, Victor. [1964] 1979. "Betwixt and Between: The Liminal Period in *Rites de Passage.*" Pp. 234–243 in W. Lessa and E. Vogt (eds.), *Reader in Comparative Religion.* 4th ed. New York: Harper and Row.

———. 1987. *The Anthropology of Performance.* New York: PAJ Publications.

Zola, Irving. 1982. *Missing Pieces: A Chronicle of Living with a Disability.* Philadelphia: Temple University Press.

CHAPTER 2

THE CULTURAL CONTEXT

Labeling the Mentally Retarded

JANE R. MERCER

Two viewpoints seem to prevail when it comes to thinking about deviance. Laymen, as well as students of the subject, blame deviant behavior either on the person or on the social environment. The medical model locates the sources of deviance in characteristics of the person. A number of sociological theories of deviant behavior locate the sources of deviance in the characteristics of people's social environments. The interactionist perspective can combine both viewpoints by arguing that deviance turns out to be the result of transactions between an individual and persons in the individual's social environment.

The interactionist perspective focuses on the official constructions of deviance that are current in different social situations, the agents of control who apply those constructions, and the responses of those who are implicated in these labels of deviance. Jane R. Mercer compares and contrasts the ways in which high-status and low-status families respond to their children if they have a low "IQ." The findings lend support to the "relativity of deviance" generalization. Thus, some families suspect that a child is "different" and seek confirmation of their suspicions from specialists. Others perceive that agents of control are imposing an official definition of deviance. These are less likely than the first set of families to accept the official construction.

The clinical perspective is the frame of reference most commonly adopted in studies of mental deficiency, mental illness, drug addiction, and other areas which the students of deviance choose to investigate.[1,2] This viewpoint is readily identified by several distinguishing characteristics.

Reprinted from Jane Mercer, "Social System Perspective and Clinical Perspective: Frames of Reference for Understanding Career Patterns of Persons Labelled as Mentally Retarded," *Social Problems*, Vol. 13, No. 1: 18–34. © 1965, The Society for the Study of Social Problems, Inc. Used by permission of the University of California Press and the author. All rights reserved.

First, the investigator accepts as the focus for study those individuals who have been labeled deviant. In so doing, he adopts the values of whatever social system has defined the person as deviant and assumes that its judgments are the valid measure of deviance. . . . Groups in the social structure sharing the values of the core culture tend to accept the labels attached as a consequence of the application of these values without serious questioning. . . .

A second distinguishing characteristic of the clinical perspective is the tendency to perceive deviance as an attribute of the person, as a meaning inherent in his behavior, appearance, or performance. Mental retardation, for example, is viewed as a characteristic of the person, a lack to be explained. This viewpoint results in a quest for etiology. Thus, the clinical perspective is essentially a medical frame of reference, for it sees deviance as individual pathology requiring diagnostic classification and etiological analysis for the purpose of determining proper treatment procedures and probable prognosis.

Three additional characteristics of the clinical perspective are the development of a diagnostic nomenclature, the creation of diagnostic instruments, and the professionalization of the diagnostic function.

When the investigator begins his research with the diagnostic designations assigned by official defining agents, he tends to assume that all individuals placed in a given category are essentially equivalent in respect to their deviance. . . . Individuals assigned to different categories of deviance are compared with each other or with a "normal" population consisting of persons who, for whatever reason, have escaped being labeled. The focus is on the individual.

Another characteristic of the clinical perspective is its assumption that the official definition is somehow the "right" definition. . . .

Finally, when deviance is perceived as individual pathology, social action tends to center upon changing the individual or, that failing, removing him from participation in society. Prevention and cure become the primary social goals. . . .

The social system [labeling] perspective, on the other hand, attempts to see the definition of an individual's behavior as a function of the values of the social system within which he is being evaluated. The professional definers are studied as one of the most important of the evaluating social systems but within the context of other social systems which may or may not concur with official definitions.

Defining an individual as mentally ill, delinquent, or mentally retarded is viewed as an interpersonal process in which the definer makes a value judgment about the behavior of the persons being defined. . . . Deviation is not seen as a characteristic of the individual or as a meaning inherent in his behavior, but as a socially derived label which may be attached to his behavior by some social systems and not by others.[3]

. . . Thus, it follows that a person may be mentally retarded in one system and not mentally retarded in another. He may change his label by changing his social group. This viewpoint frees us from the necessity of seeing the person as permanently stigmatized by a deviant label and makes it possible to understand otherwise obscure patterns in the life careers of individuals. . . . The research reported in this paper attempts to answer these questions about a group of persons who shared the common experience of having been labeled retarded by official defining agencies and placed in a public institution for the retarded. . . .

The specific question which this study seeks to investigate within the above framework is: "Why do the families of some individuals take them back home after a period of institutionalization in a hospital for the retarded while other families do not, when, according to official evaluations, these individuals show similar degrees of deviance, that is, have comparable intelligence test scores, and are of equivalent age, sex, ethnic status, and length of hospitalization?". . .

METHOD

Two groups of labeled retardates were studied. One group consisted of patients who had been released to their families from a state hospital for the retarded and the other group consisted of a matched group of patients still resident in the hospital at the time of the study.[4] . . .

FINDINGS

SOCIAL STATUS OF RELEASED PATIENTS

Several indices were used to measure the socioeconomic level of the family of each retardate. A socioeconomic index score based on the occupation and education of the head of the household, weighted according to Hollingshead's system, was used as the basic measure. In addition, the interviewer rated the economic status of the street on which the patient's home was located, rated the physical condition of the housing unit, and completed a checklist of equipment present in the household.... [T]he families of the released patients rated significantly lower than the families of the resident patients on every measure. The heads of the households in the families of released patients had less education and lower level jobs, the family residence was located among less affluent dwellings, the housing unit was in a poorer state of repair, and the dwelling was less elaborately furnished and equipped. Contrary to the pattern found in studies of those placed as mentally ill,[5] it is the "retardate" from lower socioeconomic background who is most likely to be released to his family while higher status "retardates" are more likely to remain in the hospital.

From the clinical perspective, several explanations may be proposed for these differences. It has been found in hospital populations that patients with an I.Q. below 50 are more likely to come from families which represent a cross-section of social levels, while those with an I.Q. between 50 and 70 are more likely to come from low status families.[6] Since persons with higher I.Q.'s have a higher probability of release, this could account for higher rates of release for low status persons. However, in the present study, the tested level of intelligence was equal for both groups, and this hypothesis cannot be used as an explanation.

A second possible explanation from a clinical perspective might be based on the fact that persons who have more physical handicaps tend to be institutionalized for longer periods of time than persons with few handicaps.[7] Should it be found that high status patients have more physical handicaps than low status patients, then this could account for the latter's shorter hospitalization. Data from the present sample were analyzed to determine whether there was a significant relationship between physical handicap and social status. Although released patients tended to have fewer physical handicaps than resident patients, this was irrespective of social status. When high status patients were compared with low status patients, 50% of the high status and 56% of the low status patients had no physical handicaps....

A third explanation from the clinical perspective may hinge on differences in the diagnostic categories to which retardates of different social status were assigned.... A diagnostic label of "familial" or "undifferentiated" ordinarily indicates that the individual has few or no physical stigmata and is essentially normal in body structure. All other categories ordinarily indicate that he has some type of physical symptomatology. Although released patients were more likely to be diagnosed as familial or undifferentiated than resident patients ... this, like physical handicap, was irrespective of social status. Fifty-seven per cent of the high status retardates and 69% of the low status retardates were classified as either undifferentiated or familial, a difference which could be accounted for by chance....

DIVERGENT DEFINITIONS

In analyzing social status, four types of situations were identified. The modal category for resident patients was high social status with a smaller number of resident patients coming from low status families. The modal category for released patients was low status with a smaller number of released patients coming from higher status families. If we are correct in our hypothesis (that higher release rates for low status patients are related to the fact that the family social system is structurally more distant from the core culture and that its style of life, values, and definitions of the patient are more divergent from official definitions than that of high status families), we could expect the largest differences to occur when high status resident families are compared to low status released families....

[T]hree questions [were] asked to determine the extent to which family members concurred in the official label of "retardation," the extent to which they believed the patient's condition amenable to change, and the extent to which they anticipated that the individual could live outside the hospital and, perhaps, fill adult roles. The patterns of the divergent definitions of the situation which emerged for each group are illuminating.

When asked whether *he* believed the patient to be retarded, the high status parent more frequently concurred with the definitions of the official defining agencies while the low status parent was more prone to disagree outright or to be uncertain. This tendency is especially marked when the two modal categories are compared. While 33.3% of the parents of the low status released patients stated that they did not think the patient was retarded and 25.6% were uncertain whether he was retarded, only 4.6% of the parents of high status resident patients felt he was not retarded and 20.9% were uncertain.

When parents were asked whether they believed anything could change the patient's condition, the differences between all groups were significant at the .02 level or beyond. The high status parent was most likely to believe that nothing could change his child's condition, and this was significantly more characteristic of parents whose children were still in the hospital than those who had taken their child from the hospital on both status levels.

When asked what they saw in the future for their child, all groups again differed significantly in the expected direction. The modal, high status group was least optimistic and the modal, low status group, most optimistic about the future. Fully 46% of the parents of the latter group expressed the expectation that their child would get a job, marry, and fulfill the usual adult roles while only 6.9% of the modal, high status group responded in this fashion. High status parents, as a group, more frequently see their child playing dependent roles. It is interesting to note that, although a large percentage of parents of released patients believe the patient will be dependent, they demonstrate their willingness to accept responsibility for the retarded child themselves by their responding that

they foresee him having a future in which he is dependent at home. Only 9.3% of the high status and 22.2% of the low status parents of the resident patients see this as a future prospect. Release to the family clearly appears to be contingent upon the willingness of the family to accept the patient's dependency, if they do not foresee him assuming independent adult roles.

FACTORS IN THE LABELING PROCESS

From the social system [labeling] perspective, retardation is viewed as a label placed upon an individual after someone has evaluated his behavior within a specific set of norms. Retardation is not a meaning necessarily inherent in the behavior of the individual. We have seen that the parents of low status, released patients tend to reject the label of retardation and to be optimistic about the future. We surmised that this divergent definition could well be related to factors in the process by which the child was first categorized as subnormal, such as his age at the time, the type of behavior which was used as a basis for making the evaluation, and the persons doing the labeling. Consequently, parents were asked specifically about these factors. . . .

Children from lower status families were labeled as mentally subnormal at a significantly later age than children from high status families. Seventy-nine per cent of the patients in the high status, modal group were classified as retarded by the age of six while only 36.1% of those in the low status, modal group were identified at such an early age. The largest percentage of low status retardates were first classified after they reached public school age. This indicates that relatives and friends, who are the individuals most likely to observe and evaluate the behavior of young children, seldom saw anything deviant in the early development of lower status children later labeled retarded, but that the primary groups of higher status children did perceive early deviation.

This is related to the responses made when parents were asked what first prompted someone to believe the patient retarded. The modal, high status group reported slow development in 48.8% of the cases and various types of physical symptoms in an additional 20.9%, while only 14.7% and 11.8% of the modal, low status parents gave these responses. On the other hand, 55.9% of the modal, low status group were first labeled because they had problems learning in school, while this was true of only 9.3% of the modal high status group.

When parents were asked who was the most important person influencing them in placing the child in the hospital, a parallel pattern emerged. Medical persons are the most important single group for the modal, high status persons while the police and welfare agencies loom very significant in 64.1% of the cases in the modal, low status group. These findings are similar to those of Hollingshead and Redlich in their study of paths to the hospital for the mentally ill.[8] Of additional interest is the fact that the person important in placement differentiates the low status released from the low status resident patient at the .01 level. The resident low status patient's path to the hospital is similar to that of the high status patient and markedly different from released low status persons. When authoritative figures such as police and welfare are primary forces in placement, the patient is more likely to return home.

We interpret these findings to mean that when the family—or persons whose advice is solicited by the family, i.e., medical persons—is "most important" in placing a person in a hospital for the retarded, the primary groups have themselves first defined the individual as a deviant and sought professional counsel. When their own suspicions are supported by official definitions, they are most likely to leave the patient in an institution.

Conversely, when a person is labeled retarded by an authoritative, government agency whose advice is not solicited and who, in the case of the police, may be perceived as a punishing agent, the family frequently rejects the official definition of the child as retarded and withdraws him from the institution at the first opportunity. This attitude was clearly exemplified by one mother who, when asked why the family had taken the child from the hospital, replied, "Why not? He had served his time."

The police [are more of] a factor in labeling the low status person as retarded. . . . Fifty per cent of the low status retardates had some type of police record while only 23% of the high status subnormals were known to the police. . . .

DISCUSSION AND CONCLUSIONS

The life space of the individual may be viewed as a vast network of interlocking social systems through which the person moves during the course of his lifetime. Those systems which exist close to one another in the social structure tend, because of overlapping memberships and frequent communication, to evolve similar patterns of norms. Most individuals are born and live out their lives in a relatively limited segment of this social network and tend to contact mainly social systems which share common norms. When an individual's contacts are restricted to a circumscribed segment of the structure, this gives some stability to the evaluations which are made of his behavior and to the labels which are attached to him.

However, when the person's life career takes him into segments of the social network which are located at a distance from his point of origin, as when a Mexican-American child enters the public school or a black child gets picked up by police, he is then judged by a new and different set of norms. Behavior which was perfectly acceptable in his primary social systems may now be judged as evidence of "mental retardation." At this point, he is caught up in the web of official definitions. However, because he has primary social systems which may not agree with these official labels, he may be able to return to that segment of the social structure which does not label him as deviant after he has fulfilled the minimal requirements of the official system. That is, he can drop out of school or he can "serve his time" in the state hospital and then go home. By changing his location in social space, he can change his label from "retarded" to "not much different from the rest of us." For example, the mother of a Mexican-American, male, adult patient who had been released from the hospital after being committed following an incident in which he allegedly made sexual advances to a young girl, told the author, "There is nothing wrong with Benny. He just can't read or write." Since the mother spoke only broken English, had no formal schooling, and could not read or write, Benny did not appear deviant to her. From her perspective, he didn't have anything wrong with him.

The child from a high status family has no such recourse. His primary social systems [labeling] lie structurally close to the official social systems and tend to concur on what is acceptable. Definitions of his subnormality appear early in his life and are more universal in all his social groups. He cannot escape the retarded label because all his associates agree that he is a deviant.[9]

In conclusion, tentative answers may be given to the three questions raised earlier in this discussion. "Who sees whom as retarded?" Within the social system [labeling] perspective, it becomes clear that persons who are clinically similar may be defined quite differently by their primary social systems. The person from lower status social systems is less likely to be perceived as mentally subnormal.

"What impact does this differential definition have on the life career of the person?" Apparently, these differential definitions do make a difference because the group which diverges most widely from official definitions is the group in which the most individuals are released from the institution to their families.

Finally, "What are the characteristics of the social systems which diverge most widely from official definitions?" These social systems seem to be characterized by low educational achievement, high levels of dependency, and high concentrations of ethnic minorities.

A social system perspective adds a useful dimension to the label "mental retardation" by its focus on the varied definitions which may be applied to behavior by different groups in society. For those interested in the care and treatment of persons officially labeled as mentally subnormal, it may be beneficial in some cases to seek systematically to relocate such individuals in the social structure in groups which will not define them as deviant. Rather than insisting that family members adopt official definitions of abnormality, we may frequently find it advisable to permit them to continue to view the patient within their own frame of reference and thus make it easier for them to accept him.

NOTES

1. August B. Hollingshead and Frederick C. Redlich, *Social Class and Mental Illness* (New York: John Wiley and Sons, 1958), Chapter 11.
2. H. E. Freeman and O. G. Simmons, "Social Class and Posthospital Performance Levels," *American Sociological Review* 2 (June 1959), p. 348.
3. Howard S. Becker (ed.), *The Other Side: Perspectives on Deviance* (New York: The Free Press, 1964).
4. Pacific State Hospital, Pomona, California, is a state-supported hospital for the mentally retarded with a population of approximately 3,000 patients.
5. Hollingshead and Redlich.
6. Georges Sabagh, Harvey F. Dingman, George Tarjan, and Stanley W. Wright, "Social Class and Ethnic Status of Patients Admitted to a State Hospital for the Retarded," *Pacific Sociological Review* 2 (Fall 1959), pp. 76–80.
7. G. Tarjan, S. W. Wright, M. Kramer, R. H. Person, Jr., and R. Morgan, "The Natural History of Mental Deficiency in a State Hospital. I: Probabilities of Release and Death by Age, Intelligence Quotients, and Diagnosis," *AMA J. Dis. Childr.* 96 (1958), pp. 64–70.
8. Hollingshead and Redlich.
9. Lewis Anthony Dexter, "On the Politics and Sociology of Stupidity in Our Society," in H. S. Becker (ed.), *The Other Side: Perspectives on Deviance* (New York: The Free Press, 1964), pp. 37–49.

Fecal Matters

MARTIN S. WEINBERG and COLIN J. WILLIAMS

Much deviant and/or criminal behavior occurs in public. Fighting, robbery, and shoplifting are examples. And most of these public behaviors will reflect the key element of the interactionist perspective on deviance—a transaction between self and others. When a person breaks legal, moral, and/or social rules, others will respond by labeling the actor as deviant. Most interactionist research focuses on the social conditions of the infraction and of the response. Through it all, the focus is on the actor and the social response.

In contrast to overt public acts, Martin Weinberg and Colin Williams examine the special case of private acts that become public. Their research is a good example of an analysis of deviance and the role of culture in everyday life. They ask what happens when defecation takes place when there is an audience? They find that what is ordinarily a simple act, which everyone engages in, can become a complex social matter. Variations in the actors and audience can produce significant differences in cultural meanings and, thus, the social outcomes.

Weinberg and Williams study the conditions of shame, embarrassment, and stigma a person might anticipate after a bowel movement becomes public (through loud noises, foul smells, clogged toilets, etc.). They found that heterosexual men and nonheterosexual women evince the least concern after exposure of their mishaps in toilet etiquette. On the other side of the gender and sexual identity divide, they found that heterosexual women and nonheterosexual men evinced the most concern. In each case, the nature of the audience and the anticipated social consequences influenced the degree of concern over the breach of modesty norms. For example, when the audience for heterosexual women was heterosexual men, anticipated concern increased. Here, the mismanagement of human waste called into question the cultural image of "attractiveness" they wished to maintain— of most salience as a concern when they wanted to develop a relationship with the man. The results of their study show how the cultural context, the gender and sexual identity of actors and audiences, and the nature of the social relationship shape concerns about deviance with regard to toilet matters.

. . . David Inglis (2000), [describes] the "faecal habitus" (hereafter spelled "fecal habitus") [as referring to what] . . . Western, bourgeois citizens embody as they go about correctly ridding themselves of fecal matter. Inglis (2000) sees the fecal habitus as comprised of two components. The first

Reprinted from Martin S. Weinberg and Colin J. Williams, "Fecal Matters," *Social Problems*, Aug 2005, Vol. 52, No. 3: 315–336. Reprinted by permission of the author.

component refers to a symbolic classificatory schema which variably evaluates excrement as "dirt" (both morally and hygienically). Certainly, excrement is assigned a highly emotional negative meaning in the contemporary U.S. The second component of the fecal habitus is a set of excretory practices based on such symbolic meaning. Three sets of practices exist. First are the ways in which defecation is carried out in socially acceptable ways in terms of time, location, and

use of receptacles. Second are sensory considerations and practices—those that reflect the
degree of emotional repugnance that exists for
the sounds, smells, and sights of defecation.
Third, and finally, there are verbal practices that
regulate the ways that excrement is to be named
and referred to (e.g., euphemisms and circumlo-
cutions). In general, defecation practices are
not considered a socially acceptable topic for
conversation.

Regarding the first set of practices, the habitus
enjoins that excretion should be carried out according to established times, locales, and receptacles.
Most important, it should be done in private (Kira
1967). In terms of the second and third sets, fecal
odors and sounds must also be minimized, and verbal practices must be circumspect. Thus, according
to Inglis (2000), "The imperatives of the bourgeois
faecal habitus are privacy, deodourization, and
euphemism"(pp. 53–54). Such a habitus acts
as a background against which shortcomings in
actual defecation practices are thrown into relief.
As such it provides a cultural template with regard
to which everyday social problems prevention
work is done.

Embodiment of the fecal habitus applies to
all persons. Our first task is to show how this
works in everyday life, how persons recognize the
habitus and honor its dictates. At the same time,
the fecal habitus exists in conjunction with various forms of embodiment, which gives us a second task—to examine how the habitus may be
modified to reflect such contingent phenomena.
We consider how the embodiment of social identity may play such a role. We look at two inter-
secting aspects of identity—gender and sexual
identity—and how they affect corporeal practices. In short, like Hazel Rose Markus, Patricia
R. Mullaly, and Shinobu Kitayama (1997), we see
selves as culturally specific, emerging as individuals learn and engage local cultures. Thus we
shall also ask: Is the fecal habitus differentially
experienced by men and women, heterosexuals
and non-heterosexuals? Does having different
embodied identities affect adherence to the fecal
habitus? And, if so, does this lead to greater or

lesser emotions of negative self regard? Our reasoning is based on the following.

With regard to gender, in Western societies,
emanations from the female body have long been
considered deviant and feared as a source of contamination. Menstruation has been a particular
concern so that much female embodiment stresses
practices that control "her bleeding and oozing
body" (Lee and Sasser-Coen 1996:16; also see
Fingerson 2001). Women's bowel movements,
however, may be more stigmatizing than their
menstruation. Compared to books on menstruation there is little published per se on women's
defecation other than to discuss it in the context of
modesty and the idealization of women as pure.
Sally R. Munt (1998) quotes Jonathan Swift's
1730 poem "The Lady's Dressing Room," which
satirically deals with the idea ". . . that women
don't shit . . ." (p. 201) as reflecting this idealized
view. The fear expressed is that women's fecal
odors may destroy male desire—with no mention
of men's odors destroying female desire (Miller
1997). Thus, we might expect that women's
embodiment of the fecal habitus will include a
heightened concern over controlling evidence of
their bowel movements—that given their physical
idealization the social cost will be greater. We
would expect this to be of even greater concern
when they are in the company of men.

The above reflects men's power in the gender
system which under most circumstances allows
for greater freedom of embodiment for men. This
is shown in cultural definitions of masculinity
that repudiate all that is associated with women
(Savin-Williams 2001). Thus bodily grossness
may be valued for its opposition to the manners
that femininity is thought to imply. The delight
taken in physical behaviors like burping can
indicate men's disdain for what they perceive as
feminine. Some men may adopt this form of
embodiment as an expression of their power over
women as they deliberately breach the habitus.
Such "strategic embarrassment" (Karp et al.
2004:294) is also used to socially control other
men who are seen to be straying from masculine
ideals (also see Lyman 2001).

Our argument represents an ideal case. Many men and women accept or reject the models of embodiment offered them or modify them in accordance with other identities—for example, status systems based on age, race, ethnicity and, our concern, sexual identity. By "sexual identity" we mean "the self-concept an individual organizes around . . . [a] predisposition typically labeled (in this culture) 'heterosexual,' 'gay,' 'lesbian,' or 'bisexual'" (Diamond 2003:352). Because sexual identity intersects with gender, we ask whether differences in men's and women's embodiment are the same among persons who do not define themselves as traditionally heterosexual (e.g., as gay, lesbian, bisexual). Specifically, do nonheterosexual women tend to scrutinize their body and bodily processes in the same way as straight women; do nonheterosexual men tend to be as blasé about bodily functions as straight men may be? Do any differences related to sexual identity affect the operation of the fecal habitus?

Recent work suggests that gay and lesbian embodiment is both conditioned by and resists the dominant culture. For example, Ritch Savin-Williams (2001) found that many gay men ". . . [are] repelled by . . . [straight men's] behavior, their standard of dress and cleanliness, and their barbarian nature" (p. 121). Moreover, Marc E. Mishkind, Judith Rodin, Lisa R. Silberstein, and Ruth H. Striegal-Moore (2001) say that gay subcultural norms place ". . . an elevated importance on all aspects of a man's physical self—body build, grooming, dress, [and] handsomeness" (p. 113). It seems that a new phenomenon, the "queer body"—muscled, buffed, and tanned—has become a widespread ideal among young gay men (Kiley 1998). According to Travis Kong Shiu-Ki (2004), having such a "fit" body is part of gay men's "embodied cultural capital" (p. 9). Many bisexual men are also to some extent involved in gay subcultures (Weinberg, Williams, and Pryor 1994) and may be similar to the gay men who reject certain aspects of "hegemonic masculinity" (Connell 2002:61–62). We would also note the importance of the anus as a receptive sexual orifice for some men who have sex with men. For

them, a self presentation that brackets fecal matters may be salient. We note, however, that diversity exists among men who have sex with men. For example, the influence of the metropolitan gay subculture may not reach all nonheterosexual men (see Brekhus 2003). And there is a diversity of gay subcultures that reject these subcultural themes of "gay embodiment," for example, those accepting the "bear" identity and "drag queens."

Nonheterosexual women also face images of lesbian embodiment but these tend to be unflattering (Creed 1999). One common stereotype depicts the lesbian body as "masculine," which can generate suspicion that many women athletes and a variety of masculine embodied women are lesbian (Blinde and Taub 1992). Failure to live up to heteronormativity, however, has not meant that lesbians necessarily avoid concerns about appearing attractive. Rather, Liahna Gordon (2005) has shown how participation in a lesbian subculture can foster a broader conception of attractiveness. These norms display resistance to appearance norms of the dominant culture. Weight, for example, is not as central a concern; nor is breast size or shape or indicants of disability or motherhood. In fact, these are sometimes redefined to produce an embodiment that offers alternative beauty ideals. Many bisexual women are involved in the lesbian subculture and may also adopt some of its themes (Weinberg et al. 1994), especially those that reject heterosexual embodiment. As in the case of nonheterosexual men, however, there also are nonheterosexual women who adopt a stereotypical traditional gender role.

A final consideration for the production of self-regarding emotions is the audience in whose eyes one's impression management succeeds or fails. The operation of the fecal habitus will thus be further mediated by the nature of the audience as the anticipation of deviant attributions may vary according to relational context. For example, in settings such as hospitals and old age homes, staff may be used to the "abject embodiment" of their patients so that loss of control over urination and defecation is ordinarily an unmarked event (Mitteness 1987; Waskul and van der Riet 2002).

Socio-emotional closeness may also affect reactions. Cleaning up the mess made by an aged and incontinent parent may be done with the same "suspension of disgust rules" (Miller 1997:132) as in attending to a newborn's messy diaper. Similarly, living in communal quarters that do not allow for privacy may provide a backdrop for the relaxation of the fecal habitus.

Though breaches of the fecal habitus can be downplayed through normalization and neutralization as noted above, there are also instances when such breaches are celebrated. These occur among young men in same sex settings, for example, pissing contests, lighting farts, farting contests. Attention to a breach of body boundaries is often sought to embarrass the offender and provide amusement to others. Or it can signify solidarity based on flouting authority or middle-class adult norms of propriety.

We examine the above topics and questions with our research. First we describe the nature of the study and those who participated in it. Then we discuss the embodied concerns study participants had with regard to fecal matters and their fears of being labeled deviant. We examine embarrassing and shameful experiences that ensued from breaches of the fecal habitus and the projection of incompatible selves. We consider the role of the various senses (sound, smell, and sight), the gender of the audience, and the role of the social relationship in providing a context for one's concerns. We look at social problem prevention work—the strategies used to avoid the awkward interactions that can result from being designated deviant in this way. And we look at how the intersection of one's gender and sexual identity may enter into these matters.

THE STUDY

Participants in the study are young adults in college who are at the stage of social life where they are particularly concerned with bodily issues. (A question we included in a poll of a representative sample of state residents showed that a concern with fecal matters was found more in such younger age groups.) Moreover, many of them live in public settings (e.g., dormitories, sororities) where toilet practices do not go unnoticed and are more or less accepted topics of conversation and occasions for humor. These factors may make students more reflexively aware of the fecal habitus. Whereas these living arrangements may provide a plus for a study that examines the operation of the habitus, it may compromise its representative character given that many persons may be less reflective of these matters.

The questions asked investigated their concerns and experiences surrounding fecal matters. One set of questions referred to the sound involved in having a bowel movement and asked how uncomfortable the study participants would feel if this sound was overheard by different people (e.g., a new date, a spouse/partner, a good friend, a work associate, a stranger). Where appropriate we varied the individuals posited in each relationship by gender (e.g., a woman who was a good friend, a man who was a good friend). Later, if the study participant noted differences in discomfort by gender and/or relationship, they were asked to describe what was involved in creating such a difference. We investigated their concern with the smell and sight of defecation and how their concerns were related to the particular sense involved. Additional questions referred to experiences they might have had in which the fecal habitus was cast into relief: namely, when their feces would not flush down the toilet, being flatulent in the presence of others, and having to use a public restroom to defecate. Inquiries were also made about the specific strategies employed with regard to the various senses to avoid breaching the fecal habitus.

BODY BETRAYAL AND PROXIMITY/DISTANCE

We begin by describing two common ways in which fecal matters are experienced and how they create the anticipation of embarrassment, shame, and disgust. One is "body betrayal"; the other is "proximity/distance." Body betrayal (Featherstone and Hepworth 1991) is part of a more general characteristic of embodiment. Body boundaries are highlighted by efforts to maintain the integrity of inside/outside borders against the pressures of fluids, gasses, and the like. Failing to do this can result in embarrassment when the projection of oneself as a mature and poised adult is called into question. Thus the experience of involuntary flatulence is described by one heterosexual man:

> It's not so much the action itself, as it is the reaction that passing gas gets from people. I guess the most embarrassing thing about it is the loss of control [our emphasis] in holding your gas. It just seems like in social situations . . . that you'd be able to hold your gas.

Body betrayal also casts into relief the social expectation that these boundaries *will* be controlled. Thus people feel unease over "upset stomachs" and other gastro-intestinal ailments. They are aware of their bodies as both being a container and being contained (see Falk 1994; Johnson 1987) and from which substances can demand escape. Experiencing the body this way, although a private matter, nonetheless must be articulated with the public fecal habitus. One of life's most embarrassing moments can be "having to go" in a situation where toilet facilities are unavailable or which one feels can not be reached in time. Digestive trauma is one of the things that compromises the body container and throws into relief the needs of the body. One heterosexual man related his attempt to bring the physical and the social into alignment under these conditions.

> My [digestive] system has a problem with Italian food and for my sister's last birthday we went to Olive Garden. I went walking in the mall afterwards and I had to run to the toilet and I almost did not make it. I actually sprayed a little poop just as I sat down. My family knew I was trying to run but I kept my cheeks clenched to avoid having an accident.

Clenching the sphincter muscles was the way he tried to control the body container. To feel literally driven by the body in an attempt to appropriately meet its dictates is also recounted in the following heterosexual woman's story:

> I suddenly had to go. I was really sick so I just started driving around and found a fast food restaurant and I didn't want to go in there because they might know that I didn't buy anything; like a Wal-Mart would be better. So I'm driving around and I find an Osco [drugstore] and I run to the back and they have a sign up that says no public restrooms, so I just drive around and I'm in pain and it's raining really hard and I'm totally lost and finally I figure out on the map where I am and how to get back to campus; and on the way I passed the same Wendy's and I run in and poop and run out. By the time I got to pick up my boyfriend I was so late he had already taken the bus. I was crying and had to explain to him what had happened, which was embarrassing. But he thought it was funny, mostly that I was crying.

A second way in which the embodiment of the fecal habitus can be experienced is through the failure to clearly distance oneself from one's fecal outputs. Routinely this is done through use of the flush toilet, the mechanical manifestation of the habitus. This does not always occur efficiently, resulting in too close proximity to one's fecal outputs for self and others. This can produce feelings of disgust, defined by Paul Rozin, Jonathan Haidt, and Clark McCauley (1993) as "a reaction to unwanted intimacy" (p. 576), especially to waste products of the body. Failure to clearly separate oneself from one's fecal outputs can occur in the following cases: the fecal bolus will not flush away or flushing will not remove all fecal debris—in New Zealand called "floaters" and "stripes" respectively (Longhurst 2001); a fecal smell remains for others to experience; fecal matter adheres to the body or ends up in one's clothing; fecal efforts can be overheard; flatulence can be heard and/or smelled. One heterosexual man reported the apprehension such a situation caused him:

[Embarrassing?] Leaving a skid mark in someone else's bowl and not being able to do anything about it. Like a piece of shit that is stuck to the inside of the bowl that the flushing doesn't get rid of. It was out of my control. . . . They know they didn't leave it and they could narrow it down to who it might be.

Another described the following experience as potentially shameful even though the audience was members of his family:

I was at my aunt's house. This sucks. I took the most horrible shit and the toilet wouldn't flush, and I tried several times to flush it, and pushed so hard that I broke the handle. My aunt, she didn't find out it was me, but she saw the shit and the broken handle. Because I was there, I was still a suspect, still scared of being called out in front of my entire family.

With regard to the experience of proximity, the closer the distance between the person and his or her fecal output, the greater is the blow to self presentation, and the greater the stigma. One non-heterosexual man recounted:

I thought I was going to fart while I was working [he does large landscaping projects] and when I did, shit started coming out. When it came out, it just kept coming so I ran into the cornfield, pulled my pants down and finished in my pants. I had to take them off. I left them in the field and made a pair of shorts with my shirt. And besides getting made fun of by my co-workers, I just finished my day. Well, it was only two hours. . . . To this day, they call me "diaper boy."

It is worth mentioning that it is the sense of sight that is involved in these examples. Although an obvious medium for gauging distance between a person and their fecal products, other senses can be involved too, notably smell. Producing a fecal smell through flatulence or leaving one behind after defecating can also bring others into too close contact with one's fecal output. A non-heterosexual woman recalled not being able to adequately distance herself:

Just having to go at work one time. It smelled afterwards and we didn't have any air freshener. They made fun of me for like two hours afterwards. It was like pretty embarrassing at 15. You know I worked with them and had to go to school with them the next day.

These experiences, "body betrayal" and "proximity/distance," reflect the embodiment of the fecal habitus brought to one's attention when things go awry. All these recollections show persons are aware that they should control their fecal efforts and dispose of their fecal products in a prescribed way. Failure to do so, or apprehension about the same, brings into consciousness a self that is incompatible with the one the person wishes to project; thus the anticipation or experience of embarrassment, shame, and disgust.

We next turn to a consideration of which sense is assaulted (vision, smell, or hearing) and the anticipations of deviant attributions by the study participants.

SIGHTS AND SMELLS

Modern plumbing and the imperative of "privacy" from the fecal habitus means that although we may hear and smell bowel movements, we seldom leave evidence that others can see. Seeing feces is considered particularly disgusting. For example, on a nine item Disgust Scale designed by Haidt, McCauley, and Rozin, the highest ranking item was "You see a bowel movement left unflushed in a public toilet" (Rozin et al. 1993:585). Most study participants thought it would be worse to have someone see their feces than to smell or hear their bowel movement as it was the most direct contradiction to their self presentation. One heterosexual man described this as follows:

It is more personal. They actually see the results. When they can't get any closer to knowing what you have done, you are exposed. It is defiling their vision of you; there is a certain purity that is involved with people and them seeing such a personal act—that can change or defile you in their minds. That's how deep it is.

Having one's feces seen is a situation that in addition to creating embarrassment can produce shame, in that many participants felt such an occurrence had implications for assessing their character. One heterosexual man expressed this as follows:

> If someone just hears or smells you, it is still an abstract concept of you defecating. But once they see it, the image is imprinted in their minds. . . .

This seems to be because such deviance can be directly attributed to a person—a concrete reminder that they have breached the fecal habitus and in a way that produces a high degree of disgust. A nonheterosexual man said:

> The visual impact is more powerful than the audible impact. When you've seen something, you have a visual memory and that's harder to deal with than the sound.

It is an unsought intimacy. As put by a heterosexual woman:

> Out of sight, out of mind. It's a personal thing for you to hear or smell someone going to the bathroom. It's not affecting you, but to see it face to face, it's a very different thing. You are entering someone's personal zone.

The participants saw the sight of their excrement as more destructive of self than were fecal sounds and odors. The seemingly universal nature of these reactions probably accounts for the fact that we found no related differences between the four gender-sexual identity groups. This was not because such experiences and anxieties were rare. Seventy percent of the participants said they had experienced a situation where their stools would not flush away. These experiences produced a great deal of concern over the discovery that they were the source of the excreta.

The most common strategies to remedy such a situation were reported (with about equal mention) to be continuing to flush (or putting extra water in the toilet), using a toilet plunger (if available) or some other object as a tool, or such practices as blaming others or fleeing the scene. These situations were reported to be stressful as efforts at distancing were not always immediately successful.

A nonheterosexual woman reported:

> I continued flushing until it [the stool] would move. If it didn't I'd have to put a bunch of toilet paper in there to hide the little thing. I'm not about to just leave it there for the next person. My goodness! I'd seriously flush about six times to make sure it was gone.

Putting space between the self and the fecal product was evident in the case of this heterosexual woman:

> I pretended they weren't mine. I lied and said they [the feces] were someone else's.

And a nonheterosexual man described fleeing the scene of a fecal mess with an even greater sense of urgency:

> I was in the airport . . . and I couldn't do anything, so I just washed my hands and left. . . . [My boyfriend] was waiting outside and I said, "We just need to leave." One of the airport attendants was walking into the bathroom at the time.

The above reactions flow from the anxiety felt from being unable to easily distance one's bodily products from the gaze of others. Such strategies are aimed at eliminating their association with what the fecal habitus evaluates as polluting—human excrement.

The fecal habitus also strongly enjoins us to suppress our fecal odors. We found discomfort over breaching this rule to be less than for having one's feces seen, but more than having one's fecal efforts overheard. Thus, while almost half of the participants reported anticipating the same level of discomfort over others smelling their bowel movements as they did over being overheard having them, twice as many of the remaining participants thought that it would be worse to have someone smell their fecal outputs. Again, the almost universal disgust associated with the smell of fecal odors led to no differences in this regard according to gender-sexual identity group.

Most of study participants anticipated that other persons would feel disgust over the smell of their bowel movement. The greater negative anticipation regarding smell than sound by many of the participants was attributed to the fact that smell can produce nausea, a correlate of disgust. And no one wanted to think of themselves as causing another person to feel sick. One heterosexual woman described this anticipated effect on an audience:

> [Smell] is more intense and more disgusting. It can be more embarrassing depending on how it smells. The worse it stinks, the nastier they think I am.

Another factor entering into how participants felt their self would be affected was that allowing fecal smells to escape called into question their self control. A heterosexual woman commented:

> [They think] that it stinks. Like I made the area smell bad; like it's my fault.

Both the failure to contain fecal smells and the inability to distance oneself from one's fecal outputs are shown in the shame recalled by one heterosexual man.

> In a public restroom . . . I was leaving and the other person was walking in and there was a strong smell. As I left, I made eye contact with the opposing person and there was an awkward feeling. Knowing that they will be put in a situation of discomfort because of my bowel movement. The person walking in had a look of disgust and I had a look of remorse . . . knowing that I was responsible. I could tell that they acknowledged the smell and were not pleased.

Following the imperative of "deodorization," the most frequently mentioned strategy for handling fecal smells in enclosed spaces like bathrooms was to freshen the air through the use of commercial products such as air fresheners or fragrance candles. This was followed in frequency by reports of the use of extractor fans, and, next, by continuing to flush. Lighting a match to emit sulfur and overpower the fecal smell was also mentioned as a strategy. No significant variation appeared among the gender-sexual identity groups.

SOUNDS

We did the most systematic investigation of sound. As we have described, the smell of one's bowel movement was often considered more offensive than overhearing one defecate, and the sight of their feces was considered the most disgusting and stigmatizing. In classroom discussion about the topic, however, the most salient concern verbalized by students was the fear of other students overhearing them defecate if they used on-campus toilets. They were less concerned with their feces being seen as this was a rare happenstance. On the other hand, being overheard was something that could easily occur. Humorous accounts suggested that though both sounds and smells of defecation may be equally pervasive, the former was considered more immediate and less easily distanced from.

The habitus rule of privacy means that people should take care in not allowing another person to hear them defecate. The force of the norm against fecal sounds can be understood through the answers to a question that asked, "In general, what do you think goes through other people's minds who hear you having a bowel movement?" Overall the thought most frequently offered was that other people would find it disgusting. A heterosexual woman articulated how disgust relates to a violation of privacy:

> They're grossed out. . . . It's not something you put out there; you do it in private. That's kind of the way I was raised; its expected by the culture.

As we have seen, such a response of disgust is an anticipated reaction to an unwanted intimacy occasioned by an unruly body. Even though the anticipation of disgust is common, however, we should not ignore that it may be accompanied by other expectations. Thus, some thought that having their bowel movement overheard could evoke a humorous response, especially when failure to control the body toppled the presentation of self as a poised adult. A nonheterosexual man referred directly to the loss of poise that can be central to creating embarrassment:

> *I guess [people could react to such a sound with] just some sort of laughter, because it [pooping] is universal. I think implicitly that it shows some sort of weakness. I guess it's like when you see someone fall. At the same time you see it as something you've done, you also see that they're in a vulnerable position. It's sort of humorous.*

Such anticipations may be widespread, but because we have argued that the fecal habitus is mediated by socio-cultural factors there may be variations in what is anticipated. Thus, whether the anticipated reaction was more disgust or humor was said by some to be related to the gender of the person overhearing. A heterosexual man said:

> *For guys it's kind of like a joke, like "dude that's nasty." Women would probably think it was gross. It's a social norm that women should find that disgusting, or at least should never outwardly say that they accept it or that it is not gross.*

A heterosexual woman concurred:

> *I know guys think it's funny and amusing; girls probably think it's gross. They [guys] always do that bathroom humor. . . .*

Sexual identity also mediates such expectations. Thus we found about half of the heterosexual women and the nonheterosexual men anticipating that the hearer would feel disgusted as compared to over a quarter of the heterosexual men and nonheterosexual women. A nonheterosexual man attributed his concerns to the influence of his more effeminate friends ("divas"):

> *Only around people that I'm regularly naked with would I be comfortable with them knowing what I was doing in the bathroom. I'm on the self-prescribed "pretty pill"—where you don't fart, sweat, burp, or use the bathroom. ["Pretty pill"?] That's just a social construction between some friends and I. I learned it from my diva friends.*

Nonheterosexual men who adopt such a stance not only distance themselves from their own body products but also from heterosexual men.

With regard to humor, a different pattern appears. Both heterosexual and nonheterosexual men were at least twice as likely as either group of women to think that others would find their fecal sounds humorous, which was the next most common expectation. The anticipation of humor when fecal sounds breach body boundaries thus seems more closely linked to gender than to sexual identity. In contrast, as shown, the anticipation of disgust reflects the intersection of gender and sexual identity. On the one hand, the nonheterosexual women were less likely to anticipate disgust than the heterosexual women and, on the other hand, the nonheterosexual men were more likely to anticipate disgust than the heterosexual men.

As well as the embodied nature of gender and sexual identity mediating the effects of the fecal habitus, the anticipation of embarrassment also is affected by thinking of how our gaffs and faux pas may be constructed by various audiences (see Weinberg 1968). Referring to this, one nonheterosexual woman stratified her male audiences by sexual identity:

> *If it's a straight guy, there's always that tension—some kind of male-female tension. With gay guy friends, I am comfortable. . . .*

To systematically study the audience feature of embarrassment we looked at various types of social relationships and how the degree of anticipated discomfort over fecal efforts being overheard might vary. Generally, the highest level of concern over being overheard was with the following audiences: people they were sexually attracted to but hadn't yet dated (the audience that presented participants with the greatest concern), followed by someone they just started dating, and, then, someone they knew well (but who was not a good friend) like a work associate. At a lower level of concern was a stranger, then a person they were in a significant relationship with, a good friend, and lastly (of least concern), a person they were married to (or, if nonheterosexual, were in a civil union with). The lowest level of concern contained two contrasting groups—strangers and long-term intimates—which suggests an interesting association between fecal concerns and audiences. Both groups pose little threat to one's self presentation: the former because the event will invoke only a fleeting identity, the latter because such mishaps do not overwhelm a more solid identity.

The importance of providing or maintaining a good impression in this regard was variably expressed among the different groups. Thus we found it was a salient concern among the heterosexual women. One such woman said:

> I think it is the need to impress [that lead to such concerns]. . . . It's more of an impression that you leave [with other persons]. I don't want that to be the most memorable thing that they know about me.

Heterosexual women were the most likely to anticipate that such an event could affect a relationship. This concern over incompatible images of themselves reflects the particular image that heterosexual women have been measured against, one that emphasizes purity, restraint, and "femininity." And this incompatibility was experienced as especially salient when the audience was men. Further, in response to the question asking about the gender of the hearer, we found over a quarter more of the heterosexuals (both the women and the men) said the gender of the person would make a difference; in addition, the greater discomfort was with the "other gender" among all of the groups except the nonheterosexual men who were evenly divided into

feeling more discomfort with men or women. When we analyzed why this was the case, men and women from the different groups often gave different answers. The heterosexual women's explanations were more likely to refer to a loss of attractiveness reflecting a deviation from gender ideals. One heterosexual woman said:

> With males you feel they have this image of women that they just aren't like that. You know the "women don't sweat, they glow" thing.

In the quotations that follow, gender norms were addressed by one heterosexual woman and the effect on sexual attractiveness by another.

As one said:

> If there's an opportunity for him to hear, it's not lady like at all. It's unappealing for a man to hear a strange woman poop. It's an ascribed thing; it's a social norm.

And as the other stated:

> Maybe it's that sexual image about what it is to be a woman. That women are supposed to be nonpoopers. One time one of my guy friends was like, "girls don't poop," and I was like, "I got news for you." I guess it would go back to the whole [idea of] women having to be the attractive one. Like, women wear the make-up, wear the dresses, and are the sex objects.

Some of the heterosexual men validated these women's concerns. One said:

> Women in my mind are beautiful perfect creatures that are the object of desire. . . . I don't want the image of them tainted in my mind.

Heterosexual men were more likely than the other groups to frame concerns about themselves in terms of "bad manners" in the presence of the other gender. As one heterosexual man put it:

[It's] compromising. . . . I'm a guy and I'm a pig, and a lot of girls don't like that so I try to control myself a bit. Compromising what I would normally do like keep the door open when I'm pooping.

We have argued that heterosexual women's self consciousness over fecal matters reflects the salience of "attractiveness norms." Nonheterosexual men, like the heterosexual women, were also more concerned about a loss of attractiveness. Their lack of ease stemmed from a similar emphasis on the body beautiful, but in this case, in the eyes of other nonheterosexual men. Additionally, nonheterosexual men of the type involved in this study seem less likely to be integrated into networks of hegemonic masculinity (Connell 2002) and thus heterosexual men are less likely to be their reference group.

It is also interesting that men of any sex identity who avoid this form of masculine expression may be labeled deviant because they are "not acting like men." As described by a heterosexual woman:

We had a guy who lived with us two years ago and he went to great lengths for people not to hear . . . him. He would run the water so we couldn't hear him. He went to extreme lengths. But since we hear the water running, we knew what he was doing. We were like: "He's worse than a girl."

The heterosexual men and the nonheterosexual women were less concerned with hiding that they were defecating beings. On average, they worried less about the loss of attractiveness. It appears that the greater embodiment concerns of heterosexual women and nonheterosexual men reflect a dependence on men for their personal validation as sexually attractive.

The lesser concern of heterosexual men over the embodiment of attractiveness is reinforced by the complicit masculinity (Connell 2002a) that local communities of heterosexual men can sustain. Their greater indifference to body boundaries is most clearly seen when the audience is other men. Thus the heterosexual men stand out in having less concern over their fecal sounds

than do any of the other groups. This is evident with regard to good male friends, men they know well, and male strangers. Parallel findings do not come out for either women's group (i.e., women do not show a greater comfort than men do when women are the audience—women who are good friends, who they know well, or who are strangers). Furthermore, it is not surprising that the heterosexual men also showed the least concern about having a bowel movement in a public restroom and were more likely to report being intentionally flatulent in the presence of other people. As one heterosexual man replied when asked what he thought other people would feel if they smelled his fecal gas:

Guys would say it's raunchy and then say "Nice one," because if it's strong it's more manly. You know, because women would not try to clear a room with a fart.

Thus, although many often felt constrained by the fecal habitus, young heterosexual men were the most likely to show disdain for its dictates. This finding again shows how the power of heterosexual men is exemplified through their embodiment—they feel the freedom to ignore the fecal habitus more so than persons in the other groups.

Finally, the participants' answers cite the mediating influence of the social relationship and its duration. The fecal habitus is generally reported to be of greatest salience when attracted to the person and at the beginning of a relationship. When asked if being sexually attracted to the person who hears them defecate would exacerbate their discomfort, nearly all said it would. They also noted, however, how the threshold for embarrassment can be altered over the course of a relationship. In the words of a nonheterosexual man:

There is a tendency to be watchful and careful about everything that you do—especially at the beginning of a relationship. . . . At the beginning of a relationship with an attractive person, I am uncomfortable. But after I know them, I don't care.

The longer the relationship the more it was believed to routinize the experience of the other's bodily functions. Embarrassment and shame were least likely to be reported in relationships that had become routinized or where a single event (like a fecal mishap) would probably not outweigh other aspects of a primary relationship. In the beginnings of a relationship, however, unruly bodies were seen to draw the most unwelcome attention and make incompatible selves the most evident.

We again asked participants how they complied with the fecal habitus so as to protect their body boundaries. To the question, "What things do you do, or what strategies do you engage in to avoid people from hearing you [defecate]," the strategy they mentioned most often was to produce distance by waiting until there was no audience to overhear them. A nonheterosexual woman said:

I go to the bathroom when no one's there. I go in another room if I have to fart. . . .

Of the strategies reported, waiting until no one was in a public restroom was followed in frequency by running the water [in the sink or bathtub] of a private bathroom to mask the sound. Flushing the toilet and/or waiting until other people in the public lavatory flushed were similar in frequency of mention to running the water in a private bathroom. As a heterosexual woman said:

In a public restroom I might try to choose one that I'm fairly certain will be empty but if I'm feeling particularly paranoid I might wait until someone flushes. . . .

The strength of the norms of the habitus is also reflected in accounts of how embodiment can be manipulated. For example, some persons controlled their sphincter muscles to let out gas or excrement slowly, thus decreasing the sound of their bowel movement. One heterosexual man stated:

If it is going to be loud, I would stop and go, meaning let it out in intervals so it would not be a big kerplunk sound.

Other techniques to prevent people from hearing included having a bowel movement early in the morning or late at night, going upstairs if people are downstairs (or vice versa), doing it as fast as you can, pulling out the toilet paper roll to make a cover-up noise, turning the fan on, and not using public restrooms at all.

Compliance with this aspect of the habitus was also shown to be mediated by the intersection of gender and sexual identity. The most common strategy of waiting until others were not around was mentioned by over two-thirds of the heterosexual women and the nonheterosexual men. They mentioned this about twice as often as the heterosexual men and the nonheterosexual women. The strategy of using toilet flushing to mask the sound was most likely to be practiced by the heterosexual women. These results are consistent with the findings reported earlier that show elevated concerns over fecal events among heterosexual women and nonheterosexual men.

REFERENCES

Blinde, Elaine M. and Diane E. Taub. 1992. "Women Athletes as Falsely Accused Deviants: Managing the Lesbian Stigma." *Sociological Quarterly* 33:521–33.

Brekhus, Wayne H. 2003. *Peacocks, Chameleons, Centaurs: Gay Suburbia and the Grammar of Social Identity*. Chicago: University of Chicago Press.

Connell, Robert W. 2002. "Hegemonic Masculinity." Pp. 60–62 in *Gender: A Sociological Reader*, edited by Stevi Jackson and Sue Scott. London: Routledge.

———. 2002a. "On Hegemonic Masculinity and Violence: Response to Jefferson and Hall." *Theoretical Criminology* 6:89–99.

Creed, Barbara. 1999. "Lesbian Bodies: Tribades, Tomboys, and Tarts." Pp. 111–24 in *Feminist Theory and the Body*, edited by Janet Price and Margrit Shildrick. New York: Routledge.

Diamond, Lisa M. 2003. "Was It a Phase? Young Women's Relinquishment of Lesbian/Bisexual Identities Over a 5-Year Period." *Journal of Personality and Social Psychology* 84:352–64.

Falk, Pasi. 1994. *The Consuming Body*. London: Sage.

Featherstone, Mike and Mike Hepworth. 1991. "The Mask of Aging and the Postmodern Lifecourse." Pp. 371–89 in *The Body: Social Processes and Cultural Theory*, edited by Mike Featherstone, Mike Hepworth, and Bryan S. Turner. London: Sage.

Fingerson, Laura. 2001. "Social Construction, Power, and Agency in Adolescent Menstrual Talk." Ph.D. Dissertation Thesis, Department of Sociology, Indiana University, Bloomington, IN.

Gordon, Liahna. 2005. "Lesbians' Resistance to Culturally Defined Attractiveness." Pp. 344–9 in *Deviance: The Interactionist Perspective*, ninth edition, edited by Earl Rubington and Martin S. Weinberg. Boston: Allyn and Bacon.

Inglis, David. 2000. *A Sociological History of Excretory Experience: Defecatory Manners and Toiletry Technologies*. Lewiston, NY: The Edwin Mellen Press.

Johnson, Mark. 1987. *The Body in the Mind: The Bodily Basis of Meaning, Imagination and Reason*. Chicago: University of Chicago Press.

Karp, David A., William C. Yoels, and Barbara H. Vann. 2004. *Sociology in Everyday Life*. Long Grove, IL: Waveland Press.

Kiley, Dean. 1998. "Queer Crash Test Dummies: Theory, Aging, and Embodiment Problematics." In *Looking Queer: Body Image and Identity in Lesbians, Gay, and Transgender Communities*, edited by Dawn Atkins. Binghamton, NY: Hawthorn Press.

Kira, Alexander. 1967. *The Bathroom: Criteria for Design*. Ithaca, NY: Center for Housing and Environmental Studies, Cornell University.

Lee, Janet and Jennifer Sasser-Coen. 1996. *Blood Stories: Menarche and the Politics of the Female Body in Contemporary U.S. Society*. New York: Routledge.

Longhurst, Robyn. 2001. *Exploring Fluid Boundaries*. London: Routledge.

Lyman, Peter. 2001. "The Fraternal Bond as a Joking Relationship." Pp. 157–68 in *Men's Lives*, edited by Michael Kimmel and Michael A. Messner. Boston: Allyn and Bacon.

Markus, Hazel Rose, Patricia R. Mullally, and Shinobu Kityama. 1997. "Selfways: Diversity in Modes of Cultural Participation." Pp. 13–61 in *The Conceptual Self in Context: Culture, Experience, Self-Understanding*, edited by Ulric Neisser and David A. Jopling. Cambridge: Cambridge University Press.

Miller, William Ian. 1997. *The Anatomy of Disgust*. Cambridge, MA: Harvard University Press.

Mishkind, Marc E., Judith Rodin, Lisa R. Silberstein, and Ruth H. Striegel-Moore. 2001. "The Embodiment of Masculinity: Cultural, Psychological and Behavioral Dimensions." Pp. 103–20 in *The American Body in Context*, edited by Jessica R. Johnson. Wilmington, DE: Scholarly Resources.

Mitteness, Linda. 1987. "So What Do You Expect When You're 85?: Urinary Incontinence in Late Life." *Research in the Sociology of Health Care* 6:177–219.

Munt, Sally R. 1998. "Orifices in Space: Making the Real Possible." Pp. 200–209 in *Butch/Femme: Inside Lesbian Gender*, edited by Sally R. Munt. London: Cassell.

Rozin, Paul, Jonathan Haidt, and Clark R. McCauley. 1993. "Disgust." Pp. 575–94 in *Handbook of Emotions*, edited by Michael Lewis and Jeannette M. Haviland. New York: The Guilford Press.

Savin-Williams, Ritch C. 2001. "Memories of Same-Sex Attractions." Pp. 117–33 in *Men's Lives*, edited by Michael S. Kimmel and Michael Messner. Boston: Allyn and Bacon.

Shiu-Ki, Travis Kong. 2004. "Queer at Your Own Risk: Marginality, Community and Hong Kong Gay Male Bodies." *Sexualities* 7:5–30.

Waskul, Dennis D. and Pamela van der Riet. 2002. "The Abject Embodiment of Cancer Patients: Dignity, Selfhood, and the Grotesque Body." *Symbolic Interaction* 25:487–513.

Weinberg, Martin S. 1968. "Embarrassment: Its Variable and Invariable Aspects." *Social Forces* 46:382–8.

Weinberg, Martin S., Colin J. Williams, and Douglas W. Pryor. 1994. *Dual Attraction: Understanding Bisexuality*. New York: Oxford University Press.

The Labeling of Sexual Harassment

KIRSTEN DELLINGER and CHRISTINE L. WILLIAMS

According to labeling theory, if there is no pejorative label, then, in a sociological sense, there is no deviant. So where do the labels come from, and under what circumstances are they applied? Custom can dictate what actions will be called deviant. Common law simply restates customs. Statute law, on the other hand, can prohibit conduct that custom allows. Social movements, one of the major sources of cultural change, often succeed in getting such laws passed. The women's movement succeeded in having laws passed that provided the label of sexual harassment and were meant to discourage and punish its occurrence. After passage of such laws, researchers often ask about their observance and enforcement.

Kirsten Dellinger and Christine L. Williams compared the culture in the editorial departments of two magazines. One, a sex magazine, treated women as sex objects in text, cartoons, and photographs. Its editors were equally divided between men and women. The other magazine concerned itself with feminist issues. Its editorial staff was made up entirely of women. The authors found numerous instances of behavior that met the legal criteria of sexual harassment in both editorial departments. Each department had established its own permissive culture with respect to etiquette between staff members. In the sex magazine, both men and women made jokes about sex behavior that in other workplaces would most likely have been labeled sexual harassment. In the feminist magazine, the all-woman staff established informal norms that allowed disclosures about one's sex life. Again, actions that met the legal criteria of sexual harassment did not lead to the labeling of any of the personnel. Thus, the study by Dellinger and Williams effectively demonstrates how the cultural context in which a person is located can affect the labeling of deviance.

Sexual behavior is common in workplaces, but for the most part sociologists have not paid attention to it unless sexual harassment is involved. Sexual harassment researchers have found that a large proportion of women workers have experienced behaviors that might fit the legal definition of sexual harassment—between 40 and 50 percent (Welsh 1999). But that does not mean that the women surveyed actually considered themselves to have been harassed. Even those who reported an offensive act against them, rarely answer "yes" to the survey question, "Have you ever been sexually harassed?" Why not?

At least part of the answer lies in the fact that sexual harassment is a feature of many jobs. Many women are employed in jobs where they are routinely subjected to deliberate or repeated sexual behavior that is unwelcome, as well as other sex-related behaviors that they consider hostile, offensive, or degrading. Studies of restaurant servers (Giuffre and Williams 1994; Allison

1994), amusement park attendants (Adkins 1995), nursing home aides (Foner 1994), and maquiladora workers (Salzinger 2000) demonstrate that employees in a variety of fields encounter unwanted sexual behavior as a routine feature of their jobs. They rarely label their experiences sexual harassment, however, precisely because they are institutionalized as part of their jobs. Those who refuse to put up with such requirements end up quitting or being fired, or never taking the job in the first place.

Yet not everyone who works in these jobs objects to their sexual aspects. Many people seek out and enjoy jobs that are highly sexualized. Meika Loe (1996), who studied the "Bazooms" restaurant chain, an establishment that requires waitresses to wear skimpy outfits and engage in sexual banter with customers, reported that 800 women applied for the job when she did. In a study of doctors and nurses in a teaching hospital, some high-ranking professional women claimed to enjoy the sexual elements of their jobs. A woman surgeon admitted that in the operating room, "[there's] teasing and joking and pinching and elbowing. It's fun. That's one reason people like being in that arena. That's part of the camaraderie" (Williams, Giuffre, and Dellinger 1999:86). Leslie Salzinger's (2000) study of a maquiladora plant found that women who initially resisted sexual objectification eventually became won over and gradually transformed themselves into sexual objects competing for the attentions of their male supervisors. But even in these cases, workers still draw boundary lines between sexual behaviors that they consider pleasurable, tolerable, and harassing.

In this paper, we compare two highly sexualized workplaces in the same industry, magazine publishing, to better understand how workers define sexual harassment and distinguish it from other, acceptable, forms of sexual expression. One of the organizations we studied publishes a men's pornographic magazine, and the other a feminist magazine. We use pseudonyms for each of the organizations to protect the identities of the individuals interviewed: the men's pornographic

magazine is referred to as *Gentleman's Sophisticate* and the feminist magazine as *Womyn*. The editorial departments of the two magazines are our focus.

We chose these two organizations for comparison because they are both highly sexualized but in very different ways. The magazines produced by these organizations represent distinctive ideals of sexuality: one committed to feminism, and the other to what Robert W. Connell (1995) has called "hegemonic masculinity," the structural and cultural privileging of white, heterosexual male power. In this paper, we focus on the editorial departments at the two magazines because sexuality is an especially salient issue there. Editors are responsible for all of the written content published in their magazines (except for advertisements). Because members of these workplaces explicitly deal with sexuality as part of their jobs, we anticipated that editors at *Womyn* and *Gentleman's Sophisticate* would constantly have to draw boundary lines between acceptable and unacceptable expressions of sexuality.

The different values of feminism and hegemonic masculinity contained in the magazines are reflected in the organizational cultures of the two workplaces, but in complex ways. Organizational culture can be defined as the understandings, behaviors, and symbolic forms, including totems, rituals, taboos and myths, that are shared by members of a work organization (Reskin and Padavic 1994; Trice 1993). In these workplaces, the magazines themselves are among the most important symbols of the editors' shared organizational culture. Images from the magazines are posted throughout the workplaces, and copies of current and former issues are strewn about on desks. Although not all workers admire and identify with the magazines they edit—as we will see, this is especially the case at *Gentleman's Sophisticate*—the magazines, nevertheless, represent their collective effort and symbolize the values of the organization. Organizational culture also refers to the informal, emotional, and interpersonal dynamics of work, including the norms governing sexual interactions among workers (Gherardi 1995; Hearn and Parkin 1987). As we will show, editors consider these informal norms when drawing boundary lines between acceptable and unacceptable sexual behavior. While not all members of a workplace agree in every instance when a boundary has been crossed, we argue that understanding the process whereby workers make this determination requires taking organizational culture into account.

Although these two workplaces are in privately owned companies in the same industry, located in the same city, that employ people in the same occupations (editors, assistant editors, administrative assistants, secretaries, interns), there are several structural differences between them. Most importantly, all of the 18 members of the *Womyn* editorial staff are women, while six of the 12 editors at *Gentleman's Sophisticate*, including the top managers, are men. Overall, the occupation of editing is gender balanced (*Employment and Earnings*, January 1998), but it is not unusual for organizations committed to feminism to employ only women. Some might find the comparison of an all-women work site and a gender-balanced work site to be problematic because the assumption of most research has been that sexual harassment is solely a cross-sex phenomenon. A discussion of homophobia as sexual harassment has been limited (Williams 1997). We believe the comparison between *Gentleman's Sophisticate* and *Womyn* is useful in pointing out that the nature of occupational segregation in the workplace often finds women dealing with "male cultures" or working with other women in sex-segregated settings. We rarely find men who must negotiate a "female culture." The asymmetrical nature of these cases in regard to gender composition, actually allows us to examine the most common work experiences for women as they work in male dominated settings or as they work in women-only settings. If we are to understand women's experience with sexuality and sexual harassment at work, it is essential that we compare and contrast the workplace cultures that may develop in these different settings.

The ratio of men to women in a workplace is considered by some researchers to be an important predictor of the prevalence of sexual harassment (see Welsh 1999 for an overview of debates in this literature). Some researchers argue that the number of interactions between men and women at work is predictive of the likelihood of sexual harassment (Gruber 1998; Gutek, Cohen, and Konrad 1990). The findings from these studies would suggest that it is more likely that women editors would experience sexual harassment at *Gentleman's Sophisticate* than at *Womyn*, simply because there are more men employed at *Gentleman's Sophisticate*.

Other studies have endeavored to identify features of organizational culture that are conducive to sexual harassment. Pryor and his colleagues conducted a series of experiments that found that exposure to male supervisors and peers who sexually harass increases other men's likelihood of sexually harassing women (Hulin, Fitzgerald, and Drasgow 1996; Pryor, Giedd, and Williams 1995; Pryor, LaVite, and Stoller 1993). On the other side of the coin, Gruber (1998) found that workplaces with proactive methods of sexual harassment training were much more effective in reducing hostile environment harassment than workplaces that relied solely on less aggressive "get out the word" techniques.

These studies identify specific elements of organizational culture that are linked to the frequency and type of sexual harassment likely to occur in a workplace. But they do not address the meaning of sexual harassment, and how that meaning may be shaped by organizational context. In fact, these studies, like most quantitative studies of sexual harassment, assume that there is prior consensus regarding the meaning of sexual behaviors. As Welsh (1999:173) points out, "when using survey responses, it is common for researchers to define all unwanted sexual behaviors as sexual harassment, whether the respondent defines them as such (see Gruber 1998 for a notable exception)." Qualitative research is better suited to uncovering how the meaning of sexual behaviors varies in different organizational contexts. As Salzinger (2000) shows in her ethnography of a maquiladora, in certain workplace contexts, even egregious sexual behaviors on the part of management (ogling, demands for sexual access) may be accepted by workers as reasonable or inevitable conditions of their employment.

In addition to examining how organizational culture shapes workers' responses to sexual behavior, we explore the ambiguity that often surrounds sexuality for employees (Williams 1997; Williams, Giuffre, and Dellinger 1999). Unlike most studies that focus on the presence or absence of sexual harassment, our goal is to document the process whereby individuals decide whether a certain behavior is harassing, tolerable, or pleasurable. Finally, by focusing on a sexually diverse group of workers, we consider both heterosexual and nonheterosexual interactions, an element missing from most studies of sexual harassment.

METHODS

In 1996, the first author conducted 65 in-depth interviews and 10 weeks of fieldwork at *Womyn* and *Gentleman's Sophisticate* in New York City as part of a larger study on the ways in which organizations are gendered and sexualized. *Gentleman's Sophisticate* is owned by Publisher's, Inc., which employs approximately 270 people, and Bradwell, Inc. is the publisher of *Womyn* and it employs about 170 workers. (The names of the publishers and the magazines are pseudonyms.) Interviews were conducted with editors, accountants, and administrative assistants who worked at the two magazines, including both current and former employees. The larger sample includes 45 women and 20 men. Of all the respondents, 11 are African American, six are Latina/o, two are Asian American, and 46 are white. The full sample includes 54 heterosexual men and women, two gay men, three lesbian women, three bisexual women, and three individuals who declined to give their sexual orientation.

In this article, we draw on the interviews conducted with 28 members of the editorial departments at the two magazines. The editor-in-chief at each magazine was initially interviewed and asked for permission to interview and observe in the respective editorial departments. All of the members of the editorial staff at *Womyn* (18) and all but two of the editorial staff at *Gentleman's Sophisticate* (10) agreed to be interviewed. (The two refusals were on vacation during the summer research.) Interviews were conducted in a semi-structured format, and were tape-recorded and transcribed for analysis. Most lasted one hour, and were conducted in a variety of locations: in private offices and conference rooms during the workday and in cafes or parks during lunch breaks.

These interviews were augmented by 10 weeks of participant observation at the two organizations. During August and September 1996, the first author was employed as a temporary filing clerk in the accounting department of *Womyn's* parent company, Bradwell, Inc., where she worked for approximately 20 hours a week. The rest of the workday was spent conducting interviews or observing at both magazines. While filing, she observed the day-to-day workings of the accounting department at *Womyn,* and interacted frequently with members of the *Womyn* editorial staff, located in the same building down the hall. During this time, she received permission from the editor-in-chief to attend several editorial staff meetings. In November 1996, she was granted permission to observe full-time in the editorial offices for an additional two weeks. At *Gentleman's Sophisticate,* there are no regularly scheduled staff meetings, but the first author received permission from the editor-in-chief to observe the workings of the editorial department by "shadowing" the managing editor during two work days. She also attended formal and informal company gatherings including an evening art opening held at *Gentleman's Sophisticate* and two "happy hours" after work with members of the accounting department. Fieldnotes were recorded as soon as possible after observing and interviewing at each magazine.

The fieldwork portion of the study enables us to understand individuals' experiences, feelings, and expectations regarding sexual behavior in the context of the unstated, taken-for-granted rules of behavior that govern organizational life. The combination of in-depth interviews and participant observation at both workplaces provided valuable insights into the everyday work experiences of the editorial staffs.

FINDINGS

GENTLEMAN'S SOPHISTICATE

The editorial department at *Gentleman's Sophisticate* employs six women and six men. A primary component of editors' jobs is to make decisions about the written content of the magazine. Their jobs include editing sexual advice columns, writing and copyediting captions for the euphemistically called "pictorials" or "artwork," and editing and screening sexually graphic reader mail for potential publication. To illustrate one facet of her job, one of the editors produced a letter signed, 'A Big Fan in Michigan,' who writes to the magazine each month describing his sexual practices in detail and grading the photos to determine the one he thinks deserves his monthly "Big Fan Masturbation Award." This editor decides whether or not to publish these letters.

When asked to describe her everyday work, Margaret, the managing editor, explained that among other tasks, she engages in detailed conversations about copy style:

> *Many of the conversations that we have are on when things should be capitalized or not or . . . is blow job one word or two . . . is it hyphenated or is it not hyphenated? Those are serious conversations and it's a copy style decision that needs to be made . . . and sometimes I'll just stop and say, "I cannot believe this is a discussion that we have at work!" (laughing).*

Everyone at *Gentleman's Sophisticate* has to confront the sexually explicit nature of the magazine and, consequently, of their jobs. When describing her responsibility for writing the captions beneath the sexually explicit pictorials, Tina, another woman editor, said that you just have to get used to the material and you have to have a sense of humor to deal with it:

> *It used to be so hard . . . It used to be like, torture. And now . . . you get used to what it's supposed to sound like . . . . You get used to it. So it's easier to write . . . I mean they're funny—you really have to have a sense of humor, that's the one requirement to work here. You gotta be able to have anything go off your back. Because there's just so much, you know. You gotta have a really open mind.*

When Tina started working at *Gentleman's Sophisticate,* the sexual aspect of her job felt to her like "torture." Since she was subjected to a working environment that she considered offensive and that made her uncomfortable, her experience could be interpreted as sexual harassment. But instead of labeling it sexual harassment, she eventually learned to define it as "funny"— something not to be taken seriously. The transformation of the material from "torturous" to "funny" can be understood as a form of emotional labor required of many workers at *Gentleman's Sophisticate* (Hochschild 1983). This process of identity management may be more visible in settings where workers must manage a "legitimate" identity while creating a stigmatized product (Goffman 1963). Yet all workers probably engage in emotional labor to some extent (see Leidner 1993; Pierce 1995).

Emotional labor is shaped by workplace context. At least part of the reason for Tina's growing tolerance of her sexualized work environment might be attributed to the organizational policies at *Gentleman's Sophisticate.* Workers there are required to sign an acknowledgment that states that they are aware that they "will encounter and be called upon to work with pictures and written text that involve nudity and sexually explicit material." This measure was instituted, in part, to stave off the possibility of sexual harassment lawsuits. (Loe 1996 describes a similar policy in place at the "Bazooms" restaurant chain.)

Margaret, the managing editor, explained the purpose of this requirement this way:

> *I think that's more—not to eliminate the possibility that the company could be sued because a boss is harassing a single employee, but just in general, saying that you understand this is what you are going to work on when you are here. . . . So, that's something that we really do stress to people and we send them home with copies of the magazines and make them look at it and make sure that you feel comfortable with this.*

It is interesting to note that in other contexts, workers have successfully brought "hostile environment" sexual harassment lawsuits against work organizations that permitted some employees to pin up nude centerfolds in the workplace. In a 1991 landmark case, Lois Robinson went to court after officials at the Jackonsville Shipyard ignored complaints that pornographic pictures were prominently displayed in the workplace (Petrocelli and Repa 1998). Because their jobs require them to look at nude pin-ups, workers at *Gentleman's Sophisticate* do not define it this way.

Gentleman's Sophisticate will only hire employees who can tolerate exposure to sexual materials that might offend them. This practice may discriminate against women workers if women, in general, are less able to develop this tolerance. Boswell contends that some young interns leave after two days because they can't cope with the sexual materials:

> *I've seen interns come in who are just very young. Especially women who are very young and they're here for about two days and they just like, scream and run out of the room because I don't know what they thought, but they obviously weren't thinking. "Oh, gee, I can't do this! Somebody said pussy." I mean, you know, "Oooh, there was a picture of a breast." You know, "My sister and her powerful group will not approve of me being here." I don't know what it is. But interns sometimes show up, do about two days and then just freak. But they're usually like eighteen to twenty-two and just don't have enough worldliness.*

Only those who find ways to cope with the materials stay on; those who can't are quickly weeded out. Importantly, both men and women eventually learn this tolerance; the staff of the editorial department is gender balanced. However, few editors had actually sought out the opportunity to work in the pornography industry. Members of the editorial staff came from backgrounds in journalism, publishing, or business. None of the editors were involved in the sex industry prior to working at the magazine. Moreover, when individuals applied for a job at the parent company (which we have given the pseudonym Publisher's Inc.), some were unaware that they would be working for a men's pornographic magazine. The editors claimed that they accepted a job at *Gentleman's Sophisticate* not because it is pornography, but rather because it is an internationally known publication. Many of the editors talk about a period of adjustment in which they get used to working with the sexually explicit material on a daily basis, and most say that they learn to enjoy the work. This is similar to Salzinger's (2000) study of a maquiladora in Mexico, where she witnessed the process by which women adjusted to the sexual objectification expected of them. *Gentleman's Sophisticate* provides another case of how workers who decide to stay have to find some way to adjust to the norms of their workplace.

Workers at *Gentleman's Sophisticate* often reconcile the tension they experience with sexually explicit material using humor. Humor is one of the main strategies that people use to deal with unsettling or unwanted experiences (Fitzgerald, Swan, and Fischer 1995:120). One person referred to the culture of *Gentleman's Sophisticate* as a "locker room": a place filled with bawdy jokes and sexual bantering. Most of the sexual joking at *Gentleman's Sophisticate* is about the content of the magazine itself. People joke about breast implants, ads for penis enlargements, and the impossibility of certain sexual acts that are described in letters from readers. Editors also joke about the readers who buy the magazine and enjoy it. Boswell claims that most of the editors have contempt for the readers of the magazine, believing that they are all "in federal prisons and trailer camps." In fact, none of the editors claim that they enjoy reading the magazine and looking at the pictures; they consider the overarching view of sexuality portrayed in the magazine to be narrow and outdated.

Although joking is pervasive in the editorial department, it is almost never about personal matters. Tina says joking is "just business and never personal." When Bill is asked if he ever talks about sex at work, he doesn't think to mention sexual joking about the magazine. He says, "No, not at all. I just don't want to talk about sex . . . especially with women, because everything could be misconstrued, especially in these times when people are so sensitive." But when asked if he talks about sex in regard to the magazine, he clarifies that "that" kind of joking happens "all the time":

> Oh yeah, we laugh at a lot of stuff. Some of it is so ridiculous, you know, how many positions can you come up with and have it artful? We laugh at the pictorials. We laugh at the color. We laugh at the choice of girls. Yeah, we do that a lot. Sure. But to me, that's in the abstract. . . . If I met you outside of this environment and I brought a Gentleman's Sophisticate magazine with me . . . and started talking to you about it, that would be like approaching you, hitting on you. For us, it's like an "in" thing. It's like we work here.

Working with the magazine and joking about it is an "in" thing at Gentleman's Sophisticate "as long as it is not personal." Talking about sex is fine if it is about the magazine, or if it is "abstract." If it is concrete talk about an individual's sexual behavior or desires, then it is "sensitive" and likely to be "misconstrued." Bill acknowledges that while this "abstract" sexual talk and joking is considered part of the job here, in other contexts, it might be interpreted as an inappropriate "come on" or even as sexual harassment.

On several occasions, the editors shared jokes that were "going around the office that day." During an interview with a male editor, he said,

"You'll get good and raunchy jokes and you pass those around. And the popular joke last week was . . . oh yeah, 'Why do women fake their orgasms? [Why?] Because they think we care.'"

Although the editor said that this was a very popular joke with both men and women, the joke only makes sense if told from a male point of view. The joke is "on" women for thinking that men care about their sexual pleasure. Messner (1992) has noted that male locker room jokes are almost always about degrading women. However, at Gentleman's Sophisticate, both men and women participate in this type of humor. When the first author arrived for an interview, a woman employee who escorted her to her appointment told her a blow job joke in the hallway, and then "offered" her to a man in the elevator as "his own personal girl." Thus, even though the editorial department at Gentleman's Sophisticate is not an all-male domain, the description of the culture in the editorial department as a male locker room is apt given the emphasis on the bawdy depiction and discussion of sex from a male heterosexual point of view, with most of the jokes at women's expense.

But just because the work culture is sexualized does not mean that absolutely anything goes. Boundary lines are still drawn at the organization. Margaret, the managing editor, said:

> I watched in the production room one day and one of the men who works there held open an issue of [a competing pornographic magazine] which happened to have a Black centerfold and said, "Can you imagine what our relationship would be like if you looked like this?" Comments like that are totally inappropriate. It doesn't matter that I work here. It's inappropriate and that's an inappropriate discussion to have. So I think people think they're not crossing the line just because you work here and in reality they really are. That line is still there and should still be there.

Margaret's boundary line between acceptable and harassing sexual behavior is personal sexual innuendo. In this sense, working at Gentleman's

Sophisticate may really be like the men's locker rooms where there may be lots of fantasy talk and sexual joking, but little actual emotional and personal intimacy (Curry 1991; Lyman 1987).

The racist stereotype embedded in the man's remark is also important in understanding why Margaret used this example to illustrate her boundary line. Both Margaret and the man in the production room are white. His comment insinuates that if she were Black, she would be more sexually available to him, reflecting a popular "controlling image" of Black women (Collins 2000). It is also significant that *Gentleman's Sophisticate* does not regularly publish images of women of color. From a production standpoint (one that is surely influenced by racist assumptions about sexuality in the larger culture) (West 1993), Black sexuality is defined as unacceptable. In this context, the fact that the centerfold was Black may have marked this "joke" as different from and more offensive than the regular joking about sex that occurs on a daily basis.

According to Lyman (1987) and Curry (1991), joking in all-male settings (sports locker rooms and fraternities) is a form of male bonding. The success of the male bond relies on several things: avoiding talk of personal relationships and other intimate matters, being able to put someone down (often by degrading and objectifying women and gays and lesbians), and being able to "take" a joke without losing one's cool. All-male arenas that are highly sexualized (like locker rooms or fraternities) may foster even more humorous and joking relationships than other contexts because joking is a way of releasing sexual tension, and maybe even denying its existence.

Sexual joking is enjoyed by most editors, unless it crosses the line into the personal. When this happens, editors claim that their organization responds speedily and decisively to protect those who feel victimized. Brian provided one example of this organizational commitment to protecting workers. Part of his job is fielding calls from prospective writers and models. Brian received a phone call from "Ginger Petty" who said she had been doing research on S&M and wanted to submit her work to *Gentleman's Sophisticate*. Over the course of the conversation, Ginger began telling Brian about her own sexual fantasies, and how she would like to be "disciplined" by Brian. Brian thought the incident was "hilarious" and went to tell Margaret, his boss, about it:

> *I went over to tell Margaret about the call, laughingly. Just saying, "This really takes the cake!" And she laughed, too, but she said, "You know, in truth, if it were Nicole [the other woman that was working there at the time], who'd gotten this call, I don't think I'd be laughing right now." She said, "I think I'd be concerned. It would be more than a joke, but 'assault' is the wrong word. Like a harassment type of call." But she asked me, "Do you at all feel offended or whatever?" And I said, "Please! Honestly! I mean, not even close!" But I thought it was very nice that she extended that kind of sensitivity because I could have been.*

Margaret is sensitive to the possibility that Ginger Petty's call could be harassment because it seems to cross personal boundaries. It is interesting that this workplace norm allows Margaret to consider the possibility that a man may be harassed by a woman, but Brian does not share Margaret's definition of this particular situation as sexual harassment, although he appreciates his boss's reasoning and her sensitivity.

Margaret attributes Brian's lack of concern over the incident to the fact that he is a man. Brian is also gay, and this may help to explain his decision not to label this incident as sexual harassment. He describes the environment at *Gentleman's Sophisticate* as "liberating" in many ways. He says that he enjoys the freedom of self-expression one is allowed in regards to sexuality. On the one hand, Brian reports that he is out at work and that he enjoys joking with women colleagues and "playing around a little with ideas of gender roles . . . within certain parameters." He also explains that he has learned to slip into what he calls "hyper-hetero extreme" talk around his straight friends to make them uncomfortable. He sees himself at the forefront of sexual joking and uses this talk as a way to make his straight friends "squirm." He explains,

I feel like it's a parody. I feel like I'm really making fun of them and the way they talk and they may not get it that way, but I get a kick out of teasing them and seeing that they really don't feel comfortable with it. . . . Actually, in truth, there's got to be some element of hostility in it too, for me. You know, for the years that I had to listen to this shit. For all the years that I had to swallow and maybe even make believe that it was who I was. Now, I can do it better than you can! I can teach you! And doesn't it make you squirm?

Giuffre and Williams (1994) report a similar incident in their study of sexual harassment in restaurants when a gay waiter explained that the open sexual environment allowed him to make straight co-workers uncomfortable with his sexual banter. He, too, saw this joking as a kind of payback for all the times he and other gay people had been oppressed and excluded by the norms of compulsory heterosexuality. Granted his penchant for engaging in "hyper-hetero-extreme" talk, it is understandable why Brian did not see the Ginger Petty incident as sexual harassment.

Women in other departments said they felt protected from sexual harassment owing to a powerful woman lawyer employed by the firm who they perceived as vigorously pursuing all complaints of harassment. This is consistent with Gruber's (1998) finding that sexual harassment complaints may be less frequent in workplaces with proactive sexual harassment procedures. Women employees at *Gentleman's Sophisticate* said they felt empowered to complain about any individual who crossed the line from "business sex" to "personal sex." This sense of the individual's right to personal autonomy, and protection from individual harassers, is consistent with the overarching values of free choice and individual rights which characterized the organization culture as a whole. Thus, while the norms and values of the locker room might seem to foster sexual harassment, employees in general felt that their workplace was free of sexual harassment, and that anyone who dared cross the line would be quickly reprimanded.

Some editors acknowledged that sexual harassment did sometimes occur at *Gentleman's Sophisticate*. These instances were perceived as the result of a few "Neanderthals" outside the editorial department who didn't understand the difference between joking and harassment. According to Boswell,

There's very little sexual harassment that does go on. Probably less than in other companies because again, it's not really an issue. I mean, that's not to say, I don't observe like "Troglodytes speaking coarsely with their women." But the strange thing is that other men will speak up and say, "Hey, knock it off!" or "Gentlemen, stop this!" I mean, for the most part, people cool it. . . . There's a couple of guys that roam around the office that are real sort of pigs, and classic male chauvinists, but because the company is so upwardly mobile, it's just sort of like, "Ahh, he's just a retrograde." There are a couple of people in the organization that are just sort of hardwired into their Italian-Stallion souls and they can be good about it for about a week, but sooner or later, the genetics reassert themselves and you have to slap them again. But in a company of hundreds of people, who cares?

Boswell describes the men who sexually harass women employees as throwbacks to the 1970s, a time when the magazine was at the height of its popularity. They are men who have failed to evolve with the times. Interestingly, the editors often described the readers of *Gentleman's Sophisticate* in a similar way. They, too, are considered Neanderthals stuck in another era's vision of sexuality. In both instances, the editors attempt to separate themselves from what they perceive as a lower class, unsophisticated view of sexuality and masculinity. This tension between the editors' sexual tastes and preferences, and the expressions of sexual desire represented in the magazine, reflects what Connell (1995) has characterized as a key feature of masculinity. Different forms of masculinity constantly compete for dominance; the hegemonic form of masculinity is always defined in terms of its difference from, and superiority over, alternative forms of masculinity, and all versions of femininity. Thus, the "Neanderthal" readers of *Gentleman's Sophisticate,* and the "Neanderthal" men at the organization who sexually harass women, function as foils for the men editors to define themselves as superior to other men.

By separating business sex from personal sex, the culture of the editorial department supports the idea that sexual harassment is an individual problem and not an organizational issue. Although the editors are subjected to a sexualized work environment, they rarely complain about it or label it sexual harassment. Men and women editors seem to enjoy joking in the locker room environment. Only when sexual bantering crosses over into the personal do some editors feel like they are being sexually harassed. Perhaps for this reason, editors distance themselves from the content of the magazine. Because anyone who enjoys the magazine is a retrograde, lower class "Neanderthal," an employee who took the magazine too seriously and admitted to finding it personally stimulating would likely be looked upon with suspicion by others, perhaps as the sort of "Neanderthal" likely to sexually harass women.

WOMYN

The editorial department at *Womyn* employs a staff of 18 women. Included in this number are four unpaid interns. Unlike *Gentleman's Sophisticate,* the editors at *Womyn* are not offered training in sexual harassment policy, nor are they asked to sign any acknowledgment about the sexual content of their magazine. When asked whether the company had a formal sexual harassment policy, the editor-in-chief replied, "We don't have any formal policy here at *Womyn* except we clearly, as feminists, know where we stand on the issue."

Many other members of the editorial staff seemed surprised when asked if they had a formal policy regarding sexual harassment. Most said they weren't sure and then explained that *anybody* who would choose to work at *Womyn* would simply understand that sexually harassing behavior is not tolerated. In other words, the editors saw the feminist norms and values within their workplace culture as protection against sexual harassment.

Working at *Womyn* means knowing where one stands on all sorts of important feminist issues. This feminist sensibility creates an environment where editors believe they are doing more than "just a job." Brett, a senior editor at *Womyn,* said,

> I think it's hard to work at Womyn and look at it as a job in journalism. It's more of a calling. I feel like I live it everyday . . . I don't think my work is just a piece of journalism, I think it's a piece of activism.

The motto "the personal is political" is very much alive at *Womyn.* People's personal identities are intricately tied to their work identities. This encourages the formation of intimate ties among co-workers. Natasha, a copy editor who was new to the department when she was interviewed, described the sense that when she was being welcomed to the job she was also being welcomed to a "sisterhood":

> I felt this whole school marmish excitement about the way we were speaking to one another. You know, I felt it was like, girls' novels, you know, like eighth grade girls' novels. . . . The image is patent leather shoes and girls who are pledging undying friendship. You know what I mean?

Being an editor at *Womyn* requires a certain amount of personal disclosure, often about sexual matters. Editors at *Womyn* reflect on and share their opinions about topics ranging from date rape to sexual harassment to the nature of sexual pleasure and desire. While it is necessary to consider these topics from an editorial standpoint, sexuality permeates the more informal conversations as well. People talk about their own sex lives and what they do and don't like to do in bed, as well as having serious conversations about their sexual identities and their relationships. Many women at the magazine explain that this sharing creates very close bonds among the workers that extend beyond the walls of the editorial department. This environment of trust leads to an openness about sexuality that some editors described as "dorm room" culture. Stacey describes some aspects of this dorm room:

> It's just like all of us hanging around all the time. We're so touchy. And we're always having parties just together without our partners. And so we're always dancing together and having sleep overs and stuff.

When at work, employees frequently give each other pats on the back, hugs, and the occasional back rub. There is also a great deal of joking about sex. Almost every editor repeated a joke around the office that there are three main topics of conversation: Food, Hair, and Sex. It is quite common for workers to bring snacks and treats to share that are placed for collective consumption at the so-called "trough." Offering food is an effective means of achieving integration into predominately female work groups, as the first author discovered after she donated homemade brownies to the trough (see also, Reskin and Padavic 1994).

When asked for examples of how people joke about sex at *Womyn,* Brett explains that things can get pretty explicit:

> There's always discussion of—literally—what kind of sex people do and what they like. It's very graphic sometimes. It's very technical. . . . And I do think, very much, that that has to do with an all-women staff. I think it's totally comfortable. Both straight and lesbians. It doesn't matter. Everybody talks about everything.

Another member of the staff, Samantha, reinforces the idea that *Womyn* is a very sexualized, but safe environment:

> I think this is a very sexual place in a lot of ways. And there's a lot of sexual energy in here, but it's very positive. And maybe, if it was a place where you felt threatened in some way, that the energy could be a form of harassment, you know what I mean? But it's so non-threatening.

When asked what makes it non-threatening, she replied, "For me, it's probably just the all-women environment."

According to Brett and Samantha, if the same conversations involved men, they would probably consider them sexual harassment. Once again, this indicates how social context matters in the definition of sexual harassment. It also helps to explain why the male/female ratio is an important predictor of the likelihood of experiencing sexual harassment (Gruber 1998). A feminist all-women dorm room culture that encourages personal disclosure about sex shapes the definition of sexual harassment very differently from the male-dominated locker room culture that promotes impersonal, heterosexual, and often degrading sex talk. While talk of "the personal" is taboo and possibly constitutes harassment in the locker room, it is normative and expected in the dorm room.

Some women may seek out a sex-segregated work environment in hopes of finding this pleasurable, non-threatening atmosphere. In fact, most of the editors described the dorm room environment as very liberating. Vera, a former editor, explained, "For the most part, conversations about our emotional and sexual lives are wonderful and liberating and one of the best parts of being at *Womyn.* It is special."

But even in this all-women environment, boundary lines were drawn between acceptable and unacceptable behavior. Here we focus on two examples where power dynamics between workers, especially between editors and interns, led to uncomfortable situations that the editors thought could be defined as sexual harassment.

(1) At *Womyn,* all staff members, including interns, attend and participate in editorial meetings. While internship programs are common in the magazine publishing industry, the high level of participation interns enjoy at *Womyn* seems to be quite unusual. During a staff meeting to generate ideas for a special issue on sexuality, the editor-in-chief asked the interns for their input. She wanted to draw on their experiences going off to college for the first time, dealing with boyfriends

and girlfriends, perhaps even handling date rape. When asked whether anyone was ever uncomfortable about the way people talked about sex at work, the assistant to the editor-in-chief said that after the staff meeting about the sex issue, an intern approached her and said:

> *"God, can I answer this?" You know, "I feel so embarrassed" or "I wanted to say something, but I was so embarrassed that everybody's sitting around. You know, can I talk about it?"*

The intern did not want to be forced to self-disclose. The request for information in a public forum felt impersonal to her and exploitative, like she was being used, not comforted and supported by her friends.

The interns did not describe these experiences as sexual harassment, however. At *Womyn,* workers give each other the benefit of the doubt that they know what sexual harassment is and they are opposed to it in all its manifestations. Sexual harassment is implicitly defined as something that "other" people do—not feminists. For this reason, some workers at *Womyn* may not feel empowered to complain about a co-worker's or supervisor's behavior, despite its potentially negative impact.

(2) A second incident where people expressed discomfort with sexuality at *Womyn* was linked to the ambiguous hierarchy in the editorial department. The emphasis on sisterhood in the dorm room culture can lead to confusing relationships between members of the organization who hold differing amounts of power. Kara contends that things can get a "bit odd" when people talk or joke about sex at work. When asked for an example of when things "get odd," she said:

> *The last batch of interns that we had, one of my interns hit on me—quite strongly. And that was a very uncomfortable situation. But, I think it would have been something that would not have happened at any other office. I had just come to Womyn and I wasn't as aware of the demarcation lines. It was horrifying.*

Kara explained that after a party at a co-worker's house, a few interns and other *Womyn* staff decided to go dancing. At the end of the night she and one intern were the only ones left and they decided to go to a strip show at a lesbian bar. Kara identifies herself as heterosexual and assumed that the intern she was with was heterosexual as well. Sometime that night the intern made a pass at Kara which she characterized as extremely aggressive and similar to some sexual interactions she had experienced in college "when people were half-drunk." As Kara reflected back on this night, she was clearly upset at herself for taking the intern to a bar. She felt this was completely inappropriate behavior on her part:

> *I would have never done that in another workplace. NEVER!! After it happened, I was like, "How could you not see that this was completely inappropriate behavior? You do not take your intern to [a lesbian bar with a strip show]. That is ridiculous!"*

There are many important issues that may explain why, at *Womyn,* the lines of demarcation between acceptable and unacceptable sexual expression were unclear to Kara, but one major issue seems to have impacted her definition of this situation as "horrifying": the de-emphasis on hierarchy. She says, "Here you have a very strange thing where there is a hierarchy, but we are not supposed to talk about it. We are not supposed to acknowledge it and we are all supposed to be friends."

Oerton (1996) points out that U.S. feminists have been in the forefront of creating flatter, non-hierarchical organizations as part of their effort to transform social inequality. The assumption is that when organizations lack formal hierarchies there will be an absence of gendered and sexualized inequalities. In the case of *Womyn,* a definite hierarchy exists, but its existence is informally denied. Kara implies that the invisible hierarchy at *Womyn* may have encouraged her to think it was acceptable to go out to a bar and socialize with an intern, and for the intern to believe it was acceptable to express sexual interest in Kara. But Kara believes that in a hierarchical situation, sexual relationships should not be permitted because in situations of unequal power, subordinates are vulnerable to abuses of power, including sexual harassment.

In both of these examples, the respondents identified unequal power as the defining feature of sexual harassment. Unpaid interns are seen as especially vulnerable: they fear that the dorm room disclosure of personal sexual information may be exploitative when hierarchical positions come into play, particularly in editorial meetings; or that interns may be easily taken advantage of by those who are more powerful. From the viewpoint of these editors, the key feature of sexual harassment is not that it is sexual, or even personal, but rather, that it involves the exploitation of someone in a less powerful position by someone with organizational power over them.

The dorm room culture at *Womyn* encourages open and frank discussion of sexuality. Editors are expected to discuss their sexual needs and desires. Most staff members say they enjoy the intimacy between coworkers involved in sharing and joking about personal aspects of their lives. Editors at *Womyn* did not consider sexual harassment to be a problem at their organization because there were no men in the department, and perhaps more importantly, because they shared a feminist analysis of sexual harassment as an abuse of power. In this regard, it is interesting that both of the examples of sexual harassment we described were described not by the person who was the target of the possible harassment, but by the person occupying the more powerful position who was concerned about the vulnerabilities of those less powerful. The editors at *Womyn* felt safe from sexual harassment because the norms and values of the dorm room culture supported constant vigilance against it, even by those who are in charge.

DISCUSSION

The organizational cultures of the editorial departments at *Gentleman's Sophisticate* and *Womyn* are quite distinct. Imagine that it is your first day of work as an editor at *Gentleman's Sophisticate*. Pictures of naked women are hanging on the walls, and copies of the pornographic magazine lay scattered on coffee tables and on the desks of your colleagues. Your new colleagues stop you in the hallway to tell a dirty joke. Getting "one up" on people by telling especially crude or "politically incorrect" jokes will enhance your status and put you in the "in" crowd. You are told to sign an agreement that says that you understand that exposure to sexually explicit materials will not "count" as sexual harassment in this workplace. If you are shocked or offended by this sexualized atmosphere, you have to let it "roll off your back," or else you'll probably quit or be fired. If you agree to stay on the job, you might begin to define yourself as someone who doesn't let those things bother them. But everyone— including your boss and the legal department— agrees that there is a "line" beyond which the sexual bantering becomes sexual harassment. That line is the personal, and anyone who violates it is likely to be reprimanded.

Now imagine your first day of work at *Womyn*. You learn that "Food, Sex, and Hair" are the popular topics of conversation. Office sex talk requires personal disclosure and soul-searching discussions of the political implications of your intimate sexual relationships. If you don't fully participate in this personal disclosure, you will be marginalized to some degree. You notice that your coworkers share backrubs, go out dancing together, and hold slumber parties. The topic of sexual harassment in this workplace will probably not come up, since everyone here is a feminist who presumably knows where everyone else stands on the issue. The consensus is that sexual harassment is an abuse of organizational power, meaning that the least powerful members of the organization, the interns, are the most vulnerable.

Both workplaces are sexualized, although very differently. Editors at *Womyn* would surely object to normative behaviors at *Gentleman's Sophisticate,* and vice versa. To characterize this difference we have suggested the analogy of the "locker room v. the dorm room." Because locker rooms are implicitly assumed to be male, dorm rooms, female, these gendered metaphors capture both the cultural values of the two workplaces as well as the skewed numerical proportions of men and women who work in high-level management positions in them. We have argued that these different organizational cultures help explain why workers at *Gentleman's Sophisticate* and *Womyn* define sexual behavior differently. While not all individuals at each workplace share the same interpretation of specific interactions, they do seem to share similar understandings of the meaning of sexual harassment and the difference between acceptable and unacceptable sexual behavior.

This finding has important implications for the study of sexual harassment. It challenges the validity of research that uses seemingly objective lists of unwanted sexual behaviors to gauge the prevalence of harassment (Williams 1997). The meaning of sexual harassment varies depending on organizational context. The boundary between acceptable and unacceptable sexual behavior is the result of a complex interplay between the characteristics of individual workers, the structural features of an organization, and the cultural norms in any given work place. Researchers should consider this context when measuring the prevalence of harassment. This perspective draws on a long tradition of sociologists beginning with Durkheim and later Goffman who suggest that the rituals or performances we engage in on a daily basis are complicated interactions "which hold society together, but in a stratified way" (Collins 1994:219). Perhaps the definition of sexual harassment as an illegal act has led us to assume that sexual harassment is the exception in the workplace instead of the norm. We suggest that taking a closer look at the workplace norms regarding sexuality that shape interactions and rituals at work will be a more fruitful avenue than focusing on individual behaviors or definitions of sexual harassment taken out of context.

Our research also has important insights for policy makers working to find remedies for sexual harassment. According to legal scholar Vicki Schultz (1998a, 1998b), many sexual harassment policies promote the misguided belief that all forms of sexual expression are harmful to women. In some cases, concern over sexual harassment litigation has led companies to forbid men and women from travelling together on business; in others a "five second rule" has been imposed prohibiting men from looking at women for more than five seconds at a time. These draconian measures, ostensibly imposed to "protect" women, can actually harm them by denying them equal opportunities and respect. Schultz insists that not all sexual behavior is harmful to women. She writes, "sexuality is part of the human experience, and so long as organizations still employ people rather than robots, it will continue to flourish in one form or another. And sexuality is not simply a tool of gender domination; it is also a potential source of empowerment and even pleasure for women on the job" (1998b:14). She urges courts to conduct in-depth investigations of the meaning of sexual expression in a given workplace before determining whether something is sexual harassment.

Our research supports the view that sexual behavior itself is not necessarily harmful to women. Sometimes an offensive nude pin-up is sexual harassment; sometimes it isn't. Sometimes demands for personal disclosure about sexual behavior are sexual harassment; some times they aren't. Individuals who experience unwanted sexual behavior take culture into consideration when deciding whether they have experienced sexual harassment; researchers and policy makers should do likewise.

Our research did not uncover rampant sexual harassment at *Womyn* or *Gentleman's Sophisticate,* but it did reveal the type of behaviors that the editors would consider harassment. According to Schultz, this information would be valuable to the courts if one of the editors were to file a complaint of sexual harassment against their employer. She argues that sexually explicit behavior must be examined in the "larger workplace context" to determine if it, along with any objectionable "nonsexual behavior . . . created a discriminatory work environment" (1998a:1795). She would insist that the fact that the workplaces are sexual does not in itself constitute proof that the women employed there were sexually harassed. Schultz writes, "Sex should be treated just like anything else in the workplace: Where it furthers sex discrimination, it should go. Where it doesn't, it's not the business of our civil rights laws" (1998b:15). For a finding of sexual harassment, the complainant would have to link their experience to blocked opportunities or some other form of gender discrimination.

We need more case studies of organizational sexuality in a variety of workplace settings to broaden our understanding of how organizational culture influences workplace definitions of acceptable and unacceptable sexual joking and behavior. In this study, we examined two extreme cases chosen to highlight how culture matters. But what about editors who work for other magazines which are not strongly associated with gender and sexual ideology, such as *Businessweek* and *Time*? And how do workers in other industries, like retail or computing, draw boundary lines? By examining organizational sexuality in a number of work contexts, we can begin to understand sexual harassment as part of the larger phenomenon of sexuality at work without falling into the trap of equating all sex at work with harassment. A research agenda attuned to the complex ways that organizational sexuality is put to use in the service of pleasure and discrimination will move us closer to the goal of eliminating blocked opportunities for women (and men) without reducing them to helpless victims in need of protection from sex.

REFERENCES

Adkins, Lisa. 1995. *Gendered Work: Sexuality, Family, and the Labour Market.* Buckingham, UK: Open University Press.

Allison, Anne. 1994. *Nightwork: Sexuality, Pleasure, and Corporate Masculinity in a Tokyo Hostess Club.* Chicago: The University of Chicago Press.

Collins, Patricia Hill. 2000. *Black Feminist Thought: Knowledge, Consciousness, and the Politics of Black Empowerment.* New York: Routledge.

Collins, Randall. 1994. *Four Sociological Traditions.* New York: Oxford University Press.

Connell, Robert W. 1995. *Masculinities.* Berkeley: University of California Press.

Curry, Timothy Jon. 1991. "Fraternal Bonding in the Locker Room: A Profeminist Analysis of Talk about Competition and Women." *Sociology of Sport Journal* 8:119–135.

Fitzgerald, Louise F., Suzanne Swan, and Karla Fischer. 1995. "Why Didn't She Just Report Him?: The Psychological and Legal Implications of Women's Responses to Sexual Harassment." *Journal of Social Issues* 51, 1:117–138.

Foner, Nancy. 1994. *The Caregiving Dilemma: Work in an American Nursing Home.* Berkeley: University of California Press.

Gherardi, Sylvia. 1995. *Gender, Symbolism and Organizational Cultures.* London: Sage.

Giuffre, Patti A., and Christine L. Williams. 1994. "Boundary Lines: Labeling Sexual Harassment in Restaurants." *Gender and Society* 8, 3:378–401.

Goffman, Erving. 1963. *Stigma: Notes on the Management of a Spoiled Identity.* Upper Saddle River, NJ: Prentice Hall.

Gruber, James E. 1998. "The Impact of Male Work Environments and Organizational Policies on Women's Experiences of Sexual Harassment," *Gender and Society* 12(3):301–320.

Gutek, Barbara A., Aaron Groff Cohen, and Alison M. Konrad. 1990. "Predicting Social-Sexual Behavior at Work: A Contact Hypothesis." *Academy of Management Journal* 33:560–577.

Hearn, Jeff, and Wendy Parkin. 1987. *Sex at Work: The Power and Paradox of Organization Sexuality.* New York: St. Martin's Press.

Hochschild, Arlie Russell. 1983. *The Managed Heart: Commercialization of Human Feeling.* Berkeley: University of California Press.

Hulin, Charles L., Louise F. Fitzgerald, and Fritz Drasgow. 1996. "Organizational Influences on Sexual Harassment." Pp. 127–150 in Margaret S. Stockdale (ed.), *Sexual Harassment in the Workplace: Perspectives, Frontiers, and Response Strategies.* Thousand Oaks, CA: Sage.

Leidner, Robin. 1993. *Fast Food, Fast Talk: Service Work and the Routinization of Everyday Life.* Berkeley: University of California Press.

Loe, Meika. 1996. "Working for Men—at the Intersection of Power, Gender, and Sexuality." *Sociological Inquiry* 66:399–421.

Lyman, Peter. 1987. "The Fraternal Bond as a Joking Relationship: A Case Study of the Role of Sexist Jokes in Male Group Bonding." In Michael Kimmel (ed.), *Changing Men: New Directions in Research on Men and Masculinity.* Newbury Park, CA: Sage.

Messner, Michael A. 1992. *Power at Play: Sports and the Problem of Masculinity.* Boston: Beacon Press.

Oerton, Sarah. 1996. *Beyond Hierarchy: Gender, Sexuality, and the Social Economy.* London: Taylor and Francis.

Petrocelli, William, and Barbara Kate Repa. 1998. *Sexual Harassment on the Job: What It Is and How to Stop It,* 3rd ed. Berkeley, CA: Nolo Press.

Pierce, Jennifer L. 1995. *Gender Trials: Emotional Lives in Contemporary Law Firms.* Berkeley: University of California Press.

Pryor, John B., Janet L. Giedd, and Karen B. Williams. 1995. "A Social Psychological Model for Predicting Sexual Harassment." *Journal of Social Issues* 51(1):69–84.

Pryor, John B., Christine M. LaVite, and Lynnette M. Stoller. 1993. "A Social Psychological Analysis of Sexual Harassment: The Person/Situation Interaction." *Journal of Vocational Behavior* 42:68–83.

Reskin, Barbara, and Irene Padavic. 1994. *Women and Men at Work.* Thousand Oaks, CA: Pine Forge.

Salzinger, Leslie. 2000. "Manufacturing Sexual Subjects: 'Harassment,' Desire and Discipline on a Maquiladora Shopfloor." *Ethnography* 1:67–92.

Schultz, Vicki. 1998a. "Reconceptualizing Sexual Harassment." *Yale Law Journal* 107 (6) (April): 1683–1805.

———. 1998b. "Sex Is the Least of It: Let's Focus Harassment Law on Work, Not Sex." *The Nation* (May 25) 266:11–15.

Trice, Harrison M. 1993. *Occupational Subcultures in the Workplace.* Ithaca, NY: ILR Press.

Welsh, Sandy. 1999. "Gender and Sexual Harassment." *Annual Review of Sociology* 25:169–190.

West, Cornell. 1993. *Race Matters.* New York: Vintage Books.

Williams, Christine L. 1997. "Sexual Harassment in Organizations. A Critique of Current Research and Policy." *Sexuality and Culture* 1:19–43.

Williams, Christine L., Patti Giuffre, and Kirsten Dellinger. 1999. "Sexuality in the Workplace: Organizational Control, Sexual Harassment, and the Pursuit of Pleasure." *Annual Review of Sociology* 25:73–93.

CHAPTER 3

ACCOMMODATION TO DEVIANCE

How Women Experience Battering

KATHLEEN J. FERRARO and JOHN M. JOHNSON

Conduct depends on social definitions. Before people can take action, they have to have some ideas about what kind of action to take and with whom. Some general questions the sociology of deviance asks are the following: Who creates the definitions of deviance? Who applies those definitions? What are the consequences of applying definitions? Applications of definitions and their consequences vary considerably according to the kinds of groups in which labeling and responses to deviance occur. If in some groups there is a lapse of time between repeated violations and labeling, in others there is a history of repeated violations without labeling.

Battered women are a case in point. Kathleen J. Ferraro and John M. Johnson note that the general question asked about battered women is "Why do they stay with their partners?" People outside the situation of battering are quick to define the batterer as the deviant. By contrast, battered women in the early stages of the relationship may not see the batterer's actions as deviant or may define themselves as the deviant ones. In time, over a long series of stages, some battered women are able to see the batterer as the one who is the deviant and are able to end the relationship with their partner when others assist them in redefining their situation.

. . . Marriages and their unofficial counterparts develop through the efforts of each partner to maintain feelings of love and intimacy. In modern, Western cultures, the value placed on marriage is high; individuals invest a great amount of emotion in their spouses, and expect a return on that investment. The majority of women who marry still adopt the roles of wives and mothers as primary identities, even when they work outside the home, and thus have a strong motivation to succeed in their domestic roles. Married women remain economically dependent on their husbands. In 1978, married men in the United States earned an average of $293 a week, while married women earned $167 a week (U.S. Department of Labor, 1980). Given these high expectations and dependencies, the costs of recognizing failures and dissolving marriages are significant. Divorce is an increasingly common phenomenon in the United States, but it is still labeled a social problem and is seldom

Reprinted from Kathleen Ferraro and John M. Johnson, "How Women Experience Battering: The Process of Victimization," *Social Problems*, Vol. 30, No. 3: 325–339. © 1983, The Society for the Study of Social Problems, Inc. Used by permission of the University of California Press and the author. All rights reserved.

undertaken without serious deliberations and emotional upheavals (Bohannan, 1971). Levels of commitment vary widely, but some degree of commitment is implicit in the marriage contract.

When marital conflicts emerge there is usually some effort to negotiate an agreement or bargain, to ensure the continuity of the relationship (Scanzoni, 1972). Couples employ a variety of strategies, depending on the nature and extent of resources available to them, to resolve conflicts without dissolving relationships. It is thus possible for marriages to continue for years, surviving the inevitable conflicts that occur (Sprey, 1971).

In describing conflict-management, Spiegel (1968) distinguishes between "role induction" and "role modification." Role induction refers to conflict in which "one or the other parties to the conflict agrees, submits, goes along with, becomes convinced, or is persuaded in some way" (1968:402). Role modification, on the other hand, involves adaptations by both partners. Role induction seems particularly applicable to battered women who accommodate their husbands' abuse. Rather than seeking help or escaping, as people typically do when attacked by strangers, battered women often rationalize violence from their husbands, at least initially. Although remaining with a violent man does not indicate that a woman views violence as an acceptable aspect of the relationship, the length of time that a woman stays in the marriage after abuse begins is a rough index of her efforts to accommodate the situation. In a U.S. study of 350 battered women, Pagelow (1981) found the median length of stay after violence began was four years; some left in less than one year, others stayed as long as 42 years.

Battered women have good reasons to rationalize violence. There are few institutional, legal, or cultural supports for women fleeing violent marriages. In Roy's (1977:32) survey of 150 battered women, 90 percent said they "thought of leaving and would have done so had the resources been available to them." Eighty percent of Pagelow's (1981) sample indicated previous, failed attempts to leave their husbands. Despite the development of the international shelter movement, changes in police practices, and legislation to protect battered women since 1975, it remains extraordinarily difficult for a battered woman to escape a violent husband determined to maintain his control. At least one woman, Mary Parziale, has been murdered by an abusive husband while residing in a shelter (Beverly, 1978); others have been murdered after leaving shelters to establish new, independent homes (Garcia, 1978). When these practical and social constraints are combined with love for and commitment to an abuser, it is obvious that there is a strong incentive—often a practical necessity—to rationalize violence.

Previous research on the rationalizations of deviant offenders has revealed a typology of "techniques of neutralization," which allow offenders to view their actions as normal, acceptable, or at least justifiable (Sykes and Matza, 1957). A similar typology can be constructed for victims. Extending the concepts developed by Sykes and Matza, we assigned the responses of battered women we interviewed to one of six categories of rationalization: (1) the appeal to the salvation ethic; (2) the denial of the victimizer; (3) the denial of injury; (4) the denial of victimization; (5) the denial of options; and (6) the appeal to higher loyalties. The women usually employed at least one of these techniques to make sense of their situations; often they employed two or more, simultaneously or over time.

1. *The appeal to the salvation ethic:* This rationalization is grounded in a woman's desire to be of service to others. Abusing husbands are viewed as deeply troubled, perhaps "sick," individuals, dependent on their wives' nurturance for survival. Battered women place their own safety and happiness below their commitment to "saving my man" from whatever malady they perceive as the source of their husbands' problems (Ferraro, 1979a). The appeal to the salvation ethic is a common response to an alcoholic or drug-dependent abuser. The battered partners of substance-abusers frequently describe the charming, charismatic personality of their sober mates, viewing this appealing personality as the "real man" being destroyed by disease. They then assume responsibility for helping their partners to overcome their problems, viewing the batterings they receive as an index of their partners' pathology. Abuse must be endured while helping the man return to his "normal" self. One woman said:

> I thought I was going to be Florence Nightingale. He had so much potential; I could see how good he really was, and I was going to "save" him. I thought I was the only thing keeping him going, and that if I left he'd lose his job and wind up in jail. I'd make excuses to everybody for him. I'd call work and lie when he was drunk, saying he was sick. I never criticized him, because he needed my approval.

2. *The denial of the victimizer:* This technique is similar to the salvation ethic, except that victims do not assume responsibility for solving their abusers' problems. Women perceive battering as an event beyond the control of both spouses, and blame it on some external force. The violence is judged situational and temporary, because it is linked to unusual circumstances or a sickness which can be cured. Pressures at work, the loss of a job, or legal problems are all situations which battered women assume as the causes of their partners' violence. Mental illness, alcoholism, and drug addiction are also viewed as external, uncontrollable afflictions by many battered women who accept the medical perspective on such problems. By focusing on factors beyond the control of their abuser, women deny their husbands' intent to do them harm, and thus rationalize violent episodes.

> He's sick. He didn't used to be this way, but he can't handle alcohol. It's really like a disease, being an alcoholic. . . . I think too that this is what he saw at home, his father is a very violent man, and alcoholic too, so it's really not his fault, because this is all he has ever known.

3. *The denial of injury:* For some women, the experience of being battered by a spouse is so discordant with their expectations that they simply refuse to acknowledge it. When hospitalization is not required—and it seldom is for most cases of battering[1]—routines quickly return to normal. Meals are served, jobs and schools are attended, and daily chores completed. Even with lingering pain, bruises, and cuts, the normality of everyday life overrides the strange, confusing memory of the attack. When husbands refuse to discuss or acknowledge the event, in some cases even accusing their wives of insanity, women sometimes come to believe the violence never occurred. The denial of injury does not mean that women feel no pain. They know they are hurt, but define the hurt as tolerable or normal. Just as individuals tolerate a wide range of physical discomfort before seeking medical help, battered women tolerate a wide range of physical abuse before defining it as an injurious assault. One woman explained her disbelief at her first battering:

> I laid in bed and cried all night. I could not believe it had happened, and I didn't want to believe it. We had only been married a year, and I was pregnant and excited about starting a family. Then all of a sudden, this! The next morning he told me he was sorry and it wouldn't happen again, and I gladly kissed and made up. I wanted to forget the whole thing, and wouldn't let myself worry about what it meant for us.

4. *The denial of victimization:* Victims often blame themselves for the violence, thereby neutralizing the responsibility of the spouse. Pagelow (1981) found that 99.4 percent of battered women felt they did not deserve to be beaten, and 51 percent said they had done nothing to provoke an attack. The battered women in our sample did not believe violence against them was justified, but some felt it could have been avoided if they had been more passive and conciliatory. Both Pagelow's and our samples are biased in this area, because they were made up almost entirely of women who had already left their abusers, and thus would have been unlikely to feel major responsibility for the abuse they received. Retrospective accounts of victimization in our sample, however, did reveal evidence that some women believed their right to leave violent men was restricted by their participation in the conflicts. One subject said:

> Well, I couldn't really do anything about it, because I did ask for it. I knew how to get at him, and I'd keep after it and keep after it until he got fed up and knocked me right out. I can't say I like it, but I shouldn't have nagged him like I did.

As Pagelow (1981) noted, there is a difference between provocation and justification. A battered woman's belief that her actions angered her spouse to the point of violence is not synonymous with the belief that violence was therefore *justified*. But belief in provocation may diminish a woman's capacity for retaliation or self-defense, because it blurs her concept of responsibility. A woman's acceptance of responsibility for the violent incident is encouraged by an abuser who continually denigrates her and makes unrealistic demands. Depending on the social supports available, and the personality of the battered woman, the man's accusations of inadequacy may assume the status of truth. Such beliefs of inferiority inhibit the development of a notion of victimization.

5. *The denial of options:* This technique is composed of two elements: practical options and emotional options. Practical options, including alternative housing, source of income, and protection from an abuser, are clearly limited by the patriarchal structure of Western society. However, there are differences in the ways battered women respond to these obstacles, ranging from determined struggle to acquiescence. For a variety of reasons, some battered women do not take full advantage of the practical opportunities which are available to escape, and some return to abusers voluntarily even after establishing an independent lifestyle. Others ignore the most severe constraints in their efforts to escape their relationships. For example, one resident of the shelter we observed walked 30 miles in her bedroom slippers to get to the shelter, and required medical attention for blisters and cuts to her feet. On the

other hand, a woman who had a full-time job, had rented an apartment, and had been given by the shelter all the clothes, furniture, and basics necessary to set up housekeeping, returned to her husband two weeks after leaving the shelter. Other women refused to go to job interviews, keep appointments with social workers, or move out of the state for their own protection (Ferraro, 1981b). Such actions are frightening for women who have led relatively isolated or protected lives, but failure to take action leaves few alternatives to a violent marriage. The belief of battered women that they will not be able to make it on their own—a belief often fueled by years of abuse and oppression—is a major impediment to [acknowledgment] that one is a victim and taking action.

The denial of *emotional* options imposes still further restrictions. Battered women may feel that no one else can provide intimacy and companionship. While physical beating is painful and dangerous, the prospect of a lonely, celibate existence is often too frightening to risk. It is not uncommon for battered women to express the belief that their abuser is the only man they could love, thus severely limiting their opportunities to discover new, more supportive relationships. One woman said:

> He's all I've got. My dad's gone, and my mother disowned me when I married him. And he's really special. He understands me, and I understand him. Nobody could take his place.

6. *The appeal to higher loyalties:* This appeal involves enduring battering for the sake of some higher commitment, either religious or traditional. The Christian belief that women should serve their husbands as men serve God is invoked as a rationalization to endure a husband's violence for later rewards in the afterlife. Clergy may support this view by advising women to pray and try harder to please their husbands (Davidson, 1978; McGlinchey, 1981). Other women have a strong commitment to the nuclear family, and find divorce repugnant. They may believe that for their children's sake, any marriage is better than no

marriage. One woman we interviewed divorced her husband of 35 years after her last child left home. More commonly women who have survived violent relationships for that long do not have the desire or strength to divorce and begin a new life. When the appeal to higher loyalties is employed as a strategy to cope with battering, commitment to and involvement with an ideal overshadows the mundane reality of violence.

CATALYSTS FOR CHANGE

Rationalization is a way of coping with a situation in which, for either practical or emotional reasons, or both, a battered woman is stuck. For some women, the situation and the beliefs that rationalize it, may continue for a lifetime. For others, changes may occur within the relationship, within individuals, or in available resources which serve as catalysts for redefining the violence. When battered women reject prior rationalizations and begin to view themselves as true victims of abuse, the victimization process begins.[2]

There are a variety of catalysts for redefining abuse; we discuss six: (1) a change in the level of violence; (2) a change in resources; (3) a change in the relationship; (4) despair; (5) a change in the visibility of violence; and (6) external definitions of the relationship.

1. *A change in the level of violence:* Although Gelles (1976) reports that the severity of abuse is an important factor in women's decisions to leave violent situations, Pagelow (1981) found no significant correlation between the number of years spent cohabiting with an abuser and the severity of abuse. On the contrary: the longer women lived with an abuser, the more severe the violence they endured, since violence increased in severity over time. What does seem to serve as a catalyst is a sudden change in the relative level of violence. Women who suddenly realize that battering may be fatal may reject rationalizations in order to save their lives. One woman who had been severely beaten by an alcoholic husband for many

years explained her decision to leave on the basis of a direct threat to her life:

> *It was like a pendulum. He'd swing to the extremes both ways. He'd get drunk and beat me up, then he'd get sober and treat me like a queen. One day he put a gun to my head and pulled the trigger. It wasn't loaded. But that's when I decided I'd had it. I sued for separation of property. I knew what was coming again, so I got out. I didn't want to. I still loved the guy, but I knew I had to for my own sanity.*

There are, of course, many cases of homicide in which women did not escape soon enough. In 1979, 7.6 percent of all murders in the United States where the relationship between the victim and the offender was known were murders of wives by husbands (Flanagan *et al.*, 1982). Increases in severity do not guarantee a reinterpretation of the situation, but may play a part in the process.

2. *A change in resources:* Although some women rationalize cohabiting with an abuser by claiming they have no options, others begin reinterpreting violence when the resources necessary for escape become available. The emergence of safe homes or shelters since 1970 has produced a new resource for battered women. While not completely adequate or satisfactory, the mere existence of a place to go alters the situation in which battering is experienced (Johnson, 1981). Public support of shelters is a statement to battered women that abuse need not be tolerated. Conversely, political trends which limit resources available to women, such as cutbacks in government funding to social programs, increase fears that life outside a violent marriage is economically impossible. One 55-year-old woman discussed this catalyst:

> *I stayed with him because I didn't want my kids to have the same life I did. My parents were divorced, and I was always so ashamed of that. . . . Yes, they're all on their own now, so there's no reason left to stay.*

3. *A change in the relationship:* Walker (1979), in discussing the stages of a battering relationship, notes that violent incidents are usually followed by periods of remorse and solicitude. Such phases deepen the emotional bonds, and make rejection of an abuser more difficult. But as battering progresses, periods of remorse may shorten, or disappear, eliminating the basis for maintaining a positive outlook on the marriage. After a number of episodes of violence, a man may realize that his victim will not retaliate or escape, and thus feel no need to express remorse. Extended periods devoid of kindness or love may alter a woman's feelings toward her partner so much so that she eventually begins to define herself as a victim of abuse. One woman recalled:

> At first, you know, we used to have so much fun together. He has kind've, you know, a magnetic personality; he can be really charming. But it isn't fun anymore. Since the baby came, it's changed completely. He just wants me to stay at home, while he goes out with his friends. He doesn't even talk to me, most of the time. . . . No, I don't really love him anymore, not like I did.

4. *Despair:* Changes in the relationship may result in a loss of hope that "things will get better." When hope is destroyed and replaced by despair, rationalizations of violence may give way to the recognition of victimization. Feelings of hopelessness or despair are the basis for some efforts to assist battered women, such as Al-Anon.[3] The director of an Al-Anon organized shelter explained the concept of "hitting bottom":

> Before the Al-Anon program can really be of benefit, a woman has to hit bottom. When you hit bottom, you realize that all of your own efforts to control the situation have failed; you feel helpless and lost and worthless and completely disenchanted with the world. Women can't really be helped unless they're ready for it and want it. Some women come here when things get bad, but they aren't really ready to be committed to Al-Anon. Things haven't gotten bad enough for them, and they go right back. We see this all the time.

5. *A change in the visibility of violence:* Creating a web of rationalizations to overlook violence is accomplished more easily if no intruders are present to question their validity. Since most violence between couples occurs in private, there are seldom conflicting interpretations of the event from outsiders. Only 7 percent of the respondents in Gelles' (1974) study who discussed spatial location of violence indicated events which took place outside the home, but all reported incidents within the home. Others report similar findings (Pittman and Handy, 1964; Pokorny, 1965; Wolfgang, 1958). If violence does occur in the presence of others, it may trigger a reinterpretation process. Battering in private is degrading, but battering in public is humiliating, for it is a statement of subordination and powerlessness. Having others witness abuse may create intolerable feelings of shame which undermine prior rationalizations.

> He never hit me in public before—it was always at home. But the Saturday I got back (returned to husband from shelter), we went Christmas shopping and he slapped me in the store because of some stupid joke I made. People saw it, I know, I felt so stupid, like, they must all think what a jerk I am, what a sick couple, and I thought, "God, I must be crazy to let him do this."

6. *External definitions of the relationship:* A change in visibility is usually accomplished by the interjection of external definitions of abuse. External definitions vary depending on their source and the situation; they either reinforce or undermine rationalizations. Battered women who request help frequently find others—and especially officials—don't believe their story or are unsympathetic (Pagelow, 1981; Pizzey, 1974). Experimental research by Shotland and Straw (1976) supports these reports. Observers usually fail to respond when a woman is attacked by a man, and justify nonintervention on the grounds that they assumed the victim and offender were married. One young woman discussed how lack of support from her family left her without hope:

> It wouldn't be so bad if my own family gave a damn about me. . . . Yeah, they know I'm here, and they don't care. They didn't care about me when

I was a kid, so why should they care now? I got raped and beat as a kid, and now I get beat as an adult. Life is a big joke.

Clearly, such responses from family members contribute to the belief among battered women that there are no alternatives and that they must tolerate the abuse. However, when outsiders respond with unqualified support of the victim and condemnation of violent men, their definitions can be a potent catalyst toward victimization. Friends and relatives who show genuine concern for a woman's well-being may initiate an awareness of danger which contradicts previous rationalizations.

My mother-in-law knew what was going on, but she wouldn't admit it. . . . I said, "Mom, what do you think these bruises are?" and she said, "Well, some people just bruise easy. I do it all the time, bumping into things.". . . And he just denied it, pretended like nothing happened, and if I'd said I wanted to talk about it, he'd say, "Life goes on, you can't just dwell on things.". . . But this time, my neighbor knew what happened, she saw it, and when he denied it, she said, "I can't believe it! You know that's not true!". . . and I was so happy that finally, somebody else saw what was goin' on, and I just told him then that this time I wasn't gonna come home!

Shelters for battered women serve not only as material resources, but as sources of external definitions which contribute to the victimization process. They offer refuge from a violent situation in which a woman may contemplate her circumstances and what she wants to do about them. Within a shelter, women meet counselors and other battered women who are familiar with rationalizations of violence and the reluctance to give up commitment to a spouse. In counseling sessions, and informal conversations with other residents, women hear horror stories from others who have already defined themselves as victims. They are supported for expressing anger and rejecting responsibility for their abuse (Ferraro, 1981a). The goal of many shelters is to overcome

feelings of guilt and inadequacy so that women can make choices in their best interests. In this atmosphere, violent incidents are reexamined and redefined as assaults in which the woman was victimized.

How others respond to a battered woman's situation is critical. The closer the relationship of others, the more significant their response is to a woman's perception of the situation. Thus, children can either help or hinder the victim. Pizzey (1974) found adolescent boys at a shelter in Chiswick, England, often assumed the role of the abusing father and themselves abused their mothers, both verbally and physically. On the other hand, children at the shelter we observed often became extremely protective and nurturing toward their mothers. This phenomenon has been thoroughly described elsewhere (Ferraro, 1981a). Children who have been abused by fathers who also beat their mothers experience high levels of anxiety, and rarely want to be reunited with their fathers. A 13-year-old, abused daughter of a shelter resident wrote the following message to her stepfather:

I am going to be honest and not lie. No, I don't want you to come back. It's not that I am jealous because mom loves you. It is [I] am afraid I won't live to see 18. I did care about you a long time ago, but now I can't care, for the simple reason you['re] always calling us names, even my friends. And another reason is, I am tired of seeing mom hurt. She has been hurt enough in her life, and I don't want her to be hurt any more.

No systematic research has been conducted on the influence children exert on their battered mothers, but it seems obvious that the willingness of children to leave a violent father would be an important factor in a woman's desire to leave.

The relevance of these catalysts to a woman's interpretation of violence vary with her own situation and personality. The process of rejecting rationalizations and becoming a victim is ambiguous, confusing, and emotional. We now turn to the feelings involved in a victimization.

THE EMOTIONAL CAREER
OF VICTIMIZATION

As rationalizations give way to perceptions of victimization, a woman's feelings about herself, her spouse, and her situation change. These feelings are imbedded in a cultural, political, and interactional structure. Initially, abuse is contrary to a woman's cultural expectations of behavior between intimates, and therefore engenders feelings of betrayal. The husband has violated his wife's expectations of love and protection, and thus betrayed her confidence in him. The feeling of betrayal, however, is balanced by the husband's efforts to explain his behavior, and by the woman's reluctance to abandon faith. Additionally, the political dominance of men within and outside the family mediate women's ability to question the validity of their husband's actions.

At the interpersonal level, psychological abuse accompanying violence often invokes feelings of guilt and shame in the battered victim. Men define violence as a response to their wives' inadequacies or provocations, which leads battered women to feel that they have failed. Such character assaults are devastating, and create long-lasting feelings of inferiority (Ferraro, 1979b):

> I've been verbally abused as well. It takes you a long time to . . . you may say you feel good and you may . . . but inside, you know what's been said to you and it hurts for a long time. You need to build up your self-image and make yourself feel like you're a useful person, that you're valuable, and that you're a good parent. You might think these things, and you may say them. . . . I'm gonna prove it to myself.

Psychologists working with battered women consistently report that self-confidence wanes over years of ridicule and criticism (Hilberman and Munson, 1978; Walker, 1979).

Feelings of guilt and shame are also mixed with a hope that things will get better, at least in the early stages of battering. Even the most violent man is nonviolent much of the time, so there is always a basis for believing that violence is exceptional and the "real man" is not a threat. The vacillation between violence and fear on the one hand, and nonviolence and affection on the other was described by a shelter resident:

> First of all, the first beatings—you can't believe it yourself. I'd go to bed, and I'd cry, and I just couldn't believe this was happening. And I'd wake up the next morning thinking that couldn't of happened, or maybe it was my fault. It's so unbelievable that this person that you're married to and you love would do that to you but yet you can't leave either because, ya' know, for the other 29 days of the month that person loves you and is with you.

Hope wanes as periods of love and remorse dwindle. Feelings of love and intimacy are gradually replaced with loneliness and pessimism. Battered women who no longer feel love for their husbands but remain in their marriages enter a period of emotional dormancy. They survive each day, performing necessary tasks, with a dull depression and lack of enthusiasm. While some battered women live out their lives in this emotional desert, others are spurred by catalysts to feel either the total despair or mortal fear which leads them to seek help.

Battered women who perceive their husbands' actions as life-threatening experience a penetrating fear that consumes all their thoughts and energies. The awareness of murderous intent by a presumed ally who is a central figure in all aspects of her life destroys all bases for safety. There is a feeling that death is imminent, and that there is nowhere to hide. Prior rationalizations and beliefs about a "good marriage" are exploded, leaving the woman in a crisis of ambiguity (Ridington, 1978).

Feelings of fear are experienced physiologically as well as emotionally. Battered women experience aches and fatigue, stomach pains, diarrhea or constipation, tension headaches, shakes, chills, loss of appetite, and insomnia. Sometimes, fear is expressed as a numbed shock, similar to rape trauma syndrome (Burgess and

Holmstrom, 1974), in which little is felt or communicated.

If attempts to seek help succeed, overwhelming feelings of fear subside, and a rush of new emotions are felt: the original sense of betrayal re-emerges, creating strong feelings of anger. For women socialized to reject angry feelings as unfeminine, coping with anger is difficult. Unless the expression of anger is encouraged in a supportive environment, such women may suppress anger and feel only depression (Ball and Wyman, 1978). When anger is expressed, it often leads to feelings of strength and exhilaration. Freedom from threats of violence, the possibility of a new life, and the unburdening of anger create feelings of joy. The simple pleasures of going shopping, taking children to the park, or talking with other women without fear of criticism or punishment from a husband, constitute amazing freedoms. One middle-aged woman expressed her joy over her newly acquired freedom this way:

Boy, tomorrow I'm goin' downtown, and I've got my whole day planned out, and I'm gonna do what I wanna do, and if somebody doesn't like it, to hell with them! You know, I'm having so much fun, I should've done this years ago!

Probably the most typical feeling expressed by women in shelters is confusion. They feel both sad and happy, excited and apprehensive, independent, yet in need of love. Most continue to feel attachment to their husbands, and feel ambivalent about divorce. There is grief over the loss of an intimate, which must be acknowledged and mourned. Although shelters usually discourage women from contacting their abusers while staying at the shelter, most women do communicate with their husbands—and most receive desperate pleas for forgiveness and reconciliation. If there is not strong emotional support and potential material support, such encouragement by husbands often rekindles hope for the relationship. Some marriages can be revitalized through counseling, but most experts agree that long-term batterers are unlikely to change (Pagelow,

1981; Walker, 1979). Whether they seek refuge in shelters or with friends, battered women must decide relatively quickly what actions to take. Usually, a tentative commitment is made, either to independence or working on the relationship, but such commitments are usually ambivalent. As one woman wrote to her counselor:

My feelings are so mixed up sometimes. Right now I feel my husband is really trying to change. But I know that takes time. I still feel for him some. I don't know how much. My mind still doesn't know what it wants. I would really like when I leave here to see him once in a while, get my apartment, and sort of like start over with our relationship for me and my baby and him, to try and make it work. It might. It kind of scares me. I guess I am afraid it won't. . . . I can only hope this works out. There's no telling what could happen. No one knows.

The emotional career of battered women consists of movement from guilt, shame, and depression to fear and despair, to anger, exhilaration, and confusion. Women who escape violent relationships must deal with strong, sometimes conflicting, feelings in attempting to build new lives for themselves free of violence. The kind of response women receive when they seek help largely determines the effects these feelings have on subsequent decisions.

NOTES

1. National crime survey data for 1973–76 show that 17 percent of persons who sought medical attention for injuries inflicted by an intimate were hospitalized. Eighty-seven percent of injuries inflicted by a spouse or ex-spouse were bruises, black eyes, cuts, scratches, or swelling (National Crime Survey Report, 1980).

2. Explanation of why and how some women arrive at these feelings is beyond the scope of this paper. Our goal is to describe feelings at various stages of the victimization process.

3. Al-Anon is the spouse's counterpart to Alcoholics Anonymous. It is based on the same self-help, 12-step program that A.A. is founded on.

REFERENCES

Ball, Patricia G., and Elizabeth Wyman. 1978. "Battered Wives and Powerlessness: What Can Counselors Do?" *Victimology* 2(3–4):545–552.

Beverly. 1978. "Shelter Resident Murdered by Husband." *Aegis*, (September/October):13.

Bohannan, Paul (ed.). 1971. *Divorce and After*. Garden City, New York: Anchor.

Burgess, Ann W., and Linda Lytle Holmstrom. 1974. *Rape: Victims of Crisis*. Bowie, Maryland: Brady.

Davidson, Terry. 1978. *Conjugal Crime*. New York: Hawthorn.

Ferraro, Kathleen J. 1979a. "Hard Love: Letting Go of an Abusive Husband." *Frontiers* 4(2):16–18.

———. 1979b. "Physical and Emotional Battering: Aspects of Managing Hurt." *California Sociologist* 2(2):134–149.

———. 1981a. "Battered Women and the Shelter Movement." Unpublished Ph.D. dissertation, Arizona State University.

———. 1981b. "Processing Battered Women." *Journal of Family Issues* 2(4):415–438.

Flanagan, Timothy J., David J. van Alstyne, and Michael R. Gottfredson (eds.). 1982. *Sourcebook of Criminal Justice Statistics: 1981*. U.S. Department of Justice, Bureau of Justice Statistics, Washington, DC: U.S. Government Printing Office.

Garcia, Dick. 1978. "Slain Women 'Lived in Fear.'" *The Times* (Erie, PA), June 14:B1.

Gelles, Richard J. 1974. *The Violent Home*. Beverly Hills: Sage.

———. 1976. "Abused Wives: Why Do they Stay?" *Journal of Marriage and the Family* 38(4):659–668.

Hilberman, Elaine, and Kit Munson. 1978. "Sixty Battered Women." *Victimology* 2(3–4):460–470.

Johnson, John M. 1981. "Program Enterprise and Official Cooptation of the Battered Women's Shelter Movement." *American Behavioral Scientist* 24(6):827–842.

McGlinchey, Anne. 1981. "Woman Battering and the Church's Response." Pp. 133–140 in A. R. Roberts (ed.), *Sheltering Battered Women*. New York: Springer.

National Crime Survey Report. 1980. *Intimate Victims*. Washington, DC: U.S. Department of Justice.

Pagelow, Mildred Daley. 1981. *Woman-Battering*. Beverly Hills: Sage.

Pittman, D. J., and W. Handy. 1964. "Patterns in Criminal Aggravated Assault." *Journal of Criminal Law, Criminology, and Police Science* 55(4):462–470.

Pizzey, Erin. 1974. *Scream Quietly or the Neighbors Will Hear*. Baltimore: Penguin.

Pokorny, Alex D. 1965. "Human Violence: A Comparison of Homicide, Aggravated Assault, Suicide, and Attempted Suicide." *Journal of Criminal Law, Criminology, and Police Science* 56 (December):488–497.

Ridington, Jillian. 1978. "The Transition Process: A Feminist Environment as Reconstitutive Milieu." *Victimology* 2(3–4):563–576.

Roy, Maria (ed.). 1977. *Battered Women*. New York: Van Nostrand.

Scanzoni, John. 1972. *Sexual Bargaining*. Upper Saddle River, NJ: Prentice Hall.

Shotland, R. Lance, and Margret K. Straw. 1976. "Bystander Response to an Assault: When a Man Attacks a Woman." *Journal of Personality and Social Psychology* 34(5):990–999.

Spiegel, John P. 1968. "The Resolution of Role Conflict within the Family." Pp. 391–411 in N. W. Bell and E. F. Vogel (eds.), *A Modern Introduction to the Family*. New York: Free Press.

Sprey, Jetse. 1971. "On the Management of Conflict in Families." *Journal of Marriage and the Family* 33(4):699–706.

Sykes, Gresham M., and David Matza. 1957. "Techniques of Neutralization: A Theory of Delinquency." *American Sociological Review* 22(6):667–670.

U.S. Department of Labor. 1980. *Handbook of Labor Statistics*. Washington, DC: U.S. Government Printing Office.

Walker, Lenore E. 1979. *The Battered Woman*. New York: Harper & Row.

Wolfgang, Marvin E. 1958. *Patterns in Criminal Homicide*. New York: John Wiley.

Accommodation to Madness

MICHAEL LYNCH

A general conception held by laypeople as well as sociologists is that deviance creates the need for social control. One textbook definition, for example, says deviance is a violation of norms likely to elicit negative sanctions. Such a definition, however, takes for granted a consensus on both rules and sanctions. Interactionists assume that deviance is subjectively problematic rather than objectively given. If so, then sociologists must research what happens when rules are allegedly broken.

The objectively given definition of deviance arrives at generalizations by studying people who have been apprehended and processed by the various formal agencies of social control. Michael Lynch asks a different question: How do people who are not police officers or psychiatrists deal with "difficult persons" who disrupt social order? Analyzing student papers on how people they knew dealt with makers of interpersonal troubles, Lynch shows that few of their responses could be classified as negative sanctions.

The variety of responses he describes all have the effect of protecting the selves of people in face-to-face contact with these "difficult persons," the group, and its reputation—and, in some instances, even to save the troublemaker's self. Lynch finds the common factor in these various responses to be socially organized attempts to preserve the appearance of normality for all concerned. All these efforts are intended to repair and retain the appearance of orderly social interaction.

People are committed to mental hospitals after informal efforts to accommodate them in society fail. Studies report that spouses of prospective mental patients (Cumming and Cumming, 1957; Mayo *et al.*, 1971; Sampson *et al.*, 1962; Spitzer *et al.*, 1971; Yarrow *et al.*, 1955), co-workers (Lemert, 1962), and police officers (Bittner, 1967) claim that they contact psychiatric authorities only as a last resort, when informal methods of "care" are unavailable or are overwhelmed by the extremity of the person's disorder. There is widespread reluctance, especially in lower-class families

(Hollingshead and Redlich, 1958:172–179; Myers and Roberts, 1959:213–220), to take a perspective on relational disorders which supports professional intervention and hospitalization. As a result, the population of potential mental patients is said to vastly outnumber the population of professionally treated patients (Srole *et al.*, 1962). Accommodating families can hide potential patients from official scrutiny by placing few demands upon them and allowing them to "exist as if in a one-person chronic ward, insulated from all but those in a highly tolerant household" (Freeman and Simmons, 1958:148).

Such observations suggest that a massive program of community care exists independently of formally established programs of inpatient and outpatient treatment. Countless numbers of undiagnosed, but troublesome, individuals, as well as an increasing number of diagnosed outpatients, are consigned by default to the informal care of family and community. Although the social characteristics of professionally administered mental health care institutions have been exhaustively analyzed, the practices that make up ordinary lay-operated "institutions" of care remain largely unexamined. In this study I call attention to such accommodation practices, elaborate upon previous descriptions of the practices, and present some conjectures on the social construction of the individual.

Accommodation practices are interactional techniques that people use to manage persons they view as persistent sources of trouble. Accommodation implies attempts to "live with" persistent and ineradicable troubles [1] Previous studies mention a number of accommodation practices. Lemert (1962) describes how people exclude distrusted individuals from their organization's covert activities by employing methods of "spurious interaction." Such forms of interaction are:

> . . . distinguished by patronizing, evasion, "humoring," guiding conversation onto selected topics, underreaction, and silence, all calculated either to prevent intense interaction or to protect individual and group values by restricting access to them. When the interaction is between two or more persons in the individual's presence it is cued by a whole repertoire of subtle expressive signs which are meaningful only to them. (1962:8)

Other methods for managing perceived "troublemakers" include: isolation and avoidance (Lemert, 1962; Sampson et al., 1962); relieving an individual of ordinary responsibilities associated with their roles (Sampson et al., 1962); hiding liquor bottles from a heavily drinking spouse (Jackson, 1954); and "babying" (Jackson, 1954).

Some studies (Yarrow et al., 1955) treat accommodation practices as sources of delay in the recognition and treatment of mental illness; others (Goffman, 1961, 1969; Lemert, 1962) portray them as primary constituents of "illness." Whether the studies assume a realist or a societal reaction

perspective on the nature of mental illness, they attempt to explain how persons become mental patients by reconstructing the social backgrounds of hospitalized patients. As Emerson and Messinger (1977:131) point out, retrospective analyses of the "careers" of diagnosed mental patients presuppose a specific pathological outcome to the "prepatient's" biography. To avoid this problem, social scientists need to abandon retrospective methods and analyze contemporary situations where troublesome individuals are accommodated. Such people are not yet patients, and may never attain that status. Therefore, institutional records cannot be used to locate cases for study. An appropriate way to find them is to use vernacular accounts of madness or mental illness, and to document the patterns of accommodation that others use to control such troublesome people.

THE STUDY

This study is an analysis of the results of an assignment which I gave to students in classes on the sociology of mental illness in 1981 and 1982. I instructed students to locate someone in a familiar social environment who was identified by others (and perhaps by themselves) as "crazy"; the subject need not appear "mentally ill," but need only be a *personal* and *persistent* source of trouble for others. The vast majority of the students had little trouble finding such subjects. I instructed them to interview persons who consistently dealt with the troublemaker in a living or work situation. The interviews were to focus on the practices used by others to "live with" the troublemaker from day to day. Students who were personally acquainted with the troublemaker were encouraged to refer to their own recollections and observations in addition to their interviews. They were instructed not to interview or otherwise disturb the troublemakers. Each student wrote a 5–7 page paper on accommodation practices with an appendix of notes from their interview. . . .

I have organized accommodation practices under three thematic headings: (1) practices which *isolate* the troublemaker within the group; (2) practices which *manipulate* the troublemaker's behavior, perception, and understanding; and (3) practices which members use to influence how others react to the troublemaker. The first set of practices defines and limits the troublemaker's chances for interaction, expression, and feedback within the group. The second set directs the details of the troublemaker's actions and establishes the discrepant meanings of those actions for "self" and "other." The third set includes attempts to make the troublemaker's public identity into a covert communal project.

MINIMIZING CONTACT WITH THE TROUBLEMAKER

Avoiding and *ignoring* were the two accommodation practices mentioned most often by students. Both were methods for minimizing contact with the troublemaker, and had the effect of isolating the troublemaker within the organizational network. While both were negative methods of behavior control, attenuating the troublemaker's actual and possible occasions of interaction, they worked quite differently. Avoiding limited the gross *possibility* of interaction, while ignoring worked *within* ongoing occasions of interaction to limit the interactional *reality* of the encounter. Where avoiding created an absence of encounter, ignoring created a dim semblance to ordinary interaction.

AVOIDING

In virtually every student's account, one or more of the members they interviewed mentioned that they actively avoided the troublemaker. Avoidance created an interactional vacuum around the troublemaker. Members managed to stay out of the way of the troublemaker without actually requesting or commanding the troublemaker to stay away from them. Methods of avoidance included individual and joint tactics such as "ducking into restrooms," "keeping a lookout for

her at all times," and "hiding behind a newspaper or book."

Some members were better placed than others within the structure of the organization to avoid the troublemaker. In larger organizations like fraternities and sororities, persons could stake out positions which minimized contact with the troublemaker. In more intimate circles avoidance ran more of a risk of calling attention to the *absence* of usual interactional involvement. Avoidance *did* occur in such intimate groups as families (Sampson *et al.*, 1962), but only at the cost of threatening the very integrity of the group.

IGNORING/NOT TAKING SERIOUSLY

Ignoring differed from avoiding because it entailed at least some interaction, though of an attenuated and inauthentic kind. One account described conversations with the troublemaker as being "reduced to superficial 'hellos,' most of which are directed at her feet; there is an obvious lack of eye contact." Many accounts mentioned the superficiality of interactions with troublemakers. In some cases this was accomplished by what one student called "rehearsed and phony responses" to limit the openness of their conversations to a few stock sequences.[2]

Although ignoring entailed interaction, it was like avoidance in that it circumscribed the troublemaker's interactional possibilities. Where avoidance operated to limit, in a gross way, the intersection of pathways between troublemaker and other members, ignoring operated intensively to trivialize the troublemaker's apparent involvements in group activities.[3] Bids for positive notice were ignored, and had little effect on the troublemaker's position within the group.

DIRECTLY MANAGING THE TROUBLEMAKER'S ACTIONS

Members used a number of more direct interventions to control and limit the troublemaker's behavior, including humoring, screening, taking over, orienting to local prospects of normality, and practical jokes and retaliations. While such methods had little hope of permanently modifying the behavior, they were used to curtail episodic disruptions by the troublemaker.

HUMORING

Members often used the term *humoring* to describe attempts to manage the troublemaker by maintaining a veneer of agreement and geniality in the face of actions which would ordinarily evoke protest or disgust. For example, in the case of "an obnoxiously argumentative person," members offered superficial tokens of agreement in response to even the most outlandish pronouncements for the sake of avoiding more extreme disruptions.

Humoring was often made possible through insight into recurrent features of the troublemaker's behavior. Members recognized recurrent situations in ordinary interactions which triggered peculiar reactions by the troublemaker. They developed a heightened awareness of ordinary and seemingly innocuous details of interaction which could touch off an explosive reaction. One student described how her parents managed a "crazy aunt," who she said was prone to sudden and violent verbal assaults:

> My parents avoided discussing specific topics and persons that they knew distressed her. Whenever she began talking about an arousable [sic] event or person, my parents and her husband attempted to change the subject.[4]

Although members rationalized humoring as a way "to make it easy for everybody," they did not always find it easy to withhold their reactions to interactional offenses. A student wrote about her efforts to prepare her fiancé for a first encounter with her grandmother, said to be suffering from senile dementia, Alzheimer type:

> I attempted to explain to him that he should not say anything controversial, agree with whatever she says, and generally stay quiet as much as possible. [He assured her that everything would be okay, but when he was confronted with the actual grandmother, the assurance proved quite fragile.] That encounter proved to be quite an experience for Charles—we left Grandma's house with Charles screaming back at her for his self-worth.

Other accounts mentioned the strain and difficulty of trying to humor troublemakers. They described an exceedingly fragile interactional situation which was prone to break down at any moment:

> You don't want to set him off, so you're very careful about what you do and say. You become tense trying to keep everything calm, and then something happens to screw it up anyway: The car won't start, or a light bulb blows. It's all my fault because I'm a rotten wife and mother.

Humoring often entailed obedience or deference to what members claimed (when not within earshot of the troublemaker) were outrageous or absurd demands:

> Everyone did what she asked in order to please her and not cause any bad scenes.

In some cases, members exerted special efforts or underwent severe inconvenience for the sake of a person they secretly despised. Not surprisingly, such efforts often, though not always, were exerted by persons over whom the troublemaker had formal authority. In one case the members of a crew traveling with a rock and roll band would set up the troublesome member's equipment before that of the others and set up daily meetings with him to discuss his "technical needs," while at the same time they believed it was foolish of him to demand such special attention. They described the special meetings and favors as a "bogus accommodation." In every case, whether correlated with formal divisions of authority or not, humoring contributed to the troublemaker's sense of interactional power over others.

Humoring always included a degree of duplicity in which members "kept a straight face" when interacting with the troublemaker or acted in complicity with the troublemaker's premises—premises which members otherwise discounted as delusional or absurd:

> We played along with her fantasy of a boyfriend, "John." We never said what a complete fool she was for waiting for him.

Commonly, members practiced *serial* duplicity by waiting until the troublemaker was out of earshot to display for one another's appreciation the "real" understanding they had previously suppressed:

> They pretend to know what she is talking about, they act as if they are interested . . . they make remarks when she is gone.

At other times they practiced *simultaneous* duplicity by showing interest and serious engagement to the troublemaker's face while expressing detachment and sarcasm to one another through furtive glances, gestures, and double entendres (Lemert, 1962:8):

> Those employees who she is not facing will make distorted faces and roll their eyes around to reaffirm the fact that she is a little slow. All the time this occurs Susan is totally oblivious to it, or at least she pretends to be.

In one fraternity, members devised a specific hand gesture (described as "wing flapping") which they displayed for one another when interacting with a troublemaker they called "the bird."

Members occasionally rationalized their duplicity by describing the troublemaker as a self-absorbed and "dense" person, whose lack of orientation to others provided ample opportunity for their play:

> People speak sarcastically to him, and Joe, so wrapped up in himself, believes what they are saying and hears only what he wants to hear.

SCREENING

Jackson (1954:572) reported that alcoholics' wives attempted to manage their husbands' heavy drinking by hiding or emptying liquor bottles in the house and curtailing their husbands' funds. One student described a similar practice used by friends of a person who they feared had suicidal tendencies. They systematically removed from the person's environment any objects that could be used to commit suicide.

Screening and monitoring of troublemakers' surroundings also occurred in the interactional realm. A few accounts mentioned attempts to monitor the moods of a troublemaker, and to screen the person's potential interactions on the basis of attributed mood. When one sorority's troublemaker was perceived to be especially volatile, members acted as her covert receptionists by turning away her visitors, explaining that she was not in or was ill. In this case members were concerned not only to control the potential actions of the individual, but also to conceal those actions from others, and by doing so to protect the collective "image" of their sorority from contamination.

TAKING OVER

A number of accounts mentioned efforts by members to do activities which ordinarily would be done by someone in the troublemaker's social position. Like published accounts of cases in which husbands or mothers take over the household duties of a wife (Sampson *et al.*, 1962), the apartment mates of a troublemaker washed dishes and paid bills for her "as if she wasn't there." A circle of friends insisted on driving the automobile of a man they considered dangerously impulsive. Fraternity members gradually and unofficially took over the duties of their social chairman in fear of the consequences of his erratic actions and inappropriate attire. Taking over sometimes included such intimate personal functions as grooming and dressing, as when the spouse of a drunk diligently prepared her husband for necessary public appearances.

ORIENTING TO LOCAL PROSPECTS
OF NORMALITY

Yarrow *et al.* (1955) mention that wives of mental patients sustained efforts to live with their husbands by treating interludes between episodes as the beginnings of "recovery" rather than as periods of calm before the inevitable storms. By keeping tabs on the latest developments in the troublemaker's behavior, members were often able to determine when it was "safe" to treat the troublemaker as a "normal" person. This method was not always as unrealistic as one would be led to believe from Yarrow *et al.* (1955). Since most troublemakers were viewed as persons whose difficulties, though inherent, were intermittent, living with them required knowing what to expect in the immediate interactional future:

> *I have observed the occasion when a friend at the fraternity house entered the television room and remained in the rear of the room, totally quiet, watching Danny, waiting for a signal telling him how to act. When Danny turned and spoke to him in a friendly, jovial manner, the young man enthusiastically pulled his chair up to sit next to Danny and began speaking freely.*

Members described many troublemakers as persons with likeable and even admirable qualities, whose friendship was valued during their "good times." When a member anticipated an encounter with a troublemaker, he or she wanted most of all to avoid touching off a "bad scene." The local culture of gossip surrounding a troublemaker tended to facilitate such an aim by providing a running file on the current state of his or her moods. By using the latest news members could decide when to avoid encounters and when they could approach the troublemaker without undue wariness.

PRACTICAL JOKES AND RETALIATIONS

Although direct expressions of hostility toward troublemakers were rarely mentioned, it is possible that they occurred more frequently than was admitted. Practical jokes and other forms of retaliation

were designed not to reveal their authors. The troublemaker would be "clued in" that *somebody* despised him or was otherwise "out to get" him, but he would be left to imagine just who it was. Some jokes were particularly cruel, and were aimed at the troublemaker's particular vulnerabilities. A member of a touring rock and roll band was known to have difficulty forming relationships with women:

> *They would get girls to call his room and make dates they would never keep. Apparently, the spotlight operator was the author of a series of hot love letters of a mythical girl who was following Moog [a pseudonym for the troublemaker] from town to town and would soon appear in his bedroom. The crew must have been laughing their heads off for days. Moog was reading the letters out loud in the dressing room.*

INFLUENCING THE REACTION
TO THE TROUBLEMAKER

A group of practices, instead of focusing solely on the troublemaker's interactional behavior, attempted to control others' *reactions to* and *interpretations of* that behavior. These accommodations recognized that there could be serious consequences in the reactions of outsiders—non-members—to the troublemaker. Such practices included efforts by members to control the reactions of persons outside the group; and to control assessments not only of the individual troublemaker, but of the group as well. The responsibilities for, and social consequences of, the individual's behavior were thus adopted by members as a collective project.

TURNING THE TROUBLEMAKER
INTO A NOTORIOUS CHARACTER

In stories to outsiders as well as others in the group, members were sometimes able to turn the troublemaker into a fascinating and almost admirable character. A classic case was the fraternity "animal." Although litanies of crude, offensive, and assaultive actions were recounted, the character's antics were also portrayed with evident delight. Such descriptions incorporated elements of heroism, the prowess of the brawler, or the fearlessness and outrageousness of a prankster. In one case a student reported that the fraternity troublemaker, nicknamed "the deviant," was supported and encouraged by a minority faction who claimed to an outsider that he was merely "a little wild," and that nothing was wrong with him. This faction seemed unembarrassed by, and perhaps a bit proud of, the troublemaker's "animal" qualities that others might ascribe to the fraternity as well. The quasi-heroic or comical repute of the troublemaker did not overshadow many members' distaste for the disruptions, but it did constitute a supportive moral counterpoint.

SHADOWING

In one instance a group of students living in a dorm arranged covertly to escort their troublemaker on his frequent trips to local bars. He had a reputation for drinking more than his capacity and then challenging all comers to fights. To inhibit such adventures members of the group volunteered to accompany him under various pretexts, and to quell any disputes he precipitated during the drinking sessions. In the case of the member of the rock and roll band, other members chaperoned him during interviews with media critics. When he said something potentially offensive, his chaperon attempted to turn his statement into a joke. Another account described efforts by a group to spy on a member who they believed was likely to do something rash or violent.

ADVANCE NOTICES

As Lemert (1962) points out, members often build a legacy of apocryphal stories about their troublemaker. Stories told by one member to another about the troublemaker's latest antics provided a common source of entertainment, and perhaps solidarity. Some members admitted that they could not imagine what they would talk about with one another if not the troublemaker's behavior:

> *The highlight of the day is hearing the latest story about Joanie.*

Such gleeful renditions helped to prepare nonmembers for first encounters with the troublemaker.

A few students mentioned that the troublemakers they studied appeared normal or even charming during initial encounters, but that members soon warned them to be careful about getting involved with the person. Subsequent experience confirmed the warnings, although it was difficult to discern whether this was a result of their accuracy or of the wariness they engendered.

Members of a group that included a persistently troublesome character "apologized for him beforehand" to persons who shortly would be doing business with him. They also warned women he approached that he was "a jerk." In addition to preparing such persons for upcoming encounters, the apologies and warnings carried the tacit claim that "we're not like him." This mitigated any potential contamination of the group's moral reputation.

HIDING AND DILUTING THE TROUBLEMAKER

Some fraternities and sororities institutionalized a "station" for hiding troublemakers during parties and teas where new members were recruited. Troublemakers were assigned out-of-the-way positions in social gatherings and, in some cases, were accompanied at all times by other members whose job it was to cut off the troublemaker's interaction with prospective members.

The methods used for hiding and diluting were especially artful when they included pretexts to conceal from the troublemakers that their role had been diminished. The troublemaker in the rock and roll band was said to embarrass other members with "distasteful ego tripping" on stage during public concerts. Such "ego trips" were characterized by loud and "awful" playing on his instrument and extravagant posturing in attempts to draw the audience's attention to himself. These displays were countered by the sound and light men in the crew:

> On those nights the sound man would turn up the monitors on stage so Moog sounded loud to himself and would turn down Moog in the [concert] hall and on the radio.

Simultaneously, the lighting director would "bathe him in darkness" by dimming the spotlights on him. These practices, in effect, technically created a delusional experience for the troublemaker. They produced a systematic distortion of his perception of the world and simultaneously diminished his public place in that world.

COVERING FOR/COVERING UP

Friends and intimates sometimes went to great lengths to smooth over the damages and insults done to others by the troublemaker. The husband of a "crazy woman" monitored his wife's offenses during her "episodes" and followed in the wake of the destruction with apologies and sometimes monetary reparations to offended neighbors. Similar efforts at restoring normality also occurred in immediate interactional contexts:

> Before she will even tell you her name, she is telling you how one day she was hitchhiking and was gang raped by the five men who picked her up. This caused so many problems for her that she ended up in a mental hospital and is now a lesbian. The look on people's faces is complete shock. . . . Those hearing this story for the first time will sit in shock as if in a catatonic stupor, with wide eyes and their mouths dropped open, absolutely speechless. Someone who has already heard this story will break the silence by continuing with the previous conversation, . . . putting it on extinction by ignoring it as if she never said anything.

Members sometimes conspired, ostensibly on behalf of the troublemaker, to prevent the relevant authorities from detecting the existence and extent of the troubles. One group of girls in a freshman dorm deliberately lied to hide the fact that one of their members was having great difficulty and, in their estimation, was potentially suicidal. When her parents asked how she was doing the students responded that she was doing "fine." Members tried to contain her problems and to create a "blockade" around any appearances of her problems that might attract the attentions of university authorities. Once underway, such coverups gained momentum, since the prospect of exposure increasingly threatened to make members culpable for not bringing the matter to the attention of remedial agents.

DISCUSSION

A prevailing theme in the students' accounts of accommodation practices was the avoidance of confrontation. They described confrontation as potentially "unpleasant," to be avoided even when considerable damage and hardship had been suffered:

> When students' money began disappearing from their rooms, we had a group meeting to discuss our mode of intervention. Although we all believed Chris was responsible, we did not confront her. Instead, we simply decided to make sure we locked our bedroom doors when not in our rooms.

In general, a number of reasons for avoiding confrontation were given, including the anticipation of denial by the troublemaker, fear that the troublemaker would create a "bad scene," and the belief that confrontation would make no difference in the long run.

Less direct methods were used to communicate the group's opinions to the troublemaker. Instead of telling the troublemaker in so many words, members employed a peculiar sort of gamesmanship. Systematic "leaks" were used to *barely* and *ambiguously* expose the duplicity and conspiracy, so that the troublemaker would realize something was going on, but would be unable or unwilling to accuse specific offenders. Duplicitous gestures or comments which operated *just* on the fringes of the troublemaker's awareness produced maximum impact.

The successful operation of these practices relied, in part, on the troublemaker's complicity in the conspiracy of silence:

> *Once I was in the room next door to her and the girls were imitating her. Two minutes later she walked in asking [us] to be quiet because she was trying to sleep. I thought I was going to die. Obviously Tammy realized what was going on as the walls are extremely thin; however, Tammy seems to be conspiring on the side of her "friends" to prevent any confrontation of the actual situation.*

Hostilities were therefore expressed, and retaliations achieved, often with rather specific reference to the particular offenses and their presumed source. At the same time, they remained "submerged" in a peculiar way. They were not submerged in a psychological "unconscious," since both members and troublemakers were aware of what was going on. Instead, both members and troublemakers made every effort to [ensure] that the trouble did not disturb the overtly normal interaction. "Business as usual" was preserved at the cost of keeping secret deep hostilities within the organization.

A few accounts did mention instances of explicit confrontation. However, members claimed that such confrontations did not alter troublemakers' subsequent behaviors; instead they resulted in misunderstandings or were received by troublemakers in a defensive or unresponsive way.

Efforts to remove troublemakers from organizations were rarely described, though members of the rock band eventually expelled their troublemaker after he hired a lawyer to redress his grievances against the group. In another case a fraternity "de-pledged" a new recruit who had not yet been fully initiated. In no other case was an established member removed, although numerous dramatic offenses were recounted and widespread dislike for troublemakers was commonly reported.

Taken as a whole, accommodation practices reveal *the organizational construction of the normal individual*. The individual is relied upon both in commonsense reasoning and social theory as a source of compliance with the standards of the larger society. The normal individual successfully adapts to the constraints imposed by social structure. Troublemakers were viewed as persons who, for various reasons, could not be given full *responsibility* for maintaining normality. Instead, the burden of maintaining the individual's normal behavior and appearance was taken up by others. Troublemakers were not overtly sanctioned; instead, they were shaped and guided through the superficial performances of ordinary action. Their integration into society was not a cumulative mastery learned "from inside"; it was a constant project executed by others from the "outside."

Accommodation practices allow us to glimpse the project of the self as a practical struggle. A semblance of normal individuality for troublemakers was a carefully constructed artifact produced by members. When the responsibility for normality is assumed as an individual birthright, it appears inevitable that conformity or defiance proceeds "from inside" the individual, just as it appears in common sense that gender is a natural inheritance. In the latter instance, a transsexual's unusual experience indicates the extent to which the ordinary behavior and appearance of being female is detachable from the individual's birthright, and can be explicated as a practical accomplishment (Garfinkel, 1967). Similarly, for the organizational colleagues of a troublemaker, the elements of normal individuality cannot be relied upon, but must be achieved through deliberate practice. Members together performed the work of minding the troublemaker's business, of guiding the troublemaker through normal interactional pathways, and of filling the responsibilities and appearances associated with the troublemaker's presence for others.[5]

Of course, such projects were less than successful; members complained of the undue burden, disruptions occurred despite their efforts, and the troublemaker was provided with a diminished self and a distorted reality. Perhaps all would have been better off had they "left the self inside where it belongs." Nevertheless, accommodation practices enable us to see the extent to which the division between self and other is permeable, and subject to negotiation and manipulation. We can see that individual responsibility for the conduct of affairs is separable from the actual performance of those affairs. Troublemakers were manipulated into a tenuous conformity by members who relied upon the fact that such conformity would be attributed to the individual's responsibility. The individual was thus reduced to the subject of an informal code of responsibility, separable from any substantive source of action (Goffman, 1969:357). . . .

NOTES

1. The equally interesting topic of how patients accommodate to their own disorders (Critchley, 1971:290; O. Sacks, 1974:227) is not included in this discussion of interactional practices.
2. A topic needing further study is how members use greetings and other conversational "adjacency pairs" (Sacks *et al.*, 1974) to foreclose conversation with troublemakers at the earliest convenient point, but in such a way as not to call attention to their action as a snub.
3. See Wulbert (n.d.) for a poignant discussion of trivializing practices.
4. Jefferson and Lee (1980) characterize some of the detailed ways in which participants in ordinary conversations head off "troubles talk" and transform it to "business as usual." Such procedures are much more varied and intricate than can adequately be described by such phrases as "changing the subject."
5. My discussion of the social production of the individual is heavily indebted to Pollner and Wikler's (1981) treatment of that theme. Pollner and Wikler (1981) discuss a family's efforts to construct the appearance of normality for their (officially diagnosed) profoundly retarded daughter. Not only does *normality* become a communal project in these cases, *abnormality* becomes shared as well. One student in my research described an alcoholic's family as "three characters revolving around a central theme—alcoholism."

The preoccupation with alcohol was shared along with the *denial* that the man's drinking was an official problem.

REFERENCES

Bittner, Egon. 1967. "Police Discretion in Emergency Apprehension of Mentally Ill Persons." *Social Problems* 14(3):278–292.
Critchley, MacDonald. 1971. *The Parietal Lobes*. New York: Hafner Publishing Co.
Cumming, Elaine, and John Cumming. 1957. *Closed Ranks*. Cambridge, MA: Harvard University Press.
Emerson, Robert, and Sheldon Messinger. 1977. "The Micro-politics of Trouble." *Social Problems* 25(2):121–134.
Freeman, Howard, and Ozzie Simmons. 1958. "Mental Patients in the Community: Family Settings and Performance Levels." *American Sociological Review* 23(2):147–154.
Garfinkel, Harold. 1967. *Studies in Ethnomethodology*. Upper Saddle River, NJ: Prentice Hall.
Goffman, Erving. 1961. *Asylums*. Garden City, NY: Doubleday.
———. 1969. "The Insanity of Place." *Psychiatry* 32(4):352–388.
Hollingshead, August, and Frederick Redlich. 1958. *Social Class and Mental Illness*. New York: Wiley.
Jackson, Joan. 1954. "The Adjustment of the Family to the Crisis of Alcoholism." *Quarterly Journal of Studies on Alcohol* 15(4):562–586.
Jefferson, Gail, and John Lee. 1980. "The Analysis of Conversations in Which Anxieties and Troubles Are Expressed." Unpublished report for the Social Science Research Counsel, University of Manchester, England.
Lemert, Edwin. 1962. "Paranoia and the Dynamics of Exclusion." *Sociometry* 25(1):2–20.
Mayo, Clara, Ronald Havelock, and Diane Lear Simpson. 1971. "Attitudes Towards Mental Illness among Psychiatric Patients and Their Wives." *Journal of Clinical Psychology* 27(1): 128–132.
Myers, Jerome, and Bertram Roberts. 1959. *Family and Class Dynamics*. New York: Wiley.
Pollner, Melvin, and Lynn Wikler. 1981. "The Social Construction of Unreality: A Case Study of the Practices of Family Sham and Delusion." Unpublished paper, Department of Sociology, University of California, Los Angeles.

Sacks, Harvey, Emanuel Schegloff, and Gail Jefferson. 1974. "A Simplest Systematics for the Organization of Turn Taking in Conversation." *Language* 50(4): 696–735.

Sacks, Oliver. 1974. *Awakenings*. New York: Doubleday.

Sampson, Harold, Sheldon Messinger, and Robert Towne. 1962. "Family Processes and Becoming a Mental Patient." *American Journal of Sociology* 68(1):88–98.

Spitzer, Stephan, Patricia Morgan, and Robert Swanson. 1971. "Determinants of the Psychiatric Patient Career: Family Reaction Patterns and Social Work Intervention." *Social Service Review* 45(1):74–85.

Srole, Leo, Thomas Langer, Stanley Michael, Marvin Opler, and Thomas Rennie. 1962. *Mental Health in the Metropolis: The Midtown Manhattan Study.* New York: McGraw-Hill.

Wulbert, Roland. n.d. "Second Thoughts about Commonplaces." Unpublished paper, Department of Sociology, Columbia University (circa 1974).

Yarrow, Marian, Charlotte Schwartz, Harriet Murphy, and Leila Deasy. 1955. "The Psychological Meaning of Mental Illness in the Family." *Journal of Social Issues* 11(4):12–24.

When Accommodation Breaks Down

J. SCOTT KENNEY

The interactionist perspective holds that contact with formal agencies of social control such as the criminal justice system imposes sharply defined labels more quickly and with what can be drastic consequences for the persons so labeled. As Edwin Lemert predicts, the more severe the societal reaction, the more likely persons suffer status reduction, see themselves as criminals, and adopt a deviant role. When aberrant conduct takes place in the course of everyday life, a sequence of accommodative practices ensues. Since the conventional person generally has the upper hand, the potential deviant seeks to accommodate the more powerful partner. In sequence, in order to fend off the deviant label, the persons at risk of labeling sometimes conceal symbols of their deviance. There are, of course, other possibilities because accommodative practices are always contingent on the outcome of interactive processes between the deviant and family, friends, acquaintances, strangers, and the general public.

J. Scott Kenney looks at the kinds of mutual problems that face people who have lost family members to murderers when those surviving relatives come in contact with other family members, friends, acquaintances, strangers, and the community at large. He concludes that a series of accommodations occur on the part of both parties to the encounter. When the accommodations are consensual, the bereaved party experiences social reintegration. When such practices are in conflict or break down, the most likely outcome is that the bereaved persons either are defined as "emotional deviants" or as bereaving over people who are deviants and who brought their deaths on by their own actions.

. . . Crime creates problems for people. In the past much research in this vein, particularly from the labeling perspective, has largely focused on offenders. Yet, victims of crime often experience the labeling process as well. This paper delineates the processes and consequences underlying such labeling by empirically examining the experiences of individuals who have suffered the murder of a loved one. In this way, the labeling perspective, as a theory rooted in the interactionist tradition, is broadened in a direction implicit in its philosophical antecedents. . . .

The labeling perspective is grounded in the conception that deviance is defined by social reactions, and that the frequency and character of the deviation, as well as the role of the deviant, are largely shaped by interactional response (Lemert 1951; Becker 1963). As such, it draws attention away from the idea that there is anything objective in the actions of individuals that is deviant, focusing instead on changes in social definitional processes and their consequences. Yet this perspective need not be restricted to the study of deviance.[1] Taylor, Wood, and Lichtman (1983) note the *victims* often experience negative social consequences, asserting that "interpersonal reactions to victims are at best ambivalent, and at worst hostile and rejecting" (1983:23). . . .

METHODOLOGY

The methods underlying this study were qualitative in nature. Recognizing the difficulty of accessing highly personal information from a traumatized population, I used a wide variety of direct and indirect approaches, including extensive volunteer involvement with a prominent victims' organization, advertising for interview and survey respondents with a variety of others,

reviewing published accounts, and seeking information through the legal systems.[2] Taken together, while some of these strategies were more successful than others, they ultimately resulted in a large volume of rich, qualitative data. The overwhelming majority of data fell into three general categories: (1) intensive interviews with 32 individuals; (2) mail-back surveys from 22 respondents; and (3) 108 homicide files obtained under an agreement with a Provincial Criminal Injuries Compensation Board (C.I.C.B.), including information on 145 individuals. . . .

PRESENTATION OF THE DATA

The varying social responses to survivors following a homicide interactionally shaped the course of their experiences and strongly suggested differential labeling dynamics at work. I will briefly discuss these results in three parts: (1) extended family and friends; (2) acquaintances, strangers, and the community; and (3) subjects' responses.

First, a minority of respondents experienced widespread, ongoing support from the majority of their extended family and friends.

> *I've always had people really look after me. I've never been left to do this alone—and that made a huge difference. My family and friends were there morning, noon, and night for at least two years, which made me feel good—to know that they were there for me (Survey #19: Female, age 45).*

These individuals reported a number of sympathetic, and reportedly helpful responses such as others visiting and staying, providing ongoing emotional support, handling responsibilities for them, and a wide variety of helpful communication involving the ability of others to pick up subtle cues regarding when, and how, to offer support.

Running through such responses is the implicit theme that these individuals were considered "sympathy worthy" by others (Clark 1987). On the one hand, as extended family and friends are relatively close to survivors, they may have built up, or feel it necessary to extend a wider "sympathy margin" than others, at least initially. However, as these responses were only mentioned by a minority in the sample, it may be that this also has something to do with survivors adhering to the rules of "sympathy etiquette" such as making "legitimate" claims to sympathy in "appropriate" circumstances. These matters are closely interrelated with survivors' "victim" status, and these sympathetic behaviors cannot be understood outside of this context. Indeed, in Clark's (1987) terms, such helpful responses, often extending for considerable periods of time, suggest that suffering the murder of a loved one prima facie constitutes, for these sympathizers, a legitimate claim for sympathy, and that the victim label, in some instances, even broadens their definitions of what is too long for victims to accept sympathy and their obligation to reciprocate.

It also may be argued that much of the above fits clearly into the idea of accommodation to deviance (Lynch 1983; Rubington and Weinberg 1987; Yarrow et al. 1955; Jackson 1954). Grief, in such unusual and violent circumstances, is frequently extreme and persistent (Rynearson and McCreery 1993; Knapp 1986; Klass 1988), and the data in this study certainly bore this out. Family and friends who respond to such behavior as above are attempting to make adjustments to accommodate survivors' powerful emotions without making an explicit labeling of deviance. If anything, it may be the situation that is seen as unusual, not survivors' reactions to it, which are considered normal for victims. As such, the label of victim may not only play a role in accommodation to deviance, it may indicate the entry point of a parallel labeling process revolving around the term *victim*. Accommodation in one sense is thus interchanged by labeling in the other.

On the other hand, the stigmatization of victims and the labeling of emotional deviance generally proceed when accommodation quickly breaks down, or doesn't occur in the first place. Together, these were the most common patterns, and had a far different impact on survivors' experiences.

Generally, survivors who reported a lack of support from the *majority* of their extended family and friends over time felt that this made their experience worse. One survivor noted:

The only thing I remember is that I was alone—all the time. All the time. There was nobody came around. My family hasn't been supportive. I haven't seen any of my family. None of them have come, and that hurt . . . It's been two years, and I think you are the third person that's been in this house (Interview #10: Female, age 60) (Emphasis added).

Similar comments were made by survivors about their friends:

We were ostracized in a sense. In our own minds we felt ostracized anyway by everybody we knew (Interview #14: Male, age 54) (Emphasis added).

This was a time for me to find out who my real friends were, and it sometimes hurt a lot to see that your friends are not always the ones that you had considered. It is a shock (Survey #3: Female, age 58) (Emphasis added).

These individuals reported a number of unhelpful responses including initial lack of support, rapidly disappearing support (e.g., after the funeral), inappropriate attention and harassment, widespread avoidance by others, numerous problems with communication such as others using "stock" responses and attempting to identify with their feelings, and, in some cases, overt conflict with family and friends. Taken together, these corroborate and expand, in a new empirical context, many of the problems noted by Wortman and Lehman (1983).

Most interestingly, some considered that these were the result of their being labeled as *victims*, others as *deviants*. Survivors' rationales for these responses were instructive in separating these:

Some labeled as victims asserted how many of their extended family and friends were afraid to do or say anything that might upset them further and avoided contact as a result. This involved ascriptions of sympathy worthiness, labeling as victims, but an inability to provide overt expressions of sympathy out of uncertainty as to appropriate response.

> *I know that my family just damn well didn't know how to cope and how to deal with me [sounds angry]. They were scared. In fact we talked about it. We went home and it was discussed—and they said that they had no idea. They really didn't know how to deal with me, and were afraid to even phone me [sounds tearful] (Interview #15: Female, age 49).*

> *Like my friends are afraid to keep bringing it up, and they shy away because they're afraid you're going to bring it up, cause they're afraid they're going to say something that's going to hurt you. So they shy away. Maybe they don't know that you want it. That it's all right to talk about it. So they're afraid to. I think that's what happens with a lot of them, they're afraid to start . . . Cause, I had a few people that I've bumped into, and I've said: "Oh, you haven't been around." "Well [respondent's name], it's not that we didn't want to. It's just that we just don't know what to say, and we didn't want to say the wrong thing and hurt your feelings" (Interview 21: Female, age 45).*

This was further exacerbated in some cases where family and friends were considered to be so upset about the murder themselves that seeing the survivors evoked unpleasant sympathetic outbursts among all concerned. This response exhibited an excess of sympathy for survivors labeled as "victims" whereby others became so upset that they simply couldn't handle seeing the survivors:

> *My family, for the most part, kept their distance. And, occasionally when we'd come by, they would just sob and cry, and they'd be so upset. The few that did come by, they'd just break down. Horrible. I think they felt they were just upsetting us more and would be all apologetic. Then they wouldn't come by (Interview #31: Female, age 46) (Emphasis added).*

> *Our friends? It varied. I think that the reason why some of them kind of were standoffish was because they couldn't handle it themselves. I figure that because they knew [the deceased] personally, they just couldn't handle it. It was too close to reality for them, so they kind of backed off. I was a little bit taken aback by that, and I was very hurt. It's been difficult because you really do need your friends at a time like that (Interview #1: Female, age 47).*

These responses were particularly notable among individuals previously close to respondents.

There also were survivors, initially labeled as victims, who noted how the initially sympathetic responses of others eventually gave way to privately urging them to "get on with your lives." This signifies a breakdown in others' ascriptions of sympathy worthiness and the beginning of stigmatization as "helpless victims." These are individuals who have broken one of the cardinal rules of sympathy etiquette: not to claim too much sympathy for too long.

> *We had some very close friends who came out to visit us, but after a while their recommendation to us was, "You've got to put this in the past, like, bury this right now" [sarcastically]. The closest friends we had! He'd say to me "[survivor's name], you've got to put this behind, get back to work, and you've got to get on with your life." You know, "You've got to maintain your business, you've got to . . ." and I'm not thinking any of this! (Interview #14: Male, age 54).*

Some individuals came to feel that they were stigmatized as emotional deviants by others due to inappropriate behavior in public settings. For example, some talked about how their inability to talk about subjects other than the murder, or to remain calm, drove others away and resulted in uncomfortable encounters at social events. Others talked of their own upset driving family and friends away. This is more suggestive of labeling as emotional deviants:

> *They started changing the subject a lot, so we would just pick up on it that "OK, we won't talk about this any more." We caught the vibes, right? Bad vibes. Some pulled back from us, and this continues right up to the present. Nobody really wants to talk (Interview #8: Female, age 45).*

I think if I'm showing signs of emotion, I mean showing tears or emotional stress to others, they don't feel very comfortable, because they don't know how to handle it. And so, if you are at a stage where you can't speak about your son or daughter clearly, openly, and without showing an awful lot of undue stress, it drives people away (Interview #5: Male, age 50).

Finally, some individuals were simply stigmatized as deviants. In these cases, survivors attributed others' reactions to the perceived stigma or discrediting that went along with having a murder in the family, a stigma that suggested shared deviance:

The rest of my relatives were worthless and acted like a stigma was attached to us, like something about us caused us to have a murder victim (Survey #7: Female, age 38).

Some asked me "How could you let him kill the kids?" A few other people I counted as close friends suddenly were distant. The press had picked up that when [the offender] was arrested he shouted that I had done it. Some of these "friends" seem to have doubts about my involvement (Survey #6: Female, age 37).

These were individuals who felt blamed or thought they were somehow viewed as contributing to their plight. In some cases this stigmatization referred to ostensibly questionable circumstances surrounding the murder (e.g., the murder of drug dealers; families of women who remained with abusive partners). However, this was not necessarily the case, and many may have simply been the result of individuals' attempting to apportion blame in line with a cultural belief that "people get what they deserve" (Lerner 1980). Essentially, these were individuals who broke (or were perceived to break) another cardinal rule of sympathy etiquette: not making "false claims" to sympathy.

The ultimate result of such interactions, whether motivated by stigma, uncertainty regarding how to behave, survivors' or others' own upset, or generally not wanting to further upset each other, was that survivors tended to become socially isolated when they needed support. Moreover, while this often upset them further, many chose to withdraw themselves as "people in general don't understand . . . it's too difficult" (Interview #29: Female, age 37).

Summing up this topic, survivors indicating a wide variety of perceived support from their extended families and friends reportedly fared better. These survivors reported few insensitive comments and obvious avoidance behaviors from those previously close to them, along with support and encouragement. This clearly relates to the literature on accommodation (Lynch 1983; Rubington and Weinberg 1987; Yarrow et al. 1955; Jackson 1954), but further suggests that sensitive, overt expression of sympathy worthiness associated with the label of victim played a significant role. Ultimately, such survivors tended to report milder grief experiences overall, supporting the literature suggesting that "social support is the most important factor in helping parents find new social and psychic equilibria" (Klass 1988:179).

However, the majority of survivors who experienced many of the unhelpful, unsupportive interactions with friends generally assessed themselves as faring much worse than those with perceived long-term support. Indeed, they may experience additional losses. These interactions not only gave survivors more reasons to be emotionally upset, such accumulated indignities were often interrelated with the various labels associated with survivors (Wortman and Lehman 1983). In some cases unhelpful behaviors were associated with uncertainty, unexpressed or inappropriately manifested sympathy, and the label of victim; in other cases these behaviors were associated with stigmatization as victims or deviants, or stigmatization as "emotional deviants" (Thoits 1990). Regardless of their label, such survivors were avoided, stigmatized, encountered difficulties in communication, or had increased conflicts. Moreover, survivors' resulting social and emotional isolation, which was commonly employed as a defense or reaction to this labeling, could be cited as evidence of secondary victimization (Taylor, Wood, and Lichtman 1983), secondary deviance (Lemert 1951), or secondary emotional deviance (Thoits 1990; Lemert 1951).

Next, and in contrast with their extended family and friends, respondents often noted receiving remarkable support from mere acquaintances. This included many of the matters discussed earlier, but especially emotional support.

> It was really strange because you find out who you could lean on. You know, and sometimes it's the people you least expect (Interview #16: Female, age 56).

> We found some friends that we considered to be close friends never showed up again. Yet, there were other people that came out that we had sort of considered acquaintances, and we became very close (Interview #24: Male, age 47).

It is hypothesized that acquaintances who labeled respondents as victims considered them as legitimately sympathy worthy as did sympathetic friends and family. However, their expression of sympathy was not as readily blocked by their own upset, familiarity, and personal grief.

Interestingly, respondents sometimes noted a groundswell of support from strangers in the community as well. Strangers sometimes volunteered to search for the deceased, sent cards, flowers, food, raised money, erected memorials, organized petitions, and urged respondents to take action. Two factors were associated with the wide sympathy margins ascribed to such survivors: First, either the deceased, or their survivors, were well known, had much prior community involvement, or both:

> [The deceased] had a lot of friends. She was a very popular girl. She had a lot of friends from school. And I was very active in the community. I belonged to the Optimist Club, I coached baseball, I coached hockey, and so on—so I was very active, as far as that goes, with kids and all that all the time. I worked in other various organizations, working bingos and fundraising. So, I mean, there were a lot of people that it stunned, too. Then, as the trial went

> on, they were reading the newspaper and were getting upset with what was being said, and most of the people got together and wanted to do something. So, basically that's how it started (Interview #23: Male, age 49).

The second factor was widespread media coverage sympathetic to the survivors, illustrating the impact of the mass media on sympathy margins:

> It was not until the Saturday that it made the papers. The local paper did a good story, and people started coming to the door then, and we had literally hundreds of total strangers just arriving at our door in tears, very upset. It was obviously that their prayers were with us. Food started arriving in trays, flowers, baskets of fruit, it was just incredible. From 10 a.m. to 10 p.m. there was just a steady stream of traffic, and probably thirty to forty people at all times (Interview #31: Female, age 46).

Indeed, it appeared that several respondents were cast into the role of victim advocates in such a context. One woman, who has made a career as a moral crusader for victims' rights, recounts:

> I went on the radio [to thank the community search teams]. A policeman phoned in and said "I searched for [the deceased], now what are you going to do?" And that's how I started. I wrote a petition, and this whole thing kept going and kept going. So that is how [this survivor's organization] happened. People just kept coming to us and saying "what are you going to do?" There was never a day when the phone didn't ring thirty times (Interview #17: Female, age 50).

Such widespread community support, in several cases, was the genesis of more enduring victims' rights organizations. Moreover, in such altercasting (Weinstein and Deutschberger 1963) we may see the potential social basis for such survivors' tertiary victimization (Taylor, Wood, and Lichtman 1983; Kitsuse 1980) or tertiary emotional deviance (Thoits 1990; Kitsuse 1980), where the victim role is converted into something positive, meaningful, and socially efficacious.[3]

However, in cases where the deceased and/or survivors were not well known, sympathy margins were lessened. Where interactions with the media also did not go well, there was little interest in the story, or where the press' investigation of the crime resulted in an unfavorable portrayal, the mitigating effect on sympathy margins, community support, and survivors was magnified. One woman asked: Why isn't our daughter being talked about? (Field notes: Female, age 50). Another added:

> The publicity made it worse. The fact that the murder had to deal with drug dealing made it much worse, as there was no sympathetic community support. It was almost "like AIDS" (C.I.C.B. #91: Testimony of Female, age 46).

Aside from generalized lack of sympathy, such circumstances and related statuses were frequently characterized by an increased potential for stigmatization, either as a victim, deviant, or emotional deviant. Three types of negative interaction followed. First, survivors experienced harassment:

> Like, we got obscene phone calls to the house. The minute that we became public, I got phone calls that "If you and your family had belonged to the right religion, these horrible things wouldn't happen to you. God is punishing you." We'd get phone calls like that. One day this guy phoned and asked if I was the mother of one of these children that had been murdered. I said I was, and he says "Well, would you stay on the line while I masturbate?" And like this is for real! This is going on like every hour around here. Like—not just sporadically days apart—this is for real! And it's going on constantly (Interview #15: Female, age 49).

Secondly, survivors experienced a problem with blaming, particularly in a context of ongoing speculation, innuendo, and gossip. For example, one mother comments:

> One young girl came to the funeral home. I think when you have that type of thing, some come just

to be nosy, like, to see what they can see. She had just come with these other girls, and said "Well, the little slut got what she deserved." People had to hold us back! (Interview #21: Female, age 45).

Finally, notoriety resulted in uncomfortable interactions when going about one's business in public. This became a problem for some survivors:

> You know, you're a bit of a freak for a while because people don't really understand: "Oh, that's the woman that lost her daughter." People point you out. When they hear the name, they say, "Oh, are you the [respondent's first name]?" Like, that kind of thing. And you go "No, I'm just me." I kind of lose it there (Interview #16: Female, age 56) (Emphasis in original).

A male respondent also said:

> We went on a cruise, a company cruise. When we'd come down to dinner, we'd be the last, so everyone's sitting around their tables laughing and having a good time. Whatever table we'd pick, Whew! Dead silence. In the end we sat by ourselves in the corner. Cause when you sit at a table with people who are feeling that way, I had to start the conversation, and you know what it's like to try and talk . . . I mean it's bullshit that you have to come up with these little weak things to keep the conversation going (Interview #26: Male, age 61).

Ultimately, survivors who reported encountering such negative responses from acquaintances, strangers, and the community were far more likely to feel that they were faring worse emotionally. Indeed, it could be argued that these negative interactions revictimized those who reported experiencing them, leading again to secondary victimization (Taylor, Wood, and Lichtman 1983).

Summing up, these findings regarding differential support from acquaintances, strangers, and the community are intriguing, particularly insofar that such individuals appeared in many cases to respond more sympathetically than extended family and friends. It is hypothesized that, despite agreement on the sympathy-worthiness of survivors among these groups, supportive acquaintances and strangers were not as nervous about upsetting survivors, or becoming upset themselves. Of further interest was the potential for popular protest, fed by the media, to not only provide meaningful support to survivors, but also to inculcate positive new role identities (e.g., victims' advocate) indicative of tertiary victimization (Taylor, Wood, and Lichtman 1983; Kitsuse 1980) or tertiary emotional deviance (Thoits 1990; Kitsuse 1980). Of course, the more negative interactions simply revictimized survivors, adding to the secondary labeling process noted earlier.

Turning, finally, to subjects' responses, it is important to note that survivors in the wake of a murder essentially faced one major decision: either to attempt to deal with the murder primarily on their own, or to seek out help from other individuals, groups, and institutions. Their responses generally involved an interaction between their initial, gendered orientation toward seeking help and a variety of incentives and disincentives found in social interaction. The first strategy was more frequently utilized by men, who often avoided seeking help from medical professionals, self-help, and/or victims' groups. Women appeared to be far more inclined to seek out help from others, and this was reflected in the data in their reports of far greater levels of seeking out medical and psychiatric care, involvement in victims' and self-help groups, and economic support from social service agencies when unable to maintain employment. To give just one example, a survivor, who also happens to be a practicing therapist who treats victims, stated that her clientele was approximately "one quarter men, the rest women" (Interview #6: Female, age 46).

In addition to survivors' initial orientation to seeking help, they faced a variety of incentives and disincentives to do so related to the labeling process. Frequently, there was an obvious relation between perceived or actual level of support and survivors seeking outside help. For example, there were survivors who eventually sought outside help because of increasing social isolation:

I did go to a psychiatrist on a regular basis, because [sighs] after a while your friends don't want to hear about it any more. They just don't want to talk about it, or they're uncomfortable talking to you about it (Interview #16: Female, age 56).

If it wasn't for the group, I would be so isolated, and I wouldn't have a network, and I wouldn't have . . . soul companions . . . Because our families won't let us talk about it, cause they're dealing with guilt or something of their own, and they won't allow us to really express ourselves and hear this stuff, you know? So we do it amongst ourselves (Interview #19: Female, age 53).

Conversely, others felt they did not need to seek help as they had sufficient support already:

We didn't require any counselling. We've got good family around us, and that's how we've dealt with it (Interview #24: Male, age 47).

A few times I thought I should've gone to the hospital, but I didn't want to. I'm lucky I have friends. It's nice to have a support system behind you. You know, a support system is very important to mental health (Interview #1: Female, age 47).

These examples illustrate how sympathetic labeling as victims, as in the latter case, can accommodate survivors in such a way that they are not isolated in subcultures or relegated to formal control agents. On the other hand, social stigmatization as either victims, deviants, or emotional deviants can increase survivors' chances of contact with subcultures (such as support groups), or more formal agents of social control (e.g., those in a position to apply medical labels). Yet, level of support did not tell the whole story. Going hand in hand with this, survivors also spoke of encouragement to seek help. In some cases, survivors noted that others—particularly those with whom they could identify—tactfully and altruistically encouraged them to do so:

I have a friend who lost his son—I guess it was some sort of cancer. Well, because of his loss, he had sought help with [a self-help group]. So, knowing what had happened to us, he says "I'd like to talk to you for a minute." We talked a bit, and he

went on to tell me about the group. He told me
about himself, and how his grief had been helped.
He highly recommended it, saying that he wouldn't
have survived without them. It was interesting, so I
approached my wife (Interview #4: Male, age 56).

Yet other survivors, most often men, appeared to resent such "interference" and avoided seeking help, which suggests that gender plays a role as well. Finally, as this suggests, there was the element of choice. Consider the words of the following woman who, after unsupportive interactions with her family during the funeral, and avoidance thereafter, chose to become involved in a newly formed survivors' support group:

I had people there who I could talk to, and that
was good for me. In fact, right or wrongly, I made
the decision that would be the only place I'd ever
talk about this. I would not talk to my friends or
family unless I had to. But fortunately, you know, a
survivor will find a way—and that's exactly what I
did. I felt "Hey, who needs them?" (Interview #18:
Female, age 55) (Emphasis added).

Theorists have argued that labeling can have both adaptive and maladaptive consequences (Plummer 1979:118). Here it appears that informal labeling was important in either directing survivors to therapy and self-help or "forcing" them into further social withdrawal. It should be noted that a breakdown in perceptions of sympathy-worthiness, and the corresponding aspect of the victim label, undermines accommodation. This results in either a shift in emphasis to the stigmatized, helpless side of the victim label, or the labeling of individuals as deviant, in this case emotionally deviant. Indeed, in some cases where they are not perceived as sympathy worthy at the outset, victims can be blamed and seen as deviants deserving of their fate. All of these outcomes can have a significant impact on their self-identity (Rubington and Weinberg 1987:289–384). In such cases, the concepts of secondary victimization (Taylor, Wood, and Lichtman 1983) and secondary emotional deviance (Thoits 1990; Lemert 1951), in which survivors begin to

employ their victimization, deviant behavior, or a role based upon it as a means of defense or adjustment to the problems created by this social reaction, are strongly suggested.

Finally, it is important to consider that, both within and outside their respective subcultures (Rubington 1982), these individuals sometimes embraced, at other times distanced themselves from these various roles, or aspects thereof (Goffman 1961). Indeed, it appeared that a form of self-presentation (Goffman 1959) was sometimes utilized, which I term "volitional gerrymandering."

Summing up, survivors' initial orientation to seeking help were partially rooted in traditional gender roles. However, social incentives and disincentives appeared to play a significant part in survivors' coping choices. Overall perceived level of support from family, friends, and the community, coupled with gender, the relative maintenance or breakdown of accommodation by others to the emotional upset of survivors, and individual coping choices all played a role in the evolution of survivors' interactions beyond the "unofficial" sphere, to those with more "formal" helping agents. Often, the labeling process appeared to be at work here (Plummer 1979; Lemert 1951). This was reflected in both secondary and tertiary victimization (Taylor, Wood, and Lichtman 1983; Kitsuse 1980) and corresponding aspects for deviance (Lemert 1951; Thoits 1990; Kitsuse 1980). In either case survivors employed the victim role as a shield or as a sword in interactions, as well as in their involvement with subcultures (Rubington 1982). While all of this can have a significant impact on an individual's self-concept, particularly when a "deviant identity" is being inculcated (Rubington and Weinberg 1987), one must also bear in mind the potential for self-presentation evidenced by some subjects' use of "volitional gerrymandering."[4]

DISCUSSION AND CONCLUSION

The results of this research confirm and elaborate many of the themes in the labeling literature, but extend them theoretically by identifying a parallel labeling process for victims. Moreover, the intricate interplay between this and the deviance labeling process were empirically illustrated through a study of homicide survivors.

First, the varieties of helpful interactions may be conceptualized as reflecting the sympathy margins ascribed to survivors by others (Clark 1987). In those cases where wide sympathy margins are ascribed and helpfully expressed to survivors, survivors are labelled as victims but accommodated as deviants. In these cases, it is not so much individuals' grief that is defined as deviant, but the circumstances that initiated it. Survivors are recognized as victims, not blamed as such.

Secondly, it is important to note that such labeling as victims and recognition of sympathy worthiness is often also the case when survivors do not find others' behavior helpful. In these circumstances sympathetic others either do not know what to say, avoid survivors, or express their sorrow and care for survivors in well-meaning but hurtful ways in victims' eyes. The difference between the responses of extended family and friends, on the one hand, and acquaintances, strangers, and the community, on the other, was particularly interesting. This corroborates and extends the literature on social response to victims of life crises to a new empirical context (Lepore et al. 1996; Holman and Silver 1996; Wortman and Lehman 1983; Silver and Wortman 1980; Wortman and Dunkel-Schetter 1979).

Third, it is clear that survivors are not always recognized as victims deserving of sympathy, or as such indefinitely. Sympathy margins vary in width, and are governed by the rules of sympathy etiquette. In those cases where survivors break the rules of sympathy etiquette, either by claiming too much sympathy for too long, not making legitimate claims to sympathy, and the like, they may risk stigmatization. This may take several forms as illustrated above.

The data illustrating sympathetic social support, on the one hand, and active avoidance of survivors by their extended family, friends, and members of the community, on the other, exemplified these labeling variations. This was supple-

mented by survivors' own rationales of why this occurred, including varying perceptions of stigmatization, and others' fear of upsetting them. Indeed, survivors' additional reports of poor communication and inappropriate attention such as harassment and unwelcome comments further supported these variations in labeling. Significantly, when accommodation of survivors' upset broke down in these ways, many survivors became socially isolated and utilized others' responses as a rationale and defense. This is clearly evidence of secondary victimization (Taylor, Wood, and Lichtman 1983) or secondary emotional deviance (Thoits 1990; Lemert 1951), depending on the predominant focus of the labeling.

In other cases, some survivors, such as those who became caught up with others in community protests and fighting for change, showed evidence of engaging in tertiary victimization (Taylor, Wood, and Lichtman 1983; Kitsuse 1980) or tertiary emotional deviance (Thoits 1990; Kitsuse 1980). In such cases, a new, positive self-image emerges in interaction such that victims' advocates are seen as working toward positive ends for all, using their role as a sword in the process.

Ultimately, however, once accommodation breaks down and labeling begins, regardless of whether survivors use the victim role as a shield or as a sword, this becomes relevant to the literature on subcultures (Rubington 1982) and deviant identity (Rubington and Weinberg 1987). Yet, the fact that some embraced, while others distanced themselves from these identities, and employed them selectively, suggests that volitional gerrymandering also has significance for self-presentation and micropolitics (Goffman 1959; Emerson and Messinger 1977; Clark 1990). . . .

NOTES

1. It has already been extended in the study of illness by Conrad and Schneider (1980:17–20 et. seq). As such, the parallels outlined by examining victims merely refer to one possible analogy among others. Indeed, while this paper's specific focus is on extending labeling theory, one can easily look to other theoretical

traditions, such as Parsons' (1951) work on the sick role, for additional insights.

2. These strategies included: (i) volunteering, conducting fieldwork, and doing interviews for a year with a prominent Canadian victims' organization; (ii) networking/advertising with six other Canadian victims' rights organizations for interview/survey respondents; (iii) advertising with a national U.S. support/advocacy group for the homicide bereaved for survey respondents; (iv) attending conferences, rallies, and protests on victims' issues to observe/seek respondents; (v) contacting a prominent bereavement support organization for potential subjects; (vi) contacting the provincial chapter of an organization devoted to combatting impaired driving for comparative data; (vii) subscribing to the newsletters of the above organizations; (viii) reviewing biographical and journalistic accounts of survivors' experiences; (ix) unsuccessfully attempting, through formal access to information requests, to gain access to "victim impact statements" submitted by survivors at the sentencing of offenders; and (x) writing all Criminal Injuries Compensation Tribunals in Canada for information on applications by survivors.

3. While the issue of applying the term "deviant" to those organizing lobby self-help groups may be questioned by some, this is firmly in line with how these individuals—and others—perceive them (i.e., as somehow different). However, this does not mean that they, or their emotional self-presentation, must be seen as immoral. In the words of one such man "our normals are different now."

4. The issue of whether labeling amplifies or creates victimization must be answered on two levels. On one hand, the labeling described above has been shown to have a significant effect on both subjects' self-identity and their subsequent behaviors (e.g., social withdrawal, participation in counseling, self-help, and lobbying activities, along with differential self-presentation). On the other hand, the question of whether they are more likely to be victims of future violent crimes is unclear, as it is beyond the scope of the data utilized in this study.

REFERENCES

Becker, Howard. 1963. *Outsiders: Studies in the Sociology of Deviance*. Glencoe, Illinois: The Free Press.

Clark, Candace. 1987. "Sympathy Biography and Sympathy Margin." *American Journal of Sociology* 93(2):290–321.

Clark, Candace. 1990. "Emotions and Micropolitics in Everyday Life: Some Patterns and Paradoxes of 'Place.'" In T. D. Kemper (ed.), *Research Agendas in the Sociology of Emotions*. New York: SUNY Press.

Conrad, Peter, and Joseph W. Schneider. 1980. *Deviance and Medicalization: From Badness to Sickness*. St. Louis, MO: Mosby.

Emerson, Robert M., and Sheldon L. Messinger. 1977. "The Micro-Politics of Trouble." *Social Problems* 25(2):121–134.

Goffman, Erving. 1959. *The Presentation of Self in Everyday Life*. New York: Doubleday.

Goffman, Erving. 1961. *Encounters: Two Studies in the Sociology of Interaction*. Indianapolis, IN: Bobbs-Merrill.

Holman, E. Alison, and Roxanne C. Silver. 1996. "Is It the Abuse or the Aftermath? A Stress and Coping Approach to Understanding Responses to Incest." *Journal of Social and Clinical Psychology* 15(3):318–339.

Jackson, Joan K. 1954. "The Adjustment of the Family to the Crisis of Alcoholism." *Quarterly Journal of Studies on Alcohol* 15 (December): 564–586.

Kitsuse, John I. 1980. "Coming Out All Over: Deviants and the Politics of Social Problems." *Social Problems* 28(1):1–12.

Klass, Dennis. 1988. *Parental Grief: Solace and Resolution*. New York: Springer.

Knapp, Ronald J. 1986. *Beyond Endurance: When a Child Dies*. New York: Schocken.

Lemert, Edwin M. 1951. *Social Pathology*. New York: McGraw-Hill.

Lepore, Stephen J., Camille B. Wortman, Roxanne C. Silver, and Heidi A. Wayment. 1996. "Social Constraints, Intrusive Thoughts, and Depressive Symptoms among Bereaved Mothers." *Journal of Personality and Social Psychology* 70(2): 271–282.

Lerner, Melvin J. 1980. *The Belief in a Just World: A Fundamental Delusion*. New York: Plenum.

Lynch, Michael. 1983. "Accommodation Practices: Vernacular Treatments of Madness." *Social Problems* 31(2):152–164.

Parsons, Talcott. 1951. *The Social System*. New York. The Free Press.

Plummer, Kenneth. 1979. "Misunderstanding Labelling Perspectives." Pp. 85–121 in D. Downes and P. Rock (eds.), *Deviant Interpretations*. Oxford: Martin Robertson.

Rubington, Earl. 1982. "Deviant Subcultures." Pp. 57–60. In M. Rosenberg, R. A. Stebbins, and A. Turowetz (eds.), *The Sociology of Deviance*. New York: St. Martin's Press.

Rubington, Earl, and Martin S. Weinberg. 1987. *Deviance: The Interactionist Perspective*, 5th ed. New York: Macmillan.

Rynearson, E. K., and Joseph M. McCreery. 1993. "Bereavement after Homicide: A Synergism of Trauma and Loss." *American Journal of Psychiatry* 150:258–261.

Silver, Roxanne L., and Camille B. Wortman. 1980. "Coping with Undesirable Life Events." Pp. 279–340 in J. Garber and M. E. P. Seligman (eds.), *Human Helplessness: Theory and Applications*. New York: Academic.

Taylor, Shelley E., Joanne V. Wood, and Rosemary R. Lichtman. 1983. "It Could Be Worse: Selective Evaluation as a Response to Victimization." *Journal of Social Issues* 39(2):19–40.

Thoits, Peggy A. 1990. "Emotional Deviance: Research Agendas." Pp. 180–203 in T. D. Kemper (ed.), *Research Agendas in the Sociology of Emotions*. New York: State University of New York.

Weinstein, Eugene, and Paul Deutschberger. 1963. "Some Dimensions of Altercasting." *Sociometry* 26:454–466.

Wortman, Camille B., and Christine Dunkel-Schetter. 1979. "Interpersonal Relationships and Cancer: A Theoretical Analysis." *Journal of Social Issues* 35(1):120–155.

Wortman, Camille B., and Darrin R. Lehman. 1983. "Reactions to Victims of Life Crises: Support Attempts that Fail." Pp. 463–489. In I. G. Sarason and B. R. Sarason (eds.), *Social Support: Theory, Research and Applications*. Boston: Martinus Nijhoff.

Yarrow, Marian R., Charlotte G. Schwartz, Harriet S. Murphy, and Leila Calhoun Deasy. 1955. "The Psychological Meaning of Mental Illness in the Family." *Journal of Social Issues* 11(4):12–24.

CHAPTER 4

THE ROLE OF THIRD PARTIES

The Enforcement of College Alcohol Policy

EARL RUBINGTON

Although violations of rules may be brought to anyone's attention at times, only some people are officially required to respond to them. Examples of these formal agents of social control are police and corrections officers, schoolteachers, mental hospital attendants, and supervisors in various workplaces. The situation of enforcement in which an agent comes in contact with someone thought to be a "rule breaker" can mark the beginning of a deviant social career, so a key question for students of deviance is, What happens when a rule is assumed to have been broken? Under what conditions do negative sanctions take place?

Unlike most official agents of social control, residence-hall assistants live where they work. One important part of their work is enforcement of the college's no-drinking rule. Earl Rubington examines how residence-hall assistants manage the complexities of their relations with fellow students when enforcing the college's alcohol policy. His findings support the tentative generalization that the more frequent the contact of control agents with persons under surveillance, the less likely the enforcement of the rules. As a result, at least in college residence halls, familiarity breeds leniency rather than contempt.

When law and custom are in conflict, "patterned evasion" often follows (Williams 1970). As community support for a law wanes, official enforcement becomes selective, lax, or even nonexistent. The years from 1920 to 1933, when Prohibition was the law of the land, are generally considered to provide the classic example of patterned evasion (Merz 1970). Yet since repeal of Prohibition, age-specific prohibition and patterned evasion have long coexisted.

Reprinted from Earl Rubington, "The Ethic of 'Responsible Drinking,'" *Deviant Behavior*, Vol. 17 (1996), pp. 319–335. Copyright © 1996. Reproduced by permission of Taylor & Francis, LLC, http://www.taylorandfrancis.com.

Despite laws enjoining sales, purchase, possession, or consumption of alcoholic beverages by minors, more underage youth drink today, and more of them are "binge drinkers." The law . . . [influences] youth to drink, and the lack of enforcement only makes underage drinkers indifferent to or contemptuous of the law (Mosher 1980; Engs and Hanson 1989a). Since 1987, when all 50 states raised the drinking age to 21, although teenage drinking and driving has declined, teenage drinking remains at high levels.

Whether alcohol problems on campus are more prevalent than a generation ago, college administrators seem more concerned (Engs 1977). They seek to eliminate underage drinking on campus through formulating more detailed alcohol policies, more stringent sanctions, or a combination of both. As a consequence, freshman residence halls have become the focal point for the kinds of problems that contradiction between law and its enforcement can create. The vast majority of entering 1st-year students not only are already drinking but are also quite well accustomed to obtaining alcoholic beverages with impunity (O'Hare 1990). Thus, when they enter residence halls in the fall, they experience culture shock when they learn that the college forbids them to drink on campus. Most 1st-year students believe that they have been denied their "right to drink" (Engs and Hanson 1989b) and face a conflict between how they define drinking and how their college does.

It falls to residential assistants (RAs) to enforce the policies administrators have formulated. Documenting and reporting infractions of residence hall rules are an important part of RAs' duties (Blimling and Miltenberger 1990; Upcraft 1982). Unlike other agents of control such as police officers, prison guards, mental hospital attendants, and elementary school teachers, RAs live, work, and associate with the people whom they may have to report for infractions of residence hall rules (Becker 1952; Reiss 1971; Perrucci 1974; Zimmer 1986; Lombardo 1989). Thus, the complexity of RAs' social situation makes study of their enforcement role theoretically significant.

Police officers, prison guards, mental hospital attendants, and elementary school teachers, for example, have more community support and institutional authority than RAs. Their "clients" are all subordinate to them by reason of deviant or age status. Similarly, they are socially distant from them and share few cultural values with them. And, perhaps most important, these enforcers' chances of experiencing role conflict in their work with clients are considerably less than those of RAs (Merton 1957; Goode 1960).

Unlike the above-mentioned agents, RAs live and work in the same building with freshman residents. Like them, they are also students. They share many facilities both on and off campus, are not that far apart in age, share many values, and more or less share the same drinking culture (Berkowitz and Perkins 1986). Often, they meet one another in off-campus drinking parties or when they patronize the same drinking establishments. Thus, RAs can come into frequent contact with residents in a variety of social contexts including enforcement over the course of the academic years. That the kinds of relationships that emerge out of such contacts may have some bearing on how they enforce the no-drinking rule seems reasonable. But just what kinds of influence these contacts and relationships have had on enforcement of age-specific prohibition in freshman residence halls has not drawn a lot of research attention.

Three studies give some indication of the conditions under which enforcement of college alcohol policy varies. Moffatt (1989) studied a Rutgers University residence hall floor where upper-class students lived. He found that the RA went from being a lax to a strict enforcer of the no-drinking rule when the state raised the legal drinking age to 21 (Moffatt 1989). Cohn and White carried out a field experiment at the University of New Hampshire. Comparing three kinds of disciplinary policies, they found more violations of all residence hall rules in those residence halls where residents rather than administrators formulated alcohol policy (Cohn and White 1990). Concentrating on freshman residence halls, I studied RA–resident relations when the legal drinking age was 20. Comparing two residence halls, I found that floor layout as well as RAs' own drinking patterns influenced the way RAs enforced City University's (CU's) policy (Rubington 1993a).

After the drinking age was raised to 21, I compared the frequency of alcohol violations in three CU freshman residence halls for three consecutive years (1989 to 1992). These studies yielded the following uniformities: RAs recorded most alcohol violations in the fall quarter, with 30% of those violations coming in the week before the start of classes; most alcohol violators, whether one-time or repeat, were male; and male RAs reported four males for every single female violator, whereas for female RAs the sex ratio of reported violators was three males for every two females (Rubington 1991, 1993a, 1993b).

The present paper, pooling qualitative interview data from the three previous studies, seeks to account for variations in RAs' performance as prohibition agents.

RAs' job description mandates enforcement of residence hall rules. The contradiction between drinking age laws and their enforcement makes role problems for RAs. They are well aware of the ease with which residents can obtain alcoholic beverages off campus. Such easy access to alcoholic beverages, coupled with CU's ban on alcohol in the residence halls requires a cultural compromise. Just as residents have interests in violating the no-drinking rule, so do RAs have interests in its enforcement. What those interests are and how they may be best served comes out of their work experience. Through a process of mutual socialization, they adopt enforcement styles that best serve their interests. We turn now to an examination of those experiences, the enforcement roles they adopted, and their consequences.

The Student Handbook and CU's Housing Handbook, issued to all residents of university housing, spells out the university's policy on drinking: no possession, service, sale, or consumption of alcoholic beverages by students under 21; and students of legal age may drink only in their rooms. As part of their police function, RAs report most violations during those times when they are "on duty" and have to "make rounds" of the entire building. During the year a single RA is "on duty" on weekdays (Monday, Tuesday, and Wednesday); on weekends (defined as Thursday, Friday, Saturday, and Sunday), two RAs do "double duty." RAs are on duty for approximately 10 weekdays and 3 weekends during each of the three academic quarters. On weekdays, they make rounds at 8:00, 10:00, and 12:00 at night; weekends, they add a fourth round at 1:00 a.m. On rounds, they check up

on the building and its residents, and document any violations of residence hall rules. After each round, they record infractions on "discipline cards" and make more detailed entries in a staff log. Discipline card entries contain resident's name, date, time, place, and kind of infraction; resident's attitude (cooperative or uncooperative); and the RA's initials.

The three categories of infractions (sometimes occurring in combination) are alcohol, noise, and all others. Alcohol violations include being in the presence of alcohol; underage drinking (in the lobby, corridor, bathroom, stairway, elevator, or room); alcohol possession; drunkenness; attempting to smuggle alcohol into the building; residents' guest drinking; and the like. Noise violations include loud voices, stereos, radios, or musical instruments. Other violations include hallway sports, vandalism, throwing objects out of room windows, insubordination, suspicion of marijuana use, burning incense, and the like. Over the course of a year, alcohol and noise usually account for about two-thirds of all recorded violations.

SETTING AND METHOD

These studies took place in South, East, and West Halls, three CU freshman residence halls. (Names of the persons and places, including "City University," are fictitious.) The three residence halls housed men and women on alternate floors. An upper-class student of the same gender had a single room on each floor and served as the RA. Data for the three studies came from tabulation and analysis of all infractions RAs recorded on discipline cards, examination of residence hall staff logs, some participant observation, and interviews with resident directors (RDs), graduate assistants (GAs), and RAs in each of the three study years. The analysis and interpretation in this paper [are] based primarily on interviews with RAs. In the interview quotes that follow, R = residential assistant, D = residence director, and G = graduate assistant.

BECOMING A RESIDENTIAL ASSISTANT

RAs constitute the first line of defense of college alcohol policy. In the course of making rounds, RAs confront residents in situations that may require action on their part. In time, they develop their own style, a term RAs use when discussing their work as prohibition agents. Stages in RA careers and development of their styles follow below.

RAs AS RESIDENTS

CU requires that RAs have some prior experience as residents in a college residence hall. Most had been residents in one of CU's freshman residence halls. RAs who drank as freshmen reported a variety of experiences with their floor RAs. Most reported that their RAs were quite lax in enforcement of the no-drinking rule. Some reported RAs' collusion in alcohol violations.

A few recalled being "written up" for alcohol violations when they were freshmen, but most reported that they drank in the residence hall with impunity. One male said he got drunk once a week throughout the year without ever being written up. Others recalled their RAs inviting them into their room for a drink, or joining in a drinking party already going on in the informant's room. Still others noted that when the RA on rounds came upon them drinking in their rooms, he or she simply closed the door. One informant noted that the RA simply had them "dump" the beer (pour contents in sink or toilet bowl). And one female said that her RA used to call up on the phone to warn them when the RA on duty was making rounds. Thus RAs as freshmen were socialized to a number of ideas about drinking in the residence halls. Their freshman experiences showed them that drinking was ubiquitous, its enforcement lax.

FORMAL AND INFORMAL TRAINING

Both in the week before freshmen arrive and then later throughout the academic year, RAs attend training sessions, mainly lectures on a variety of subjects. The closest thing to "hands-on" experience that participants recalled was role-playing, which took place the week before classes started. It involved new RAs getting some idea of what went on behind closed doors. They had to knock on a resident's door, identify themselves as the RA, and request permission to enter. Once inside, they confronted veteran RAs acting as residents of the room and simulating one of the many kinds of situations they could expect to deal with once the fall quarter started. Underage drinking, domestic disputes, insubordination, suicidal residents, and the smell of marijuana were but a few of the surprises veteran RAs had in store for them. After the new RA responded to the situation, the veterans suggested other ways he or she could have handled the situation or commended the new RA for what he or she did.

In the early weeks of the quarter, veteran RAs sometimes accompany 1st-year RAs when they are making rounds. One source of informal training comes from observing how veterans manage confrontations with residents. Discussion with them after the fact also provides information for novice RAs on how to act should they come upon similar situations. In time, RAs fashion their own particular style by blending or avoiding techniques veteran RAs employ. Being matter-of-fact or strictly business, using humor to defuse situations, and taking charge more quickly are only some of the points RAs made in interviews. Some noted that with experience they managed confrontations with less time and effort.

THE FIRST FLOOR MEETING

In the first week of the fall quarter, RDs meet with all residents of the building and orient them to Big Town, CU, and residence hall rules. They point out that underage students cannot have alcohol in their rooms and cannot drink; and they tell them that anyone who breaks the rules will be subject to sanctions. Later, RAs hold their own first floor meetings. After mutual introductions, they also inform their residents about CU's alcohol policy.

At these meetings, RAs present their views about alcohol policy in one of four ways: tacit, proscriptive, conditional, or prescriptive. The few RAs who take the tacit route say nothing at all about the subject. Presumably, they believe that the RD has said all that needs to be said on the subject. A somewhat larger number of RAs are proscriptive. On the subject of alcohol and other drugs, they are both succinct and specific: They simply say: "Don't do it here." Most RAs, however, are conditional in their alcohol policy orientations. The way R-4 stated alcohol policy to her floor was typical. She said: "I don't see it, smell it, or hear it. [Hear it?] Quarters [a drinking game played with quarters], opening cans. The implied message is if I don't see it, smell it, or hear it, there's nothing I can do about it." First-year RAs were more apt to be prescriptive. Some wondered if they had sent mixed messages to their residents. For example, R-2 said: " 'I know you're gonna be drinking. It's gonna happen. Be quiet. Be in control. Don't let it get out of hand.' Some may have thought that validated drinking. Some took it that way."

RAs have notions on how to present themselves as rule enforcers at the start of the fall quarter. At the outset, some present themselves as sticklers. R-7 pointed out: "I decided to tell them that I was going to be strict, sort of scare them. Common sense says it's easier to go from hard to soft than from soft to hard. It's harder to get tough. . . . I'm majoring in marketing. It's only common sense to start with a higher price, then mark it down."

But, on the whole, RAs have a different relationship with the residents of their own floors than with residents of the other floors in the building. For one thing, they live on their own floors. They do not make scheduled rounds on their floor except when on duty. Although they do write up residents of their own floor, they are more lenient when disciplining them; they are more apt to use informal rather than formal means of social control. But, at the same time, they have to be somewhat concerned about the behavior of their own residents. For instance, RAs are subject to periodic performance reviews and evaluation by their RDs. "Problem floors" as well as "troublemakers" get labeled quickly after just a few rounds. Disorder, vandalism, noise, trash in the hallways, and numerous write-ups reflect on the floor RA's competence and affect his or her performance evaluation as well as reputation with fellow RAs. A "wild floor" makes for considerable work for all the other RAs when they have to make rounds. These RAs sometimes let the RA who has made extra work for them know how they feel; through direct comments or indirectly, in the staff log.

MAKING ROUNDS

RAs are most likely to come upon alcohol violations when making rounds. If they see people drinking in hallways or in their rooms, or if they hear loud voices or stereos coming from a room, they confront residents. Confrontation requires them to knock on the door, identify themselves as the RA, and request permission to enter. Once inside, if they see open cans of beer, people holding cans, or people drinking from containers, they ask all present for their IDs. After restoring order, they go downstairs to fill out discipline cards. They enter all names from the IDs on the cards along with the violations, and they enter the same information in the staff log.

The first time RAs make rounds, they experience some anxiety; but in a very short time it becomes, as one of them described it, "second nature." Confrontations with residents, of course, are not always matters of routine. RAs are expected to remain cool, assertive, and in control of the situation rather than become angry or excited. However, numerous contingencies attend RA–resident confrontations. As G-1 said: "You never know what you'll find once they open the door." A number of RAs have pointed out that residents become upset simply because RAs have intervened in their activities. These enforcement encounters generate understanding on not only how residents feel about being written up, but also how RAs themselves feel about writing up residents.

Thus, enforcement can be problematic for RAs. It soon becomes incumbent on them to fashion their own personal solutions to problems of their identity as RAs, situation control, and exercise of authority.

RAs expressed dislike about having to write up residents, having to document violations in accordance with Housing Office requirements. In addition to disliking the idea in general, some said they really didn't enjoy "getting people in trouble." Many residents, for example, took being written up quite personally and claimed that the RA was "out to get them." RAs reported that they often went out of their way the following morning to say hello to residents they had written up the night before. Greeting them as if nothing had happened, they sought to communicate that they had been "only doing their job." Whereas some residents came to understand, others did not. They showed their animosity by refusing to return the greeting.

DEVELOPMENT OF A STYLE

Over time, RAs solve problems of confrontation by developing what they call their "style." As experience with enforcing rules becomes routine, RAs opt for one of three styles: strict ("by-the-book"), moderate ("in between"), or lenient ("laid-back").

RAs who are "by-the-book" approach all encounters as if the matter were "cut and dried." They have a no-nonsense, matter-of-fact approach; take command of a situation immediately; collect IDs rapidly; are strictly business, quick, and cool. For the most part, they are rule-oriented. RAs who are "laid-back" are more apt to give residents the benefit of the doubt. More often situation-oriented, they will find a way to restore order without having to write residents up if possible. RAs who are "in between" are more often person-oriented. If residents are cooperative in a confrontation and do not give them a "hard time," they may manage a situation without necessarily documenting a violation of residence hall rules. But, as is generally the case with police–citizen contacts, disrespect guarantees being written up (Westley 1970; Reiss 1971; Black 1978). D-1 summarized the three types of RA styles when she said that "there are RAs who write up everything they see, RAs who will give a person a chance, and RAs who ignore everything."

RAs evolve their own styles out of a combination of observation, experience, and discussion with other RAs. R-2, for example, blended the styles of the two other veteran RAs, becoming an "in between." He said: "I hang around more with R-10 and R-11. R-10 gives more leeway, he deals personally, he's a humanist, he's friends with his residents, he's a fun guy. R-11, he's by-the-book: This is the policy, that's it. I learned from them. I relied on them. I found a middle ground." But here R-2 was talking about developing a style for dealing with his own floor.

Making rounds, however, brings RAs into more fleeting contacts with residents of a whole building on the dozen or more times they make rounds in the course of a quarter. These contacts necessarily turn on whether there has been a violation of the rules, which requires RAs to assert their authority, take charge, and alter the situation. Breaking up drinking parties, getting people in a room to leave, quieting residents, and getting them to dump the beer are just some examples. What is quite clear is that most RAs handle residents of their own floors differently. As R-12 said: "You use your discretion. I treat guys on my floor different from the rest of the building."

As previously noted, what makes RAs different from other control agents is that they live and work in the same place with people they may have to report for violating rules. During the course of an academic year they can make contact with residents of the whole building, but they are much more likely to come into frequent contact with residents of their own floor. The more frequent the contact between people, the more likely that something like friendship may develop (Homans 1951). Some RAs commented, for example, that visiting residents in their room and accepting a slice of pizza may set up expectations for special consideration at some later time. R-14 dropped in to visit a friend on her floor. Her friend's boyfriend was present, drinking a beer. R-14 had the boyfriend dump the beer, which upset her friend. Some RAs are aware of the need, as they put it, to "walk the line" between being a friend and being an RA. The friend–RA or cop–counselor conflict has been a problem for RAs ever since the establishment of the position (Upcraft 1982).

But if all RAs work in the same building, particularly when they are "on duty," they live on their home floors. As R-24 said: "I have to live with these guys for the rest of the year." And so variation in violation sites can make for variations in enforcement styles. RAs enforce rules on their home floors as well as on all floors and locations within the building, but once home floor versus all other floors is taken into account the site of enforcement makes for variations in styles of enforcement.

First, there are RAs who are "by-the-book" on all floors, their own as well as others. They know the rules, and when in the presence of a violation they write up the violator no matter who he or she is or where the violation took place. These sticklers can be generalists or specialists. R-15 considered making noise a more serious violation than drinking in one's room; he specialized in writing up residents for noise violations. Most violators he cited were residents of his floor. R-3 and R-16, both former problem drinkers, on the other hand, were specialists in writing up residents for alcohol violations whether on their home floors or on any of the others. But whether generalists or specialists, pure "by-the-book" RAs are paragons of consistency in the enforcement of residence hall rules. Most pure "by-the-book" RAs in this study were either seniors or veteran RAs, and more of them were women.

Next are those RAs who are "laid-back" with respect to their home floors but "by-the-book" when dealing with residents of any of the other floors. D-2 said: "R-17 is most lax enforcing rules on his floor. He loves his floor; they can do no wrong. But he's very consistent when enforcing rules off his floor." Other residence hall staff agreed that RAs are less strict with residents of their own floor. R-18 exemplified reluctance to document infractions on one's own floor. She acknowledged that when making "double-duty" rounds, she always stayed in the background when they got to her floor and let the other RA write up any of her residents. Being "laid-back" with one's own floor and "by-the-book" with all other floors is probably the typical enforcement style.

RAs who are "laid-back" on all floors are least frequent but most notorious. There are three degrees of "laid-backness": lenient, lax, and absent. Generally, the overly lenient lean more in the direction of friend rather than RA when it comes to confrontations with residents, irrespective of floors. This means that most of the time such an RA gives the resident the benefit of the doubt. Walking by an open door and seeing a student drinking, the RA may just close the door. Coming upon a student standing or walking in the corridor with an open beer in his or her hand, the RA may suggest that the person go to his or her room and close the door. On occasion, such an RA may ask the resident to dump a beer without later recording the incident on a discipline card and noting it on the staff log. The distinction between the lenient and the lax is that lenient RAs see the violation but do not treat it as such, whereas lax RAs go out of their way not to see any violations that require documenting. G-1 once accompanied R-5 on rounds. He was amazed at R-5's selective inattention. R-5 was a master at "looking the other way."

Laxity on the home floor can also come about when RAs have "lost control" of their floor. Overidentification with residents, coupled with an inability to accept identity as an RA and to exercise the authority that goes with the position, produces loss of control. D-1 pointed out R-19 as a good example of an RA who had lost control of his floor. Residents of his floor were written up for numerous trash, vandalism, noise, and alcohol violations. When I interviewed R-19 later, he said that his first two alcohol write-ups had made him most uncomfortable. He went on to say: "I was a freshman once. How do I get off getting them in trouble when I did the same things?" And later in that same interview he acknowledged that "I am more lax on my own floor."

Absence produces the third degree of "laid-backness." Occasionally RAs are off their floors for extended periods if they are holding another job, or are spending much of their time with a boyfriend or girlfriend. Extended absence produces the situation of "when the cat's away, the mice will play," as R-20 put it. A classic example of absence was R-21: Although he served as RA for an entire academic year, he wrote only one violation for that year. In turn, his floor was known as the wildest. The other seven RAs all wrote up a considerable number of violations whenever they made rounds on R-21's floor.

The last category consisted of RAs who were "in betweens." RAs who called themselves "in betweens" were most conscious of what they called "gray areas." They said that all RAs varied in their personal tolerances for alcohol and for noise. And some "in betweens" acknowledged that their mood sometimes influenced whether they wrote up a resident for a violation. The few "in betweens" were most apt to be women who made fine distinctions about incidents that came to their attention. These few were usually seniors and/or veteran RAs.

After a while, both residents and RAs become aware of these varied styles of enforcement among RAs. Consistency in rule enforcement can well become an issue, as it was in East Hall in the 1989–1990 academic year, when the "by-the-books" lined up against the "laid-backs" and the "in betweens."

"LIGHTENING UP"

During interviews, RAs either volunteered information or answered questions on how they as well as residents may have changed over the course of the academic year. On changes in residents' drinking, RAs gave one of four answers: Most drinking took place during the fall quarter (the "rite of passage" argument), during winter quarter (the "cabin fever" argument), during spring quarter (the "spring fever" argument), or at the beginning and end of each quarter (the "tension release" argument).

RAs said their own behavior changed with the quarters for one of three reasons: They "lightened up," they became apathetic, or they "burned out."

Typically, they complained of "living in a fishbowl," of lacking privacy. Although part of their job was surveillance, they deplored the fact that they "were always being watched." Informants often said that, whereas they had lightened up, it was usually the other RAs who had become apathetic or were burnouts. Over time, costs of rule enforcement began to outweigh its benefits. Yet despite variations in enforcement styles as well as lightening up as the year went on, in serving their own particular enforcement interests, RAs managed to collaborate in fashioning a common understanding of what the term "responsible drinking" came to mean in residence hall life.

THE ETHIC OF "RESPONSIBLE DRINKING"

Keeping the peace in CU residence halls depends on the ethic of "responsible drinking." For alcohol educators, responsible drinking means persons understand the action of alcohol, know their limits, make informed choices when they drink, and are prepared to take the consequences of their drinking, whatever they may be (Weisheit 1990). Responsible drinking means something entirely different to residence hall staff.

They take it as inevitable that freshmen are going to drink, that there is no stopping them. They claim that most freshmen drink, that many of them have fake IDs. They see empty cans and bottles in the trash cans. Many residents tell them about their drinking experiences. They overhear conversations in the building about parties, escapades, incidents, and hangovers. They see or hear residents vomiting in the bathroom at night or early in the morning. They come to know those rare residents who do not get out of bed until midafternoon. They know of vandalism, verbal or physical assaults that sometimes follow drinking, and occasions when they or other RAs have had to call campus police to deal with unruly, insubordinate residents. They know of cases of alcohol poisoning.

For RAs, drinking is a problem only if it makes trouble for them. Thus, those residents who drink behind closed doors, with few people in the room and voices or stereos lowered, have learned how to "drink responsibly." They are not, in D-1's words, "calling attention to themselves." G-4 said that when having an administrative meeting with residents she sometimes asked them why they hadn't considered "closing the door and turning it down."

At the beginning of the fall quarter, RAs are "gung ho," eager, enthusiastic. In line with Housing Office's suggestion that they start out tough as top sergeants, they come on in early confrontations as "hard-asses." They employ more aggressive tactics on rounds. They intimidate residents who try to sneak alcohol into the building. Since the development of the student rights movement, staff are not permitted to examine gym, duffel, or hockey bags, or to open the refrigerators that many students have in their rooms, or to enter rooms without residents' permission. Nevertheless, in the beginning of the year, they ask students if they may see what's in their bags or in their refrigerators. They always catch naive 1st-year students who are unaware of their rights. Once caught with unopened bottles or cans, residents must either remove them from the building or dump them while RAs watch.

The aggressive drive in the early weeks of the fall quarter probably discourages some residents from drinking in the residence halls. These early weeks also constitute a mutual testing period; residents and RAs alike negotiate over the definition and enforcement of the no-drinking rule. Over time, RAs spell out their definition of the rule. Agreement with their terms constitutes the ethic of "responsible drinking." "Responsible drinking" means drinking that goes on behind closed doors and makes no public trouble. Drinking that is not disorderly, disruptive, or destructive is considered responsible. For example, although the Housing Handbook lists public drunkenness as a violation, RAs don't write up residents who return to the residence hall intoxicated after a night's drinking if they can make it to their rooms without making a disturbance.

RAs interviewed attributed the marked decline in alcohol violations to the workings of the agreement. RAs said residents learned what they could and could not get away with. If for many this meant not drinking in the building, for others it meant learning the best times and places for sneaking alcohol in, adjusting their drinking to the RAs' cycle of rounds, finding out which RAs were hard on alcohol violations and which were not, becoming aware that they did not have to say what was in bags or refrigerators, and opening doors slowly when RAs knocked so as to conceal open containers. For most, it meant becoming more discreet when they did drink in the residence hall. And the reciprocal of the exercise of residents' discretion was the gradual relaxation of strict enforcement of the no-drinking rule by the RAs.

The ratio of actual to reported alcohol violations, of course, can never be known. Some RAs exaggerate the frequency of clandestine drinking. R-23 estimated that "we only catch about 30% of them." R-24 said that if she were to write up all the violations that came to her attention, they would probably total around 30 after all of her three rounds. Exaggerated or not, these estimates suggest that RAs' compliance with the terms of the unwritten agreement, that is, the ethic of "responsible drinking," keeps the peace in CU's freshman residence halls.

DISCUSSION

RAs face a particular role problem. On the one hand, the university asks them to enforce a rule inside the residence hall that is violated regularly outside. On the other hand, RAs live, work, and study among the very people who are subject to the rule they are required to enforce. Central to their dilemma is the social fact that those who enforce an unpopular rule can become as unpopular as, if not more so than, the rule itself. Enforcement of the rule creates the friend–RA role conflict endemic to the position of RA.

RAs' styles evolve out of the interests they believe enforcement will best serve. Those interests come to shape the stance they take in resolving the friend–RA conflict. Thus, those RAs who are "by-the-book" when making rounds on all floors as well as enforcing rules on their home floor resolve conflict by being strictly RAs. Their strict and regular enforcement symbolizes the relational distance they keep between themselves and all residents.

Those RAs who are "laid-back" with their own floors while being "by-the-book" on all the other floors tailor their enforcement efforts to the degree of social distance between them and residents: formal control for "strangers" (residents of the other floors), informal control for residents of their own floor. They "walk the line" between being the RA and being a friend because they believe they know their residents better than the pure "by-the-book" RAs know theirs. Informal control does the least damage to their relations with their residents. It takes two to make a role conflict. Although their residents would prefer them as friends, they teach their residents that they can be friends who also can be RAs when circumstances require it.

"Laid-back" RAs, whether on home floors or others, seek to be friends to everyone, authorities to none. Finally, those RAs who are neither friend nor RA to anyone are that way because they are rarely around. RAs of all degrees of "laid-backness" lose control of their floors, only making more enforcement work for all the other RAs when they make rounds.

The failure of the "laid-backs" to comply with the ethic of "responsible drinking" becomes a special residence hall form of patterned evasion. Then the other RAs have to redefine the situation by their more consistent enforcement of the residence hall drinking norm when they make their rounds. Residents with interests in defying the rules are left with two choices: drink outside the building or drink only when strict RAs are not making rounds. And to the extent that they don't call attention to themselves, they too are complying with the ethic of responsible drinking.

REFERENCES

Becker, Howard S. 1952. "The Career of the Chicago Public School Teacher." *American Journal of Sociology* 57:470–477.

Berkowitz, Alan D., and H. Wesley Perkins. 1986. "Resident Advisers as Role Models: A Comparison of Drinking Patterns of Resident Advisers and Their Peers." *Journal of College Student Personnel* 27:146–153.

Black, Donald J. 1978. "The Social Organization of Arrest." Pp. 154–160 in E. Rubington and M. S. Weinberg (eds.), *Deviance: The Interactionist Perspective,* 2nd ed. New York: Macmillan.

Blimling, Gregory S., and Lawrence J. Miltenberger. 1990. *The Resident Assistant.* Dubuque, IA: Kendall/Hunt.

Cohn, Ellen, and Susan White. 1990. *Legal Socialization: A Study of Norms and Roles.* New York: Springer-Verlag.

Engs, Ruth C. 1977. "The Drinking Patterns and Problems of College Students." *Journal of Studies on Alcohol* 38:2144–2156.

Engs, Ruth C., and David J. Hanson. 1989a. "University Students' Drinking Patterns and Problems: Examining the Effects of Raising the Purchase Age." *Public Health Reports* 103:667–673.

Engs, Ruth C., and David J. Hanson. 1989b. "Reactance Theory: A Test with Collegiate Drinking." *Psychological Reports* 64:1083–1086.

Goode, William J. 1960. "A Theory of Role Strain." *American Sociological Review* 25:483–496.

Homans, George C. 1951. *The Human Group.* New York: Harcourt Brace.

Lombardo, Lucien X. 1989. *Guards Imprisoned: Correctional Officers at Work.* Cincinnati: Anderson.

Merton, Robert K. 1957. "The Role-Set: Problems in Sociological Theory." *British Journal of Sociology* 8:106–120.

Merz, Charles. 1970. *The Dry Decade.* Seattle, WA: University of Washington Press.

Moffatt, Michael. 1989. *Coming of Age in New Jersey: College and American Culture.* New Brunswick, NJ: Rutgers University Press.

Mosher, James F. 1980. "The History of Youthful-Drinking Laws: Implications for Current Policy." Pp. 11–38 in H. Wechster (ed.), *Minimum Drinking-Age Laws.* Lexington, MA: Lexington Books.

O'Hare, T. M. 1990. "Drinking in College: Consumption Patterns, Problems, Sex Differences and Legal Drinking Age." *Journal of Studies on Alcohol* 51: 536–541.

Perrucci, Robert. 1974. *Circle of Madness*. Upper Saddle River, NJ: Prentice Hall.

Reiss, Albert J. 1971. *The Police and the Public*. Chicago: University of Chicago Press.

Rubington, Earl. 1990. "Drinking in the Dorms: The Etiquette of RA–Resident Relations." *Journal of Drug Issues* 20:451–461.

Rubington, Earl. 1991. "Drinking Sanctions and Freshman Residence Halls: An Exploratory Case Study." *Contemporary Drug Problems* 18:373–387.

Rubington, Earl. 1993a, August. "Drinking Sanctions and Freshman Residence Halls, 1989–1992." Paper delivered at the annual meeting of the Society for the Study of Social Problems, Arlington, VA.

Rubington, Earl. 1993b. "College Drinking and Social Control." *Journal of Alcohol and Drug Education* 39:56–65.

Upcraft, Lee. 1982. *Residence Hall Assistants in College*. San Francisco: Jossey-Bass.

Weisheit, Richard A. 1990. "Contemporary Issues in the Prevention of Adolescent Alcohol Abuse." Pp. 194–207 in D. A. Ward (ed.), *Alcoholism: Introduction to Theory and Treatment*. Dubuque, IA: Kendall/Hunt.

Westley, William. 1970. *Violence and the Police*. Cambridge, MA: MIT Press.

Williams, Robin M. 1970. *American Society*. New York: Alfred A. Knopf.

Zimmer, Lynn. 1986. *Women Guarding Men*. Chicago: University of Chicago Press.

Paranoia and the Dynamics of Exclusion

EDWIN M. LEMERT

One of the core values of American culture is individualism. Related to this is the value placed on effort. Thus, people succeed or fail on the basis of their individual efforts. In accounting for deviance, the individualist scheme of interpretation spills over: Deviance is seen to stem from the person's character rather than from a complex pattern of interactions with other people.

A familiar example of the individualist scheme of interpretation is the popular application of the psychiatric term "paranoid" in everyday life. Paranoids, it is said, are typically extremely suspicious persons who view the social world as a great conspiracy with everybody plotting against them. The consensus is that this is a completely distorted view of the real world and by itself sufficient proof that the problem is "in their head" rather than in their social circle.

Edwin M. Lemert, after interviewing a number of mental patients who had been classified as paranoids and then studying the history of their exclusion in the workplace, developed an interactionist account for the circumstances under which the definition, interpretation, and actions against them occurred. He found the paranoids were not deluded—people, in fact, had conspired against them. In all cases, groups in the workplace, after collectively defining them as "difficult persons," formed coalitions to exclude these individuals from membership in the broader workplace social circle. In responding to this process of mutual alienation and estrangement, these patients had assumed the role and status of the "paranoid."

The paranoid process begins with persistent interpersonal difficulties between the individual and his family, or his work associates and superiors, or neighbors, or other persons in the community. These frequently or even typically arise out of bona fide or recognizable issues centering upon some actual or threatened loss of status for the individual. This is related to such things as the death of relatives, loss of a position, loss of professional certification, failure to be promoted, age and physiological life cycle changes, mutilations, and changes in family and marital relationships. The status changes are distinguished by the fact that they leave no alternative acceptable to the individual, from whence comes their "intolerable" or "unendurable" quality. For example: the man trained to be a teacher who loses his certificate, which means he can never teach; or the man of 50 years of age who is faced with loss of promotion which is a regular order of upward mobility in an organization, who knows that he can't "start over"; or the wife undergoing hysterectomy, which mutilates her image as a woman.

In cases where no dramatic status loss can be discovered, a series of failures often is present, failures which may have been accepted or adjusted to, but with progressive tension as each new status situation is entered. The unendurability of the current status loss, which may appear unimportant to others, is a function of an intensified commitment, in some cases born of an awareness that there is a quota placed on failures in our society. Under some such circumstances, failures have followed the person, and his reputation as a "difficult person" has preceded him. This means that he often has the status of a stranger on trial in each new group he enters, and that the groups or organizations willing to take a chance on him are marginal from the standpoint of their probable tolerance for his actions.

Reprinted from "Paranoia and the Dynamics of Exclusion," *Sociometry*, Vol. 25, No. 1 (March 1962), pp. 7–15, by permission of the author and the American Sociological Association.

The behavior of the individual—arrogance, insults, presumption of privilege and exploitation of weaknesses in others—initially has a segmental or checkered pattern in that it is confined to status-committing interactions. Outside of these, the person's behavior may be quite acceptable—courteous, considerate, kind, even indulgent. Likewise, other persons and members of groups vary considerably in their tolerance for the relevant behavior, depending on the extent to which it threatens individual and organizational values, impedes functions, or sets in motion embarrassing sequences of social actions. In the early generic period, tolerance by others for the individual's aggressive behavior generally speaking is broad, and it is very likely to be interpreted as a variation of normal behavior, particularly in the absence of biographical knowledge of the person. At most, people observe that "there is something odd about him," or "he must be upset," or "he is just ornery," or "I don't quite understand him" [1].

At some point in the chain of interactions, a new configuration takes place in perceptions others have of the individual, with shifts in figure-ground relations. The individual, as we have already indicated, is an ambiguous figure, comparable to textbook figures of stairs or outlined cubes which reverse themselves when studied intently. From a normal variant the person becomes "unreliable," "untrustworthy," "dangerous," or someone with whom others "do not wish to be involved." An illustration nicely apropos of this came out in the reaction of the head of a music department in a university when he granted an interview to a man who had worked for years on a theory to compose music mathematically:

> When he asked to be placed on the staff so that he could use the electronic computers of the University I shifted my ground . . . when I offered an objection to his theory, he became disturbed, so I changed my reaction to "yes and no."

As is clear from this, once the perceptual reorientation takes place, either as the outcome of continuous interaction or through the receipt of biographical information, interaction changes qualitatively. In our words it becomes *spurious,* distinguished by patronizing, evasion, "humoring," guiding conversation onto selected topics, underreaction, and silence, all calculated either to prevent intense interaction or to protect individual and group values by restricting access to them. When the interaction is between two or more persons it is cued by a whole repertoire of subtle expressive signs which are meaningful only to them.

The net effects of spurious interaction are to:

1. stop the flow of information to ego;
2. create a discrepancy between expressed ideas and affect among those with whom he interacts;
3. make the situation or the group image an ambiguous one for ego, much as he is for others.

Needless to say this kind of spurious interaction is one of the most difficult for an adult in our society to cope with, because it complicates or makes decisions impossible for him and also because it is morally invidious.[1]

The process from inclusion to exclusion is by no means an even one. Both individuals and members of groups change their perceptions and reactions, and vacillation is common, depending upon the interplay of values, anxieties and guilt on both sides. Members of an excluding group may decide they have been unfair and seek to bring the individual back into their confidence. This overture may be rejected or used by ego as a means of further attack. We have also found that ego may capitulate, sometimes abjectly, to others and seek group reentry, only to be rejected. In some cases compromises are struck and a partial reintegration of ego into informal social relations is achieved. The direction which informal exclusion takes depends upon ego's reactions, the degree of communication between his interactors, the composition and structure of the informal groups, and the perceptions of "key others" at points of interaction which directly affect ego's status.

ORGANIZATIONAL CRISIS AND FORMAL EXCLUSION

Thus far we have discussed exclusion as an informal process. Informal exclusion may take place but leave ego's formal status in an organization intact. So long as this status is preserved and rewards are sufficient to validate it on his terms, an uneasy peace between him and others may prevail. Yet ego's social isolation and his strong commitments make him an unpredictable factor; furthermore the rate of change and internal power struggles, especially in large and complex organizations, means that preconditions of stability may be short-lived.

Organizational crises involving a paranoid relationship arise in several ways. The individual may act in ways which arouse intolerable anxieties in others, who demand that "something be done." Again, by going to higher authority or making appeals outside the organization, he may set in motion procedures which leave those in power no other choice than to take action. In some situations ego remains relatively quiescent and does not openly attack the organization. Action against him is set off by growing anxieties or calculated motives of associates—in some cases his immediate superiors. Finally, regular organizational procedures incidental to promotion, retirement or reassignment may precipitate the crisis.

Assuming a critical situation in which the conflict between the individual and members of the organization leads to action to formally exclude him, several possibilities exist. One is the transfer of ego from one department, branch or division of the organization to another, a device frequently resorted to in the armed services or in large corporations. This requires that the individual be persuaded to make the change and that some department will accept him. While this may be accomplished in different ways, not infrequently artifice, withholding information, bribery, or thinly disguised threats figure conspicuously among the means by which the transfer is brought about. Needless to say, there is a limit to which transfers can be employed as a solution to the problem, contingent upon the size of the organization and the previous diffusion of knowledge about the transferee.

Solution number two we call encapsulation, which, in brief, is a reorganization and redefinition of ego's status. This has the effect of isolating him from the organization and making him directly responsible to one or two superiors who act as his intermediators. The change is often made palatable to ego by enhancing some of the material rewards of his status. He may be nominally promoted or "kicked upstairs," given a larger office, or a separate secretary, or relieved of onerous duties. Sometimes a special status is created for him.

This type of solution often works because it is a kind of formal recognition by the organization of ego's intense commitment to his status and in part a victory for him over his enemies. It bypasses them and puts him into direct communication with higher authority who may communicate with him in a more direct manner. It also relieves his associates of further need to connive against him. This solution is sometimes used to dispose of troublesome corporation executives, high-ranking military officers, and academic *personae non gratae* in universities.

A third variety of solutions to the problem of paranoia in an organization is outright discharge, forced resignation or non-renewal of appointment. Finally, there may be an organized move to have the individual in the paranoid relationship placed on sick leave, or to compel him to take psychiatric treatment. The extreme expression of this is pressure (as on the family) or direct action to have the person committed to a mental hospital.

The order of the enumerated solutions to the paranoid problem in a rough way reflects the amount of risk associated with the alternatives, both as to the probabilities of failure and of damaging repercussions to the organization. Generally, organizations seem to show a good deal of resistance to making or carrying out decisions which require expulsion of the individual or forcing

hospitalization, regardless of his mental condition. One reason for this is that the person may have power within the organization, based upon his position, or monopolized skills and information,[2] and unless there is a strong coalition against him the general conservatism of administrative judgments will run in his favor. Herman Wouk's novel of *The Caine Mutiny* dramatizes some of the difficulties of cashiering a person from a position of power in an essentially conservative military organization. An extreme of this conservatism is illustrated by one case in which we found a department head retained in his position in an organization even though he was actively hallucinating as well as expressing paranoid delusions. Another factor working on the individual's side is that discharge of a person in a position of power reflects unfavorably upon those who placed him there. Ingroup solidarity of administrators may be involved, and the methods of the opposition may create sympathy for ego at higher levels.

Even when the person is almost totally excluded and informally isolated within an organization, he may have power outside. This weighs heavily when the external power can be invoked in some way, or when it automatically leads to raising questions as to the internal workings of the organization. This touches upon the more salient reason for reluctance to eject an uncooperative and retaliatory person, even when he is relatively unimportant to the organization. We refer to a kind of negative power derived from the vulnerability of organizations to unfavorable publicity and exposure of their private lives that are likely if the crisis proceeds to formal hearings, case review or litigation. This is an imminent possibility where paranoia exists. If hospital commitment is attempted, there is a possibility that a jury trial will be demanded, which will force leaders of the organization to defend their actions. If the crisis turns into a legal contest of this sort, it is not easy to prove insanity, and there may be damage suits. Even if the facts heavily support the petitioners, such contests can only throw unfavorable light upon the organization.

THE CONSPIRATORIAL NATURE
OF EXCLUSION

A conclusion from the foregoing is that organizational vulnerability as well as anticipations of retaliations from the paranoid person lay a functional basis for conspiracy among those seeking to contain or oust him. Probabilities are strong that a coalition will appear within the organization, integrated by a common commitment to oppose the paranoid person. This, the exclusionist group, demands loyalty, solidarity and secrecy from its members; it acts in accord with a common scheme and in varying degrees utilizes techniques of manipulation and misrepresentation.

Conspiracy in rudimentary form can be detected in informal exclusion apart from an organizational crisis. This was illustrated in an office research team in which staff members huddled around a water cooler to discuss the unwanted associate. They also used office telephones to arrange coffee breaks without him and employed symbolic cues in his presence, such as humming the *Dragnet* theme song when he approached the group. An office rule against extraneous conversation was introduced with the collusion of supervisors, ostensibly for everyone, actually to restrict the behavior of the isolated worker. In another case an interview schedule designed by a researcher was changed at a conference arranged without him. When he sought an explanation at a subsequent conference, his associates pretended to have no knowledge of the changes.

Conspiratorial behavior comes into sharpest focus during organizational crises in which the exclusionists who initiate action become an embattled group. There is a concerted effort to gain consensus for this view, to solidify the group and to halt close interaction with those unwilling to completely join the coalition. Efforts are also made to neutralize those who remain uncommitted but who can't be kept ignorant of the plans afoot. Thus an external appearance of unanimity is given even if it doesn't exist.

Much of the behavior of the group at this time is strategic in nature, with determined calculations as to "what we will do if he does this or that." In one of our cases, a member on a board of trustees spoke of the "game being played" with the person in controversy with them. Planned action may be carried to the length of agreeing upon the exact words to be used when confronted or challenged by the paranoid individual. Above all there is continuous, precise communication among exclusionists, exemplified in one case by mutual exchanging of copies of all letters sent and received from ego.

Concern about secrecy in such groups is revealed by such things as carefully closing doors and lowering of voices when ego is brought under discussion. Meeting places and times may be varied from normal procedures; documents may be filed in unusual places and certain telephones may not be used during a paranoid crisis.

The visibility of the individual's behavior is greatly magnified during this period; often he is the main topic of conversation among the exclusionists, while rumors of the difficulties spread to other groups, which in some cases may be drawn into the controversy. At a certain juncture steps are taken to keep the members of the ingroup continually informed of the individual's movements and, if possible, of his plans. In effect, if not in form, this amounts to spying. Members of one embattled group, for example, hired an outside person unknown to their accuser to take notes on a speech he delivered to enlist a community organization on his side. In another case, a person having an office opening onto that of a department head was persuaded to act as an informant for the nucleus of persons working to depose the head from his position of authority. This group also seriously debated placing an all-night watch in front of their perceived malefactor's house.

Concomitant with the magnified visibility of the paranoid individual come distortions of his image, most pronounced in the inner coterie of exclusionists. His size, physical strength, cunning, and anecdotes of his outrages are exaggerated, with a central thematic emphasis on the fact that he is dangerous. Some individuals give cause for such beliefs in that previously they have engaged in violence or threats, others do not. One encounters characteristic contradictions in interviews on this point, such as: "No, he has never struck anyone around here—just fought with the policemen at the State Capitol," or "No, I am not afraid of him, but one of these days he will explode."

It can be said parenthetically that the alleged dangerousness of paranoid persons storied in fiction and drama has never been systematically demonstrated. As a matter of fact, the only substantial data on this, from a study of delayed admissions, largely paranoid, to a mental hospital in Norway, disclosed that "neither the paranoiacs nor paranoids have been dangerous, and most not particularly troublesome" [4]. Our interpretation of this, as suggested earlier, is that the imputed dangerousness of the paranoid individual does not come from physical fear but from the organizational threat he presents and the need to justify collective action against him.

However, this is not entirely tactical behavior—as is demonstrated by anxieties and tensions which mount among those in the coalition during the more critical phases of their interaction. Participants may develop fears quite analogous to those of classic conspirators. One leader in such a group spoke of the period of the paranoid crisis as a "week of terror," during which he was wracked with insomnia and "had to take his stomach pills." Projection was revealed by a trustee who, during a school crisis occasioned by discharge of an aggressive teacher, stated that he "watched his shadows," and "wondered if all would be well when he returned home at night." Such tensional states, working along with a kind of closure of communication within the group, are both a cause and an effect of amplified group interaction which distorts or symbolically rearranges the image of the person against whom they act.

Once the battle is won by the exclusionists, their version of the individual as dangerous becomes a crystallized rationale for official action. At this point misrepresentation becomes part of a more deliberate manipulation of ego. Gross misstatements, most frequently called "pretexts," become justifiable ways of getting his cooperation, for example, to get him to submit to psychiatric examination or detention preliminary to hospital commitment. This aspect of the process has been effectively detailed by Goffman, with his concept of a "betrayal funnel" through which a patient enters a hospital [5]. We need not elaborate on this, other than to confirm its occurrence in the exclusion process, complicated in our cases by legal strictures and the ubiquitous risk of litigation.

THE GROWTH OF DELUSION

The general idea that the paranoid person symbolically fabricates the conspiracy against him is in our estimation incorrect or incomplete. Nor can we agree that he lacks insight, as is so frequently claimed. To the contrary, many paranoid persons properly realize that they are being isolated and excluded by concerted interaction, or that they are being manipulated. However, they are at a loss to estimate accurately or realistically the dimensions and form of the coalition arrayed against them.

As channels of communication are closed to the paranoid person, he has no means of getting feedback on consequences of his behavior, which is essential for correcting his interpretations of the social relationships and organization which he must rely on to define his status and give him identity. He can only read overt behavior without the informal context. Although he may properly infer that people are organized against him, he can only use confrontation or formal inquisitorial procedures to try to prove this. The paranoid person must provoke strong feelings in order to receive any kind of meaningful communication from others—hence his accusations, his bluntness, his insults. Ordinarily this is non-deliberate; nevertheless, in one complex case we found the person consciously provoking discussions to get readings from others on his behavior. This man said of himself: "Some people would describe me as very perceptive, others would describe me as very imperceptive."

The need for communication and the identity which goes with it does a good deal to explain the preference of paranoid persons for formal, legalistic, written communications, and the care with which many of them preserve records of their contacts with others. In some ways the resort to litigation is best interpreted as the effort of the individual to compel selected others to interact directly with him as equals, to engineer a situation in which evasion is impossible. The fact that the person is seldom satisfied with the outcome of his letters, his petitions, complaints and writs testifies to their function as devices for establishing contact and interaction with others, as well as "setting the record straight." The wide professional tolerance of lawyers for aggressive behavior in court and the nature of Anglo-Saxon legal institutions, which grew out of a revolt against conspiratorial or star-chamber justice, mean that the individual will be heard. Furthermore his charges must be answered; otherwise he wins by default. Sometimes he wins small victories, even if he loses the big ones. He may earn grudging respect as an adversary, and sometimes shares a kind of legal camaraderie with others in the courts. He gains an identity through notoriety. . . .

NOTES

1. The interaction in some ways is similar to that used with children, particularly the *"enfant terrible."* The function of language in such interactions was studied by Sapir [2] years ago.
2. For a systematic analysis of the organizational difficulties in removing an "unpromotable" person from a position see [3].

REFERENCES

1. Cumming, Elaine, and John H. Cumming. 1957. *Closed Ranks.* Cambridge, MA: Harvard Press, Chapter 6.
2. Sapir, Edward. 1915. "Abnormal Types of Speech in Nootka." *Canada Department of Mines, Memoir 62* (5).
3. Levenson, Bernard. 1961. "Bureaucratic Succession." Pp. 362–395 in Amitai Etzioni (ed.), *Complex Organizations.* New York: Holt, Rinehart and Winston.
4. Ödegard, Örnulv. 1958. "A Clinical Study of Delayed Admissions to a Mental Hospital." *Mental Hygiene,* 42:66–67.
5. Goffman, Erving. 1959. "The Moral Career of the Mental Patient." *Psychiatry* 22:127 ff.

The Moral Career of the Mental Patient

ERVING GOFFMAN

Textbooks on psychiatry distinguish neurosis from psychosis. Generally, neurotics make much trouble for themselves but little or none for others, are not dangerous to others, and can function in daily life. Generally, psychotics make as much trouble for others as they do for themselves, are often a danger to themselves as well as to others, and are less able to take care of themselves. Public opinion concurs with professional judgment but adds to it the important dimensions of fear, anxiety, and ambivalence. Lay and expert judgment concur that the most severely impaired are rightly confined to mental hospitals.

Erving Goffman counters this view with his own conception of three stages a person goes through as a "mental patient": prepatient, inpatient, and ex-patient. Some degree of impairment in everyday life may be a condition for becoming a mental patient. But the sufficient condition according to him is the marshalling together of a team of laypersons as well as professional agents of social control who in concert facilitate the person's entry into the mental hospital. Hence, severity of impairment is of considerably less importance than the social organization of what he calls an *alienative coalition*. Once again, the social reaction to a pattern of behavior assumes considerably more importance than the pattern of behavior in its own right when a person becomes labeled as a deviant.

Traditionally the term *career* has been reserved for those who expect to enjoy the rises laid out within a respectable profession. The term is coming to be used, however, in a broadened sense to refer to any social strand of any person's course through life. The perspective of natural history is taken: unique outcomes are neglected in favor of such changes over time as are basic and common to the members of a social category, although occurring independently to each of them. Such a career is not a thing that can be brilliant or disappointing; it can no more be a success than a failure. In this light, I want to consider the mental patient, drawing mainly upon data collected during a year's participant observation of patient social life in a public mental

Reprinted from "The Moral Career of the Mental Patient," *Psychiatry: Journal for the Study of Interpersonal Processes*, Vol. 22 (May 1959), pp. 123–135, by special permission of the author and The William Alanson White Psychiatric Foundation, Inc. Copyright © 1959 by The William Alanson White Psychiatric Foundation, Inc.

hospital,[1] wherein an attempt was made to take the patient's point of view.

One value of the concept of career is its two-sidedness. One side is linked to internal matters held dearly and closely, such as image of self and felt identity; the other side concerns official position, jural relations, and style of life, and is part of a publicly accessible institutional complex. The concept of career, then, allows one to move back and forth between the personal and the public, between the self and its significant society, without having overly to rely for data upon what the person says he thinks he imagines himself to be.

This paper, then, is an exercise in the institutional approach to the study of self. The main concern will be with the *moral* aspects of career—that is, the regular sequence of changes that career entails in the person's self and in his framework of imagery for judging himself and others.[2]

The category "mental patient" itself will be understood in one strictly sociological sense. In this perspective, the psychiatric view of a person becomes significant only insofar as this view itself alters his social fate—an alteration which seems to become fundamental in our society when, and only when, the person is put through the process of hospitalization.[3] I therefore exclude certain neighboring categories: the undiscovered candidates who would be judged "sick" by psychiatric standards but who never come to be viewed as such by themselves or others, although they may cause everyone a great deal of trouble;[4] the office patient whom a psychiatrist feels he can handle with drugs or shock on the outside; the mental client who engages in psychotherapeutic relationships. And I include anyone, however robust in temperament, who somehow gets caught up in the heavy machinery of mental hospital servicing. In this way the effects of being treated as a mental patient can be kept quite distinct from the effects upon a person's life of traits a clinician would view as psychopathological.[5] Persons who become mental hospital patients vary widely in the kind and degree of illness that a psychiatrist would impute to them, and in the attributes by which laymen would describe them. But once started on the way, they are confronted by some importantly similar circumstances and respond to these in some importantly similar ways. Since these similarities do not come from mental illness, they would seem to occur in spite of it. It is thus a tribute to the power of social forces that the uniform status of mental patient cannot only assure an aggregate of persons a common fate and eventually, because of this, a common character, but that this social reworking can be done upon what is perhaps the most obstinate diversity of human materials that can be brought together by society . . . .[6]

The career of the mental patient falls popularly and naturalistically into three main phases: the period prior to entering the hospital, which I shall call the *prepatient phase;* the period in the hospital, the *inpatient phase;* the period after discharge from the hospital, should this occur, namely, the *ex-patient phase.*[7] This paper will deal only with the first . . . [phase].

THE PREPATIENT PHASE

A relatively small group of prepatients come into the mental hospital willingly, because of their own idea of what will be good for them, or because of wholehearted agreement with the relevant members of their family. Presumably these recruits have found themselves acting in a way which is evidence to them that they are losing their minds or losing control of themselves. This view of oneself would seem to be one of the most pervasively threatening things that can happen to the self in our society, especially since it is likely to occur at a time when the person is in any case sufficiently troubled to exhibit the kind of symptom which he himself can see. As Sullivan described it,

> *What we discover in the self-system of a person undergoing schizophrenic changes or schizophrenic processes, is then, in its simplest form, an extremely fear-marked puzzlement, consisting of the use of rather generalized and anything but exquisitely refined referential processes in an attempt to cope with what is essentially a failure at being human—a failure at being anything that one could respect as worth being.*[8]

Coupled with the person's disintegrative reevaluation of himself will be the new, almost equally pervasive circumstance of attempting to conceal from others what he takes to be the new fundamental facts about himself, and attempting to discover whether others too have discovered them.[9] Here I want to stress that perception of losing one's mind is based on culturally derived and socially engrained stereotypes as to the significance of symptoms such as hearing voices, losing temporal and spatial orientation, and sensing that one is being followed, and that many of the most spectacular and convincing of these symptoms in some instances psychiatrically signify merely a temporary emotional upset in a stressful situation, however terrifying to the person at the time. Similarly, the anxiety consequent upon this perception of oneself, and the strategies devised to reduce this anxiety, are not a product of abnormal psychology, but would be exhibited by any person socialized into our culture who came to conceive of himself as someone losing his mind. Interestingly, subcultures in American society apparently differ in the amount of ready imagery and encouragement they supply for such self-views, leading to differential rates of *self*-referral; the capacity to take this disintegrative view of oneself without psychiatric prompting seems to be one of the questionable cultural privileges of the upper classes.[10]

For the person who has come to see himself—with whatever justification—as mentally unbalanced, entrance to the mental hospital can sometimes bring relief, perhaps in part because of the sudden transformation in the structure of his basic social situations; instead of being to himself a questionable person trying to maintain a role as a full one, he can become an officially questioned person known to himself to be not so questionable as that. In other cases, hospitalization can make matters worse for the willing patient, confirming by the objective situation what has theretofore been a matter of the private experience of self.

Once the willing prepatient enters the hospital, he may go through the same routine of experiences as do those who enter unwillingly. In any case, it is the latter that I mainly want to consider, since in America at present these are by far the more numerous kind.[11] Their approach to the institution takes one of three classic forms: they come because they have been implored by their family or threatened with the abrogation of family ties unless they go "willingly"; they come by force under police escort; they come under misapprehension purposely induced by others, this last restricted mainly to youthful prepatients.

The prepatient's career may be seen in terms of an extrusory model; he starts out with relationships and rights, and ends up, at the beginning of his hospital stay, with hardly any of either. The moral aspects of this career, then, typically begin with the experience of abandonment, disloyalty, and embitterment. This is the case even though to others it may be obvious that he was in need of treatment, and even though in the hospital he may soon come to agree.

The case histories of most mental patients document offense against some arrangement for face-to-face living—a domestic establishment, a work place, a semipublic organization such as a church or store, a public region such as a street or park. Often there is also a record of some *complainant,* some figure who takes that action against the offender which eventually leads to his hospitalization. This may not be the person who makes the first move, but it is the person who makes what turns out to be the first effective move. Here is the *social* beginning of the patient's career, regardless of where one might locate the psychological beginning of his mental illness.

The kinds of offenses which lead to hospitalization are felt to differ in nature from those which lead to other extrusory consequences—to imprisonment, divorce, loss of job, disownment, regional exile, noninstitutional psychiatric treatment, and so forth. But little seems known about these differentiating factors; and when one studies actual commitments, alternate outcomes frequently appear to have been possible. It seems true, moreover, that for every offense that leads to an effective complaint, there are many psychiatrically similar ones that never do. No action is taken; or action is taken which leads to other extrusory outcomes; or ineffective action is taken, leading to the mere pacifying or putting off of the person who complains. Thus, as Clausen and Yarrow have nicely shown, even offenders who are eventually hospitalized are likely to have had a long series of ineffective actions taken against them.[12]

Separating those offenses which could have been used as grounds for hospitalizing the offender from those that are so used, one finds a vast number of what students of occupation call career contingencies.[13] Some of these contingencies in the mental patient's career have been suggested, if not explored, such as socioeconomic status, visibility of the offense, proximity to a mental hospital, amount of treatment facilities available, community regard for the type of treatment given in available hospitals, and so on.[14] For information about other contingencies one must rely on atrocity tales: a psychotic man is tolerated by his wife until she finds herself a boyfriend, or by his adult children until they move from a house to an apartment; an alcoholic is sent to a mental hospital because the jail is full, and a drug addict because he declines to avail himself of psychiatric treatment on the outside; a rebellious adolescent daughter can no longer be managed at home because she now threatens to have an open affair with an unsuitable companion; and so on. Correspondingly there is an equally important set of contingencies causing the person to bypass this fate. And should the person enter the hospital, still another set of contingencies will help determine when he is to obtain a discharge—such as the desire of his family for his return, the availability of a "manageable" job, and so on. The society's official view is that inmates of mental hospitals are there primarily because they are suffering from mental illness. However, in the degree that the "mentally ill" outside hospitals numerically approach or surpass those inside hospitals, one could say that mental patients *distinctively* suffer not from mental illness, but from contingencies.

Career contingencies occur in conjunction with a second feature of the prepatient's career— *the circuit of agents*—and agencies—that participate fatefully in his passage from civilian to patient status.[15] Here is an instance of that increasingly important class of social system whose elements are agents and agencies, which are brought into systemic connection through having to take up and send on the same persons. Some of these agent-roles will be cited now, with the understanding that in any concrete circuit a role may be filled more than once, and a single person may fill more than one of them.

First is the *next-of-relation*—the person whom the prepatient sees as the most available of those upon whom he should be able to most depend in times of trouble; in this instance the last to doubt his sanity and the first to have done everything to save him from the fate which, it transpires, he has been approaching. The patient's next-of-relation is usually his next of kin; the special term is introduced because he need not be. Second is the *complainant*—the person who retrospectively

appears to have started the person on his way to the hospital. Third are the *mediators*—the sequence of agents and agencies to which the prepatient is referred and through which he is relayed and processed on his way to the hospital. Here are included police, clergy, general medical practitioners, office psychiatrists, personnel in public clinics, lawyers, social service workers, school teachers, and so on. One of these agents will have the legal mandate to sanction commitment and will exercise it, and so those agents who precede him in the process will be involved in something whose outcome is not yet settled. When the mediators retire from the scene, the prepatient has become an inpatient, and the significant agent has become the hospital administrator.

While the complainant usually takes action in a lay capacity as a citizen, an employer, a neighbor, or a kinsman, mediators tend to be specialists and differ from those they serve in significant ways. They have experience in handling trouble, and some professional distance from what they handle. Except in the case of policemen, and perhaps some clergy, they tend to be more psychiatrically oriented than the lay public, and will see the need for treatment at times when the public does not.[16]

An interesting feature of these roles is the functional effects of their interdigitation. For example, the feelings of the patient will be influenced by whether or not the person who fills the role of complainant also has the role of next-of-relation—an embarrassing combination more prevalent, apparently, in the higher classes than in the lower.[17] Some of these emergent effects will be considered now.[18]

In the prepatient's progress from home to the hospital he may participate as a third person in what he may come to experience as a kind of *alienative coalition*. His next-of-relation presses him into coming to "talk things over" with a medical practitioner, an office psychiatrist, or some other counselor. Disinclination on his part may be met by threatening him with desertion, disownment, or other legal action, or by stressing the joint and explorative nature of the interview. But typically the next-of-relation will have set the interview up, in the sense of selecting the professional, arranging for time, telling the professional something about the case, and so on. This move effectively tends to establish the next-of-relation as the responsible person to whom pertinent findings can be divulged, while effectively establishing the other as the patient. The prepatient often goes to the interview with the understanding that he is going as an equal of someone who is so bound together with him that a third person could not come between them in fundamental matters; this after all, is one way in which close relationships are defined in our society. Upon arrival at the office the prepatient suddenly finds that he and his next-of-relation have not been accorded the same roles, and apparently that a prior understanding between the professional and the next-of-relation has been put in operation against him. In the extreme but common case the professional first sees the prepatient alone, in the role of advisor, while carefully avoiding talking things over seriously with them both together.[19] And even in those nonconsultative cases where public officials must forcibly extract a person from a family that wants to tolerate him, the next-of-relation is likely to be induced to "go along" with the official action, so that even here the prepatient may feel that an alienative coalition has been formed against him.

The moral experience of being third man in such a coalition is likely to embitter the prepatient, especially since his troubles have already probably led to some estrangement from his next-of-relation. After he enters the hospital, continued visits by his next-of-relation can give the patient the "insight" that his own best interests were being served. But the initial visits may temporarily strengthen his feeling of abandonment; he is likely to beg his visitor to get him out or at least to get him more privileges and to sympathize with the monstrousness of his plight—to which the visitor ordinarily can respond only by trying to maintain a hopeful note, by not "hearing" the requests, or by assuring the patient that the medical authorities know about these things and are

doing what is medically best. The visitor then nonchalantly goes back into a world that the patient has learned is incredibly thick with freedom and privileges, causing the patient to feel that his next-of-relation is merely adding a pious gloss to a clear case of traitorous desertion.

The depth to which the patient may feel betrayed by his next-of-relation seems to be increased by the fact that another witnesses his betrayal—a factor which is apparently significant in many three-party situations. An offended person may well act forbearantly and accommodatively toward an offender when the two are alone, choosing peace ahead of justice. The presence of a witness, however, seems to add something to the implications of the offense. For then it is beyond the power of the offended and offender to forget about, erase, or suppress what has happened; the offense has become a public social fact.[20] When the witness is a mental health commission as is sometimes the case, the witnessed betrayal can verge on a "degradation ceremony."[21] In such circumstances, the offended patient may feel that some kind of extensive reparative action is required before witnesses, if his honor and social weight are to be restored.

Two other aspects of sensed betrayal should be mentioned. First, those who suggest the possibility of another's entering a mental hospital are not likely to provide a realistic picture of how in fact it may strike him when he arrives. Often he is told that he will get required medical treatment and a rest, and may well be out in a few months or so. In some cases they may thus be concealing what they know, but I think, in general, they will be telling what they see as the truth. For here there is a quite relevant difference between patients and mediating professionals; mediators, more so than the public at large, may conceive of mental hospitals as short-term medical establishments where required rest and attention can be voluntarily obtained, and not as places of coerced exile. When the prepatient finally arrives he is likely to learn quite quickly, quite differently. He then finds that the information given him about life in the hospital has had the effect of his having put up less resistance to entering than he now sees he would have put up had he known the facts. Whatever the intentions of those who participated in his transition from person to patient, he may sense they have in effect "conned" him into his present predicament.

I am suggesting that the prepatient starts out with at least a portion of the rights, liberties, and satisfactions of the civilian and ends up on a psychiatric ward stripped of almost everything. The question here is *how* this stripping is managed. This is the second aspect of betrayal I want to consider.

As the prepatient may see it, the circuit of significant figures can function as a kind of *betrayal funnel*. Passage from person to patient may be effected through a series of linked stages, each managed by a different agent. While each stage tends to bring a sharp decrease in adult free status, each agent may try to maintain the fiction that no further decrease will occur. He may even manage to turn the prepatient over to the next agent while sustaining this note. Further, through words, cues, and gestures, the prepatient is implicitly asked by the current agent to join with him in sustaining a running line of polite small talk that tactfully avoids the administrative facts of the situation, becoming, with each stage, progressively more at odds with these facts. The spouse would rather not have to cry to get the prepatient to visit a psychiatrist; psychiatrists would rather not have a scene when the prepatient learns that he and his spouse are being seen separately and in different ways; the police infrequently bring a prepatient to the hospital in a strait jacket, finding it much easier all around to give him a cigarette, some kindly words, and freedom to relax in the back seat of the patrol car; and finally, the admitting psychiatrist finds he can do his work better in the relative quiet and luxury of the "admission suite" where, as an incidental consequence, the notion can survive that a mental hospital is indeed a comforting place. If the prepatient heeds all of these implied requests and is reasonably decent about the whole thing, he can travel the whole circuit from home to hospital without forcing anyone to look directly at what is happening or to deal with the raw emotion that his situation might well cause him to express. His showing consideration for those who are moving him toward the hospital allows them to show consideration for him, with the joint result that these interactions can be sustained with some of the protective harmony characteristic of ordinary face-to-face dealings. But should the new patient cast his mind back over the sequence of steps leading to hospitalization, he may feel that everyone's *current* comfort was being busily sustained while his long-range welfare was being undermined. This realization may constitute a moral experience that further separates him for the time from the people on the outside.[22]

I would now like to look at the circuit of career agents from the point of view of the agents themselves. Mediators in the person's transition from civil to patient status—as well as his keepers, once he is in the hospital—have an interest in establishing a responsible next-of-relation as the patient's deputy or *guardian*; should there be no obvious candidate for the role, someone may be sought out and pressed into it. Thus while a person is gradually being transformed into a patient, a next-of-relation is gradually being transformed into a guardian. With a guardian on the scene, the whole transition process can be kept tidy. He is likely to be familiar with the prepatient's civil involvements and business, and can tie up loose ends that might otherwise be left to entangle the hospital. Some of the prepatient's abrogated civil rights can be transferred to him, thus helping to sustain the legal fiction that while the prepatient does not actually have his rights he somehow actually has not lost them.

Inpatients commonly sense, at least for a time, that hospitalization is a massive unjust deprivation, and sometimes succeed in convincing a few persons on the outside that this is the case. It often turns out to be useful, then, for those identified with inflicting these deprivations, however justifiably, to be able to point to the cooperation and agreement of someone whose relationship to the patient places him above suspicion, firmly defining him as the person most likely to have the patient's personal interest at heart. If the guardian is satisfied with what is happening to the new inpatient, the world ought to be.[23]

Now it would seem that the greater the legitimate personal stake one party has in another, the better he can take the role of guardian to the other. But the structural arrangements in society which lead to the acknowledged merging of two persons' interests lead to additional consequences. For the person to whom the patient turns for help—for protection against such threats as involuntary commitment—is just the person to whom the mediators and hospital administrators logically turn for authorization. It is understandable, then, that some patients will come to sense, at least for a time, that the closeness of a relationship tells nothing of its trustworthiness.

There are still other functional effects emerging from this complement of roles. If and when the next-of-relation appeals to mediators for help in the trouble he is having with the prepatient, hospitalization may not, in fact, be in his mind. He may not even perceive the prepatient as mentally sick, or, if he does, he may not consistently hold to this view.[24] It is the circuit of mediators, with their great psychiatric sophistication and their belief in the medical character of mental hospitals, that will often define the situation for the next-of-relation, assuring him that hospitalization is a possible solution and a good one, that it involves no betrayal, but is rather a medical action taken in the best interests of the prepatient. Here the next-of-relation may learn that doing his duty to the prepatient may cause the prepatient to distrust and even hate him for the time. But the fact that this course of action may have had to be pointed out and prescribed by professionals, and be defined by them as a moral duty, relieves the next-of-relation of some of the guilt he may feel.[25] It is a poignant fact that an adult son or daughter may be pressed into the role of mediator, so that the hostility that might otherwise be directed against the spouse is passed on to the child.[26]

Once the prepatient is in the hospital, the same guilt-carrying function may become a significant part of the staff's job in regard to the next-of-relation.[27] These reasons for feeling that he himself has not betrayed the patient, even though the patient may then think so, can later provide the next-of-relation with a defensible line to take when

visiting the patient in the hospital and a basis for hoping that the relationship can be re-established after its hospital moratorium. And of course this position, when sensed by the patient, can provide him with excuses for the next-of-relation, when and if he comes to look for them.[28]

Thus while the next-of-relation can perform important functions for the mediators and hospital administrators, they in turn can perform important functions for him. One finds, then, an emergent unintended exchange or reciprocation of functions, these functions themselves being often unintended.

The final point I want to consider about the prepatient's moral career is its peculiarly *retroactive* character. Until a person actually arrives at the hospital there usually seems no way of knowing for sure that he is destined to do so, given the determinative role of career contingencies. And until the point of hospitalization is reached, he or others may not conceive of him as a person who is becoming a mental patient. However, since he will be held against his will in the hospital, his next-of-relation and the hospital staff will be in great need of a rationale for the hardships they are sponsoring. The medical elements of the staff will also need evidence that they are still in the trade they were trained for. These problems are eased, no doubt unintentionally, by the case-history construction that is placed on the patient's past life, this having the effect of demonstrating that all along he had been becoming sick, that he finally became very sick, and that if he had not been hospitalized much worse things would have happened to him—all of which, of course, may be true. Incidentally, if the patient wants to make sense out of his stay in the hospital, and, as already suggested, keep alive the possibility of once again conceiving of his next-of-relation as a decent, well-meaning person, then he too will have reason to believe some of this psychiatric workup of his past.

Here is a very ticklish point for the sociology of careers. An important aspect of every career is the view the person constructs when he looks backward over his progress; in a sense, however, the whole of the prepatient career derives from this reconstruction. The fact of having had a prepatient career, starting with an effective complaint, becomes an important part of the mental patient's orientation, but this part can begin to be played only after hospitalization proves that what he had been having, but no longer has, is a career as a prepatient . . . .

NOTES

1. The study was conducted during 1955–56 under the auspices of the Laboratory of Socio-environmental Studies of the National Institute of Mental Health. I am grateful to the Laboratory Chief, John A. Clausen, and to Dr. Winfred Overholser, Superintendent, and the late Dr. Jay Hoffman, then First Assistant Physician of Saint Elizabeth's Hospital, Washington, D.C., for the ideal cooperation they freely provided. A preliminary report is contained in Goffman, "Interpersonal Persuasion," pp. 117–193; in *Group Processes: Transactions of the Third Conference,* edited by Bertram Schaffner; New York, Josiah Macy, Jr. Foundation, 1957. A shorter version of this paper was presented at the Annual Meeting of the American Sociological Society, Washington, D.C., August, 1957.

2. Material on moral career can be found in early social anthropological work on ceremonies of status transition, and in classic social psychological descriptions of those spectacular changes in one's view of self that can accompany participation in social movements and sects. Recently new kinds of relevant data have been suggested by psychiatric interest in the problem of "identity" and sociological studies of work careers and "adult socialization."

3. This point has recently been made by Elaine and John Cumming, *Closed Ranks;* Cambridge, Commonwealth Fund, Harvard Univ. Press, 1957; pp. 101–102. "Clinical experience supports the impression that many people define mental illness as 'That condition for which a person is treated in a mental hospital.' . . . Mental illness, it seems, is a condition which afflicts people who must go to a mental institution, but until they do almost anything they do is normal." Leila Deasy has pointed out to me the correspondence here with the situation in white-collar crime. Of those who are detected in this activity, only the ones who do not manage to avoid going to prison find themselves accorded the social role of the criminal.

4. Case records in mental hospitals are just now coming to be exploited to show the incredible amount of trouble a person may cause for himself and others before anyone begins to think about him psychiatrically, let alone take psychiatric action against him. See John A. Clausen and Marian Radke Yarrow, "Paths to the Mental Hospital," *J. Social Issues* (1955) 11:25–32; August B. Hollingshead and Frederick C. Redlich, *Social Class and Mental Illness;* New York, Wiley, 1958; pp. 173–174.

5. An illustration of how this perspective may be taken to all forms of deviancy may be found in Edwin Lemert, *Social Pathology;* New York, McGraw-Hill, 1951; see especially pp. 74–76. A specific application to mental defectives may be found in Stewart E. Perry, "Some Theoretic Problems of Mental Deficiency and Their Action Implications," *Psychiatry* (1954) 17: 45–73; see especially p. 68.

6. [Goffman developed this point more fully as follows.] Whatever . . . the various patient's psychiatric diagnoses, and whatever the special ways in which social life on the "inside" is unique, the researcher can find that he is participating in a community not significantly different from any other he has studied. Conscientious objectors who voluntarily went to jail sometimes arrived at the same conclusion regarding criminal inmates. See, for example, Alfred Hassler, *Diary of a Self-made Convict;* Chicago, Regnery, 1954; p. 74.

7. This simple picture is complicated by the somewhat special experience of roughly a third of ex-patients—namely, readmission to the hospital, this being the recidivist or "repatient" phase.

8. Harry Stack Sullivan, *Clinical Studies in Psychiatry,* edited by Helen Swick Perry, Mary Ladd Gavel, and Martha Gibbon; New York, Norton, 1956; pp. 184–185.

9. This moral experience can be contrasted with that of a person learning to become a marihuana . . . [user], whose discovery that he can be "high" and still "op" effectively without being detected apparently leads to a new level of use. See Howard S. Becker, "Marihuana Use and Social Control," *Social Problems* (1955) 3:35–44; see especially pp. 40–41.

10. See Hollingshead and Redlich, *op. cit.,* p. 187, Table 6, where relative frequency is given of self-referral by social class grouping.

11. The distinction employed here between willing and unwilling patients cuts across the legal one, of voluntary and committed, since some persons who are glad to come to the mental hospital may be legally committed, and of those who come only because of strong familial pressure, some may sign themselves in as voluntary patients.

12. Clausen and Yarrow, *op. cit.*

13. An explicit application of this notion to the field of mental health may be found in Edwin M. Lemert, "Legal Commitment and Social Control," *Sociology and Social Research* (1946) 30:370–378.

14. For example, Jerome K. Meyers and Leslie Schaffer, "Social Stratification and Psychiatric Practice: A Study of an Outpatient Clinic," *Amer. Sociological Rev.* (1954) 19:307–310. Lemert, see footnote 5; pp. 402–403. *Patients in Mental Institutions, 1941;* Washington, D.C., Department of Commerce, Bureau of the Census, 1941; p. 2.

15. For one circuit of agents and its bearing on career contingencies, see Oswald Hall, "The Stages of a Medical Career," *Amer. J. Sociology* (1948) 53:327–336.

16. See Cumming and Cumming, *op. cit.;* p. 92.

17. Hollingshead and Redlich, *op. cit.;* p. 187.

18. For an analysis of some of these circuit implications for the inpatient, see Leila C. Deasy and Olive W. Quinn, "The Wife of the Mental Patient and the Hospital Psychiatrist," *J. Social Issues* (1955) 11:49–60. An interesting illustration of this kind of analysis may also be found in Alan G. Gowman, "Blindness and the Role of Companion," *Social Problems* (1956) 4:68–75. A general statement may be found in Robert Merton, "The Role Set: Problems in Sociological Theory," *British J. Sociology* (1957) 8:106–120.

19. I have one case record of a man who claims he thought *he* was taking his wife to see the psychiatrist, not realizing until too late that his wife had made the arrangements.

20. A paraphrase from Kurt Riezler, "The Social Psychology of Shame," *Amer. J. Sociology* (1943) 48:458.

21. See Harold Garfinkel, "Conditions of Successful Degradation Ceremonies," *Amer. J. Sociology* (1956) 61:420–424.

22. Concentration camp practices provide a good example of the function of the betrayal funnel in inducing cooperation and reducing struggle and fuss, although here the mediators could not be said to be acting in the best interests of the inmates. Police picking up persons from their homes would sometimes joke good-naturedly and offer to wait while coffee was being served. Gas chambers were fitted out like delousing rooms, and victims taking off their clothes were told to note where they were leaving them. The sick, aged, weak, or insane who were selected for extermination were sometimes driven away in Red Cross ambulances to camps referred to by terms such as "observation hospital." See David Boder, *I Did Not Interview the Dead;* Urbana, Univ. of Illinois Press, 1949; p. 81; and Elie A. Cohen, *Human Behavior in the Concentration Camp;* London, Cape, 1954; pp. 32, 37, 107.

23. Interviews collected by the Clausen group at NIMH suggest that when a wife comes to be a guardian the responsibility may disrupt previous distance from in-laws, leading either to a new supportive coalition with them or to a marked withdrawal from them.

24. For an analysis of these nonpsychiatric kinds of perception, see Marian Radke Yarrow, Charlotte Green Schwartz, Harriet S. Murphy, and Leila Calhoun Deasy, "The Psychological Meaning of Mental Illness in the Family," *J. Social Issues* (1955) 11:12–24; Charlotte Green Schwartz, "Perspectives on Deviance—Wives' Definitions of Their Husbands' Mental Illness," *Psychiatry* (1957) 20:275–291.

25. This guilt-carrying function is found, of course, in other role-complexes. Thus, when a middle-class couple engages in the process of legal separation or divorce, each of their lawyers usually takes the position that his job is to acquaint his client with all of the potential claims and rights, pressing his client into demanding these, in spite of any nicety of feelings about the rights and honorableness of the ex-partner. The client, in all good faith, can then say to self and to the ex-partner that the demands are being made only because the lawyer insists it is best to do so.

26. Recorded in the Clausen data.

27. This point is made by Cumming and Cumming, see *op. cit.;* p. 129.

28. There is an interesting contrast here with the moral career of the tuberculosis patient. I am told by Julius Roth that tuberculous patients are likely to come to the hospital willingly, agreeing with their next-of-relation about treatment. Later in their hospital career, when they learn how long they yet have to stay and how depriving and irrational some of the hospital rulings are, they may seek to leave, be advised against this by the staff and by relatives, and only then begin to feel betrayed.

PART TWO

THE FORMAL REGULATION OF DEVIANCE

In addition to typing on an informal, interpersonal level, much typing of deviants occurs on a formal or official level. In fact, complex societies such as ours invariably include formal agencies whose role it is to seek out, identify, and regulate deviance. Such agencies include the police, the courts, the federal Drug Enforcement Administration, the Department of the Treasury (whose agents deal with smuggling), the Department of Homeland Security, county and state health and welfare agencies—the list could go on and on. When these agencies of social control take action against someone adjudged deviant, the effects can be dramatic. These may include a formal confirmation of deviant typing, induction into a deviant role, and launching on a deviant career. This turning point in the deviant's life can also bring about a radical redefinition of self. What the deviant may experience as a unique personal crisis, however, is usually merely organizational routine for the agent and the agency.

The controls that such agents and agencies can impose differ significantly from those available to lay people. In terms of power, for example, the political state stands behind many agencies, while informal labelers may be no more powerful than the deviant. Likewise, the agents' control is usually legitimized by the state, whereas labeling by other people may simply represent an opposing set of norms. Finally, agents of social control usually operate according to an elaborate set of rules that provide standardized ways of dealing with deviants; other people's actions against the deviant need not be based on any plan at all.

AGENCIES AND THEIR THEORIES

A special perspective, composed of rules, beliefs, and practices, underlies the formal processing of deviants. In the course of their work with deviant clients, agents of social control come to adopt this perspective. As they become more familiar with the agency's perspective, agents find that they can process their deviant clients more efficiently. As these conceptions become routine for agents, their processing of deviants also takes on a routine character.

Agencies of control also often put forth claims as to why they should be the sole organization to handle deviance and how they would go about regulating the social deviants who come to their official attention. Common to all of these agencies and organizations is their ideology. All of these special ideologies have three major ideas: etiology, or how people become deviants; treatment rationale, or how the agency processes its deviant clientele; and justification, or the basis of the agency's claim for expertise in regulating deviance.

The growth and expansion of agents and agencies within the institutions of religion, criminal justice, and medicine have only added to the relativization of deviance. In addition, they have fueled increasing conflicts between agencies concerning jurisdiction over and theories about particular types of deviance. In addition to professional specialization, two other developments add to the complexity of organized responses to deviance. One is the privatization of police and corrections. The other is the spread of numerous mutual-help movements that have fashioned themselves after the model of Alcoholics Anonymous.

ORGANIZATIONAL PROCESSING OF DEVIANTS

Once persons have been socially designated as deviants, they can be subject to two kinds of organizational processing. In the first instance, they have allegedly violated the law or breached taken-for-granted rules of interpersonal conduct. They can come to the attention of the formal agencies of criminal justice or institutions of mental health. In the second instance, they have broken the rules of some complex organization in which they are an employer, employee, member, student, or client. Complex organizations, such as colleges, corporations, and schools, have their own internal agencies of control, primarily to respond to organizational troublemakers.

Despite the differences in the degrees of deviance and the ways in which deviants come to be clients of these two types of agencies, both kinds of agencies face similar problems. Hard-pressed to perform their work, often because of the number of clients, agents of control devise a shared perspective. This perspective evolves primarily through close and frequent interaction with colleagues. Not only does the agent's perspective help in categorizing the people who have come to the attention of the agency, but it also helps in specifying which agent should do what and when, and how and why action should be taken in the course of the client's contact with the agency. Perhaps most important of all are those unwritten rules, derived from the perspective, that prescribe the kinds of treatment the clients may or may not receive. In effect, an etiquette of agency-client relations obtains. A good example is when urban school officials selectively enforce the school dress code, defining and disciplining minority student violators differently than the other student violators. In addition, the fusion of agent's and agency goals often plays a major part in the organizational processing of clients through intake, screening, and agency action, as well as after discharge. As a consequence, the variety of agency labels of deviance go a long way toward simplifying the work of agents at the same time that they are assigning clients to a deviant status.

THE EFFECTS OF CONTACT WITH CONTROL AGENTS

When a person comes into contact with an agency of social control, the agency may view the person solely in terms of a deviant label. Initial contact with such an agency may suffice to call into question the person's "good name." Offenders, after processing through the agencies of criminal justice, can suffer diminished legitimate life chances amid the reinforcement of a criminal social definition and come to see themselves in the same way as the agencies do. Similarly, people who have contact with a health agency (e.g., individuals who have a sexually transmitted infection) may come to see themselves through the health agency's eyes as being irresponsible or immoral because of obtaining a particular infection. Additional contact may give the person a definitely bad social reputation. Thus deviant typing may not end with the person's experience with a given agency. When meeting a stranger, for example, people look for information to help them type the stranger. If they find out that a person has been in a prison or mental hospital, they may type the person primarily on the basis of that past experience, assuming that a person who has had contact with an agency of social control is likely to repeat the behavior that originally led to that contact. Accordingly, laypeople feel less inclined to trust such a person. The agency perspective is so powerful that a deviant label, once formally applied, can long outlive any evidentiary basis. Once formally labeled, the so-called deviant becomes socially constructed as being the kind of person who probably did perform the imputed behaviors, or at least would if given a chance. Both the deviant and others may then organize their social relations around this belief.

CHAPTER 5

AGENCIES AND THEIR THEORIES

Case Routinization in Investigative Police Work

WILLIAM B. WAEGEL

In everyday life, people sometimes come into contact with specific instances of deviance. Some but not necessarily all of these contacts may be crises for them. By contrast, what may be a crisis for laypeople in everyday life turns out to be routine for agents of social control. Their official task is to process cases of deviant behavior that come before them. The sheer number of clients with whom agents come into frequent contact generates a need for classification. Agents classify the cases that come before them in accordance with organizational requirements, informal work norms, and status concerns. To manage the many cases they have to deal with, they devise interpretations that give rise to recipes for handling cases in the most efficient manner for themselves as well as for the agency in which they work.

William B. Waegel shows how detectives produce reports and arrests that meet supervisors' demands and enhance their own chances for promotion. They classify cases in accordance with the chances that arrests are likely or unlikely to be made. According to detectives' routine conceptions, 10 percent of burglary cases are likely to produce an arrest, while 90 percent are unlikely to. Thus, in the absence of solid information, detectives frequently suspend cases because they are unlikely to produce arrests. They fit these cases to the constructed stereotypes they have fashioned (often without any basis in fact) to expedite their goals and the agency's.

In the police department studied,[1] detectives face two practical problems which substantially shape the manner in which cases are handled. They must satisfy the paperwork demands of the organization (referred to as "keeping the red numbers

down") by classifying each case and producing a formal investigative report within two weeks after the case is assigned. Sanctions may be applied to those who fail to meet deadlines and who thus accumulate too many "red numbers." At the same time, the detectives are under the same pressure as other employees: they must produce. Specifically, detectives believe they must produce an acceptable level of arrests which will enhance their chances of remaining in the detective division and gaining promotion. While no arrest quota is formalized in the division, there is a shared belief that one should produce roughly two to three lock-ups per week. This arrest level is a practical concern for the detective because most wish to remain in the division and avoid transfer "back to the pit" (i.e., back into uniform in the patrol division). Moreover, the position of detective holds the highest status of any assignment in the department, and a transfer, therefore, generally entails a loss of status.

For the vast majority of cases handled, no explicit procedures exist to indicate what must be done on the case and how to go about doing it. As detectives go about the ordinary business of investigating and processing cases, they can select strategies ranging from a *pro forma* victim interview comprising the total investigative activity devoted to the case, to a full-scale investigation involving extensive interviewing, physical evidence, the use of informants, interrogation, surveillance, and other activities. The selection of a particular handling strategy in most cases is an informal process and not the direct result of formal organizational policy or procedure. This process of selection is grounded in practical solutions to concrete problems faced by the detective; it consists of an assignment of meaning to persons and events in ways that are regarded as proper because they have "worked" in previous cases.

A great deal of actual detective work may thus be seen as a process of mapping the features of a particular case onto a more general and commonly recognized *type* of case. The present work suggests that a detective's interpretation, classification, and handling of cases is guided by a set of occupationally shared typifications. The categorization schemes used by detectives center around specific configurations of information regarding the victim, the offense, and possible suspects. Information pertaining to these three elements constitutes the meaningful unit that detectives deal with: the case.

The most basic dimension of case categorization is that of the routine versus the nonroutine. Where a particular configuration of information regarding the victim, the offense, and possible suspects appears, the competent detective understands the case as a routine one—as an instance of a familiar type—and particular handling strategies are deemed appropriate. Such cases contrast with those which are viewed as nonroutine: that is, where no general type is available to which the case reasonably corresponds, and where the case is vigorously investigated and the detective attends to the unique features of the case. Case routinization is most characteristic for burglaries, which comprise the bulk of cases handled by detectives, but it is also exhibited in the handling of many assault, robbery, rape, and homicide cases.

The categorization schemes used by detectives are derived from concrete experiences in working cases and are continually assessed for their relevance, adequacy, and effectiveness in handling one's caseload. It is because typificatory schemes serve as a solution to practical problems commonly faced by all detectives that they learn to share most of the content of these schemes. Both through direct experience in working cases and through interaction with other members, the detective learns to categorize and handle cases in ways that are regarded as proper by other detectives.

Routine case imageries serve as resources upon which detectives may draw to construct a solution to their problem of interpreting, investigating, and resolving their cases. The features of a specific case are compared with routine case imagery in a process of interpretive interplay. In some instances a correspondence is readily apparent, in others a fit is forced by the detective, and in still others the features of a specific case render the use of the typical imagery inappropriate. The interpretation and handling of a case may also change over the case's history; a routine case may come to be treated as nonroutine upon the receipt of additional information, and vice versa.

THE ORGANIZATIONAL CONTEXT OF CASE ROUTINIZATION

In the department studied, detectives have no formal guidelines for allocating time and effort to different cases and there is little effective monitoring of daily activities by supervisors.[2] In conducting their work, detectives are, however, guided and constrained by two organizational imperatives: 1) the requirement to submit investigative reports, and 2) the requirement to produce arrests. In other words, the work is not organized by formal rules, but rather by the kinds of outcomes that are expected. Both of these expected outcomes generate practical problems leading to routinized solutions.

An investigative report must be produced for each case assigned, and its submission within the prescribed time limit is viewed as a fundamental constraint on how vigorously different cases can be investigated. Departmental policy indicates that each investigative report submitted must be reviewed and signed by a supervisory lieutenant. However, in practice, these reports are often given only a cursory glance, and seldom is the content of a report questioned or challenged by a lieutenant. The primary concern of the supervisor is that the submission of reports comply with time deadlines.

The potential a case appears to hold for producing an arrest also has an important impact on how the case will be handled. Most detectives believe that the number of arrests they produce will be used as a basis for evaluating performance and, therefore, will affect decisions regarding promotions and transfers. Attempts to cope with the practical problems of meeting paperwork demands, while at the same time producing a satisfactory number of arrests, creates a situation in which one burglary case involving a $75 loss may receive less than five minutes' investigative effort, yet another case with an identical loss may be worked on exclusively for two or three full days. These two concerns constitute central features of the work setting which structure case handling.

PAPERWORK

Formal organizational procedure demands that a case be investigated, classified, and a report produced within a specified time period after it is assigned. Detectives experience paperwork requirements and deadlines as central sources of pressure

and tension in their job, and stories abound concerning former detectives who "could handle the job but couldn't handle the paperwork."

Most cases are assigned during the daily roll-call sessions. At this point, the information about the incident consists of an original report written by a patrol officer and any supplemental reports submitted by personnel in the evidence detection unit. Each case is stamped with a "red number" which supervisors use to monitor compliance with report deadlines.

Ordinary cases require the submission of two reports within specific time periods. A brief first-day report, consisting essentially of an interview with the victim, is formally required the day after the case is assigned. However, this deadline is generally ignored by supervisors and first-day reports are seldom submitted. The more meaningful deadline for detectives is the fourteen-day limit for the submission of an investigative report. Here, the detective must provide a detailed accounting of the activities undertaken in investigating the incident and assign an investigative status to the case. Compliance with this second deadline is closely monitored; every Sunday a lieutenant draws up a list of each detective's overdue red numbers, and this list is read at the next roll call along with a caution to keep up with one's paperwork.

In the investigative report, the detective must classify the status of the investigation as suspended, closed arrest, or open. The ability to manipulate information about cases to fit them into these categories is of the utmost importance to detectives, for it is through such strategic manipulations that they are able to manage their caseloads effectively.

Of the total cases handled by a detective, a substantial majority are classified as suspended. This means that the steps already taken in the investigation (which may consist merely of a telephone interview with the victim) have not uncovered sufficient information to warrant continued investigation of the incident. Any number of acceptable reasons for suspending a case may be offered, ranging from a simple statement that the victim declines to prosecute up to a fairly elaborate report detailing contacts with the victim, the entry of serial numbers of stolen articles into the computerized crime files, the usefulness of evidence obtained from the scene, and a conclusion that the case must be suspended because there are no further investigative leads. Over 80 percent of the burglary cases assigned in the city are suspended; this percentage drops considerably for robbery cases and even more for assault, rape, and homicide cases.[3]

An investigation is classified as closed when one or more arrests have been made pertaining to the incident and the detective anticipates no additional arrests. A case is classified as open when an investigation extends beyond the fourteen-day limit but it is expected that an arrest eventually will be made. Generally, only major cases may remain classified as open after the fourteen-day investigative period.

PRODUCING ARRESTS

As organizations become more bureaucratized and their procedures more formalized, there evolves a general tendency to develop quantitative indices or measures of individual performance. In the department studied, most detectives believe that the crude number of lock-ups they make is used as a basis for assessing their performance and competence in doing investigative work. Every arrest a detective makes is entered into a logbook, which is available for inspection by superiors and from which they can compare each detective's arrest level with that of others.

Ambitious detectives in particular are very conscious of producing a steady stream of arrests, feeling that this is an effective way to achieve recognition and promotion. One young detective boasted:

I've made over forty lock-ups since the beginning of the year and eleven in April alone. Since I don't really have a godfather in here, I gotta depend on making good lock-ups if I'm gonna make sergeant.

This detective's use of the term "godfather" reveals a widely shared belief that some individuals are promoted not because of their performance but because they have a friend or relative in a position of power within the department.

Skimming off selected cases from one's workload is widely practiced as a means of achieving a steady stream of arrests. The practice of skimming refers to 1) selectively working only those cases that appear potentially solvable from information contained in the original report, and 2) summarily suspending the remainder of one's ordinary cases. Supervisors are certainly aware of both aspects of this practice, but they recognize its practical value in producing arrests. Moreover, supervisors, to a greater extent than working detectives, find their performance assessed in crude quantitative terms, and they are likely to be questioned by superiors if arrest levels begin to drop sharply. Supervisors support the practice of skimming even though they recognize that it ensures that a majority of ordinary cases will never receive a thorough investigation. The pragmatic work orientation of detectives is further revealed in the lack of attention given to conviction rates by both detectives and supervisors. Competence and productivity are judged by the arrests made, not by the proportion of cases which survive the scrutiny of the judicial process.

The recognition of potentially productive cases and of their utility in effectively managing one's caseload is among the earliest skills taught to the neophyte in the detective division. Moreover, newcomers are taught that their work on burglary cases is the primary basis upon which their performance will be judged. In a sizeable percentage of crimes against persons, the perpetrator is readily identified from information provided by the victim. Since no great investigative effort or acumen is involved, the same credit is not accorded an arrest in this type of case as in burglary cases. Detectives are expected to produce a steady flow of "quality" arrests: that is, arrests involving some effort and skill on the part of the investigator. Straightforward assault cases involving acquainted parties, for example, are often handed out by supervisors along with a remark such as "Here's an easy one for you."

INTERPRETING CASES

The preceding observations have suggested that detectives are constrained in their conception and handling of cases not by the formal organization of their work or by supervisory surveillance, but rather by the bureaucratic pressure of writing reports and producing the proper number and quality of arrests. The process of interpreting cases in accordance with these pragmatic concerns may now be considered.

Data derived from observation of detective-victim interviews and from written case reports provide a basis for examining the interpretive schemes used by detectives. In the victim interview, the kinds of questions asked and the pieces of information sought out reveal the case patterns recognized as routine for the different offenses commonly encountered.[4] However, in attempting to make sense of the incident at hand, detectives attend to much more than is revealed in their explicit communications with the victim. Interpretation of the case is also based upon understanding of the victim's lifestyle, racial or ethnic membership group, class position, and possible clout or connections—especially as these factors bear upon such concerns as the likelihood of the victim inquiring into the progress of the investigation, the victim's intentions regarding prosecution, and the victim's competence and quality as a source of information.

The interpretive schemes employed also receive partial expression in the written investigative reports which must be produced for each case. These reports contain a selective accounting of the meaning assigned to a case, the information and understandings upon which this interpretation is based, and the reasonableness of the linkage between this particular interpretation of the case and the handling strategy employed.[5]

Several important features of the process of interpreting cases as routine or nonroutine may be seen in the following incidents.

CASE 1: ATTEMPTED HOMICIDE

A radio call was broadcast that a shooting had just occurred on the street in a working-class residential area. The victim, a white male, was still conscious when the detectives arrived, although he had been severely wounded in the face by a shotgun blast. He indicated that he had been robbed and shot by three black males, and provided a vague description of their appearance and clothing. This description was broadcast, an area search was initiated, the crime scene was cordoned off, and a major investigation was begun.

The following morning, the victim's employer brought into question the account of the incident that had been provided. He indicated his belief that the incident involved a "lover's triangle" situation between the victim, a male acquaintance of the victim, and a woman. All three were described as "hillbillies." The three parties were interviewed separately and each denied this version of the incident. After further questioning, the victim finally admitted that the story concerning three black males was false, but would say nothing more about the incident. Articles of the woman's clothing believed to show bloodstains and a weapon believed to have been used were obtained, but crime lab analysis would take at least three weeks. The case was now interpreted as a routine "domestic shooting" and little additional effort was devoted to it.

CASE 2: BURGLARY

A detective parked his car in front of an address in a public housing project and pulled out the original burglary report. A new member of the prosecutor's office was riding along to observe how detectives work. The detective read over the report, and after hesitating for awhile decided to go into the residence. He explained to the prosecutor that the loss was an inexpensive record player and added, "This one's a pork chop, like most of the burglaries we get. But we gotta go and interview the victim before suspending it." The detective asked the victim if she knew who might have committed the burglary or if she had heard about anyone committing burglaries in the area. Negative replies followed both questions. The entire encounter with the victim lasted less than two minutes.

CASE 3: ASSAULT AND ROBBERY

A robbery squad detective was waiting for two victims to come in the hall to be interviewed. Both were black, middle-aged, center-city residents who were described by the detective as "dead-end alcoholics." They had been robbed in their residence by a young male who had forced his way in, taken $20 from the pair, and cut the female victim on the hand with a knife. The victims were able to provide the detective with the name of their assailant, and they both picked his photograph out of a number of pictures they were shown. Several minutes later the detective handed them a photograph of a different individual, asking, "Are you sure this is the guy who robbed you?" After inspecting the picture they replied that they knew this person as well but he had not been the one who robbed them. At this point, the detective sat down and took a formal statement from the victims.

When the victims had left, the detective explained his views and usual handling of such "ghetto robberies": "In a case like this, what can we do? To tell you the truth, the only way this kind of thing is going to stop is for the victims or somebody they know to kill this guy off. My involvement in this case is minimal. If the two victims, those two old drunks, if they sober up and if they show up in court, we'll see how they do there. It's up to them here and not up to me."

CASE 4: BURGLARY

A detective entered the center-city residence of a burglary victim in a block where about one-fourth of the row houses were vacant. He examined a large hole in a basement wall that had been made to gain entry, and then sat down to compile a list of articles that had been stolen. The victim had literally been cleaned out, losing every easily transportable item of value she had owned. The woman explained that she worked during the day, that this was the fifth time she had been burglarized in the past four years, and that her coverage had been dropped by the insurance company. She added that she lived in the house for 21 years and was not about to move, and then asked, "What can I do to keep this from happening again?" The detective replied: "Ma'am, I don't know what to tell you. You're the only white family on this block. Most of the people around here work during the daytime, and a lot of these people, even if they saw somebody coming out of your house with some of your stuff, they're not going to call the cops anyhow. That's the way it is around here. It's a shame, but that's the way it is." The detective entered the serial numbers of some of the stolen articles into the computerized stolen property files, "to cover myself, just in case." The written report indicated that the pawn shop sheets had been checked but in fact this step was not taken. When the report deadline approached, the case was suspended.

CASE 5: HOMICIDES

Two homicides had occurred over the weekend. On Monday morning two detectives who were working on the different cases were discussing the status of their investigations. One detective, who was investigating a shooting death that occurred in a crowded bar in the presence of 100 persons, noted that he was on the verge of making a lockup even though none of the witnesses present had voluntarily come forward. The other detective was investigating the bludgeoning death of a male homosexual whose body had been found by firemen called to extinguish a small fire in the victim's residence. There were as yet no suspects in the case. The second detective took offense to remarks made by the other comparing the lack of progress in the second case to the nearly completed investigation in the barroom case. The second detective remarked, "Anybody can handle a killing like you've got. What we've got here is a murder, not a killing."

The above incidents illustrate detectives' use of a body of accumulated knowledge, beliefs, and assumptions which lead to the interpretation of certain case patterns as common, typical, and routine. Cases are interpreted primarily using conceptions of 1) how identifiable the perpetrators seem to be; 2) the normal social characteristics of the victims; and 3) the settings involved, and behavior seen as typical in such settings. A detective's initial efforts on a case tend to focus on these three aspects, in the process of assigning meaning to the case and selecting an appropriate strategy for handling it.

1. Conceptions of how different kinds of offenses are typically committed—especially how identifiable the perpetrators seem to be—are routinely used in interpreting incidents. These imageries are specifically relevant to a detective's practical concerns. The ordinary burglary (Cases 2 and 4) is seen as involving a crude forced entry at a time of day or at a location where it is unlikely that anyone will witness the perpetrator entering or exiting. A burglary victim's ability or inability to provide information identifying a probable perpetrator constitutes the single feature of burglary cases which is given greatest interpretive significance. In roughly 10 percent of these cases, the victim provides the name of a suspected perpetrator (commonly an ex-boyfriend, a relative, or a neighboring resident), and vigorous effort is devoted to the case. For the remaining burglary cases, the initial inclination is to treat them as routine incidents deserving of only minimal investigative effort. In these routine cases the victim's race and class position have a decisive impact on whether the case will be summarily suspended or whether some minor investigative activities will be undertaken to impress the victim that "something is being done."

On the other hand, assault, rape, and homicide cases commonly occur in a face-to-face situation which affords the victim an opportunity to observe the assailant. Further, detectives recognize that many personal assault offenses involve acquainted parties. The earliest piece of information sought out and the feature of such cases given the greatest interpretive significance is whether the offense occurred between parties who were in some way known to one another prior to the incident. The interpretation and handling of the shooting incident in Case 1 changed markedly when it was learned that the victim and suspect were acquainted parties and that the offense reasonably conformed to a familiar pattern of domestic assaults. Where the victim and perpetrator are acquainted in assault, rape, and homicide cases, the incident is seen as containing the core feature of the routine offense pattern for these cases. In such incidents a perfunctory investigation is usually made, for the identity of the perpetrator generally is easily learned from the victim or from persons close to the victim.

The barroom homicide in Case 5 was termed a "killing" and viewed as a routine case because the victim and perpetrator were previously acquainted and information linking the perpetrator to the crime could be easily obtained. The term "murder" is reserved for those homicides which do not correspond to a typical pattern.

A somewhat different pattern follows in the category of incidents which detectives refer to as "suspect rapes." Victims having certain social characteristics (females from lower-class backgrounds who are viewed as having low intelligence or as displaying some type of mental or emotional abnormality) are viewed as most likely to make a false allegation of rape. Where a victim so perceived reports a sexual assault by a person with whom she had some prior acquaintance, the initial orientation of the detective is to obtain information which either negates the crime of rape (the complainant actually consented) or warrants reducing the charge to a lesser offense. Where the victim and assailant were not previously acquainted, the case receives a vigorous investigative effort. The level of police resources devoted to the case varies according to the race and social standing of the victim.

2. Conceptions of the normal social characteristics of victims are also central to case routinization.

Victims having different social characteristics are regarded as being more or less likely to desire or follow through with prosecution in the case, to be reliable sources of information about it, and to inquire as to the outcome of the investigation.

The treatment of the assault and robbery in Case 3 illustrates how a case may be interpreted and handled primarily in terms of the victim's class position, race, and presumed lifestyle and competencies. The case was cleared by arrest on the basis of information provided by the victims, but the handling of this "ghetto robbery" involved little actual police effort. No attempt was made to locate witnesses, gather evidence from the crime scene, or otherwise strengthen the case against the accused.

Poor and working-class people who are regarded as unlikely to make inquiries regarding the handling and disposition of the case are seen as typical of victims in the category of routine burglaries. Case 2 illustrates how the interpretation of an incident may be accomplished solely on the basis of information contained in the patrol report and prior to an actual interview with the victim. The interview was structured in this case by the detective's expectation of its outcome.

Case 4 illustrates how inconsistent elements in an otherwise routine pattern (in this instance the victim's social status and apparent interest in the handling of the case) are managed to suit the purposes of the detective. Detectives speak of a case "coming back on them" if a respectable victim contacts superiors regarding progress in the case when the incident has received little or no investigative effort. Informing the victim that the case was not solvable largely because of her neighbor's attitudes enabled the detective to suspend the case with minimal problems.

3. Routinization formulas, finally, contain conceptions of the settings in which different kinds of offenses normally occur and the expected behavior of inhabitants of those settings. While assumptions about victims and perpetrators are derived in part from the nature of the offense involved, the physical and social setting where the incident occurred also contributes to a detective's understanding of

these parties. The fact that the burglary in Case 2 occurred in a particular public housing project told the detective much of what he felt he had to know about the case. It should be noted that none of these perceptions were communicated to the prosecutor observing the detective work; they were part of the taken-for-granted background upon which the detective based his handling of the case.

With regard to actual and potential *witnesses,* however, a detective's assumptions and beliefs are based primarily on the offense setting, if the witness is seen as a normal inhabitant of that setting. (This latter qualification simply recognizes that detectives attribute different inclinations and sentiments to social workers or salesmen who may have witnessed an incident than to residents of the area who may have witnessed a crime.)

The impact of territorial conceptions may be seen in the handling of Case 4. Routine burglaries occur mainly in low-income housing projects, residences in deteriorating center-city areas or, less frequently, in commercial establishments in or near these locations. Residents of these areas are considered unlikely to volunteer that they have witnessed a crime. Although official investigative procedure dictates that neighboring residents be interviewed to determine whether they saw or heard anything that might be of value to the investigation, this step was not undertaken in Cases 2 or 4 because it was assumed that the residents would be uncooperative.

Routine cases, then, may be seen as having two components, one at the level of consciousness and cognition, and the other at the level of observable behavior. A detective's interpretation of a case as routine involves an assessment of whether sufficient correspondence exists between the current case and some typical pattern to warrant handling it in the normal way. The criterion of sufficient correspondence implies that not all the elements of the typical pattern need be present for a detective to regard a case as a routine one. Common elements are viewed and used as resources which may be drawn upon selectively in accordance with one's practical concerns and objectives. Further, when certain elements in a case appear inconsistent with the typical pattern, there is a tendency to force and manage a sufficient fit between the particular and the typical in ways that help detectives deal with their caseload management problems and constraints.

These features of the interpretation process mean that the assessments of the routine or nonroutine nature of a case take on more of the character of a dichotomy than a continuum. Once an assessment is made, the case will be handled by means of prescribed formulas unless additional information changes the interpretation. It must be emphasized that the routinization process is not a matter of automatic or unreflective mapping of case features onto more general conceptions of criminal incidents. The interpretation of any particular case is shaped by a detective's understandings of what is required and expected and of how to manage these concerns effectively.

CASE HANDLING

Case handling normally proceeds in accordance with informal understandings shared among detectives. Routine case patterns are associated with prescribed handling recipes. It is critical to an understanding of investigative police work that interpretation of criminal incidents as routine or nonroutine largely determines which cases will be summarily suspended, which will be investigated, and how vigorous or extensive that investigation will be.

The characteristic behavioral element of a routine case is an absence of vigorous or thorough investigative effort. Two distinct sets of circumstances are ordinarily encountered in routine cases which lead to such a superficial or cursory investigative effort. The first, most common in burglary and robbery cases, is that the available information concerning the incident is seen as so meager or of so little utility that the possibility of making a quick arrest is virtually nonexistent. Viewing the case as nonproductive, and not wishing to expend effort on cases for which there are no formal rewards, the detective produces a brief investigative report detailing the routine features of the incident, concludes the case summary with "N.I.L." (no investigative leads were found), and classifies it as a suspended case.

The second set of circumstances associated with an absence of vigorous investigative effort involves assault, rape, and homicide cases which require some investigation because of their seriousness and the possibility of scrutiny by the judicial process. However, in many such incidents the facts of the case are so obvious and straightforward that little actual investigative work needs to be done. In these three types of offenses the victim and perpetrator are often known to one another, and it is not at all uncommon for the victim to name the assailant as soon as the police arrive. Cases in which a spouse or lover is still standing by the victim with weapon in hand when the police arrive, or in which the victim names the perpetrator before expiring, are not unusual. In essence, such cases are solved without any substantial police investigation. The detective is obligated to produce a comprehensive report on the incident, and the investigation is generally classified as closed in this report if the perpetrator has been apprehended. Indeed, in such obvious and straightforward cases the detective's only difficult task may be that of locating the perpetrator.[6]

Handling recipes associated with routine cases have a practical and instrumental character, reflecting the objective circumstances surrounding the investigation of many criminal events. After all, in the great majority of burglary cases the probability of ascertaining the identity of the perpetrator is rather small. Yet, handling recipes reflect certain *beliefs* and *assumptions* on the part of detectives concerning such matters as a victim's willingness to cooperate fully in the case, whether persons in particular sections of the city are likely to volunteer information about a crime, or the kind of impression a victim or witness would make in court. Such beliefs and assumptions constitute integral features in the construction of cases as routine or nonroutine, and they represent a pivotal linkage between specific features of cases and particular handling recipes.

The following incident illustrates the extent to which case handling may be guided by the detective's beliefs and assumptions about the nature of an incident and the parties involved:

CASE 6

A detective was assigned a case in which a man had stabbed his common-law wife in the arm with a kitchen knife. The patrol report on the incident indicated that the woman had been taken to City Hall to sign an arrest warrant, while the man had been arrested by patrol officers on the charge of felony assault and released on his own recognizance. Nominally, the detective was required to collect additional information and evidence relating to the incident and to write a detailed and comprehensive report which would be used in prosecuting the case. However, the detective's interpretation of the incident, based on his understanding of the area in which it occurred and the lifestyles of the persons involved, led him to view any further investigative effort on his part as futile. He remarked: "These drunks, they're always stabbing one another over here. Then you see 'em the next day and they're right back together again. She won't show up in court anyhow. Why waste my time and everybody else's on it." The handling of the case involved only the production of a brief report which concluded: "The victim in this complaint wishes no further investigation by the police department. This complaint is to be classified as closed."

The interpretive schemes used by detectives are not based solely on their experiences as police investigators, but also on their accumulated experiences as everyday social actors; they thus reflect commonsense social knowledge. Categorizations made by detectives about race, class, ethnicity, sex, and territory parallel wider cultural evaluations of morality and worth. None of the features of the formal organization of detective work substantially reduces this reliance on commonsense knowledge and its typical biases, prejudices, and interpretations.

SUMMARY AND IMPLICATIONS

Some general features of case routinization may now be noted in an attempt to clarify the interpretive activities through which detectives achieve order and predictability in their handling of cases and their encounters with victims and other relevant actors.

1. Shortly after receipt of a case, specific pieces of information are sought out and attended to for use in assessing the typicality of the incident. That is, the fundamental case-working orientation of detectives involves an attempt to establish commonalities between an actual case and typical case patterns. Incidents having typical features are interpreted and constructed as some variety of routine case. The orientation to typify and routinize cases is partly traceable to bureaucratic pressures and constraints to meet paperwork deadlines and produce a certain quantity and quality not of convictions but of arrests.

2. The interpretation of an incident is accomplished by attending to case features having commonly recognized utility as indicators of the type of case at hand. Detectives use such routinization schemes unless some problematic feature of an actual case brings into question their applicability and appropriateness. The interpretation of a case as routine or nonroutine essentially determines whether the case will be quickly closed or suspended or whether it will receive a more vigorous and extensive investigation. However, this initial assignment of meaning is provisional and subject to revision or modification upon receipt of additional information. Most importantly, the handling of cases is directed by these informal categorization schemes and is not the result of formal organizational policy or procedures. These schemes constitute a taken-for-granted background of decision making.

3. The interpretive schemes shared by detectives represent "successful" solutions to common practical problems, based on experience and shared understandings about the nature of urban crime and about types of urban residents, lifestyles, and territories. These understandings are rooted in socially distributed as well as role-specific knowledge, for both provide a basis for constructing solutions to work problems. Occupationally specific knowledge provides a set of instructions for interpreting case patterns in ways which enable a detective to successfully manage organizational constraints and demands. Commonsense social knowledge provides an understanding of the typical characteristics, attitudes, and action patterns of persons encountered. Identities may be readily assigned to persons by drawing on this stock of knowledge. Such identity assignments structure case handling along race, class, age, sex, and territorial lines in ways that are intended to minimize case handling problems. Because of this reliance on general social knowledge, the treatment of different types of urban residents tends to reflect wider cultural evaluations of social worth.

4. The essential nature of these interpretive processes is phenomenological rather than mechanical or rule-guided. In formulating a particular case, the operative process involves a determination of whether sufficient correspondence exists between the actual case and the paradigmatic case to warrant handling the incident in routine, low-effort ways. Sufficient correspondence assessments are accomplished in ways that serve the practical purposes of detectives, especially those of paperwork compliance and productivity.

5. Accordingly, routine cases are not constituted as a single determinant pattern. A variety of combinations of case features may result in routine handling of the case. For each offense, a core feature or set of features gets maximum interpretive significance. When a core feature is recognized in a particular case, other features which are ambiguous or even contradictory tend to be interpreted in a manner consistent with the identified core feature. Additional interpretive features, particularly the social status of the victim, are used as resources in selecting a safe and workable handling strategy.

6. In highly routinized case patterns, there is a tendency to squeeze great indicativeness out of a few case features. Detectives often rely upon assumptions to add detail to a case rather than actually gather information to further specify the type of case at hand. In other words, it is frequently taken for granted that certain investigative procedures will have predictable outcomes. Frequently, this process manifests itself in the fudging, doctoring, and manipulation of formal organizational reports.

It is likely that interpretive schemes having similar features will be found in all bureaucratically organized enterprises where large numbers of clients or cases are processed (e.g., social service centers, public hospitals, and other agencies in the criminal justice system). Whenever we find an organizational setting where members deal with similar events time and again, and where there are no features in the formal organization of the work which act to counter stereotyping, we may expect to find routinization schemes in use. These schemes will be used to categorize the population and apply standard patterns of treatment to each category.

These observations have significant implications for the study of decision making by legal agents. Decision making by bureaucratic agents inevitably involves discretion on the part of the agent who must fit general rules to particular cases. This discretionary latitude will be reflected in different forms of decision making in different kinds of organizational settings. The work of Roth (1977), Scheff (1978), Sudnow (1965), and others suggests that caseload size, amount of information readily available about the person or event, the nature of the body of knowledge used, and the expectation of future interaction with the person are crucial features governing the nature of the decision-making process. Where caseloads are high, continued interaction is not anticipated, minimal information is available, and the body of knowledge used by the agent is imprecise—stereotypes tend to become the operative and binding basis for decision making. Accordingly, detective work, presentence casework, public defender work, and medical practice in clinics or emergency rooms may be seen as lying toward the end of a continuum where typifications act as essentially final judgments.

At the other end of the continuum are settings where caseload sizes are smaller, more detailed information about the person is available, future interaction is anticipated, and decision making is grounded in a more substantial body of knowledge. In such settings, typificatory schemes are likely to be used only as provisional hypotheses, to be amplified and modified over the course of the encounter. Thus in probation work, some types of social service work, and the practice of general medicine, we might expect to find interaction only tentatively structured by stereotypic understandings. As interaction proceeds in these latter settings, typifications will begin to fade in importance as the basis for decision making.

NOTES

1. The description and the analysis presented here are based on nine months of participant observation field work in a city police detective division. Further information about access agreements, characteristics of the city and department, the field role adopted, and problems encountered during the research is available from the author.

2. An exception to this general observation occurs where a supervisor imposes a "major case" definition on an incident. In highly publicized or nonroutine homicide or rape cases, especially those involving higher status victims, a supervisor frequently takes an active part in the investigation and more closely monitors and directs the activities of detectives. With regard to the influence of the victim's social status on case handling, see Wilson's (1968:27) analysis of police perceptions of the legitimacy of complaints made by middle-class versus lower-class victims.

3. Official nationwide clearance rates are listed as 17.6% for burglary, 27.3% for robbery, 63.4% for felonious assault, 51.1% for rape, and 79.9% for homicide (Hindelang *et al.*, 1977).

4. Cf. Sudnow's (1965) argument that public defenders use their first interview with a client to gain an initial

sense of the defendant's place in the social structure as well as the typicality or lack thereof of the offense with which the person has been charged.

5. Garfinkel (1967:186–207) argues that organizational records are not to be treated as accurate or mirror reflections of the actual handling of a client or case by organizational members. However, these records can be employed to examine how members go about constructing a meaningful conception of a client or case and use it for their own practical purposes. Any valid sociological use of such records requires detailed knowledge on the part of the researcher regarding the context in which the records are produced, background understandings of members, and organizationally relevant purposes and routines.

6. Reiss (1971) makes a similar observation. He found that a great deal of detective work in the department studied merely involves attempting to locate identified perpetrators. The Rand survey of investigative practices in 153 police departments draws conclusions similar to those presented here. It was found that substantially more than half of all serious reported crimes receive no more than superficial attention from investigators (Greenwood and Petersilia, 1975).

REFERENCES

Garfinkel, Harold. 1967. *Studies in Ethnomethodology.* Upper Saddle River, NJ: Prentice Hall.

Greenwood, Peter W., and Joan Petersilia. 1975. *The Criminal Investigation Process,* Volume I. Santa Monica, CA: The Rand Corporation.

Hindelang, M., M. Gottfredson, C. Dunn and N. Parisi. 1977. *Sourcebook of Criminal Justice Statistics.* Washington, DC: National Criminal Justice Information and Statistics Service.

Reiss, Albert. 1971. *Police and the Public.* New Haven: Yale University Press.

Roth, Julius. 1977. "Some Contingencies of the Moral Evaluation and Control of Clients." *American Journal of Sociology* 77 (October):830–856.

Scheff, Thomas. 1978. "Typification in Rehabilitation Agencies." Pp. 172–175 in E. Rubington and M. S. Weinberg (eds.), *Deviance: The Interactionist Perspective.* New York: Macmillan.

Sudnow, David. 1965. "Normal Crimes: Sociological Features of the Penal Code in a Public Defender's Office." *Social Problems* 12 (3):255–276.

Wilson, James Q. 1968. *Varieties of Police Behavior.* Cambridge, MA: Harvard University Press.

Control Agents and the Creation of Deviant Types

KATHRYN J. FOX

A division of labor specifies what institution of social control will respond to an alleged violation of norms. The nature of the control that is anticipated as being the necessary one determines the institution to which it is assigned. Criminal justice takes charge when it is assumed that an offender could have controlled his or her conduct but chose not to. Health agencies assume responsibility when offenders are assumed to be unable to control their conduct. Social welfare agencies respond when offenders are assumed to have had neither choice nor control. Subsequently, the criminal justice system confines and punishes the persons found guilty of crimes. Health agencies treat offenders whose putative illness is believed to have caused their violations. Social welfare agencies help or support those seen as having been victimized by social or natural disasters. These social definitions regarding personal control further shape the production and use of constructions of the deviance by control agents within these institutions of social control.

Kathryn J. Fox studied a treatment unit for violent offenders in a Vermont prison. She spells out some of the conditions and consequences of a particular construction of deviance. Caseworkers held that errors in thinking always preceded violent behavior. In twice-weekly group meetings, two caseworkers and eight inmates met to go over inmates' past and present instances of rule-breaking. Workers had inmates search in both talk and writing for their errors in thought. Many inmates saw this search as an attempt to cram many varieties of behavior into one narrow category. When they resisted the workers' interpretation of their actions, workers simply interpreted their resistance as but another instance of errors in their thinking. Whenever inmates became angry in the group meetings, workers took their anger as evidence confirming their overarching conception of a "criminal type." Fox's study calls attention to an irony of formal social control: Agency staff tend to induce behavior in their interactions with inmates, patients, or clients that can confirm their stereotypes of deviants.

The institutional production of social types and identities has been studied extensively throughout various parts of the criminal justice system by early ethnomethodologists and others (Cicourel 1968; Quinney 1970; Skolnick 1966; Sudnow 1965). In other institutional settings, researchers

Reprinted from Kathryn J. Fox, "Reproducing Criminal Types: Cognitive Treatment for Violent Offenders in Prison," *The Sociological Quarterly*, Vol. 40, No. 3, Summer 1999, pp. 435–453. Copyright © 1999 by The Midwest Sociological Society. Reprinted by permission of Blackwell Publishing and the author.

have documented the significance of interactional dynamics between "expert" (or official) agents and clients. Agents rely on representations of particular types and, in turn, interpret clients' actions as evidence of the veracity of the construction (Frohmann 1991; Garfinkel 1967; Goffman 1961; Holstein 1992, 1993; Loseke 1989; Maynard 1984; Miller 1991, 1992; Pfohl 1978). These studies share an interest in the ways in which "collective representations" (Durkheim 1953) of particular "types" of people influence officials' and helping professionals' actions and, as such, have power in producing realities. These representations can help to manufacture a "social type"—a reductionist characterization that subsumes diverse client experiences into a narrow interpretation of those experiences (Holstein 1992; Loseke 1989, 1992; Miller 1992). Often these typologies are built into the institutional rhetoric, having "political consequences" insofar as they express the intersection of power and knowledge (Edelman 1977, p. 59). . . .

I observed the construction of criminal "types" in a cognitive therapy program for violent offenders in prison. The Cognitive Self-Change (CSC) program, which is in operation in several Vermont correctional facilities, maintains that violent offenders' "cognitive distortions" explain their criminality. The program works with violent offenders to reorient their "thinking" about or perceptions of their own lives and selves. . . .

METHODS

I observed CSC group meetings for approximately eight months, conducted formal and informal interviews with inmates and facilitators, and participated in CSC training sessions. In addition, I formally interviewed two administrators in the Vermont Department of Corrections and informally interviewed several program facilitators. The majority of the findings presented here come from observation of group sessions, focusing on dialogue among facilitators and participants in the CSC program. . . .

THE TALK OF CSC

The CSC groups I attended were held in a regional correctional facility that housed both men and women at various security levels. Each group consisted of eight inmate participants and two cofacilitators. A few facilitators were subcontractors who worked in mental health fields. However, most CSC facilitators were correctional caseworkers and probation/parole officers. According to a

program designer, the "use of authority is the keystone piece"—a concept that reveals the function of employing correctional workers as group facilitators.

Participation in the CSC program was voluntary, yet an inmate would not be eligible for early release without completing the program, so nearly all chose to participate. This paradox of voluntary coercion (Peyrot 1985) created a situation in which, as the program designer said, "They're going to try to please us and they're going to show their resentment at the same time." This context allowed anger to fester and find expression, and, in turn, reinforced an interpretation of criminals as having distinctively derelict, aggressive thought processes.

Meetings were held twice a week and lasted for an hour and a half each. In each group, inmates reflected upon their criminal histories and current, as well as past, situations that put them "at risk" for violence. Every session began with a "check-in" in which each inmate reported a recent risky situation that either could have or did prompt an angry or aggressive response. The inmates were asked to report the situation "objectively"; thus, the requisite format insisted that they refrain from evaluative language. For example, an inmate phrased a situation "someone snapped at me for no reason" and was informed that her phrasing included an unnecessary judgment. The group analyzed each situation for the thoughts, feelings, attitudes, and beliefs that surrounded it. Inmates were asked to report several different thoughts and feelings to learn how to identify the ones that preceded and motivated anger and/or violence. Thoughts were often "fuck this" or "I can't believe this shit." Feelings were usually reported as "anger, frustration, irritation, upset," and so on. A "good" check-in identified the "risk" for "going off on someone" that may be involved in particular ways of thinking, as well as some intervention thoughts to help deescalate a situation. Intervention thoughts were often of the variety "it's not worth doing more time."

Some meeting sessions focused exclusively on check-ins, depending upon how long they took and the extent to which other matters arose. Check-ins might fill the entire meeting if facilitators challenged participants' characterization of the situation. For example, if a report of a "situation" involved a lengthy explanation of what others were doing "to" the inmate, facilitators would be prompted to point out the error in that kind of thinking. Usually, after check-ins, a particular individual might post a thinking report (similar to a written check-in on a risky situation or crime) for the group to help analyze for life patterns or to question the integrity of the account. The facilitators might challenge the objectivity of the account if, for example, the report focused heavily on the inmate's own victimization. Or perhaps one inmate might present his or her "Fearless Criminal Inventory" (FCI), which is supposed to be an honest and thoughtful history of one's rule-breaking behaviors, beginning with the earliest one and including rule breaking in prison. FCIs included the reasons behind their actions and the consequences of them in hopes of finding a similar theme or pattern that motivated a particular individual's criminal impulses. In sum, the CSC program concentrated exclusively on the connection between thoughts (and their relationship to feelings, attitudes, and beliefs) and actions; as such, reports of rule-breaking behaviors by inmates were decontextualized from situations and rearticulated as the product of thinking errors characteristic of criminals.

In the group sessions, facilitators instructed participants in the language of the CSC program. Inmates needed to recast their crimes within the sanctioned interpretive and linguistic framework (Pollner and Stein 1994). For example, inmates selected "patterns" from a list that best explained their personal thought processes. The list described the typical "thinking errors" of criminal personalities; for instance, among the most popular ones were "victim stance" (feeling victimized by others), "justification," "power thrust" (needing power and control over others), and "failure to consider others." Intervention thoughts for avoiding future crimes, especially violent ones, were designed based upon inmates' understandings of their life patterns.

The CSC program literature stressed that the program did not insist that inmates change, rather that they demonstrate that they know *how* to change—which meant that they must explain how they *could* intervene in their thought process. One facilitator confided: "I'm saying, 'I'm not trying to tell you how you should think and feel'—at least that's my disclaimer. I'm not sure if it'll hold up or not." Some facilitators believed strongly that the CSC program was merely an educational tool to provide skills that inmates either chose to employ or not; others stated that the program indeed insisted that inmates' beliefs were wrong and must be changed, at least superficially to meet the "competencies" of the program. Another facilitator explained, "You can't just *say* certain thoughts—you gotta say what we want."

Participants were evaluated on their performance according to the program standards and must have completed the competencies (identifying and intervening in risky thoughts) that were measured by in-group participation, written assignments, and the adequacy of their "relapse prevention" plans. In this sense, true rehabilitation was not forced, but some recognized effort toward that end was required for positive evaluation. As one facilitator explained, "There are no wrong beliefs—there *are* wrong ones for making it through the program." In fact, one participant was suspended from the group because "he's not buying it." In this respect, "buying" the CSC rhetoric was demanded; rejection of the dictated moral standard reflected pathology and reproduced it (Henry and Milovanovic 1996; Miller and Rose 1994). . . .

CREATING CRIMINAL TYPES

The CSC program was designed to treat violent offenders by targeting their distinctive thought patterns. The rhetoric drew heavily upon Samuel Yochelson and Stanton E. Samenow's (1976) research on criminal personalities. Thus, CSC reduced inmates' experiences into ideal-typical criminal patterns by interpreting their actions and words according to a particular schematic representation of criminals. Although a recent move has attempted to eliminate the terms "error" and "distortion" from the program's language, pathology was implied (and the terms are still used). In asking inmates to reflect upon their "core patterns" of thought that precede violent actions and asking explicitly that they devise new ways of thinking, program participation informed inmates that their *thinking* was different and troubling. In this respect, the CSC program relied on and reinforced a construction of a type of person—criminal type—that was evident in the interactions of group meetings.

Group thinking reports and journal assignments focused on "mind-sets" or particular ways of seeing the world that led to a cycle of violence. Many thinking reports concentrated on the ways in which their thoughts motivated feelings of anger and how beliefs and attitudes supported such thoughts. Yet often the inmates' thoughts were about how their victims deserved what they got or that correctional personnel victimized them. Facilitators insisted that inmates' complaints about mistreatment in prison or unfair prosecution or sentencing were reflective of their "thinking patterns." For example, in one group, inmates complained about the behavior of prison guards and the facilitator suggested this kind of sentiment reflected a "mind-set." An inmate responded: "If you have so many inmates telling you that guards are out to get them, how can that be a mind-set?" After the facilitator explained how this same mind-set shared by inmates was what landed them all in prison, the inmate joked, "I guess the mind is a terrible thing."

In another example, an inmate was asked to consider: "When I have these thoughts, someone gets hurt." He responded, "There isn't anything in my life that goes like that," continuing that his thoughts do not explain his violence. He was eventually given a negative evaluation for program performance because he could not meet the basic competency, which was to connect *thoughts* to risk for violence. Insofar as inmates' counterclaims were treated as illegitimate by facilitators, they referred to a representation of criminal thinking as a particular variety of thought: "distorted concrete thinking." In reality contests such as these, inmates' versions could not be sustained, but were, rather, co-opted in the process of recontextualization. The simplicity of the CSC program's premises was regarded as one of its strengths—it was relatively easy to implement. However, as one facilitator lamented to me, "[CSC] doesn't consider the forces outside the person—it assumes that thinking alone causes behavior—there's more to it than that!"

In reducing the complexity of inmates' life situations to a simple equation between malleable thoughts and actions, the program depended upon the judgments handed down by the courts. As one facilitator said, "I start with the premise that they're a lying sack of shit because I can't retry the case." In this sense, then, the assumption of pathology (or immorality) was built into the program—after all, it was a correctional treatment program. Pathology was reproduced by eliminating other possible explanations.

DECONTEXTUALIZING CRIMINALITY

In order to construct criminality as evidence of a "type," situational explanations for crimes had to be dismissed. Most of the time, inmates claimed that their violence was provoked or somehow prompted by circumstances beyond their control. Such accounts echo Sykes and Matza's (1957) "techniques of neutralization" used by delinquents to deflect a deviant identity. For instance, inmates' claims that someone else started a fight represented "denial of responsibility," and claims that their victims deserved what they got exemplified "denial of the victim." Their techniques of neutralization were social explanations that conflicted with the notion of a criminal personality. Deviance was situational, according to inmates. Yet, in order for CSC to work, criminal acts must be disembodied from their circumstances and be considered outside of contexts. As an administrator said: "There's a difference between the *reason* for what they did and what they did." He went on to say that CSC was only interested in what the offenders did. In this sense, the group process could be seen as one that *de*contextualized inmates' behaviors and treated them as objectively deviant.

A sample exchange in a group meeting illustrated this point. Pete was discussing a written thinking report (for which he had been evaluated negatively) on a violent situation. He was supposed to describe the situation "objectively":

PETE: The situation was: I had been drinking, getting drunk, with my girlfriend and she pissed me off so I went to bed. I was sleeping and my girlfriend punched me in the balls so I broke her jaw. Then you said I didn't need to put so much here.

FACILITATOR: We don't need an explanation—like this getting drunk and all that—just what you did: you broke her jaw.

PETE: I was sleeping and my girlfriend punched me in the balls and I broke her jaw. Is that acceptable?

FACILITATOR: I don't know if I'd use the word acceptable. . . .

The negotiation of reality that took place in this incident reflected Pete's subtle attempt to "minimize" his violence (Potter 1996, p. 187). Pete's reluctance to exclude explanatory information from his description demonstrated his efforts to "soften" the violence (Potter 1996, p. 191). A major goal of the CSC program was to make offenders accountable for their crimes—thus, these attempts to minimize were thwarted.

Also striking in this example is the way in which the facilitator asked Pete to eliminate from the discussion the context in which the act took place. Pete was then asked to reduce the situation more, excluding the part about his being attacked first. In this sense, the only aspect of the situation of interest in the group process was the act of breaking a woman's jaw. Insofar as the act was discussed, dissected, and analyzed out of context, the actor was reconfigured in another context—that of his own violent nature. In a delicate way, the description of violence was maximized. Out of context, it seemed that Pete broke a woman's jaw for no apparent reason—as such, he fit neatly into

a descriptive type of a violent person. This is not meant to suggest that Pete's violence was justified in or out of context but rather to highlight the process by which criminal acts of all kinds were viewed in a vacuum in CSC.

Interestingly, the inmates' accounts were often somewhat sociological. Inmates reported acting out in school after being labeled "stupid" because of a learning disability; they explained their stealing as a result of poor employment opportunities and their violent episodes as consequences of inadequate verbal skills. In this respect, inmates stressed the social (structural) context of their criminality. Yet their discourse of social causation was a target for treatment in CSC and served as proof of extreme criminal thinking: claiming victimization. The institutional discourse of CSC needed a construction of inmates as pathological; incarceration could not be justified and rehabilitation makes no sense without such a construction. The program itself could not be validated or sustained without manufacturing evidence of criminal thinking.

REPRODUCING ERRONEOUS THINKING

The construction of criminal thinking as erroneous was the fulcrum of the CSC program. Thus, errors in thinking were the cornerstone of interpretations of inmates' thoughts. These distortions in thought were tied into the ideology of moral autonomy: any claims inmates might make about the ways they were constrained or compelled by others in their actions were treated as distortions. As a facilitator explained: "Bare bones: you gotta take responsibility for [your] offense." In addition, regardless of others' actions, inmates needed to fit their own actions and thoughts into a pattern suggestive of pathology. For example, Todd was discussing a recent situation in jail: another inmate failed to refill the coffeepot after emptying it. Todd stated that this incident fit the thinking error paraphrased as "failure to consider others." A facilitator responded:

FACILITATOR: Does that pattern fit?
TODD: It fits the person who emptied the coffeepot and didn't fill it back up.

FACILITATOR: Could it ever fit you?

TODD: Now that I think about it, it could be, like when I steal from someone else.

FACILITATOR: Then write that down for your relapse plan.

This is not to imply that stealing represented something other than a "failure to consider others." But the interactions between facilitators and inmates were devised to reorient inmates' interpretations, to examine their own responsibility for their actions, to shift the blame onto themselves.

Inmates' counterclaims in reality contests were regarded as indicative of how entrenched their thought patterns were. In this sense, claims as to one's "change" or rehabilitation actually reinforced the rhetorical claims of the facilitators. In other words, extreme resistance represented typical criminal thinking, as did ready capitulation. Because criminal thinking was the target, some resistance was expected, and was targeted as well. In an exchange with two facilitators, Todd stated:

TODD: I have a dilemma because my way[s] of thinking's changed and I know I gotta show you that but I don't get into beefs anymore—I'm above all that.

FACILITATOR: Don't show us that you've changed your thinking, show us that you have interventions.

COFACILITATOR: [incredulously] Yeah, how did you change your thinking?

TODD: You're saying someone can't change their thinking?

COFACILITATOR: Well, we think you may *respond* differently now.

In this exchange, Todd's suggestion that he thought "differently" than he did before was greeted with suspicion. In this sense, the program's discourse assumed that criminals retained their core thinking patterns—which were distorted—but that they could train themselves to intervene with some new thoughts. The rhetoric seemed contradictory: inmates could not change their thinking but they may devise *new* thinking.

Yet even interventions that inmates devised were often deemed characteristic of criminal thinking. In an exchange with a facilitator, Jens recounted an incident he had with a prison guard:

FACILITATOR: What thoughts did you have?

JENS: I start to get irritated because it's my pattern—I gotta be in control.

FACILITATOR: What are your thoughts becoming next [in the situation]?

JENS: Dehumanizing thoughts, you know, I can't say because there's a lady present [referring to me]. I start formulating plans for getting even, for revenge. For me, I always gotta get my words in, so walking away for me is a big intervention.

FACILITATOR: Walking away and getting the last word—are they similar?

JENS: Yeah, failure to consider others, to look at their side of the story.

FACILITATOR: You're thinking what now? [referring to the time of the incident]

JENS: "F—— off."

FACILITATOR: So you get the final word?

JENS: For me, I've always been drawn to confrontation.

FACILITATOR: Walking away—is it at all high risk?

JENS: Well, it's payback for his behavior, you know, like pride. I take pride in what I do.

FACILITATOR: So it *is* risky. It's getting even. So is that an intervention?

JENS: No, intervention was nowhere on my mind I guess when I walked out.

Implicit in this exchange was the presumption that even when inmates believed they were devising "real" interventions—and even when the intervention "worked" in averting violence—their intervening behaviors emanated from the criminal thought patterns that were so much a part of them. They were responsible for getting angry in the first place.

In another example, an inmate was upset over a meeting with his caseworker, and he intervened in his anger by working on his relapse plan:

FACILITATOR: Intervention should be working on the angry part. It's supposed to help you deal with the anger, not the caseworker. It's about *you*.

COFACILITATOR: "Cognitive" means thinking, changing your thinking so you're less risky. It's not a problem-solving course, it's about how can you change your thinking.

Regardless of others' actions toward participants, the "problem" and target of intervention was their response: their angry thoughts. Thus, anger was never justified for inmates, but was a normal emotion for others—inmate anger was evidence of faulty, pathological thinking. The inherent tautology in this model helped to sustain and (re)produce angry criminal "types."

REPRODUCING ANGRY CRIMINALS

CSC discourse incorporated and reified cultural conceptions of criminality. According to Alison Young (1996, pp. 1–2), the popular imagery of crime is comprised of a "binary logic of representation." Thus, crime is reduced to opposing poles: rational/irrational, responsible/irresponsible, victims/victimizers, prosocial/antisocial, and so on. In such a scheme, this reductionist logic played out in globalizing identities; in other words, a person was constructed as either one ideal type or another (see also Best 1997).

Stuart Henry and Dragan Milovanovic (1996, p. 178) stated that, "the dichotomous separation between law-abiding and law-breaking behavior is an artifact of the conventional criminologist." Indeed, the Cognitive Self-Change program was adapted from social scientific research on criminal personalities. Within the rhetoric of CSC, dichotomies of erroneous/correct thinking and anger/rationality were enforced and, in that sense,

had a disciplinary effect (Foucault 1977; Rose 1988). The dichotomies became ideological, disciplining tools with a reflexive relationship to the larger system of social control. They may be cultural artifacts of an established psychological paradigm, but they were animated in microinteractions that again provided fuel for the legitimacy of the ideology of social control.

Let us look at anger as our illustration. Within CSC, inmates were regarded as victimizers, never victims. In addition, inmates' opposition to the representations of criminality in the program was interpreted as evidence of their extreme anger that motivated their violent behavior. Angel complained that his probation officer requested more "thinking reports" on his convicted crime. Angel reported this "high-risk situation" during check-in since he was angry—he was certain she had several copies in her file already,

FACILITATOR: What were your thoughts?

ANGEL: My risky thoughts were "fuck her, fuck this. I don't f'ing care. It's a buncha BS." Then, "Well, I better do it or else I ain't getting out. I gotta satisfy them. Don't do it and I stay here or do it and get out." But I was trying to figure out why she was doing this to me.

FACILITATOR: Why she's doing it to you? Do you think she would have asked that of anyone or just you?

ANGEL: Well, I don't know. I just know she has [the thinking reports].

FACILITATOR: What are your core patterns?

ANGEL: Anger, power thrust. . . .

FACILITATOR: Your core pattern is anger—it seems you got there pretty quickly.

ANGEL: Yeah, but I didn't express it. I went to my bunk and sorted it out in my head.

FACILITATOR: But inside your head would have been an interesting thing to see. It probably would have been X-rated.

ANGEL: Yeah.

In this complex example, the facilitator initially probed to see if the inmate was grasping onto a belief that he was being "singled out" or victimized, as this was regarded as the most typical pattern. In addition, Angel described how his interventions worked to calm him down. Yet the facilitator seized upon the fact that he questioned his parole officer's motives. Although Angel explained that he did not express his anger, he was still responsible for his "criminal" thinking. Being angry was associated with erroneous thought patterns or "core" patterns that globally defined the inmate. As such, Angel's anger was of a fundamentally different nature than that of other noncriminal types: his anger was illegitimate and pathological.

In private discussions about inmate resistance to the discourse of CSC, facilitators would dismiss prisoners' complaints as "typical criminal kind of thinking." Particularly obstinate inmates were regarded as embodiments of "the culture" of prison in their antagonism toward corrections (Irwin 1987; Wieder 1974). There were several occasions in which inmates complained about the rigid requirements, for example, for expressing their beliefs in short "bumper sticker" phrases and the like. Each time, facilitators relied upon a characterization of inmates as angry or resistant to authority to marginalize their protests. For example, in one exchange, Calhoun suggested that "I don't need a piece of paper to tell me I can drive" was an appropriate intervention for the times he felt tempted to drive without a license. The facilitator challenged him:

FACILITATOR: That's more of a belief, isn't it?
CALHOUN: Whatever.
FACILITATOR: See, I am thinking of you in Phase 3 [aftercare group for released inmates], the providers don't know a thing about your past.
CALHOUN: So? This is for us, not for you!
FACILITATOR: Well, you'll need to demonstrate that you can intervene.
CALHOUN: Oh man! That's what I'm doing! [Then Calhoun suggested alternative interventions, such as "my freedom is more important."]

FACILITATOR: Those are goals. Maybe the intervention [thought] would look like "remember past."
CALHOUN: You can't get that from what I just said? You mean to tell me you guys are that fucking stupid? All right then, I'll need another page eight to write this so you people can understand.

Calhoun's intervention thoughts were of dubious quality based on the standards required. Interestingly, though, his resistance was mostly centered on the arbitrary format requirements the facilitator enforced. However, after the meeting, the facilitators discussed Calhoun's bad "attitude" and chalked up his complaints to his "anger." Thus, his objections were dismissed as illegitimate because they were simply indicative of his criminal anger.

In another example, an inmate argued that since his return to prison was for a nonviolent offense, he should not be required to complete the CSC program (which was explicitly designed for violent offenders). The lengthy exchange between Doug and a facilitator was instructive:

FACILITATOR: It's not just a violent offender program—it's for criminal thinking—like "I can break this rule."
DOUG: But if it's all that, why would I have to take a separate drug and alcohol program?
FACILITATOR: Did you recently get some bad news?
DOUG: No, it's just that. . . .
FACILITATOR: Did you recently get some bad news?
DOUG: [angrily] No! I see what you're getting at!
FACILITATOR: What is it you're really saying?
DOUG: I just don't see why I am in a violent offender program. . . .
FACILITATOR: What is it you're really saying?
DOUG: Look, I did some drinking. I didn't do a violent offense!
FACILITATOR: That's only part of it. The other part is that we make decisions, like the decision to

drink, based on what's going on up here [points to head]. So part of it is to teach you not to be violent by developing an awareness of how you're thinking about things so you can catch yourself. Like the decision you made to drink again: something was behind that.

DOUG: It wasn't violent though.

FACILITATOR: But your body gives you signals about your patterns.

In this interaction, Doug's concern about his forced participation in a drug and alcohol program was ignored and interpreted as evidence of his anger. He then became angry at the suggestion that his complaint was "about" something else. He was later characterized as "an angry dude" by the facilitators. This example demonstrates the reproductive aspect of the rhetoric of CSC. Built upon assumptions of violent criminals as essentially angry, the insistence on that interpretation produced anger that reinforced the representation (Young 1995). In fact, during one meeting, Doug seemed unusually happy, and the facilitator said later that he must have been smoking marijuana.

When inmates expressed resentment over their treatment by individuals in the Department of Corrections, these claims were marginalized as well. In another exchange with Doug, the facilitator asked:

FACILITATOR: When your P.O. [parole officer] gave you a negative recommendation [for parole], what were you thinking about her?

DOUG: I know her game. I knew it right off. I always thought she was a piece of shit and I planned to tell her that when I saw her.

FACILITATOR: Was that high risk [of violence] for you?

DOUG: No. I wasn't going to do anything except tell her off.

FACILITATOR: [pause] I notice your shirt says "Slap-a-[whore] tribe." Somebody that would wear a shirt like that—that's quite a statement. What did you think of [your P.O.]?

DOUG: Nothing.

FACILITATOR: You were just this calm, cool, and collected guy?

DOUG: Well, what am I gonna do—call her a bunch of names?

FACILITATOR: You said you were.

DOUG: Look, I told her I drank and she picked up the telephone and called parole. . . . Maybe it was something just to give her something to do, to make her book of work on me look good, like she's doing something.

FACILITATOR: It wouldn't have anything to do with the way you present yourself?

DOUG: No! Fuck it. Screw it. You got everything you need to know. What do you want to pick at?

FACILITATOR: You're angry today.

DOUG: I am just sick of everything—this revolving door into here.

One could argue that the message on the inmate's shirt spoke volumes about his perspective toward women. In addition, he seemed confused about whether or not he was planning to behave aggressively toward his parole officer. However, through a series of pointed questions, the facilitator implied that the inmate was angry, aggressive toward women, and responsible for his probation officer's decision to "violate" him for transgressing—all of which may well have been true. However, through a discursive technique, Doug was constructed interactionally. The representation of "calm, cool, collected guy" was used as a "contrast structure" (Smith 1990) to shore up the absurdity of this image of the inmate, discursively constructing him as essentially angry.

In addition, the path that the questions took led the inmate to become angry, which would later be interpreted as a sign that the facilitator had "touched a nerve." Touching a nerve meant that the core truth had been probed. In this sense, then, expressions of anger toward the line of reasoning a facilitator pursued were regarded as evidence of the righteousness of that reasoning. As such, reality was not negotiated so much as persuaded and enforced.

DEMANDING REALIGNMENT

Clearly, facilitators' assumptions about the essential anger of inmates helped to arouse sufficient anger among participants to bolster the construction. In addition, facilitators subtly demanded realignment to the program's representation of them as "angry criminals" by insisting that there was more anger than inmates admitted. In this exchange, an inmate described her thoughts about a situation in which a prison official reneged on a promise to let her daughter visit:

ANNIE: I did my end of the bargain. [She's] not doing hers.
FACILITATOR: Something else is going on in that head of yours—those are awfully tame [thoughts]. If I couldn't see my kid for three weeks, I'd be thinking, "This is bullshit. The bitch isn't keeping her end of the bargain."
ANNIE: I was thinking that in the unit.

This seemed to satisfy the facilitator. Interestingly, the facilitator admitted to having similar thoughts as those that would be classified as distorted. However, her anger was normalized, while the inmate's was pathological. In another exchange, again the facilitator insisted the inmate's thoughts were too "tame." When Annie replied that she was trying to suppress her angry thoughts, which would be considered "prosocial" behavior, her strategy was regarded as evidence of her simmering anger.

In a different example of realignment, a facilitator was trying to persuade an inmate to see himself in the thinking errors list. One thinking error stated, "The criminal believes that he is a good and decent person. He rejects the thought that he is a criminal." An inmate had referred to this error in a thinking report, describing how he was, in fact, a good person and was not what he considered a "criminal." He said that a criminal was "a thief who steals for drugs." He was told that he misunderstood the point of the assignment—that he should have reflected upon "hurtful, destructive" things he'd done. Todd became frustrated because he was trying to do what he understood the assignment to be:

TODD: What do you want me to put here?
FACILITATOR: Whatever you want.
TODD: Obviously not.

They discussed the crime for which he was convicted.

FACILITATOR: Do you think that's criminal?
TODD: Yeah, I guess. But what do you want [for the assignment]?
FACILITATOR: "A thief" is someone else, it's not you. It's supposed to be about you.
COFACILITATOR: How are *you* criminal?
TODD: I reject the thought of being a criminal. That's what it says [on the thinking errors list]. That's what I do.

In this instance, the inmate thought he was supposed to write down the patterns that apply to his thoughts—he believed he was a good person. However, he did not perceive this to be an error. Later, when he again insisted that he was not a criminal because he had only one conviction, a facilitator replied, "It does make it difficult when your view is that you're innocent." In this sense, he was asked to internalize a "criminal" identity, to accept that his thoughts were merely "typical" criminal ones, thereby adopting his essential criminality as "master status" (Becker 1963). Acknowledging the criminality of his act was the first step in the process of talking him into being a criminal *person;* his resistance to the label was seen as a rejection of a criminal identity. Clinging to the belief that he was essentially a decent person was deemed erroneous and further evidence of how deeply ingrained his criminal thinking was.

In another important way, the inmate was asked to align himself externally with the ideology of the program. Although ostensibly the target of intervention was the inmate's "mind," the only resources available for making change in group sessions were interactional devices such as writing and speaking (Young 1995). A facilitator said, "You gotta fake it till you make it," meaning that inmates had to try using the terms and concepts to demonstrate that they "know *how* to change"—in hopes that eventually inmates would realize it works. Because this interpretive lens shaped the interactions between facilitators and inmates and was built into the rhetoric of "thinking errors," resistance was regarded as extreme criminal thinking (or "concrete thinking"). If an inmate refused to cooperate even after being sanctioned on occasion, his or her cognitive ability may be questioned; one inmate was so resistant to the concepts endorsed in the program that his mental capacity became suspect. The facilitators could not comprehend why he would choose not to "fake it" and become an "expedient confessor" (Scott 1969), given the potential consequence of suspension from the group and a stalled prison release. An exchange in a group meeting demonstrated this point:

FACILITATOR: You gotta get past this, "This isn't gonna work" stuff.

LEE: So what you're saying is that I shouldn't be honest. I should tell you what you wanna hear?

FACILITATOR: Well, by telling us what we want to hear, you're gonna *know* what we want. . . .

LEE: I don't have a clue what you want!

In this example, the facilitator suggested that a demonstrated ability to provide the facilitators with "what they want to hear" would show competency in understanding the program. Resistance, or a reluctance to "try," was perceived as extreme willfulness—a typical criminal pattern. "Trying" was measured by attempts to utilize the terms and complete the assignments properly. Whenever inmates would ask about the possibility of failing the program, they were told that "it's not like school, no pass or fail." An inmate responded: "You say it's not like school, but why does our R.P. [relapse prevention plan] have to be accepted by you, by whoever? What standard do you use? If it's our thinking, there's no way you can grade it." At times like these,

when arguments between inmates and facilitators became circular, facilitators would refer to "the program" and its requirements. Occasionally when inmates objected to the language of "thinking errors" or "criminal personalities," a facilitator would say something like "it's from a book by some psychologists!" in order to reify the program's relevance.

OBJECTIFYING DISCOURSE

Using an "objectifying discourse" (Smith 1990, p. 4) to silence resistance, CSC rhetoric reinforced its own scientific frame. The objectivist language of "cognitive distortions," "criminal personalities," and the like rhetorically produced angry types of criminals. Thus, the taken-for-granted social facts of criminality were constituted through practices of rehabilitation (Pollner 1987). Anger was evidence of subjectivity, whereas inmates were asked to read their lives objectively. Objectivity was presumed to be the property of facilitators in their abilities to see inmates' deluded criminal thinking. In a training session for CSC facilitators, an instructor insisted "You're the experts, not them," and:

> We're a step ahead of the game, right? That we can see their risk more clearly than they do. And that's not surprising because we're more objective about it and they've got, they're more close to this and defensive and the rest of that stuff.

It is clear that objectivity and rationality were preferred interpretive frames, and "criminal" anger was irrational and overly subjective. Thus, anger was a fundamental ingredient in constructing criminals as "other" types with inappropriate thoughts.

Objectivity was measured by the degree to which inmates conformed to the paradigm of the CSC program. Inmates who resisted continually, charging that the program was "bullshit" and that their thinking was undistorted, were not evaluated positively for release. In time, most inmates recognized their "choice" to serve their maximum sentence and began to adopt the language of the program. In this sense, participants in CSC were "talked into being" (Heritage 1984, p. 290) pathological types by conforming their interpretations and rearticulating their lives to fit the "narrative map" (Pollner and Stein 1994) provided.

Donileen R. Loseke (1989) argued that the production of people as types places them "within particular moral universes, which simultaneously constructs such persons as residing within particular universes of 'sympathy-worthiness' or 'condemnation-worthiness.'" Insofar as inmates inhabited a "condemnation-worthy" category, CSC imposed this moral order through rhetorical strategies and interpretations. Moral universes were mystified by the objectivist language of "cognition." For instance, the program literature emphasized that the logic of CSC eschews moral judgment and privileges an objective approach to treatment. However, in an argument with a facilitator, an inmate claimed that his crime was the result of self-defense, which he said was "the nature of human beings." The facilitator responded, "No, we've progressed past that—maybe not in your world, maybe that's the problem." In this example, the inmate's entire "world" was indicted as being regressive. Interestingly, the facilitator acknowledged the distinction between subcultural values and those endorsed by the CSC program, yet the "problem" was in reconciling the inmate's values—indeed, his view, of human nature—with those of the program. This is part of what was implied by the concept of "cognitive self-change"—borrowing from the 1960s film *Cool Hand Luke*—inmates had to "get their minds right." Within CSC, fundamental change was invisible; rather, change was measured in "verbal behavior" that reinforced criminal typification (Young 1995, p. 187).

DISCUSSION

Although other studies have documented the interactional production of types in human service settings, analyzing CSC unearths greater implications in several respects. First, CSC represents but one theory about the nature of criminality—that of a distinct criminal "personality." The specific nature of inmate pathology may vary in therapeutic approaches, but correctional ideology regards inmates as some version of immoral, irrational, irresponsible, or ill. Incarceration cannot be rationalized without some accompanying ideology of the "otherness" of inmates (Foucault 1977, 1980a; Irwin 1987; Sloop 1996). Thus, the institution relies upon the enforcement and support of its underlying premises one way or another. Whatever the construct of the essence of criminality, the "type" is constructed and reified, in part, out of institutional necessity.

Second, the creation and reproduction of types is an animating process. This is not meant to suggest that typologies or knowledges determine social practices—rather that the facilitators' activities (derived from legitimated knowledge) build and fortify existing ideologies (Garfinkel 1967). The process is interactive and dynamic. Sue Fischer and Alexandra Dundas Todd (1986, p. xiii) describe a "contextual web" in which interactions occur in the center and spread out to the organizational structure that shapes them. The larger context is refined by the microinteractions and "folds back again to shape interactions and communication." Insofar as resistant interactions solidify the "truth" of the institution's intervention paradigm, the creative and interactive relationship between the institution and its many actors is evident.

Third, intervention into socially problematic behavior is justified by an ideology of pathology, one that may be supported by social scientistic theories (Rose 1988, 1996). The CSC program is an example of the use of criminological research on criminal types. Criminology, by virtue of its focus on the study of criminals' alleged distinctiveness, can be used as an "alibi" to sustain social control ideologies (Foucault 1980b, p. 47). Thus, the ideology of pathology is enforced in a "disciplinary discourse" (Henry and Milovanovic 1996, p. 197) that merges criminology and crime control in ways of talk.

In micropolitical exchanges in CSC, the nature of the individual criminal self is negotiated and contested. Inmates are enjoined to take part in this reproductive project. In this sense, their subjectivity is constituted by an *inter*subjective process (Foucault 1983, 1988; Garland 1997). Not only are convicted violent offenders sentenced to incarceration, they are subject to a rhetorical process in which their minds are penetrated and treated as objects for intervention. As a professional discursive technology, CSC incites "troubles talk" and, as such, manufactures criminality, by constructing criminals as objects of power (Miller and Silverman 1995). Through such talk, not only are inmates' actions challenged, but their inner selves (or their "will" as the program literature puts it) as well.

Thus, as an example of cognitive social control, the CSC program powerfully represents how an interpretation of inmates as pathological is impervious to contrary evidence—inmates' actions are reinterpreted to fit the category of deviant (Fox 1999). An overt context of control shapes the interactions such that counterrhetorics are marginalized; the institution sets the parameters within which new selves can be created. Insofar as power is accomplished through discourse, the micropolitics of CSC groups reveal larger processes embodied in the rehabilitative "talk" about criminal types (Foucault 1980a, 1980b).

Finally, inmates employ rhetorical devices to try to "normalize" their activities, formulating their accountability in particular ways (Potter 1996). A construction of individuals as determined by external forces would undermine the CSC program's logic; thus, lay sociological accounts by inmates are refuted. In essence, external causation discourses are silenced by individualistic, pathologizing ones. Indeed, CSC engages in a process that actively delegitimates social explanations. The implications for sociological perspectives in crime control/talk are obvious—sociology's influence may be limited in institutions charged with regulating human behavior. Correctional philosophy has been characterized of late by a psychologistic paradigm,

presumably reflecting the cultural dominance of those disciplines (Rose 1996; Simon and Feeley 1995). However, for agencies involved in the management of human behavior, the benefit of relying on "psy" disciplines may be that pathological types continue to be (re)produced.

REFERENCES

Becker, Howard. 1963. *Outsiders: Studies in the Sociology of Deviance.* New York: Free Press.

Best, Joel. 1997. "Victimization and the Victim Industry." *Society* 34:9–17.

Cicourel, Aaron V. 1968. *The Social Organization of Juvenile Justice.* London: Heinemann.

Durkheim, Emile. 1953. *Sociology and Philosophy.* Translated by D. F. Pocock. Glencoe, IL: Free Press.

Edelman, Murray. 1977. *Political Language: Words That Succeed and Policies That Fail.* New York: Academic Press.

Fischer, Sue, and Alexandra Dundas Todd. 1986. "Introduction: Communication in Institutional Contexts: Social Interaction and Social Structure." Pp. ix–xviii in S. Fischer and A. Dundas Todd (eds.), *Discourse and Institutional Authority: Medicine, Education, and Law.* Norwood, NJ: Ablex.

Foucault, Michel. 1977. *Discipline and Punish: The Birth of the Prison.* New York: Vintage.

———. 1980a. *The History of Sexuality Vol I.* New York: Vintage/Random House.

———. 1980b. *Power/Knowledge.* New York: Pantheon Books.

———. 1983. "The Subject and Power." Pp. 208–226 in 2nd ed., H. L. Dreyfus and P. Rabinow (eds.), *Michel Foucault.* Chicago: University of Chicago Press.

———. 1988. "Technologies of the Self." Pp. 16–49 in L. H. Martin, H. Gutman, and P. H. Hutton (eds.), *Technologies of the Self.* Amherst: University of Massachusetts Press.

Fox, Kathryn J. 1999. "Changing Violent Minds: Discursive Correction and Resistance in the Cognitive Treatment of Violent Offenders in Prison." *Social Problems* 46:88–103.

Frohmann, Lisa. 1991. "Discrediting Victims' Allegations of Sexual Assault: Prosecutorial Accounts of Case Rejections." *Social Problems* 38: 213–226.

Garfinkel, Harold. 1967. *Studies in Ethnomethodology.* Upper Saddle River, NJ: Prentice Hall.

Garland, David. 1997. " 'Governmentality' and the Problem of Crime: Foucault, Criminology, Sociology." *Theoretical Criminology* 1:173–214.

Goffman, Erving. 1961. *Asylums.* Garden City, NY: Anchor Books.

Henry, Stuart, and Dragan Milovanovic. 1996. *Constitutive Criminology: Beyond Postmodernism.* London: Sage.

Heritage, John C. 1984. *Garfinkel and Ethnomethodology.* Cambridge, MA: Polity Press.

Holstein, James A. 1992. "Producing People: Descriptive Practices in Human Service Work." Pp. 23–40 in G. Miller (ed.), *Current Research on Occupations and Professions.* Greenwich, CT: JAI Press.

———. 1993. *Court-Ordered Insanity: Interpretive Practice and Involuntary Commitment.* Hawthorne, NY: Aldine de Gruyter.

Irwin, John. 1987. *The Felon.* Berkeley: University of California Press.

Loseke, Donileen R. 1989. "Creating Clients." Pp. 173–193 in J. A. Holstein and G. Miller (eds.), *Perspectives on Social Problems Vol. 1.* Greenwich, CT: JAI Press.

———. 1992. *The Battered Woman and Shelters: The Social Construction of Wife Abuse.* Albany: State University of New York Press.

Maynard, Douglas. 1984. *Inside Plea Bargaining.* New York: Plenum Press.

Miller, Gale. 1991. *Enforcing the Work Ethic.* Albany: State University of New York Press.

———. 1992. "Human Service Practice as Social Problems Work." *Current Research on Occupations and Professions* 7:3–21.

Miller, Gale, and David Silverman. 1995. "Troubles Talk and Counseling Discourse: A Comparative Study." *The Sociological Quarterly* 36:725–747.

Miller, Peter, and Nikolas Rose. 1994. "On Therapeutic Authority: Psychoanalytic Expertise under Advanced Liberalism." *History of the Human Sciences* 7:29–64.

Peyrot, Mark. 1985. "Coerced Voluntarism: The Micropolitics of Drug Treatment." *Urban Life* 13:343–365.

Pfohl, Stephen J. 1978. *Predicting Dangerousness.* Lexington, MA: Lexington Books.

Pollner, Melvin. 1987. *Mundane Reason: Reality in Everyday and Sociological Discourse.* Cambridge: Cambridge University Press.

Pollner, Melvin, and Jill Stein. 1994. "Narrative Maps of Social Worlds: The Voice of Experience in Alcoholics Anonymous." *Symbolic Interaction* 19:203–223.

Potter, Jonathan. 1996. *Representing Reality: Discourse, Rhetoric, and Social Construction.* London: Sage.

Quinney, Richard. 1970. *The Social Reality of Crime.* Boston: Little, Brown.

Rose, Nikolas. 1988. "Calculable Minds and Manageable Individuals." *History of the Human Sciences* 1:179–200.

———. 1996. *Inventing Our Selves: Psychology, Power, and Personhood.* Cambridge: Cambridge University Press.

Scott, Robert A. 1969. *The Making of Blind Men: A Study of Adult Socialization.* New York: Russell Sage Foundation.

Simon, Jonathan and Malcolm M. Feeley. 1995. "True Crime: The New Penology and Public Discourse on Crime." Pp. 147–180 in T. G. Blomberg and S. Cohen (eds.), *Punishment and Social Control: Essays in Honor of Sheldon L. Messinger.* Hawthorne, NY: Aldine de Gruyter.

Skolnick, Jerome H. 1966. *Justice without Trial: Law Enforcement in Democratic Society.* New York: Wiley.

Sloop, John M. 1996. *The Cultural Prison: Discourse, Prisoners, and Punishment.* Tuscaloosa: University of Alabama Press.

Smith, Dorothy E. 1990. *The Conceptual Practices of Power: A Feminist Sociology of Knowledge.* Boston: Northeastern University Press.

Sudnow, David. 1965. "Normal Crimes: Sociological Features of the Penal Code in a Public Defender's Office." *Social Problems* 12:255–276.

Sykes, Gresham M., and David Matza. 1957. "Techniques of Neutralization: A Theory of Delinquency." *American Sociological Review* 22:664–670.

Wieder, D. Lawrence. 1974. *Language and Social Reality: The Case of Telling the Convict Code.* The Hague: Mouton.

Yochelson, Samuel, and Stanton E. Samenow. 1976. *The Criminal Personality.* New York: J. Aronson.

Young, Alison. 1996. *Imagining Crime: Textual Outlaws and Criminal Conversations.* London: Sage.

Young, Allan. 1995. *The Harmony of Illusions: Inventing Post-Traumatic Stress Disorder.* Princeton, NJ: Princeton University Press.

Experts on Battered Women

DONILEEN R. LOSEKE and SPENCER E. CAHILL

People create deviant categories and theories about the people to whom they are applied. These categorizations and conceptualizations can vary in different cultures and historical periods. The rise, fall, and recreation of deviant categories and perspectives turn out to be increasingly characteristic. More often than not, these new deviant categories are the work of social movements, which are coalitions of people and organizations that seek to produce social change. Sometimes such movements have an interest in defining a pattern of social behavior as deviant and requiring the intervention of "experts" to understand and change the behavior.

A paradox of the work of such social movements is the emergence of a social construction that, on the one hand, simplifies the complexity of the behavior under review and, on the other hand, claims that only the "experts" they designate are capable of changing the behavior the movement has reconceptualized. The movement may disregard diversity among the persons categorized by their deviant category or the fact that, for many of these people, the behavior is not most correctly characterized as being pathological.

Donileen R. Loseke and Spencer E. Cahill show how the rebirth of feminism as a social movement gave rise to a new conception of the victims of domestic violence. In essence, a new deviant social type emerged—"battered women who remain with their mates." Such a decision on the part of battered women was viewed by the "experts" as an unreasonable one. A theory was constructed that suggested that what could be considered pathological traits on the part of the women is what explained the continuation of their relationships with these men. Loseke and Cahill view this conceptualization by the "experts" as based on folklore rather than empirical evidence and as being one that created a new clientele for their services. In its place, the authors present a theory that does not characterize battered women who remain with their mates as being pathological, unusual, or deviant.

During the 1970s, women's movement activists succeeded in focusing public attention on the topic of wife assault.[1] While the phenomenon itself was not new, contemporary feminists were the first to argue that wife assault was not merely a private trouble but a social issue as well. They asserted that public attention and resources were required in order to assist the immediate victims of this social malaise, "battered women."

While the feminist ideals underlying the movement for battered women suggested that victims of wife assault could be the only "experts" regarding their problems (Ridington, 1977–78; Segovia-Ashley, 1978; Warrior, 1978),[2] ironically, but not surprisingly, the movement was accompanied by the emergence of experts on battered women.[3] By the late 1970s, these self-identified experts were speaking on behalf of battered women to the media, in government hearings (U.S. Commission on Civil Rights, 1978;

U.S. House of Representatives, 1978), and in legal proceedings (Jones, 1980:296). A diverse group, these experts share neither a common vocabulary of discourse nor a common ideological perspective; some but not all explicitly state an allegiance to the feminist ideals underlying the movement for battered women.[4] They include academics (sociologists, psychologists, legal scholars), social service providers (social workers, nurses, lawyers, shelter workers), political activists, and journalists. Their claims to expertise are based on either intellectual study (Bass and Rice, 1979; Dobash and Dobash, 1979; Gelles, 1976; Ferraro and Johnson, 1983; Hofeller, 1982; Langley and Levy, 1977; Morgan, 1982; Pagelow, 1981a,b; Roy, 1977; Truninger, 1971), practical experience in social service provision (Fleming, 1979; Hendrix et al., 1978; Pizzey, 1979; Rounsaville, 1978; Shainess, 1977), or both (Hilberman, 1980; McShane, 1979; Walker, 1979, 1983).

Despite this diversity, the experts on battered women share a fundamentally important belief. As members of what Berger and Berger (1983:38) call the "knowledge class," these experts believe that their understandings should be used to educate and assist those who are less knowledgeable and fortunate. Among experts on battered women, this belief in the necessity of expert intervention in others' everyday matters is reflected in their common, overriding concern with a particular issue: Why do battered women remain in relationships with abusive mates? This question has been the explicit and almost sole concern of two books (Pagelow, 1981a; Walker, 1979), four academic journal articles (Bass and Rice, 1979; Ferraro and Johnson, 1983; Gelles, 1976; Pagelow, 1981b), and five chapters in larger works or edited volumes (Davidson, 1978; Dobash and Dobash, 1979; Langley and Levy, 1977; Martin, 1976, 1979).

This paper also considers the question "why do they stay?" However, we focus not on the behaviors of battered women *per se,* but on the experts. We look at how, by both asking and answering this question, the experts have constructed a new category of deviance: battered women who remain with their mates.[5] Three interrelated questions are also addressed. First, we analyze the question itself to see what asking it implies about battered women. Second, we examine the general character of the experts' responses to this question. Third, we consider the quality of the evidence offered by the experts in support of these responses. Initially, we suggest an alternative vocabulary for battered women's motives.

SOCIOLOGICAL IMPLICATIONS OF THE QUESTION

The question "why do they stay?" implicitly defines the parameters of the social problem of battered women. By asking this question, the experts imply that assaulted wives are of two basic types: those who leave their mates and those who do not. Not only are possible distinctions among assaulted wives who remain with their mates implicitly ignored, but so too are the unknown number of assaulted wives who quickly terminate such relationships. By focusing attention on those who stay, the experts imply that assaulted wives who remain with their mates are more needy and deserving of public and expert concern than those who do not. In fact, some of the experts have explicitly defined battered women as women who *remain* in relationships containing violence (Ferraro and Johnson, 1983; Pizzey, 1979; Scott, 1974; Walker, 1979).

Moreover, the experts' common and overriding concern with the question of why assaulted wives stay reveals their shared definition of the normatively expected response to the experience of battering. To ask why assaulted wives remain with their mates is to imply that doing so requires explanation. In general, as Scott and Lyman (1968) have noted, normatively expected behavior does not require explanation. It is normatively unanticipated, untoward acts which require what Scott and Lyman term an "account." By asking why battered women stay, therefore, the experts implicitly define leaving one's mate as the normatively expected response to the experience of wife assault. Staying, on the other hand, is implicitly defined as deviant, an act "which is perceived (i.e., recognized) as violating expectations" (Hawkins and Tiedeman, 1975:59).

In other words, once the experts identify a woman as battered, normative expectations regarding marital stability are reversed. After all, separated and divorced persons are commonly called upon to explain why their relationships "didn't work out" (Weiss, 1975). It is typically marital stability, "staying," which is normatively expected and marital instability, "leaving," which requires an account. However, as far as the experts on battered women are concerned, once wife assault occurs, it is marital stability which requires explanation.

In view of the experts' typifications of relationships within which wife assault occurs, this reversal of normative expectations seems only logical. Although research indicates that the severity and frequency of wife assault varies considerably across couples (Straus *et al.*, 1980), the experts stress that, *on the average,* wife assault is more dangerous for victims than is assault by a stranger (U.S. Department of Justice, 1980). Moreover, most experts maintain that once wife assault has occurred within a relationship it will become more frequent and severe over time (Dobash and Dobash, 1979), and few believe that this pattern of escalating violence can be broken without terminating the relationship.[6] It is hardly surprising, therefore, that the experts on battered women define "leaving" as the expected, reasonable, and desirable response to the experience of wife assault.[7] Staying, in contrast, is described as "maladaptive choice behavior" (Waites, 1977–78), "self-destruction through inactivity" (Rounsaville, 1978), or, most concisely, "deviant" (Ferraro and Johnson, 1983). For the experts, battered women who remain with their mates pose an intellectual puzzle: Why are they so unreasonable? Why do they stay?

To ask such a question is to request an account. Experts who provide answers to this question are, therefore, offering accounts on behalf of battered women who remain with their mates. According to Scott and Lyman (1968), two general types of accounts are possible: justifications and excuses. A justification is an account which acknowledges the actor's responsibility for the behavior in question but challenges the imputation of deviance ("I did it, but I didn't do anything wrong"). An excuse, on the other hand, acknowledges the deviance of the behavior in question but relieves the actor of responsibility for it ("I did something wrong, but it wasn't my fault").

Clearly, these different types of accounts elicit different kinds of responses. If the behavior in question is socially justifiable, then the actor was behaving reasonably, as normatively expected. The actor's ability or competence to manage everyday affairs without interference is not called into question (Garfinkel, 1967:57). In contrast, excusing behavior implies that the actor cannot manage everyday affairs without interference. Although the behavior is due to circumstances beyond the actor's control, it is admittedly deviant. By implication, assistance from others may be required if the actor is to avoid behaving similarly in the future. In order to fully understand the experts' responses to battered women who remain with their mates it is necessary, therefore, to determine which type of account they typically offer on behalf of such women.

THE EXPERTS' ACCOUNTS

Experts on battered women are a diverse group. This diversity is reflected in the emphasis each expert places on various accounts, in the number of accounts offered, and in how series of accounts are combined to produce complex theoretical explanations. Despite such diversity, however, there is a sociologically important similarity among the experts' accounts. None of the experts argues that "staying" is justifiable. "Staying" is either explicitly or implicitly defined as unreasonable, normatively unexpected, and, therefore, deviant. By implication, the accounts offered by the experts are excuses for women's deviant behavior, and they offer two basic types.[8] Battered women are said to remain with their mates because of external constraints on their behavior or because of internal constraints. In either case, the accounts offered by the experts acknowledge the deviance of staying but relieve battered women of responsibility for doing so.

EXTERNAL CONSTRAINTS

Almost all contemporary experts on battered women maintain that staying is excusable due to external constraints on women's behavior (Dobash and Dobash, 1979; Freeman, 1979; Langley and Levy, 1977; Martin, 1976; Pagelow, 1981a,b; Pizzey, 1979; Ridington, 1977–78; Roy, 1977; Shainess, 1977).

> *Why does she not leave? The answer is simple. If she has children but no money and no place to go, she has no choice. (Fleming, 1979:83)*

Clearly, such accounts are based on the assumption that battered women who stay are economically dependent upon their mates. If a woman has no money and no place to go, she cannot be held responsible for the unreasonable act of staying. She has no choice.

Although this excuse is the most prevalent in the literature on battered women, further elaboration is necessary. In its simplest form, such an account can be easily challenged: What about friends, family, the welfare system, and other social service agencies? In response to such challenges, experts must offer accounts which will excuse women for not taking advantage of such assistance. Experts meet these challenges with at least two further accounts of external constraints. First, experts claim that most battered women are interpersonally isolated. Even if they are not, family and friends are said to typically blame women for their problems instead of providing assistance (Carlson, 1977; Dobash and Dobash, 1971; Fleming, 1979; Hilberman and Munson, 1977–78; Truninger, 1971). Second, experts claim that social service agencies typically provide little, if

any, assistance. In fact, experts maintain that the organization of agencies (bureaucratic procedures and agency mandates to preserve family stability) and the behavior of agency personnel (sexism) discourage battered women who attempt to leave (Bass and Rice, 1979; Davidson, 1978; Dobash and Dobash, 1970; Higgins, 1978; Martin, 1976, 1978; McShane, 1979; Pizzey, 1979; Prescott and Letko, 1977; Truninger, 1971). In other words, the experts maintain that battered women can expect little assistance in overcoming their economic dependency. According to the experts, the excuse of economic dependency should be honored given the additional excuses of unresponsive friends, family, and social service agencies.

Although the external constraint type of excuse acknowledges that staying is unreasonable, it relieves battered women of the responsibility for doing so. Battered women who remain with their mates are portrayed as "more acted upon than acting" (Sykes and Matza, 1957:667). The implication, of course, is that women would leave (i.e., they would be reasonable) if external constraints could be overcome. The experts provide a warrant, therefore, for intervention in battered women's everyday affairs. In order to act reasonably and leave, battered women must overcome the external constraint of economic dependency which they cannot do without the assistance of specialized experts.

Despite the prevalence of external constraint accounts in the literature on battered women, most experts consider such excuses insufficient. Instead of, or in addition to, such accounts, the experts maintain that battered women face a second type of constraint on their behavior. Although few contemporary experts argue that women stay because they enjoy being the objects of abuse, that they are masochistic, the experts do maintain that battered women face various "internal constraints."[9]

INTERNAL CONSTRAINTS

Some experts have proposed that biographically accumulated experiences may lead women to define violence as "normal" and "natural" (Ball,

1977; Gelles, 1976; Langley and Levy, 1977; Lion, 1977). Likewise, according to some experts, women define violence as a problem only if it becomes severe and/or frequent "enough" (Carlson, 1977; Gelles, 1976; Moore, 1979; Rounsaville and Weissman, 1977–78).[10] If violence is not subjectively defined as a "problem," then women have no reason to consider leaving.

For the most part, experts have focused their attention on documenting internal constraints which are said to prevent women from leaving their mates *even when* violence is subjectively defined as a problem. Experts suggest two major sources of such internal constraints: femininity and the experience of victimization.

To many experts, the primary source of internal constraints is the femininity of battered women. Attributes commonly regarded as "feminine" are automatically attributed to battered women, especially when these characteristics can conceivably account for why such women might remain with their mates. For example, women who stay are said to be emotionally dependent upon their mates (Dobash and Dobash, 1979; Fleming, 1979; Freeman, 1979; Langley and Levy, 1977; Moore, 1979; Pizzey, 1979; Roy, 1977); to have a poor self-image or low self-esteem (Carlson, 1977; Freeman, 1979; Langley and Levy, 1977; Lieberknecht, 1978; Martin, 1976; Morgan, 1982; Ridington, 1977–78; Star *et al.*, 1979; Truninger, 1971); and to have traditional ideas about women's "proper place."[11] In isolation or in combination, these so-called feminine characteristics are said to internally constrain women's behavior. According to the experts, women find it subjectively difficult to leave their mates even when violence is defined as a problem.

Internal constraints are also said to follow from the process of victimization itself. According to the experts, battered women not only display typically feminine characteristics, but they also develop unique characteristics due to the victimization process. For example, some experts have argued that once a woman is assaulted she will fear physical reprisal if she leaves (Lieberknecht,

1978; Martin, 1979; Melville, 1978). Other physical, emotional, and psychological after-effects of assault are also said to discourage battered women from leaving their mates (Moore, 1979; Roy, 1977). Indeed, battered women are sometimes said to develop complex psychological problems from their victimization. These include the "stress-response syndrome" (Hilberman, 1980), "enforced restriction of choice" (Waites, 1977–78), "learned helplessness" (Walker, 1979), or responses similar to those of the "rape trauma syndrome" (Hilberman and Munson, 1977–78). A symptom common to all such diagnostic categories is that sufferers find it subjectively difficult to leave their mates.

As with external constraint excuses, these internal constraint accounts also acknowledge the deviance of remaining in a relationship containing violence while, at the same time, relieving battered women of responsibility for doing so. They function in this way, as excuses, because the various internal constraints attributed to battered women are identified as beyond their personal control. Clearly, battered women are not responsible for their gender socialization or for the physical violence they have suffered. In other words, both external and internal constraint accounts portray battered women who stay with their mates as more acted upon than acting. What women require, "for their own good," is assistance in overcoming the various barriers which prevent them from acting reasonably. Thus, both types of accounts offered by the experts on behalf of battered women who stay provide grounds for expert intervention in these women's everyday affairs.

As Scott and Lyman (1968) have pointed out, the criteria in terms of which accounts are evaluated vary in relation to the situation in which they are offered, the characteristics of the audience, and the identity of the account provider. In the present context, the identity of the account provider is of particular interest. When experts provide accounts which implicitly serve to promote their right to intervene in others' affairs, an important evaluative criterion is the quality of supportive evidence they offer. Experts who speak on behalf of others are expected to do so on the basis of uncommon knowledge. If, therefore, the evidence which the experts offer in support of their accounts for why battered women stay fails to confirm the expectation of uncommon knowledge, then their claim to be speaking and acting on such women's behalf is open to question.

THE EVIDENCE FOR EXPERTS' ACCOUNTS

How do experts obtain their knowledge about the experiences and behavior of battered women? In order to explore the experts' claim to uncommon knowledge, we address three questions: From whom is evidence obtained (the issue of generalizability)? By what means is evidence obtained (the issue of validity)? How consistently does the evidence support the accounts offered (the issue of reliability)?

1) GENERALIZABILITY

Experts on battered women claim to have knowledge of the experiences and behavior of women who remain in relationships containing violence. Yet, while there is general agreement that many battered women suffer in silence, with few exceptions the experts have studied only those assaulted wives who have come to the attention of social service agencies, many of whom have already left their mates.[12] Women who contact social service agencies have decided that they require expert intervention in their private affairs, and there is good reason to believe that such women differ from women who have *not* sought assistance.

The decision to seek professional help is typically preceded by a complex process of problem definition, and this process is invariably more difficult and of longer duration when the problem involves the behavior of a family member (Goffman, 1969; Schwartz, 1957; Weiss, 1975; Yarrow *et al.*, 1955). Regardless of the nature of the problem, this definitional process seems to follow a fairly predictable pattern. Only as a

last resort are professional helpers contacted (Emerson and Messinger, 1977; Kadushin, 1969; Mechanic, 1975). Since it is primarily the experiences of women who have reached the end of this help-seeking process which provide evidence for experts' accounts, the generalizability of this evidence is questionable.

2) VALIDITY

When not simply stating their own perceptions of battered women, experts obtain their evidence in one of two ways. They sometimes question other experts and they sometimes directly question women. Clearly, others' perceptions, whether expert or not, are of uncertain validity. However, even the evidence based on battered women's responses to the question "why do you stay?" is of doubtful validity.

To ask a battered woman to respond to this question is to request that she explain her apparently deviant behavior. This leaves her two alternatives. She can either justify her staying ("I love him"; "he's not all bad"; "the kids need him") or she can excuse her behavior. Since experts have predefined staying as undeniably deviant, it is unlikely that they will honor a justification. Indeed, some experts on battered women have explicitly characterized justifications for staying as "rationalizations," accounts which are self-serving and inaccurate (Ferraro and Johnson, 1983; Waites, 1977–78). Given the experts' presuppositions about the behavior of "staying" and the typical desire of persons to maintain "face" (Goffman, 1955), it is likely that the only accounts the experts will honor—excuses—are subtly elicited by the experts who question battered women. If this is so, then the experts, by asking women why they remain with their mates, have merely constructed an interactional situation which will produce evidence confirming the accounts they offer on women's behalf.[13]

It is hardly surprising, therefore, that the experts on battered women offer remarkably similar accounts of why women stay. This is particularly visible in the evidence which supports the external constraint accounts. By almost exclusively interviewing women who turn to inexpensive or free social service agencies and then constructing an interactional situation which is likely to elicit a particular type of account, experts practically ensure that their presuppositions about external constraints are confirmed.[20] In brief, the validity of the experts' evidence is doubtful.

3) RELIABILITY

Relying primarily on evidence from interviewing and observation, the experts on battered women offer amazingly similar accounts of why women remain. There are, however, many ways to obtain evidence. The question at hand is whether evidence gained from interviewing and observation is similar to evidence obtained using other methods.

If the economic dependency (external constraint) excuse is to avoid challenge, it must be supplemented by the additional excuses of unresponsive friends, family members, and social service agencies. Yet, evidence to support these supplementary external constraint excuses is less than overwhelming. In fact, some evidence undermines the excuse that social service agencies and providers discourage battered women from leaving their mates. Pagelow (1981a) found little relationship between her measures of "agency response" and the amount of time battered women had remained with their mates. Hofeller (1982) found that many battered women self-reported being either "completely" or "somewhat" satisfied with the efforts of social service agencies on their behalf.[21]

As with the excuse of unresponsive social service agencies, available evidence conflicts with various internal constraint accounts offered by the experts. For example, available evidence does not support assertions that battered women hold traditional beliefs about "women's proper place," or that these beliefs internally constrain women from leaving their mates. Walker (1983) reports that battered women perceive themselves to be *less* traditional than "other women," and the results of experimental studies conducted by

Hofeller (1982) and Rosenbaum and O'Leary (1981) indicate that women who have *not* been victims of wife assault hold more traditional attitudes than women who are victims. Moreover, Pagelow (1981a) reports that her measures of "traditional ideology" did not help explain the length of time battered women remained with their mates.

The experts have also maintained that the low self-esteem assumed to be common to women in general is exacerbated by the process of victimization, producing a powerful internal constraint on the behavior of battered women. Yet in their now classic review of research evidence regarding sex differences in self-esteem, Maccoby and Jacklin (1974:15) labelled as a popular myth the commonsense deduction that "women, knowing that they belong to a sex that is devalued, . . . must have a poor opinion of themselves." Contrary to this commonsense deduction, sex differences in self-esteem have rarely been found in experimental studies, and when they have, women's self-esteem is often higher than men's. In addition, at least two studies contained in the literature on battered women refute the statement that battered women have lower self-esteem than women who have not experienced assault. Walker (1983) found that battered women reported their self-esteem as higher than that of "other women," and Star (1978) found that shelter residents who had *not* experienced wife assault scored lower on an "ego-strength" scale than residents who had been assaulted.

In short, the evidence provided to support expert claims about battered women is, by scientific standards, less than convincing. In fact, it appears as if the experts' accounts are presupposed and then implicitly guide both the gathering and interpretation of evidence. In constructing their accounts, the experts have employed the commonsense practice of automatically attributing to individual women (in this case, battered women) sets of traits based on their sex. As females, battered women are automatically assumed to be economically and emotionally dependent upon their mates, to have low self-esteem, and to hold traditional attitudes and beliefs. Methodologies which might yield conflicting evidence are seldom used, and when seemingly conflicting evidence is uncovered it is often explained away. For example, Walker (1983:40) implicitly argues that battered women have an inaccurate perception of themselves. She interprets the finding that battered women consider themselves to be in control of their own behavior as a "lack of acknowledgement that her batterer *really* is in control" (emphasis added). Likewise, Pagelow (1981a) discredits seemingly conflicting evidence by challenging her own measures; the presupposed accounts are not questioned. In other words, the interpretive force of the "master status" of sex "overpowers" evidence to the contrary (Hughes, 1945:357). What the experts on battered women offer in support of their accounts for why women remain is not uncommon knowledge, therefore, but professional "folklore" which, however sophisticated, remains folklore (Zimmerman and Pollner, 1970:44).

This does not mean that evidence which conflicts with the experts' accounts is itself above question. On the contrary, the generalizability, reliability, and validity of conflicting evidence are also problematic. For example, both Pagelow (1981a) and Star (1978) used paper and pencil tests, and both studies were primarily concerned with residents of shelters in urban southern California. Likewise, Walker's (1979, 1983) findings are based primarily on clinical records of an unrepresentative group of women, and evidence regarding self-esteem is primarily derived from experimental studies involving only college students.

The sociologically intriguing issue is not, however, the "truthfulness" of accounts. In a diverse society, a variety of different vocabularies of motive (Mills, 1940) are available for making sense out of the complex interrelationships between actor, biography, situation, and behavior. Under such circumstances, "what is reason for one man is mere rationalization for another" (Mills, 1940:910). Any attempt to ascertain battered women's "true" motives would therefore be an exercise in what Mills termed "motive-mongering."

What is of sociological interest is that the experts' accounts are not based upon uncommon knowledge but upon commonsense deductions best described as folklore. Clearly, this should raise questions about both the experts' claim to be speaking on battered women's behalf and their claim to have the right to intervene in such women's private affairs.

Given the experts' claim to be speaking and acting in battered women's "best interests," the sociologically important issue is the relative plausibility of the particular vocabulary of motive used by the experts. According to the experts, their primary concerns are the condemnation and elimination of wife assault, tasks which are likely to require specialized expertise. The vocabulary of motive which supports this agenda is one of highlighting "constraints" on women's behavior which must be overcome in order for them to behave reasonably—that is, in order for them to leave. But such a vocabulary is not the only plausible way to make sense of women's behavior.

AN ALTERNATIVE VOCABULARY OF MOTIVE

Prior to the 1970s, the problems of battered women received little attention. In contrast, the contemporary experts have portrayed women as little more than victims. The tendency has been to define both battered women and their relationships with their mates almost exclusively in terms of the occurrence and effects of physical and emotional assault. Battered women are simply defined as assaulted wives who remain with assaultive mates (Ferraro and Johnson, 1983; Pizzey, 1979; Scott, 1974; Walker, 1979), and their relationships are portrayed as no more than victimizing processes. Such a focus leads to what Barry (1979) has termed "victimism," knowing a person only as a victim. One effect of the victimism practiced by the experts on battered women is that possible experiential and behavioral similarities between battered women and other persons are overlooked. It is simply assumed that the occurrence and experience of assault clearly distinguish battered women and their relationships from individuals in cross-sex relationships which do not contain violence. However, even a cursory review of the sociological literature on marital stability and instability suggests that, at least in regard to their reluctance to leave their mates, battered women are quite similar to both other women and to men.

This literature consistently indicates that marital stability often outlives marital quality. Goode (1956) found that such stability was only sometimes due to the obvious, objective costs of terminating the relationship ("external constraints"). Contrary to predictions that relationships will terminate when apparent "costs" outweigh apparent "benefits," it is not at all unusual for relationships to be sustained even when outsiders perceive costs to be greater than benefits. Although experts on battered women have argued that leaving a relationship means that a woman's status will change from "wife" to "divorcee" (Dobash and Dobash, 1979; Truninger, 1971), a variety of family sociologists have noted that terminating a relationship is far more complex than is suggested by the concept of "status change." Over time, marital partners develop an "attachment" to one another (Weiss, 1975), a "crescive bond" (Turner, 1970), a "shared biography" (McLain and Weigert, 1979). As a result, each becomes uniquely irreplaceable in the eyes of the other. Such a personal commitment to a specific mate has been found to persist despite decreases in marital partners' liking, admiration, and/or respect for one another (Rosenblatt, 1977; Weiss, 1975). Battered women who remain in relationships which outsiders consider costly are not, therefore, particularly unusual or deviant.

Moreover, the sociological literature on marital stability and instability suggests that the process of separation and divorce, what Vaughan (1979) terms "uncoupling," is typically difficult. One indication of the difficulty of this process is the considerable time uncoupling often takes (Cherlin, 1981; Goode, 1956; Weiss, 1975). It is also typical for a series of temporary separations to

precede a permanent separation (Lewis and Spanier, 1979; Weiss, 1975; Vaughan, 1979). In brief, the lengthy "leaving and returning" cycle said to be characteristic of battered women is a typical feature of the uncoupling process. Further, the guilt, concern, regret, bitterness, disappointment, depression, and lowered perception of self attributed to battered women are labels for emotions often reported by women and men in the process of uncoupling (Spanier and Castro, 1979; Weiss, 1975).

Although the experts attribute unusual characteristics and circumstances to battered women who remain with their mates, the reluctance of battered women to leave can be adequately and commonsensically expressed in the lyrics of a popular song: "Breaking up is hard to do." It can also be expressed in the more sophisticated vocabulary of sociological psychology: Individuals who are terminating intimate relationships "die one of the deaths that is possible" for them (Goffman, 1952). The sociological literature on marital stability and instability does suggest, therefore, an alternative to the vocabulary of battered women's motives provided by the experts on battered women. Because a large portion of an adult's self is typically invested in their relationship with their mate, persons become committed and attached to this mate as a uniquely irreplaceable individual. Despite problems, "internal constraints" are experienced when contemplating the possibility of terminating the relationship with the seemingly irreplaceable other. Again, if this is the case, then women who remain in relationships containing violence are not unusual or deviant; they are typical.

Some experts on battered women have reported evidence which supports this alternative characterization of the motives of women who remain. Gayford (1975) reports that half of his sample of battered women claimed to be satisfied with their relationships, and Dobash and Dobash (1979) note that, apart from the violence, battered women often express positive feelings toward their mates. Moreover, Ferraro and Johnson (1983) report that battered women typically believe that their mates are the only person they could love, and Walker (1979) reports that battered women often describe their mates as playful, attentive, exciting, sensitive, and affectionate. Yet, because of the victimism they practice, experts on battered women often fail to recognize that such findings demonstrate the multi-dimensionality of battered women's relationships with their mates. Indeed, some of these experts have explicitly advised that battered women's expressions of attachment and commitment to their mates not be believed:

> The statement that abused wives love their husbands need not be taken at face value. It may represent merely a denial of ambivalence or even unmitigated hatred. (Waites, 1977–78:542)

> The only reasons the woman does not end the marriage are dependence—emotional or practical—and fear of change and the unknown. These are often masked as love or so the woman deludes herself. (Shainess, 1977:118)

Such expressions of commitment and attachment are *justifications* for why a person might remain with their mate. To honor such a justification would be to acknowledge that staying in a relationship which contains violence is not necessarily deviant. In order to sustain their claim to expertise, therefore, the experts on battered women cannot acknowledge the possible validity of this alternative, "justifying" vocabulary of motive even when it is offered by battered women themselves. In other words, the experts discredit battered women's interpretations of their own experiences. The justifications offered by battered women are reinterpreted by the experts as merely "symptoms" of the Stockholm Syndrome (Ochlberg, 1980), of an "addiction" which "must be overcome" (Waites, 1977–78), or as the "miracle glue" which "binds a battered woman to her batterer" (Walker, 1979:xvi). By reinterpreting the justifications of battered women in these ways, the experts sustain their claim that such women require the assistance of specialized experts.

CONCLUSIONS

This case study of the social construction of deviance by a group of experts illustrates how members of the knowledge class create a new clientele for their services. In effect, experts discredit the ability of a category of persons to manage their own affairs without interference. The actors in question are portrayed as incapable of either understanding or controlling the factors which govern their behavior. In order for them to understand their experiences and gain control over their behavior, by implication, they require the assistance of specialized experts. Because the category of actors which compose such a clientele are characterized as unreasonable and incompetent, any resistance they offer to the experts' definitions and intervention is easily discredited. For example, battered women's attempts to justify staying with their mates are often interpreted by the experts as further evidence of such women's unreasonableness and incompetence. Experts are able to sustain their claims to be speaking and acting on others' behalf, therefore, despite the protests of those on whose behalf they claim to be speaking and acting.

We do not mean to suggest that experts' potential clientele do not benefit from experts' efforts. For example, the experts on battered women have played a major role in focusing public attention on the plight of the victims of wife assault. In doing so, they have helped to dispel the popular myth that these women somehow deserved to be assaulted. In turn, this has undoubtedly encouraged the general public, the police, the courts, and various social service agencies to be more responsive and sensitive to the needs of such women. Yet, battered women may pay a high price for this assistance.

The experts on battered women define leaving one's mate as the normatively expected, reasonable response to the experience of wife assault. By implication, staying with one's mate after such an experience requires explanation. In order to explain this unreasonable response, the experts have provided accounts, that is, ascribed motives to battered women which excuse such deviance. As Blum and McHugh (1971:106) have noted, "observer's ascription of motive serves to formulate . . . persons." In offering accounts on behalf of battered women who stay, the experts propose a formulation of the type of persons such women are. For example, the experts characterize this type of person as "oversocialized into feminine identity" (Ball and Wyman 1977–78), "bewildered and helpless" (Ball, 1977), "immature" and lacking clear self-identities (Star *et al.*, 1979), "overwhelmingly passive" and "unable to act on their own behalf" (Hilberman and Munson, 1977–79), and cognitively, emotionally, and motivationally "deficient" (Walker, 1977–78). Moreover, these women are described as suffering from either the "battered wife syndrome" (Morgan, 1982; Walker, 1983) or the "adult maltreatment syndrome" in Section 995.8 of the International Classification of Diseases. They are "society's problem" (Martin, 1978). Clearly, the categorical identity of battered women is a deeply discrediting one. As Hawkins and Tiedeman (1975) have noted, such typifications of persons by experts often have significant, practical consequences. The experts' descriptions of such "types" often serve as "processing stereotypes" which influence the perceptions and responses of social service providers. Indeed, Loseke (1982) documented how the experts' typifications of battered women served as a processing stereotype which influenced workers' perceptions and service provision at a shelter for battered women.

In summary, once a woman admits that she is a victim of wife assault, her competence is called into question if she does not leave. She is defined as a type of person who requires assistance, a person who is unable to manage her own affairs. As a result, the experts on battered women have constructed a situation where victims of wife assault may lose control over their self-definitions, interpretations of experience, and, in some cases, control over their private affairs. In a sense, battered women may now be victimized twice, first by their mates and then by the experts who claim to speak on their behalf.

NOTES

1. Consistent with the literature under review, we use the terms *marriage* and *wife* in a purely sociological, rather than legal, sense. *Marriage* refers to any continuing, cross-sex relationship and *wife* to a female participant in such a relationship.
2. For a history of the feminist-identified battered women's movement see Schechter (1983).
3. Straus (1974) has argued that three social factors combined in the 1970s to bring the topic of family violence to the attention of academics: the emergence of a politically vocal women's movement, public concern about all forms of violence, and the decline of consensus models of society.
4. See Wardell *et al.* (1983) for a discussion of disagreements among those who state an allegiance to feminist ideals.
5. See Morgan (1981), Wardell *et al.* (1983), and Stark and Flitcraft (1983) for discussions of how experts have shaped public understandings of the phenomenon of wife assault.
6. There has been little systematic study of the possibility of change in relationships. Walker (1979) reports that her pessimism is based on clinical experience. See Coleman (1980) for a more optimistic prognosis.
7. Of course, this commonsense deduction is also based on the common, although often unspoken, assumption that humans are "rational actors." If the basis of human motivation is a desire to maximize rewards and minimize costs, then why would a battered woman remain in such an obviously "costly" relationship?
8. A third type of explanation for why victims of wife assault remain with their mates is seldom found in the literature on battered women and, therefore, will not be reviewed here. This type of explanation is based on a systems theory analysis of family interactions. Straus (1974) suggests the empirical applicability of such an approach, and Denzin (1983) provides a phenomenological foundation. Erchak (1981) used this approach to explain the maintenance of child abuse, and Giles-Sims (1983) has used this to explain the behavior of battered women.
9. Theories focusing on feminine masochism have been proposed by Snell *et al.* (1964) and Gayford (1975). Waites (1977–78) suggested that the "appearance" of masochism results from "enforced restriction of choice." Most experts argue that the concept of masochism is not applicable to battered women (Breines and Gordon, 1983).

10. Empirical testing of the association between leaving and childhood experiences has not confirmed this theory (Pagelow, 1981a; Star, 1978; Walker, 1977–78). Likewise, empirical testing of the association between leaving and "severity/frequency" has also not supported theory. See Pagelow (1981b) for a complete discussion.

11. "Traditional ideology" includes such beliefs as: divorce is a stigma (Dobash and Dobash, 1979; Langley and Levy, 1977; Moore, 1979; Roy, 1977); the children need their father (Dobash and Dobash, 1979); the woman assumes responsibility for the actions of her mate (Fleming, 1979; Langley and Levy, 1977; Martin, 1976); or feels embarrassed about the family situation (Ball and Wyman, 1977–78; Fleming, 1979; Hendrix et al., 1978).

12. Exceptions are Gelles (1976), Hofeller (1982), and Rosenbaum and O'Leary (1981), who included matched samples of persons not receiving services, and Prescott and Letko (1977), who used information from women who responded to an advertisement in Ms. magazine.

13. The situation is more complicated when women who have left are asked why did you stay? Or, as Dobash and Dobash (1979:147) asked: "why do you think you stayed with him as long as you did?" In such situations, the question asks women to retrospectively reconstruct their personal biographies based on their current circumstances and understandings.

14. However, Rounsaville (1978) found that "lack of resources" did not distinguish between women who had left and women who had not left.

15. The "satisfaction" of victims with social services varies considerably by the type of agency (Hofeller, 1982; Prescott and Letko, 1977).

REFERENCES

Ball, Margaret. 1977. "Issues of Violence in Family Casework." *Social Casework* 58(1):3–12.

Ball, Patricia G., and Elizabeth Wyman. 1977–78. "Battered Wives and Powerlessness: What Can Counselors Do?" *Victimology* 2(3,4):545–552.

Barry, Kathleen. 1979. *Female Sexual Slavery.* New York: Avon.

Bass, David, and Janet Rice. 1979. "Agency Responses to the Abused Wife." *Social Casework* 60 (June):338–342.

Berger, Brigitte, and Peter L. Berger. 1983. *The War over the Family.* New York: Anchor.

Blum, Alan F., and Peter McHugh. 1971. "The Social Ascription of Motives." *American Sociological Review* 36 (February):98–109.

Breines, Wini, and Linda Gordon. 1983. "The New Scholarship on Family Violence." *Signs* 8 (Spring): 490–531.

Carlson, Bonnie E. 1977. "Battered Women and Their Assailants." *Social Work* 22 (November):455–460.

Cherlin, Andrew J. 1981. *Marriage, Divorce, Remarriage.* Cambridge, MA: Harvard University Press.

Coleman, Karen Howes. 1980. "Conjugal Violence: What 33 Men Report." *Journal of Marital and Family Therapy* 6 (April): 207–214.

Davidson, Terry. 1978. *Conjugal Crime.* New York: Hawthorne.

Denzin, Norman K. 1983. "Towards a Phenomenology of Family Violence." *Paper presented at the meetings of the American Sociological Association.* Detroit, August.

Dobash, R. Emerson, and Russell Dobash. 1979. *Violence against Wives: A Case against the Patriarchy.* New York: Free Press.

Emerson, Robert M., and Sheldon L. Messinger. 1977. "The Micro-politics of Trouble." *Social Problems* 25 (December):121–134.

Erchak, Gerald M. 1981. "The Escalation and Maintenance of Child Abuse: A Cybernetic Model." *Child Abuse and Neglect* 5:153–157.

Ferraro, Kathleen J., and John M. Johnson. 1983. "How Women Experience Battering: The Process of Victimization." *Social Problems* 30 (February): 325–339.

Fleming, Jennifer Baker. 1979. *Stopping Wife Abuse.* New York: Anchor Books.

Freeman, M. D. A. 1979. *Violence in the Home.* Westmead, England: Saxon House.

Garfinkel, Harold. 1967. *Studies in Ethnomethodology.* Upper Saddle River, NJ: Prentice Hall.

Gayford, J. J. 1975. "Wife Battering: A Preliminary Survey of 100 Cases." *British Medical Journal* 1:194–197.

Gelles, Richard J. 1976. "Abused Wives: Why Do They Stay?" *Journal of Marriage and the Family* 38(4):659–668.

Giles-Sims, Jean. 1983. *Wife Battering: A Systems Approach.* New York: Guilford Press.

Goffman, Erving. 1952. "On Cooling the Mark Out: Some Aspects of Adaptation to Failure." *Psychiatry* 15 (November): 451–463.

————. 1955. "On Face-Work: An Analysis of Ritual Elements in Social Interaction." *Psychiatry* 18 (August):213–231.

————. 1969. "Insanity of Place." *Psychiatry* 32 (November):352–388.

Goode, William J. 1956. *After Divorce.* Glencoe, IL: Free Press.

Hawkins, Richard, and Gary Tiedeman. 1975. *The Creation of Deviance: Interpersonal and Organizational Determinants.* Columbus, OH: Charles E. Merrill.

Hendrix, Melva Jo, Gretchen E. LaGodna, and Cynthia A. Bohen. 1978. "The Battered Wife." *American Journal of Nursing* 78 (April):650–653.

Higgins, John G. 1978. "Social Services for Abused Wives." *Social Casework* 59 (May):266–271.

Hilberman, Elaine. 1980. "Overview: The 'Wife-Beater's Wife' Reconsidered." *American Journal of Psychiatry* 137 (November).1336–1346.

Hilberman, Elaine, and Kit Munson. 1977–78. "Sixty Battered Women." *Victimology* 2(3,4):460–470.

Hofeller, Kathleen H. 1982. *Social, Psychological, and Situational Factors in Wife Abuse.* Palo Alto, CA: R. and E. Associates.

Hughes, Everett. 1945. "Dilemmas and Contradictions of Status." *American Journal of Sociology* 50 (March):353–359.

Jones, Ann. 1980. *Women Who Kill.* New York: Holt, Rinehart and Winston.

Kadushin, Charles. 1969. *Why People Go to Psychiatrists.* New York: Atherton.

Langley, Roger, and Richard C. Levy. 1977. *Wife Beating: The Silent Crisis.* New York: Pocket Books.

Lewis, Robert A., and Graham B. Spanier. 1979. "Theorizing about the Quality and Stability of Marriage." Pp. 268–294 in W. R. Burr, R. Hill, F. I. Nye, and I. L. Reiss (eds.), *Contemporary Theories About the Family,* Volume 1. New York: Free Press.

Lieberknecht, Kay. 1978. "Helping the Battered Wife." *American Journal of Nursing* 78 (April):654–656.

Lion, John R. 1977. "Clinical Aspects of Wifebattering." Pp. 126–136 in Maria Roy (ed.), *Battered Women: A Psychosociological Study of Domestic Violence.* New York: Van Nostrand.

Loseke, Donileen R. 1982. "Social Movement Theory in Practice: A Shelter for Battered Women." Unpublished Ph.D. dissertation, University of California, Santa Barbara.

Maccoby, Eleanor Emmons, and Carol Nagy Jacklin. 1974. *The Psychology of Sex Differences.* Stanford, CA: Stanford University Press.

McLain, Raymond, and Andrew Weigert. 1979. "Toward a Phenomenological Sociology of Family: A Programmatic Essay." Pp. 160–205 in W. R. Burr, R. Hill, F. I. Nye, and I. L. Reiss (eds.), *Contemporary Theories About the Family,* Volume 2. New York: Free Press.

McShane, Claudette. 1979. "Community Services for Battered Women." *Social Work* 24 (January):34–39.

Martin, Del. 1976. *Battered Wives.* San Francisco: Glide Publications.

————. 1978. "Battered Women: Society's Problem." Pp. 111–142 in J. Roberts Chapman and M. Gates (eds.), *The Victimization of Women.* Beverly Hills, CA: Sage.

————. 1979. "What Keeps a Woman Captive in a Violent Relationship? The Social Context of Battering." Pp. 33–58 in D. M. Moore (ed.), *Battered Women.* Beverly Hills, CA: Sage.

Mechanic, David. 1975. "Sociocultural and Social-Psychological Factors Affecting Personal Responses to Psychological Disorder." *Journal of Health and Social Behavior* 16(4):393–404.

Melville, Joy. 1978. "Women in refuges." Pp. 293–310 in J. P. Martin (ed.), *Violence and the Family.* New York: John Wiley.

Mills, C. Wright. 1940. "Situated Actions and Vocabularies of Motive." *American Sociological Review* 5 (December): 904–913.

Moore, Donna M. 1979. "An Overview of the Problem." Pp. 7–32 in D. M. Moore (ed.), *Battered Women.* Beverly Hills, CA: Sage.

Morgan, Patricia A. 1981. "From Battered Wife to Program Client: The State's Shaping of Social Problems." *Kapitalistate* 9:17–40.

Morgan, Steven M. 1982. *Conjugal Terrorism: A Psychological and Community Treatment Model of Wife Abuse.* Palo Alto, CA: R. and E. Associations.

Ochberg, F. M. 1980. "Victims of Terrorism." *Journal of Clinical Psychiatry* 41:73–74.

Pagelow, Mildred Daley. 1981a. *Woman-Battering: Victims and Their Experiences.* Beverly Hills, CA: Sage.

————. 1981b. "Factors Affecting Women's Decisions to Leave Violent Relationships." *Journal of Family Issues* 2 (December):391–414.

Pizzey, Erin. 1979. "Victimology Interview: A Refuge for Battered Women." *Victimology* 4(1):100–112.

Prescott, Suzanne, and Carolyn Letko. 1977. "Battered Women: A Social Psychological Perspective." Pp. 72–96 in Maria Roy (ed.), *Battered Women: A Psychosociological Study of Domestic Violence.* New York: Van Nostrand.

Ridington, Jillian. 1977–78. "The Transition Process: A Feminist Environment as Reconstructive Milieu." *Victimology* 2(3,4):563–575.

Rosenbaum, Alan, and K. Daniel O'Leary. 1981. "Marital Violence: Characteristics of Abusive Couples." *Journal of Consulting and Clinical Psychology* 49(l):63–71.

Rosenblatt, Paul C. 1977. "Needed Research on Commitment in Marriage." Pp. 73–86 in G. Levinger and H. L. Raush (eds.), *Close Relationships: Perspectives on the Meaning of Intimacy.* Amherst: University of Massachusetts.

Rounsaville, Bruce J. 1978. "Theories in Marital Violence: Evidence from a Study of Battered Women." *Victimology* 2(1,2):11–31.

Rounsaville, Bruce, and Myrna M. Weissman. 1977–78. "Battered Women: A Medical Problem Requiring Detection." *International Journal of Psychiatry in Medicine* 8(2):191–202.

Roy, Maria. 1977. "A Current Survey of 150 Cases." Pp. 25–44 in M. Roy (ed.), *Battered Women: A Psychosociological Study of Domestic Violence.* New York: Van Nostrand.

Schechter, Susan. 1983. *Women and Male Violence.* Boston: South End Press.

Schwartz, Charlotte Green. 1957. "Perspectives on Deviance: Wives' Definitions of Their Husbands' Mental Illness." *Psychiatry* 20(3):275–291.

Scott, Marvin B., and Stanford M. Lyman. 1968. "Accounts." *American Sociological Review* 33 (December):46–62.

Scott, P. D. 1974. "Battered Wives." *British Journal of Psychiatry* 125 (November):433–441.

Segovia-Ashley, Marta. 1978. "Presentation of Marta Segovia-Ashley." Pp. 98–107 in U.S. Commission on Civil Rights (ed.), *Battered Women: Issues, of Public Policy.* Washington, DC: U.S. Commission on Civil Rights.

Shainess, Natalie. 1977. "Psychological Aspects of WifeBattering." Pp. 111–118 in M. Roy (ed.), *Battered Women: A Psychosociological Study of Domestic Violence.* New York: Van Nostrand.

Snell, John E., M. D. Richard, J. Rosenwald, and Ames Robe. 1964. "The Wifebeater's Wife." *Archives of General Psychiatry* 11 (August):107–112.

Spanier, Graham, and Robert F. Castro. 1979. "Adjustment to Separation and Divorce: An Analysis of 50 Case Studies." *Journal of Divorce* 2 (Spring):241–253.

Star, Barbara. 1978. "Comparing Battered and Non-battered Women." *Victimology* 3(1,2): 32–44.

Star, Barbara, Carol G. Clark, Karen M. Goetz, and Linda O'Malia. 1979. "Psychosocial Aspects of Wife Battering." *Social Casework* 60 (October): 479–487.

Stark, Evan, and Anne Flitcraft. 1983. "Social Knowledge, Social Policy, and the Abuse of Women: The Case Against Patriarchal Benevolence." Pp. 330–348 in D. Finkelhor, R. J. Gelles, G. T. Hotaling, and M. A. Straus (eds.), *The Dark Side of Families.* Beverly Hills, CA: Sage.

Straus, Murray A. 1974. "Forward." Pp. 13–17 in Richard J. Gelles. *The Violent Home.* Beverly Hills, CA: Sage.

Straus, Murray A., Richard J. Gelles, and Suzanne Steinmetz. 1980. *Behind Closed Doors: Violence in the American Home.* New York: Anchor.

Sykes, Gresham, and David Matza. 1957. "Techniques of Neutralization: A Theory of Delinquency." *American Sociological Review* 22 (December): 664–669.

Truninger, Elizabeth. 1971. "Marital Violence: The Legal Solutions." *Hastings Law Journal* 23 (November):259–276.

Turner, Ralph. 1970. *Family Interaction.* New York: John Wiley.

U.S. Commission on Civil Rights (ed.). 1978. *Battered Women: Issues of Public Policy.* Washington, DC: U.S. Commission on Civil Rights.

U.S. Congress: House of Representatives. 1978. *Research into Violent Behavior: Domestic Violence.* Hearings Before the Sub-Committee on Domestic and International Scientific Planning, Analysis and Cooperation of the Committee on Science and Technology. 95th Congress, 2nd Session. January 10–12. Washington, DC: U.S. Government Printing Office.

U.S. Department of Justice. 1980. *Intimate Victims: A Study of Violence Among Friends and Relatives.* Washington, DC: U.S. Government Printing Office.

Vaughan, Diane. 1979. "Uncoupling: The Process of Moving from One Lifestyle to Another." *Alternative Lifestyles* 2 (November):415–442.

Waites, Elizabeth A. 1977–78. "Female Masochism and the Enforced Restriction of Choice." *Victimology* 2(3,4):535–544.

Walker, Lenore E. 1977–78. "Battered Women and Learned Helplessness." *Victimology* 2(3,4): 525–534.

———. 1979. *The Battered Woman.* New York: Harper and Row.

———. 1983. "The Battered Woman Syndrome Study." Pp. 31–48 in D. Finkelhor, R. J. Gelles, G. T. Hotaling, and M. A. Straus (eds.), *The Dark Side of Families.* Beverly Hills, CA: Sage.

Wardell, Laurie, Dair L. Gillespie, and Ann Leffler. 1983. "Science and Violence against Wives." Pp. 69–84 in D. Finkelhor, R. J. Gelles, G. T. Hotaling, and M. A. Straus (eds.), *The Dark Side of Families.* Beverly Hills, CA: Sage.

Warrior, Betsy. 1978. *Working on Wife Abuse.* 46 Pleasant Street, Cambridge, MA: privately published manual.

Weiss, Robert. 1975. *Marital Separation.* New York: Basic Books.

Yarrow, Marian Radke, Charlotte Green Schwartz, Harriet S. Murphy, and Leila Calhoun Deasy. 1955. "The Psychological Meaning of Mental Illness in the Family." *Journal of Social Issues* 11(4):12–24.

Zimmerman, Don, and Melvin Pollner. 1970. "The Everyday World as a Phenomenon." Pp. 80–104 in Jack Douglas (ed.), *Understanding Everyday Life.* Chicago: Aldine.

CHAPTER 6

ORGANIZATIONAL PROCESSING OF DEVIANTS

Discipline in an Urban School

EDWARD W. MORRIS

Common sense argues that an act of deviance is what causes social control. Interactionists, however, argue that the interrelationship between deviance and social control is more complex. For example, there may be a selective perception of deviance and, therefore, a differential enforcement of the rules. One instance is where an organization makes assumptions about race, class, and gender that guide the officials in their social reactions. Thus, agents of social control may try to control the behavior of one gender more than another and of members of a particular class and/or ethnicity more than another. This usually privileges the dominant group(s) and reproduces the dominant modes of comportment in the society.

Edward W. Morris's study of the enforcement of the dress code in an urban middle school is a case in point. The school he studied prescribed a strict dress code and then set about enforcing it. But, as Morris points out, school officials and teachers had a shared perspective that led to a pattern of selective perception and enforcement. Latino and African American boys were more likely to be labeled deviant and punished more severely for dress code violations, as were African American and Latina girls. By contrast, white and Asian American boys and girls were less often assigned a deviant status for such breaches and less severely punished. Many times their infractions were ignored by the school staff.

Being punished for what was for them typical street dress only antagonized African American and Latino boys. In the end, many of them become alienated from the school. School staff interpreted their noncompliance as resistance to their authority. Many of the teachers felt that their efforts to get these students to dress and speak "properly" would help the students, most of whom came from poor families, to acquire the social skills necessary for upward mobility. The result, however, was a telling instance of where well-intentioned social control only engendered more resistance and, at the same time, reinforced race, class, and gender stereotypes.

Virtually every day that I conducted research at Matthews Middle School,[1] a predominately minority, urban school, I heard an adult admonishing a student "Tuck in that shirt!" The prevalence of this phrase represents the connections among dress, behavior, and discipline that composed a primary but unofficial emphasis at the school. In this article I incorporate the theoretical concepts of cultural capital and bodily discipline to analyze this concern with student dress and comportment. I show how educators identified students deemed deficient in cultural capital, especially regarding manners and dress, and attempted to reform these perceived deficiencies through regulating their bodies. This process differed by race, class, and gender as interconnected, rather than distinct, concepts. Perceptions of race, class, and gender guided educators' assumptions of which students lacked cultural capital and which students required disciplinary reform. Although many school officials viewed this discipline as a way of teaching valuable social skills, it appeared instead to reinforce race, class, and gender stereotypes and had the potential to alienate many students from schooling. . . .

I explore the relationship among race, class, gender, bodily display, and discipline. . . . Using observational and interview data from an urban middle school in Texas, I expand our view of this problem to include the educational experiences of African American girls, Latino boys, and white and Asian American girls and boys. I examine how educators' assumptions about these students drove the different ways they disciplined their bodies, especially in dress and manners. School officials tended to interpret African American girls as not "ladylike" and Latino boys as oppositional and potentially dangerous, and disciplined these students regularly. White and Asian American students, by contrast, were seen as less problematic, even though they lived in the

Reprinted from Edward W. Morris, " 'Tuck in That Shirt!' Race, Class, Gender and Discipline in an Urban School," *Sociological Perspectives*, Vol. 48, No. 1: 25–48. © 2005, Pacific Sociological Association. Used by permission of the University of California Press and the author. All rights reserved.

same low-income area, and these students often avoided discipline. I suggest that educators' responses to students based on intersections of race, class, and gender resulted in disciplinary practices that could inadvertently maintain these areas of educational inequality.

METHODS

The data come from ethnographic research conducted at Matthews Middle School, located in a large Texas city. According to school records while I was there, the student body of Matthews was 47 percent African American, 40 percent Latino, 9 percent Asian American, and 4 percent white. The school was located in a predominantly poor and working-class area, and 60 percent of its students received free or reduced lunch, indicating economic disadvantage. The faculty consisted of approximately sixty teachers, administrators, and aides. According to records, the faculty was roughly two-thirds black and one-third white. The principal was an African American woman. The middle school encompassed the seventh and eighth grades and had a student population of more than one thousand. . . .

The classes and students I tutored varied but focused primarily on helping with writing, at the behest of the school. Tutoring allowed me to converse with several students (I tutored roughly 15 students one-on-one and more than 40 in group settings and in classrooms), without interviewing them formally. I observed or spoke with nearly every teacher at Matthews during my time there, and many students and teachers became familiar with me. I typically recorded classroom and lunchroom interactions and assemblies directly in a small notebook as they occurred. I conducted a student survey in order to learn how students identified themselves racially.[2] I also conducted fourteen semistructured interviews with teachers and administrators. I tape-recorded two of these interviews, but because of the uneasiness this caused the interviewees, I wrote down the other interviews as they occurred. When I could only remember the gist of what was said, I did not record this as a quote. Thus the quotes given below are not verbatim but are reasonably accurate. . . .

FINDINGS

THE IMPORTANCE OF DRESS AT MATTHEWS

Matthews was a public school but required students to wear uniforms based on the school colors—navy blue, red, or white shirts, and navy blue or khaki shorts or pants. Girls could wear navy blue or khaki skirts or skorts (half skirt, half shorts) that fell below the knee. Most sneakers and dress shoes were allowed, except sandals and boots. The school expected students to have their shirts tucked in at all times. According to teachers, the movement for uniforms at Matthews began about eight years before I started my fieldwork. Teachers told me that this was a collaborative effort between parents and the school, and the few parents I spoke with supported the uniforms. Similar to many urban schools, the uniform dress code at Matthews was intended to decrease gang activity (to rid the school of the "flying colors," according to one teacher) and make student poverty less visible. The regulation of the dress code, however, was a constant source of conflict between teachers and students.

Teachers' profound interest in instilling discipline through dress was reflected in their nearly ubiquitous calls to "tuck in that shirt!" This phrase is peppered throughout my field notes, and although adherence to the dress code was not an initial concern of my study, I soon found it emblematic of the school's exhaustive focus on bodily discipline. According to the principal, a survey of teachers conducted by the school just before I arrived found that dress code violations and discipline problems were among the top issues teachers wanted improved. Indeed, like other urban schools that require uniforms, teachers and administrators at Matthews linked the dress code to student discipline and order in general (Stanley 1996).

Beyond the uniforms, the school sought to discipline the kids[3] into wearing clothing considered appropriate on nonuniform school days and events. This discipline served as part of a hidden curriculum, emphasizing strict regulation of dress for working-class students whom adults thought did not possess knowledge of "appropriate" manners and clothing. In addition, . . . instructions in how to dress well typically fell along gendered lines. A black administrator named Ms. Adams, for example, instructed a group of girls, most of whom were black, in how to dress for one formal event by warning, "Don't come in here with no hoochie-mama dress all tight up on your butt!" (Fieldnotes, 4/12/01). I also observed other school officials, all of them African American women, critiquing girls (who were almost always African American as well), for wearing "hoochie-mama" clothing. These adults appeared to identify the styles of black girls in particular as overly sexual and sought to reform them (see also Collins 1990, 1998).

However, concerns over clothing and appearance were not just directed toward girls. Adults also feared that boys, especially black and Hispanic boys, might wear something considered inappropriate to formal events, such as oversized pants that sagged below the waist. Several African American men and women at the school encouraged boys to dress like "gentlemen," even giving some practical advice such as not wearing white socks with a suit. In this sense, these boys appeared to educators to display "marginalized masculinities," interpreted as overly coarse and aggressive (Connell 1995). Educators aimed to reform these styles and behaviors into what were perceived to be mainstream masculine forms. School officials viewed the gendered prescription of dress for both girls and boys as a central part of teaching the students appropriate manners. In this process, they distinguished "street" styles, which they deemed brash, from "appropriate," conservative styles of dress and behavior. . . .

Many adults thought that teaching students "the rules" of dress and manners, including adherence to the dress code, was an important way to prepare students for future success. School officials viewed their discipline of students' bodies, especially in appropriately masculine and feminine ways, as transmitting cultural capital—modeling the type of dress and conduct that could be linked to upward mobility.[4]

However, school officials did not appear concerned with the dress and manners of all students in the same way. Disciplinary action differed according to how perceptions of race and class interacted with perceptions of masculinity and femininity. In my observations, disciplinary focus at Matthews took three general forms, which I discuss in detail below. First, educators were concerned with "ladylike" behavior and dress, especially for African American girls. Second, educators were concerned with threatening and oppositional behavior and dress, especially for African American and Latino boys (because Ferguson [2000] has already provided an in-depth account of the disciplinary experiences of African American boys, I focus on the discipline directed at Latino boys below). Third, many school officials assumed that some students, especially white and Asian American students, required little guidance or discipline in their behavior and dress. Fourth, I consider how these disciplinary patterns may have provoked alienation and resistance from many of the students targeted for reform.

ACTING LIKE A YOUNG LADY: RACE AND PERCEPTIONS OF FEMININITY

Aside from "Tuck in that shirt!" the most often used phrase that I recorded in my fieldnotes was some variation on "Act like a young lady!" Adults invariably directed this reprimand at African American girls; I never recorded it directed at Latina girls, Asian American girls, or white girls (although members of these groups did receive other reprimands). Adults occasionally instructed boys (primarily black boys) in how to act like "gentlemen," but this was far less common and was never used as a reprimand. Teachers and administrators used the phrase "Act like a young lady" to instruct black girls in how to sit and get up properly, dress appropriately, and speak quietly, as the following excerpt illustrates.

As the students are working on Texas Assessment of Academic Skills (the state achievement test) worksheets, Brittany, a black girl wearing dark blue shorts and a white shirt, gets up from her desk to get a tissue. The action seems perfectly innocuous to me, but Ms. Taylor, a black teacher, sees something unacceptable in it. Before Brittany can get to the tissue box, Ms. Taylor makes her go back to her seat, sit down, and then get up "like a young lady." Brittany seems rather confused by this and seems about to protest but eventually obeys with some huffing. She gets up much slower this time and with her legs closer together, looking at Ms. Taylor the whole time for assurance that everything is correct. Ms. Taylor says, "Thank you, Brittany." And Brittany proceeds to get her tissue while still looking rather perplexed. (Fieldnotes, 3/21/01, 1:00)

In a subsequent interview I conducted with Ms. Taylor, a veteran teacher, she explained why she considered it necessary to teach some girls "ladylike" behavior, as she did with Brittany:

I talk to them about how a lady talks and walks—I used to put books on their heads, so they would learn to stand straight and sit straight, with no slouching. I've had to say things like "Close your legs—ladies don't sit like that." But there is a lack of parental involvement, and they are not taught these things. Some come in here as young ladies already, but some have to learn. (3/27/02)

According to my observations, the girls adults thought needed to learn this ladylike behavior tended to be African American. One first-year teacher, a black man named Mr. Neal, told me in a conversation that black girls in particular required instruction in acceptable manners:

Mr. Neal talks to me about how important he thinks it is for black, urban youth to learn how to express themselves in acceptable ways, like through video and film. He tells me: "Like the black girls here—they lack social skills. The way they talk, it's loud and combative. They grow up in these rough neighborhoods, and that's how they act to survive. We need to teach them more social skills because that's one of the big problems now." (Fieldnotes, 3/6/02)

Mr. Neal's statement echoes Grant's (1984) finding that teachers tend to focus on improving the social skills of black girls. As he mentions, many teachers, both black and white, interpreted black girls as overly "loud" and aggressive. This was one of the main ways adults thought these girls deviated from their model of ideal feminine behavior, and it often stimulated reprimands:

> I am walking outside among the portable buildings that are used as classrooms while the school building is under construction. It is between classes, and the kids are running around to find their friends, and laughing boisterously, as usual. A group of three black girls runs by Mr. Henry, a black male teacher, laughing loudly. This upsets him and he scolds them as they leave. "Hey! You need to act like young ladies!" (Fieldnotes, 5/11/01, 10:30)

In this passage, Mr. Henry is offended not only by the volume of the girls' laughter but also by the speed of their movements. He implies through his gendered scolding of this behavior that the girls would conduct themselves in a more acceptable and gender-appropriate manner if they slowed and controlled their bodily movements and spoke quietly. Adults did not often demand that boys (of any racial-ethnic background) exert similar control over themselves. I witnessed no admonitions to "act like young gentlemen!" for example. Thus, similar to Martin (1998), I find that school officials restricted the movements of girls more than boys and encouraged girls to exert greater control over their bodies. While most of the children in Martin's (1998) study were white, however, my findings from Matthews indicate that adults directed these bodily restrictions at black girls far more than at white, Asian American, or Latina girls (discussed below). Race appeared to shape the perception of femininity. Educators tended to read the behavior of black girls as more stereotypically masculine than feminine and attempted to discipline them into exhibiting behavior closer to stereotypical femininity.

Interestingly, however, this concern with the gendered comportment of black girls did not seem to affect teachers' perceptions of them academically. Although black girls were frequently disciplined, they were not viewed as particularly "bad." They were overrepresented in pre-Advanced Placement classes, and teachers frequently described them in "regular" classes as among their best students. In fact, stereotypically masculine behavior, such as the boldness many adults interpreted as "loud," often seemed to benefit black girls in the classroom. As Mr. Wilson, a veteran white teacher, said in describing some of the best students in his class, "The black girls up there I don't worry about, they can fend for themselves—they're loud, but they're a sharp bunch and do their work" (Fieldnotes, 10/3/01). Although many adults viewed training girls to "act like young ladies" as putting them on the path to upward mobility, their discipline of black girls seemed to curtail some of the very behaviors that led to success in the classroom. Despite adults' good intentions, this disciplinary pattern could actually serve to solidify racial and gender inequality by restricting the classroom input and involvement of black girls.

SYMBOLIZING OPPOSITION: RACE, MASCULINITY, AND STYLE

In contrast to girls, adults saw many boys at Matthews as "bad" and occasionally threatening. This was particularly true for Latino and African American boys. In my observations, members of these groups were the most likely to "get in trouble." Unlike that for most girls, this discipline often entailed stern reprimands and referrals to the office for punishment. My findings of the negative disciplinary experiences of African American boys match those of Ferguson (2000). However, I found that school officials at Matthews also considered many *Latino* boys equally if not more dangerous and subjected them to constant surveillance and bodily discipline. The discipline directed at Latino boys was strongly mediated by their presentation of self, however, especially through their choice of clothing, hairstyle, and response to authority (Bettie 2000; Goffman 1973; West and Fenstermaker 1995). Teachers interpreted Hispanic students who projected a "street" persona through their dress and behavior as indifferent to school. Markers of this persona included gang-related dress such as colored shoelaces, colored or marked belts, or a white T-shirt or towel slung over a particular shoulder. However, other markers of this street style were less directly related to gang involvement, such as baggy Dickies brand pants, shaved or slicked-back hair, or refusal to keep the shirt tucked in. Many of these markers appeared instead to reflect a working-class identity.

Latino boys provoked fear in many teachers, especially when the boys were suspected of gang involvement. One white teacher, for example, referred to a group of Hispanic boys she called "gangsters" as "the type that would get back at you" (Fieldnotes, 5/13/02). Although many adults and students told me that most kids affiliated with gangs at the school were wannabes rather than full-fledged members, and I never witnessed any gang violence on or near school grounds, teachers viewed any "gang-related" students as potentially dangerous and disciplined them accordingly. Students suspected of being in gangs were almost always Latinos and were monitored closely by adults, especially in terms of their dress:

> *Mr. Pham, an Asian American teacher, is over-seeing a class made up of students from different classes who have finished TAAS [Texas Assessment of Academic Skills] testing early. The kids are very unruly, and few heed Mr. Pham's directions for silent reading. During the course of this "class," Mr. Pham reprimands several Latino and African American boys but not girls. Carlos, a Latino boy that another teacher told me is affiliated with the Crips, a large and popular gang, has been sent to the office. Toward the end of class he returns, and in a show of defiance, immediately untucks his shirt. Mr. Pham eventually notices and tells him to tuck it back in. Carlos complies somewhat, tucking half of it in. As the class draws to a*

> *close, Carlos walks by Mr. Pham and fakes like he will hit him. Mr. Pham seems to not notice amid all the other activity. After class I talk to Mr. Pham about Carlos causing so much trouble. Mr. Pham says, "Yeah, well he's in a gang. I won't back down to him, though." (Fieldnotes, 4/26/01, 9:45)*

Although many of the students at Matthews resisted the dress code prescription to tuck in their shirts, it was the resistance of Latinos that was viewed as especially threatening and oppositional. As Mr. Wilson told me, "The gang influence is bad among these Hispanics" (Fieldnotes, 10/3/01). Many teachers expressed a similar view of Latinos, constructing the group as exotic and untrustworthy and connecting them to negative gang activity.

For example, many school officials interpreted types of clothing as gang related when worn by Latino boys. Ms. McCain, a white fourth-year teacher, expressed this view when asked in an interview how she identified gang members: "Like if one of my Hispanic boys is wearing all blue—blue shirt and blue pants. The Crips, they wear blue rag." Many students, irrespective of race or gender, wore blue clothing at Matthews, occasionally all blue. Yet Ms. McCain implied that she interprets such clothing to indicate gang membership only when worn by Latino boys. The combination of race and gender with dress in this case could signal the difference between a potentially dangerous student and a harmless one.

Some Hispanic boys at the school were indeed involved with gangs, including the Crips, and announced this verbally as well as through their bodily displays. But outright gang members constituted only a small percentage of Latino boys at the school. I also knew of Asian boys and Hispanic girls who were involved in gangs, for instance, but teachers did not generalize that these groups of students, defined by race and gender, were dangerous. In addition, many adults viewed Latino boys in general as having the potential for gang involvement or violence, even if they did not openly display gang markers. For example, in another class I observed with Mr. Pham, he reprimanded a Latino boy who was wrestling with another boy. The Latino boy protested, saying he did not think he was hurting the other boy. Mr. Pham told him to stop anyway and added, "One day you're gonna hurt someone and not know it and go to jail." This particular Latino boy did not wear any salient markers of gang affiliation typically used at the school. However, Mr. Pham still interpreted his actions as overly aggressive and warned that they could one day land him in jail.

Discipline and surveillance were especially directed at Hispanic boys who projected various elements of a "street" persona. This persona did not necessarily include direct gang markers but almost always included wearing baggy Dickies brand pants. Many Latino and African American boys preferred this brand of pants and shorts and usually wore them oversized and low on their hips. The choice of Dickies by these students suggests a working-class-based, "tough" identity because the brand is primarily marketed as men's blue-collar work clothing (see Hebdige 1979 for a discussion of other styles of clothing and class identity). Many adults at Matthews, such as Ms. Boyd, an African American fifth-year teacher, interpreted Dickies negatively: "You know how they wear these baggy Dickies pants and stuff—you know where that comes from? It's like how they dress in prison. A lot of them see their older brothers or whatever in prison and that's what they pattern themselves after" (Fieldnotes, 4/20/01). For Ms. Boyd, Dickies represented oppositional values. Interestingly, I rarely saw white students wearing Dickies, and only a few Asian students wore them. The brand was overwhelmingly preferred by black and Latino students, usually boys. This parallels Ferguson's (2000) finding that school officials viewed many black boys as "bound for jail." My findings from Matthews expand this view to include Hispanic boys and highlight how something as simple as a style of pants can indicate potential criminality when worn by black or Latino boys.

However, bodily display, especially clothing choice, had a major influence on how educators viewed and treated Latino boys. The few Latino boys who wore Dockers brand pants and dark sneakers or dress shoes and kept their shirts tucked in signaled to teachers that they were good students. One Hispanic student of this type was named Thomas. Thomas projected a middle-class, "schoolboy" persona through his Dockers pants, tucked-in shirt, and parted hair (see also Ferguson 2000). Although I heard him called a "little nerd" by some of his classmates, he received positive reactions from teachers in class. Thomas was rambunctious and did have a few referrals to the assistant principal's office. However, these referrals were not for severe and persistent behavior, and teachers did not interpret Thomas's actions as threatening.

Thomas serves as an example of how Latino boys, largely through their dress and manners, could signal to school officials that they were conscientious students and came from middle-class backgrounds. These students paralleled the African American boys that Ferguson (2000) terms "Schoolboys" because of their strict adherence to school rules (in contradistinction to boys considered "Troublemakers"). At Matthews I noticed a similar split between those considered "schoolboys" and "bad boys" among Latino students.[5] I suggest that this dichotomous view stemmed largely from educators' perceptions of social class. Teachers seemed to hold more polarized views of the potential class backgrounds of Latino students than they did for other students. Many told me that the Hispanic students' backgrounds could be relatively wealthy and upwardly mobile or very disadvantaged. A veteran white teacher named Ms. Phillips, for instance, explained in our interview that she thought many of the school's Hispanic students were middle class or at least stable working class and in a better economic situation than most of the white students: "I'm pretty sure most of the white kids who go here live in apartments, and are poor like a lot of the other kids. Now, if you drive through the neighborhood just down from here—the one with all the houses—its's all Hispanic. A lot of the Hispanic families here are homeowners."

I found that many Latino students at Matthews actively "performed" (Bettie 2000) class identity and membership, especially through their dress. A middle-class performance displayed the students' possession of cultural capital in the form of dress and grooming, indicating a middle-class or upwardly mobile background and mitigating the discipline they received. Although Latino boys in general were viewed as potentially problematic, social class–oriented signals, in the form of clothing and manners, could ameliorate the negative perceptions associated with being male and Hispanic.

At the same time, any display of a working-class street style by Latinos could lead educators to perceive them as oppositional. This was true for boys as well as girls but appeared less acute for girls. Latinas who displayed a street style could be disciplined and seen as "bad" but not as dangerous as Latinos who displayed this style. Teachers suggested that although they believed many of the Latinas were connected to gangs, they did not see them as "ringleaders" or instigators of trouble in classrooms, or as overly aggressive. Some teachers even tried to protect Hispanic girls from boys they suspected of gang activity. Mr. Wilson told me, for example, that he tried to separate the Hispanic boys and girls in one of his classes because he thought that the girls "wanted to do their work": "I try to give them as much positive reinforcement as possible, so they don't get under the influence of those boys" (Fieldnotes, 10/3/01). Teachers could view Latinas exhibiting a street style as oppositional, but they did not see this as the tendency for Latinas in general. By contrast, they did view many Latino boys as inclined to opposition and having the potential to influence others in that same way. Thus, race- and class-oriented style did not really compromise femininity for Latinas or lead adults to view them as resistant, but these factors had important implications for perceptions of masculinity for Latino boys.

SELF-DISCIPLINE AND BENIGN RESISTANCE: RACE, CLASS, AND GENDER IN THE PERCEPTION OF ACCEPTABLE BEHAVIOR

Matthews had a small minority of white students and a larger minority of Asian American students. I almost never saw these students disciplined in terms of dress or manners, even when I observed clear violations.[6] School officials appeared to view Asian students at the school through the lens of the "model-minority" stereotype of high academic achievement and discipline (see Lee 1994, 1996). I never saw Asian American girls disciplined for behavior or dress; in many ways these girls exemplified the educators' ideal self-disciplined student. I rarely observed school officials discipline Asian American boys. Behaviors for which adults frequently rebuked African American and Latino boys (e.g., getting out of their seats without permission, being loud) often went unnoticed when engaged in by Asian American boys. Further, some Asian American boys exhibited behavior and dress almost identical to that considered dangerous and gang affiliated when engaged in by Latino boys, but the Asian Americans were still considered good students.

A Pakistani student named Roshan, for example, dressed in a street-based style that included baggy Dickies pants. Roshan could be quite disruptive in classes and received some discipline, but educators did not describe him as "bad," and I never saw him referred to the assistant principal's office (for serious infractions). Roshan often dressed in all blue, and I observed him hanging out with kids that teachers considered gang affiliated. In fact, one day when I was helping Roshan write a paper, he calmly informed me that he was indeed involved with a gang (Fieldnotes, 4/15/02). Thus, even when Asian American boys such as Roshan exhibited specific markers associated with gang affiliation, and in his case actually did have some involvement in gangs, educators still did not view them as threatening or dangerous, especially compared to Latino boys.

Adults rarely disciplined white girls or boys, although, as was the case for Latinos, this was strongly mediated by race- and class-based performance. Some white students, through their interactive style, choice of clothing, and friendship groups, signaled a type of street persona similar to many other students. This persona incorporated styles of dressing and speaking commonly associated with urban black youth. Although I never saw these white students wear Dickies pants, some wore gold chains outside their shirts, like many of the black and Latino students, and used expressions and spoke in a cadence similar to many black students at the school, what many might call "Black English" or "ebonics" (Labov 1972). Students affecting this persona tended to receive more disciplinary action than other whites.

One example is Lisa, whom I originally considered white, then multiracial, and then white again based on her survey response of just "White." I had difficulty classifying Lisa racially because she often wore her dark hair in styles similar to many black girls at the school, such as cornrows, she tended to hang out with black girls, and she spoke in a rhythm similar to her black friends. Teachers occasionally monitored and regulated Lisa's comportment, such as when she gave a class presentation.

Lisa, who has her hair styled like many of the black girls in a sort of bun on top of her head, and is dressed up, goes next. The teacher, a black woman named Ms. Lewis, again tells the class how important it is to "look nice" when doing a presentation for a job. She gives Lisa quite a bit of coaching, including making her take off her jacket: "You do not wear a jacket giving a presentation for a job unless it is part of your outfit." Lisa reluctantly takes the jacket off. Then Ms. Lewis tells her, "Take your hand off your hip, and stand up at the front—don't slouch." Ms. Lewis also asks why Lisa's parent didn't come (students were given extra credit if they brought their parent[s] to see their presentation). Lisa says she doesn't know. She then starts her presentation, which she goes through quickly. She speaks in a

slight southern/black cadence—different from other white students I've seen at the school but also different from the black students—sort of in between. (Fieldnotes, 11/14/01, 9:10)

Lisa certainly received bodily discipline in this instance, which differed from what I observed with other white girls. The "coaching" of Lisa's behavior parallels what I witnessed with many black girls and appears to be an attempt to instill in Lisa knowledge of how to conduct herself in a business setting. However, this discipline differed from that directed at the black girls in that the adult did not label Lisa's actions specifically "unladylike." Ms. Lewis, like most of Lisa's teachers, did not seem to assume she really lacked knowledge of how to "act like a young lady." Although Lisa dressed and acted in ways virtually indistinguishable from many black girls at the school, adults did not interpret her behaviors as overly bold or aggressive. Lisa's whiteness, however nonstereotypical, seemed to indicate adequate femininity in itself.

The same class contained another white student who spoke in a style similar to many black students at the school. This student, a large boy with light brown hair named Jackson, marked "White" on his survey and in the "Other" space wrote in "white chocolate." Jackson very much portrayed this "white chocolate" racial identity. He hung out with black students, used Black English in his speech, and wore long gold chains outside his shirt. Although Jackson often wore his pants or shorts well below his waist and rarely tucked in his shirt, I never saw him scolded for it. He did "get in trouble" frequently for other reasons, however, such as in this interaction with Ms. Lewis from the same class period discussed above.

After a few presentations at the beginning that Ms. Lewis seemed satisfied with, the rest have not pleased her—many students had multiple misspellings and failed to follow directions. Ms. Lewis is particularly angry with Jackson for his. She has already scolded him and moved him away from the class for causing a disruption.

I notice as he moves, Jackson is wearing a large gold chain on the outside of his shirt and that his shirt is not tucked into his long baggy shorts. No one has told him to tuck it in. As Jackson starts his presentation, his clothes contrasting with many of the other students who have dressed up for their presentations, he tells Ms. Lewis, "I ain't finish." Ms. Lewis tells him to do it anyway. He attempts to but has not done most of the things she asked for. Ms. Lewis scolds Jackson for this, and he talks back, saying, "I told you I ain't finish yet." Ms. Lewis responds, "But why did you tell me it was done last week when you weren't doing anything?" Jackson tries to mount a weak defense: "It was—I just had it somewhere else." Ms. Lewis tells Jackson to see her after class but later forgets about it, and he goes free.

Teachers often reprimanded Jackson like this for not doing his work or being insolent. However, as in the example above, they tended to not monitor or correct his clothing or mannerisms. Similarly, school officials did not appear to perceive Jackson as particularly "bad" or threatening. In fact, although some teachers watched Jackson closely during assemblies, he was allowed to walk around rather freely and stand near the teachers at the same time that they often admonished other students, to "Get in your seat!" or "Tuck in that shirt!" Jackson's whiteness seemed to make his technically deviant (according to school rules) dress and behavior appear harmless and benign to many school officials.

In her study of the disciplinary experiences of black children, Ferguson (2000:72) states, "The closer to whiteness, to the norm of bodies, language, emotion, the more these children *are* self-disciplined and acceptable members of the institution." In my observations, students such as Jackson and Lisa performed identities that deviated from stereotypical whiteness despite their white skin and despite their categorization of themselves as white on a survey form. Perhaps because these students lived in this working-class, predominantly minority urban neighborhood, they reflected and aligned themselves with their experience in this context, which produced an

alternative projection of whiteness. However, although this performance tended to slightly differentiate these students from other white students in terms of discipline, their whiteness still afforded them less concern and monitoring from teachers than that directed at most African American and Latino students, especially in terms of manners and dress. This provided white students with latent racial benefits, something scholars have referred to as "white privilege" (Fine et al. 1997; McIntosh [1988] 1998). Whiteness, even when expressed through a streetwise demeanor in the working-class context of Matthews, was still considered quietly central and normative. . . .

CONCLUSION

Schools teach children many lessons. These lessons often transgress the formal elements of overt curricula and instruct children how to speak, what to wear, how to move their bodies, and, ultimately, how to inhabit different race, class, and gender positions. At Matthews, school officials helped implement and regulate dress and manners out of an expressed, genuine desire to help students.[7] Left hidden, however, were the assumptions of which students needed this discipline, and in what form. . . .

My study suggests that race, class, and gender profoundly alter each other in framing perceptions of different students, which translates into different methods of regulating and shaping their behaviors. Examining organizational discipline at these intersections is crucial to developing a more nuanced understanding of the role of schools in producing and reproducing social inequalities.

For instance, in my observations the "blackness" of students seemed to indicate aggression and forcefulness. When combined with gender, this influenced perceptions of masculinity and femininity. As a result, adults not only viewed black boys as dangerously masculine, as Ferguson (2000) finds, but also viewed black girls as inadequately feminine. This perception of black girls influenced educators to restrict behaviors perceived as loud and aggressive, even though these very behaviors aided black girls in the classroom. Although not always producing the intended results, the discipline adults directed at black girls aimed to mold these energetic girls into models of quiet compliance and deference. . . .

For Latinos in this urban, southwestern setting, "brownness" worked somewhat differently when combined with gender and social class perceptions. School officials did not view Latinas as inadequately feminine but did view many Latino boys as potentially aggressively masculine, similar to popular culture characterizations of dangerous Latino masculinity (see Fregoso 1993:29). Latino boys in this setting endured adult assumptions that because of their race and gender, they had the potential for danger and should be monitored and disciplined accordingly. Overcoming this assumption required displays of cultural capital from Latino boys in the form of dress and manners not required of other students especially white and Asian American students, whose race often seemed to represent cultural capital in itself (see also Lareau and Horvat 1999). Through these displays, Latino boys could signal a middle-class background, which reduced the surveillance and discipline directed at them. By contrast, adults viewed Latinos and Latinas who displayed a non-middle-class "street-based" persona as oppositional. The negative perceptions of this class-based display were especially acute for Latino boys, however. Thus, for Latino boys in particular, adults' perceptions of their class could alter perceptions of their race and masculinity.

When adopted by white and Asian American students, a street-based style elicited some discipline but seemed to be less menacing to educators. In this way, race modified perceptions of class- and gender-based behavior. Even when these students affected a street style almost identical to that of black and Latino youth, educators typically interpreted white and Asian American boys as harmless and white girls as well mannered. "Whiteness" and "Asianness," although partially qualified by class-based performative

display, appeared to indicate docility and normative masculinity and femininity. Educators assumed at the outset that white and Asian American students did not need disciplinary reform, which only solidified their connection to educationally valuable forms of cultural capital in dress and manners. . . .

Rather than create opportunities for advancement, the emphasis on regulating students into embodying dominant modes of dress and comportment only seems to bolster perceptions of poor and minority youth as flawed in some way. Schools employing disciplinary regimes steeped in race, class, and gender assumptions (however well intentioned) risk pushing many students away and, ironically, reproducing the very inequalities they are attempting to change. This study suggests that to truly advance toward equality of opportunity, schools and society should seek to value, rather than reform, marginalized forms of style and appearance.

NOTES

1. A pseudonym, as are all names in this analysis.
2. The survey asked students to circle all that apply from the following choices: African American/Black; Latino/Hispanic; Asian; White/Anglo; Native American; or "Other," which provided space for them to write in their own choice.
3. I occasionally refer to adolescents as "kids" because that is how teachers often referred to them and how they often referred to themselves (see also Thorne 1993).
4. This interest in gender-specific manners—particularly when invoked by black teachers—perhaps stemmed from the influence of African American fraternities, sororities, and other social clubs that have historically emphasized social etiquette.
5. To be sure, there were black boys who were considered "school-oriented" and "street-oriented" at Matthews as well. However, educators seemed to especially identify this distinction among Latinos, many of whom could be considered extremely polite and from upwardly mobile backgrounds and others of whom could be considered among the most dangerous students in the school. This polarity did not appear to exist for black students; compared to Latinos, few were

described as middle class, and fewer were also described as threatening gang members.

6. One could argue that this stems from the fewer numbers of white and Asian American students at the school and that I was simply less likely to encounter discipline aimed at these students. However, as this article is part of a broader research plan focusing on white students in this predominantly racial-ethnic minority school, I purposely observed more classes and interactions involving white students than other students. It is possible that I missed some instances of discipline aimed at Asian American students, but this is highly unlikely in the case of white students.

7. While certainly strict, Matthews's climate was not one of harsh and severe discipline, such as that described by Anyon (1997) in her study of an urban school. Indeed, many adults as Matthews, including the principal, expressed a desire to create a caring, family atmosphere at the school.

REFERENCES

Anyon, Jean. 1980. "Social Class and the Hidden Curriculum of Work." *Journal of Education* 162:67–92.

Bettie, Julie. 2000. "Women without Class: *Chicas, Cholas*, Trash, and the Presence/Absence of Class Identity." *Signs* 26:1–35.

Collins, Patricia Hill. 1990. *Black Feminist Thought: Knowledge, Consciousness, and the Politics of Empowerment*. New York: Routledge.

———. 1998. *Fighting Words: Black Women and the Search for Justice*. Minneapolis: University of Minnesota Press.

Connell, R. W. 1995. *Masculinities*. Berkeley: University of California Press.

Ferguson, Ann Arnett. 2000. *Bad Boys: Public Schools in the Making of Black Masculinity*. Ann Arbor: University of Michigan Press.

Fine, Michele, L. Weis, L. Powell, and L. Mun Wong, eds. 1997. *Off White: Readings on Race, Power, and Society*. New York: Routledge.

Foley, Douglas E. 1990. *Learning Capitalist Culture: Deep in the Heart of Tejas*. Philadelphia: University of Pennsylvania Press.

Foucault, Michel. [1977] 1995. *Discipline and Punish*, 2d ed. Trans. A. Sheridan, New York: Vintage.

Fregoso, Rosa Linda. 1993. *The Bronze Screen: Chicana and Chicano Film Culture*. Minneapolis: University of Minnesota Press.

Gilmore, Perry. 1985. "'Gimme Room': School Resistance, Attitude, and Access to Literacy." *Journal of Education* 167:111–28.

Goffman, Erving. 1973. *The Presentation of Self in Everyday Life*. New York: Overlook Press.

Grant, Linda. 1984. "Black Females' 'Place' in Desegregated Classrooms." *Sociology of Education* 57:98–111.

Hebdige, Dick. 1979. *Subculture: The Meaning of Style*. London: Routledge.

Labov, W. 1972. *Language in the Inner City: Studies in the Black English Vernacular*. Philadelphia: University of Pennsylvania Press.

Lareau, Annette and Erin McNamara Horvat. 1999. "Moments of Social Inclusion and Exclusion: Race, Class, and Cultural Capital in Family-School Relationships." *Sociology of Education* 72:37–53.

Lee, Stacey J. 1994. "Behind the Model-Minority Stereotype: Voices of High- and Low-Achieving Asian American Students." *Anthropology and Education Quarterly* 25:413–29.

———. 1996. *Unraveling the "Model Minority" Stereotype: Listening to Asian American Youth*. New York: Teachers College Press.

Lewis, Amanda E. 2003. *Race in the Schoolyard: Negotiating the Color Line in Communities and Classrooms*. New Brunswick, NJ: Rutgers University Press.

Martin, Karin A. 1998. "Becoming a Gendered Body: Practices of Preschools." *American Sociological Review* 63:494–511.

McIntosh, Peggy. [1988] 1998. "White Privilege and Male Privilege: A Personal Account of Coming to See Correspondences through Work in Women's Studies." Pp. 94–105 in *Race, Class, and Gender*, (eds.) M. L. Andersen and P. H. Collins. Boston: Wadsworth.

Stanley, M. Sue. 1996. "School Uniforms and Safety." *Education and Urban Society* 28:424–36.

Thorne, Barrie. 1993. *Gender Play: Girls and Boys in School*. New Brunswick, NJ: Rutgers University Press.

West, Candace and Sarah Fenstermaker. 1995. "Doing Difference." *Gender and Society* 9:8–37.

Sexual Assault

LISA FROHMANN

Whether cases that come to a prosecutor's attention ever get to trial depends on how prosecutors define the situation. If defendants wish they could drop out of the system of criminal justice, prosecutors seek not only to remain in the system but also to move up in it. To achieve personal as well as organizational goals, prosecutors have to take into account what detectives have told them as well as to anticipate how a judge or jury will respond to the cases they bring to court. To achieve both personal and organizational goals of reducing the number of cases brought to trial and of moving cases brought to successful conclusion requires considerable discretion in evaluating the evidence in potential cases.

Lisa Frohmann shows that prosecutors rise or fall in accordance with bureaucratic measures of performance: the number of cases not brought to trial and the conviction rates of those cases that have been brought to trial. To meet these goals, prosecutors develop an interpretive scheme that classifies complainants according to the degree of consistency in their reported complaint and their social character. Only those sexual assault cases brought by women whom they consider "good witnesses" will be brought to trial, for only "good witnesses" will make a good impression on judges or juries.

Case screening is the gateway to the criminal court system. Prosecutors, acting as gatekeepers, decide which instances of alleged victimization will be passed on for adjudication by the courts. A recent study by the Department of Justice (Boland et al. 1990) suggests that a significant percentage of felony cases never get beyond this point, with only cases characterized as "solid" or "convictable" being filed (Mather 1979; Stanko 1981, 1982). This paper examines how prosecutors account for the decision to reject sexual assault cases for prosecution and looks at the centrality of discrediting victims' rape allegations in this justification.

A number of studies on sexual assault have found that victim credibility is important in police decisions to investigate and make arrests in sexual assault cases (LaFree 1981; Rose and Randall 1982; Kerstetter 1990; Kerstetter and Van Winkle 1990). Similarly, victim credibility has been shown to influence prosecutors' decisions at a number of stages in the handling of sexual assault cases (LaFree 1980, 1989; Chandler and Torney 1981; Kerstetter 1990).

Much of this prior research has assumed, to varying degrees, that victim credibility is a phenomenon that exists independently of prosecutors' interpretations and assessments of such credibility. Particularly when operationalized in terms of quantitative variables, victim credibility is treated statistically as a series of fixed, objective features of cases. Such approaches neglect the processes whereby prosecutors actively assess and negotiate victim credibility in actual, ongoing case processing.

An alternative view examines victim credibility as a phenomenon constructed and maintained through interaction (Stanko 1980). Several qualitative studies have begun to identify and analyze these processes. For example, Holmstrom and Burgess's (1983) analysis of a victim's experience with the institutional handling of sexual assault cases discusses the importance of victim credibility through the prosecutor's evaluation of a complainant as a "good witness." A "good witness" is someone who, through her appearance and demeanor, can convince a jury to accept her account of "what happened." Her testimony is "consistent," her behavior "sincere," and she cooperates in case preparation. Stanko's (1981, 1982) study of felony case filing decisions similarly emphasizes prosecutors' reliance on the notion of the "stand-up" witness—someone who can appear to the judge and jury as articulate and credible. Her work emphasizes the centrality of victim credibility in complaint-filing decisions.

In this article I extend these approaches by systematically analyzing the kinds of accounts prosecutors offer in sexual assault cases to support their complaint-filing decisions. Examining the justifications for decisions provides an understanding of how these decisions appear rational, necessary, and appropriate to decision-makers as they do the work of case screening. It allows us to uncover the inner, indigenous logic of prosecutors' decisions and the organizational structures in which those decisions are embedded (Garfinkel 1984).

I focus on prosecutorial accounting for case rejection for three reasons. First, since a significant percentage of cases are not filed, an important component of the case-screening process involves case rejection. Second, the organization of case filing requires prosecutors to justify case rejection, not case acceptance, to superiors and fellow deputies. By examining deputy district attorneys' (DDAs') reasons for case rejection, we can gain access to what they consider "solid" cases, providing further insight into the case-filing process. Third, in case screening, prosecutors orient to the rule—when in doubt, reject. Their behavior is organized more to avoiding the error

of filing cases that are not likely to result in conviction than to avoiding the error of rejecting cases that will probably end in conviction (Scheff 1966). Thus, I suggest that prosecutors are actively looking for "holes" or problems that will make the victim's version of "what happened" unbelievable or not convincing beyond a reasonable doubt, hence unconvictable (see Miller 1970; Neubauer 1974; and Stanko 1980, 1981 for the importance of conviction in prosecutors' decisions to file cases). This bias is grounded within the organizational context of complaint filing.

DATA AND METHODS

The research was part of an ethnographic field study of the prosecution of sexual assault crimes by deputy district attorneys in the sexual assault units of two branch offices of the district attorney's offices in a metropolitan area on the West Coast.[1] . . .

THE ORGANIZATIONAL CONTEXT OF COMPLAINT FILING

Several features of the court setting that I studied provided the context for prosecutors' decisions. These features are prosecutorial concern with maintaining a high conviction rate to promote an image of the "community's legal protector," and prosecutorial and court procedures for processing sexual assault cases.

The promotion policy of the county district attorney's (DA's) office encourages prosecutors to accept only "strong" or "winnable" cases for prosecution by using conviction rates as a measure of prosecutorial performance. In the DA's office, guilty verdicts carry more weight than a conviction by case settlement. The stronger the case, the greater likelihood of a guilty verdict, the better the "stats" for promotion considerations. The inducement to take risks—to take cases to court that might not result in conviction—is tempered in three ways: First, a pattern of not-guilty verdicts is used by the DA's office as an indicator of prosecutorial incompetency. Second, prosecutors are given credit for the number of cases they reject as a recognition of their commitment to the organizational concern of reducing the case load of an already overcrowded court system. Third, to continually pursue cases that should have been rejected outright may lead judges to question the prosecutor's competence as a member of the court.

Sexual assault cases are among those crimes that have been deemed by the state legislature to be priority prosecution cases. That is, in instances where both "sex" and "nonsex" cases are trailing (waiting for a court date to open), sexual assault cases are given priority for court time. Judges become annoyed when they feel that court time is being "wasted" with cases that "should" have been negotiated or rejected in the first place, especially when those cases have been given priority over other cases. Procedurally, the prosecutor's office handles sexual assault crimes differently from other felony crimes. Other felonies are handled by a referral system; they are handed from one DDA to another at each stage in the prosecution of the case. But sexual assault cases are vertically prosecuted; the deputy who files the case remains with it until its disposition, and therefore is closely connected with the case outcome.

ACCOUNTING FOR REJECTION BECAUSE OF "DISCREPANCIES"

Within the organizational context, a central feature of prosecutorial accounts of case rejection is the discrediting of victims' allegations of sexual assault. Below I examine two techniques used by prosecutors to discredit victim's complaints: discrepant accounts and ulterior motives.

USING OFFICIAL REPORTS AND RECORDS TO DETECT DISCREPANCIES

In the course of reporting a rape, victims recount their story to several criminal justice officials. Prosecutors treat consistent accounts of the incident over time as an indicator of a victim's credibility. In the first example two prosecutors are discussing a case brought in for filing the previous day.

> *DDA TAMARA JACOBS: In the police report she said all three men were kissing the victim. Later in the interview she said that was wrong. It seems strange because there are things wrong on major events like oral copulation and intercourse . . . , for example whether she had John's penis in her mouth. Another thing wrong is whether he forced her into the bedroom immediately after they got to his room or, as the police report said, they all sat on the couch and watched TV. This is something a cop isn't going to get wrong, how the report started. (Bay City)*

The prosecutor questions the credibility of the victim's allegation by finding "inconsistencies" between the complainant's account given to the police and the account given to the prosecutor. The prosecutor formulates differences in these accounts as "discrepancies" by noting that they involve "major events"—events so significant no one would confuse them, forget them, or get them wrong. This is in contrast to some differences that may involve acceptable, "normal inconsistencies" in victims' accounts of sexual assault. By "normal inconsistencies," I mean those that are expected and explainable because the victim is confused, upset, or shaken after the assault.

The DDA also discredited the victim's account by referring to a typification of police work. She assumes that the inconsistencies in the accounts could not be attributed to the incorrect writing of the report by the police officer on the grounds that they "wouldn't get wrong how the report started." Similarly, in the following example, a typification of police work is invoked to discredit the victim's account. Below the DDA and IO [investigating officer] are discussing the case immediately after the victim interview.

> *DDA SABRINA JOHNSON: [T]he police report doesn't say anything about her face being swollen, only her hand. If they took pictures of her hand, wouldn't the police have taken a picture of her face if it was swollen? (Bay City)*

The prosecutor calls the credibility of the victim's complaint into question by pointing to a discrepancy between her subsequent account of injuries received during the incident and the notation of injuries on the police reports taken at the time the incident was reported. Suspicion of the complainant's account is also expressed in the prosecutor's inference that if the police went to the trouble of photographing the victim's injured hand they would have taken pictures of her face had it also shown signs of injury.

In the next case the prosecutor cites two types of inconsistencies between accounts. The first set of inconsistencies is the victim's accounts to the prosecutor and to the police. The second set is between the account the victim gave to the prosecutor and the statements the defendants gave to the police. This excerpt was obtained during an interview.

> DDA TRACY TIMMERTON: *The reason I did not believe her [the victim] was, I get the police report first and I'll read that, so I have read the police report which recounts her version of the facts but it also has the statement of both defendants. Both defendants were arrested at separate times and give separate independent statements that were virtually the same. Her story when I had her recount it to me in the DA's office, the number of acts changed, the chronological order of how they happened has changed.* (Bay City)

When the prosecutor compared the suspects' accounts with the victim's account, she interpreted the suspects' accounts as credible because both of their accounts, given separately to police, were similar. This rests on the assumption that if suspects give similar accounts when arrested together, they are presumed to have colluded on the story, but if they give similar accounts independent of the knowledge of the other's arrest, there is presumed to be a degree of truth to the story. This stands in contrast to the discrepant accounts the complainant gave to law enforcement officials and the prosecutor.

USING OFFICIAL TYPIFICATIONS OF RAPE-RELEVANT BEHAVIOR

In the routine handling of sexual assault cases prosecutors develop a repertoire of knowledge about the features of these crimes.[2] This knowledge includes how particular kinds of rape are committed, post-incident interaction between the parties in an acquaintance situation, and victims' emotional and psychological reactions to rape and their effects on victims' behavior. The typifications of rape-relevant behavior are another resource for discrediting a victim's account of "what happened."

Typifications of Rape Scenarios

Prosecutors distinguish between different types of sexual assault. They characterize these types by the sex acts that occur, the situation in which the incident occurred, and the relationship between the parties. In the following excerpt the prosecutor discredits the victim's version of events by focusing on incongruities between the victim's description of the sex acts and the prosecutor's knowledge of the typical features of kidnap-rape. During an interview a DDA described the following:

> DDA TRACY TIMMERTON: *[T]he only act she complained of was intercourse, and my experience has been that when a rapist has a victim cornered for a long period of time, they engage in multiple acts and different types of sexual acts and very rarely do just intercourse.* (Bay City)

The victim's account is questioned by noting that she did not complain about or describe other sex acts considered "typical" of kidnap-rape situations. She only complained of intercourse. In the next example the DDA and IO are talking about a case involving the molestation of a teenage girl.

> DDA WILLIAM NELSON: *Something bothers me, all three acts are the same. She's on her stomach and has her clothes on and he has a "hard and long penis." All three times he is grinding his penis into*

her butt. It seems to me he should be trying to do more than that by the third time. (Center Heights)

Here the prosecutor is challenging the credibility of the victim's account by comparing her version of "what happened" with his typification of the way these crimes usually occur. His experience suggests there should be an escalation of sex acts over time, not repetition of the same act.

Often the typification invoked by the prosecutor is highly situational and local. In discussion a drug-sex-related rape in Center Heights, for example, the prosecutor draws on his knowledge of street activity in that community and the types of rapes that occur there to question whether the victim's version of events is what "really" happened. The prosecutor is describing a case he received the day before to an investigating officer there on another matter.

DDA KENT FERNOME: I really feel guilty about this case I got yesterday. The girl is 20 going on 65. She is real skinny and gangly. Looks like a cluckhead [crack addict]—they cut off her hair. She went to her uncle's house, left her clothes there, drinks some beers and said she was going to visit a friend in Center Heights who she said she met at a drug rehab program. She is not sure where this friend Cathy lives. Why she went to Center Heights after midnight, God knows? It isn't clear what she was doing between 12 and 4 a.m. Some gang bangers came by and offered her a ride. They picked her up on the corner of Main and Lincoln. I think she was turning a trick, or looking for a rock, but she wouldn't budge from her story. . . . There are lots of conflicts between what she told the police and what she told me. The sequence of events, the sex acts performed, who ejaculates. She doesn't say who is who. . . . She's beat up, bruises on face and a laceration on her neck. The cop and doctor say there is no trauma—she's done by six guys. That concerns me. There is no semen that they see. It looks like this to me—maybe she is a strawberry, she's hooking or looking for a rock, but somewhere along the line it is not consensual. . . . She is [a] real street-worn woman. She's not leveling with me—visiting a woman with

an unknown address on a bus in Center Heights— I don't buy it. . . . (Center Heights)

The prosecutor questioned the complainant's reason for being in Center Heights because, based on his knowledge of the area, he found it unlikely that a woman would come to this community at midnight to visit a friend at an unknown address. The deputy proposed an alternative account of the victim's action based on his knowledge of activities in the community—specifically, prostitution and drug dealing—and questioned elements of the victim's account, particularly her insufficiently accounted for activity between 12 and 4 a.m., coming to Center Heights late at night to visit a friend at an unknown address, and "hanging out" on the corner.

The DDA uses "person-descriptions" (Maynard 1984) to construct part of the account, describing the complainant's appearance as a "cluckhead" and "street-worn." These descriptions suggest she was a drug user, did not have a "stable" residence or employment, and was probably in Center Heights in search of drugs. This description is filled in by her previous participation in "a drug rehab program," the description of her activity as "hanging out" and being "picked up" by gang bangers, and a medical report which states that no trauma or semen was found when she was "done by six guys." Each of these features of the account suggests that the complainant is a prostitute or "strawberry" who came to Center Heights to trade sex or money for drugs. This alternative scenario combined with "conflicts between what she told the police and what she told me" justify case rejection because it is unlikely that the prosecutor could get a conviction.

The prosecutor acknowledges the distinction between the violation of women's sexual/physical integrity—"somewhere along the line it is not consensual"—and prosecutable actions. The organizational concern with "downstream consequences" (Emerson and Paley, 1992) mitigate against the case being filed.

Typifications of Post-incident Interaction

In an acquaintance rape, the interaction between the parties after the incident is a critical element in assessing the validity of a rape complaint. As implied below by the prosecutors, the typical interaction pattern between victim and suspect after a rape incident is not to see one another. In the following cases the prosecutor challenges the validity of the victims' allegations by suggesting that the complainants' behavior runs counter to a typical rape victim's behavior. In the first instance the parties involved in the incident had a previous relationship and were planning to live together. The DDA is talking to me about the case prior to her decision to reject.

> DDA SABRINA JOHNSON: *I am going to reject the case. She is making it very difficult to try the case. She told me she let him into her apartment last night because she is easily influenced. The week before this happened [the alleged rape] she agreed to have sex with him. Also, first she says "he raped me" and then she lets him into her apartment. (Bay City)*

Here the prosecutor raises doubt about the veracity of the victim's rape allegation by contrasting it to her willingness to allow the suspect into her apartment after the incident. This "atypical" behavior is used to discredit the complainant's allegation.

In the next excerpt the prosecutor was talking about two cases. In both instances the parties knew each other prior to the rape incident as well as having had sexual relations after the incident. As in the previous instance, the victims' allegations are discredited by referring to their atypical behavior.

> DDA SABRINA JOHNSON: *I can't take either case because of the women's behavior after the fact. By seeing these guys again and having sex with them they are absolving them of their guilt. (Bay City)*

In each instance the "downstream" concern with convictability is indicated in the prosecutor's

talk—"She is making it very difficult to try the case" and "By seeing these guys again and having sex with them they are absolving them of their guilt." This concern is informed by a series of common-sense assumptions about normal heterosexual relations that the prosecutors assume judges and juries use to assess the believability of the victim: First, appropriate behavior within ongoing relationships is noncoercive and nonviolent. Second, sex that occurs within the context of ongoing relationships is consensual. Third, if coercion or violence occurs, the appropriate response is to sever the relationship, at least for a time. When complainants allege they have been raped by their partner within a continuing relationship, they challenge the taken-for-granted assumptions of normal heterosexual relationships. The prosecutors anticipate that their challenge will create problems for the successful prosecution of a case because they think that judges and jurors will use this typification to question the credibility of the victim's allegation. They assume that the triers of fact will assume that if there is "evidence" of ongoing normal heterosexual relations—she didn't leave and the sexual relationship continued—then there was no coercive sex. Thus the certitude that a crime originally occurred can be retrospectively undermined by the interaction between complainant and suspect after the alleged incident. Implicit in this is the assumed primacy of the normal heterosexual relations typification as the standard on which to assess the victim's credibility even though an allegation of rape has been made.

Typifications of Rape Reporting

An important feature of sexual assault cases is the timeliness in which they are reported to the police (see Torrey, forthcoming). Prosecutors expect rape victims to report the incident relatively promptly: "She didn't call the police until four hours later. That isn't consistent with someone who has been raped." If a woman reports "late," her motives for reporting and the sincerity of her allegation are questioned if they fall outside the typification of officially recognizable/explainable reasons for late reporting. The typification is characterized by the features that can be explained by Rape Trauma Syndrome (RTS). In the first excerpt the victim's credibility is not challenged as a result of her delayed reporting. The prosecutor describes her behavior and motives as characteristic of RTS. The DDA is describing a case to me that came in that morning.

> *DDA TAMARA JACOBS: Charlene was in the car with her three assailants after the rape. John (the driver) was pulled over by the CHP [California Highway Patrol] for erratic driving behavior. The victim did not tell the officers that she had just been raped by these three men. When she arrived home, she didn't tell anyone what happened for approximately 24 hours. When her best friend found out from the assailants (who were mutual friends) and confronted the victim, Charlene told her what happened. She then reported it to the police. When asked why she didn't report the crime earlier, she said that she was embarrassed and afraid they would hurt her more if she reported it to the police. The DDA went on to say that the victim's behavior and reasons for delayed reporting were symptomatic of RTS. During the trial an expert in Rape Trauma Syndrome was called by the prosecution to explain the "normality" and commonness of the victim's reaction. (Bay City)*

Other typical motives include "wanting to return home first and get family support" or "wanting to talk the decision to report over with family and friends." In all these examples, the victims sustained injuries of varying degrees in addition to the trauma of the rape itself, and they reported the crime within 24 hours. At the time the victims reported the incident, their injuries were still visible, providing corroboration for their accounts of what happened.

In the next excerpt we see the connection between atypical motives for delayed reporting and ulterior motives for reporting a rape allegation. At this point I focus on the prosecutors' use of typification as a resource for discrediting the victim's account. I will examine ulterior motives as a

technique of discrediting in a later section. The deputy is telling me about a case she recently rejected.

> *DDA SABRINA JOHNSON: She doesn't tell anyone after the rape. Soon after this happened she met him in a public place to talk business. Her car doesn't start, he drives her home and starts to attack her. She jumps from the car and runs home. Again she doesn't tell anyone. She said she didn't tell anyone because she didn't want to lose his business. Then the check bounces, and she ends up with VD. She has to tell her fiancé so he can be treated. He insists she tell the police. It is three weeks after the incident. I have to look at what the defense would say about the cases. Looks like she consented, and told only when she had to because of the infection and because he made a fool out of her by having the check bounce. (Bay City)*

The victim's account is discredited because her motives for delayed reporting—not wanting to jeopardize a business deal—fall outside those considered officially recognizable and explicable.

Typifications of Victim's Demeanor

In the course of interviewing hundreds of victims, prosecutors develop a notion of a victim's comportment when she tells what happened. They distinguish between behavior that signifies "lying" versus "discomfort." In the first two exchanges the DDA and IO cite the victim's behavior as an indication of lying. Below, the deputy and IO are discussing the case immediately after the intake interview.

IO NANCY FAUTECK: I think something happened. There was an exchange of body language that makes me question what she was doing. She was yawning, hedging, fudging something.

DDA SABRINA JOHNSON: Yawning is a sign of stress and nervousness.

IO NANCY FAUTECK: She started yawning when I talked to her about her record earlier, and she stopped when we finished talking about it. (Bay City)

The prosecutor and the investigating officer collaboratively draw on their common-sense knowledge and practical work experience to interpret the yawns, nervousness, and demeanor of the complainant as running counter to behavior they expect from one who is "telling the whole truth." They interpret the victim's behavior as a continuum of interaction first with the investigating officer and then with the district attorney. The investigating officer refers to the victim's recurrent behavior (yawning) as an indication that something other than what the victim is reporting actually occurred.

In the next excerpt the prosecutor and IO discredit the victim's account by referencing two typifications—demeanor and appropriate rape-victim behavior. The IO and prosecutor are telling me about the case immediately after they finished the screening interview.

IO DINA ALVAREZ: One on one, no corroboration.

DDA WILLIAM NELSON: She's a poor witness, though that doesn't mean she wasn't raped. I won't file a one-on-one case.

IO DINA ALVAREZ: donI don't like her body language.

DDA WILLIAM NELSON: She's timid, shy, naive, virginal, and she didn't do all the right things. I'm not convinced she is even telling the truth. She's not even angry about what happened to her. . . .

DDA WILLIAM NELSON: Before a jury if we have a one on one, he denies it, no witnesses, no physical evidence or medical corroboration they won't vote guilty.

IO DINA ALVAREZ: I agree, and I didn't believe her because of her body language. She looks down, mumbles, crosses her arms, and twists her hands.

DDA WILLIAM NELSON: . . . She has the same mannerisms and demeanor as a person who is lying. A jury just won't believe her. She has low self-esteem and self-confidence. . . . (Center Heights)

The prosecutor and IO account for case rejection by characterizing the victim as unbelievable and the case as unconvictable. They establish their disbelief in the victim's account by citing the victim's actions that fall outside the typified notions of believable and expected behavior—"she has the same mannerisms and demeanor as a person who is lying," and "I'm not convinced she is even telling the truth. She's not even angry about what happened." They assume that potential jurors will also find the victim's demeanor and post-incident behavior problematic. They demonstrate the unconvictability of the case by citing the "holes" in the case—a combination of a "poor witness" whom the "jury just won't believe" and "one on one," with no "corroboration" and a defense in which the defendant denies anything happened or denies it was nonconsensual sex.

Prosecutors and investigating officers do not routinely provide explicit accounts of "expected/honest" demeanor. Explicit accounts of victim demeanor tend to occur when DDAs are providing grounds for discrediting a rape allegation. When as a researcher I pushed for an account of expected behavior, the following exchange occurred. The DDA had just concluded the interview and asked the victim to wait in the lobby.[3]

IO NANCY FAUTECK: Don't you think he's credible?

DDA SABRINA JOHNSON: Yes.

LF: What seems funny to me is that someone who said he was so unwilling to do this talked about it pretty easily.

IO NANCY FAUTECK: Didn't you see his eyes, they were like saucers.

DDA SABRINA JOHNSON: And [he] was shaking too. (Bay City)

This provides evidence that DDAs and IOs are orienting to victims' comportment and could provide accounts of "expected/honest" demeanor if necessary. Other behaviors that might be included in this typification are the switch from looking at to looking away from the prosecutor when the victim begins to discuss the specific details of the rape itself; a stiffening of the body and tightening of the face as though to hold in tears when the victim begins to tell about the particulars of the incident; shaking of the body and crying when describing the details of the incident; and a lowering of the voice and long pauses when the victim tells the specifics of the sexual assault incident.

Prosecutors have a number of resources they call on to develop typification related to rape scenarios and reporting. These include how sexual assaults are committed, community residents and activities, interactions between suspect and defendants after a rape incident, and the way victims' emotional and psychological responses to rape influence their behavior. These typifications highlight discrepancies between prosecutors' knowledge and victims' accounts. They are used to discredit the victims' allegation of events, justifying case rejection.

As we have seen, one technique used by prosecutors to discredit a victim's allegations of rape as a justification of case rejection is the detection of discrepancies. The resources for this are official documents and records and typifications of rape scenarios and rape reporting. A second technique prosecutors use is the identification of ulterior motives for the victim's rape allegation.

ACCOUNTING FOR REJECTION BY "ULTERIOR MOTIVE"

Ulterior motives rest on the assumption that a woman consented to sexual activity and for some reason needed to deny it afterwards. These motives are drawn from the prosecutor's knowledge of the victim's personal history and the community in which the incident occurred. They are elaborated and supported by other techniques and knowledge prosecutors use in the accounting process.

I identify two types of ulterior motives prosecutors use to justify rejection: The first type suggests the victim has a reason to file a false rape complaint. The second type acknowledges the legitimacy of the rape allegation, framing the motives as an organizational concern with convictability.

KNOWLEDGE OF VICTIM'S CURRENT CIRCUMSTANCES

Prosecutors accumulate the details of victims' lives from police interviews, official documents, and filing interviews. They may identify ulterior motives by drawing on this information. Note that unlike the court trial itself, where the rape incident is often taken out of the context of the victim's life, here the DDAs call on the texture of a victim's life to justify case rejection. In an excerpt previously discussed, the DDA uses her knowledge of the victim's personal relationship and business transactions as a resource for formulating ulterior motives for the rape allegation—disclosure to her fiancé about the need to treat a sexually transmitted disease, and anger and embarrassment about the bounced check. Both of these are motives for making a false complaint. The ulterior motives are supported by the typification for case reporting. Twice unreported sexual assault incidents with the same suspect, a three-week delay in reporting, and reporting only after the fiancé insisted she do so are not within the typified behavior and reasons for late reporting. Her atypical behavior provides plausibility to the alternative version of the events—the interaction was consensual and only reported as a rape because the victim needed to explain a potentially explosive matter (how she contracted venereal disease) to her fiancé. In addition she felt duped on a business deal.

Resources for imputing ulterior motives also come from the specifics of the rape incident. Below, the prosecutor's knowledge of the residents and activities in Center Heights supply the reason: the type of activity the victim wanted to cover up from her boyfriend. The justification for rejection is strengthened by conflicting accounts between the victim and witness on the purpose for being in Center Heights. The DDA and IO are talking about the case before they interview the complainant.

DDA WILLIAM NELSON: A white girl from Addison comes to buy dope. She gets kidnapped and raped.

IO BRANDON PALMER: She tells her boyfriend and he beats her up for being so stupid for going to Center Heights. . . . The drug dealer positively ID's the two suspects, but she's got a credibility problem because she said she wasn't selling dope, but the other two witnesses say they bought dope from her. . . .

LF: I see you have a blue sheet [a sheet used to write up case rejections] already written up.

IO BRANDON PALMER: Oh yes. But there was no doubt in my mind that she was raped. But do you see the problems?

DDA WILLIAM NELSON: Too bad because these guys really messed her up. . . . She has a credibility problem. I don't think she is telling the truth about the drugs. It would be better if she said she did come to buy drugs. The defense is going to rip her up because of the drugs. He is going to say, isn't it true you had sex with these guys but didn't want to tell your boyfriend, so you lied about the rape like you did about the drugs, or that she had sex for drugs. . . . (Center Heights)

The prosecutor expresses doubt about the victim's account because it conflicts with his knowledge of the community. He uses this knowledge to formulate the ulterior motive for the victim's complaint—to hide from her boyfriend the "fact" that she was trading sex for drugs. The victim, "a white girl from Addison," alleges she drove to Center Heights "in the middle of the night" as a favor to a friend. She asserted that she did not come to purchase drugs. The DDA "knows" that white people don't live in Center Heights. He assumes that whites who come to Center Heights, especially in the middle of the night, are there to buy drugs or trade sex for drugs. The prosecutor's scenario is strengthened by the statements of the victim's two friends who accompanied her to Center Heights, were present at the scene, and admitted buying drugs. The prosecutor frames the ulterior motives as an organizational concern with defense arguments and convictability. This concern is reinforced by citing conflicting accounts between witnesses and the victim. He does not suggest that the victim's allegation was false—"there was no doubt in my mind that she was raped"; rather, the case isn't convictable—"she has a credibility problem" and "the defense is going to rip her up."

CRIMINAL CONNECTIONS

The presence of criminal connections can also be used as a resource for identifying ulterior motives. Knowledge of a victim's criminal activity enables prosecutors to "find" ulterior motives for her allegation. In the first excerpt the complainant's presence in an area known by police as "where prostitutes bring their clients" is used to formulate an ulterior motive for her rape complaint. This excerpt is from an exchange in which the DDA was telling me about a case he had just rejected.

> *DDA WILLIAM NELSON: Young female is raped under questionable circumstances. One on one. The guy states it is consensual sex. There is no corroboration, no medicals. We ran the woman's rap sheet, and she has a series of prostitution arrests. She's with this guy in the car in a dark alley having sex. The police know this is where prostitutes bring their customers, so she knew she had better do something fast unless she is going to be busted for prostitution, so, lo and behold, she comes running out of the car yelling "he's raped me." He says no. He picked her up on Long Beach Boulevard, paid her $25 and this is "where she brought me." He's real scared, he has no record. (Center Heights)*

Above, the prosecutor, relying on police knowledge of a particular location, assumes the woman is a prostitute. Her presence in the location places her in a "suspicious" category, triggering a check on her criminal history. Her record of prostitution arrests is used as the resource for developing an ulterior motive for her complaint: To avoid being busted for prostitution again, she made a false allegation of rape. Here the woman's record of prostitution and the imminent possibility of arrest are used to provide the ulterior motive to discredit her account. The woman's account is further discredited by comparing her criminal history—"a series of prostitution arrests" with that of the suspect, who "has no record," thus suggesting that he is the more credible of the two parties.

Prosecutors and investigating officers often decide to run a rap sheet (a chronicle of a person's arrests and convictions) on a rape victim. These decisions are triggered when a victim falls into certain "suspicious" categories, categories that have a class/race bias. Rap sheets are not run on women who live in the wealthier parts of town (the majority of whom are white) or have professional careers. They are run on women who live in Center Heights (who are black and Latina), who are homeless, or who are involved in illegal activities that could be related to the incident.

In the next case the prosecutor's knowledge of the victim's criminal conviction for narcotics is the resource for formulating an ulterior motive. This excerpt was obtained during an interview.

> DDA TRACY TIMMERTON: *I had one woman who had claimed that she had been kidnapped off the street after she had car trouble by these two gentlemen who locked her in a room all night and had repeated intercourse with her. Now she was on a cocaine diversion [a drug treatment program where the court places persons convicted of cocaine possession instead of prison], and these two guys' stories essentially were that the one guy picked her up, they went down and got some cocaine, had sex in exchange for the cocaine, and the other guy comes along and they are all having sex and all doing cocaine. She has real reason to lie, she was doing cocaine, and because she has then violated the terms of her diversion and is now subject to criminal prosecution for her possession of cocaine charge. She is also supposed to be in a drug program which she has really violated, so this is her excuse and her explanation to explain why she has fallen off her program. (Bay City)*

The prosecutor used the victim's previous criminal conviction for cocaine and her probation conditions to provide ulterior motives for her rape allegation—the need to avoid being violated on probation for the possession of cocaine and her absence from a drug diversion program. She suggests that the allegation made by the victim was false.

Prosecutors develop the basis for ulterior motives from the knowledge they have of the victim's personal life and criminal connections. They create two types of ulterior motives, those that suggest the victim made a false rape complaint and those that acknowledge the legitimacy of the complaint but discredit the account because of its unconvictability. In the accounts prosecutors give, ulterior motives for case rejection are supported with discrepancies in victims' accounts and other practitioners' knowledge.

CONCLUSION

Case filing is a critical stage in the prosecutorial process. It is here that prosecutors decide which instances of alleged victimization will be forwarded for adjudication by the courts. A significant percentage of sexual assault cases are rejected at this stage. This research has examined prosecutorial accounts for case rejection and the centrality of victim discreditability in those accounts. I have elucidated the techniques of case rejection (discrepant accounts and ulterior motives), the resources prosecutors use to develop these techniques (official reports and records, typifications of rape-relevant behavior, criminal connections, and knowledge of a victim's personal life), and how these resources are used to discredit victims' allegations of sexual assault.

This examination has also provided the beginnings of an investigation into the logic and organization of prosecutors' decisions to reject/accept cases for prosecution. The research suggests that prosecutors are orienting to a "downstream" concern with convictability. They are constantly "in dialogue with" anticipated defense arguments and anticipated judge and juror responses to case testimony. These dialogues illustrate the intricacy of prosecutorial decision-making. They make visible how prosecutors rely on assumptions about relationships, gender, and sexuality (implicit in this analysis, but critical and requiring of specific and explicit attention) in complaint filing of sexual assault cases. They also make evident how the processes of distinguishing truths from untruths and the practical concerns of trying cases are central to these decisions. Each of these issues, in all its complexity, needs to be examined if we are to understand the logic and organization of filing sexual assault cases.

The organizational logic unveiled by these accounts has political implications for the prosecution of sexual assault crimes. These implications are particularly acute for acquaintance rape situations. As I have shown, the typification of normal heterosexual relations plays an important role in assessing these cases, and case conviction is key to filing cases. As noted by DDA William Nelson: "There is a difference between believing a woman was assaulted and being able to get a conviction in court." Unless we are able to challenge the assumptions on which these typifications are based, many cases of rape will never get beyond the filing process because of unconvictability.

NOTES

1. To protect the confidentiality of the people and places studied, pseudonyms are used throughout this article.
2. The use of practitioners' knowledge to inform decision making is not unique to prosecutors. For example, such practices are found among police (Bittner 1967; Rubinstein 1973), public defenders (Sudnow 1965), and juvenile court officials (Emerson 1969).
3. Unlike the majority of rape cases I observed, this case had a male victim. Due to lack of data, I am unable to tell if this made him more or less credible in the eyes of the prosecutor and police.

REFERENCES

Bittner, Egon A. 1967. "The Police on Skid-Row: A Study of Peace Keeping." *American Sociological Review* 32:699–715.

Boland, Barbara, Catherine H. Conly, Paul Mahanna, Lynn Warner, and Ronald Sones. 1990. *The Prosecution of Felony Arrests, 1987.* Washington, DC: Bureau of Justice Statistics, U.S. Department of Justice.

Chandler, Susan M., and Martha Torney. 1981. "The Decision and the Processing of Rape Victims through the Criminal Justice System." *California Sociologist* 4:155–169.

Emerson, Robert M. 1969. *Judging Delinquents: Context and Process in Juvenile Court.* Chicago: Aldine Publishing Co.

Emerson, Robert M., and Blair Paley. 1992. "Organizational Horizons and Complaint-Filing." In K. Hawkins (ed.), *The Uses of Discretion.* Oxford: Oxford University Press.

Garfinkel, Harold. 1984. *Studies in Ethnomethodology.* Cambridge, England: Polity Press.

Holmstrom, Lynda Lytle, and Ann Wolbert Burgess. 1983. *The Victim of Rape: Institutional Reactions.* New Brunswick, NJ: Transaction Books.

Kerstetter, Wayne A. 1990. "Gateway to Justice: Police and Prosecutorial Response to Sexual Assaults against Women." *Journal of Criminal Law and Criminology* 81:267–313.

Kerstetter, Wayne A., and Barrik Van Winkle. 1990. "Who Decides? A Study of the Complainant's Decision to Prosecute in Rape Cases." *Criminal Justice and Behavior* 17:268–283.

LaFree, Gary D. 1980. "Variables Affecting Guilty Pleas and Convictions in Rape Cases: Toward a Social Theory of Rape Processing." *Social Forces* 58:833–850.

———. 1981. "Official Reactions to Social Problems: Police Decisions in Sexual Assault Cases." *Social Problems* 28:582–594.

———. 1989. *Rape and Criminal Justice: The Social Construction of Sexual Assault.* Belmont, CA: Wadsworth Publishing Co.

Mather, Lynn M. 1979. *Plea Bargaining or Trial? The Process of Criminal-Case Disposition.* Lexington, MA: Lexington Books.

Maynard, Douglas W. 1984. *Inside Plea Bargaining: The Language of Negotiation.* New York: Plenum Press.

Miller, Frank. 1970. *Prosecution: The Decision to Charge a Suspect with a Crime.* Boston: Little, Brown.

Neubauer, David. 1974. *Criminal Justice in Middle America.* Morristown, NJ: General Learning Press.

Rose, Vicki M., and Susan C. Randall. 1982. "The Impact of Investigator Perceptions of Victim Legitimacy on the Processing of Rape/Sexual Assault Cases." *Symbolic Interaction* 5:23–36.

Rubinstein, Jonathan. 1973. *City Police*. New York: Farrar, Straus & Giroux.

Scheff, Thomas. 1966. *Being Mentally Ill: A Sociological Theory*. Chicago: Aldine Publishing Co.

Stanko, Elizabeth A. 1980. "These Are the Cases That Try Themselves: An Examination of the Extra-Legal Criteria in Felony Case Processing." Presented at the Annual Meetings of the North Central Sociological Association, December. Buffalo, NY.

——. 1981. "The Impact of Victim Assessment on Prosecutor's Screening Decisions: The Case of the New York District Attorney's Office." *Law and Society Review* 16:225–239.

——. 1982. "Would You Believe This Woman? Prosecutorial Screening for 'Credible' Witnesses and a Problem of Justice." Pp. 63–82 in N. H. Rafter and E. A. Stank (eds.), *Judge, Lawyer, Victim, Thief*. Boston: Northeastern University Press.

Sudnow, David. 1965. "Normal Crimes: Sociological Features of the Penal Code in a Public Defenders Office." *Social Problems* 12:255–276.

Torrey, Morrison. Forthcoming. "When Will We Be Believed? Rape Myths and the Idea Coming of a Fair Trial in Rape Prosecutions." *U.C. Davis Law Review*.

Mental Illness Assumptions in Commitment Hearings

JAMES A. HOLSTEIN

Agents of social control—for example, court personnel—have to decide what to do with the cases that are brought before them. Information on which to base their decisions stems from a number of sources: the "record" that candidates for commitment bring in, what other people have done about them to get to the point of this decision, what people say about them, and how these patients answer the questions the decision maker puts to them. Over time, personnel have considerable experience with a range of cases. In the end, however, the set of background assumptions that they make about typical cases frames the kinds of interpretations they make and the decisions they reach.

James A. Holstein shows that judges in civil commitment hearings believe that people brought before them for possible commitment to a mental hospital are in fact mentally ill. Although courts generally depend upon independent, objective evidence in order to make decisions, judges in these hearings interpret answers to their questions as symptoms of illness rather than making an unbiased judgment. Because of the presumption of incompetence, they commit to institutions those candidate patients who have no one to take care of them, while discharging those who have people who can care for them. In either instance, their decisions sustain dependence and are more apt to train people to play the role of mental patient than to train them to be independent and self-reliant citizens.

Challenges to the assumption that a candidate mental patient's[1] psychiatric condition is the basis for involuntary mental hospitalization have commanded considerable sociological attention for more than two decades. Indeed, a persistent controversy (see Scheff, 1974; Gove, 1980, 1982;

Horwitz, 1979) has revolved around the "societal reaction" or "labeling theory" argument that involuntary hospitalization depends upon conditions external to the individual rather than on a person's *intrapersonal* mental disorders. From this perspective, involuntary commitment is better explained by contingencies affecting societal response to those seen as deviant than by the putative deviant's mental condition (Scheff, 1964, 1966, 1974; Wilde, 1968; Wenger and Fletcher, 1969). Proponents of the opposing "psychiatric" or "medical" model of mental illness have steadfastly argued that commitment is a response to the genuine presence of mental disorder; they hold that psychiatric disturbance more than social contingencies determines hospitalization (Gove, 1970, 1980).

A sociological understanding of the involuntary commitment process does not require a resolution to this debate. Indeed, it may be rendered moot if one takes seriously a more analytically promising mandate to study how *imputations* of deviance are central to the process through which putative deviants are progressively identified, differentiated, and sanctioned (Kitsuse, 1980). This approach treats forms of behavior (or psychiatric conditions) per se as meaningless and sociologically irrelevant. Rather, it seeks to discover how relevant actors formulate, utilize, and accomplish imputations, depictions, and other representations of these behaviors and conditions in dealing with and talking about candidate deviants.

From the earliest (Scheff, 1964) to more contemporary studies of civil commitment (Warren, 1982; Hiday, 1983; Holstein, 1984, forthcoming), observers have consistently noted that authorized decision makers presume that candidate mental patients are *in fact* mentally ill. Psychiatrists called to testify routinely offer diagnoses of mental illness, and decision makers form their own commonsense opinions of candidate patients'

mental condition, often guided (if not dictated) by these diagnoses. It has been less appreciated, however, that for those making commitment decisions these assessments of mental illness are experienced as objective, literal, factual (if occasionally problematic) descriptions. In this respect then it is analytically irrelevant whether or not mental illness "really exists" in any specific case; decision makers take its factual status for granted *for all practical purposes*. "Mental illness" thus has an experientially consequential place in the commitment process, its impact deriving from decision makers' *belief* in its existence and not from any necessarily "factual" conditions.

In this article I will analyze how such assumptions and imputations—that candidate patients are in fact mentally ill—are used in and affect decisions about whether or not to hospitalize. This analytic task requires specific examination of the ways in which these attributions are incorporated into the practical work and commonsense procedures (Garfinkel, 1967) of relevant decision makers. Such an approach thus both reaffirms and advances the fundamental mandate of the societal reaction perspective to investigate the *processes* by which persons come to be identified, defined, and consequentially reacted to as deviant (Kitsuse, 1962).[2]

BACKGROUND AND SETTINGS

This study is based on fieldwork in several mental health and legal settings. Extensive observations and interviews were conducted in Metropolitan Court[3] in California from 1982 to 1984, focusing on habeas corpus hearings through which persons hospitalized on an initial 14-day commitment seek their release (see Holstein, 1984, and Warren, 1982, for further details of this court and the organization of its activities). This court hears only mental health–related cases. More limited observations and formal interviews were conducted in four other jurisdictions across the United States from 1983 through 1986.[4] Laws and procedures in these five sites were generally similar, with several consequential exceptions to be noted below.

Candidate patients in Metropolitan Court are represented by legal counsel—nearly always a public defender—while the county district attorney's office argues for commitment. Hearings, conducted in a public courtroom, vary in length and typically include testimony by the certifying doctor[5] (with cross-examination) and the candidate patient (with cross-examination). Rarely are other witnesses called. Judges freely interact with witnesses and attorneys, commenting and questioning to elicit whatever information they need to resolve a case. The other settings were generally similar, although several hearings I observed were closed to the public and a few were conducted very informally in noncourtroom settings. Regardless of physical setting, hearing interactions followed the same general format.

The civil commitment laws in the five study sites varied somewhat in their literal wording, but were similar in actual use. California's Lanterman-Petris-Short Act requires that both mental illness and danger to self or others or grave disability be established in order to commit someone involuntarily. A person is gravely disabled if as a result of mental disorder he or she is unable to provide for basic personal needs of food, clothing, and/or shelter. Two other jurisdictions have essentially the same commitment requirements, but the terminology *grave disability* is not a formal legal designation. The remaining jurisdictions make no provision for grave disability as a legal basis for commitment; danger to self or others are the only formally recognized grounds. In actual practice, however, someone considered unable to provide necessary food, clothing, shelter, or medical care due to mental illness would be judged a danger to self. Consequently, these communities can and do hospitalize persons based on a de facto grave disability provision as well.[6]

Cases concerned with grave disability or its practical equivalent are by far the most common commitment cases. Warren (1977), for example, reported that 74% of the cases she studied were

adjudicated on this basis. During my own observations, over 90% of the candidate patients appearing in jurisdictions maintaining an explicit grave disability provision had been certified as gravely disabled by the doctor requesting hospitalization. In the other jurisdictions the large majority of cases observed also revolved around grave disability-type issues. My discussion, therefore, focuses mainly on hearings concerned with grave disability-type issues due to their sheer frequency and the clear importance of disability judgments to the commitment process.

In grave disability hearings, the most consequential issue is typically the "tenability" of candidate patients' living situtations in the community (Holstein, 1984). Judges generally orient their decision making to the answers they assemble to the following question: Can the candidate patient establish a community living situation that can contain the intra- and interpersonal havoc that is believed to be associated with mental illness? Grave disability is not established simply by reference to a person's psychiatric symptoms or even general incompetencies in caring for himself or herself. Rather, it is a characterization of the condition of a person who is judged incapable of managing a life in some imaginable community living context that might contain, accommodate, and shelter a mentally disturbed person. As such, the living situation—its tenability—is of as much concern as is the candidate patient himself or herself.

In part this orientation is due to the adoption of reformed commitment laws that promote noninstitutional remedies for problems seen as mental illness. New statutes explicitly introduce hospitalization criteria beyond psychiatric diagnosis to promote treatment in the least restrictive environment available. Commitment thus requires evidence of both mental problems and inability to function as competent community members. But it would oversimplify the commitment decision-making process to conceptualize it as the *separate* resolution of the issues of candidate patients' mental health or illness, on the one hand, and their disability or dangerousness on the other. Rather, assessments of candidate patients' mental condition and appraisals of their competence and/or dangerousness are *reflexively* related so that each is practically established only in light of the other.

JUDGES' MENTAL ILLNESS ASSUMPTIONS

Judges—indeed most courtroom personnel involved in commitment cases—anticipate that nearly everyone brought before the court is severely disturbed. In part this anticipation recognizes the requisite diagnoses of pathology that must accompany recommendations to hospitalize. Routine relations between courts that handle mental health–related cases and doctors providing psychiatric evaluations develop so that it is rare to find a person advancing to candidacy for involuntary hospitalization without a psychiatric diagnosis of severe mental illness. These diagnoses are seldom challenged; rarely does a candidate patient or his or her counsel argue that a psychiatric *diagnosis* is incorrect, although they frequently question the *implications* that doctors draw from the diagnoses they reach. This tendency continually reaffirms judges' notion that civil commitment cases *always* involve persons with psychiatric troubles.

Perhaps as important as psychiatric input are judges' direct encounters with candidate patients. Those who frequently hear civil commitment cases are convinced that their experience cultivates a certain diagnostic acuity. One judge from a rural jurisdiction indicated that he "could tell if a person is mentally unbalanced—or if he should be in a hospital—as well as any psychiatrist after all the years I've been doing these hearings." And judges' experiences convince them that candidate patients brought before them are truly disturbed. One Metropolitan Court judge stated that "I know all these people, every one of them have problems. That's why they're here. Most of them are very, very sick." A judge from another jurisdiction somewhat less tactfully summarized a generally held opinion that "every one of them that comes through here is crazy in one way or another."

While it is possible that comparison of the instant case with the typically experienced "case stream" (Emerson, 1983) of mental health cases may produce a sense that the candidate patient being evaluated is not a "normal" case and may not be as mentally impaired as most, the imputation of mental illness is seldom overthrown in its entirety.[7] The condition may be seen as less severe or less "case relevant" but it is rarely converted to a judgment of "not mentally ill."

Judges also assume that candidate patients' illness is chronic and view their lives as ongoing mental illness "careers." They believe that a candidate patient has a history of hospitalization and/or contact with other agents in the mental health care system, and are thoroughly convinced that a person will not be involved in a civil commitment hearing the first time he or she experiences psychological distress or encounters mental health authorities. Judges thus assume that people who appear before them are *severely* ill, that this illness has been repeatedly confirmed elsewhere, and a number of other less coercive and restrictive interventions have been tried and have failed.

While these assumptions exist almost apart from the evidence provided about any particular candidate patient, they should not be understood as mere personal bias or prejudgment toward the mentally ill. Judges' evaluations reflect an organizational practice of responding not to individuals per se, but to *cases* within a "case set" (Emerson, 1983, 1985). As in a variety of social control settings (Dingwall et al., 1983; Emerson, 1985), prior screening is assumed, presumably at several decision points, so judges feel confident that any case sent forward merits serious attention. Indeed, much research has shown that both law enforcement and mental health personnel employ a justificatory decision logic that frames civil commitment as a remedy of "last resort" (Emerson, 1981; Emerson and Pollner, 1976; Warren, 1982; Bittner, 1967). Judges appear keenly aware of this and assume that the court is, in a sense, insulated by several layers of organizational procedures to which apparently disturbed persons are subjected before involuntary commitment is sought. This use of organizationally embedded (Gubrium, forthcoming) background knowledge leads judges to focus on candidate patients not in terms of the more particularistic qualities of individual candidate patients' *minds* but as *cases with known organizational backgrounds*.

In typifying persons as cases of mental illness, however, judges in no way yield responsibility for deciding the commitment issue. Mental status may be largely "taken for granted," but judges vigorously assert their warrant to determine its meaning within the context of tenability assessments and commitment decisions.

Beyond assuming mental illness, judges also feel there is little chance for a candidate patient's recovery or cure. They believe symptoms arise and abate in a cycle of acute psychological disturbance, temporary remission, then relapse. While judges' prognoses are rather pessimistic, they nonetheless believe that various psychiatric treatments and therapies can be beneficial, if only in containing symptoms of distress. But they are also aware of the shortcomings and side effects of most conventional treatments. In particular, most judges feel that psychotropic medications can stabilize behavior in a variety of acute episodes and also prolong periods of remission. Still, most believe that medications do not cure symptoms but merely control them temporarily. Therefore, judges are extremely concerned that the mentally ill regularly take their medications, and typically seek assurance that reliable assistance is available to maintain an effective chemotherapy regimen.

ASSUMPTION OF MENTAL ILLNESS AS A PERVASIVE INTERPRETIVE SCHEME

In insisting that judges routinely presume that candidate patients are mentally ill, I am calling attention to the fact that judges in these circumstances do not view the presence of mental illness as problematic, as an issue that must be focused on, explicitly inquired into, and conclusively established during the court hearing. Psychiatric condition is *not* a matter of *foreground* attention

in these respects; rather, the imputation of psychiatric disorder provides a distinctive and pervasive *background* against which all other assessments and evaluations are made. The assumption of mental illness thus serves as a scheme of interpretation (Schutz, 1962) that imposes a particular *context* upon all other information regarding the candidate patient, embedding knowledge of and judgments about the person and his or her behavior in a particular body of commonsense knowledge about mentally ill persons.

As judges impute mental illness, they implicitly structure how they interpret candidate patients' behavior generally. "Mental illness" becomes an organizing framework through which candidate patients' behavior comes to be meaningfully construed. That behavior, viewed as a product of mental illness, then serves further to document the presence of the illness itself. Thus descriptions of candidate patients as mentally ill and subsequent interpretations of their behavior are reflexively related, standing in a fundamentally dialectical relation to one another. The underlying pattern or structure—mental illness—provides the basis for interpreting actions in a meaningful, distinctive way. These actions, so interpreted, in turn serve to document, substantiate, and sustain the underlying pattern (Garfinkel, 1967).

Judges' commitment decisions are always made within the context that ascriptions of mental illness provide. Candidate patients and their behavior are seen against this background so that anything said or done is viewed as the claim or behavior of a "crazy person." Cast in this light, their testimony and behavior is always suspect. Their credibility is constantly challenged and their claimed capabilities discounted. Behavior that might pass for "normal" or "competent" is regarded as artificial or transitory. And, of special consequences, the assumption of mental illness fundamentally shapes judges' evaluations of the tenability of living situations—the issue on which most commitment hearings center. Indirectly, then, the candidate patient's imputed mental status has a strong bearing on how judges make commitment decisions, as the following sections demonstrate.

CANDIDATE PATIENT CREDIBILITY

Perhaps the greatest consequence of judges' assumption that candidate patients are mentally ill is the manner in which this belief consistently undermines candidate patients' credibility. As a Metropolitan Court judge related, "You have to be very careful about what you believe and what you don't. It's not that they're lying. They just don't know what the truth is. They aren't too keen on reality, if you know what I mean." Of course, this handicaps candidate patients when they are called upon to testify because all their accounts and explanations are suspect as claims made by crazy people, claims not to be trusted or believed. Even candidate patients' statements regarding "factual" information are more likely to be disbelieved, suspected, or discounted than statements made by other witnesses.

Harris Charles, for example, indicated under cross-examination that he lived in the Marriott Plaza hotel. He said that a friend had been paying for his room for the past few months. When asked the friend's name, Mr. Charles declined to reveal it, claiming that his friend was a "philanthropist" who wanted to remain anonymous: "He doesn't want to be exposed to all those people who would be begging for his help."

In explaining his subsequent finding of grave disability, the judge noted that Mr. Charles would benefit from hospitalization because "he has no place to stay on a consistent basis." The judge's inquiry into the factual status of these claims involved asking the certifying psychiatrist where Mr. Charles lived, to which the psychiatrist replied, "Apparently nowhere that we can establish." The judge continued, "He could give you no address?" to which the psychiatrist replied, "Nothing whatsoever, except the Marriott Plaza." "That story about the hotel and the philanthropist was just too crazy," the judge explained later. The judge contended he had no reason to believe such a "wild story": "There's no way in the world a guy like that could live there. If that's the best story he can come up with, I've got to assume he's got no place to go. The psychiatrist says the same thing.

It's a fabrication of a disturbed mind." This example makes clear the relative credibility attributed to so-called mentally ill candidate patients and another witness. Judges' assumption of mental illness makes the evaluation of such instances of conflicting testimony a choice between honoring the claims of a "sane" person (who is frequently a psychiatric professional) or those of a "madman." While the choice is not automatic, the mere imputation of mental disturbance severely disadvantages the candidate patient.

The manner in which Mr. Charles's testimony was discounted reveals another subtle consequence of judges' assumption of psychiatric disorder. Rather than viewing Charles's claim as a *report*—albeit fraudulent—about his place of residence, this testimony was understood as a *symptom* of Charles's illness, "a fabrication of a disturbed mind." This practical distinction between report and symptom casts candidate patients' talk and behavior as outward signs of their "known" underlying trouble. In this case, what might otherwise pass for rationally motivated (but deceitful) action or description comes to be seen as a sign revealing the condition such action or description attempts to dismiss. Taken to the extreme, any claim of normalcy or mental health may be apprehended as a symptom rather than a report, and thus be discounted, because it reveals the candidate patient's failure to comprehend and acknowledge the fact of his or her illness—actions clearly symptomatic of that very illness.

This situation is not unlike those mental patients encounter elsewhere in the mental health care system. There is ample documentation, for example, of the extent to which their claims are routinely discounted in a variety of treatment settings (Goffman, 1961; Rosenhan, 1973). A significant difference here is that this is allegedly a legal setting in which matters of fact are to be impartially and concretely established. All witnesses, including candidate patients, are sworn to tell the truth, yet it is uniquely assumed that these persons are incapable of valid testimony. But their assumed misrepresentation of the facts is not punished through contempt citations (as one presumably should be punished for lying while under oath), because such false claims are treated as symptoms of illness, not rationally calculated deceit. So, while candidate patients have their testimony automatically discredited and their freedom jeopardized as a result, their assumed mental illness does protect them from the consequences of willful violation of legal constraints.

CANDIDATE PATIENT PERFORMANCE

During the courtroom hearing judges typically assess candidate patients' social and interactional competence. They look beyond the mere content of official testimony to all other observable behavior that they treat as relevant decision-making data. Thus how the candidate patients comport themselves, how they respond to questioning and conduct themselves while being examined by counsel, and even how they act when not directly involved in the courtroom proceedings are matters of practical interest for judges as they consider not so much what persons claim about themselves, but rather what they reveal through their current behavior. Indeed, candidate patients are "on trial" the entire day in court, not just the few minutes spent on the witness stand, and are seldom "offstage" because any observable behavior is treated as somehow indicative of their mental or interactional competence.[8]

In a sense, commitment proceedings orient as much to what candidate patients do *in the hearing setting* as they do to information concerning prior incidents or behaviors that mobilized commitment actions. Judges are not evaluating "sanity" per se, because they are certain that candidate patients are "insane," but they do want to establish firsthand how well candidate patients respond to the demands of community living. An Eastern Court judge indicated that he thought that formal courtroom hearings were essential to the commitment process, not just for legal reasons, but because they provided the opportunity to "check out" and "test" the candidate patient's ability to function outside the sheltered world of the mental hospital or community mental health center. "We give them a chance to prove themselves," he noted, "by letting them defend themselves. If they can't manage to show me that they can handle themselves, then I'm not gonna release them."

Much of the so-called testing takes the form of apparent checks on "reality orientation," a practice argued to be common in civil commitment proceedings (Scheff, 1964; Warren, 1982). In Metropolitan Court, in particular, judges repeatedly ask questions that demand factual information from the candidate patient: "What day is it?" "Where are you right now?" "How do you get to your mother's house from Southpark?" "What is 50 plus 35?" One might argue, however, that many of these questions are not asked to evaluate a candidate patient's "reality orientation" as much as they are intended to reveal the person's current ability to locate himself or herself in the community, proceed to intended destinations, and conduct the routine transactions of everyday life required by release into the community. These may be conceived as very practical questions, their importance deriving from a mundane or literal interpretation of their significance. Correct answers document a sort of competence in community living; incorrect responses indicate that the person would have difficulty negotiating life outside an institution and not *necessarily* a faulty grasp of "reality."[9]

Such evaluations of responses to these questions are dictated by the presumption of mental illness, which demands locating the cause of any displayed incompetence *within* the candidate patient and his or her *psychiatric condition*. An incorrect answer will be cited as a symptom, both a product and a document of a disturbed mind; other possible reasons for a wrong answer go unconsidered. For example, a Metropolitan Court judge refused to consider the possibility that Jefferson Smith's inability to state his mother's address might be due to his recent arrival in town, or his recent 10-day hospitalization in which he was heavily medicated, or even his nervousness about appearing in court—all possible explanations suggested by Smith's attorney. Instead the judge offered the following: "This man's mental condition interferes with his ability to do the day-to-day functions that he has to do if he wants to live with his family. His psychosis has impaired his memory. . . . He's lost. He can't look out for himself." The assumption that Smith was mentally ill precludes assigning other cause (including simple ignorance) for his misstatement of the address. Thus those *situational* explanations that relieve the "normal" actor from responsibility for many minor transgressions in the course of everyday life are invalid when evaluating the meaning of a "mentally ill" person's mistakes. The assumption of mental illness insinuates that good cause for perceived incompetence can be found in the candidate patient's "sick" mind. External causes need not be seriously considered.

Despite assuming that persons sought to be committed are mentally disturbed, judges believe that most candidate patients are conscious of their courtroom demeanor. "Let's face it," noted an Eastern Court judge, "they're on their best behavior. They're doing everything they can to hide their condition." They are viewed as intentionally concealing or containing the symptoms that judges assume lurk just below any facade of normalcy that may be temporarily sustained. Composed, situationally appropriate demeanor and organized, articulate testimony are routinely discounted, if not disregarded, as valid indicators of competence because judges assume they are little more than "acting" or "performances" that quickly evaporate once the candidate patient lets down his or her guard. Judges reveal their belief that candidate patients' courtroom behavior is often deceiving through statements such as, "That one almost slipped right by us," or "He was really trying hard to hold his act together, but he just couldn't keep it up." Marie Albeck, for example, testified in an articulate and rational manner, giving every indication of interactional competence, even by the admission of the judge who ruled her gravely disabled. Yet her composed demeanor was seen as ephemeral, merely a temporary departure from, or disguise for, the chaotic behavior of the mentally ill person she was "known" to be. Said the judge, "She's really disturbed, but she doesn't always show it. She's so sick that she tries to hide her illness even when people just want to help her. We know it can't last." Even her "good behavior"—interpreted as a calculated yet pathological departure from the typical—was used to document her psychiatric disturbance. Once assumed, mental illness remains an almost incorrigible (Pollner, 1974) description of persons sought to be committed.

Conversely, any behavior that might be interpreted as symptomatic of mental illness is readily viewed as indicative of the candidate patient's true condition. Indeed, any slipup may be viewed as the mere "tip of the iceberg" of deranged behavior that can be caused by mental illness. Judges, then, consider much behavior to be motivated, manipulative self-presentation (Goffman, 1959), while also believing that they must see beneath mere appearance to the "true" nature and condition of the persons brought before them.

Medication and Performance

The fact that most involuntary commitment hearings are held while candidate patients are undergoing institutional evaluation and treatment further colors judges' interpretations of what these persons say and do. Most candidate patients are receiving psychotropic medications at the time of their hearings. While judges clearly do not believe such medications cure mental illness, they do believe such medications can be effective in containing or suppressing symptoms. Whatever rational, composed, "appropriate" behavior candidate patients might display is often attributed to their medications. And because they are assumed to be mentally ill and mental illness is assumed to have visible symptoms, any absence of symptoms is attributed to the drugs. As one judge noted:

These people are very, very sick. And without their medications they don't stand a chance. Usually the medications give them a chance to pull themselves together, get things under control. But they need to stay on them. It's the only way they can maintain. This last fellow today seemed very together, but take him off meds and he's in his own world again. He can do just fine—like today—if he'll just take his meds.

Thus candidate patients find themselves in the precarious position of receiving causal credit for all "inappropriate" behavior, but "appropriate" or "competent" behavior is attributed to medications. Under such circumstances, it is sometimes difficult to convince a judge that hospitalization is unnecessary because, even when no symptoms are apparent or when visible symptoms seem innocuous, one's fundamental competence is continually suspect.

Negative Cases

There are, of course, instances when candidate patients' testimony or performances are not discounted. While these may be due to extraordinary displays of competence by candidate patients, they are more likely to result from some violation of organizational procedure or expectation by the *sponsors* of commitment. For example, in Metropolitan Court, psychiatrists (or occasionally representatives of the district attorney's office) who are inexperienced with commitment cases may seek hospitalization in violation of either explicit or implicit commitment criteria. They may believe that a candidate patient's florid symptoms or disturbed behavior so warrants hospitalization that less restrictive treatment alternatives are not pursued before commitment proceedings are initiated. If this becomes apparent to a judge, all assumptions about the case—and hence the candidate patient—may be suspended. The usual attribution of mental illness may be tentative or problematic, thus allowing testimony and behavior to be seen against a new background, through a different interpretive framework.

Consider the case of Janet Conrad, a 22-year-old white female whose family had engaged a psychiatrist in private practice, Dr. Ryan, to involuntarily hospitalize her. According to her family,

Janet had been very depressed, then had become delusional and agitated. In response to commands "from inside her head," Janet had tried to kill the family dog and threatened some neighborhood children. The family also claimed that Janet had repeatedly been uncontrollable in public places and finally had to be physically removed from a local shopping mall and transported to a psychiatric facility by the police due to bizarre and threatening behavior. She had been held there over the weekend, and after a psychiatric evaluation the Conrad parents asked Dr. Ryan to pursue more extended hospitalization.

At the hearing, his first in Metropolitan Court, Dr. Ryan sought Janet's involuntary commitment, arguing that he had diagnosed her as "schizophrenic" and that she was gravely disabled as well as dangerous to herself and others. After seeking some clarifications regarding Ryan's recommendation, the judge asked how long Janet had been under Ryan's care and what her history of outpatient psychiatric treatment had been. He was somewhat surprised to hear that Ryan had been brought onto the case only recently and that Janet had no treatment history. She had previously seen the Conrad family physician to discuss her feelings of "agitation" but he had done nothing more than prescribe a mild sedative. At this point the judge launched a rather extended lecture on the mandate of community mental health care, then aggressively requestioned Dr. Ryan regarding his commitment recommendation when so many alternatives had not been explored. Ryan reiterated his belief that Janet's symptoms were so bad and her behavior so bizarre and uncontrollable that institutional control and monitoring [were] clearly indicated, especially in light of her parents' request.

Janet Conrad's testimony was agitated but coherent. She admitted to hearing voices but claimed that she was not going to listen to them in the future. She repeatedly denied the need for psychiatric care but acknowledged that she could use some help "to make her feel better." The judge asked her if she would be willing to see a counselor at a community mental health center, if she would agree to take medications if they were prescribed for her, and if she would move in with her parents "until she was feeling like herself again." She reluctantly agreed to all three stipulations, although she claimed she didn't want to live at home and continued to assert that she was not the only one that needed help: "This whole mess is crazy. I'll go to the shrink if you say so, but why are you just picking on me?"

The judge released Janet Conrad with the following explanation:

> *This woman obviously needs help, but I think she can get it without hospitalizing her at this time. She says she can keep her act together on her own, so I'll trust her to keep her promise to get the kind of care she needs and give her a chance. . . . If this doesn't work out, we can always bring you back here, young lady. Let's not let your emotional problems get out of hand. You get help, so we don't have to force it on you.*

Later, the judge indicated that he was ambivalent about releasing a woman whose family sought her hospitalization but felt there was insufficient evidence to warrant Janet's commitment: "She's got troubles, no doubt about that, but it's not clear that she can't overcome them. Sometimes we have to find out if they can really manage or not."

Janet Conrad's case was uncharacteristic in that a violation of the court's expectation of prior processing dislodged the typical interpretive framework through which candidate patients are evaluated. While the judge still thought that Janet was mentally ill, he apparently bracketed this assumption because it was not supported by a typical organizational and remedial history. Consequently, the judge was willing to honor Janet's claims to a much greater extent than usual. Her promises regarding management of her life in the community were not immediately dismissed because her credibility was not completely undermined by assumed psychiatric disorder. It is not that the judge doubted the psychiatric diagnosis so much as he was not yet convinced that the disorder was socially disabling, Janet's case having already departed from the ordinary.

Typical assumptions about a case are apparently rendered problematic to the extent that features of the instant case cannot be articulated with the "normal case." Thus judges' commitment decisions are not shaped so much by a predisposition to hospitalize as much as they are by their assumption about the typical course of psychiatric disturbance and its treatment, coupled with a practical understanding of its effects on one's ability to function in community settings. When that assumption is altered, the ensuing interpretation of matters at hand may change, as might the contingent decision.

TENABLE LIVING ARRANGEMENTS

Concern for a candidate patient's ability to function in the community focuses commitment decision making on *both* psychiatric disturbance and the person's proposed community living circumstances. In assessing grave disability judges try to establish whether or not the person released will maintain reliable access to basic necessities such as food, clothing, and shelter, be supervised by a competent "caretaker," and participate in an ongoing treatment regime (Holstein, 1984). Such tenability assessments are distinctively shaped by judges' assumption that a living situation must be proven viable *for a mentally ill person*, thus merging evaluation of personal capabilities and the adequacy of proposed living situations. As a result judges tend to view as problematic a variety of situations and living arrangements that might otherwise be seen as tenable. In their practical decision making, judges presume a tenable living situation must accommodate, contain, and control the havoc that is assumed to accompany mental illness. They consequently may attend to the situation's ability to deal with instability, vulnerability, irresponsibility, dangerousness, and erratic or bizarre behavior even if the candidate patient in question has given no concrete evidence of acting in these ways.

As noted earlier, when viewed against the assumption of mental illness, candidate patients' claims regarding viable living arrangements are viewed with suspicion. In addition to skepticism toward the very existence of such situations, judges are also reluctant to concede their adequacy for accommodating released patients assumed to be still "mentally ill." The practicalities of how candidate patients will support themselves are always a concern because it is assumed that mental illness renders its victims too unstable, unreliable, and incompetent to make and manage money. Judges assume the mentally ill behave erratically and are likely to lose jobs, even those marginal and menial jobs that they might most likely fill. Consequently, financial support based on employment is considered highly vulnerable, and living arrangements dependent upon holding a job are clearly untenable. Conversely, candidate patients who claim to support themselves on some sort of entitlement assistance (for example, social security, Supplemental Security Income, Social Security Disability Insurance, unemployment insurance, veteran's benefits, and so on) are considered more financially stable; their living situations are more viable because they are, in a sense, financially protected from the uncertainties that accompany mental illness.

Consider the Eastern Court case of Ned Yost, a 27-year-old white male who had been hospitalized after being arrested for causing a public disturbance in an all-night doughnut shop. At his commitment hearing Yost testified that he had been supporting himself by working as a busboy. The restaurant had agreed to participate in a locally sponsored vocational rehabilitation program and hired Yost upon his completion of the program's job training. Yost gave the judge the name and address of the restaurant and said that his supervisor could be called to verify his employment. Yost indicated that he had the job for almost three months and previously held several jobs of this nature. He was making the minimum wage, but was working enough hours to earn over $100 weekly, after taxes. This was enough to live on, he claimed, because he paid only $276 a month for rent and received free meals on the job.

At the hearing, no attempt was made to contact Yost's employer or anyone from the vocational

rehabilitation program. Yost was committed, with the explanation that his financial situation was too precarious to be considered viable. The judge argued:

> The option of living outside [of the hospital] at the present time isn't very realistic. He is in no condition to fend for himself, support himself. If I release Mr. Yost, he will surely lose his job, just go out and do something to get fired. His behavior is too unpredictable. And when he loses the job, where will he be? Nowhere. I just can't release him to face that prospect. He's better off getting the help he needs in the hospital.

In contrast, the same judge released several candidate patients whose only claim of support was that they received SSI or veteran's benefits. In all the jurisdictions studied, judges regularly cited dependable income from such sources in justification of returning persons to the community, but I never observed the release of a person who claimed that he or she would hold a job as his or her source of support.

The assumption of mental illness also colors the way in which judges evaluate the adequacy of other basic necessities. The sources of such necessities were considered vulnerable to the extent that the candidate patient's assumed mental illness might be able to affect them. Living arrangements, for example, are untenable if seen as easily disrupted by disturbed or erratic behavior. Thus persons who rent apartments on their own (even if they can document their ability to pay rent) are more likely to be committed than are persons who live in some structured or institutionalized setting over which they exercise no responsibility or control. Renting, judges believe, requires meeting financial obligations and observing both formal and informal rules of apartment life. Judges feel these seemingly mundane and minimal obligations are likely to pose major difficulties for mentally ill persons. They suspect that candidate patients will almost certainly disrupt the situation, thus jeopardizing their living arrangements and effectively depriving themselves of the adequate shelter required for their release. Thus it is not the living situation per se that is judged appropriate or deficient. Rather, judges base tenability assessments on how well a housing situation can provide for the very special needs of persons presumed to be mentally ill. This presumption, then, imposes evaluative criteria upon judges' tenability assessments that render many "conventional" housing arrangements untenable.

Other aspects of tenability assessments are similarly influenced. The adequacy of a caretaker, for example, is judged in terms of those capabilities required to deal with a potentially erratic, disruptive, violent person—even though no formal psychiatric prognosis suggests that such behavior is likely. Or a candidate patient's pledge to adhere to a program of psychiatric care will be treated as a worthless promise due to the person's impaired mental capacity. Robert Castillo's case illustrates these processes. Castillo, a 37-year-old Chicano, was judged gravely disabled in Metropolitan Court after he repeatedly came to the attention of the police for "threatening and harassing" people in his neighborhood. The judge's account for his ruling emphasized the lack of a competent caretaker to monitor Castillo's daily activities or ensure his continued outpatient treatment. While the judge indicated that Castillo's wife tried her best to keep track of him, he also noted that she was away from home at her job a good portion of the day:

> *A guy like this may seem to be just fine one minute, then go off the deep end the next. If there's no one there watching all the time, who's gonna step in and take over when he loses his senses? Somebody has got to be constantly on guard.*

The judge assumed that Castillo was mentally ill and prone to unpredictable swings that called for especially rigorous supervision; these assumptions, not direct testimony about his psychological state, supported the characterization of Castillo as gravely disabled.

The assumption of mental illness also caused the judge to question Castillo's commitment to getting psychiatric care:

> *He needs treatment—regular medication—but he doesn't recognize that. In his mental state, he doesn't think he needs help. So he can't be trusted, and if she's [Mrs. Castillo] not around, who's gonna get him to the clinic? Who's gonna give him his meds? He says he'll take them now, but what about next week when he says he's better, when his delusions make him think that he feels ok and doesn't need them?*

By assuming Castillo is psychiatrically disturbed, and characterizing the symptoms of that disturbance as he does, the judge sees no hope for community treatment in the present circumstances. When one believes that mental illness causes its victims to be oblivious to their own needs, one can never trust such a person to seek psychiatric help. And when an individual is assumed to be mentally ill, others (especially judges) are likely to interpret any report by that person of a subjective sense of well-being, improvement, or remission as misapprehension, delusion, or irrationality—one further symptom of psychiatric disorder.

Certainly not all candidate patients are committed, even though they are assumed to be mentally ill. Release merely requires convincing a judge that an appropriate situation is available for the "mentally ill" person in question. In a sense, this calls for producing a match between candidate patient needs and the accommodations a situation provides (Holstein, forthcoming). This match is an accomplishment of the persons arguing the case at hand, so the demands of a particular person and the capabilities of a particular caretaker or household may be explicitly contested and negotiated as the "facts" of the case are established. Whereas Mrs. Castillo was depicted as an inadequate match to her husband's supervisorial needs, other cases may produce descriptions of household settings that can better accommodate the demands of candidate patients who wish to reside there. For example, "family rhetoric" (Gubrium and Lynott, 1985; Gubrium and Holstein, forthcoming) may depict a household composed of capable and loving caretakers for a person characterized as placing few demands on their management abilities. Release might be forthcoming in such a case. Commitment, then, is never a foregone conclusion, even though mental illness ascriptions dictate stringent criteria for determining a living situation's tenability.

CONCLUSION: THE IRONY OF COMMITMENT CRITERIA

Judges routinely ascribe mental illness to those whose hospitalization is sought through involuntary commitment. I have not questioned the validity or warrant of this imputation because members of the decision-making setting treat it as valid and correct. By focusing on *members'* use of and orientation to practical psychiatric assessments, the "actuality" of mental illness is rendered inconsequential in light of its experiential reality. Mental illness ascriptions implicitly structure judges' evaluations of candidate patients' testimony, behavior, and community living arrangements, and in many respects "straitjacket" candidate patients' attempts to establish their own competence or the tenability of their proposed living situations. Commitment decisions are thus profoundly responsive to the background assumption of mental illness.

Since hospitalization is forestalled only with a convincing argument that a candidate patient will live in a community situation that can accommodate and contain a person *who is mentally ill*, a tenable living situation, for judges' practical decision-making purposes, becomes one that approximates in many ways the structured and encompassing institutionalized setting represented by the mental hospital. This tendency ironically twists the logic and implementation of "deinstitutionalized" mental health care that undergirds most reformed commitment legislation. In place of dehumanizing total institutions (Goffman, 1961) that isolate mental patients from nearly all social contact and reinforce passive and dependent behavior patterns, the community mental health movement promotes treatment of mental patients in more natural community settings.

Such placement seeks to capitalize on a wide range of healthful influences thought to be inherent in community living, influences that might render mental patients better able to manage themselves and approach some minimal level of normal functioning (Kirk and Thierren, 1975).

But when judges' involuntary commitment decisions are premised on a distinctive set of assumptions about mental illness and a derived set of assumptions about tenability, candidate patients who claim living arrangements apparently most consonant with those mandated by deinstitutionalization become those *least likely to be released*. Specifically, persons wishing to live in community circumstances that might require independent living skills or normal social functioning are unlikely to be released because such circumstances would be viewed as *untenable* "for mentally ill persons." In contrast, candidate patients who appear more willingly dependent upon other persons and institutions to supervise all aspects of their daily lives are *more likely to avoid commitment*. Judges' persistent belief in candidate patients' mental illness thus minimizes the likelihood that a person with the desire and opportunity to live in more "conventional" circumstances requiring initiative, responsibility, and control will be allowed to do so. In this respect reformed commitment procedures within the community mental health care movement promote the hospitalization of many persons who are among the most willing and perhaps the most capable of living independently in community settings, while those released are typically the ones most willing to accept virtual custodial treatment in an alternative setting.

In effect, contemporary commitment decision making promotes a system of "community custody" (Scull, 1981). This no doubt contributes to what Warren (1981) has labeled the "transinstitutionalism" of both treatment and social control by requiring that community settings housing released candidate patients still be required to constrain and control the havoc-wreaking symptoms of mental illness that are assumed to follow these persons into their lives beyond the hospital.

Release from commitment thus takes on the same character that Kirk and Thierren (1975: 212) note in the deinstitutionalization movement in general, where "the return of patients to the community has, in many ways, extended the philosophy of custodialism into the community rather than ending it at the gates of the state hospital."

NOTES

1. All persons whose commitment is being considered in the proceedings studied here will be called *candidate patients*, although in most cases they are already patients who have been hospitalized and are now seeking their release. For example, in California's habeas corpus proceedings, their status is technically that of petitioner because they have been hospitalized and now seek their release through legal review. I use this convention to minimize the terminological confusion of these persons with "petitioners" who file petitions seeking the involuntary hospitalization of others.

2. At the same time, it might also help us better understand the findings Gove (1982) cites as the "undoing of labeling theory" in such a way as to acknowledge the apparently strong correlation between psychiatric diagnoses and hospitalizations, yet maintain the integrity of the societal reaction point of view.

3. Names of all persons and places have been fictionalized.

4. See Holstein (1984) for further descriptions of the settings studied here.

5. Generally this person is a psychiatrist, although occasionally a psychologist or medical doctor (M.D.) will be called to testify. In the other jurisdictions, psychiatrists were also the most commonly called as expert witness, but psychologists and M.D.s testified in a greater percentage of cases. Since their testimony appears to be similarly received, I will, for the sake of convenience, refer to this group as "psychiatrists," even though this may not literally be the case.

6. As a matter of convenience, I will extend the use of the term *grave disability* to all other settings.

7. In sites other than Metropolitan Court, judges hear non–mental health cases as the majority of their caseloads. For them, the case stream of all cases seen may make it seem even more apparent that candidate mental patients are mentally ill because they stand out in greater contrast to the non–mentally ill persons who more regularly appear in courts. Thus judges in these courts may develop a great deal of confidence in their "diagnostic capabilities" (that is, their ability to differentiate the sane from the insane) even though they have less experience dealing with mental health matters than do Metropolitan Court judges.

8. This is especially true of Metropolitan Court, where most candidate patients are bussed in from distant psychiatric wards between 8 and 10 a.m. and remain in the court building until the end of the day's hearings, when they are returned to their wards if they have not been released.

9. While judges may hear these answers very pragmatically, psychiatrists are still inclined to use them as evidence of underlying mental disorientation. Thus the "reality testing" that Scheff (1964) has described may in part be a product of professional and organizational location.

REFERENCES

Bittner, E. 1967. "Police Discretion in Apprehending the Mentally Ill." *Social Problems* 14:278–292.

Dingwall, R., J. M. Eekelaar, and T. Murray. 1983. *The Protection of Children: State Intervention and Family Life.* Oxford, England: Basil Blackwell.

Emerson, R. M. 1981. "On Last Resorts." *American Journal of Sociology* 87:1–22.

Emerson, R. M. 1983. "Holistic Effects in Social Control Decision-Making." *Law and Society Review* 17: 425–455.

Emerson, R. M. 1985. "Detecting the 'Real Reason' for Referrals." Presented at the annual meetings of the Law and Society Association, San Diego.

Emerson, R. M., and M. Pollner. 1976. "Mental Hospitalization and Assessments of Untenability." Presented at the annual meeting of the Society for the Study of Social Problems, New York.

Garfinkel, H. 1967. *Studies in Ethnomethodology.* Upper Saddle River, NJ: Prentice Hall.

Goffman, E. 1959. *The Presentation of Self in Everyday Life.* Garden City, NY: Doubleday.

Goffman, E. 1961. *Asylums.* Garden City, NY: Doubleday.

Gove, W. R. 1970. "Societal Reaction as an Explanation of Mental Illness: An Evaluation." *American Sociological Review* 35:863–884.

Gove, W. R. (ed.). 1980. "Labelling and Mental Illness: A Critique," in *The Labeling of Deviance: Evaluating a Perspective.* Newbury Park, CA: Sage.

Gove, W. R. (ed.). 1982. "The Current Status of the Labelling Theory of Mental Illness," in *Deviance and Mental Illness*. Newbury Park, CA: Sage.

Gubrium, J. (forthcoming). "Organizational Embeddedness and Family Life," in T. Brubaker (ed.), *Older Families and Long-Term Care*. Newbury Park, CA: Sage.

Gubrium, J., and J. A. Holstein. 1988. "Experiential Location and Method in Family Studies." *Journal of Marriage and the Family*.

Gubrium, J., and R. J. Lynott. 1985. "Family Rhetoric as Social Order." *Journal of Family Issues* 6:129–152.

Hiday, V. A. 1983. "Judicial Decisions in Civil Commitment: Facts, Attitudes and Psychiatric Recommendations." *Law and Society Review* 17:517–530.

Holstein, J. A. 1984. "The Placement of Insanity: Assessments of Grave Disability and Involuntary Commitment Decisions." *Urban Life* 13:35–62.

Holstein, J. A. (forthcoming). "Producing Gender Effects: Gender Depictions and Accommodations in the Involuntary Mental Hospitalization Process." *Social Problems*.

Horwitz, A. V. 1979. "Models, Muddles, and Mental Illness Labelling." *Journal of Health and Social Behavior* 20:296–300.

Kirk, S., and M. E. Thierren 1975. "Community Mental Health Myths and the Fate of Former Hospitalized Patients." *Psychiatry* 38:209–217.

Kitsuse, J. I. 1962. "Societal Reactions to Deviant Behavior: Problems of Theory and Method." *Social Problems* 9:247–256.

Kitsuse, J. I. 1980. "The 'New Conception of Deviance' and Its Critics," in W. Gove (ed.), *The Labeling of Deviance*. Newbury Park, CA: Sage.

Pollner, M. 1974. "Mundane Reasoning." *Philosophy of the Social Sciences* 4:35–54.

Rosenhan, D. L. 1973. "On Being Sane in Insane Places." *Science* 179:250–258.

Scheff, T. J. 1964. "The Societal Reaction to Deviance: Ascriptive Elements in the Psychiatric Screening of Mental Patients in a Midwestern State." *Social Problems* 11:401–413.

Scheff, T. J. 1966. *Being Mentally Ill: A Sociological Theory*. Chicago: Aldine.

Scheff, T. J. 1974. "The Labelling Theory of Mental Illness." *American Sociological Review* 39: 444–452.

Schutz, A. 1962. *The Problem of Social Reality*. The Hague: Martinus Nijhoff.

Scull, A. 1981. "A New Trade in Lunacy." *American Behavioral Scientist* 24:741–754.

Warren, C. A. B. 1977. "Involuntary Commitment for Mental Disorder: The Application of California's Lanterman-Petris-Short Act." *Law and Society Review* 11:629–649.

Warren, C. A. B. 1981. "New Forms of Social Control: the Myth of Deinstitutionalization." *American Behavioral Scientist* 24:724–740.

Warren, C. A. B. 1982. *The Court of Last Resort*. Chicago: University of Chicago Press.

Wenger, D., and C. R. Fletcher. 1969. "The Effect of Legal Counsel on Admissions to a State Mental Hospital: A Confrontation of Professions." *Journal of Health and Social Behavior* 10:66–72.

Wilde, W. 1968. "Decision-Making in a Psychiatric Screening Agency." *Journal of Health and Social Behavior* 9:215–221.

CHAPTER 7

THE EFFECTS OF CONTACT
WITH CONTROL AGENTS

The Saints and the Roughnecks

WILLIAM J. CHAMBLISS

Organizational processing, whether in the criminal justice or health care systems, tends to produce some taken-for-granted assumptions about all of the people processed. These assumptions are frequently held just as often by laypeople as by professionals. It is believed that persons processed by these systems share a set of common characteristics. They are alike, not only in the offenses they have committed but in other significant social respects as well. In turn, they are markedly dissimilar from all members of conventional society.

William J. Chambliss, in a study of two different high school gangs, finds variations in social responses to deviance that attest to the power and consequences of social reputation. Reputation is made up of one's past of alleged performance, social responses, and expectations for future performance. Although both of the gangs studied engaged in the same frequency of deviance, one gang received considerable official social control attention while the other one did not. In time, members of the two gangs lived up to the community's differential predictions about their future after graduation from high school. In this case study, the subsequent careers of both gangs turned out to be examples of a self-fulfilling prophecy—what people believe to be real will be real in its consequences.

Eight promising young men—children of good, stable, white upper-middle-class families, active in school affairs, good pre-college students— were some of the most delinquent boys at Hanibal High School. While community residents and parents knew that these boys occasionally sowed

Reprinted from "The Saints and the Roughnecks" by William J. Chambliss, *Society*, Vol. 11, No. 1 (November/December 1973), pp. 24–31 excerpted. Copyright © 1973 by Transaction Publishers. Reprinted by permission of the publisher.

a few wild oats, they were totally unaware that sowing wild oats completely occupied the daily routine of these young men. The Saints were constantly occupied with truancy, drinking, wild driving, petty theft and vandalism. Yet not one was officially arrested for any misdeed during the two years I observed them.

This record was particularly surprising in light of my observations during the same two years of another gang of Hanibal High School students, six lower-class white boys known as the

Roughnecks. The Roughnecks were constantly in trouble with police and community even though their rate of delinquency was about equal with that of the Saints. What was the cause of this disparity? The result? The following consideration of the activities, social class and community perceptions of both gangs may provide some answers.

THE SAINTS FROM MONDAY TO FRIDAY

The Saints' principal daily concern was with getting out of school as early as possible. The boys managed to get out of school with minimum danger that they would be accused of playing hookey through an elaborate procedure for obtaining "legitimate" release from class. The most common procedure was for one boy to obtain the release of another by fabricating a meeting of some committee, program or recognized club. . . .

Having escaped from the concrete corridors the boys usually went either to a pool hall on the other (lower-class) side of town or to a cafe in the suburbs. Both places were out of the way of people the boys were likely to know (family or school officials), and both provided a source of entertainment. . . .

THE SAINTS ON WEEKENDS

On weekends, the automobile was even more critical than during the week, for on weekends the Saints went to Big Town—a large city with a population of over a million, 25 miles from Hanibal. Every Friday and Saturday night most of the Saints would meet between 8:00 and 8:30 and would go into Big Town. Big Town activities included drinking heavily in taverns or nightclubs, driving drunkenly through the streets, and committing acts of vandalism and playing pranks.

By midnight on Fridays and Saturdays the Saints were usually thoroughly high, and one or two of them were often so drunk they had to be carried to the cars. Then the boys drove around town, calling obscenities to women and girls;

occasionally trying (unsuccessfully so far as I could tell) to pick girls up; and driving recklessly through red lights and at high speeds with their lights out. Occasionally they played "chicken." One boy would climb out the back window of the car and across the roof to the driver's side of the car while the car was moving at high speed (between 40 and 50 miles an hour); then the driver would move over and the boy who had just crawled across the car roof would take the driver's seat.

Searching for "fair game" for a prank was the boys' principal activity after they left the tavern. The boys would drive alongside a foot patrolman and ask directions to some street. If the policeman leaned on the car in the course of answering the question, the driver would speed away, causing him to lose his balance. The Saints were careful to play this prank only in an area where they were not going to spend much time and where they could quickly disappear around a corner to avoid having their license plate number taken.

Construction sites and road repair areas were the special province of the Saints' mischief. A soon-to-be-repaired hole in the road inevitably invited the Saints to remove lanterns and wooden barricades and put them in the car, leaving the hole unprotected. The boys would find a safe vantage point and wait for an unsuspecting motorist to drive into the hole. Often, though not always, the boys would go up to the motorist and commiserate with him about the dreadful way the city protected its citizenry.

Leaving the scene of the open hole and the motorist, the boys would then go searching for an appropriate place to erect the stolen barricade. An "appropriate place" was often a spot on a highway near a curve in the road where the barricade would not be seen by an oncoming motorist. The boys would wait to watch an unsuspecting motorist attempt to stop and (usually) crash into the wooden barricade. With saintly bearing the boys might offer help and understanding. . . .

The boys had a spirit of frivolity and fun about their escapades. They did not view what they were engaged in as "delinquency," though it surely was by any reasonable definition of that word. They simply viewed themselves as having a little fun and who, they would ask, was really hurt by it? The answer had to be no one, although this fact remains one of the most difficult things to explain about the gang's behavior. Unlikely though it seems, in two years of drinking, driving, carousing and vandalism no one was seriously injured as a result of the Saints' activities.

THE SAINTS IN SCHOOL

The Saints were highly successful in school. The average grade for the group was "B," with two of the boys having close to a straight "A" average. Almost all of the boys were popular and many of them held offices in the school. One of the boys was vice-president of the student body one year. Six of the boys played on athletic teams. . . .

Teachers and school officials saw no problem with any of these boys and anticipated that they would all "make something of themselves."

How the boys managed to maintain this impression is surprising in view of their actual behavior while in school. Their technique for covering truancy was so successful that teachers did not even realize that the boys were absent from school much of the time. Occasionally, of course, the system would backfire and then the boy was on his own. A boy who was caught would be most contrite, would plead guilty and ask for mercy. He inevitably got the mercy he sought.

Cheating on examinations was rampant, even to the point of orally communicating answers to exams as well as looking at one another's papers. Since none of the group studied, and since they were primarily dependent on one another for help, it is surprising that grades were so high. Teachers contributed to the deception in their admitted inclination to give these boys (and presumably others like them) the benefit of the doubt. . . .

One exception to the gang's generally good performance was Jerry, who had a "C" average in his junior year, experienced disaster the next year

and failed to graduate. Jerry had always been a little more nonchalant than the others about the liberties he took in school. Rather than wait for someone to come get him from class, he would offer his own excuse and leave. Although he probably did not miss any more classes than most of the others in the group, he did not take the requisite pains to cover his absences. Jerry was the only Saint whom I ever heard talk back to a teacher. Although teachers often called him a "cut up" or a "smart kid," they never referred to him as a troublemaker or as a kid headed for trouble. It seems likely, then, that Jerry's failure his senior year and his mediocre performance his junior year were consequences of his not playing the game the proper way (possibly because he was disturbed by his parents' divorce). His teachers regarded him as "immature" and not quite ready to get out of high school.

THE POLICE AND THE SAINTS

The local police saw the Saints as good boys who were among the leaders of the youth in the community. Rarely, the boys might be stopped in town for speeding or for running a stop sign. When this happened the boys were always polite, contrite and pled for mercy. As in school, they received the mercy they asked for. None ever received a ticket or was taken into the precinct by the local police.

The situation in Big City, where the boys engaged in most of their delinquency, was only slightly different. The police there did not know the boys at all, although occasionally the boys were stopped by a patrolman. Once they were caught taking a lantern from a construction site. Another time they were stopped for running a stop sign, and on several occasions they were stopped for speeding. Their behavior was as before: contrite, polite and penitent. The urban police, like the local police, accepted their demeanor as sincere. More important, the urban police were convinced that these were good boys just out for a lark.

THE ROUGHNECKS

Hanibal townspeople never perceived the Saints' high level of delinquency. The Saints were good boys who just went in for an occasional prank. After all, they were well dressed, well mannered and had nice cars. The Roughnecks were a different story. Although the two gangs of boys were the same age, and both groups engaged in an equal amount of wild-oat sowing, everyone agreed that the not-so-well-dressed, not-so-well-mannered, not-so-rich boys were heading for trouble. Townspeople would say, "You can see the gang members at the drugstore night after night, leaning against the storefront (sometimes drunk) or slouching around inside buying cokes, reading magazines, and probably stealing old Mr. Wall blind. When they are outside and girls walk by, even respectable girls, these boys make suggestive remarks. Sometimes their remarks are downright lewd."

From the community's viewpoint, the real indication that these kids were in for trouble was that they were constantly involved with the police. Some of them had been picked up for stealing, mostly small stuff, of course, "but still it's stealing small stuff that leads to big time crimes." "Too bad," people said. "Too bad that these boys couldn't behave like the other kids in town; stay out of trouble, be polite to adults, and look to their future."

The community's impression of the degree to which this group of six boys (ranging in age from 16 to 19) engaged in delinquency was somewhat distorted. In some ways the gang was more delinquent than the community thought; in other ways they were less.

The fighting activities of the group were fairly readily and accurately perceived by almost everyone. At least once a month, the boys would get into some sort of fight, although most fights were scraps between members of the group or involved only one member of the group and some peripheral hanger-on. Only three times in the period of observation did the group fight together [against others]. . . .

More serious than fighting, had the community been aware of it, was theft. Although almost everyone was aware that the boys occasionally stole things, they did not realize the extent of the activity. . . .

The thefts ranged from very small things like paperback books, comics and ballpoint pens to expensive items like watches. The nature of the thefts varied from time to time. The gang would go through a period of systematically lifting items from automobiles or school lockers. Types of thievery varied with the whim of the gang. Some forms of thievery were more profitable than others, but all thefts were for profit, not just thrills. . . .

Over the period that the group was under observation, each member was arrested at least once. Several of the boys were arrested a number of times and spent at least one night in jail. While most were never taken to court, two of the boys were sentenced to six months incarceration in boys' schools.

THE ROUGHNECKS IN SCHOOL

The Roughnecks' behavior in school was not particularly disruptive. During school hours they did not all hang around together, but tended instead to spend most of their time with one or two other members of the gang who were their special buddies. Although every member of the gang attempted to avoid school as much as possible, they were not particularly successful and most of them attended school with surprising regularity. . . .

Teachers saw the boys the way the general community did, as heading for trouble, as being uninterested in making something of themselves. Some were also seen as being incapable of meeting the academic standards of the school. Most of the teachers expressed concern for this group of boys and were willing to pass them despite poor performance, in the belief that failing them would only aggravate the problem.

The group of boys had a grade point average just slightly above "C." No one in the group failed either grade, and no one had better than a "C" average. They were very consistent in their achievement or, at least, the teachers were consistent in their perception of the boys' achievement.

Two of the boys were good football players. Herb was acknowledged to be the best player in the school and Jack was almost as good. Both boys were criticized for their failure to abide by training rules, for refusing to come to practice as often as they should, and for not playing their best during practice. What they lacked in sportsmanship they made up for in skill, apparently, and played every game no matter how poorly they had performed in practice or how many practice sessions they had missed.

TWO QUESTIONS

Why did the community, the school and the police react to the Saints as though they were good, upstanding, nondelinquent youths with bright futures but to the Roughnecks as though they were tough, young criminals who were headed for trouble? Why did the Roughnecks and the Saints in fact have quite different careers after high school—careers which, by and large, lived up to the expectations of the community?

The most obvious explanation for the differences in the community's and law enforcement agencies' reactions to the two gangs is that one group of boys was "more delinquent" than the other. Which group *was* more delinquent? The answer to this question will determine in part how we explain the differential responses to these groups by the members of the community and, particularly, by law enforcement and school officials.

In sheer number of illegal acts, the Saints were the more delinquent. They were truant from school for at least part of the day almost every day of the week. In addition, their drinking and vandalism occurred with surprising regularity. The Roughnecks, in contrast, engaged sporadically in delinquent episodes. While these episodes were frequent, they certainly did not occur on a daily or even a weekly basis. . . .

There are really no clear-cut criteria by which to measure qualitative differences in antisocial behavior. The most important dimension of the difference is generally referred to as the "seriousness" of the offenses.

If seriousness encompasses the relative economic costs of delinquent acts, then some assessment can be made. The Roughnecks probably stole an average of about $5.00 worth of goods a week. Some weeks the figure was considerably higher, but these times must be balanced against long periods when almost nothing was stolen.

The Saints were more continuously engaged in delinquency but their acts were not for the most part costly to property. Only their vandalism and occasional theft of gasoline would so qualify. Perhaps once or twice a month they would siphon a tankful of gas. The other costly items were street signs, construction lanterns and the like. All of these acts combined probably did not quite average $5.00 a week, partly because much of the stolen equipment was abandoned and presumably could be recovered. The difference in cost of stolen property between the two groups was trivial, but the Roughnecks probably had a slightly more expensive set of activities than did the Saints.

Another meaning of seriousness is the potential threat of physical harm to members of the community and to the boys themselves. The Roughnecks were more prone to physical violence; they not only welcomed an opportunity to fight; they went seeking it. In addition, they fought among themselves frequently. Although the fighting never included deadly weapons, it was still a menace, however minor, to the physical safety of those involved.

The Saints never fought. They avoided physical conflict both inside and outside the group. At the same time, though, the Saints frequently endangered their own and other people's lives. They did so almost every time they drove a car, especially if they had been drinking. Sober, their driving was risky; under the influence of alcohol it was horrendous. In addition, the Saints endangered the lives of others with their pranks. Street excavations left unmarked were a very serious hazard. . . .

VISIBILITY

Differential treatment of the two gangs resulted in part because one gang was infinitely more visible than the other. This differential visibility was a direct function of the economic standing of the families. The Saints had access to automobiles and were able to remove themselves from the sight of the community. In as routine a decision as where to go to have a milkshake after school, the Saints stayed away from the mainstream of community life. Lacking transportation, the Roughnecks could not make it to the edge of town. The center of town was the only practical place for them to meet since their homes were scattered throughout the town and any noncentral meeting place put an undue hardship on some members. Through necessity the Roughnecks congregated in a crowded area where everyone in the community passed frequently, including teachers and law enforcement officers. They could easily see the Roughnecks hanging around the drugstore.

The Roughnecks, of course, made themselves even more visible by making remarks to passersby and by occasionally getting into fights on the corner. Meanwhile, just as regularly, the Saints were either at the cafe on one edge of town or in the pool hall at the other edge of town. Without any particular realization that they were making themselves inconspicuous, the Saints were able to hide their time-wasting. Not only were they removed from the mainstream of traffic, but they were almost always inside a building.

On their escapades the Saints were also relatively invisible, since they left Hanibal and travelled to Big City. Here, too, they were mobile, roaming the city, rarely going to the same area twice.

DEMEANOR

To the notion of visibility must be added the difference in the responses of group members to outside intervention with their activities. If one of the Saints was confronted with an accusing policeman, even if he felt he was truly innocent of a wrongdoing, his demeanor was apologetic and penitent. A Roughneck's attitude was almost the polar opposite. When confronted with a threatening adult authority, even one who tried to be pleasant, the Roughneck's hostility and disdain were clearly observable. Sometimes he might attempt to put up a veneer of respect, but it was thin and was not accepted as sincere by the authority. . . .

BIAS

Community members were not aware of the transgressions of the Saints. Even if the Saints had been less discreet, their favorite delinquencies would have been perceived as less serious than those of the Roughnecks.

In the eyes of the police and school officials, a boy who drinks in an alley and stands intoxicated on the street corner is committing a more serious offense than is a boy who drinks to inebriation in a nightclub or a tavern and drives around afterwards in a car. Similarly, a boy who steals a wallet from a store will be viewed as having committed a more serious offense than a boy who steals a lantern from a construction site. . . .

Visibility, demeanor and bias are surface variables which explain the day-to-day operations of the police. Why do these surface variables operate as they do? Why did the police choose to disregard the Saints' delinquencies while breathing down the backs of the Roughnecks?

The answer lies in the class structure of American society and the control of legal institutions by those at the top of the class structure. Obviously, no representative of the upper class drew up the operational chart for the police which led them to look in the ghettos and on streetcorners—which led them to see the demeanor of lower-class youth as troublesome and that of upper-middle-class youth as tolerable. Rather, the procedures simply developed from experience—experience with irate and influential upper-middle-class parents insisting that their son's vandalism was simply a prank and his drunkenness only a momentary "sowing of wild oats"—experience with cooperative or indifferent, powerless, lower-class parents who acquiesced to the laws' definition of their son's behavior.

ADULT CAREERS OF THE SAINTS AND THE ROUGHNECKS

. . . Seven of the eight members of the Saints went on to college immediately after high school. Five of the boys graduated from college in four years. The sixth one finished college after two years in the army, and the seventh spent four years in the air force before returning to college and receiving a B.A. degree. Of these seven college graduates, three went on for advanced degrees. One finished law school and is now active in state politics, one finished medical school and is practicing near Hanibal, and one boy is now working for a Ph.D. The other four college graduates entered submanagerial, managerial or executive training positions with larger firms. . . .

Some of the Roughnecks have lived up to community expectations. A number of them were headed for trouble. A few were not.

Jack and Herb were the athletes among the Roughnecks and their athletic prowess paid off handsomely. Both boys received unsolicited athletic scholarships to college. After Herb received his scholarship (near the end of his senior year), he apparently did an about-face. His demeanor became very similar to that of the Saints. Although he remained a member in good standing of the Roughnecks, he stopped participating in most activities and did not hang on the corner as often. . . .

Two of the boys never finished high school. Tommy left at the end of his junior year and went to another state. That summer he was arrested and placed on probation on a manslaughter charge. Three years later he was arrested for murder; he pleaded guilty to second degree murder and is serving a 30-year sentence in the state penitentiary.

Al, the other boy who did not finish high school, also left the state in his senior year. He is serving a life sentence in a state penitentiary for first degree murder.

Wes is a small-time gambler. He finished high school and "bummed around." After several years he made contact with a bookmaker who employed him as a runner. Later he acquired his own area and has been working it ever since. . . .

REINFORCEMENT

The community responded to the Roughnecks as boys in trouble, and the boys agreed with that perception. Their pattern of deviancy was reinforced, and breaking away from it became increasingly unlikely. *Once the boys acquired an image of themselves as deviants* [italics added], they selected new friends who affirmed that self-image. As that self-conception became more firmly entrenched, they also became willing to try new and more extreme deviances. With their growing alienation came freer expression of disrespect and hostility for representatives of the legitimate society. This disrespect increased the community's negativism, perpetuating the entire process of commitment to deviance. Lack of a commitment to deviance works the same way. In either case, the process will perpetuate itself unless some event (like a scholarship to college or a sudden failure) external to the established relationship intervenes. For two of the Roughnecks (Herb and Jack), receiving college athletic scholarships created new relations and culminated in a break with the established pattern of deviance. . . .

Selective perception and labelling—finding, processing and punishing some kinds of criminality and not others [italics added]—means that visible, poor, nonmobile, outspoken, undiplomatic "tough" kids will be noticed, whether their actions are seriously delinquent or not. Other kids, who have established a reputation for being bright (even though underachieving), disciplined and involved in respectable activities, who are mobile and monied, will be invisible when they deviate from sanctioned activities. They'll sow their wild oats—perhaps even wider and thicker than their lower-class cohorts—but they won't be noticed. When it's time to leave adolescence most will follow the expected path, settling into the ways of the middle class, remembering fondly the delinquent but unnoticed fling of their youth. The Roughnecks and others like them may turn around, too. It is more likely that their noticeable deviance will have been so reinforced by police and community that their lives will be effectively channeled into careers consistent with their adolescent background.

Medical Diagnosis and the Reinforcement of Deviant Labels

ADINA NACK

The interactionist perspective holds that both a person's self and a person's social role arise in the course of social interaction. Thus, parents train their female children to act like young women, and in time these youngsters come to see themselves in this way and to behave accordingly. By the same token, deviant selves and roles also arise in social interaction. For example, frequent association with persons already well established in deviant roles can influence individuals to see themselves in new ways. Sometimes even more dramatic transformations can come about through contact with formal agents such as criminal justice or medical personnel. As labeling theory argues, such agents can apply, or exacerbate the effects of, deviant labels.

Adina Nack shows that women who have contracted a sexually transmitted infection can place themselves in the tribe of women considered "bad girls" or "fallen women." She shows the role that physicians can play in this process. In the "diagnostic encounter," physicians can make explicit by their words and actions the violation of gender norms their patients had held implicitly about other women who are labeled "bad girls" or "fallen women."

Drawing on illness narratives of forty-three women living with genital herpes and/or HPV [the virus that causes genital warts], this article

Reprinted from Adina Nack, "Bad Girls and Fallen Women: Chronic STD Diagnoses as Gateways to Tribal Stigma," *Symbolic Interaction*, Vol. 25, No. 4: 463–485. © 2002, Society for the Study of Symbolic Interaction. Used by permission of the University of California Press and the author. All rights reserved.

addresses the following six questions: How do women come to learn the sexual and moral criteria of feminine "goodness" and "badness"? What are the gendered lessons they learn about the status implications of contracting an STD [sexually transmitted disease]? How do women make sense of being diagnosed with a chronic STD? How does a woman's prediagnostic view of herself as a sexual being serve to contextualize her experiences of diagnostic stigma? What intrapersonal challenges are posed by internalizing diagnostic stigma? Finally, what are the macrolevel public health implications for socially constructing and interactionally reinforcing the idea that STD-infected girls and women are "bad"? In exploring these questions, this article illuminates important facets of stigma, with a focus on diagnostic encounters as the beginnings of event series that will ultimately shape the women's redefinitions of their sexual selves and social relationships.

. . . I analyzed the data according to the principles of grounded theory, using constant comparative methods to adjust analytic categories to fit emerging theoretical concepts (Glaser 1978; Glaser and Strauss 1967). Initially, I used introspection (Ellis 1991) to hypothesize stages of how the sexual self was transformed by a chronic STD. Over time, I verified some categories and discarded others as data patterns reappeared. With each interview, I clustered subjects' experiences around particular stages to assess the validity of my initial model. The resulting evolutionary analysis was what Wiseman (1970) called a "total pattern"—a sequence of events that held true for the group studied. . . . This article focuses on the women's creations of meaning during diagnostic encounters, "a realm that has special meaning, and in which a particular language of reality is binding" (Radley 1994:99).

STD DIAGNOSES . . .

When asked to describe their diagnostic encounters, the women first recalled different degrees of "diagnostic shock" (Charmaz 2000), depending on whether they had noticed symptoms before the medical visit. They then described the emotional impact of finding out that something was seriously wrong with their bodies. Similar to the chronically ill men studied by Charmaz (1994), diagnoses triggered "identity dilemmas" for the majority of the women. What kind of women

were they to have contracted an STD? How did they now feel about themselves as sexual beings? What were the social implications of their new sexual health statuses?

At this point in their moral careers, most of the women could be categorized as fairly *discreditable* (Goffman 1963): by virtue of patient confidentiality, each woman was only explicitly discredited to her practitioner. My analysis, however, hones in on their *perceptions* of stigma, "what the putatively stigmatized think others think of them and 'their kind' and about how these others might react to disclosure" (Schneider and Conrad 1981:212). As the women entered the *diagnostic crisis* stage, many had their worst fears confirmed and began the process of defining the meanings and consequences of now "official" STD statuses.

PREDIAGNOSTIC LESSONS: CULTURAL MESSAGES ABOUT STDS

The social history of sexual disease in the United States reflects a tradition not only of assigning moral responsibility to those infected with STDs but also of differentially assigning moral stigma on the basis of gender, race, and class (e.g., Brandt 1987; Luker 1998). The social hygiene movement of the Progressive Era saw physicians and female moral reformers combine forces to more explicitly shape the moral boundaries of sexual behavior under the justification of public health. However, these boundaries were gendered with regard to venereal disease. A doctrine of physical *necessity* justified men's forays into promiscuity. In contrast, "the cowardly and cruel theory of innate depravity has been industriously disseminated as applying to 'fallen women.'. . . [M]en, the stronger, have remained free from blame; women, the weaker, have lived under a curse" (Dock 1910:60).

Following a modified life history format for interviews, I asked the women to discuss when they had first learned about sex in general and STDs in particular. I also asked them to relate any sexual or STD-related gossip, rumors, or jokes they had heard before their own STD diagnosis. My goal was to discover the processes through which each of them had learned to think about sexual norms and values and how they learned to assign symbolic meanings to girls and women who contracted STDs. "Since definitions of illness are ultimately cultural products, their meanings are influenced by social attitudes and cultural stereotypes" (Grove, Kelly, and Liu 1997:318). To analyze the intrapersonal impacts of STD diagnoses on these women, I had to first understand their prediagnostic heuristics.

"Suzy Rottencrotch" and Other Members of the Tribe

When I asked each woman to reflect on what she had learned about sexually diseased women, all conveyed similar imagery. Analytically, I conceptualized this pattern as the definitional building blocks for a gendered experience of tribal stigma. The women's stories of how they learned to think about women with STDs served to construct a *stigma theory,* "an ideology to explain [the stigmatized individual's] inferiority and account for the danger [that individual] represents" (Goffman 1963:5). According to the data, the women assigned auxiliary traits of promiscuity, dirtiness, low class, and irresponsibility to the "type" of woman who would contract an STD. As Goffman (1963) noted, stigma theory often incorporates rationalizations of animosity toward stigmatized individuals based on status differences, such as social class.

Historically, public opinion and public health campaigns have targeted sexually active, working class, and racial or ethnic minority women as the "vectors and vessels" of sexual disease (Davidson 1994; Luker 1998; Mahood 1990). For example, those in the lower economic classes, particularly women, have been viewed as transmitters of disease to wealthier classes. Several of the women described racial and socioeconomic dimensions of the bad girls tribe. Rhonda, a twenty-three-year-old Cuban American working-class administrative assistant, described how she

had conceptualized women with STDs before her first herpes outbreak. She painted a picture of poverty and substance abuse: "She'd be dirty. . . . I guess I would picture somebody who's really skinny, like sickly skinny, and just not clean. She'd probably have cold sores . . . like a crackhead." Jasmine, a twenty-year-old white upper-middle-class undergraduate had the perspective of a privileged upbringing and added an educational component to tribal membership: "People [who get STDs] are dirty or just not as intelligent. You know, not smart enough to be safe." Haley, a twenty-two-year-old white upper-middle-class undergraduate, added irresponsibility as a tribal trait. She had learned to assume that a woman who contracts an STD "isn't responsible, just going out and partying, and just not really caring about what they're doing and not watching out for themselves[,] . . . someone who doesn't even know what they're doing half the time." Monica, a twenty-one-year-old white middle-class undergraduate, added a racial dynamic to the social construction of this social class of women. Her high school health class featured "teenage mothers" as guest speakers to educate girls about the price of female sexuality. All of these teen moms were African Americans or Latinas from economically disadvantaged areas. As a white teenager from a middle-class home, Monica remarked that she felt "removed" from the risk of joining their ranks because these girls were "different in all those ways."

The age at which moral meanings became attached to STDs was fairly consistent among participants. While a few of the women recalled overhearing others' comments about STDs during childhood, all cited junior high or middle school as the time when their sexual health ideologies took shape. When asked what ideas they had about people with STDs during junior high and high school, all of the women described a consistent stereotype. Cleo, a thirty-one-year-old white middle-class graduate student, remembered how her high school health teacher had presented STDs as "awful" and "bad," so she "thought that only bad people had STDs." Kayla, a twenty-two-year-old white working-class undergraduate, told of having learned myths about the character blemishes of dishonesty and treachery embedded in stories about sexually diseased women who lied to their partners about their sexual health statuses and risked infecting them.

Because of religious lessons about sex, many of the women had learned to associate premarital sex and promiscuity with sin. For example, all twelve of the women who described themselves as having been raised Catholic recalled learning that STDs were connected to deficiencies in spiritual "goodness" that are manifested as "bad" behavioral choices. As an adolescent, Francine, a forty-three-year-old white middle-class health educator, remembered her Catholic school showing a sex education movie that gave her "the message that there's something very bad about having sex." She recalled, "That film showed sexuality being a temptation of the devil." In her social construction of sexuality, STDs became the mark of the sinner. Ingrid, a twenty-three-year-old white middle-class undergraduate, had learned from a nun, her Catholic school teacher in seventh grade, that she "didn't have to worry about STDs because [she was] a good Catholic." Implicit in this lesson was the message that those who contracted STDs were lacking in piety and moral fortitude. Such lessons were not limited to Catholicism: all of the remaining thirty-one women, raised in variety of faiths, used derogative adjectives to describe the explicit and implicit lessons from their childhood and adolescence about people with STDs.

The women's agreement on the trait of promiscuity was unanimous. Before contracting HPV, Cleo, thirty-one years old, had believed that "you had to be really promiscuous to get an STD." In high school, Ingrid learned the connection between being a *bad girl* and having an STD when she befriended a girl who had been "forced into prostitution at age eleven and had contracted several STDs, including syphilis and gonorrhea." In college, Tanya, a twenty-seven-year-old white upper-middle-class graduate student, also learned to connect STD status with being a woman who

"slept around a lot." When rumors got out that a female student (named Dee) had herpes, she and others mocked this woman by calling her "ST. Dee or V. Dee" and by ostracizing her from their social group. Being excluded from desirable social groups was another price to pay for being labeled a bad girl.

Tasha, a thirty-year-old white middle-class graduate student, clarified the gendered aspect of promiscuity when recounting the myths she had learned: men contracted STDs "from wanton women," not vice versa. Diana, a forty-five-year-old African American upper-middle-class professional, had had a similar attitude as a teenager: "I didn't think that I would ever be around anybody who would have something like that. You know, just kind of scum of the earth people had it . . . like, men who hung out with prostitutes." Hence, the double standard of STD morality: good men can be infected, but any woman with an STD is a bad woman. Ingrid, twenty-three years old, confirmed the inequity evident in standards of sexual morality. She recalled one female classmate in junior high who was not known to be sexually active but "was considered a slut just because she grew boobs." Thus this classmate served as a tease to the unrequited desires of her male peers. Highlighting the gendered nature of this category, she talked about a boy of the same age who was sexually active and positively regarded by peers as "the shit."

One woman described how military institutions clarify the rules of membership for this tribe. Chris, a forty-year-old white professional, recounted a tale of the infamous "Suzy Rottencrotch," a fictional character created by the military to exemplify the sexually diseased woman. Her former husband had shared with her his experiences with U.S. military programs on STD prevention. According to him, the programs relied heavily on the legend of Suzy, a loose woman/prostitute who would tempt men on leave to stray from their "good wives" who were faithfully chaste (and "clean") back home. This example clarifies how Suzy and her kind represent a different breed of women, the polar opposite in a moral dichotomy of female tribes: the "bad" versus the "good."

Contemporary U.S. ideologies of feminine sexual morality shaped interpersonal interactions in which the women learned symbolic meanings and consequences of STD infection for girls and women, in contrast to that of boys and men. *Bad* girls and *fallen* women were described as having gained their stigmatized affiliation by breaking the feminine moral code of their antithesis, the *good* girls or women. "The stigma attached to venereal disease then is generated not by who the person is, but rather by what the person no longer is" (Fox and Edgely 1983:70). Is a woman with an STD no longer "good"? This question would become personal and highly relevant in the context of receiving herpes and HPV diagnoses.

PATIENT-PRACTITIONER INTERACTIONS

The diagnosis itself is key to the moral careers of women with STDs because it can be taken as "evidence" that they possess attributes that differentiate them from other women, other *good* women. As Frank (1998) noted, "deep" illness experiences can trigger alterations in identity, and Kelly (1992) connected awareness of illness not only to identity transformation but also to social status degradation. Chronic and serious illness increases the possibility for affected individuals to become self-aware "that these differences are undesirable in themselves and likely to be appraised by others as undesirable" (Kelly 1992:397).

Medical Meanings of Diagnoses

Few studies examine microlevel interactions in sexual health services, especially from patients' perspectives. Such studies have the potential to illuminate issues at the interface between medical practitioners and patients, such as the prevalence of "moral evaluations" of patients (Roth 1972). All of the women studied viewed their practitioners' deliveries of their diagnoses as formative in how they initially processed medical and symbolic meanings of their STDs. The content and

style of practitioners' diagnostic presentations varied and, in different ways, served to exacerbate or diminish the women's perceptions of stigma.

A key factor that shaped the medical meanings of the diagnosis was whether the practitioner had presented accurate information about transmission, treatment, and prognosis. During interviews, the women assessed their practitioners' degree of accuracy in retrospect, as most had researched their diseases or sought out second opinions after receiving their initial diagnoses. In all, twenty-four women reported feeling initially devastated by the physiological implications of how STDs had *permanently* harmed their bodies.[1] Practitioners had reinforced their concerns that their infections meant permanent damage. For example, Summer, a twenty-year-old Native American working-class clerical worker, remembered the exam when she was diagnosed with genital warts. For her, the most horrible part was her practitioner explaining to her that it was not curable. Several of these women asked their practitioners directly to clarify the chronic nature and the implications of their diagnoses. In one case, Gita, a twenty-three-year-old Persian American middle-class professional, admitted that she "freaked out" when she was diagnosed with genital warts. She asked her practitioner, "Is this a lifetime thing? Am I gonna have another [outbreak]? I felt very unsure." Implicit in the incurable nature of these diseases was the long-term responsibility of being contagious. Haley, twenty-two years old, also remembered being more upset by the idea of infecting others than by the fact that HPV was incurable. When her practitioner told her that she could transmit genital warts to sexual partners, Haley recalled feeling "bad": "What made me feel worse than knowing that I had it was that I had the capability of giving it to somebody else."

In contrast to the above women, the other nineteen women in this study left their diagnostic interactions feeling less stigma of bodily abomination because their practitioners had helped them to see that their chronic STDs were, to some degree, manageable physical conditions. Sandy, a twenty-one-year-old white middle-class undergraduate, saw a practitioner who told her that her cervical HPV infection was not only treatable but also statistically "normal"—a fact she found very comforting. Elle, a thirty-two-year-old white working-class graduate student, had a doctor who helped her to understand that although herpes may not be curable, the outbreaks may decrease in severity and duration over time. Her practitioner also detailed treatment options that could alleviate symptoms and shorten the length of outbreaks.

Other practitioners in this subgroup fostered a lack of knowledge that served equally (if not genuinely) well in minimizing health fears. Many of the women felt calm after receiving STD diagnoses because their practitioners had not fully explained the chronic nature of the infections. In a few cases, practitioners gave significantly incorrect information about the contagious aspects of the STDs in their diagnostic interactions with patients. Helena, a thirty-one-year-old Greek American middle-class graduate student, received incorrect and incomplete information about HPV and "almost felt like [the practitioner] was going to treat the warts, and then everything was going to be fine . . . because nothing else was really explained." Several practitioners left their patients with similar false senses of well-being; they told the women that their HPV infections were not serious because the virus could not be transmitted to male partners.[2] Previous health research has found that many HPV patients "were initially informed that they had a 'virus' or 'condyloma.' The sexual route of transmission and the implications of the disease were not even mentioned" (Keller, Egan, and Mims 1995:358). My data confirm this finding and reveal that in such cases this lack of information reduced the women's initial perceptions of diagnostic stigma.

Moral Meanings of Diagnoses

Analyses show that while practitioners played important roles in shaping the medical meanings of STD diagnoses, they had less affect on the symbolic meanings. Not even the most compassionate and knowledgeable practitioner succeeded in undoing the years of socialization that had shaped their patients' perceptions that STDs were associated with the lower social *caste* of immoral and promiscuous women. However, sixteen of the women reported having received diagnoses from practitioners who acted in ways that exacerbated the women's fears of being seen as less than or worse than "good" women.

For this subgroup, the demeanor, actions, and language of their practitioners revealed judgment and condemnation of female patients with STDs. Diagnostic interactions with moralizing practitioners generated an immediate realization of the demoralizing interpersonal implications of having an STD.[3] In some cases, the participant perceived general disgust and revulsion toward them on the part of practitioners. For example, Chris, a forty-year-old who had scheduled a gynecological appointment because of a painful first herpes outbreak, described her doctor's interactions with her as if he were a car mechanic assessing a vehicle whose irresponsible owner had created a horrible problem. "He just looked at my crotch and said, 'Yep, that's herpes,' and sort of *slammed* my knees back together, like, Let's close this back up, like a car—slam the hood down! Don't want to see anymore of this one." In another case of perceived tactile communication of disgust, Julia, a fifty-year-old white middle-class professional, observed her doctor "pulling back" when he examined her, "like he didn't really want to touch my leg, like I was contaminated merchandise."

Practitioners also expressed negative feelings verbally about the women to whom they delivered news of a serious shift in health status. Louise, a twenty-eight-year-old white middle-class graduate student, received a harsh HPV diagnosis over the telephone. "He was very accusatory, like now I was this big pain in the ass for having a bad pap smear. . . . I got him on the phone, and he's like, You have cancerous growth all over your cervix: it's everywhere. It's probably HPV. You probably picked it up from some guy." Not only had her doctor described a very significant part of her body as ravaged by cancer, but he had also marked her as promiscuous. Her case illustrates how swiftly a woman can first face the stigma of bodily abomination and then rapidly feel the stain of blemished character and tribal stigma.

In some of these cases, the women perceived their practitioners as doubting both their morality and their intelligence. Such encounters left the women feeling like their characters had been doubly tarnished. When Jasmine, twenty years old, saw a gynecologist for her first outbreak of external genital warts she recalled her doctor asking, "Well, you've had unsafe sex?" She remembered: "[I felt] like I wanted to pull out my SAT scores and tell her, 'Just look—I'm not stupid!'" Looking back on her diagnosis, she admonished, "Someone in the health field should be objective about it and should be there to help you and to answer questions and not say, 'You've done the wrong thing.'" When Violet, a thirty-five-year-old white engineer, was given an HPV diagnosis, her nurse reprimanded, "You should use condoms," in response to Violet's disclosure that she had many casual partners whose STD status she did not know. Violet, whose nurse had labeled her promiscuous and stupid for not practicing safer sex, resented the nurse's choice to go "off on a moralistic trip." Essentially, these practitioners encouraged their patients to reduce their moral identities to those of women neither good enough nor smart enough to avoid getting spoiled by STDs. Violet's and the other women's concerns of being viewed as women of poor character reflect larger fears of being socially "reclassified" as belonging to a different and lesser category of women.

The interactions of these sixteen women with practitioners magnified concerns they already had about how others would react on learning about, seeing, or feeling their STD symptoms. This subgroup of women logically concluded that if a medical practitioner, whose training presumably stressed objectivity, could blithely assassinate their characters, then those beyond the walls of the examination room might dole out even harsher judgments. We must note that twenty-seven women described their practitioners as ranging from "kind" to "matter-of-fact" and did not feel that their practitioners actively reinforced the negative stereotypes of promiscuity or immorality. However, prediagnostic lessons about bad girls and fallen women provided the contextual backdrop for all of the women's sexual-self assessments during the diagnostic stage of their moral careers.

CONTEXTS OF DIAGNOSTIC MEANING

Previous research asserts that STD stigma "represents a total social identity, an identity devoid of qualities which would attract desirable persons" (Fox and Edgely 1983:70). Receiving medical results and confirmation of an official diagnosis, these women faced the challenge of whether to revise their *actual* social identities into that of fallen women. Though 75 percent of the women described feeling that their newly diagnosed bodies were "dirty," each woman's unique sexual-historical framework served to filter the amount of tribal stigma she internalized.

Romantic Relationship Status

Although practitioners served the role of the first "other" who discredited their STD statuses, most of the women's immediate stigma management concerns shifted from the real interactions with their practitioners to the imagined interactions with significant others. Relationship status—whether the women were single, casually dating, or in a committed romantic relationship—influenced how they imagined their STDs might affect their social status. They described how they began to evaluate internally potential ramifications in the medical office, after the practitioners had presented the diagnosis. The women employed a process of self-reflexivity and began to imagine how others, especially current and future sexual partners, might view them in light of their new STD status.

The women in committed intimate relationships felt buffered from the full effect of shame and fear of moral condemnation. For almost half of the women, long-term and monogamous relationships acted as shields from judgment, easing the moral shock of an STD diagnosis. Amelia knew that she could "talk about anything," including her cervical HPV diagnosis, with her fiancé because he was "very sexually secure." Similarly, Sierra, a twenty-three-year-old white administrative assistant, felt that having a boyfriend tempered her genital warts diagnosis: "I think I'm really fortunate in that I'm in a relationship right now that's absolutely amazing. . . . I also feel like he and I are pretty long term." Robin, a twenty-one-year-old white undergraduate, remembered her boyfriend as having a positive attitude: "I was really lucky to be with someone that was secure in how he felt about me. . . . And I think he was like 'we both have it,' it wasn't like one person did and one person didn't." She was grateful to have his support at the time of her diagnosis. By having partners reaffirm their worth, these women felt absolved from moral condemnation to some extent.

A few of the women expressed relief that they had not been dating casually at the time of diagnosis because that allowed them to delay the additional stress of being morally judged by a new partner. Sandy, at twenty-one, was "glad to be single" and did not plan on dating any time soon because she wanted to get treated and put the STD "behind" her without having to deal with possible rejection. Mary, a fifty-one-year-old white lower-middle class widow, had "not had sex" since her diagnosis with genital warts. She wanted to avoid the "humiliation" of talking about her STD. Being single and celibate seemed to provide less of an immorality "buffer" than having a committed relationship. However, the women perceived celibacy as offering less risk of moral scorn than casual dating. These findings speak to high levels of concern about the social ramifications of possibly being perceived by others as a *bad* girl or *fallen* woman.

Prediagnostic "Good" Girl Status

The culture had taught these women to evaluate the moral status of other women through assessments of their sexual behaviors. Hence they found themselves struggling to ascertain the relevancy of prediagnostic tales about the type of women who contracted STDs. They described looking to their unique sexual narratives for answers to how they had come to "earn" this mark of immorality. Thirty-five of the women saw themselves as having far too limited levels of sexual experience and, in turn, far too high sexual morality to "deserve" their infections. Examples of these women were Monica, twenty-two, who contracted external HPV as a "technical" virgin (i.e., skin-to-skin transmission occurred without penetrative intercourse), and Ingrid, twenty-three, who contracted cervical HPV from her first sexual partner.

A few of the women verbalized the question Why me? when they struggled with STD stereotypes of immorality. Helena, thirty-one, recalled postdiagnosis emotions and questions: "I just came home from the doctor, and I felt so dirty—why was this happening to me?" Rebecca, a fifty-six-year-old white upper-middle-class professional, was shaken when she was diagnosed with herpes: "All of a sudden, it *did* have something to do with me—my first reaction was, 'Who, me?' "

Several of the women recalled their earlier conceptions of bad girls and fallen women as they tried to discern what their diagnoses meant for their symbolic status as women. Louise, twenty-eight years old, related that she received her cervical HPV diagnosis over the telephone and immediately thought that this meant she was a "slut." However, she was conflicted about this: "I haven't had that many sexual partners. I've been fairly careful. . . . Who could I have gotten it from?" Likewise, Hillary, a twenty-two-year-old white middle-class undergraduate, could not believe that she had contracted HPV: "I just thought [STDs] happened to promiscuous, slutty people." Haley, twenty-two years old, also diagnosed as an undergraduate, described feeling jarred and distracted during her diagnostic encounter as she struggled with the contrast between who she thought she was and the type of people she thought got STDs: "I was pretty overwhelmed. . . . I have this disease, but I never thought I would get it. I never thought I would be one of *those* people. And here I am." In contrast to Haley's surprise, Jenny, an eighteen-year-old white upper-middle-class undergraduate, described how receiving her cervical HPV diagnosis caused her to reflect on how she could have been so naive as to have believed she was one of the "good girls." As the practitioner delivered the diagnosis, "Well, I kinda felt like a slut. . . . I wasn't thinking that when I got to ten, or however many people I had sex with, that I would look back and be like, Oh, my god—I've had sex with ten people!" Anne, a twenty-eight-year-old lower-middle-class graduate student, expanded on the dissonance she experienced:

I feel kind of slimy sometimes when I think about it. Like only slimy people get things like that, and I don't think of myself as slimy. So it's—yeah. It kind of doesn't fit, in a way, with my whole conception of myself. I never thought of myself as someone who would get a sexually transmitted infection and I definitely didn't—still it doesn't sit well with my image of myself.

For this subgroup of women, previous "good" moral identities clashed and created intrapersonal conflict over the potential shift to the lesser status of being "bad" and immoral. Having learned consistent messages about STDs equaling promiscuity and promiscuity equaling *bad* girl or *fallen woman,* the women perceived their diagnostic encounters as unwarranted and unexpected threats. The curse of two tribes assumed sudden relevance, and the idea of being demoted from good girl to "Suzy Rottencrotch" horrified them.

Prediagnostic "Bad" Girl Status

In contrast to the majority, eight of the women perceived their diagnoses as minimally stigmatizing with regard to social identity because they had already experienced the initial shame and loss of status when previous sexual traumas had, in effect, barred them from viewing themselves as "good." For example, Violet, thirty-five, had survived incest and several sexual assaults that had led her to see herself as "totally tainted" before her HPV was diagnosed. She also saw herself as an "awful slut" who had spent her undergraduate years "sport-fucking," a term she defined as "making guys beg for casual sex." Similarly, Julia, fifty, viewed "getting raped" as making her "feel a little looser about having intercourse." She had thought that trying to view her sexual self as good had no point, "'cause I've been raped and I'm not a virgin anymore." Having come of age in the early 1960s, she had learned that being a "good girl" required virginity. Violet's and Julia's stories exemplify the double bind for women: whether she sees herself as the object or subject of sexual trauma the resulting blow to social identity remains the same.

Several women claimed agency and contended that they had *earned* tribal stigma before being diagnosed with herpes or HPV. Rhonda, twenty-three, saw herself through her Cuban mother's judgmental eyes as a daughter who had done a "series of bad things," including the Catholic sin of terminating a pregnancy—a crisis that she believed held far greater moral and emotional consequences. She reiterated the stereotype of the "promiscuous slut" and confirmed, "I guess I did see myself that way." Likewise, Amelia, twenty-six, reflected on her days as the "school slut" who was always worried about getting pregnant and was not surprised to find out she had contracted an STD. Natasha, a twenty-year-old white middle-class undergraduate, also saw herself as fitting the STD stereotype of "someone who'd slept around with a lot of people" and felt she "deserved" her genital warts infection. All women in this subgroup viewed their past social identities as completely congruous with being at risk for contracting an STD. As these women had judged themselves as promiscuous and sexually unhealthy before receiving an official STD diagnosis, their diagnostic encounters did not add a tribal stigma but merely confirmed their preexisting membership.

Prediagnostic Rejection of the Tribal Dichotomy

One exception to either of the aforementioned subgroups is Elle, the thirty-two-year-old white working-class graduate student. She did not describe her herpes diagnosis as having threatened her sexual self with tribal stigma. Although she had described being aware of the stereotype that women with STDs were "skanks," she had come to view STDs as "a probability issue" for anybody having sex. She viewed her practitioner as "very normalizing and very optimistic." She credited her positive perception of the moral and health implications of genital herpes to the kind nature and educational stance of her practitioner. Theoretically, her case exemplifies the context of entering the STD diagnostic encounter having already embraced a deviant belief system with regard to gendered norms of sexual conduct.

Goffman (1963:6) noted, "It seems possible for an individual to fail to live up to what we effectively demand of him, and yet be relatively untouched by this failure; insulated by his alienation, protected by identity beliefs of his own, he feels that he is a full-fledged normal human being, and that we are the ones who are not quite human." While Elle's herpes diagnosis signifies that she has failed to meet the normative standards for feminine "goodness," she represents the special type of individual described above. She revealed in her interview that she identified as "queer," reported bisexual experiences, and identified as a member of a sadomasochistic subculture. Elle had insulated herself from the STD-related tribal stigma by having embraced membership in deviant tribes that rejected mainstream norms of sexual morality.

Her example points to an important question: Is it possible to immunize female patients from the threat of tribal stigma? The answer might lie in (1) socializing girls and women to reject the double standard of sexual morality and (2) training sexual health practitioners to explicitly destigmatize STDs and affirm patients' self-worth during diagnostic interactions. The challenge of investigating this theory would be to generate a sizable sample of women with STDs who meet the criteria.

CONCLUSION

Taking a firsthand, experiential perspective, this qualitative research fills some gaps in understanding the gender discourses and interactional processes at work in shaping symbolic meanings and psychosocial consequences of STD diagnoses for women. Through STD diagnostic interactions, these women experienced the fragility and fluidity of the female sexual self. Although Goffman (1963) does not distinguish tribal stigma as one that applies to gender "tribes," my data suggest that STD tribal stigma affects women at the intrapersonal level during diagnostic encounters.[4] Cultural scripts of femininity structure a tribal dichotomy that defines what it means to be a sexual woman. Deviation from the "good girl" script threatens demotion to an unsavory social caste. Tribal stigma can result from a relatively discreditable STD diagnosis because maintaining the good girl status is inherently unstable.

Invoking Goffman's (1963) differentiation between *the discredited* and *the discreditable,* the only arena in which the women I studied were explicitly discredited was in the doctor's office, where their records contained documentation of diagnoses, treatments, and follow-up exams. The women with internal or cervical HPV could "pass" for healthy even when naked and engaged in sexual intercourse. The women with external HPV and genital herpes could pass whenever they were asymptomatic. Given the potential to remain discreditable in most relationships, why did they experience blemished characters and feel threatened by tribal stigma? I attribute these differences to the specific sociohistorical construction of non-HIV STDs such that women, rather than gay men or intravenous drug users, are posited as the root of these diseases.

Expanding tribal stigma to intrapersonal realms frames my analysis of why and how women with chronic STDs may be vulnerable to its effects. Medical sociologists have not typically found evidence of tribal stigma in individuals whose disorders are easily hidden. In reference to individuals with discreditable conditions such as Parkinson's disease, urinary or bowel incontinence, Charmaz (2000:285) found that "guilt and shame increase when chronically ill people view themselves as socially incompetent." Women with chronic STDs do not exhibit public signs of bodily abomination; yet many experienced feelings of social incompetence in that they fear having jeopardized their status as "good" women.

The master status of gender interacts with STD stereotypes to magnify the experience of STD stigmata for women. In a society that ideologically structures women as a tribe divided over sexual morality, a master health status of being STD infected stigmatizes a woman both morally and socially. Is there a function served by this ideology? If one views sexuality as "socially organized and critically structured by gender inequality" (Walby 1990:121), then a gender-based ideology of double standards for sexual morality functions to legitimate the social-sexual power of men. Researchers studying the gendered implications of STD infections have confirmed that women experience greater degrees of stigmatization and ostracism than do men (Pitts, Bowman, and McMaster 1995). Many cultures construct male promiscuity as evidence of positive masculine traits: "Popular ideas about STDs suggest little stigma is attached to male infection. Having an STD is almost regarded as a rite of passage into manhood, proof of sexual activity: 'A bull is not a bull without his scars'" (Bassett and Mhloyi 1991:143).

This study points to the fact that this ideology also has an impact on practitioner-patient sexual health interactions. My research supports Lock's (2000:266) idea that medical agents often act in the best interest of the socially dominant: "It is with special emphasis on ethnicity and gender differences, that the well-being of some individuals may be exploited in any given society for the sake of those with power." Feminist scholars have long criticized Western medicine as a significant contributor to sexist ideologies (e.g., Delaney, Lupton, and Toth 1988; Ehrenreich and English 1973). This research highlights how the majority of male and female sexual health practitioners do not work to dismantle an ideology that promotes gender inequality. A comparable study of men with chronic STDs would be able to test the hypothesis that the gender of the patient correlates with the degree to which the patient perceives an STD diagnosis as stigmatizing. . . .

NOTES

1. Because of the chronic nature of both viral infections, many patients perceived their physical symptoms as permanent during diagnostic encounters. A forthcoming manuscript addresses how these perceptions often changed after treatments eliminated or lessened symptoms.
2. A woman may be infected with more than one strain of HPV, such that diagnosis of a cervical infection does not rule out the possibility of having a future outbreak of external warts or transmitting the infection to a male partner.
3. As practitioner-patient interactions often magnified STD stigmata, I allude to "dos and don'ts" of practitioner interaction style. This is, however, the focus of a forthcoming article.
4. A forthcoming manuscript explains how the majority of the women overcome STD tribal stigma through critical self-analysis and antisexist re-visioning of an ideology of sexual morality.

REFERENCES

Bassett, M. T., and M. Mhloyi. 1991. "Women and AIDS in Zimbabwe: The Making of an Epidemic." *International Journal of Health Services* 21:143–156.

Brandt, Allan M. 1987. *No Magic Bullet: A Social History of Venereal Disease in the United States since 1880.* New York: Oxford University Press.

Charmaz, Kathy. 1994. "Identity Dilemmas in Chronically Ill Men." *Sociological Quarterly* 35:269–288.

———. 2000. "Experiencing Chronic Illness." Pp. 277–292 in G. L. Albrecht, R. Fitzpatrick, and S. C. Scrimshaw (eds.), *Handbook of Social Studies in Health and Medicine.* London: Sage.

Davidson, Roger. 1994. "Venereal Disease, Sexual Morality, and Public Health in Interwar Scotland." *Journal of the History of Sexuality* 5(2):267–294.

Delaney, Janice, Mary Jane Lupton, and Emily Toth. 1988. *The Curse: A Cultural History of Menstruation*. Urbana: University of Illinois Press.

Dock, Lavinia. 1910. *Hygiene and Morality: A Manual for Nurses and Others, Giving an Outline of the Medical, Social and Legal Aspects of the Venereal Diseases*. New York: G. P. Putnam's Sons.

Ehrenreich, Barbara, and Deirdre English. 1973. "Witches, Midwives, and Nurses." *Monthly Review* 25(5):25–40.

Ellis, Carolyn. 1991. "Sociological Introspection and Emotional Experience." *Symbolic Interaction* 14(1):23–50.

Fox, Elaine, and Charles Edgely. 1983. "Effects of Non-physical Stigma in Venereal Disease." *Free Inquiry in Creative Sociology* 11(1):68–72.

Frank, Arthur. 1998. "Just Listening: Narrative and Deep Illness." *Families Systems & Health* 16(3):197–216.

Glaser, Barney G. 1978. *Theoretical Sensitivity*. Mill Valley, CA: Sociological Press.

Glaser, Barney G., and Anselm L. Strauss. 1967. *The Discovery of Grounded Theory: Strategies for Qualitative Research*. Chicago: Aldine.

Goffman, Erving. 1963. *Stigma: Notes on the Management of Spoiled Identity*. Upper Saddle River, NJ: Prentice Hall.

Grove, Kathleen A., Donald P. Kelly, and Judith Liu. 1997. "But Nice Girls Don't Get It: Women, Symbolic Capital, and the Social Construction of AIDS." *Journal of Contemporary Ethnography* 26(3):317–337.

Keller, Mary L., Judith J. Egan, and L. Ferns Mims. 1995. "Genital Human Papillomavirus Infection: Common but Not Trivial." *Health Care for Women International* 16:351–364.

Kelly, Michael. 1992. "Self, Identity and Radical Surgery." *Sociology of Health & Illness* 14(3): 390–415.

Lock, Margaret. 2000. "Accounting for Disease and Distress: Morals of the Normal and Abnormal." Pp. 259–276 in G. L. Albrecht, R. Fitzpatrick, and S. C. Scrimshaw (eds.), *Handbook of Social Studies in Health and Medicine*. London: Sage.

Luker, Kristin. 1998. "Sex, Social Hygiene, and the State: The Double-Edged Sword of Social Reform." *Theory and Society* 27(5):601–634.

Mahood, Linda. 1990. "The Magdalene's Friend: Prostitution and Social Control in Glasgow, 1869–1890." *Women's Studies International Forum* 13(1–2):49–61.

Pitts, Marian, Margaret Bowman, and John McMaster. 1995. "Reactions to Repeated STD Infections: Psychosocial Aspects and Gender Issues in Zimbabwe." *Social Science and Medicine,* 40(9): 1299–1304.

Radley, Alan. 1994. *Making Sense of Illness. The Social Psychology of Health and Disease*. London: Sage.

Roth, Julius A. 1972. "Some Contingencies of the Moral Evaluation and Control of Clientele: The Case of Hospital Emergency Staff." *American Journal of Sociology* 77(5):839–856.

Schneider, Joseph W., and Peter Conrad. 1981. "Medical and Sociological Typologies: The Case of Epilepsy." *Social Science and Medicine* 3(1):211–219.

Walby, Syliva. 1990. *Theorizing Patriarchy*. Oxford: Basil Blackwell.

Wiseman, Jacqueline P. 1970. *Stations of the Lost*. Chicago: University of Chicago Press.

The Positive Consequences of Stigma

NANCY J. HERMAN and CHARLENE E. MIALL

Early interpreters of labeling theory stressed the negative consequences of official labeling. Some interpreters actually conceived of it as a theory of stigma determinism. Once people had been processed by some agency of social control, they had no choice but to become the kind of people the agency said they now were. It was as if they were being cast in a play. Thus, they took on the role, status, and self-conception implicit in the part the control agency had cast them. In effect, the people processed by these agencies and their agents now saw themselves through agency eyes and became the kinds of people that they were said to be.

Nancy J. Herman and Charlene E. Miall's case study explores how ex-psychiatric patients and involuntarily childless women responded to being processed in treatment agencies and how they responded to the stigmatizing label of "mental patient" or "infertile." If stigma determinism held for all such labeled persons, then all mental patients and infertile women, once labeled, would experience a lowering of their self-esteem and an increase in their deviant behavior directly proportional to their lowered self-esteem. In contrast, Herman and Miall found a number of outcomes that they define as the "positive consequences of stigma." The label provided an explanation of their conduct to others. By lowering what others expected from them, it also was able to increase their sense of competence. It often engendered a number of opportunities and exempted them from what are defined as "normal" social roles. Finally, in many cases, it not only drew their families closer to them but enabled them to gain a better understanding of themselves.

INTRODUCTION

The labeling theory perspective stresses the importance of studying social definitions and the social processes by which actions and individuals are labeled or defined as deviant. The significance of labeling resides in the stigma that accompanies the label. Stigmatizing labels may produce the deviant behavior that is being condemned, and individuals may become the very thing that they are labeled

Reprinted from Nancy J. Herman and Charlene E. Miall, "The Positive Consequences of Stigma: Two Case Studies in Mental and Physical Disability," *Qualitative Sociology*, Vol. 13, No. 3 (1990), pp. 251–269. Copyright © 1990 Springer Science and Business Media. Reprinted with kind permission from Springer Science and Business Media and the authors.

(Becker, 1973; Lemert, 1972; Manning, 1975; Tannenbaum, 1938). This may occur as a consequence of social rejection which encourages maladaptive withdrawal into deviant subcultures.

Theorists, however, have argued that labeling may have both adaptive and maladaptive consequences (Plummer, 1979:118). Prior to the emergence of the labeling perspective, Parsons (1951:239–294) noted that the development of a strong defensive morale within deviant subcultures was a secondary gain for individuals involved in deviant behavior. More recently, others have argued that stigmas or identity marks themselves may be exploitable and used for secondary gains (cf. Gramling and Forsyth, 1987; Lorber, 1967; and Schur, 1979). Notably, systematic examination of the positive social and social psychological effects of possessing a stigma or identity mark is lacking.

Most sociological research on mental and physical disability using a labeling theory approach has focused on the negative consequences of possessing a stigmatizing attribute (cf. Davis, 1961; Gove, 1976:68; and Hanks and Poplin, 1981:322).[1] However, labeling behavior as disability may legitimate incapacity, reduce role strain, and provide the disabled with adaptive opportunities (cf. Haber and Smith 1971:95). We consider two substantively different deviant and stigmatized populations—ex-psychiatric patients and involuntarily childless women—and explore whether stigma has positive consequences for these individuals.[2] Using their meanings, we document the experiences defined as positive and construct three generic categories of positive consequences of stigma. . . .

METHODOLOGY, SETTING, AND SAMPLES

Descriptive data were gathered on the nature of deinstitutionalized patient life over a period of four years by means of participant observation, informal, and semi-formal interviewing techniques with 285 chronic and non-chronic ex-psychiatric patients in Southern Ontario, Canada.[3] Qualitative data were collected at drop-in facilities for ex-patients, self-help group meetings such as "Recovery Inc.," at activist group headquarters, at sheltered workshops for the emotionally disturbed, at non-sheltered places of employment, at a psychiatric hospital canteen, in coffee shops, at boarding and nursing homes, and, in general, where subjects "hung out."

A disproportionate, stratified random sample of 285 former mental patients was drawn from a listing which included all psychiatric clients discharged from a government psychiatric facility in Southern Ontario between 1975 and 1981; all patients discharged from psychiatric wards in several general hospital facilities; those treated as outpatients between 1978 and 1981 in community psychiatric clinics; and all clients treated privately

by a psychiatric team associated with a university hospital.[4]

The sample of 285 was disproportionately stratified to include six subgroups divided according to age, chronicity, and type of hospitalization. Comparisons were made among elderly, middle-aged, and young long-term male and female ex-patients; and elderly, middle-aged, and young short-term male and female ex-patients.[5] Initial interviews were done at home or after group meetings, were unstructured and open-ended, and lasted approximately one and a half hours. Subjects were subsequently asked if the researcher could accompany them to the various functions and activities in which they were involved. Many subjects sponsored the researcher into various ex-patient groups, which facilitated participant observation with ex-psychiatric patients interacting with other ex-patients and "normal" societal members.

Qualitative data were gathered on involuntarily childless women in Southern Ontario over a period of two years.[6] In order to obtain participants, a snowball sampling technique was used. Volunteers were recruited through social work agencies, adoptive parent groups, and through other research participants. The very secretive processes surrounding infertility (Miall, 1986) and the institutional confidentiality surrounding adoption (Miall, 1987) made it very difficult to obtain a sample of participants. Respondents were included if they had a desire for children and experienced infertility in past and present relationships.[7]

A pre-tested, standardized open-ended interview was conducted with 30 involuntarily childless women. Given recruitment problems, a questionnaire identical to the interview schedule was completed by 41 other subjects who would not agree to be interviewed but who were willing to complete the questionnaire. Questions were based on previous academic work on adoption, more than one and a half years of participant observation in an infertility self-help group, discussions with infertile adoptive parents, and anecdotal literature on infertility and adoption. Interviews lasted from two and a half to four hours.

The women ranged in age from 25 to 45, were well educated, from middle to upper class backgrounds, white, and Protestant, although 16 respondents were Jewish. In this sample, 58 (82%) had adopted children and 13 (18%) were in the process of adopting for the first time. In sociodemographic terms, the respondents were similar to those surveyed by Bachrach (1983) in the United States.

EX-PSYCHIATRIC PATIENTS: THE EXPERIENCE OF STIGMA

Using the same sample, Herman has examined perceptions of mental illness as stigma, deviant identities, information/stigma management techniques, and identity transformation (cf. Herman, 1986, 1988, 1989, 1990). The data indicate that 98% of the sample categorize mental illness in negative terms and have learned the social meaning of their "failing" through formal societal reaction, official labeling, and institutional processing; direct, negative, disvaluing post-treatment experiences with others; a combination of societal reaction, institutional processing and negative experiences with "normals"; or through self-labeling (cf. Link, 1987; Link et al., 1987; Link et al., 1989).

To avoid potential or further stigma, chronic and non-chronic ex-psychiatric patients develop and use "defensive" and "offensive" strategies of stigma management (cf. Link and Cullen, 1986). Defensive strategies include institutional retreatism, societal retreatism, capitulation, passing, and subcultural participation—strategies having negative implications for identity transformation. Offensive strategies include selective concealment, therapeutic disclosure, preventive disclosure, and political activism, strategies having positive implications for identity transformation and the resumption of normal roles, identities, and statuses.

INVOLUNTARILY CHILDLESS WOMEN: THE EXPERIENCE OF STIGMA

Estimates of involuntary childlessness range from 1 in 5 (Burgwyn, 1981; Kraft et al., 1980) to 1 in 10 couples (Mosher, 1982).[8] Within western

nations, 10% to 15% of the population may be infertile (National Center for Health Statistics, 1985). Western cultural norms and values encourage reproduction and celebrate parenthood, particularly for women. Sociologists characterize childlessness, whether voluntary or involuntary, as a form of deviant behavior because it violates rules of acceptable conduct (Miall, 1985, 1986; Veevers, 1972).

Using the same sample, Miall (1986) examined involuntary childlessness as a stigmatizing attribute and discovered that the women studied feel stigmatized by their inability to reproduce. Nearly all categorize infertility as representing failure or an inability to "work" normally. These women have also provided detailed descriptions of real sanctions related to their childlessness (Miall, 1985). Their sexuality, femininity, and psychological health [have] been subject to question. In addition, infertile women are often divorced by their husbands, may not receive an equal share in the wills of relatives, are excluded from groups of mothers and children, and subjected to negative comments on an on-going basis, all because of their inability to reproduce.

Infertile couples who wish to rear children often resort to adoption. In western society, biological kinship ties are valued such that the lack of a blood tie between an adoptive mother and her children might also be discrediting. To explore the stigma potential of adoptive parent status, respondents were asked to detail their perceptions of societal beliefs about adoption. The beliefs generated contained strong elements of stigmatization based on the absence of a blood tie.[9] These women also experienced formal and informal social sanctions related to their adoptive parent status (Miall, 1987).

When compared with ex–psychiatric patients, similarities emerge in how involuntarily childless women learn the social meaning of their "failing."

Childless women experienced direct, negative, disvaluing experiences with "normals" during and after treatment for infertility, and during and after the adoption of their children. They also engaged in self-labeling apart from formal or informal processing.

To avoid potential or further stigma from others, infertile women who adopt also employ selective concealment, therapeutic disclosure, and preventive disclosure—strategies having positive implications for identity transformation (Miall, 1986, 1989).

POSITIVE RESPONSES TO STIGMA

Versions of labeling theory that focus on social reactions to deviance have been criticized for their neglect of the perceptions, interpretations, and behavior of the deviant actor (cf. Rogers and Buffalo, 1974); and their tendency to conceptualize the labeled individual as overly passive (cf. Davis, 1975). Warren and Johnson (1972:76) argue that labeling theorists have thrown out all concern with "the deviant being of the deviant" and what such a being means to the individual concerned. To correct this omission, they suggest a focus on "the everyday social reality of the individual social actor and his interpretations of that reality" (Warren and Johnson, 1972:82). As authors, we have extensively documented the negative social psychological and "real" consequences, such as restriction on rights and limitation on life chances, that occur to individuals who have been labeled mentally ill or infertile. We do not, however, only presuppose negative experiences with stigma. Rather we focus on the meanings and interpretations, both positive and negative, that our respondents bring to their life experiences. Using these meanings, we document, in this paper, those experiences defined as positive and construct three generic categories of positive consequences of stigma.

CHRONIC AND NON-CHRONIC EX-PSYCHIATRIC PATIENTS

Several authors have established the profound negative effects of the stigma of mental illness—for example, limits on future participation in society;

problems re-establishing normal social roles and identities; and employment difficulties (Herman, 1987, 1988, 1989, 1990; Link, 1987; Link et al., 1987, 1989). G. Herman's data indicate, however, that certain positive consequences result from labeling, institutional processing and treatment, and subsequent stigmatization. These positive consequences are that: (1) labeling provides ex-patients with legitimation for their post- and some pre-treatment behavior; (2) it exempts them from usual role obligations and relieves ex-patients from taxing, onerous duties; (3) it provides ex-patients, in their own terms, with certain adaptive opportunities; (4) in some cases, it leads to stronger familial ties (cf. Link et al., 1989); and (5) for some, it serves as a personal growth experience.

Approximately one half of the chronic ex-patients felt being diagnosed and treated for mental illness provided them with an identity that legitimated most or all of their post-hospital deviant behavior. As one young chronic male stated:

> This is how it is. You're an ex-nut. Society has this image of you, that you're at any moment going to do something "crazy." They almost expect it of you. And this is really great. Because if you want to go up to a woman and grab her tits or touch her ass, or even if I rip off a TV and get caught, all's I have to explain is that I'm a nut that's been let out. It tells them that I'm not in my right mind, so they don't go too hard on me. Being mental gives you just the excuse you need!

Another ex-patient explained how she "got away" with committing deviant acts following release from the hospital:

> I know that having mental illness is a bitch. I've gone through hell at times, but it does have its certain benefits. Like, if you hate someone's guts or if they've treated you meanly, you can get back at them without fear of retaliation. I had this neighbor who used to constantly pick on me and be sarcastic. He always used to be on his porch staring. One day, when I was sure he was watching, I undid my jeans and "mooned" him with my big ass. Ordinarily, I wouldn't have been able to

get away with this act, but my mother explained to the man later that I was "mentally ill and we have to expect that she may do strange things from time to time."

Twelve percent of the sample also indicated that being defined as mentally ill provided justification for previous bizarre acts:

When I was finally hospitalized and they diagnosed my condition, my family absolved me from a lot of the things I had done in the past. They didn't realize that I smashed things and hit people because I was "sick" . . . that I was psychotic, and neither did I.

One third of the ex-patients remarked that awareness of their stigmatizing attribute exempted them from many social role obligations (cf. Haber and Smith, 1971) and excused them from taxing, onerous duties (cf. Sagarin, 1975; Scheff, 1981). One female ex-patient observed:

Being crazy does have its benefits. Like people don't expect the same things from you. You don't have to perform up to certain standards like you would if you hadn't had the breakdown. You don't have to be as responsible, to meet certain obligations, to be the ideal mother, et cetera.

Ex-psychiatric patients also feel that the stigma of mental illness provides them with certain adaptive opportunities. Through participation in deviant subcultures, 42% of the chronic ex-patients learned how to capitalize on their stigmatizing attribute and "make it on the outside." Ex-patients learned where, how, and when they could pick up "quick cash," "free eats," and where to get a "free place to crash."[10] One young male ex–psychiatric patient stated:

There are certain advantages. Being a mental means that there are people and places out there that are dying to "help you." You know, like social agencies, churches, and so-called "do-gooders" in society. Some will give you a few bucks; others will give you a hot meal. You quickly find out

where they are, hand them a line, and they fork over. It's better than working for a living.

A second female ex-patient, who called herself a "professional crazy," explained how she used the system to her advantage and capitalized on her stigmatized identity:

I'm actually better off now than before I was hospitalized. Such mental illness is the shits, but you can benefit from the status too. I learned from the others that I can sell my "meds" to Dirk on Jackson Street. He usually gives me about ten bucks. I also learned which fast food joints hand out free food, so I'm eating better than ever; and if I want to make some real money, I just have to act sorrowful on some street in "Streetsville" and hold out my hand and tell 'em that I need money to help with my treatment. . . . One week, I made a hundred bucks.

The data indicate that, in the actors' terms, being labeled with a stigmatizing attribute generates certain opportunities that might otherwise not be available.

In terms of other gratifications, stronger familial relationships arose. Thirty-eight percent of the chronic and non-chronic ex-patients felt that having been labeled and treated for mental illness solidified and strengthened social relationships with family members.[11] Link et al. (1989) noted a similar phenomenon with relatives who were members of the patient's household. As one middle-aged male stated:

Things never used to be good between my family and me. There was no true genuine affection and caring. We used to fight a lot . . . big blow ups. No one pulled together. But since my sickness, things have really changed. Pop and my sisters and me are now on better terms. Tragedy can really bring people together.

Similarly, another ex-patient noted the strengthening of family ties:

I'm now sixty-two years old. Having mental illness is no picnic, don't get me wrong, but it did *something so wonderful for me. It brought my family together as a unit. They rallied around me. We all banded together the way it's supposed to be.*

For others, being labeled and treated for mental illness functioned as a growth experience. Although experiencing great frustration, anxiety, and pain, approximately 33% of chronic and non-chronic ex-patients felt they had grown from their social experiences within and outside of the hospital. Similarly, Warren (1987:227) has noted that her respondents attributed positive changes to themselves and to their marriages following hospitalization for mental illness. One ex-patient spoke of the acquired ability to engage in self-reflective activities, a consequence of hospitalization but not necessarily stigma:

> *Through the psychotherapy and shrink sessions, I must say that I did learn a lot—in particular about who I am, and why I do the things I do. Before my treatment, I was never the kind of guy to stop and think about things—what the hell is it that I'm doing and why? But now I do this on a regular basis. Sometimes, it's extremely painful, but ultimately, it's very enlightening.*

Another ex-patient commented on how she "grew" from direct negative post-hospital experiences with "normals" who stigmatized her:

> *Once I was let out, friends, people just shunned me, or they acted as if I couldn't be trusted with their kids, or with a knife or something. Before my hospitalization, how people treated me or what they thought of me was absolutely important to me. I was very insecure and had a low opinion of myself. Through this fucking ordeal, I came to the realization that what others think is not important, it's how I think about myself that counts. I realized through all of this that I can stand on my own two feet.*

To conclude, the possession of the discreditable label of mental illness has positive consequences such as legitimating subsequent deviant acts, exempting individuals from social role obligations and taxing duties, providing opportunities and gratifications, strengthening family relationships, and providing positive growth experiences.

INVOLUNTARILY CHILDLESS WOMEN

As already noted, involuntarily childless couples experience profound negative social psychological consequences and "real" sanctioning from others when they fail to reproduce. However, the infertile women studied by Miall also experienced certain positive consequences as a result of labeling and stigmatization. The positive consequences of being labeled infertile included: (1) legitimation of the childless role particularly as it pertained to interaction with family and friends; and (2) legalization of the disabled role within adoption agencies. The experience of stigma associated with being infertile and an adoptive parent also resulted in (3) personal growth as subjectively defined by the respondents; (4) the strengthening of dyadic ties; (5) opportunities for heightened interpersonal interaction with others; and (6) opportunities for career growth and change.

In terms of role legitimation, respondents diagnosed as infertile spoke of the relief they felt when others learned that their childlessness was involuntary and not by choice. Veevers (1979:4–5) has already concluded that childlessness in general is subject to stigmatization and voluntary childlessness most of all. Whereas the involuntarily childless are stigmatized by their "physical blemish," the childless by choice are stigmatized by their "moral blemish." Respondents reluctant to reveal their infertility shared this sentiment, noting feelings of frustration and hurt when others assumed they didn't *want* children. As one woman observed:

> *I know at one point I overheard someone saying, "Oh, they're too selfish, they're too interested in going on fancy holidays. Material things, that's why they're not having children." It was so untrue and it hurt.*

These women subsequently used the infertile label to avoid being labeled voluntarily childless—something the childless by choice have been known to do (cf. Veevers, 1980). As one respondent put it:

We had been married five years when we decided to start our family. Up to that point, we'd been getting hints but we always ignored them. We'd have our family when we were ready, right? Well, we didn't because we found out we couldn't and it was terrible. . . . His mother was always commenting on how many trips we were taking, the money we were spending on ourselves. Finally I had enough and told her that there was nothing we could do about it. The experience was negative, there's no getting around that but at least she didn't bug me anymore.

The use of the infertile label to deflect criticism about childlessness served as a "medical disclaimer"; that is, respondents presented a ". . . blameless, beyond-my-control medical interpretation" as a way ". . . to reduce the risk that more morally disreputable interpretations might be applied by naive others" (Schneider and Conrad, 1980:41). As another woman observed:

If the reason [for childlessness] is not an anatomical reason or a reason for which they can't find a reason, I think people will chime in with, "Well, maybe you're not doing it right" and you don't want to leave yourself open to that [sic].

Thus, assuming the stigmatizing infertile label relieved respondents of the burden of being perceived as childless by choice, sexually incompetent, or both.

Similarly, a medical diagnosis of infertility legitimated respondents in the eyes of adoption agencies. In the United States and Canada, many adoption agencies require documented medical proof of infertility in order for couples to be considered for infants. Given that legal definitions of disability made with reference to medical, psychological, and social criteria can have the force of law, the infertile label facilitated access to help-giving agencies.

Being diagnosed as infertile and experiencing the stigma accompanying the label also generated other opportunities and gratifications. Several respondents spoke of the personal growth they experienced as a consequence of surviving this major life crisis. As one woman noted:

Well, I'm more confident. . . . I'm more able to help others now I think because I've taken courses on group leadership, sensitivity training and so on, things I would probably not have become involved in otherwise. My outlook has broadened. I'm more sympathetic to others now.

Other respondents referred to stronger relationships as benefits arising from infertility and stigmatization and subsequent adoption. As another woman observed:

I think the biggest thing that we've got out of [it] is that it has made our marriage stronger. We feel we went through a hell of a lot to get to that point and I've said it to my husband, I wouldn't change a thing.

The desire to avoid or lessen stigma arising from infertility prompted these respondents to seek out adoption as a means to obtain children to raise. Although not a positive consequence of stigma per se, official agency processing mitigated feelings of inadequacy engendered by infertility by providing respondents with legitimation as potential parents.[12] As one adoptive mother observed:

I'm not as much of a failure as I thought I was. I can't have my own children but at least they think I'm good enough to adopt. . . . Adoption has helped. It's not been the whole answer but it certainly has helped by being accepted, by being deemed a good parent in their eyes.

Miall (1987) has already documented the stigma and social sanctioning that can accompany adoptive parent status. Among the benefits perceived by respondents to be linked to adoption were opportunities for heightened interpersonal experiences with others "sharing the fate"; and initiatives for career growth and change. As one adoptive mother noted:

> *I behave quite differently with other adoptive parents. We share the situation, we can discuss how other people react and achieve that understanding and rapport we can't get elsewhere. We know the secrets of adoption, we know about the love, the feelings that those other people can't understand. It's liberating.*

As another adoptive mother observed, the experience of infertility and the pain which accompanies it resulted in a career change:

> *I've had a real career change as a result of my infertility and adoption. I'm doing a degree in counselling and hope to continue to work in this area. I'm a helper now and a role model. I'm more sensitive to others regardless of what kind of life crisis they're going through.*

Although not an obvious consequence of the experience of stigma itself, another respondent observed:

> *It's interesting you know because one area of the law that sort of perked my interest was juvenile and adoption legal work. I tend to spend more time studying it where I might otherwise not have done.*

To conclude, involuntarily childless women, when given the opportunity, were able to provide detailed information on the positive gratifications and opportunities arising from possessing a stigmatizing attribute. The relevance of these findings with ex-psychiatric patients and involuntarily childless women for labeling theory will now be considered.

DISCUSSION AND CONCLUSIONS

Previous research on labeling theory has tended to focus on the negative consequences of labeling an individual as deviant. These studies have suggested that deviants are more acted upon than acting and even when consideration has been given to strategies for managing stigma, these have focused also on managing negative consequences.[13] It is apparent from the data presented in this paper, however, that in the areas of mental and physical disability, deviants are active in refuting labels, in transforming stigma into something positive, and in utilizing stigmatizing identity marks for secondary gains—in other words, exploiting stigma for positive gains.

In the case of ex–psychiatric patients, the possession of a stigmatizing attribute legitimated pre- and post-treatment deviant behavior; exempted these individuals from normal social roles and obligations; provided opportunities and rewards (as they defined them); strengthened familial ties; and facilitated personal growth experiences.

Similarly, involuntarily childless women labeled infertile were able to legitimate their childless role; legalize a disabled role within adoption agencies with resultant access to services; experience personal growth through the management of stigma; strengthen dyadic ties; enjoy heightened interpersonal social interaction with others like-situated; and explore new opportunities for career growth not previously considered.

Using these two substantive cases, we have clearly demonstrated the positive consequences actors derive from being labeled discreditable through mental illness or infertility. We wish now to propose an addition to the literature on stigma by establishing a three-fold generic categorization of positive consequences of stigma. These generic categories are: (1) therapeutic opportunities; (2) personal growth experiences; and (3) interpersonal opportunities.

In recent years, scholars have argued for a renewed focus on generic concepts in ethnographic research (cf. Couch, 1984; Lofland, 1970; Miyomato, 1959; Prus, 1985). An emphasis on examining parallel processes and concepts across different social contexts and types of social actors can maximize conceptual development. Future research on other deviant populations might fruitfully benefit from an examination of the three-fold generic categorization of positive consequences of stigma advanced here.

TABLE 7.1 A Typology of Consequences of Stigma

CONSEQUENCES OF STIGMA	TYPE OF LABELING	
	Negative	*Positive*
Negative	Adversely affects self-images and identities; acts as a "master status," limiting future participation in society	Emotional stress, strain, and pressures
Positive	Personal growth experiences, therapeutic opportunities, interpersonal opportunities	Elevated self-images, self-esteems

In more general terms we also wish to extend the analysis of responses to labeling by considering not only positive and negative responses to negative labeling, but also positive and negative responses to positive labeling. By combining the dimensions of positive and negative labeling with the dimensions of positive and negative consequences of stigma, we may establish a four-fold classificatory system or typology of stigma and responses to it. (See Table 7.1.)

Labeling an individual in a negative fashion, whether it be homosexual, thief, or child molester, may have negative consequences in that the label may act as a "master status" (Becker, 1973), limiting the person's future participation in society. Although the deviant may seek moral reinstatement into society, others see and treat the person only in terms of the deviant status. Resumption of normal roles and statuses is inhibited. Symbolic reorganization of self occurs wherein the reactions of others create for the individual the experience of viewing the self as disvalued and deviant. The individual may be unable to act except in relation to the imputed self and its concomitant disvalued, degrading status. Normal channels being blocked off, prevented from resuming normal social roles and status, the individual may ultimately become confirmed in a deviant role.

Second, labeling an individual in a negative manner may have positive consequences for the individual and, paradoxically, for society at large. As we have demonstrated in this paper, the possession of a discrediting attribute can be a positive experience dependent on actor definitions and actions. Positive consequences can include therapeutic opportunities, personal growth experiences, and interpersonal opportunities for the individual. On the other hand, Warren (1974) has noted that labeling an individual deviant may in fact conventionalize deviant behavior and return the individual to a more acceptable way of acting, a positive consequence from a societal viewpoint.

Third, labeling an individual in a positive fashion may also have certain negative social psychological implications. For example, labeling a child as a star baseball player, a future Wayne Gretzky, or a person as exceptionally bright may place a great deal of stress and strain on the individual. Others may establish standards and expectations which may or may not be realistic for the positively labeled individual to live up to. Failing to meet expectations set and experiencing the disappointment of others may also result in self-devaluation and withdrawal from normal social roles and statuses.

Fourth, labeling individuals in a positive manner may generate positive consequences or benefits. Indeed, self-fulfilling prophecy is a well established principle in the social psychological literature. The deviance literature has limited this principle, however, to the examination of negative labels. Positive labeling can result in elevated self-image and self-esteem and facilitate access to valued statuses in society. We strongly suggest that future research on labeling should consider the dimensions outlined in this typology, considering both the positive and negative consequences which can follow from positive and negative labeling.

Finally, we contend that sociologists, as members of the larger society, have focused almost exclusively on the disadvantaged status of deviants. There is no doubt that the "normal" world is powerful and individuals (deviants) who are denied full participation in it actively suffer as a result. Our attempts as sociologists to act as advocates for deviants, however, to take on an "underdog" ideological stance, may in fact be conceptually and methodologically flawed. Specifically, unstated assumptions about the relative merits or benefits of social worlds introduce biases in data collection that are reflected in the negative, suffering, disadvantaged slant of much of our research on deviant groups.

We have clearly demonstrated with our research groups that, given the opportunity, the so-called disadvantaged are able to establish positive effects or benefits of being labeled—effects or benefits that are real for them regardless of the observer's interpretations of their status or situation. Indeed, being labeled, prevented from reassuming normal roles and statuses, and forced into subcultures may provide individuals with alternate roles and statuses that are equally or even more satisfying to them and may provide them with the most intense, intimate social exchanges that they will ever know. We so-called normals, by contrast, may in fact be disadvantaged in that in our significant relationships we will never experience the intensity and understanding of those of the deviant, nor the opportunities for change. From a humanistic point of view, we, as sociologists, should not close the door to that possibility.

NOTES

1. Theoretical arguments about the stigmatized status of the disabled have been advanced by Freidson (1966); Safilios-Rothschild (1970); and Scheff (1966, 1967, and 1975).

2. The severe negative consequences arising from the possession of these stigmatizing attributes are discussed in Herman (1986, 1987, 1988, and 1990) and Miall (1984, 1985, and 1986).

3. The term "chronic" is not defined in diagnostic terms (e.g., manic-depressive); but in terms of duration, continuity, frequency, and type of hospitalization. It refers to individuals institutionalized in a psychiatric facility for two years or more, on a continual basis, or on five or more occasions. Non-chronic refers to those individuals hospitalized in general hospital facilities or psychiatric institutions for less than two years, on a discontinuous basis, or on less than five occasions.

4. Initially, 300 persons were selected for study. However 15 subjects were not included because of refusal, death, inability to locate, or bureaucratic mixups.

5. Age was trichotomized so that elderly included 60 years or over, middle-aged was 30 to 59 years, and young was 16 to 29 years. Hospitalization included individuals treated primarily in a general hospital psychiatric ward, and institutionalization included individuals treated primarily within government psychiatric facilities.

6. Despite two years of concerted effort, the researcher was unable to recruit sufficient men to compare responses to infertility and adoption. Men may regard infertility as more stigmatizing than women (Miall, 1986) or may regard infertility and adoption as "women's" issues.

7. Subclassifications controlling for age, education, occupation, religion, ethnicity, duration of marriage, and presence of adopted children did not yield significant differences in responses on infertility and adoption.

8. From a social psychological viewpoint, the essential component in defining individuals as involuntarily childless is not their biological status as fertile or infertile, but their psychological preference to procreate and their inability in present circumstances to do so.

9. These beliefs were that the biological tie is important in bonding and love, and therefore, bonding and love in adoption are second-best; adopted children are second rate because of their unknown genetic past; and adoptive parents are not "real" parents (cf. Miall, 1987).

10. Membership in a subculture was, of course, partially dependent on the stigma drawing ex-patients together. Through this subcultural participation, ex-patients learned to pick up quick cash by selling their bodies and their medication, where to sell, and how

much to ask. The dichotomy between an actor's and an observer's interpretation of lived reality is clearly illustrated here. Whereas respondents saw this as a positive aid to survival possible only because of access to the ex-patient subculture, others might regard this as a negative consequence of stigmatization. Indeed despite the possibility of benefiting from stigma, in real terms these ex-patients remained in a devalued position. Dear (1987), for example, has linked deinstitutionalization to homelessness.

11. It may be that stronger family ties also result from the "courtesy stigma" experienced by family members when a relative is diagnosed as mentally ill. A "courtesy stigma" is a "situationally induced social construct rather than a constant attribute of the person" (Birenbaum, 1975:348; Goffman, 1963), and this shared sense of stigma may bring the family closer together.

12. Adoption agency processing can also induce deep feelings of stigma in infertile couples (cf. Miall, 1987, 1989).

13. While this paper provides ethnographic information on substantive gratifications and opportunities associated with being labeled mentally ill or infertile, such positive consequences have been documented by a few notable others with respect to other deviant populations (Gramling and Forsyth, 1987; Hanks and Poplin, 1981). Stigma management techniques identified in the literature include selective concealment, passing, capitulation, preventive disclosure, political activism, and conventionalization. See, for example, Edgerton (1967); Goffman (1963); Herman (1986, 1987); Scott and Lyman (1968); Schneider and Conrad (1980).

REFERENCES

Bachrach, Christine. 1983. "Children in Families: Characteristics of Biological, Step-, and Adopted Children." *Journal of Marriage and the Family* 45:171–179.

Becker, Howard. 1973. *Outsiders: Studies in the Sociology of Deviance.* Rev. ed. New York: Free Press.

Birenbaum, Arnold. 1975. "On Managing a Courtesy Stigma." Pp. 347–357 in F. Scarpitti and P. McFarlane (eds.), *Deviance: Action, Reaction, Interaction.* Reading, MA: Addison-Wesley.

Burgwyn, Diana. 1981. *Marriage without Children.* New York: Harper & Row.

Couch, Carl. 1984. "Symbolic Interaction and Generic Sociological Principles." *Symbolic Interaction* 7:1–14.

Davis, Fred. 1961. "Deviance Disavowal: The Management of Strained Interaction by the Visibly Handicapped." *Social Problems* 9:120–132.

Davis, Nanette. 1975. *Sociological Constructions of Deviance.* Dubuque, IA: W. C. Brown Company.

Dear, Michael. 1987. *Landscapes of Despair: From Deinstitutionalization to Homelessness.* Princeton, NJ: Princeton University Press.

Edgerton, Robert. 1967. *The Cloak of Competence: Stigma in the Lives of the Mentally Retarded.* Berkeley: University of California Press.

Freidson, Elliot. 1966. "Disability as Social Deviance." Pp. 71–99 in M. Sussman (ed.), *Sociology and Rehabilitation.* Washington, DC: American Sociological Association.

Goffman, Erving. 1963. *Stigma.* Upper Saddle River, NJ: Prentice Hall.

Gove, Walter. 1976. "Social Reaction Theory and Disability." Pp. 51–71 in G. Albrecht (ed.), *The Sociology of Physical Disability and Rehabilitation.* Pittsburgh, PA: University of Pittsburgh Press.

Gramling, Robert, and Craig Forsyth. 1987. "Exploiting Stigma." *Sociological Forum* 2:401–415.

Haber, Lawrence, and Richard Smith. 1971. "Disability and Deviance: Normative Adaptations of Role Behavior." *American Sociological Review* 36: 87–97.

Hanks, Michael, and Dennis Poplin. 1981. "The Sociology of Physical Disability: A Review of Literature and Some Conceptual Perspectives." *Deviant Behavior* 2:309–328.

Herman, Nancy. 1986. "Crazies in the Community: An Ethnographic Study of Ex-psychiatric Clients in Canadian Society—Stigma, Management Strategies, and Identity Transformation." Ph.D. dissertation, McMaster University, Hamilton, Ontario, Canada.

Herman, Nancy. 1987. "The 'Mixed Nutters' and 'Looney Tuners': The Emergence, Development, Nature and Functions of Two Informal Deviant Subcultures of Chronic Ex-psychiatric Patients." *Deviant Behavior* 8:235–258.

Herman, Nancy. 1988. "The Chronic Elderly Mentally Ill in Canada." Pp. 111–121 in B. Havens and E. Rathbone-McCuan (eds.), *The North American Elders: A Comparison of U.S. and Canadian Issues.* New Haven, CT: Greenwood Press.

Herman, Nancy. 1989. "Mental Hospital Depopulation in Canada: Patient Perspectives." *Canadian Journal of Psychiatry* 34:386–391.

Herman, Nancy. 1990. *Crazies in the Community: An Ethnographic Study of the Post-hospital Worlds of Chronic and Non-chronic Ex-patients.* Dix Hills, NY: General Hall.

Kraft, Adrienne, Joseph Palombo, Dorena Mitchell, Catherine Dean, Steven Meyers, and Anne Wright-Schmidt. 1980. "The Psychological Dimensions of Infertility." *American Journal of Orthopsychiatry* 50:618–628.

Lemert, Edwin. 1972. *Human Deviance, Social Problems, and Social Control,* 2nd ed. Upper Saddle River, NJ: Prentice-Hall.

Link, Bruce. 1987. "Understanding Labeling Effects in the Area of Mental Disorders: An Assessment of the Effects of Expectations of Rejection." *American Sociological Review* 52:96–112.

Link, Bruce, and Francis Cullen. 1986. "Contact with the Mentally Ill and Perceptions of How Dangerous They Are." *Journal of Health and Social Behavior* 27:289–302.

Link, Bruce, Francis Cullen, James Frank, and John Wozniak. 1987. "The Social Rejection of Former Mental Patients: Understanding Why Labels Matter." *American Journal of Sociology* 92: 1461–1500.

Link, Bruce, Francis Cullen, Elmer Struening, Patrick Shrout, and Bruce Dohrenwend. 1989. "A Modified Labeling Theory Approach to Mental Disorders." *American Sociological Review* 54:400–423.

Lofland, John. 1970. "Interactionist Imagery and Analytic Interruptus." Pp. 35–45 in T. Shibutani (ed.), *Human Nature and Collective Behavior: Papers in Honor of Herbert Blumer.* Upper Saddle River, NJ: Prentice Hall.

Lorber, Judith. 1967. "Deviance as Performance: The Case of Illness." *Social Problems* 14:302–310.

Manning, Peter. 1975. "Deviance and Dogma." *The British Journal of Criminology* 15:1–20.

Miall, Charlene. 1984. "Women and Involuntary Childlessness: Perceptions of Stigma Associated with Infertility and Adoption." Ph.D. dissertation, York University, Toronto, Ontario, Canada.

Miall, Charlene. 1985. "Perceptions of Informal Sanctioning and the Stigma of Involuntary Childlessness." *Deviant Behavior* 6:383–403.

Miall, Charlene. 1986. "The Stigma of Involuntary Childlessness." *Social Problems* 33:268–282.

Miall, Charlene. 1987. "The Stigma of Adoptive Parent Status: Perceptions of Community Attitudes toward Adoption and the Experience of Informal Social Sanctioning." *Family Relations* 36:34–39.

Miall, Charlene. 1989. "Authenticity and the Disclosure of the Information Preserve: The Case of Adoptive Parenthood." *Qualitative Sociology* 12:279–302.

Miyamato, S. Frank. 1959. "The Social Act: Re-examination of a Concept." *Pacific Sociological Review* 2:51–55.

Mosher, William. 1982. "Infertility Trends among U.S. Couples: 1965–1976." *Family Planning Perspectives* 14:22–27.

Nagi, Saad. 1966. "Some Conceptual Issues in Disability and Rehabilitation." Pp. 100–113 in M. Sussman (ed.), *Sociology and Rehabilitation.* Washington, DC: American Sociological Association.

National Center for Health Statistics. 1985. "Fecundity and Infertility in the United States, 1965–82." *Advance Data from Vital and Health Statistics,* No. 104, DHHS Pub. No. (PHS) 85–1250. Public Health Service. Hyattsville, MD. February.

Parsons, Talcott. 1951. *The Social System.* New York: Free Press.

Plummer, Kenneth. 1979. "Misunderstanding Labeling Perspectives." Pp. 85–121 in D. Downes and P. Rock (eds.), *Deviant Interpretations.* Oxford: Martin Robertson & Company.

Prus, Robert. 1985. "Generic Sociology: Maximizing Conceptual Development in Ethnographic Research." Paper presented at the Qualitative Research Conference: An Ethnographic-Interactionist Perspective. University of Waterloo, Waterloo, Ontario, Canada. May.

Rogers, Joseph, and M. D. Buffalo. 1974. "Fighting Back: Nine Modes of Adaptation to a Deviant Label." *Social Problems* 22:101–118.

Safilios-Rothschild, Constantina. 1970. *The Sociology and Social Psychology of Disability and Rehabilitation.* New York: Random House.

Sagarin, Edward. 1975. *Deviants and Deviance.* New York: Praeger.

Scheff, Thomas. 1966. *Being Mentally Ill: A Sociological Theory.* Chicago: Aldine.

Scheff, Thomas. 1967. *Mental Illness and Social Processes.* New York: Harper & Row.

Scheff, Thomas. 1975. *Labeling Madness.* Upper Saddle River, NJ: Prentice Hall.

Scheff, Thomas. 1981. "Cultural Stereotypes and Mental Illness." Pp. 84–88 in E. Rubington and M. Weinberg (eds.), *Deviance: The Interactionist Perspective.* New York: Macmillan.

Schneider, Joseph, and Peter Conrad. 1980. "In the Closet with Illness: Epilepsy, Stigma Potential and Information Control." *Social Problems* 28:32–44.

Schur, Edwin. 1979. *Interpreting Deviance.* New York: Harper & Row.

Scott, Marvin, and Stanford Lyman. 1968. "Accounts." *American Sociological Review* 33:46–62.

Tannenbaum, Frank. 1938. *Crime and the Community.* Boston: Ginn.

Veevers, Jean. 1972. "The Violation of Fertility Mores: Voluntary Childlessness as Deviant Behavior." Pp. 571–592 in C. Boydell, C. Grindstaff and P. Whitehead (eds.), *Deviant Behavior and Societal Reaction.* Toronto: Holt, Rinehart & Winston.

Veevers, Jean. 1979. "Voluntary Childlessness: A Review of Issues and Evidence." *Marriage and Family Review* 2:1–26.

Veevers, Jean. 1980. *Childless by Choice.* Toronto: Butterworth.

Warren, Carol. 1974. "The Use of Stigmatizing Social Labels in Conventionalizing Deviant Behavior." *Sociology and Social Research* 58:303–311.

Warren, Carol. 1987. *Madwives: Schizophrenic Women in the 1950's.* London: Rutgers University Press.

Warren, Carol, and John Johnson. 1972. "A Critique of Labeling Theory from the Phenomenological Perspective." Pp. 69–92 in R. Scott and J. Douglas (eds.), *Theoretical Perspectives on Deviance.* New York: Basic Books.

PART THREE

RELATIONS AMONG DEVIANTS

Despite popular stereotype, deviant careers are not unilinear; nor do they have fixed and inevitable stages. Some people who commit deviant acts may never be typed as deviant or may discontinue those acts, while others may become "hard-core" career deviants. Even those who do become career deviants may do so through widely different routes. Thus, there is no single natural history of deviant careers; there are many career histories. One hypothetical deviant career might proceed as follows. A person lives in a culture where certain acts are viewed as deviant. This person is believed, rightly or wrongly, to have committed such deviance. Someone (e.g., teacher, neighbor) types the person as a certain type of deviant. The person comes to the attention of an official agency (e.g., juvenile authorities) and becomes an official case. This social processing propels the person into organized deviant life (e.g., the person is now a "hoodlum"—ostracized by "good kids" and accepted only in disreputable circles). Finally, in self-redefinition, the person assumes the deviant role (i.e., actually becomes a "hood"), thus confirming the initial typing.

This, however, is only one developmental model. Another hypothetical deviant career (which is probably more characteristic of certain kinds of deviance such as professional crime) might proceed along opposite lines. First, the person defines himself or herself as a certain kind of deviant, then enters a deviant world to confirm that identity, comes to official notice, becomes an official case, and engages in more persistent and patterned deviations, thus, reinforcing the system of social types. Still other types of deviant careers may require different models. Deviant careers vary so widely that a person might enter the deviance process at any one of the various stages and move forward, backward, or out of the process completely.

Perhaps a visual image will help. Suppose we visualize deviant careers as a long corridor. Each segment of the corridor represents one stage in a deviant career, with doors that allow people to directly enter into or exit from that stage. Some people can enter the deviance corridor from a side door, without previous experience in a deviant career. Others can leave by a side door, thus terminating their deviant careers. Finally, there are some who will enter at one end of the corridor and proceed through all the stages to the other end. The following diagram shows how the traffic of deviance may flow.

The dotted lines represent the invisible boundaries marking stages of a person's deviant career. At each of these symbolic boundaries there are defining agents who speed certain people farther along the corridor and usher others out the side doors or back to where they started.

The Deviance Corridor

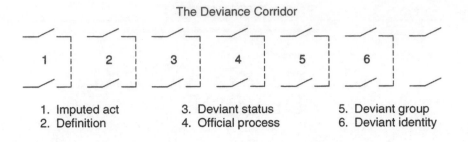

1. Imputed act   3. Deviant status   5. Deviant group
2. Definition   4. Official process   6. Deviant identity

The rate and direction of a person's progress through the corridor are based largely on the person's responses to others' symbolic definitions of him or her. In addition to conventional people, those who type and respond to the deviant often include members of a deviant group; thus, these people can be an important influence in solidifying a person's deviant career.

The fact that a person has been assigned a deviant label does not mean that she or he will automatically be drawn into a deviant group. Nonetheless, dilettantes in deviance and career deviants alike are likely to become involved with a deviant group at some time. Thus, Part Three of this book examines the social organization of deviants. It then goes on to examine how people enter deviant worlds and how they learn their traditions. Finally, it considers social diversity within deviant worlds.

THE SOCIAL ORGANIZATION OF DEVIANCE

A deviant group is apt to come into being when people are in contact with one another, suffer a common fate, and have common interests. These common interests generally arise from their social situation and are shared because these people face more or less the same dilemma.

The general dilemma for the persons who ultimately become involved in deviant groups is that they want to carry out activities that the society labels deviant but at the same time they want to avoid punishment. When people become aware that they share this interest, a group to support this deviance can arise. For example, in their leisure time, members of athletic teams often group together socially and create a subculture in which to engage in clandestine social deviance. Thus, they may participate in deviant activities without suffering social punishment, such as deviant labeling and negative sanctions.

When the people are especially concerned with pursuing their activities, the deviant group forms on the basis of a common attraction; an example would be the gay subculture. In contrast, when people are thrust together because of official typing, the deviant group forms on the basis of shared punishment; the prison subculture is one example. Finally, persons engaging in solitary deviance like self-injurers are less likely to make common cause with other solitary self-injurers.

ENTRY AND ACCULTURATION

Entry refers to the ways in which a person comes to participate in and gain admittance to a deviant group. *Acculturation* refers to the new ways and meanings a person acquires from it. Entry can be clearly defined (where a person clearly is or is not a member), or it can be rather loose in character. Likewise, acculturation can be highly specialized or casual and offhand. Like colleges, groups vary in how hard they are to get into and how hard they are to stay in. Much depends on the complexity of the activities involved, on how much commitment others in the group expect from newcomers, and on how much they must rely on them for their own safety and welfare. With a team of pickpockets, for example, entry and socialization are rigorous. On the other hand, admission and social-ization to a skid row bottle gang are relatively simple. Here all a person needs is a few coins to "go in on a bottle," and there is relatively little to learn. The culture of the street, which many inner-city black youth learn, is more involved than what is acquired in a bottle gang.

SOCIAL DIVERSITY

Deviance can be carried out in environments that are more or less secure and are, thus, more or less likely to protect the deviant from social troubles. For example, college stu-dents typically use cocaine in groups that control the time, place, and circumstance of use. As a result, such college users are less likely to get into trouble than are street users. The street user is more likely to use cocaine in a less secure environment—using at uncontrolled times and in uncontrolled places and circumstances—and consequently is more likely to encounter trouble. Some deviants also become highly involved in deviant groups, but this is not true for all deviants. Within a particular group, some people may be highly immersed while others (e.g., weekend visitors) may participate only occasionally. Also, some forms of deviance lend themselves to more involvement than do others. Because they have to be highly mobile, check forgers, for example, may be marginal to any kind of social group, conventional or deviant. Skid row drunks, on the other hand, are freer to immerse themselves in a deviant group. In addition, people who are covert (e.g., people in the "closet") are generally less engulfed in an unconventional way of life and engage in the unconventional world sporadically and secretly. Those who are more overt (e.g., gay activists) ordinarily find themselves more involved in an unconventional way of life that stipulates a regular schedule of activities and a circle of intimate acquaintances. The kind of social career that members have after they become involved in a deviant group depends on the nature of the group's major activities, the degree of the member's involvement with the group, and the member's experiences with negative social reactions.

Sanctions that deviants bring against one another are important. Social control oper-ates in deviant ways of life just as it does in the conventional world. How well do these unconventional groups control their members? In general, it seems that members are sub-ject to more social control in some groups (e.g., organized crime) than in others (e.g., skid row). Also, it seems that within a group more social control is exerted over some members (e.g., a novice) than over others (e.g., a leader in the group).

Groups have beliefs, values, and norms that are supposed to regulate conduct. These prescriptions contribute to a form of social order. Deviant groups vary in the extent to which they organize their activities and define them by rules: some have elaborate rules that specify beliefs and actions; others have simpler codes. A simple, tightly organized code leads to one set of consequences; a complex, loosely organized code to another. In addition, some deviant groups have rules and beliefs that protect and dignify their members, while others spawn normlessness, induce exploitation, and set members against one another.

Within a group some members show more commitment to the deviant way of life than do others. How dependent the person is on the group, the person's identity, and how much the person shares the viewpoints of others in the group all seem to be factors influencing a person's commitment to the group.

CHAPTER 8

THE SOCIAL ORGANIZATION OF DEVIANCE

Types of Relationships

JOEL BEST and DAVID F. LUCKENBILL

Deviants are often persons who frequently break rules, are assigned a deviant status, perform the related role, and see themselves as deviants. There are various networks of social relationships in which deviant persons can be involved. It is important to pay attention to these networks, the frequency of deviations, and the types of deviations (instrumental or expressive). The number of deviant persons involved, their relations with nondeviant people, and the stability of their deviant careers all vary with the networks in which the deviant transactions are implicated.

Joel Best and David F. Luckenbill note that deviations are both the process and product of social organization. They point out that deviant transactions involving force, fraud, or consent vary in the ways they are socially organized. In turn, the regularity, rewards, and costs of these transactions also vary in the ways they have been organized socially. The authors present a number of generalizations from their conceptual scheme concerning the effects of sophistication in forms of deviant organization.

Ethnographic research on particular social scenes provides data for general, grounded theories (Glaser and Strauss, 1967). For the study of deviance, field studies have supplied the basis for the development of general theories of the social psychology of deviance (Goffman, 1963; Lofland, 1969; Matza, 1969). However, while several reports about specific forms of deviance focus on social organization (Einstader, 1969; McIntosh,

Reprinted from Joel Best and David F. Luckenbill, "Social Organization of Deviants," *Social Problems*, Vol. 28, No. 1: 14–31. © 1980, The Society for the Study of Social Problems, Inc. Used by permission of the University of California Press and the authors. All rights reserved.

1971; Mileski and Black, 1972; Shover, 1977; Zimmerman and Wieder, 1977), there is no satisfactory general theory of the social organization of deviance.

Sociologists of varying perspectives have debated the nature of social organization among juvenile delinquents, professional criminals, organized criminals, and white-collar criminals. Others have developed typologies of deviants that include social organizational features (Clinard and Quinney, 1973; Gibbons, 1965, 1977; Miller, 1978). However, these treatments of social organization suffer from several flaws. First, they are often too narrow, focusing on a single type of deviance, such as burglary or more broadly, crime. Second, they usually are content with describing the organizational forms of different types of deviance. They fail to locate such forms along a dimension of organization or examine the consequences of organizational differences for deviants and social control agents. Third, they typically confuse two different bases for analyzing social organization: a general theory must distinguish between the social organization of *deviants* (the patterns of relationships between deviant actors) and the social organization of *deviance* (the patterns of relationships between the various roles performed in deviant transactions).

In this paper, we present a framework for understanding the social organization of deviants.[1] By examining reports of field research, several forms of social organization are identified and located along a dimension of organizational sophistication. Then some propositions are developed regarding the consequences of organizational variation for deviants and social control agents. Finally, some implications for the study of social organization are considered.

FORMS OF DEVIANT ORGANIZATION

The social organization of deviants refers to the structure or patterns of relationships among deviant actors in the context of deviant pursuits. The social organization of deviants varies along a dimension of sophistication. Organizational sophistication involves the elements of complexity,

coordination and purposiveness (cf. Cressey, 1972). Organizations vary in the complexity of their division of labor including the size of membership, degree of stratification, and degree of specialization of organizational roles. Organizations also vary in their coordination among roles including the degree to which rules, agreements, and codes regulating relationships are formalized and enforced. Finally, organizations vary in the purposiveness with which they specify, strive toward, and achieve their objectives. Forms of organization which display high levels of complexity, coordination, and purposiveness are more sophisticated than those forms with lower levels.

Research reports suggest that deviants organize in several identifiable ways along the dimension of sophistication. Beginning with the least sophisticated, we will discuss five forms: loners, colleagues, peers, mobs, and formal organizations. These organizational forms can be defined in terms of four variables: (1) whether the deviants associate with one another; (2) whether they participate in deviance together; (3) whether their deviance requires an elaborate division of labor; and (4) whether their organization's activities extend over time and space (see Table 8.1). *Loners* do not associate with other deviants, participate in shared deviance, have a division of labor, or maintain their deviance over extended time and space. *Colleagues* differ from loners because they associate with fellow deviants. *Peers* not only associate with one another, but also participate in deviance together. In *mobs*, the shared participation requires an elaborate division of

TABLE 8.1 Characteristics of Different Forms of the Social Organization of Deviants

	TYPE OF ORGANIZATION				
VARIABLE	Loners	Colleagues	Peers	Mobs	Formal Organizations
Mutual association	−	+	+	+	+
Mutual participation	−	−	+	+	+
Division of labor	−	−	−	+	+
Extended organization	−	−	−	−	+

labor. Finally, *formal organizations* involve mutual association and participation, an elaborate division of labor, and deviant undertakings extended over time and space.

The descriptions of these forms of organization must be qualified in two ways. First, the forms are presented as ideal types. There is variation among the types of deviants within each form, as well as between one form and another. The intent is to sketch out the typical features of each form, recognizing that particular types of deviants may not share all of the features of their form to the same degree. Organizational sophistication can be viewed as a continuum, with deviants located between, as well as on, the five points. Describing a number of forms along this continuum inevitably understates the complexities of social life. Second, the descriptions of these forms draw largely from field studies of deviance in the contemporary United States, and attempt to locate the deviants studied along the dimension of organizational sophistication. A particular type of deviant can be organized in various ways in different societies and at different times. The references to specific field studies are intended to place familiar pieces of research within this framework; they are not claims that particular types of deviants invariably organize in a given way.

LONERS

Some deviants operate as individuals. These loners do not associate with other deviants for purposes of sociability, the performance of deviant activities, or the exchange of supplies and information. Rather, they must supply themselves with whatever knowledge, skill, equipment, and ideology their deviance requires. Loners lack deviant associations, so they cannot receive such crucial forms of feedback as moral support or information about their performance, new opportunities, or changes in social control strategies. They often enter deviance as a defensive response to private troubles (Lofland, 1969). Because their entry does not require contact with other deviants, as

long as they can socialize themselves, loners frequently come from segments of the population which are less likely to be involved in the more sophisticated forms of deviance; it is not uncommon for loners to be middle-aged, middle-class, or female. Because their deviance often is defensive, and because they lack the support of other deviants, loners' careers typically are short-lived. Examples of loners include murderers (Luckenbill, 1977), rapists (Amir, 1971), embezzlers (Cressey, 1953), check forgers (Lemert, 1967:99–134; Klein and Montague, 1977), physician narcotic addicts (Winick, 1961), compulsive criminals (Cressey, 1962), heterosexual transvestites (Buckner, 1970), amateur shoplifters (Cameron, 1964), some gamblers (Lesieur, 1977), and many computer criminals (Parker, 1976).[2]

COLLEAGUES

Like loners, colleagues perform as individuals. Unlike loners, however, colleagues associate with others involved in the same kind of deviance. Colleagues thus form a simple group which provides important services for members. First, colleagues often socialize newcomers, providing training in deviant skills as well as an ideology which accounts for and justifies their deviance. Association also offers sociability among members with whom one's deviant identity need not be concealed: an actor can take down his or her guard without fear of discovery by agents of social control (Goffman, 1959, 1963). Also, association provides a source of information about ways to obtain deviant equipment, new techniques, new opportunities for engaging in deviance, and strategies for avoiding sanctioning. Colleagues learn and are held to a loose set of norms which direct conduct in both deviant and respectable activities. "Don't inform on a colleague" and "Never cut in on a colleague's score" exemplify such norms. The moral climate established by these expectations increases the stability of colleagues' social scene. At the same time, only some deviant activities and some people are suited for such a loose form of organization.

A successful career as a colleague depends ultimately on the individual's performance when operating alone. As a result, newcomers often sample the scene and, when they encounter difficulties, drift away. Only the more successful colleagues maintain extended deviant careers. Some examples of colleagues include most prostitutes (Hirschi, 1962; Bryan, 1965, 1966), pimps (Milner and Milner, 1972), and pool hustlers (Polsky, 1967).

PEERS

Like colleagues, peers associate with one another and benefit from services provided by their fellows. Peers are involved in the socialization of novices, considerable sociable interaction, and the maintenance of a loose, unwritten code of conduct to be followed by individuals who wish to remain in the peer group. Unlike colleagues, peers participate in deviant acts together; they are involved in deviant transactions at the same time and in the same place. In some cases, such mutual participation is required by the nature of the deviant activity. This is exemplified in the performance of homosexual acts, or in the "task force raids" where a collection of young men engages in simple acts of violence such as gang fighting or rolling drunks (Cressey, 1972). In other cases, mutual participation is required because peers form a network for supplying one another with essential goods and services, as found in the distribution of illicit drugs. In either event, peers interact basically as equals; there is a minimal division of labor and specialized roles are uncommon. Although individuals pass through these social scenes, peer groups often are quite stable, perhaps because peer groups solve structural problems within society for their members. Two common varieties of deviant peers are young people who have not yet entered integrated adult work roles, and those who frequent a deviant marketplace and depend on their contacts with one another for the satisfaction of illicit needs. Examples of peers include hobos (Anderson, 1923), homosexuals (Humphreys, 1970; Mileski and Black, 1972; Warren, 1974), group-oriented gamblers (Lesieur, 1977), swingers (Bartell, 1971), gang delinquents (Shaw, 1930; Matza, 1964; Rosenberg and Silverstein, 1969), motorcycle outlaws (Thompson, 1966), skid row tramps (Wiseman, 1970; Rubington, 1978), and illicit drug users (Blumer, 1967; Carey, 1968; Feldman, 1968; Stoddart, 1974).

MOBS

Mobs are small groups of professional or career deviants organized to pursue specific, profitable goals.[3] Their deviance requires the coordinated actions of members performing specialized roles—a more sophisticated division of labor than that found among peers. Thus, work is divided among confidence artists (the inside man and the outside man), pickpockets (the tool and the stall), or card and dice hustlers (the mechanic and the shootup man; Maurer, 1962, 1964; Prus and Sharper, 1977). Ordinarily, at least one of the roles in the mob is highly skilled, requiring considerable practice and training to perfect. This training (normally via apprenticeship), the need for on-the-job coordination, and the common practice of traveling from city to city as a mob lead to intensive interaction between mobsters. Elaborate technical argots develop, as well as elaborate codes specifying mobsters' obligations to each other.

Mobs have complex links to outsiders. They are organized to accomplish profitable yet safe crimes. McIntosh (1971) describes the historical shift from craft thieving, where mobs develop routine procedures for stealing relatively small sums from individuals, to project thieving, where larger amounts are taken from corporate targets using procedures specifically tailored to the particular crime. In either case, mob operations are planned and staged with an eye toward avoiding arrest. Also, mobs may attempt to neutralize the criminal justice system by bribing social control agents not to make arrests, "fixing" those cases where arrests take place, or making restitution to victims in return for dropped charges. Mobs also have ties to others who purchase stolen goods, provide legal services, and supply information and deviant equipment. Finally, a network of sociable and business contacts ties mobs to one another, enabling strategic information to spread quickly. These arrangements ensure that mobs can operate at a consistently profitable level with minimal interference. Consequently, the careers of individual mobsters, as well as those of specific mobs, seem to be more stable than those of deviants organized in less sophisticated ways.[4] Examples of mobs are the groups of professional criminals specializing in confidence games (Sutherland, 1937; Maurer, 1962), picking pockets (Maurer, 1964), shoplifting (Cameron, 1964), armed robbery (Einstader, 1969; Letkemann, 1973), burglary (Shover, 1977), and card and dice hustling (Prus and Sharper, 1977).

FORMAL ORGANIZATIONS

Formal organizations of deviants differ from mobs in the scope of their actions.[5] Normally they involve more people, but, more importantly, their actions are coordinated to efficiently handle deviant tasks on a routine basis over considerable time and space. While mobsters work as a group in a series of episodic attacks, formal organizations are characterized by delegated responsibility and by routine and steady levels of productivity. In many ways, formal organizations of deviants share the features which characterize such respectable bureaucracies as military organizations, churches, and business firms. They have a hierarchical division of labor, including both vertical and horizontal differentiation of positions and roles and established channels for vertical and horizontal communication. A deviant formal organization may contain departments for planning, processing goods, public relations and rule enforcement, with positions for strategists, coordinators, accountants, lawyers, enforcers, and dealers in illicit goods. There may be recruitment policies for filling these diversified positions, and entry into the organization may be marked by a ritual ceremony of passage. Formal organizations usually have binding, but normally unwritten, rules and codes

for guiding members in organizational action, and these rules are actively enforced.

Formal organizations of deviants can make large profits by operating efficiently. At the same time, they must protect themselves from harm or destruction. As in less sophisticated forms of organization, loyal members are expected to maintain the group's secrets. In addition, deviant formal organizations attempt to locate power in the office, rather than in an individual charismatic leader. Although charismatic leadership obviously plays a part in some deviant formal organizations, the successful organization is able to continue operations when a leader dies or is arrested. Finally, deviant formal organizations typically invest considerable energy in neutralizing the criminal justice system by corrupting both high- and low-level officials. The scope and efficiency of their operations, their organizational flexibility, and their ties to agencies of social control make formal organizations of deviants extremely stable. Examples of such deviant formal organizations include very large urban street gangs (Keiser, 1969; Dawley, 1973), smuggling rings (Green, 1969), and organized crime "families" (Cressey, 1969; Ianni, 1972).

THE SIGNIFICANCE OF THE SOCIAL ORGANIZATION OF DEVIANTS

The identification and description of these different organizational forms permit a comparative analysis. What are the consequences of organizing as loners, colleagues, peers, mobs, or formal organizations? A comparison suggests that the sophistication of a form of deviant social organization has several consequences for both deviants and social control agents. Five propositions can be advanced.

I. *The more sophisticated the form of deviant organization, the greater its members' capability for complex deviant operations.* Deviant activities, like conventional activities, vary in their complexity. The complexity of a deviant operation refers to the number of elements required to carry it through; the more component parts to an activity, the more complex it is.[6] Compared to simple activities, complex lines of action demand more careful preparation and execution and take longer to complete. The complexity of a deviant activity depends upon two identifiable types of elements. First, there are the *resources* which the actors must be able to draw upon. Some activities require that the deviant utilize special knowledge, skill, equipment, or social status in order to complete the operation successfully, while simple acts can be carried out without such resources. Second, the *organization of the deviant transaction* affects an activity's complexity.[7] Some deviant acts can be accomplished with a single actor, while others require two or more people. The actors in a transaction can share a common role, as in a skid row bottle gang, or the transaction may demand different roles, such as offender and victim or buyer and seller. Furthermore, the degree to which these roles must be coordinated, ranging from the minimal coordination of juvenile vandals to the precision routines performed by mobs of pickpockets, varies among situations. The more people involved, the more roles they perform; and the more coordination between those roles, the more complex the deviant transaction's organization. The more resources and organization involved in a deviant operation, the more complex the operation is.

In general, deviants in more sophisticated forms of organization commit more complex acts.[8] The deviant acts of loners tend to be simple, requiring little in the way of resources or organization. Although colleagues work apart from one another, they generally share certain resources, such as shared areas. The hustlers' pool hall and the prostitutes' red light district contain the elements needed to carry out deviant operations, including victims and clients. Peers may interact in situations where they are the only ones present, performing complementary or comparable roles, as when two people engage in homosexual intercourse or a group of motorcycle outlaws makes a "run." Peers also may undertake activities which involve nonmembers,

as when members of a delinquent gang rob a passerby. The activities carried out by mobs involve substantially more coordination among the members' roles. In an armed robbery, for instance, one member may be assigned to take the money, while a second provides "cover" and a third waits for the others in the car, ready to drive away on their return. Finally, the activities of formal organizations tend to be particularly complex, requiring substantial resources and elaborate organization. Major off-track betting operations, with staff members at local, district, and regional offices who carry out a variety of clerical and supervisory tasks on a daily basis, represent an exceedingly complex form of deviance.

The relationship between the sophistication of organization and the complexity of deviant activities is not perfect. Loners can engage in acts of considerable complexity, for example. The computer criminal who single-handedly devises a complicated method of breaking into and stealing from computerized records, the embezzler who carries through an elaborate series of illicit financial manipulations, and the physician who juggles drug records in order to maintain his or her addiction to narcotics are engaged in complex offenses requiring substantial resources. However, these offenses cannot be committed by everyone. These loners draw upon resources which they command through their conventional positions, turning them to deviant uses. The computer criminal typically is an experienced programmer, the embezzler must occupy a position of financial trust, and the physician has been trained in the use of drugs. Possessing these resources makes the loner's deviance possible. Thus, the more concentrated the resources necessary for a deviant operation, the less sophisticated the form of organization required. However, when resources are not concentrated, then more sophisticated forms of organization are necessary to undertake more complex deviant operations.

Sophisticated forms of deviant organization have advantages beyond being able to undertake complex operations by pooling resources distributed among their members. Some deviant activities require a minimal level of organization; for example, homosexual intercourse demands the participation of two parties. In many other cases, it may be possible to carry out a deviant line of action using a relatively unsophisticated form of organization, but the task is considerably easier if a sophisticated form of organization can be employed. This is so because more sophisticated forms of deviant organization enjoy several advantages: they are capable of conducting a larger number of deviant operations; the operations can occur with greater frequency and over a broader range of territory; and, as discussed below, the members are better protected from the actions of social control agents. Of course, sophisticated organizations may engage in relatively simple forms of deviance, but the deviant act is often only one component in a larger organizational context. Taking a particular bet in the policy racket is a simple act, but the racket itself, handling thousands of bets, is complex indeed. Similarly, a murder which terminates a barroom dispute between two casual acquaintances is very different from an execution which is ordered and carried out by members of a formal organization, even though the two acts may appear equally simple. In the latter case, the killing may be intended as a means of maintaining discipline by demonstrating the organization's ability to levy sanctions against wayward members.

II. *The more sophisticated the form of deviant organization, the more elaborate the socialization of its members.* Neophyte deviants need to acquire two types of knowledge: (1) they must learn how to perform deviant acts, and how to gain appropriate *skills and techniques;* (2) they must develop a *cognitive perspective,* a distinctive way of making sense of their new, deviant world (cf. Shibutani, 1961:118–127). Such a perspective includes an ideology which accounts for the deviance, the individual's participation in deviance, and the organizational form, as well as a distinctive language for speaking about these and other matters.

As forms of deviant organization increase in sophistication, socialization becomes more elaborate. Loners do not depend upon other deviants for instruction in deviant skills or for a special cognitive perspective; they learn through their participation in conventional social scenes. Murderers, for instance, learn from their involvement in conventional life how to respond in situations of interpersonal conflict, and they employ culturally widespread justifications for killing people (Bohannon, 1960; Wolfgang and Ferracuti, 1967). Embezzlers learn the technique for converting a financial trust in the course of respectable vocational training, adapting justifications such as "borrowing" from conventional business ideology (Cressey, 1953). In contrast, colleagues teach one another a great deal. Although pool hustlers usually know how to shoot pool before they enter hustling, their colleagues provide a rich cognitive perspective, including a sense of "we-ness," some norms of behavior, a system for stratifying the hustling world, and an extensive argot (Polsky, 1967).[9] Peers receive similar training or, in some cases, teach one another through a process of emerging norms (Turner, 1964). Juvenile vandals, for example, can devise new offenses through their mutually constructed interpretation of what is appropriate to a particular situation (Wade, 1967). Sometimes, the knowledge peers acquire has largely symbolic functions that affirm the group's solidarity, as when a club of motorcycle outlaws devises a written constitution governing its members (Reynolds, 1967:134–136). In mobs and formal organizations, the cognitive perspective focuses on more practical matters; their codes of conduct specify the responsibilities members have in their dealings with one another, social control agents and others. Greater emphasis is also placed on the acquisition of specialized skills, with an experienced deviant coaching an apprentice, frequently over an extended period of time.

Two circumstances affect the socialization process in different forms of deviant organization. First, the sophistication of the organization affects the scope and style of the training process. The amount of training tends to increase with the sophistication of the organization. The skills required to perform deviant roles vary, but there is a tendency for more sophisticated forms of organization to incorporate highly skilled roles. Further, the more sophisticated forms of organization often embody cognitive perspectives of such breadth that the deviant must acquire a large body of specialized knowledge. In addition, the socialization process tends to be organized differently in different forms of deviant organization. While loners serve as their own agents of socialization, and colleagues and peers may socialize one another, mobs and formal organizations almost always teach newcomers through apprenticeship to an experienced deviant. Second, the socialization process is affected by the newcomer's motivation for entering deviance. Loners, of course, choose deviance on their own. In the more sophisticated forms, newcomers may ask for admission, but they often are recruited by experienced deviants. While peers may recruit widely, as when a delinquent gang tries to enlist all of the neighborhood boys of a given age, mobs and formal organizations recruit selectively, judging the character and commitment of prospective members and sometimes demanding evidence of skill or prior experience. For loners, entry into deviance frequently is a defensive act, intended to ward off some immediate threat. Peers, on the other hand, often are using deviance to experience stimulation; their deviance has an adventurous quality (Lofland, 1969). In contrast, mobs and formal organizations adopt a more professional approach: deviance is instrumental, a calculated means of acquiring economic profits.[10] These differences in the scope of socialization, the way the process is organized, and the neophyte's motivation account for the relationship between sophistication of organization and the elaborateness of the socialization.

III. *The more sophisticated the form of deviant organization, the more elaborate the services provided its members.* Every social role poses practical problems for its performers. In some cases these problems can be solved by providing the actors with supplies of various sorts. Actors may require certain *equipment* to perform a role. They may also need *information* about their situation in order to coordinate their behavior with the ongoing action and successfully accomplish their part in an operation. One function of deviant social organization is to solve such practical problems by supplying members with needed equipment and information. More sophisticated forms of social organization are capable of providing more of these services.

Deviants differ in their requirements for equipment. Some need little in the way of equipment; a mugger may be able to get by with a piece of pipe. In other cases, deviants make use of specialized items which have few, if any, respectable uses (e.g., heroin or the booster boxes used in shoplifting).[11] Most loners require little equipment. When specialized needs exist, they are met through conventional channels accessible to the deviants, as when a physician narcotic addict obtains illicit drugs from hospital or clinic supplies. Colleagues also supply their own equipment, for the most part, although they may receive some assistance; pool hustlers, for example, provide their own cues, but they may rely on financial backers for funding. Peers adopt various patterns toward equipment. In some cases, peer groups develop to facilitate the distribution and consumption of deviant goods, such as illicit drugs. In other instances, peers use equipment as a symbol of their deviant status, as when gang members wear special costumes. The equipment used by mobsters is more utilitarian; many of their trades demand specialized tools, for safe-cracking, shoplifting, and so forth. In addition to a craftsman's personal equipment, the mob may require special materials for a specific project. Norms often exist that specify the manner in which these equipment purchases will be financed. In still other instances, some mobsters with expensive pieces of equipment may cooperate with several different mobs who wish to make use of them (such as the "big store" which is centrally located for the use of several confidence mobs). Formal organizations also have extensive equipment requirements. Because their operations extend over considerable time, formal organizations may find it expedient to invest in an elaborate array of fixed equipment. Off-track bookmaking, for example, may involve the purchase or rental of offices, desks, calculators, computer lines, special telephone lines, office supplies, and automobiles. Special staff members may have the responsibility for maintaining this equipment (Bell, 1962:134). In addition, some formal organizations are involved in producing or distributing deviant equipment for the consumption of other deviants; drug smuggling offers the best example.

Deviants need information in order to determine their courses of action. To operate efficiently, they need to know about new opportunities for deviant action; to operate safely, they need to know about the movements of social control agents. The more sophisticated forms of organization have definite advantages in acquiring and processing information. Loners, of course, depend upon themselves for information; opportunities or threats outside their notice cannot be taken into account. Colleagues and peers can learn more by virtue of their contacts with the deviant "grapevine," and they may have norms regarding a member's responsibility to share relevant information. In mobs, information is sought in more systematic ways. In the course of their careers, mobsters develop perceptual skills, enabling them to "case" possible targets (Letkemann, 1973). In addition, some mobs rely on outsiders for information; spotters may be paid a commission for pointing out opportunities for theft. A formal organization can rely upon its widely distributed membership for information and its contacts with corrupted social control agents.

The degree to which deviants need special supplies varies with the requirements of their operations, the frequency with which they interact with victims or other nondeviants, and their visibility to social control agents. Supplies other than equipment and information may be required in some instances. However, for most supply problems, sophisticated forms of social organization enjoy a comparative advantage.

IV. *The more sophisticated the form of deviant organization, the greater its members' involvement in deviance.* Complex deviant operations require planning and coordinated action during the deviant act. Socialization and supply also involve interaction among an organization's members. More sophisticated forms of deviant organization, featuring complex operations and elaborate socialization and supply, are therefore more likely to involve intensive social contact with one's fellow deviants. Furthermore, because deviants face sanctions from social control agents and respectable people, their contacts with other deviants are an important source of social support. The differences in the ability of forms . . . [of] social organization to provide support for their members have important social psychological consequences for deviants' careers and identities.

The dimensions of deviant careers vary from the form of deviant organization. Longer deviant careers tend to occur in more sophisticated forms of organization. For naive loners, deviance can comprise a single episode, a defensive act to ward off an immediate threat. For systematic loners, and many colleagues and peers, involvement in deviance is limited to one period in their life. Prostitutes grow too old to compete in the sexual marketplace, delinquents move into respectable adult work roles, and so forth. Members of mobs and formal organizations are more likely to have extended careers. Where the roles are not too physically demanding, deviance can continue until the individual is ready to retire from the work force (Inciardi, 1977). Deviant careers also vary in the amount of time they demand while the individual is active; some kinds of deviance take up only a small portion of the person's hours, but other deviant roles are equivalent to full-time, conventional jobs. Although the relationship is not perfect, part-time deviance is associated with less sophisticated forms of deviant organization.[12]

Social organization is also related to the relative prominence of the deviant identity in the individual's self-concept. Individuals may view their deviance as tangential to the major themes in their lives, or as a central focus, an identity around which much of one's life is arranged. The latter pattern is more likely to develop in sophisticated forms of deviant organization, for, as Lofland (1969) points out, several factors associated with deviant social organization facilitate the assumption of deviant identity, including frequenting places populated by deviants, obtaining deviant equipment, and receiving instruction in deviant skills and ideology. These factors also would appear to be associated with the maintenance of deviance as a central identity. Loners seem especially adept at isolating their deviance, viewing it as an exception to the generally conventional pattern their lives take. This is particularly true when the deviance was initially undertaken to defend that conventional life style from some threat. Even when an individual is relatively committed to deviance, normal identities can serve as an important resource. In his discussion of the World War II underground, Aubert (1965) notes that normal identities served to protect its members. In the same way, an established normal status shields the deviant from the suspicion of social control agents and, if the members refrain from revealing their conventional identities to one another, against discovery brought about by deviant associates who invade their respectable lives. Such considerations seem to be most important in middle-class peer groups organized around occasional leisure-time participation in a deviant marketplace, such as homosexuality and swinging.[13] Other deviants, particularly members of mobs and formal organizations, may associate with their fellows away from deviant operations, so that both their work and their sociable interaction take place among deviants. This is also true for peer groups that expand into "communities" and offer a wide range of services to members. Active members of urban gay communities can largely restrict their contacts to other homosexuals (Harry and Devall, 1978; Wolf, 1979). In these cases there is little need to perform conventional roles, aside from their obvious uses as concealment, and the deviant identity is likely to be central for the individual.

The degree to which an individual finds a deviant career and a deviant identity satisfying depends, in part, on the form of deviant organization of which he or she is a part. As in any activity, persons continue to engage in deviance only as long as the rewards it offers are greater than the rewards which could be obtained through alternative activities. The relevant rewards vary from one person to the next and from one type of deviance to another; a partial list includes money, physical and emotional satisfaction, valued social contacts, and prestige. Because the relative importance of these rewards varies with the individual, it is impossible to measure the differences in rewards between forms of deviant organization. There is some evidence that monetary profits are generally higher in more sophisticated forms of deviant organization. While an occasional loner can steal a very large sum through an embezzlement or a computer crime, most mobs can earn a reasonably steady income, and rackets run by formal organizations consistently bring in high profits. A more revealing measure of satisfaction is career stability; members of more sophisticated forms of deviant organization are more likely to remain in deviance. Loners' careers are short-lived, even when they are involved in systematic deviance. Lemert's (1967) account of the failure of professional forgers to remain at large suggests that the lack of social support is critical. As noted above, persons frequently drift out of their roles as colleagues and peers when other options become more attractive. The long-term careers of members of mobs and formal organizations suggest that these forms are more likely to satisfy the deviant.[14]

V. The more sophisticated the form of deviant organization, the more secure its members' deviant operations. The social organization of deviants affects the interaction between deviants and social control agents. This relationship is complicated because increased sophistication has consequences which would seem to make social control effects both easier and more difficult. On the one hand, the more sophisticated the deviant organization, the greater its public visibility and its chances of being subject to social control actions. Because more sophisticated forms of organization have more complex deviant operations, there are more people involved with the organization as members, victims, customers, and bystanders. Therefore, there are more people capable of supplying the authorities with information about the identities, operations, and locations of organizational members. On the other hand, more sophisticated forms of organization are more likely to have codes of conduct requiring their members to be loyal to the organization and to maintain its secrets. Further, more sophisticated forms of organization command resources which can be used to protect the organization and its members from social control agents. While highly sophisticated organizations find it more difficult to conceal the fact that deviance is taking place, they often are more successful at shielding their members from severe sanctions.

NOTES

1. A second paper, in preparation, will discuss the social organization of deviance.
2. Following Lemert (1967), loners can be subdivided into naive loners, for whom deviance is an exceptional, one-time experience, and systematic loners, whose deviance forms a repeated pattern. Lemert's analysis of the problems confronting systematic check forgers, who have trouble maintaining a deviant identity with little social support, suggests that systematic loners may have particularly unstable careers.
3. The term "mob," as it is used here, is drawn from the glossary in Sutherland: "A group of thieves who work together; same as 'troupe' and 'outfit' " (1937:239; cf. Maurer, 1962, 1964). A more recent study uses the term "crew" (Prus and Sharper, 1977).
4. Although the mob is able to accomplish its ends more efficiently, the same tasks are sometimes handled by loners. For example, see Maurer (1964:166–168) and Prus and Sharper (1977:22).
5. Our use of the term "formal organization" is not meant to imply that these organizations have all of the characteristics of an established bureaucracy. Rather, "formal" points to the deliberately designed structure of the organization—a usage consistent with Blau and Scott (1962:5).
6. The complexity of a deviant activity must be distinguished from two other types of complexity. First, the definition of organizational sophistication, given above,

included the complexity of the division of labor among the deviants in a given organizational form as one criterion of sophistication. Second, the complexity of an activity should not be confused with the complexity of its explanation. A suicide, for example, can be easily accomplished, even though a complex social-psychological analysis may be required to explain the act.
7. This point illustrates the distinction, made earlier, between the social organization of deviance (the pattern of relationships between the roles performed in a deviant transaction) and the social organization of deviants (the pattern of relationships between deviant actors). The former, not the latter, affects an activity's complexity.
8. In most cases, loners do not possess the resources required for more than one type of complex deviance; physicians, for instance, are unable to commit computer thefts. In contrast, members of more sophisticated forms of organization may be able to manage several types of operations, as when a mob's members shift from picking pockets to shoplifting in order to avoid the police, or when an organized crime family is involved in several different rackets simultaneously (Maurer, 1964; Ianni, 1972:87–106).
9. Within a given form of organization, some cognitive perspectives may be more elaborate than others. While pool hustlers have a strong oral tradition, founded on the many hours they share together in pool halls, prostitutes have a relatively limited argot. Maurer (1939) argues that this is due to the restricted contact they have with one another during their work.
10. Here and elsewhere, colleagues represent a partial exception to the pattern. Colleagues resemble members of mobs and formal organizations in that they adopt an instrumental perspective, view deviance as a career, are socialized through apprenticeship to an experienced deviant, and accept deviance as a central identity. While peers have a more sophisticated form of organization, their mutual participation in deviance is based on their shared involvement in an illicit marketplace or leisure-time activity. In contrast, colleagues usually are committed to deviance as means of earning a living.

Yet, because colleagues share a relatively unsophisticated form of organization, they labor under restrictions greater than those faced by mobs and formal organizations. Socialization is of limited scope; call girls learn about handling money and difficult clients, but little about sexual skills (Bryan, 1965). The code of conduct governing colleagues is less encompassing and less binding than those for more sophisticated forms, and the deviance of colleagues is usually less profitable. The absence of the advantages associated with organizational sophistication leads colleagues, despite their similarities to mobs and formal organizations, into an unstable situation where many individuals drift away from deviance.

11. Sometimes such equipment is defined as illicit, and its possession constitutes a crime.

12. Two reasons can be offered to explain this relationship. If a type of deviance is not profitable enough to support the individual, it may be necessary to take other work, as when a pool hustler moonlights (Polsky, 1967). Also, many loners have only a marginal commitment to deviance and choose to allocate most of their time to their respectable roles. This is particularly easy if the form of deviance requires little time for preparation and commission.

13. Swingers meeting new couples avoid giving names or information which could be used to identify them (Bartell, 1971:92–95); and Humphreys (1970) emphasizes that many tearoom participants are attracted by the setting's assurance of anonymity.

14. During their careers, deviants may shift from one organizational form or one type of offense to another. The habitual felons interviewed by Petersilia et al. (1978) reported that, while many of their offenses as juveniles involved more than one partner (presumably members of a peer group), they preferred to work alone or with a single partner on the crimes they committed as adults. The most common pattern was for juveniles who specialized in burglaries to turn to robbery when they became adults.

REFERENCES

Amir, Menachem. 1971. *Patterns in Forcible Rape.* Chicago: University of Chicago Press.

Anderson, Nels. 1923. *The Hobo.* Chicago: University of Chicago Press.

Aubert, Vilhelm. 1965. *The Hidden Society.* Totowa, NJ: Bedminster.

Bartell, Gilbert. 1971. *Group Sex.* New York: New American.

Bell, Daniel. 1962. *The End of Ideology,* Rev. ed. New York: Collier.

Blau, Peter M., and W. Richard Scott. 1962. *Formal Organizations.* San Francisco: Chandler.

Blumer, Herbert. 1967. *The World of Youthful Drug Use.* Berkeley: University of California Press.

Bohannon, Paul. 1960. *African Homicide and Suicide.* Princeton, NJ: Princeton University Press.

Bryan, James H. 1965. "Apprenticeships in Prostitution." *Social Problems* 12:287–297.

———. 1966. "Occupational Ideologies and Individual Attitudes of Call Girls." *Social Problems* 13: 441–450.

Buckner, H. Taylor. 1970. "The Transvestic Career Path." *Psychiatry* 33:381–389.

Cameron, Mary Owen. 1964. *The Booster and the Snitch.* New York: Free Press.

Carey, James T. 1968. *The College Drug Scene.* Upper Saddle River, NJ: Prentice-Hall.

Clinard, Marshall B., and Richard Quinney. 1973. *Criminal Behavior Systems: A Typology,* 2nd ed. New York: Holt, Rinehart and Winston.

Cressey, Donald R. 1953. *Other People's Money.* New York: Free Press.

———. 1962. "Role Theory, Differential Association, and Compulsive Crimes." Pp. 443–467 in A. M. Rose (ed.), *Human Behavior and Social Processes.* Boston: Houghton Mifflin.

———. 1969. *Theft of the Nation.* New York: Harper & Row.

———. 1972. *Criminal Organization.* New York: Harper & Row.

Dawley, David. 1973. *A Nation of Lords.* Garden City, NY: Anchor.

Einstader, Werner J. 1969. "The Social Organization of Armed Robbery." *Social Problems* 17:64–83.

Feldman, Harvey W. 1968. "Ideological Supports to Becoming and Remaining a Heroin Addict." *Journal of Health and Social Behavior* 9: 131–139.

Gibbons, Don C. 1965. *Changing the Lawbreaker.* Upper Saddle River, NJ: Prentice Hall.

———. 1977. *Society, Crime, and Criminal Careers,* 3rd ed. Upper Saddle River, NJ: Prentice-Hall.

Glaser, Barney G., and Anselm L. Strauss. 1967. *The Discovery of Grounded Theory.* Chicago: Aldine.

Goffman, Erving. 1959. *The Presentation of Self in Everyday Life.* Garden City, NY: Anchor.

———. 1963. *Stigma.* Upper Saddle River, NJ: Prentice Hall.

Green, Timothy. 1969. *The Smugglers.* New York: Walker.

Harry, Joseph, and William B. Devall. 1978. *The Social Organization of Gay Males.* New York: Praeger.

Hirschi, Travis. 1962. "The Professional Prostitute." *Berkeley Journal of Sociology* 7:33–49.

Humphreys, Laud. 1970. *Tearoom Trade*. Chicago: Aldine.

Ianni, Francis A. J. 1972. *A Family Business*. New York: Sage.

Inciardi, James A. 1977. "In Search of the Class Cannon." Pp. 55–77 in R. S. Weppner (ed.), *Street Ethnography*. Beverly Hills, CA: Sage.

Keiser, R. Lincoln. 1969. *The Vice Lords*. New York: Holt, Rinehart and Winston.

Klein, John F., and Arthur Montague. 1977. *Check Forgers*. Lexington, MA: Lexington Books.

Lemert, Edwin M. 1967. *Human Deviance, Social Problems, and Social Control*. Upper Saddle River, NJ: Prentice Hall.

Lesieur, Henry R. 1977. *The Chase*. Garden City, NY: Anchor.

Letkemann, Peter. 1973. *Crime as Work*. Upper Saddle River, NJ: Prentice Hall.

Lofland, John. 1969. *Deviance and Identity*. Upper Saddle River, NJ: Prentice Hall.

Luckenbill, David F. 1977. "Criminal Homicide as a Situated Transaction." *Social Problems* 25:176–186.

Matza, David. 1964. *Delinquency and Drift*. New York: Wiley.

———. 1969. *Becoming Deviant*. Upper Saddle River, NJ: Prentice Hall.

Maurer, David W. 1939. "Prostitutes and Criminal Argots." *American Journal of Sociology* 44: 346–350.

———. 1962. *The Big Con*. New York: New American.

———. 1964. *Whiz Mob*. New Haven, CT: College and University Press.

McIntosh, Mary. 1971. "Changes in the Organization of Thieving." Pp. 98–133 in S. Cohen (ed.), *Images of Deviance*. Baltimore: Penguin.

Mileski, Maureen, and Donald J. Black. 1972. "The Social Organization of Homosexuality." *Urban Life and Culture* 1:131–166.

Miller, Gale. 1978. *Odd Jobs: The World of Deviant Work*. Upper Saddle River, NJ: Prentice Hall.

Milner, Christina, and Richard Milner. 1972. *Black Players*. Boston: Little, Brown.

Parker, Donn B. 1976. *Crime by Computer*. New York: Scribner's.

Petersilia, Joan, Peter W. Greenwood, and Marvin Lavin. 1978. *Criminal Careers of Habitual Felons*. Santa Monica, CA: Rand.

Polsky, Ned. 1967. *Hustlers, Beats, and Others*. Chicago: Aldine.

Prus, Robert C., and C. R. D. Sharper. 1977. *Road Hustler*. Lexington, MA: Lexington Books.

Reynolds, Frank. 1967. *Freewheelin' Frank*. New York: Grove.

Rosenberg, Bernard, and Harry Silverstein. 1969. *Varieties of Delinquent Experience*. Waltham, MA: Blaisdell.

Rubington, Earl. 1978. "Variations in Bottle-Gang Controls." Pp. 383–391 in E. Rubington and M. S. Weinberg (eds.), *Deviance: The Interactionist Perspective*, 3rd ed. New York: Macmillan.

Shaw, Clifford R. 1930. *The Jack-Roller*. Chicago: University of Chicago Press.

Shibutani, Tamotsu. 1961. *Society and Personality*. Upper Saddle River, NJ: Prentice Hall.

Shover, Neal. 1977. "The Social Organization of Burglary." *Social Problems* 20:499–514.

Stoddart, Kenneth. 1974. "The Facts of Life about Dope." *Urban Life and Culture* 3:179–204.

Sutherland, Edwin H. 1937. *The Professional Thief*. Chicago: University of Chicago Press.

Thompson, Hunter S. 1966. *Hell's Angels*. New York: Ballantine.

Turner, Ralph H. 1964. "Collective Behavior." Pp. 382–425 in R. E. L. Faris (ed.), *Handbook of Modern Sociology*. Chicago: Rand McNally.

Wade, Andrew L. 1967. "Social Processes in the Act of Juvenile Vandalism." Pp. 94–109 in M. B. Clinard and R. Quinney (eds.), *Criminal Behavior Systems: A Typology*. New York: Holt, Rinehart and Winston.

Warren, Carol A. B. 1974. *Identity and Community in the Gay World*. New York: Wiley.

Winick, Charles. 1961. "Physician Narcotic Addicts." *Social Problems* 9:174–186.

Wiseman, Jacqueline P. 1970. *Stations of the Lost*. Upper Saddle River, NJ: Prentice Hall.

Wolf, Deborah G. 1979. *The Lesbian Community*. Berkeley: University of California Press.

Wolfgang, Marvin E., and Franco Ferracuti. 1967. *The Subculture of Violence*. London: Tavistock.

Zimmerman, Don H., and D. Lawrence Wieder. 1977. "You Can't Help but Get Stoned." *Social Problems* 25:198–207.

Self-Injurers as Loners

PATRICIA A. ADLER and PETER ADLER

When people talk about their personal problems, they find others who have the same kind of problems. In time, they may evolve a collective solution to their once private problems—a subculture. Then they can organize their deviance with the support of this subculture, and it can also help them in coping with their problems. Participants can now pursue unconventional values in the company of like-minded others and derive status, rewards, and self-esteem for acting differently than most other people.

Patricia A. Adler and Peter Adler did a study of young people who purposely injure themselves—namely, cut or burn themselves to relieve loneliness, sadness, and depression. In contrast to the subcultural organization of deviance described above, these self-injurers socially organize their deviance alone rather than with others. These adolescents hold conventional values, feel ashamed, and conceal as best they can the evidence of their self-inflicted injuries. They don't talk about what they do and, generally, avoid social congress with similar deviants. This is similar to the social organization of other forms of loner deviance—sexual asphyxia, anorexia and bulimia, embezzling, rape, and physician and pharmacist drug addiction.

Research in the sociology of deviance has characterized different types of deviant acts by the social organization of participants. Best and Luckenbill (1982) have suggested that some deviants organize and commit their acts as loners, without the support of fellow deviants. According to this definition, loners such as sexual asphyxiates (O'Halloran and Dietz 1993; Lowery and Wetli 1982), anorectics and bulimics (Gordon 1990; McLorg and Taub 1987; Way 1995), embezzlers (Cressey 1971), rapists (Scully and Marolla 1984; Stevens 1999), and physician (Winick 1964) and pharmacist drug addicts (Dabney and Hollinger 1999) do not know other individuals who participate in their form of deviance, or if they do, they generally do not congregate with these people and do not discuss their deviance together. This relative isolation requires loner deviants to move into their

Reprinted from "Self-Injurers as Loners," *Constructions of Deviance: Social Power, Context, and Interaction,* pp. 337–344, by permission of the authors. Copyright Patricia A. Adler and Peter Adler.

norm violations on their own, without the help and support of others. They must decide to do their deviance themselves and figure out on their own how to do it. Without the company of others, they lack the benefits of a deviant subculture from which to draw rationalizations and justifications that might help them neutralize their acts. Of all forms of deviants, loners are characterized as those most entrenched in the normative subculture and are most likely, then, to view their deviant acts through a conventional value system.

In this paper we examine people who self-injure, either by cutting, burning, or branding, the majority in the former category. The research draws on 25 in-depth interviews with self-injurers conducted between 2001 and 2004. Participants ranged in age from 16 to 35 and had mostly, but not entirely, given up the behavior. Most self-injury occurred when people were in middle and high school, with only a smattering of individuals continuing past that age. Nearly three-quarters of the people we interviewed were women, and all were white. Subjects were gathered through a convenience sample of individuals who heard, usually on one of our campuses, that we were interested in talking with people about their self-injury. Those who were interested came forward and contacted us by email, asking for an interview. All of the interviews were conducted on campus in our faculty offices, many with college students, friends of students, university employees, or local high school students. If there is a bias in this self-selected sample, it may be that these people do not represent the most severe segment of self-injurers. Conversations with friends and acquaintances who worked in hospital emergency rooms as well as articles and books about self-injury (Conterio and Lader 1998; Favazza 1996; Favazza and Conterio 1989; Harris 2000; Strong 1998) indicate that some people perform more damaging acts of mutilation on themselves than the people with whom we spoke. Our sample, however, likely represents the majority of self-injurers.

Not all of the self-injurers we interviewed were loners. Some cut, branded, burned, or electroshocked themselves in the company of others. The social dynamics and meanings of this kind of self-injury were dramatically different from those in the loner group. In this paper we focus only on the loners, who comprised nearly 80 percent of our sample. We outline the characteristics of loners and describe the way our self-injurers correspond to or differ from Best and Luckenbill's (1982) ideal typical model.

THE SOCIAL ORGANIZATION OF SOLITARY DEVIANCE

People became involved in self-injury as loners for a variety of reasons, including depression, malaise, alienation, and rebellion. For these young people, self-injury provided a form of comfort that assisted them during a stressful period of their lives.

FORMULATING DEVIANT IDEOLOGY

As loners, people who self-injure were on their own in formulating the meanings and set of rationalizations legitimating their deviance. They often

drew on their respectable training and experiences, not only to develop their techniques but to develop their rationales as well. We see this in the rationalizations of convicted rapists (Stevens 1999; Scully and Marolla 1984), for instance, where the men commonly denied the violent and forced nature of their acts and suggested instead that their victims precipitated or desired the incidents. Rapists drew on cultural myths, learned-hypermasculinity, and their sense of righteous entitlement to justify their behavior. Self-injurers had a much more difficult time giving social meanings and legitimacy to their acts, which were often, especially initially, unclear and undefined. Natalie, a 19-year-old college sophomore, discussed how she viewed her self-injury:

> I guess at first I didn't think much about it. I knew that it was a source of relief for me, and that was all that mattered to me. And, of course, over time when it becomes more of an issue, and people start noticing it, and other people maybe start commenting on it. And then I had to start thinking more about it and what I was really doing and the consequences and what it meant. And I guess just the way that I thought about it was, at first, I was glad that I was able to do it because it made me feel better.

After some time they developed personally acceptable views of their deviance. Some people focused on their neatness, that they were able to do it without making a mess. For others, control was the issue: they could control where their hurt would be. A common feature that many self-injurers shared was their relationship to the pain. Dana, a 19-year-old college sophomore, talked about her pain:

> The thing with emotional pain—you can't see it! It's all inside. I keep it bottled up inside 90 percent of the time, and people can never, like, quantify emotional pain because it's all inside. And so I try to put a picture to that. That's how much I hurt; I did that to myself. Those cuts, that pain, came from inside here. It's kind of a representation of . . . I mean, no cut on my body will ever embody what I feel inside, but it's a start.

Kyle, a 20-year-old junior, described how he would say to himself when he was ready to begin an episode of branding, "It's time for some pain."

SOCIAL ISOLATION

For loners, self-injury deviance was personal. Part of the reason they stayed to themselves was that they viewed their behavior as private, not to be shared with others. Unlike people such as embezzlers or pharmacist drug addicts, who had no special feeling of personal intensity about committing their deviant acts, self-injurers, like many sexual asphyxiates (O'Halloran and Dietz 1993), needed the focus and concentration of being alone while they were engaged in their deviance. It was all about them, and they were focused so completely on themselves while in the act that it would detract from what they could get out of the experience if they did it in the company of others. Dana discussed the feeling she had about her inner-directedness:

> When I hurt like that, I get really self-involved. I get my blinders on. I'm all about me, and don't disturb me . . . so that if someone was cutting themselves in my house, even though I do it, I'd be uncomfortable. It's my thing, you know? I'm in control.

When presented with the opportunity to meet or interact with other people who self-injured, many cutters withdrew from or avoided the interactions. While some knew others who self-injured or were introduced to the idea by knowing others who did it, they generally did not want to form a subculture of self-injurers and did not want to know or be responsible for others. When approached in high school by a classmate who tried to bond with her over their cutting, Mandy, an 18-year-old college freshman, rejected these overtures:

> It scared me, I think, more than anything, because I didn't want to be the person she depended on because I didn't feel ready for that. I still wouldn't, even if she came to me today and said that she needed something. I would be like, "I'm sorry."

One of the primary reasons people self-injured was that they were lonely and depressed. Episodes of self-injury tended to occur when people were away from the company of friends and family, often in the afternoons after school or at night. They had time to sit around and reflect, and they felt bad. In thinking back on high school, many people noted this as a period in their lives where they spent a lot of time alone. It is ironic that while people self-injured to avert their feelings of loneliness and depression, their self-injury could exacerbate this condition. This often occurred when they held themselves back from being with people in situations where their scars would be noticeable. Janice flunked physical education, and endured the ignorant jeers of her classmates for it, because she did not want to let the scars on her legs show. Alice described a negative consequence she incurred as a result of her cutting:

> Sometimes I would just, I would not go with my friends to a hot tub at a hotel or something. We were all having a good time, but I would stay up in the room by myself. And then I'd end up in tears up there because I was so frustrated with myself and with the fact that I have to live with that.

PRACTICAL PROBLEMS

Lacking a deviant subculture, self-injurers often found themselves on their own in coping with the practical problems posed by their deviance. Many of them worried about how to deal with these issues. Dana recalled a conversation she had with a therapist who pointed out some of the auxiliary issues she might have to deal with in the future if she continued with her cutting:

> The practical side to it—how am I going to explain these cuts all over myself in the summer, to my friends? Am I going to go to a job interview with a big scar or a cut on my arm? And that really freaked me out—I don't want anyone to know; no one can know, no!

Many were unable to anticipate what people might say to them or ask them, and they had no ready response when confronted by others. Prior to 1996 questions about scars were not as great a problem, because people could easily explain them away with almost any ridiculous answer, and nobody questioned them. Alice talked about the kind of carte blanche she had as a 12- and 13-year-old to cut without being challenged:

> You know, sometimes stuff that didn't even need to appear very realistic, but people believed it because why wouldn't they? I don't think that many people thought about it when they saw cuts, what if that's self-inflicted?

This all changed, however, when self-injury began to be more widely recognized and people became more suspicious. Longer-term cutters, whose parents had become aware of their behavior, were watched very carefully and often quizzed about their scars. This led them to move their cutting away from their hands and arms to less visible bodily locations such as their stomachs and the inside of their thighs.

In contrast to other forms of loner behavior such as sexual asphyxia (Lowery and Wetli 1982), where participants often shared their knowledge with a nonparticipant who assisted them in their deviance and also helped them keep it secret, self-injurers lacked this type of support. Cutters and burners sometimes told their closest friends or boyfriends about their behavior, but these others usually tried to get them to desist, rather than aiding them. Amy, a 19-year-old young woman working part-time in a hospital while attending community college, recalled that as a burner during high school, she had a boyfriend who cut himself and twice did it when he called her on the phone. Trying to convince him to stop, she said that she would burn herself if he cut himself. Although he denied cutting during the conversations, she felt she could tell from the quivering tone of his voice and the lags in their talk that he was incurring pain. Following through on her threat, she burned herself with a lighter (her preferred method), but this proved ineffective in restraining him. This dual self-injury happened

once again, when they both were interrupted by a girlfriend of Amy's who came in, figured out what was going on, grabbed the phone, somehow got in the middle, and stopped them both. Maggie, a 19-year-old college sophomore, described the way a friend of hers who self-injured relied on her for help in restraining herself:

> She'd call me once in a while and be like, "I'm gonna." I told her not to do it, I told her to call me or do something, so she'd call me sometimes and be like, "I'm in the bath," and I'd be like, "I'm coming to get you," or we'd talk for a long time if I wasn't in a position where I could leave.

NORMATIVE SOCIALIZATION

Another ironic juxtaposition about loners is that according to Best and Luckenbill (1982), they are socialized by society, not by fellow deviants, yet they choose deviance. They choose deviance not because they want to contradict their socialization but because they face situations where respectable courses of action are unattractive or unsatisfactory. Dana described the nature of her inner ambivalence:

> It's not, and I'm not, like, and I never really argue with myself, like, I really want to cut myself but I shouldn't, you know? If I really want to, I do, because it's not all the time, so when it does, I just do it because I'm desperate to feel better, so it's never like, I never, I'm never at war with how I should deal with it, like "Oh, I really want to do it, where's the knife," and my other side being like, "Dana, don't do that." It's always like, one or the other. If I have the urge, I will.

As a result, people who self-injured often condemned their behavior and felt ashamed of themselves. Lisa, a 20-year-old college sophomore, talked about how she viewed her deviance:

> Oh yeah. I was ashamed of myself because it's disgusting and it's not normal, which is OK, but it's just bad to do, I think, to yourself, especially if it's because someone else is hurting you or some

other reason. People that do it because someone else is doing it and get a high from it, I think that's sick, too.

STRAIN

Without the support of fellow deviants, loners are unstable in their deviance, as Best and Luckenbill (1982) have suggested, and they have more difficulty sustaining their deviance over extended periods of time. Ellen compared the isolation of her cutting with other forms of individual deviance such as eating disorders:

> *Women hear it all the time. Not so much with cutting, but with bulimia—you hear about it all the time happening, and percentages, and how many women are bulimic and how many women are anorexic. So therefore you, you not necessarily find a common bond with other people, but more like, you know, you know that other people do it. You know that you're not weird doing it. It's not like that with cutters.*

For people who self-injured, there was often a structural strain between their normative expectations and their deviant behavior. Some wanted to rebel, yet they did not want to rebel too far. One young woman found an intermediate point for balancing this strain where she could burn herself occasionally but never so much that it endangered her access to the benefits of conventional society. Like many self-injurers, she "drifted" (Matza, 1964) in deviance, keeping one foot firmly anchored in legitimacy while she dabbled in deviance, able to return to a normative lifestyle without unduly damaging her identity.

Another form of strain experienced by loners arose from their lack of fellow deviants who might share their perspectives and reaffirm the meaning of their deviance. A few people we met did have contact with other self-injurers. None cut together, but they had some limited contact. Maggie described the sense of contact she got from two other cutters she knew, one whom she described as a leader and the other as a copycat:

> *I don't think they ever sat down and said, "Let's cut together," but I know they discussed it, and they were like, "Oh, I use a razor; what do you use?" you know? And I know they had conversations— while I was never, you know, directly involved in the conversations, I know they happened because of what they said. If I was with one or the other, they would say something that would make me think that they discuss this with each other.*

When self-injurers moved away from these relationships, no matter how superficial, they noted how strongly they felt their absence. Lilly, a 21-year-old college senior, traced the demise of her high school cutting to moving to another school where she was away from the presence of a cutting acquaintance. By her own admission, they had not talked about it much. At most they occasionally said things to each other such as, "Had a bad night last night," and this would signify a cutting incident. But in the new environment, she really noted the absence of this support:

> *It wasn't that we relied on each other so much. Not at all. But somehow when I was at the new school and she wasn't there, I suddenly felt her absence a lot. It was like it had been propping me up more than I realized. Without her there, I moved away from those thoughts and those feelings and got into a new life easier.*

Most loners, then, lacking this kind of support, had difficulty sustaining their behavior over extended periods of time.

DISCUSSION

As loners, self-injurers represent the least organizationally sophisticated form of deviant association. They are on their own without the benefits of fellow deviants to either assist them in their deviant acts or to keep them company in their private backstage moments when they are not engaged in deviance. They thus lack not only the human resources to mount intricate deviant capers characterized by multiple members and differential role specialization but also the basic rudiments of deviant camaraderie to provide social support; a guide to core deviant norms and values; an ideology that offers rationalizations and neutralizations legitimating their deviant acts; information diffusal providing practical, legal, and medical advice; subcultural jargon and stories to enrich the deviant experience; and a system of status stratification to help them measure participants against each other. Although they become absorbed in their deviance, they often find themselves lonely.

REFERENCES

Best, Joel, and David F. Luckenbill. 1982. *Organizing Deviance*. Upper Saddle River, NJ: Prentice Hall.

Conterio, Karen, and Wendy Lader. 1998. *Bodily Harm: The Breakthrough Treatment Program for Self-Injurers*. New York: Hyperion.

Cressey, Donald R. 1971. *Other People's Money: A Study in the Social Psychology of Embezzlement*. Belmont, CA: Wadsworth.

Dabney, Dean A., and Richard C. Hollinger. 1999. "Illicit Prescription Drug Use Among Pharmacists: Evidence of a Paradox of Familiarity." *Work and Occupations* 26(1): 77–107.

Favazza, Armand R. 1996. *Bodies Under Siege: Self-Mutilation and Body Modification in Culture and Psychiatry*, 2nd ed. Baltimore: Johns Hopkins University Press.

Favazza, Armand R., and Karen Conterio. 1989. "Female Habitual Self-Mutilators." *Acta Psychiatrica Scandinavica* 79(3):283–89.

Gordon, Richard. 1990. *Anorexia and Bulimia: Anatomy of a Social Epidemic*. Cambridge, MA: Basil Blackwell.

Harris, Jennifer. 2000. "Self Harm: Cutting the Bad Out of Me." *Qualitative Health Research*. March 10(2):164–73.

Lowery, Shearon A., and Charles V. Wetli. 1982. "Sexual Asphyxia: A Neglected Area of Study." *Deviant Behavior* 4:19–39.

Matza, David. 1964. *Delinquency and Drift*. New York: Wiley.

McLorg, Penelope A., and Diane E. Taub. 1987. "Anorexia and Bulimia: The Development of Deviant Identities." *Deviant Behavior* (8):177–89.

O'Halloran, Ronald L., and Park Elliott Dietz. 1993. "Autoerotic Fatalities with Power Hydraulics." *Journal of Forensic Sciences*, JFSCA 38(2): 359–64.

Scully, Diana, and Joseph Marolla. 1984. "Convicted Rapists' Vocabulary of Motive: Excuses and Justifications." *Social Problems* 31(5):530–44.

Stevens, Dennis J. 1999. *Inside the Mind of a Serial Rapist*. San Francisco: Austin & Winfield.

Strong, Marilee. 1998. *A Bright Red Scream: Self-Mutilation and the Language of Pain*. New York: Penguin Putnam.

Way, Karen. 1995. "Never Too Rich . . . or Too Thin: The Role of Stigma in the Social Construction of Anorexia Nervosa." Pp. 91–113 in Donna Maurer and Jeffrey Sobal (eds.), *Eating Agendas: Food and Nutrition as Social Problems*. Hawthorne, NY: Aldine de Gruyter.

Winick, Charles. 1964. "Physician Narcotic Addicts." Pp. 261–80 in Howard S. Becker (ed.), *The Other Side: Perspectives on Deviance*. New York: Free Press.

Collegiate Rugby and Subcultural Deviance

KENNETH B. MUIR and TRINA SEITZ

In recent years campus authorities have shown increased concern about deviant behavior on campus. Such acts can be either against the public order (drunkenness, disorderly conduct), against persons (rape, assault), or against property (vandalism, malicious destruction). Much of the deviance on campus consists of a sole individual engaging in such behavior.

In contrast, Kenneth B. Muir and Trina Seitz describe deviance that is prescribed by a particular group (in this case a college rugby team) for specific times, places, and circumstances. Unlike the typical "individual" forms of deviance, this deviance can be described as collective and subcultural. The deviant activities take place before, during, and after games. Muir and Seitz report no carry-over. The collective subcultural deviance ends when the rugby season ends.

The core features of this athletic subculture center on the symbols of masculinity, misogyny, and homophobia. Rugby culture exaggerates male values, such as toughness, stoicism, and domination as exhibited in considerable public success in sexual conquest, courage, and violence. Alongside of their overemphasis on public displays of male power, however, occurs the persistent denigration of women and less virile men. Songs, T-shirts, and bumper stickers advertise the exaggerated "virtues" of rugby players.

The deviant acts committed within the collegiate rugby subculture are ritualistic in nature. The behaviors exhibited by these athletes appear to be learned once they have gained entry into the subculture, and are reminiscent of fraternity initiation rites or other similar degradation ceremonies (see Garfinkel 1956; Jones 2000). In addition, these activities are almost exclusively a group phenomenon; the extant literature indicates that these athletes rarely commit or participate in these deviant acts independent of their rugby subculture. These behaviors may range from rather benign activities, such as the boisterous singing of sexually explicit songs and physical horseplay, to more serious conduct involving binge drinking, vandalizing public property, the infliction of injury, and indecent exposure (Sheard and Dunning 1973). Finally, much of the deviance committed by those in the rugby subculture is often perceived as temporary or short-lived behavior.

This study is a heuristic, descriptive endeavor that explores a variety of deviant behaviors committed by male collegiate rugby players within the context of their athletic subculture. The notions of homophobia, misogyny, and machismo are presented as the ideological catalysts that guide a majority of these ritualized performances. While the athletes themselves largely perceive their deviant conduct as ephemeral, the behaviors nevertheless have crucial manifest and latent functions for the group and its individual members.

METHOD

This study is based on active and non-active participant observations of more than 50 male collegiate rugby teams in both competitive and noncompetitive environments in the southeast region of the United States. Over the course of a four-year period, data were collected via the utilization of field notes that documented both observed behavior and information gleaned from players during unstructured, informal interviews. Unsolicited commentaries and dialogue between players and their associates were recorded, as these peripheral conversations lend valuable insight into the players' justifications and motivations for engaging in the behavior.[1]

THE EVOLUTION OF RUGBY AS A DEVIANT ETHOS

For many devotees, rugby is far more than a mere game—it is an organized activity that affords its members the opportunity for social interaction. More often than not, this interaction culminates in ritualistic acts of functional or positive deviance before, during, and after the match. In short, the subculture of collegiate rugby functions as a figurative proving ground for excessive bravado and audacity. Athletes amplify their masculine attributes through participation in a variety of activities unique to the subculture, often at the expense of women, homosexuals, and less virile teammates.

   . . . Collegiate rugby players often cultivate an aura of hooliganism, alcohol abuse, and sexual conquest. These behaviors are generally loathed by conventional society, but are accepted and usually expected by the players and their associates within the subculture. In an attempt to perpetuate this aura of bravado, players, coaches, administrators, and even associates proudly don T-shirts and display bumper stickers with such slogans as, "Rugby Players Eat Their Dead," "Rugby: Where Men Are Men and So Are the Women," "Terrorists Beware: Rugby Player Onboard," and the ubiquitous "Give Blood, Play Rugby."

RITUAL, COHESION, AND FUNCTIONAL NECESSITY

The function of ritualistic behavior in society has significant sociological import. In keeping with the traditional Durkheimian perspective (1912–1965), rituals serve to maintain group cohesiveness, a sense of commonality, and a focus on an ideology or object much more significant than the individual (Collins and Makowsky 1989). Deviance, or the manner and style in which the deviance is performed, has its own importance in maintaining group cohesiveness, as Hebdige (1991) notes:

> Style in subculture is, then, pregnant with significance. Its transformations go "against nature," interrupting the process of "normalization." As such, they are gestures, movements towards a speech which offends the "silent majority," which challenges the principle of unity and cohesion, which contradicts the myth of consensus (p. 18).

Those within the group generally view the manifest functions of deviant subcultural rituals as positive. Indeed, these nonconventional behaviors maintain the cohesiveness of the group, reaffirm the legitimacy of its existence, and provide members with a sense of shared identity and purpose. As such, these seemingly nonfunctional ceremonies are what Goffman (1959) referred to as functional necessities. While the behavior may appear odious to the external audience, it must be evaluated with the inherent exigencies of the group in mind (Collins and Makowsky 1989). Nearly all subcultural enclaves create and maintain distinctive norms, values, and beliefs that are perceived as vital for the survival of the group. Moreover, these groups place a great deal of importance on their members' voluntary willingness to abide by these expectations. In this regard, participation in the group's ritual is viewed as altruistic; the more closely the individual's behavior parallels the philosophies of the group, the higher the degree of adulation and acceptance.

. . . For the male rugby player, his image in the context of the subculture is largely dependent upon the degree to which his behavior equals the expectations of his cohort; the more crude his behavior with regard to women or homosexuals, the less likely his actions will be negatively sanctioned by his peers. In contrast, hesitation to adhere to the group's norms and values will likely be met with ostracism, verbal harassment, or worse.

These androcentric rituals may simultaneously function as one of the many means by which society's sex-role expectations are reinforced in the individual. While subcultural camaraderie and sex-role socialization are both significant components in the lives of male athletes, these rituals are not without negative or latent consequences.

One such consequence is the paradoxical conundrum that emerges in the minds of young men who subscribe to these rigid societal definitions of masculinity. Young male athletes are encouraged to exhibit aggressive yet emotionally distant personae; as Gilder (1995) noted, "The sex that is the more competitive will tend to win more competitions" (in Petrikin, 1995; 95–6). If men desire to transcend these socially ascribed expectations, they do so at their own peril. Kupers and Letich (1995) observed:

> Many of us would like to cross the lines of traditional masculinity, the lines one does not cross if one wants to avoid being perceived as unmanly. There is always the risk that, if a man relaxes his guard, and displays too much tenderness, or if he is too willing to cop his foibles, then he will be mocked by other men. So, as adults, we don't touch each other (except in those exuberant post-touchdown moments) (p. 175).

Finally, the participation in and promotion of activities directly grounded in homophobic or misogynistic ideologies function to perpetuate the notions of male superiority, the devaluation of women, and the intolerance of men who fail to exhibit traditional expectations of masculinity.

RUGBY DEVIANCE AS LEARNED BEHAVIOR

The rugby subculture itself provides the individual with a secondary or reference group, which, in turn, reinforces his behavior with either rewards or some type of sanction. In this case, the reinforcement is largely social—as previously noted, most if not all of the deviance observed occurred exclusively within a group setting. Independent of his rugby subculture, the athlete appears to receive no reinforcement for engaging in the behavior because its meaning or function is largely irrelevant in his conventional social environments.

OBSERVATIONS

More often than not, the deviance committed by the athletes under study was ephemeral in nature, and appeared to serve as a cathartic respite from their conventional daily routines. It was common for these young men to return to their normal academic agendas or other activities a short time after games and the ensuing post-match celebrations. In fact, players frequently brought work clothes with them to the matches; immediately after the game-related activities, players changed out of their athletic gear and went directly to work or to other prearranged college functions.

It also became apparent during the span of this research that the male collegiate rugby subculture shares both striking similarities and vast differences with noncollegiate male subcultural milieus such as exotic gentlemen's clubs and private health and fitness facilities. For instance, the collegiate rugby players often have a central location similar to a fraternity house in which several players will live together. These rugby houses serve as the central meeting place for team social gatherings, post-game parties, and disseminating any information pertinent to future matches or practices.

Similarly, private gentlemen's clubs and health facilities equally serve as common locations for engaging in male camaraderie. Quite often, men will gather in these environments to recreate, bond, and occasionally discuss business-related matters. What differentiates the rugby environment from other exclusively male domains is largely logistical. Whereas noncollegiate men's spheres provide only brief opportunities for socialization, the rugby house is far more central to the very existence and survival of the subculture.

DEVIANCE AND THE IDEOLOGY OF MACHISMO

Collegiate rugby players engage in the sport for various reasons. A great number of players, however, play or associate themselves with collegiate rugby because of the aura of machismo that envelopes the sport. Considered an exaggerated form of masculinity, machismo can include the amplification of prescribed masculine attributes such as sexual prowess and conquest, excessive alcohol consumption, displays of courage or violence, and the prolific use of vulgarity. The concept of machismo is common in the realm of sport where athletes exhibit similar forms of exaggerated posturing. For instance, Weinstein, et al. (1995) noted that pre-professional hockey coaches viewed their players as more athletically competent if the athletes engaged in physical altercations above and beyond those required during the course of a game.

In contrast, rugby players differentiate themselves from other athletes such as hockey, football, and lacrosse players by noting that their chosen sport eschews all but the bare minimum of padding or protective gear. Quite often, collegiate rugby athletes refer to lacrosse players as "pricks with sticks." The use of protective gear by football players, for instance, became fodder for a popular T-shirt that circulated throughout the rugby subcultures under study here. The phrase "Pads Are for Pussies, Blood Is for Men" was clearly emblazoned across the front, communicating a less-than-subtle reference to menstruation. The cartoon caricature on the shirt depicted a rugby player with a soiled tampon flung over his shoulder, further exemplifying the toughness (and misogyny) expected of collegiate rugby players.

Injuries also are considered badges of honor among these athletes. In one instance, a rugby player suffered a large abrasion on his neck during a match. After the game he proudly pointed to the wound and remarked, "Look, my first injury! Isn't it cool?" This player's remark is a fitting example of the assertions of Brown (2002), who noted that suffering and the endurance of an excessive amount of pain reinforce the notion that heterosexual masculinity, sexiness, and bravado are partially gauged by one's ability to tolerate and prevail over injury.

Nelson (1994) further noted that sports violence plays an integral role in maintaining male supremacy in society as a whole. In addition, he added that sports violence (and by extension, violent innuendos directed toward homosexuals and women) is perceived as acceptable both on and off the field:

> Nowhere are masculinity and misogyny so entwined as on the rugby field. At the post-game parties that are an integral part of the rugby culture, drunken men sing songs that depict women as loathsome creatures with insatiable sexual appetites and dangerous sexual organs. Men sing of raping other men's girlfriends and mothers. Rape is also depicted as a joke (Nelson 1994.88).

The consumption of alcohol is a central activity within many male-dominated subcultures, including men's collegiate sports. Collective consumption is a means by which masculine hegemony is achieved within the context of the group; even in advertisements, alcohol is the vehicle by which social prescriptions of masculinity are transmitted and reaffirmed to prospective consumers (Gough and Edwards 1998; Hunt and Waldorf 2000; Lemle and Mishkind 1989; Smith 2002). At practices and during drills and exercises, the players under study often were overheard discussing their sexual conquests of the previous evening. These conversations almost always revolved around the amount of alcohol consumed during the night, as well as the successful or unsuccessful sexual conquests by fellow teammates at post-match parties. Players who failed to have a sexual encounter with a female, or who became physically ill because of excessive consumption, were openly ridiculed in front of their teammates.

One collegiate team regularly performed a pre-game ritual involving the chugging of beer. Players stood on the sidelines and, on a pre-determined signal, opened a can of beer and drank (chugged) it as fast as possible. The players would then sprint onto the field to begin the game. As one player related afterward, the object was not necessarily to determine who could drink the beer the fastest, but rather who would vomit the earliest during the course of the game. If a player did become physically ill (and in each instance one or more did), the player's teammates would cheer and taunt him at the stoppage of play.

It is common to hear both coaches and players insult one another during practices or during games. Typically, these insults involve the use of demeaning, feminized language (see Schacht 1997). Opponents and teammates alike that do not meet the criteria for acceptable standards of machismo are oftentimes overtly labeled as "sissies," "fags," or "pussies"; players who are called such names during a game or practice frequently become targets for physical violence by other players. At times, this ridicule resembles ribbing or just good-natured fun, but the underlying message is clear—those individuals who have an abundance of sexual conquests and who can hold their liquor or beer are to be admired and emulated.

Schacht (1994) noted that on the playing field, code words for specific rugby plays are patently obscene and would not be tolerated in most social circles; a similar trend was observed during this research. In one instance, a player called out a signal near a group of several dozen spectators comprised mostly of college students and players' parents. The player's audible signal consisted of a reference to Jesus and the Virgin Mary engaging in sexual intercourse. The obscene signal was greeted with cheers by some of the players, with laughter by some of the college-age

spectators, and with horror by the players' parents watching the match. At half-time, several parents and other spectators asked that the referee immediately take action to halt further such behavior. When the captain of the offending team was apprised of the parents' request, his reply was, "Fuck 'em if they can't take a joke."

DEVIANCE AND THE IDEOLOGY OF MISOGYNY

The post-match party is a key event at which a good portion of rugby deviance may be observed. It is usually at these celebrations where the majority of misogynistic-driven behaviors emerge, often in the presence of female associates who have accompanied the players to the celebration. The post-game festivities traditionally begin when both the home and visiting teams congregate at a local rugby house; opponents are first treated to free food and beer, and then join the host team in party games, pranks, dances, and the singing of traditional rugby songs (see Schacht 1997).

One frequently observed ritual was the Zulu Warrior Dance, a performance intended as a mockery of female erotic dancers (see Dunning 1986). New players who scored their first goal (or try) in the earlier match were often goaded to perform this dance, which involved the player (or Zulu) stripping naked while fellow revelers doused him with beer. Once the player was completely nude, he was required to run (or streak) through the group while being cheered on by both men and women. Players recently joining the team were most often targeted for participation in these displays of nudity, which were not just limited to semi-private venues such as rugby houses. On several occasions, the Zulu dance was performed in both public bars and restaurants, often with the tacit approval of the proprietors. Players who refused to participate in this ritual were oftentimes forcibly disrobed and were the brunt of ostracism and harassment for weeks afterward.

Similar to the Zulu Warrior Dance is another nudity ritual known as Father Abraham. One new player, who had earlier voiced his desperation to become part of the group, volunteered for this activity. As his fellow players would complete a verse to the song, the new player removed an article of clothing, which quickly culminated in full nudity. During this strip-tease ritual, the player would hand articles of clothing to his mother and sister, who happened to be in attendance. His mother later remarked, "I certainly wasn't expecting that!"

Women who attend these post-game functions are not always ancillary associates. Women also become actively involved in the nudity rituals, but are typically treated as the subjugated foci of male entertainment. At many parties following the match, a rugby "queen" is elected. The selection of the "queen" often is based on the players' perceptions of whether the woman will remove any or all of her clothing while the male participants sing to her. In nearly every incident observed, the woman was hoisted on the shoulders of two players while one person led the group in a song denigrating the woman's physical features.

If the "queen" was an unwilling participant, players placated her by handing her cups of beer or other alcoholic beverages. She was then encouraged to douse the singing men while they chanted, "Show us your tits!" and "Skin to win!" Comments such as these were almost always fueled by the hopes that the woman would eventually disrobe, at least partially. If the "queen" did not accommodate the male revelers, she was often booed and soaked with beer at the conclusion of the song. Schacht (1997) observed some disquieting effects that these rituals can have upon some of the women involved. At one rugby party, a young woman became noticeably upset by the derogatory nature of the songs. He noted, "The woman was so upset she began to cry. She continued to cry for several more minutes and then left, apparently by herself" (Schacht 1997:339).

In one instance, a college woman who had been chosen "queen" removed her shirt and bra for the cheering singers. Other women joined in removing their shirts and bras as well, which could be interpreted as an effort to gain acceptance into the deviant subculture. Women's behavior changed dramatically, however, if they began dating a player. Because the spouses or girlfriends of rugby players are considered "off-limits" to the offensive rituals within the subculture, many of the players' intimate partners would exit to another room with other non-participating women and rejoin the party once the rituals ceased. The reactions of women attending rugby matches and the post-match parties were somewhat intriguing. When asked for her reaction to a particularly offensive rugby song entitled "The S&M Man," a young woman responded, "Oh, they don't mean anything by it. They're just having fun." This appeared to be the typical reaction, as most women apparently accepted the deviant behavior as short-term, and approached the deviancy itself as a sexual "sport" in which they could become active participants.[2]

DEVIANCE AND THE IDEOLOGY OF HOMOPHOBIA

Homophobia is a salient theme within both collegiate and non-collegiate male athletic subcultures (Dundes and Stein 1985; Pronger 1999). This ideology is especially palpable when evaluating the ritualistic behaviors of rugby players, both on and off the field. The players observed during the course of this research often taunted their opponents with calls of "faggot" or "queer," but were only sporadically sanctioned by the referee with a penalty of "conduct detrimental to the spirit of the game."[3] This process of feminizing an opponent through language was aptly explained by Pronger (1999), who noted that humiliating or otherwise taunting an adversary is simply rooted in the desire to win and the aversion to losing. However, the concepts of winning and losing are situated in a sexualized domain; winning is viewed as a dominant (or penetrating) act, and losing is perceived as a submissive (penetrated) feminine act. Thus, the demeaning homophobic dialogue between adversaries is a constant struggle where power differentials (masculine versus feminine) are maintained.

Traditional rugby songs not only focused on the sexual conquest or denigration of women; they also served as vehicles for perpetuating the notions of ideal masculinity vis-a-vis effeminate or less-virile men. While singing at post-game parties, players would alter their voices and exaggerate feminine gestures. This behavior oftentimes included lisping and holding one's wrist limply, usually to the laughter and applause of those observing the behavior.

DISCUSSION

The deviance observed during the course of this research included both criminal and non-criminal activities. Furthermore, these behaviors were found to be largely group phenomena, uniquely ritualistic, and ephemeral in nature. Notions of machismo, misogyny, and homophobia perpetuated a vast majority of the deviance, and more often than not these ideologies operated dialectically rather than independent of one another. It also was apparent that these behaviors, whether occurring in competitive or non-competitive environments, functioned to provide the players with a sense of belonging, unity, and purpose within the context of the subculture.

The question . . . remains as to what extent, if at all, these ideologies are internalized within the individual once he exits the rugby subculture. As a general rule, male collegiate rugby players place a great deal of importance on their involvement within the subculture, but do not appear to integrate this behavior into their conventional social lives outside the subculture. Therefore, while these athletes can learn behaviors conducive to the goals and identity of the group, they may believe that these deviant acts, and the ideologies supporting them, are detrimental to their lives external of the subculture. Because of the ephemeral nature of the deviance, it is quite possible that the subculture simply functions as a temporary locus of resistance to the growing appeal of non-traditional masculine qualities such as exhibiting emotion or displaying affect and weakness (see Kupers and Letich 1995).

NOTES

1. The first author's access to the rugby subculture under study arose from his direct involvement in multiple rugby organizations as a player, coach, administrator, and referee.
2. Aside from women in general, female rugby players are not immune from the misogynistic onslaught exhibited and communicated by their male counterparts. Women rugby players are often referred to as "dykes on spikes," fitting both the misogynistic and homophobic notions referred to throughout this research.
3. Rules that rugby players adhere, or are supposed to adhere, are referred to as "laws." Law 10 sanctioning foul play allows the referee wide latitude in suspending a player from a match or dismissing the player from the match for gross or repeated violations of law.

REFERENCES

Brown, Jeffrey A. 2002. "The Tortures of Mel Gibson: Masochism and the Sexy Male Body." *Men and Masculinities* 5(2):123–143.

Collins, Randall, and Michael Makowsky. 1989. *The Discovery of Society*, 4th ed. New York: Random House.

Dundes, Alan, and Howard F. Stein. 1985. "The American Game of 'Smear the Queer' and the Homosexual Component of Male Competitive Sport and Warfare." *The Journal of Psychoanalytic Anthropology* 8(3):115–29.

Dunning, Eric. 1986. "Sport as a Male Preserve: Notes on the Social Sources of Masculine Identity and Its Transformations." *Theory, Culture and Society* 3(1):79–90.

Durkheim, Emile. 1912–1965. *The Elementary Norms of Religious Life*. New York: Free Press.

Garfinkel, Harold. 1956. "Conditions of Successful Degradation Ceremonies." *American Journal of Sociology* 61(2):420–4.

Gilder, George. 1995. "The Glass Ceiling Is Not What Limits Women at Work." Pp. 122–128 in *Male-Female Roles: Opposing Viewpoints*, edited by J. Petrikin. San Diego, CA: Greenwood Press.

Goffman, Erving. 1959. *Presentation of Self in Everyday Life*. Garden City, New York: Anchor.

Gough, Brendan, and Gareth Edwards. 1998. "The Beer Talking: Four Lads, A Carry Out, and the

Reproduction of Masculinities." *The Sociological Review* 46(3):409–35.

Hebdige, Dick. 1991. *Subculture: The Meaning of Style*. London, New York: Routledge.

Hunt, Geoffrey, and Dan Waldorf. 2000. "Drinking, Kicking Back, and Gang Banging: Alcohol, Violence, and Street Gangs." *Free Inquiry in Creative Sociology* 28(1):3–12.

Jones, Ricky L. 2000. "The Historical Significance of Sacrificial Ritual: Understanding Violence in the Modern Black Fraternity Pledge Process." *The Western Journal of Black Studies* 24(2):112–23.

Kupers, Terry A., and Larry Letich. 1995. "Men Need to Form Close Male Friendships." Pp. 174–79 in *Male-Female Roles: Opposing Viewpoints* [The Opposing Viewpoints Series], edited by J. Petrikin. San Diego, CA: Greenwood Press.

Lemle, Russell, and Marc E. Mishkind. 1989. "Alcohol and Masculinity." *Journal of Substance Abuse Treatment* 6(4):213–22.

Nelson, Mariah Burton. 1994. *The Stronger Women Get, the More Men Love Football: Sexism and the American Culture of Sport*. New York: Harcourt, Brace, and Co.

Petrikin, Jonathan S. 1995. *Male-Female Roles: Opposing Viewpoints* [Opposing Viewpoints Series]. San Diego, CA: Greenhaven Press, Inc.

Pronger, Brian. 1999. "Outta My Endzone: Sport and the Territorial Anus." *Journal of Sport and Social Issues* 23(4):373–89.

Schacht, Steven P. 1994. "The Sadomasochistic Ritual of Male Rugby Players and the Social Construction of Gender Hierarchies." Paper presented at the annual meeting of the North American Society for the Sociology of Sport, Toledo, Ohio, Nov. 1992.

———. 1997. "Feminist Fieldwork in the Mysogynist Setting of the Rugby Pitch: Temporarily Becoming a Sylph to Survive and Personally Grow." *Journal of Contemporary Ethnography* 23(3):338–63.

Sheard, Kenneth G., and Eric G Dunning. 1973. "The Rugby Football Club as a Type of 'Male Preserve': Some Sociological Notes." *International Review of Sport Sociology* 8(3–4): 5–24.

Smith, Tyson. 2002. "The Social Construction of Masculinity in Jim Beam's 'Real Friends, Real Bourbon' Advertising Campaign." Paper presented at the 65th Annual Southern Sociological Society Meetings, Baltimore, Maryland, April, 2002.

Weinstein, Marc D., Michael D. Smith, and David L. Wiesenthal. 1995. "Masculinity and Hockey Violence." *Sex Roles* 33(11–12):831–47.

CHAPTER 9

ENTRY INTO DEVIANT GROUPS

Becoming a Nudist

MARTIN S. WEINBERG

Sociologists focus considerable attention on experiences people have in groups. One of their major concerns is establishing the influence of group membership on conduct. But people must first become members of a particular group. Since the costs of membership in deviant groups may seem to outweigh the benefits, questions arise as to what might attract people to deviant groups, under what circumstances they have their initial experiences in such groups, and under what conditions and at what costs they continue their involvement.

Martin S. Weinberg asks, why do people go to a nudist camp for the very first time? How do they decide to continue their association with people who are nude in the company of others? His work suggests a set of generalizations that help account for both initial entry into other deviant groups and continued affiliation after the initial experience. Initial association with a deviant group quickly dissipates anxiety and replaces it with the rewards of fellowship. Fellowship strengthens the bonds to unconventionality. At the same time, it weakens social ties to certain members of the conventional world, in turn reinforcing the ties to the unconventional group.

In order to better understand deviant lifestyles and the meanings they have for those engaged in them, it is often useful to conceptualize a lifestyle as a career, consisting of various stages. We can then study the interpersonal processes that draw and sustain people at each of these various stages. In this way, we can appreciate the motivations, perceptions, and experiences that characterize involvement in that way of life at various points in time—e.g., these may differ for novices, "veterans," etc.

Using such a career model, this paper deals with the interpersonal processes and phases involved in nudist camp membership. Specifically, it deals with the processes by which people come to contemplate a visit to a nudist camp, attend for the first time, and then continue attending over a period of time. The data come from three sources—101 interviews with nudists in the Chicago area; two successive summers of participant observation in nudist camps; and 617 mailed questionnaires completed by nudists located throughout the United States and Canada.[1]

Reprinted by special permission of The William Alanson White Psychiatric Foundation, Inc., from *Psychiatry: Journal for the Study of Interpersonal Processes*, Vol. 29, No. 1 (February 1966), pp. 15–24. Copyright © 1966 by The William Alanson White Psychiatric Foundation, Inc.

PRENUDIST ATTITUDES TOWARD NUDISM

Most people seldom give much thought to the subject of nudism.[2] Responses in the interviews indicated that nudism is not a prominent object of thought even for many persons who will later become nudists. Thus when nudist members were asked what they had thought of nudism before visiting a camp, many stated that they had never really given it any thought. Until their initial experience, the interviewees' conceptions of nudism had been vague stereotypes, much like those held by the general public. In the words of a now active nudist:

> *I never gave it too much thought. I thought it was a cult—a nut-eating, berry-chewing bunch of vegetarians, doing calisthenics all day, a gymno-physical society. I thought they were carrying health to an extreme, being egomaniacs about their body.*

Many of those who had thought about the subject conceived of nudist camps as more exclusive, luxurious, and expensive than they actually are. Others had different conceptions:

> *I'm afraid I had the prevailing notion that they were undignified, untidy places populated (a) by the very poor, and (b) by languishing bleached blonds, and (c) by greasy, leering bachelors.*

Table 9.1 sums up the attitudes that nudists reported themselves to have taken before their affiliation.

THE INITIAL INTEREST IN NUDISM

If prenudist attitudes are of the nature indicated by Table 9.1, how does one become interested enough to make a first visit to a nudist camp? As shown in Table 9.2, the highest percentage of men mentioned magazines as the source of their interest, and the next largest source was other persons (exclusive of parents or parents-in-law). For women, the pattern was different; the highest percentage were first informed about nudism by their husbands. In 78 percent of the families, the husband had been more interested in visiting a camp.

TABLE 9.1 Prenudist Attitudes Toward Nudism[*]

ATTITUDE	PERCENTAGE OF INTERVIEWEES
Positive	35
Live and let live	16
Negative	19
Very negative	1
Does not know	29

[*]For coding purposes, "positive" was defined as a desire to participate in nudism or to become a nudist. "Live and let live" included those who did not desire participation in nudism, but did not think ill of those who did participate; however, some of these respondents would have imposed social distance from nudists, and some would not.

In all other cases both spouses had equally wanted to go. There were no cases in which the wife had wanted to go more than the husband.

The fact that the overwhelming majority of women became interested in nudism through their relationships with other people, rather than through the mass media which played such an important part with men, was reflected in the finding that interpersonal trust had to be sustained in order to evoke the women's interest.[3] This was indicated in the content of many interviews. The interviews also indicated that commonsense justifications and "derivations"[4] were important in overcoming the women's anxieties.

TABLE 9.2 Source of Initial Interest in Nudism

SOURCE	MALE	FEMALE
Magazines	47%	14%
Movies	6	6
Newspapers	6	0
Spouse	0	47
Parents or parents-in-law	2	8
Other person	31	23
Medical advice from physician	0	2
Other source	8	0

The following quotation is from an interview with a woman who became interested in nudism after being informed about it by a male friend. Here she was describing what her feelings would have been prior to that time. (In this quotation, as in others in this paper, *Q* is used to signify a neutral probe by the interviewer that follows the course of the last reply—such as "Could you tell me some more about that?" or "How's that?" or "What do you mean?" Other questions by the interviewer are given in full.)

> . . . *[Whether or not I would go to a nudist camp would] depend on who asked me. If a friend, I probably would have gone along with it. . . . [Q] If an acquaintance, I wouldn't have been interested. [Q] I don't know, I think it would depend on who was asking me to go. [Q] If it was someone you liked or had confidence in, you'd go along with it. If you didn't think they were morally upright you probably wouldn't have anything to do with it.*

A man described how he had persuaded his wife to become interested in nudism:

> *I expected difficulty with my wife. I presented it to her in a wholesome manner. [Q] I had to convince her it was a wholesome thing, and that the people there were sincere. . . . [Q] That they were sincere in efforts to sunbathe together and had only good purposes in mind when they did that. [Q] All the things that nudism stands for: a healthy body and a cleansed mind by killing sex curiosities.*

The anxieties that enter into the anticipation of public nudity were described in the following interview excerpts:

> *I was nervous. . . . [Q] It's different. It's not a daily practice. . . . I'm heavy, that added to the nervousness.*

> *They said they were ashamed of their builds. They think everyone there is perfection. [Q] They think everyone will look at them.*

> *He [a friend] said he'd never go, but that he could understand it. He saw nothing wrong in it. [Q] He said he wouldn't want other men looking at his wife.*

Even though they had enough confidence to make the decision to visit a camp, the respondents did not necessarily anticipate becoming nudists themselves. For many the first trip was merely a joke, a lark, or a new experience, and the main motivation was curiosity. They visited the camp as one might make a trip to the zoo, to see what it was like and what kind of characters would belong to such a group. There was also curiosity, on the part of many of the respondents, about seeing nude members of the opposite sex.

> *The original thought was that we were going to see a bunch of nuts. It was a joke going out there.*

> *I thought they must be a little nutty. Eccentric. I didn't think there'd be so many normal people. . . . [Q] I felt that people that are nudists are a little bohemian or strange. [Q] I don't feel that way now. I thought we'd be the only sane people there. I thought it was kind of an adventure. . . . [Q] I like feeling I'm doing something unusual that no one knows about. It's a big secret. . . . [Q] The novelty, the excitement of driving up in the car; no one knew we were going. . . .*

Table 9.3 presents the motivations given by interviewees for their first trip to a nudist camp.

TABLE 9.3 Motivations for the First Visit to a Nudist Camp

MOTIVATION	MALE	FEMALE
Curiosity over what it was like	33%	25%
Sexual curiosity	16	2
To satisfy spouse or relative	2	38
Combination of curiosity and to satisfy spouse	0	13
For relaxation	2	4
For health	12	6
To sunbathe	8	2
To make friends	6	0
Other	21	10

THE FIRST VISIT

The first trip to camp was frequently accompanied by extreme nervousness. Part of this might be attributed simply to the experience of entering a new group. The visitors did not know the patterns common to the group, and they were uncertain about their acceptance by group members. For example, a nudist said, referring to his participation in a nudist camp in which he was not well known:

> *I guess I'm a little nervous when I get there, 'cause I'm not recognized as a member of the group.*[5]

But, in the instance of a first visit to a nudist camp, this anxiety on entering a new group was considerably heightened by the unknown nature of the experience that lay ahead. Mead, in his discussion of the "social psychology of the act," has described how people, in planning an action, imaginatively rehearse it and its anticipated consequences.[6] The nudist camp, however, presents a totally unfamiliar situation; the person planning a visit has no past of similar situations, and usually no one has effectively described the situation to him in advance. This gap in effective imagination produces apprehension, anxiety, and nervousness.

> *[On the trip up] I was very nervous. [Q] Because the idea was foreign. [Q] . . . The unknown factor. Just seeing a lot of people without clothes on is an unusual situation. Different or new experiences make one nervous.*

> *You're nervous and apprehensive. You don't know what to expect. . . . I was very nervous. . . . I thought of everything under the sun. . . . I didn't know what to expect.*

> *I felt a little inferior at first, because I had no knowledge of nudist camps. . . . I started to enjoy myself, but I couldn't quite feel comfortable. [Q] In the nude. In front of a lot of people. A lack of confidence, self-confidence. [Q] By not having a complete knowledge. I really didn't know what to expect.*

> *I was afraid of the unknown. I didn't know what to expect. If we had known nudists, I wouldn't have had those fears.*

In most instances, the initial nervousness dissipated soon after the newcomer's arrival. Forty-six percent of the interviewees said that they were not nervous at all after arriving at camp. An additional 31 percent felt at ease in less than three hours. Thus most visitors adjusted rapidly to the nudist way of life. Seventy-one percent of those interviewed reported that *no* major adjustment was necessary. Sixteen percent of the residual group reported that undressing for the first time, or becoming used to being nude, was the only adjustment. Of these people who had to adjust, only 15 percent found the adjustment to be difficult.

> *I really was afraid and shy and I didn't feel too well. We had discussed going, but when the time came to go I couldn't sleep that night. . . . Once we got nude then everything just seemed to come natural. I was surprised at how at ease I felt.*

A variety of other response patterns, which I shall not discuss in detail, were characteristic of the initial visit. For example, one pattern related to the visitor's socioeconomic position.[7] Because facilities in many camps are relatively primitive, those used to more comfortable circumstances were likely to be disappointed. One professional man said:

> *I was disappointed to see it was as rustic and unkempt as it was. . . . If people wore clothes and nothing else changed it would be a fourth-class resort. [Q] Everything there is shabby and not well cared for.*

THE ADOPTION OF NUDISM AS A WAY OF LIFE

COACHING AND SOCIAL VALIDATION

The newcomers to camps received no formal indoctrination in the nudist perspective, but acquired it almost imperceptibly as the result of a subtle social process. Informal coaching, either prior to or after arrival, appears to have eased adjustment problems.[8]

My husband said the men are gentlemen. He told me I'd have fun, like play in the sun, play games, and swim.

She didn't want to undress. . . . [Q] I tried to talk to her and her husband did; she finally got convinced. [Q] I told her you feel better with them off, and that no one will pay any attention.

The consensus of 95 percent of the interviewees was that, as one of them put it, "Things run along very smoothly when you first become a nudist." Asked if they ever had any doubts that becoming a nudist was the right decision, once they had made up their minds, 77 percent reported that they had never had any doubts. Fourteen percent had doubts at the time of the interview. The following quotations illustrate the process of social validation that tends to quell doubts:[9]

I do and I don't [have doubts], because of my religion. [Q] Nobody knows about it, and I wonder about that. [Q] Whether it's the right thing. But as I read the pamphlets [nudist literature] I realize it's up to the individual. God made Adam and Eve and they had no clothes. You don't have to be ashamed of your body. Some are fat and some are thin, but it doesn't matter; it's your personality that matters. I don't know, if my minister found out, I'd defend it. We don't use bad language. Sometimes I wonder, but down underneath I think it's all right. We've just been taught to hide our bodies. Sometimes I wonder, but then I think what the pamphlets say. [Q: At what time do you have these doubts?] When I'm in church. [Q] Yes, when I get to thinking about religion. Not very often. Sometimes I just wonder. [Q: Do you ever have these doubts while at camp?] No, I forget about everything. I'm having too much fun. I remind myself that this is something good for the children. My children won't become Peeping Toms or sex maniacs.

[At first] I felt ridiculous. I thought all those people looked so funny. [Q: Why's that?] All your life you've seen people with their clothes on; now they all have them off. After a while, you feel ridiculous with your clothes on. [Q] I liked the people. They were all very nice. They came from nice families.

It couldn't just be something anyone would do, or just people from a lower class.

The nudist way of life becomes a different reality, a new world:

It seems like a different world from the world we live in every day. No washing, ironing, worries. You feel so free there. The people are friendly there, interested in each other. But not nosy. You can relax among them more easily than in the city.

And this new reality imposes a different meaning on the everyday life of the outside world:

My daughter told us today the boys and girls don't sit together at school, but it makes no difference to her. Several times they're out playing and the boys get excited when they see their panties. My children don't understand that. They have a different state of mind toward different sexes.

MOTIVES FOR BECOMING A NUDIST

Persons who became nudists—that is, became members of a camp and conceived of themselves as nudists—usually demonstrated an autonomy of motives,[10] in the sense that their motives for doing so differed from their motives for first visiting a camp. That is to say, participation in different stages of the "nudist career" were usually characterized by different sets of motives. Hence the curiosity that had often been the overriding motive for initial visits was satisfied, and the incentive for affiliating with a nudist camp was based on the person's experiences at the camp, experiences which may not have been anticipated before visiting the camp.[11] It should be noted, however, that the decision was sometimes prompted by the owner's insistence that visitors join if they wished to return. As Table 9.4 shows, there was a considerable change, after the first visit, in the pattern of male versus female desire to attend the camp.

TABLE 9.4 Comparative Desires of Male and Female Members of Couples to Visit a Nudist Camp[*]

	MALE WANTED TO GO MORE	MALE AND FEMALE WANTED TO GO EQUALLY	FEMALE WANTED TO GO MORE
First visit	79%	21%	0%
Return visits	40	51	9

[*]Two unmarried couples are included in these data.

The following quotations are illustrative of the autonomous motives of respondents for the first and subsequent visits:

[Q: What was your main reason for wanting to attend camp the first time?] Curiosity. [Q] To see how people behave under such circumstances, and maybe also looking at the girls. [Q] Just that it's interesting to see girls in the nude. [Q: What is the main reason you continue to attend?] I found it very relaxing. [Q] It's more comfortable to swim without a wet suit, and not wearing clothes when it's real warm is more comfortable and relaxing.

[I went up the first time] to satisfy my husband. He wanted me to go and I fought it. But he does a lot for me, so why not do him a favor. [She had told him that people went to nudist camps only for thrills and that she would divorce him before she would go. Although he talked her into it, she cried all the way to camp. Asked why she continued to attend, she looked surprised and replied:] Why, because I thoroughly enjoy it!

This last quotation describes a common pattern for women, which appears also in the following recollection:

[I went the first time] because my husband wanted me to go. [Q: What is the main reason that you continue to attend?] Because we had fun . . . and we met a lot of nice people.

The interviewees were asked what they liked most about nudism, with the results shown in

TABLE 9.5 What Interviewees Liked Most about Nudism

	PERCENT OF SAMPLE MENTIONING THE ITEM
Friendliness, sociability	60
Relaxation, getting away from the city	47
Enjoyment of outdoors and sports	36
Freedom	31
Sunbathing	26
Physical health	26
Children becoming informed about the human body	11
Mental health	8
Economical vacations	4
Family recreation, keeping family together	4
Seeing people nude	1
Other aspects	15

Table 9.5. Three of the benefits cited are of special sociological interest—the concept of nudist freedom, the family-centered nature of the recreation, and the emphasis on friendliness and sociability.

"Freedom"

Echoing the nudist ideology, many respondents mentioned "freedom"—using the term in various contexts—as a major benefit. There were varied definitions of this freedom and its meaning for the participant. Some defined it in terms of free body action, of being unhindered by clothing.

Nudism . . . gives me an opportunity to be in the sunshine and fresh air. Also to take a swim nude gives me free expression of body. [Q] I'm not hindered by clothes, a freedom of body movement and I can feel the water all over my body.

Nothing was binding; no socks, no tight belt, nothing clothing-wise touching me.

You don't have garter belts or bras. Your body can breathe.

With perspiration your clothes start to bind and you develop rashes. [Q] You just feel more relaxed when you're nude, and more comfortable from hot, sticky clothing.

Others interpreted freedom from clothing in a different way:

Freedom from a convention of society. It's a relief to get away from it. [Q] A physical relief in that wearing clothes is something you must do. I hate wearing a choking tie at a dinner party, but I have to because it is a society convention.

You don't have to dress appropriate for the occasion. You aren't looking for the smartest slacks and sports clothes.

The freedom. . . . You don't have to worry about the way you're dressed. You don't try to outdo someone with a thirty-dollar bathing suit.

For others, freedom meant the absence of routine and restraint:

A nudist camp has a lot more freedom [than a summer resort]. You do just as you want. . . . [Q] Just to do what you want to do, there is nothing you have to do. At a resort you have to participate in activities.

The freedom. [Q] You can do as you please. [Q] I can read or just lay in the sun.

The freedom. [Q] You can go any place you want in the camp. You can walk anywhere nude.

The range of conceptions of freedom is indicated by the following examples:

I felt free in the water. No one staring at you.

I like the complete freedom of . . . expression. With nudist people, I find them more frank and outspoken, not two-faced. You don't have to be cagey and worry about saying the wrong thing.

Feeling free with your body. [Q] I can't really explain it. Feeling more confident, I guess.

The varying constructions of nudist freedom support Schutz's model of man as a commonsense actor.[12] According to Schutz, man lives very naively in his world; clear and distinct experiences are mixed with vague conjectures, and "cookbook" descriptions of experiences are uncritically adopted from others. When these standard descriptions are vague, and are called into question—for example, by an interviewer who asks what is meant by "freedom"—a wide variety of constructions is elicited from respondents. Nudists, as devotees to a "cause," resemble other commonsense actors in their frequent inability to understand their stock answers critically.

Family Cohesion

As shown in Table 9.5, some respondents gave, as the feature of nudism they like most, its function in providing family recreation. One of the interview sample expressed this as follows:

Nudism tends to keep the family together. In the nonnudist society the family tends to split into different organizations; all have different interests. You can still do different things in camp, but you still have a common interest. And all your plans are made together.

One would expect that nudism would lead to family cohesiveness, as a result of this common interest, and also as a result of a tendency for the family members to conceal their nudist involvements in their dealings with the outside world. In regard to the element of secrecy, Simmel has pointed out how a group's intensified seclusion results in heightened cohesiveness.[13] Participation in nudism did not, however, always lead to increased family cohesiveness. For example, if one spouse did not appreciate the experience, the family's continued participation resulted in increased strain. And although nudist ideology claims that nudist participation brings the family closer together, 78 percent of the interviewees, and 82 percent of the questionnaire respondents, reported no change in their family relationships.

Relationships with Others

Friendliness and sociability were the characteristics of the nudist experience mentioned most often by interviewees. In addition, nudists extended the concept of "family" to include fellow nudists; they cited a "togetherness" that is rare in the clothed society. Some insight into this cohesiveness was displayed in the following remarks by an interviewee:

> Camaraderie and congeniality . . . come in any minority group that supports an unpopular position. [Q] Feelings develop by these in-groups because you are brought together by one idea which you share. On the street you may run into people you share no ideas with.

The interviewees were asked how the camp situation would change if everything remained constant except that clothes were required. Most of them anticipated that their bond would be dissolved.

> They would lose the common bond. They have a bond that automatically is a bond. They are in a minority. They are glad you're here. You are welcome there; they're glad you're one of us.
>
> I think the people would be less friendly. When you're all nude you feel the same as them. You all came here to be nude. . . . [Q] Everybody feels the other is the same; you have something in common to be doing this unusual thing.

A number of interviewees, supporting the nudist contention that social distinctions diminish in the nudist camp, believed that class distinctions would reappear if clothing were donned.[14] A 19-year-old respondent cited both class and age distinctions:

> You would have . . . your classes, and age. [Q] I wouldn't feel as close to B and G.

> There is a great age difference. Knowing them this way, though, gives us a common bond. You just don't think about their ages or anything else about them.

Several blue-collar workers remarked that one of the things they liked about nudism was that, without their uniforms or customary clothes, they and their families could associate with a better class of people. Status striving decreases with the removal of these important props of impression management.

> [If everyone in the camp wore clothes] everything I detest about country clubs I've seen would immediately become manifest. Namely: (1) social climbing with all its accompanying insincerity and ostentation; (2) wolves tracking down virgins; (3) highly formalized activities such as golf; (4) gambling and drinking; (5) embarrassment of having to swim under the appraising gaze of a gallery full of people sipping cocktails. This is the paradox, the curious thing; it doesn't embarrass me to swim at . . . [a nudist camp] whereas I can't be coaxed into the swimming pool at the country club in my hometown. [Q] I think that the reason is the fact that so much in that country club is so calculated to make tableaux or pictures, in which only the young and the handsome can really be a part. That's terribly true.

Another interviewee, when asked what he liked most about social nudism, replied:

> It is the best way to relax. [Q] Once you take your clothes off, people are on the same basis. [Q] Everyone is a person. There are no distinctions between a doctor or a mechanic because of clothing. [Q] . . . It's hard to describe. It's just that all have an equal basis, no distinctions because of clothing. That helps you to relax.

Although these statements may be somewhat idealized, the nudist camp does effectively break down patterns common to country clubs, resorts, and other settings in the outside society. Sex, class, and power lose much of their relevance in the nudist camp, and the suspension of the barriers they create effects a greater unity among the participants. This is not to say, however, that there is no social hierarchy—a point to which I shall return shortly.

The suspension of clothing modesty reinforces the atmosphere of "one big family" in another way. Clothing modesty is a *ceremony* of everyday life that sustains a nonintimate definition of relationships, and with its voluntary suspension relationships are usually defined as closer in character. However, for this to occur, trust must not be called into question, and each person must take for granted that he is differentiated from other social objects. Camp relationships usually meet these conditions. For example, they are differentiated from relationships elsewhere; being undressed in front of others is still out of the ordinary, since nudists do not appear nude among outsiders.

The social effect was significant enough to prompt members to describe the nudist way of life as a discovery that had brought new meaning to their lives. The experience provided many of them with "a sense of belonging." As one respondent put it:

> ... you feel like you're part of a whole family. You feel very close. That's how I feel.

The feeling of being part of "one big family" was, of course, more common to the smaller camps. But even in the large camps, participants in camp activities felt themselves to be a part of a special group.

As I have suggested, however, the "togetherness" of nudists is exaggerated. Personality clashes, cliques, and intergroup disagreements exist, and social stratification remains in evidence. In the words of an unmarried neophyte:

> Sometimes I think there is a hierarchy at ... [a large nudist camp]. [Q] In any organization there are cliques. [Q] These cliques I believe are formed by seniority. [Q] Those who have been there the longest. [Q: What makes you think

this?] Something that is in the air. [Q] Just an impression you get. It's hard to say; it's just a feeling. [Q] As a newcomer I felt not at ease. [Q] There is an air of suspicion; people are not really friendly. [Q] They are not really unfriendly, just suspicious, I suppose, of single men. ... They suspect single men are coming for Peeping Tom purposes. [Q] Just to see the nude women. ... Single men, I think, are the lowest class at camp.

This attitude was borne out in the interviews with other single men; rarely did they describe nudism in *gemeinschaftlich* terms. The meaning of a person's experiences still depends on his social position.

Furthermore, it is doubtful that many people find a Utopia in nudism. The nudists interviewed were asked how seriously they felt that they would be affected if nudist camps were closed. As Table 9.6 shows, 30 percent of the interviewees considered that they would be relatively unaffected. When they were asked to identify their three best friends, almost half of the interviewees did not name another nudist.[15] Table 9.7 details this information, as well as the degree of social involvement with other nudists, as rated by coders.

TABLE 9.6 The Degree to Which the Closing of Nudist Camps Would Affect Interviewees*

CLOSING CAMPS WOULD AFFECT RESPONDENT	PERCENT OF RESPONDENTS
Very much	43
Somewhat	26
Not too much	17
Not at all	13

*Vague categories, such as those presented in this table, were occasionally used for their descriptive value in grossly delineating some point. In this case, respondents were asked to classify themselves (after completing their open-end response). In other cases, the coders used a large group of indicators in constructing such gross scales. Although these scales lacked intrinsic rigor, reliability between coders was high.

TABLE 9.7 Social Involvement with Other Nudists*

	DEGREE OF SOCIAL INVOLVEMENT						
Best Friends Who Are Nudists	Very Low	Moderately Low	Neither High nor Low	Moderately High	Very High		Totals
None	13	9	12	5	7	46	(47%)
One	3	2	6	9	5	25	(26%)
Two		1	3	3	10	17	(18%)
Three					9	9	(9%)
Total	16	12	21	17	31	97	(100%)
	(16%)	(12%)	(22%)	(18%)	(32%)		

*The data on the number of best friends who are nudists were drawn from the replies of interviewees. The degree of social involvement was rated by coders on the basis of the following instructions: Code the degree of social involvement with nudists throughout the year on the basis of answers to Question 40 (b and c). Think of this as a scale or continuum. (1) Very low involvement (no contact at all); (2) moderately low involvement (just write or phone occasionally); (3) neither low nor high involvement (get together every couple of months—or attend New Year's party or splash party together); (4) moderately high involvement (visit once a month); (5) very high involvement (visit every week or two).

NUDISTS AND THE CLOTHED SOCIETY

Nudists envision themselves as being labeled deviant by members of the clothed society. In both the interviews and the questionnaires, the respondents were asked to conceptualize the view of nudists taken by the general public, and by their parents. No consistent difference was found between the views of the two groups, as described by the nudists.[16] Approximately one-third of the respondents conceptualized a live-and-let-live attitude on the part of parents and public. Two-thirds conceptualized a negative or very negative attitude.

> They think we're fanatics. [Q] That we go over-board or something. That we're out of line.

> If I went by what the guys say at work, you'd have to be pretty crazy, off your head a little bit. [Q] They think you almost have to be . . . a sex fiend or something like that. They think there's sex orgies, or wife-swapping, or something.

> They think we're a bunch of nuts. [Q] They just think that anyone who runs around without clothes

is nuts. If they stopped to investigate, they'd find we weren't.

> People think the body should be clothed and not exposed at any time. They associate that with vulgarity, indecency, and abnormality. [Q] Vulgarity is something that is unacceptable to the general public. [Q] Indecency in this respect would be exposing portions of the body which normally we hide. [Q] Abnormality? Well, the general public feels it's abnormal for the body to be undressed around other people, in a social group.

The fact that nudists were able to participate in a group which they viewed as stigmatized (and also the sense of belonging they claimed to have found in nudism) suggested that nudists might be isolated in the larger society. If they were isolated they could more easily participate in such a deviant group, being insulated from social controls.

A comparison of nudist interviewees with a sample of the general population[17] did show the nudists to fall substantially below the general population in frequency of informal association,[18] as shown in Table 9.8. Further, while members of

TABLE 9.8 Frequency of Informal Group Participation

	NUDISTS	GENERAL POPULATION
At least twice a week	17%	30%
Every 4 or 5 days	4	35
Once a week	12	16
Less often or never	67	19

TABLE 9.10 Social Isolation of Nudists According to Their Length of Time in Nudism

DEGREE OF SOCIAL ISOLATION*	YEARS IN NUDISM			
	1–2	3–5	6–9	10 and Over
Moderately or very isolated	22%	38%	44%	54%
Neither isolated nor active	39	31	25	35
Very or moderately active	39	31	32	12

*As rated by coders.

the general population got together most often with relatives, nudists got together most often with friends,[19] as Table 9.9 indicates. The fact that 34 percent of the nudist sample got together with relatives less than once a month may reflect a considerable insulation from informal controls, since it is relatives who would probably provide the greatest pressure in inhibiting participation in such deviant groups.[20]

The degree to which nudists were isolated in the clothed society was found to be related to the length of time they had been nudists. As shown in Table 9.10, the longer a person had been in nudism, the more likely he was to be isolated. This may be interpreted in different ways. For example, there may be a tendency to become more isolated with continued participation, perhaps to avoid sanctions. (Yet, in regard to formal organizations nudists did *not* drop out or become less active.) Or, in the past it is likely that nudism was considered even more deviant than it is today and therefore it may have appealed primarily to more isolated types of people.

Regardless of which interpretation is correct, as previously discussed, many nudists found a sense of belonging in nudism.[21]

People are lonely. It gives them a sense of belonging.

Until I started going out . . . [to camp] I never felt like I was part of a crowd. But I do out there. I was surprised. [Q] Well, like I said, I was never part of a crowd. . . . I had friends, but never outstanding. My wife and I were [camp] King and Queen.

However, while the nudist experience helps solve this life problem for some, it creates this same problem for others. For the latter group, nudism may only ease the problem that it creates— that is, the isolation that results from concealing one's affiliation with a deviant group.[22]

TABLE 9.9 Frequency of Association with Several Types of Informal Groups

	RELATIVES		FRIENDS		NEIGHBORS		CO-WORKERS	
	Nudists	General Population	Nudists	General Population	Nudists	General Population	Nudists	General Population
At least once a week	38%	51%	49%	29%	26%	30%	17%	13%
A few times a month	16	13	21	20	11	9	10	8
About once a month	11	13	8	19	6	9	7	15
Less often	34	23	20	32	56	52	63	65

NOTES

1. Interviews were the primary source of data, and all of the quotations and quantifications in this paper, unless otherwise specified, are drawn from interviews. All known nudists in the vicinity of Chicago were contacted for an interview; the mean interview time was three and one-half hours. Approximately one hundred camps were represented in the interviews and questionnaires. A detailed discussion of my methodology may be found in "Sex, Modesty, and Deviants," Ph.D. Dissertation, Northwestern University, June 1965.

2. This statement is based on the results of a questionnaire study of social response to nudism.

3. My thanks are due to James L. Wilkins for initially pointing this pattern out in his analysis of the additional data on the response of college students to nudists.

4. For a discussion of Pareto's concept of derivation, see Talcott Parsons, *The Structure of Social Action* (second edition); Glencoe, Ill., Free Press, 1949; p. 198 *ff.*

5. It is this very fact of an established social system, however, that prevents a disruption of social order in nudist camps. Traditions and norms are stabilized, and even neophytes who think of themselves as leader-types are forced to fall into the pattern or be rejected. (For a small-group experiment that studies this phenomenon, see Ferenc Merei, "Group Leadership and Institutionalization," *Human Relations* [1949] 2.23–39.) In another paper I have shown how some of these traditions function to sustain a nonsexual definition of the nudist situation. See Martin S. Weinberg, "Sexual Modesty, Social Meanings, and the Nudist Camp," *Social Problems* (1965) 12:311–318.

6. Anselm Strauss, editor, *The Social Psychology of George Herbert Mead;* Chicago, Univ. of Chicago Press, 1956; p. xiii.

7. At the time of the interviews, the interviewers, making a commonsense judgment, placed 54 percent of the nudist respondents in the lower-middle class. This was the modal and median placement.

8. For a discussion of "coaching" relationships, see Anselm Strauss, *Mirrors and Masks: The Search for Identity;* New York, Free Press, 1959; pp. 109–118.

9. By "social validation," I mean the process by which the subjective comes to be considered objective—that is, true. The views of others (especially those considered to have more extensive knowledge) provide a social yardstick by which to measure truth. Pareto reaches a similar view of objectivity. Note the following statement: ". . . we apply the term 'logical actions' to actions

that logically conjoin means to ends not only from the standpoint of the subject performing them, but from the standpoint of other persons who have more extensive knowledge—in other words, to actions that are logical both subjectively and objectively in the sense just explained." See Vilfredo Pareto, *The Mind and Society,* Vol. 1; New York, Harcourt, Brace, 1935; p. 77.

10. This concept was developed by Gordon Allport, "The Functional Autonomy of Motives," *Amer. J. Psychology* (1937) 50:141–156.

11. Attendance is usually confined to summer weekends, and sexual curiosity may arise again between seasons.

12. See Alfred Schutz, "The Dimensions of the Social World," in *Collected Papers, II: Studies in Social Theory,* edited by Arvid Broderson; The Hague, Martinus Nijhoff, 1964; p. 48 *ff.*

13. Kurt H. Wolff, *The Sociology of Georg Simmel;* New York, Free Press, 1950; see Part IV.

14. For discussions of clothes as "sign equipment," see Erving Goffman, "Symbols of Class Status," *British J. Sociology* (1951) 2:294–304; and *The Presentation of Self in Everyday Life;* Garden City, N.Y., Doubleday, 1959; p. 24 *ff.* Also see Gregory Stone, "Appearance and the Self," in *Human Behavior and Social Processes: An Interactionist Approach,* edited by Arnold Rose; Boston, Houghton Mifflin, 1962; pp. 86–118.

15. Although 59 percent of the interviewees had been nudists for over two years, and 27 percent of this group had been nudists for over ten years, involvement did not appear to be particularly high. Also, an estimated 17 percent of the membership drops out every year.

16. Although a positive versus negative differentiation of parents and general public was not found, there was a difference in the character of the typifications involved. In the case of parents, the typifications were derived from a history of experiences with an acting personality and were relatively concrete. In contrast, typifications of the general public were highly anonymous. Because such a collectivity could never be experienced directly, there was a much larger region of taken-for-granteds. This is due to the great number of substrata typifications underlying the general whole. This phenomenon is discussed by Alfred Schutz (see note 12).

17. In this comparison, Axelrod's data on a sample of the general population in the Detroit area were used. See Morris Axelrod, "Urban Structure and Social Participation," *Amer. Sociol. Review* (1956) 21:13–18.

18. A major limitation in this comparison, however, is that Axelrod has collapsed frequencies of association

that are less than once a week into the category of "less often or never."

19. Axelrod finds this greater participation with friends only for members of his sample with high income or high educational or social status.

20. Also the absolute frequency of association with friends includes association with nudist friends. This reduces the apparent social-control function of their friendship associations.

Curiously, members of the nudist sample belonged to more formal organizations than did members of Axelrod's sample of the general population. The comparison was as follows: Membership in no group— general population, 37 percent; nudists, 18 percent.

One group—general population, 31 percent; nudists, 27 percent. Two groups—general population, 16 percent; nudists, 19 percent. Three groups—general population, 8 percent; nudists, 16 percent. Four or more groups— general population, 8 percent; nudists, 21 percent. This may indicate that the segmental nature of many of these associations precludes a strong social-control function as well as a satisfaction of social needs.

21. Some nudists also viewed themselves as members of an elite, superior to clothed society because they had suspended the body taboo.

22. For a discussion of information control, see Erving Goffman, *Stigma: The Management of Spoiled Identity;* Upper Saddle River, N.J., Prentice Hall, 1963; pp. 41–104.

Getting into Gangs

MARTIN SANCHEZ JANKOWSKI

Traditional theories on why youth in low-income neighborhoods join gangs center on community, family, opportunities, and status. Youth join gangs because of (1) absence of community controls, (2) broken homes and the absence of primary group controls, (3) few opportunities to obtain money legitimately, and (4) chances to achieve status through gang membership.

Martin Sanchez Jankowski, after a field study of numerous gangs, argues that these theories ultimately fail as explanations of gang affiliation because of their tendency to stress one factor. He points out that there are a variety of reasons for joining, staying in, leaving, and rejoining groups.

Just as youth seek out gangs in the hope of becoming members, gangs, as social organizations, actively recruit and select candidates for membership from time to time. In addition, there are both variations in the times that youth seek membership and the times that gangs actively recruit.

Because motives for joining and styles of recruitment vary in accordance with candidates' needs and gang needs, the nature of the interaction changes as members of each category redefine their situation.

Earlier, I argued that one of the most important features of gang members was their defiant individualist character. I explained the development

of defiant individualism by locating its origins in the material conditions—the competition and conflict over resource scarcity—of the low-income neighborhoods of most large American cities. These conditions exist for everyone who lives in such neighborhoods, yet not every young person joins a gang. Although I have found that nearly all those who belong to gangs do exhibit defiant individualist traits to some degree, not all those who possess such traits join gangs. This . . . [section] explores who joins a gang and why in more detail.

Many studies offer an answer to why a person joins a gang, or why a group of individuals start a gang. These studies can be divided into four groupings. First, there are those that hold the "natural association" point of view. These studies argue that people join gangs as a result of the natural act of associating with each other.[1] Their contention is that a group of boys, interrelating with each other, decide to formalize their relationship in an attempt to reduce the fear and anxiety associated with their socially disorganized neighborhoods. The individual's impetus to join is the result of his desire to defend against conflict and create order out of the condition of social disorganization.

The second group of studies explains gang formation in terms of "the subculture of blocked opportunities": gangs begin because young males experience persistent problems in gaining employment and/or status. As a result, members of poor communities who experience the strain of these blocked opportunities attempt to compensate for socioeconomic deprivation by joining a gang and establishing a subculture that can be kept separate from the culture of the wider society.[2]

The third group of studies focuses on "problems in identity construction." Within this broad group, some suggest that individuals join gangs as part of the developmental process of building a personal identity or as the result of a breakdown in that process.[3] Others argue that some individuals from low-income families have been blocked

from achieving social status through conventional means and join gangs to gain status and self-worth, to rebuild a wounded identity.[4]

A recent work by Jack Katz has both creatively extended the status model and advanced the premise that sensuality is the central element leading to the commission of illegal acts. In Katz's "expressive" model, joining a gang, and being what he labels a "badass," involves a process whereby an individual manages (through transcendence) the gulf that exists between a sense of self located within the local world (the here) and a reality associated with the world outside (the there). Katz argues that the central elements in various forms of deviance, including becoming involved in a gang and gang violence, are the moral emotions of humiliation, righteousness, arrogance, ridicule, cynicism, defilement, and vengeance. "In each," he says, "the attraction that proves to be most fundamentally compelling is that of overcoming a personal challenge to moral—not material—existence."[5]

Most of these theories suffer from three flaws. First, they link joining a gang to delinquency, thereby combining two separate issues. Second, they use single-variable explanations. Third, and most important, they fail to treat joining a gang as the product of a rational decision to maximize self-interest, one in which both the individual and the organized gang play a role. This is especially true of Katz's approach, for two reasons. First, on the personal level, it underestimates the impact of material and status conditions in establishing the situations in which sensual needs/drives (emotions) present themselves, and overestimates/exaggerates the "seductive" impact of crime in satisfying these needs. Second, it does not consider the impact of organizational dynamics on the thought and action of gang members.

In contrast, the data presented here will indicate that gangs are composed of individuals who join for a variety of reasons. In addition, while the individual uses his own calculus to decide whether or not to join a gang, this is not the only deciding factor. The other deciding factor is whether the gang wants him in the organization.

Like the individual's decision to join, the gang's decision to permit membership is based on a variety of factors. It is thus important to understand that who becomes a gang member depends on two decision-making processes: that of the individual and that of the gang.

THE INDIVIDUAL AND THE DECISION TO BECOME A MEMBER

Before proceeding, it is important to dismiss a number of the propositions that have often been advanced. The first is that young boys join gangs because they are from broken homes where the father is not present and they seek gang membership in order to identify with other males—that is, they have had no male authority figures with whom to identify. In the ten years of this study, I found that there were as many gang members from homes where the nuclear family was intact as there were from families where the father was absent.[6]

The second proposition given for why individuals join gangs is related to the first: it suggests that broken homes and/or bad home environments force them to look to the gang as a substitute family. Those who offer this explanation often quote gang members' statements such as "We are like a family" or "We are just like brothers" as indications of this motive. However, I found as many members who claimed close relationships with their families as those who denied them.

The third reason offered is that individuals who drop out of school have fewer skills for getting jobs, leaving them with nothing to do but join a gang. While I did find a larger number of members who had dropped out of school, the number was only slightly higher than those who had finished school.

The fourth reason suggested, disconfirmed by my data, is a modern version of the "Pied Piper" effect: the claim that young kids join gangs because they are socialized by older kids to aspire to gang membership and, being young and impressionable, are easily persuaded. I found on the contrary that individuals were as likely to join when they were older (mid to late teens) as when they were younger (nine to fifteen). I also found significantly more who joined when they were young who did so for reasons other than being socialized to think it was "cool" to belong to a gang. In brief, I found no evidence for this proposition.

What I did find was that individuals who live in low-income neighborhoods join gangs for a variety of reasons, basing their decisions on a rational calculation of what is best for them at that particular time. Furthermore, I found that they use the same calculus (not necessarily the same reasons) in deciding whether to stay in the gang, or, if they happen to leave it, whether to rejoin.

REASONS FOR DECIDING TO JOIN A GANG

Most people in the low-income inner cities of America face a situation in which a gang already exists in their area. Therefore the most salient question facing them is not whether to start a gang or not, but rather whether to join an existing one. Many of the reasons for starting a new gang are related to issues having to do with organizational development and decline—that is, with the existing gang's ability to provide the expected services, which include those that individuals considered in deciding to join. . . . This section deals primarily, although not exclusively, with the question of what influences individuals to join an existing gang. However, many of these are the same influences that encourage individuals to start a new gang.

MATERIAL INCENTIVES

Those who had joined a gang most often gave as their reason the belief that it would provide them with an environment that would increase their chances of securing money. Defiant individualists constantly calculate the costs and benefits associated with their efforts to improve their financial well-being (which is usually not good). Therefore, on the one hand, they believe that if they engage in economic ventures on their own, they will, if successful, earn more per venture than if they acted as part of a gang. However, there is also the belief that if one participates in economic ventures with a gang, it is likely that the amount earned will be more regular, although perhaps less per venture. The comments of Slump, a sixteen-year-old member of a gang in the Los Angeles area, represent this belief:

Well, I really didn't want to join the gang when I was a little younger because I had this idea that I could make more money if I would do some gigs [various illegal economic ventures] on my own. Now I don't know, I mean, I wasn't wrong. I could make more money on my own, but there are more things happening with the gang, so it's a little more even in terms of when the money comes in. . . . Let's just say there is more possibilities for a more steady amount of income if you need it.

It was also believed that less individual effort would be required in the various economic ventures in a gang because more people would be involved. In addition, some thought that being in a gang would reduce the risk (of personal injury) associated with their business ventures. They were aware that if larger numbers of people had knowledge of a crime, this would increase the risk that if someone were caught, others, including themselves, would be implicated. However, they countered this consideration with the belief that they faced less risk of being physically harmed when they were part of a group action. The comments of Corner, a seventeen-year-old resident of a poor Manhattan neighborhood, represent this consideration. During the interview, he was twice approached about joining the local gang. He said:

I think I am going to join the club [gang] this time. I don't know, man, I got some things to decide, but I think I will. . . . Before I didn't want to join because when I did a job, I didn't want to share it with the whole group—hell, I was never able to make that much to share. . . . I would never have got enough money, and with all those dudes [other members of the gang] knowing who did the job,

you can bet the police would find out. . . . Well, now my thinking is changed a bit 'cause I almost got hurt real bad trying something the other day and so I'm pretty sure I'll join the gang 'cause there's more people involved and that'll keep me safer. [He joined the gang two weeks later.]

Others decided to join the gang for financial security. They viewed the gang as an organization that could provide them or their families with money in times of emergency. It represented the combination of a bank and a social security system, the equivalent of what the political machine had been to many new immigrant groups in American cities.[7] To these individuals, it provided both psychological and financial security in an economic environment of scarcity and intense competition. This was particularly true of those who were fifteen and younger. Many in this age group often find themselves in a precarious position. They are in need of money, and although social services are available to help during times of economic hardship, they often lack legal means of access to these resources. For these individuals, the gang can provide an alternative source of aid. The comments of Street Dog and Tomahawk represent these views. Street Dog was a fifteen-year-old Puerto Rican who had been in a New York gang for two years:

Hey, the club [the gang] has been there when I needed help. There were times when there just wasn't enough food for me to get filled up with. My family was hard up and they couldn't manage all of their bills and such, so there was some lean meals! Well, I just needed some money to help for awhile, till I got some money or my family was better off. They [the gang] was there to help. I could see that [they would help] before I joined, that's why I joined. They are there when you need them and they'll continue to be.

Tomahawk was a fifteen-year-old Irishman who had been in a gang for one year:

Before I joined the gang, I could see that you could count on your boys to help in times of need and that meant a lot to me. And when I needed money, sure enough they gave it to me. Nobody else would have given it to me; my parents didn't have it, and there was no other place to go. The gang was just like they said they would be, and they'll continue to be there when I need them.

Finally, many view the gang as providing an opportunity for future gratification. They expect that through belonging to a gang, they will be able to make contact with individuals who may eventually help them financially. Some look to meet people who have contacts in organized crime in the hope of entering that field in the future. Some hope to meet businessmen involved in the illegal market who will provide them with money to start their own illegal businesses. Still others think that gang membership will enable them to meet individuals who will later do them favors (with financial implications) of the kind fraternity brothers or Masons sometimes do for each other. Irish gang members in New York and Boston especially tend to believe this.

RECREATION

The gang provides individuals with entertainment, much as a fraternity does for college students or the Moose and Elk clubs do for their members. Many individuals said they joined the gang because it was the primary social institution of their neighborhood—that is, it was where most (not necessarily the biggest) social events occurred. Gangs usually, though not always, have some type of clubhouse. The exact nature of the clubhouse varies according to how much money the gang has to support it, but every clubhouse offers some form of entertainment. In the case of some gangs with a good deal of money, the clubhouse includes a bar, which sells its members drinks at cost. In addition, some clubhouses have pinball machines, soccer-game machines, pool tables, [Ping-Pong] tables, card tables, and in some cases a few slot machines. The clubhouse acts as an incentive, much like the lodge houses of other social clubs.[8]

The gang can also be a promoter of social events in the community, such as a big party or dance. Often the gang, like a fraternity, is thought of as the organization to join to maximize opportunities to have fun. Many who joined said they did so because the gang provided them with a good opportunity to meet women. Young women frequently form an auxiliary unit to the gang, which usually adopts a version of the male gang's name (e.g., "Lady Jets"). The women who join this auxiliary do so for similar reasons—that is, opportunities to meet men and participate in social events.[9]

The gang is also a source of drugs and alcohol. Here, most gangs walk a fine line. They provide some drugs for purposes of recreation, but because they also ban addicts from the organization, they also attempt to monitor members' use of some drugs.[10]

The comments of Fox and Happy highlight these views of the gang as a source of recreation.[11] Fox was a twenty-three-year-old from New York and had been in a gang for seven years:

> *Like I been telling you, I joined originally because all the action was happening with the Bats [gang's name]. I mean, all the foxy ladies were going to their parties and hanging with them. Plus their parties were great. They had good music and the herb [marijuana] was so smooth. . . . Man, it was a great source of dope and women. Hell, they were the kings of the community so I wanted to get in on some of the action.*

Happy was a twenty-eight-year-old from Los Angeles, who had been a gang member for eight years:

> *I joined because at the time, Jones Park [gang's name] had the best clubhouse. They had pool tables and pinball machines that you could use for free. Now they added a video game which you only have to pay like five cents for to play. You could do a lot in the club, so I thought it was a good thing to try it for awhile [join the gang], and it was a good thing.*

A PLACE OF REFUGE AND CAMOUFLAGE

Some individuals join a gang because it provides them with a protective group identity. They see the gang as offering them anonymity, which may relieve the stresses associated with having to be personally accountable for all their actions in an intensely competitive environment. The statements of Junior J. and Black Top are representative of this belief. Junior J. was a seventeen-year-old who had been approached about becoming a gang member in one of New York's neighborhoods:

> I been thinking about joining the gang because the gang gives you a cover, you know what I mean? Like when me or anybody does a business deal and we're members of the gang, it's difficult to track us down 'cause people will say, oh, it was just one of those guys in the gang. You get my point? The gang is going to provide me with some cover.

Black Top was a seventeen-year-old member of a Jamaican gang in New York:

> Man, I been dealing me something awful. I been doing well, but I also attracted me some adversaries. And these adversaries have been getting close to me. So joining the brothers [the gang] lets me blend into the group. It lets me hide for awhile, it gives me refuge until the heat goes away.

PHYSICAL PROTECTION

Individuals also join gangs because they believe the gang can provide them with personal protection from the predatory elements active in low-income neighborhoods. Nearly all the young men who join for this reason know what dangers exist for them in their low-income neighborhoods. These individuals are not the weakest of those who join the gang, for all have developed the savvy and skills to handle most threats. However, all are either tired of being on the alert or want to reduce the probability of danger to a level that allows them to devote more time to their effort to secure more money. Here are two representative comments of individuals who joined for this reason. Chico was a seventeen-year-old member of an Irish gang in New York:

> When I first started up with the Steel Flowers, I really didn't know much about them. But, to be honest, in the beginning I just joined because there were some people who were taking my school [lunch] money, and after I joined the gang, these guys laid off.

Cory was a sixteen-year-old member of a Los Angeles gang:

> Man I joined the Fultons because there are a lot of people out there who are trying to get you and if you don't got protection you in trouble sometimes. My homeboys gave me protection, so hey, they were the thing to do. . . . Now that I got some business things going I can concentrate on them and not worry so much. I don't always have to be looking over my shoulder.

A TIME TO RESIST

Many older individuals (in their late teens or older) join gangs in an effort to resist living lives like their parents'. As Joan Moore, Ruth Horowitz, and others have pointed out, most gang members come from families whose parents are underemployed and/or employed in the secondary labor market in jobs that have little to recommend them.[12] These jobs are low-paying, have long hours, poor working conditions, and few opportunities for advancement; in brief, they are dead ends.[13] Most prospective gang members have lived through the pains of economic deprivation and the stresses that such an existence puts on a family. They desperately want to avoid following in their parents' path, which they believe is exactly what awaits them. For these individuals, the gang is a way to resist the jobs their parents held and, by extension, the life their parents led. Deciding to become a gang member is both a statement to society ("I will not take these jobs passively") and an attempt to do whatever can be done to avoid such an outcome. At the very least, some of these individuals view being in a gang as a temporary reprieve from having to take such jobs, a postponement of the inevitable. The comments of Joey and D. D. are representative of this group. Joey was a nineteen-year-old member of an Irish gang in Boston:

> *Hell, I joined because I really didn't see anything in the near future I wanted to do. I sure the hell didn't want to take that job my father got me. It was a shit job just like his. I said to myself, "Fuck this!" I'm only nineteen, I'm too young to start this shit. . . . I figured that the Black Rose [the gang] was into a lot of things and that maybe I could hit it big at something we're doing and get the hell out of this place.*

D. D. was a twenty-year-old member of a Chicano gang in Los Angeles:

> *I just joined the T-Men to kick back [relax, be carefree] for awhile. My parents work real hard and they got little for it. I don't really want that kind of job, but that's what it looked like I would have to take. So I said, hey, I'll just kick back for a while and let that job wait for me. Hey, I just might make some money from our dealings and really be able to forget these jobs. . . . If I don't [make it, at least] I told the fuckers in Beverly Hills what I think of the jobs they left for us.*

People who join as an act of resistance are often wrongly understood to have joined because they were having difficulty with their identity and the gang provided them with a new one. However, these individuals actually want a new identity less than they want better living conditions.

COMMITMENT TO COMMUNITY

Some individuals join the gang because they see participation as a form of commitment to their community. These usually come from neighborhoods where gangs have existed for generations. Although the character of such gangs may have changed over the years, the fact remains that they have continued to exist. Many of these individuals have known people who have been in gangs, including family members—often a brother, but even, in a considerable number of cases, a father and grandfather. The fact that their relatives have a history of gang involvement usually influences these individuals to see the gang as a part of the tradition of the community. They feel that their families and their community expect them to join, because community members see the gang as an aid to them and the individual who joins as meeting his neighborhood obligation. These attitudes are similar to attitudes in the larger society about one's obligation to serve in the armed forces. In a sense, this type of involvement represents a unique form of local patriotism. While this rationale for joining was present in a number of the gangs studied, it was most prevalent among Chicano and Irish gangs. The comments of Dolan and Pepe are representative of this line of thinking. Dolan was a sixteen-year-old member of an Irish gang in New York:

> *I joined because the gang has been here for a long time and even though the name is different a lot of the fellas from the community have been involved in it over the years, including my dad. The gang has helped the community by protecting it against outsiders so people here have kind of depended on it. . . . I feel it's my obligation to the community to put in some time helping them out. This will help me to get help in the community if I need it some time.*

Pepe was a seventeen-year-old member of a Chicano gang in the Los Angeles area:

> *The Royal Dons [gang's name] have been here for a real long time. A lot of people from the community have been in it. I had lots of family in it so I guess I'll just have to carry on the tradition. A lot of people from outside this community wouldn't understand, but we have helped the community whenever they've asked us. We've been around to help. I felt it's kind of my duty to join 'cause everybody expects it. . . . No, the community doesn't mind that we do things to make some money and*

raise a little hell because they don't expect you to put in your time for nothing. Just like nobody expects guys in the military to put in their time for nothing.

In closing this section on why individuals join gangs, it is important to reemphasize that people choose to join for a variety of reasons, that these reasons are not exclusive of one another (some members have more than one), that gangs are composed of individuals whose reasons for joining include all those mentioned, that the decision to join is thought out, and that the individual believes this was best for his or her interests at the moment.

ORGANIZATIONAL RECRUITMENT

Deciding whether or not to join a gang is never an individual decision alone. Because gangs are well established in most of these neighborhoods, they are ultimately both the initiators of membership and the gatekeepers, deciding who will join and who will not.

Every gang that was studied had some type of recruitment strategy. A gang will frequently employ a number of strategies, depending on the circumstances in which recruitment is occurring. However, most gangs use one particular style of recruitment for what they consider a "normal" period and adopt other styles as specific situations present themselves. The three most prevalent styles of recruitment encountered were what I call the fraternity type, the obligation type, and the coercive type.

THE FRATERNITY TYPE OF RECRUITMENT

In the fraternity type of recruitment, the gang adopts the posture of an organization that is "cool," "hip," the social thing to be in. Here the gang makes an effort to recruit by advertising through word of mouth that it is looking for members. Then many of the gangs either give a party or circulate information throughout the neighborhood, indicating when their next meeting will be held and that those interested in becoming members are invited. At this initial meeting, prospective members hear a short speech about the gang and its rules. They are also told about the gang's exploits and/or its most positive perks, such as the dances and parties it gives, the availability of dope, the women who are available, the clubhouse, and the various recreational machinery (pool table, video games, bar, etc.). In addition, the gang sometimes discusses, in the most general terms, its plans for creating revenues that will be shared among the general membership. Once this pitch is made, the decision rests with the individual. When one decides to join the gang, there is a trial period before one is considered a solid member of the group. This trial period is similar, but not identical, to the pledge period for fraternities. There are a number of precautions taken during this period to check the individual's worthiness to be in the group. If the individual is not known by members of the gang, he will need to be evaluated to see if he is an informant for one of the various law enforcement agencies (police, firearms and alcohol, drug enforcement). In addition, the individual will need to be assessed in terms of his ability to fight, his courage, and his commitment to help others in the gang.

Having the *will* to fight and defend other gang members or the "interest" of the gang is considered important, but what is looked upon as being an even more important asset for a prospective gang member is the *ability* to fight and to carry out group decisions. Many researchers have often misinterpreted this preference by gangs for those who can fight as an indication that gang members, and thus gangs as collectives, are primarily interested in establishing reputations as fighters.[14] They interpret this preoccupation as being based on adolescent drives for identity and the release of a great deal of aggression. However, what is most often missed are the functional aspects of fighting and its significance to a gang. The prospective member's ability to fight well is not looked upon by the organization simply as an additional symbol of status. Members of gangs want to know if a potential member can fight because if any of them are caught in a situation where they are required to fight, they want to feel confident that everyone can carry his or her own responsibility. In addition, gang members want to know if the potential gang member is disciplined enough to avoid getting scared and running, leaving them vulnerable. Often everyone's safety in a fight depends on the ability of every individual to fight efficiently. For example, on many occasions I observed a small group of one gang being attacked by an opposing gang. Gang fights are not like fights in the movies: there is no limit to the force anybody is prepared to use—it is, as one often hears, "for all the marbles." When gang members were attacked, they were often outnumbered and surrounded. The only way to protect themselves was to place themselves back to back and ward off the attackers until some type of help came (ironically, most often from the police). If someone cannot fight well and is overcome quickly, everyone's back will be exposed and everyone becomes vulnerable. Likewise, if someone decides to make a run for it, everyone's position is compromised. So assessing the potential member's ability to fight is not done simply to strengthen the gang's reputation as "the meanest fighters," but rather to strengthen the confidence of other gang members that the new member adds to the organization's general ability to protect and defend the collective's interests. The comments of Vase, an eighteen-year-old leader of a gang in New York, highlight this point:

> When I first started with the Silk Irons [gang's name], they checked me out to see if I could fight. After I passed their test, they told me that they didn't need anybody who would leave their butts uncovered. Now that I'm a leader I do the same thing. You see that guy over there? He wants to be in the Irons, but we don't know nothing about whether he can fight or if he got no heart [courage]. So we going to check out how good he is and whether he going to stand and fight. 'Cause if he ain't got good heart or skills [ability to fight], he could leave some of the brothers [gang members] real vulnerable and in a big

> mess. And if [he] do that, they going to get their asses messed up!

As mentioned earlier, in those cases where the gang has seen a prospective member fight enough to know he will be a valuable member, they simply admit him. However, if information is needed in order to decide whether the prospective gang member can fight, the gang leadership sets up a number of situations to test the individual. One favorite is to have one of the gang members pick a fight with the prospective member and observe the response. It is always assumed that the prospective member will fight; the question is, how well will he fight? The person selected to start the fight is usually one of the better fighters. This provides the group with comparative information by which to decide just how good the individual is in fighting.[15] Such fights are often so intense that there are numerous lacerations on the faces of both fighters. This test usually doubles as an initiation rite, although there are gangs who follow up this test phase with a separate initiation ritual where the individual is given a beating by all those gang members present. This beating is more often than not symbolic, in that the blows delivered to the new members are not done using full force. However, they still leave bruises.

Assessing whether a prospective gang member is trustworthy or not is likewise done by setting up a number of small tests. The gang members are concerned with whether the prospective member is an undercover agent for law enforcement. To help them establish this, they set up a number of criminal activities (usually of medium-level illegality) involving the individual(s); then they observe whether law enforcement proceeds to make arrests of the specific members involved. One gang set up a scam whereby it was scheduled to commit an armed robbery. When a number of the gang members were ready to make the robbery, the police came and arrested them—the consequence of a new member being a police informer. The person responsible was identified and punished. Testing the trustworthiness of new recruits proved to be an effective policy because later the gang was able to pursue a much more lucrative illegal venture without the fear of having a police informer in the organization.

Recruiting a certain number of new members who have already established reputations as good fighters does help the gang. The gang's ability to build and maintain a reputation for fighting reduces the number of times it will have to fight. If a gang has a reputation as a particularly tough group, it will not have as much trouble with rival gangs trying to assume control over its areas of interest. Thus, a reputation acts as an initial deterrent to rival groups. However, for the most part, the gang's concern with recruiting good fighters for the purpose of enhancing its reputation is secondary to its concern that members be able to fight well so that they can help each other.

Gangs who are selective about who they allow in also scrutinize whether the individual has any special talents that could be useful to the collective. Sometimes these special talents involve military skills, such as the ability to build incendiary bombs. Some New York gangs attempted to recruit people with carpentry and masonry skills so that they could help them renovate abandoned buildings.

Gangs that adopt a "fraternity recruiting style" are usually quite secure within their communities. They have a relatively large membership and have integrated themselves into the community well enough to have both legitimacy and status. In other words, the gang is an organization that is viewed by members of the community as legitimate. The comments of Mary, a fifty-three-year-old garment worker who was a single parent in New York, indicate how some community residents feel about certain gangs:

> There are a lot of young people who want in the Bullets, but they don't let whoever wants to get in in. Those guys are really selective about who they want. Those who do get in are very helpful to the whole community. There are many times that they have helped the community . . . and the community appreciates that they have been here for us.

Gangs that use fraternity style recruitment have often become relatively prosperous. Having built up the economic resources of the group to a level that has benefited the general membership, they are reluctant to admit too many new members, fearing that increased numbers will not be accompanied by increases in revenues, resulting in less for the general membership. Hackman, a twenty-eight-year-old leader of a New York gang, represented this line of thought:

> Man, we don't let all the dudes who want to be let in in. We can't do that, or I can't, 'cause right now we're sitting good. We gots a good bank account and the whole gang is getting dividends. But if we let in a whole lot of other dudes, everybody will have to take a cut unless we come up with some more money, but that don't happen real fast. So you know the brothers ain't going to dig a cut, and if it happens, then they going to be on me and the rest of the leadership's ass and that ain't good for us.

THE OBLIGATION TYPE OF RECRUITMENT

The second recruiting technique used by gangs is what I call the "obligation type." In this form, the gang contacts as many young men from its community as it can and attempts to persuade them that it is their duty to join. These community pressures are real, and individuals need to calculate how to respond to them, because there are risks if one ignores them. In essence, the gang recruiter's pitch is that everyone who lives in this particular community has to give something back to it in order to indicate both appreciation of and solidarity with the community. In places where one particular gang has been in existence for a considerable amount of time (as long as a couple of generations), "upholding the tradition of the neighborhood" (not that of the gang) is the pitch used as the hook. The comments of Paul and Lorenzo are good examples. Paul was a nineteen-year-old member of an Irish gang in New York:

> Yeah, I joined this group of guys [the gang] because they have helped the community and a lot of us have taken some serious lumps [injuries] in doing

that. . . . I think if a man has any sense of himself, he will help his community no matter what. Right now I'm talking to some guys about joining our gang and I tell them that they can make some money being in the gang, but the most important thing is they can help the community too. If any of them say that they don't want to get hurt or something like that, I tell 'm that nobody wants to get hurt, but sometimes it happens. Then I tell them the bottom line, if you don't join and help the community, then outsiders will come and attack the people here and this community won't exist in a couple of years.

Lorenzo was a twenty-two-year-old Chicano gang member from Los Angeles. Here he is talking to two prospective members:

I don't need to talk to you dudes too much about this [joining a gang]. You know what the whole deal is, but I want you to know that your barrio [community] needs you just like they needed us and we delivered. We all get some battle scars [he shows them a scar from a bullet wound], but that's the price you pay to keep some honor for you and your barrio. We all have to give something back to our community.[16]

This recruiting pitch is primarily based on accountability to the community. It is most effective in communities where the residents have depended on the gang to help protect them from social predators. This is because gang recruiters can draw on the moral support that the gang receives from older residents.

Although the power of this recruiting pitch is accountability to the community, the recruiter can suggest other incentives as well. Three positive incentives generally are used. The first is that gang members are respected in the community. This means that the community will tolerate their illegal business dealings and help them whenever they are having difficulty with the police. As Cardboard, a sixteen-year-old member of a Dominican gang, commented:

Hey, the dudes come by and they be putting all this shit about that I should do my part to protect the community, but I told them I'm not ready to join

up. I tell you the truth, I did sometimes feel a little guilty, but I still didn't think it was for me. But now I tell you I been changing my mind a little. I thinking more about joining. . . . You see the dudes been telling me the community be helping you do your business, you understand? Hey, I been thinking, I got me a little business and if they right, this may be the final straw to get me, 'cause a little help from the community could be real helpful to me. [He joined the gang three weeks later.]

The second incentive is that some members of the community will help them find employment at a later time. (This happens more in Irish neighborhoods.) The comments of Andy, a seventeen-year-old Irish-American in Boston, illustrate this view:

The community has been getting squeezed by some developers and there's been a lot of people who aren't from the community moving in, so that's why some of the Tigers [gang's name] have come by while we've been talking. They want to talk to me about joining. Just like they been saying, the community needs their help now and they need me. I really was torn because I thought there might be some kind of violence used and I don't really want to get involved with that. But the other day when you weren't here, they talked to me and told me that I should remember that the community remembers when people help and they take care of their own. Well, they're right, the community does take care of its own. They help people get jobs all the time 'cause they got contacts at city hall and at the docks, so I been thinking I might join. [He joined three weeks later.]

The third incentive is access to women. Here the recruiter simply says that because the gang is a part of the community and is respected, women look up to gang members and want to be associated with them. So, the pitch continues, if an individual wants access to a lot of women, it will be available through the gang. The comments of Topper, a fifteen-year-old Chicano, illustrate the effectiveness of this pitch:

Yeah, I was thinking of joining the Bangers [a gang]. These two homeboys [gang members] been coming to see me about joining for two months now. They've been telling me that my barrio really needs me and I should help my people. I really do want to help my barrio, but I never really made up my mind. But the other day they were telling me that the mujeres [women] really dig homeboys because they do help the community. So I was checking that out and you know what? They really do! So, I say, hey, I need to seriously check the Bangers out. [One week later he joined the gang.]

In addition to the three positive incentives used, there is a negative one. The gang recruiter can take the tack that if a prospective member decides not to join, he will not be respected as much in the community, or possibly even within his own family. This line of persuasion can be successful if other members of the prospective recruit's family have been in a gang and/or if there has been a high level of involvement in gangs throughout the community. The suggestion that people (including family) will be disappointed in him, or look down on his family, is an effective manipulative tool in the recruiting process in such cases. The comments of Texto, a fifteen year old Chicano, provide a good example:

I didn't want to join the Pearls [gang's name] right now 'cause I didn't think it was best for me right now. Then a few of the Pearls came by to try to get me to join. They said all the stuff about helping your barrio, but I don't want to join now. I mean I do care about my barrio, but I just don't want to join now. But you heard them today ask me if my father wanted me to join. You know I got to think about this, I mean my dad was in this gang and I don't know. He says to me to do what you want, but I think he would be embarrassed with his friends if they heard I didn't want to join. I really don't want to embarrass my dad, I don't know what I'm going to do. [He joined the gang one month later.]

The "obligation method of recruitment" is similar to that employed by governments to secure recruits for their armed services, and it meets with only moderate results. Gangs using this method realized that while they would not be

able to recruit all the individuals they made contact with, the obligation method (sometimes in combination with the coercive method) would enable them to recruit enough for the gang to continue operating.

This type of recruitment was found mostly, although not exclusively, in Irish and Chicano communities where the gang and community had been highly integrated. It is only effective in communities where a particular gang or a small number of gangs have been active for a considerable length of time.

THE COERCIVE TYPE OF RECRUITMENT

A third type of recruitment involves various forms of coercion. Coercion is used as a recruitment method when gangs are confronted with the need to increase their membership quickly. There are a number of situations in which this occurs. One is when a gang has made a policy decision to expand its operations into another geographic area and needs troops to secure the area and keep it under control. The desire to build up membership is based on the gang's anticipation that there will be a struggle with a rival gang and that, if it is to be successful, it will be necessary to be numerically superior to the expected adversary.

Another situation involving gang expansion also encourages an intense recruitment effort that includes coercion. When a gang decides to expand into a geographic area that has not hitherto been controlled by another gang, and is not at the moment being fought for, it goes into the targeted area and vigorously recruits members in an effort to establish control. If individuals from this area are not receptive to the gang's efforts, then coercion is used to persuade some of them to join. The comment of Bolo, a seventeen-year-old leader of a New York gang, illustrates this position:

Let me explain what just happened. Now you might be thinking, what are these dudes doing beating up on somebody they want to be in their gang? The answer is that we need people now, we can't be waiting till they make up their mind. They don't have to stay for a long time, but we need them now. . . . We don't like to recruit this way 'cause it ain't good for the long run, but this is necessary now because in order for us to expand our business in this area we got to get control, and in order to do that we got to have members who live in the neighborhood. We can't be building no structure to defend ourselves against the Wings [the rival gang in the area], or set up some communications in the area, or set up a connection with the community. We can't do shit unless we got a base and we ain't going to get any base without people. It's that simple.

A third situation where a gang feels a need to use a coercive recruiting strategy involves gangs who are defending themselves against a hostile attempt to take over a portion of their territory. Under such conditions, the gang defending its interests will need to bolster its ranks in order to fend off the threat. This will require that the embattled gang recruit rapidly. Often, a gang that normally uses the fraternity type of recruitment will be forced to abandon it for the more coercive type. The actions of these gangs can be compared to those of nation-states when they invoke universal conscription (certainly a form of coercion) during times when they are threatened and then abrogate it when they believe they have recruited a sufficient number to neutralize the threat, or, more usually, when a threat no longer exists. The comments of M. R. and Rider represent those who are recruited using coercion. M. R. was a nineteen-year-old ex–gang member from Los Angeles:[17]

I really didn't want to be in any gang, but one day there was this big blowout [fight] a few blocks from here. A couple of O Streeters [gang's name] who were from another barrio came and shot up a number of the Dukes [local gang's name]. Then it was said that the O Streeters wanted to take over the area as theirs, so a group of the Dukes went around asking people to join for awhile till everything got secure. They asked me, but I still didn't want to get involved because I really didn't want to get killed over something that I had no interest in. But they said they wanted me and if I didn't join

and help they were going to mess me up. Then the next day a couple of them pushed me around pretty bad, and they did it much harder the following day. So I thought about it and then decided I'd join. Then after some gun fights things got secure again and they told me thanks and I left.

Rider was a sixteen-year-old member of an Irish gang from New York:

Here one day I read in the paper there was fighting going on between a couple of gangs. I knew that one of the gangs was from a black section of the city. Then some of the Greenies [local Irish gang] came up to me and told me how some of the niggers from this gang were trying to start some drugs in the neighborhood. I didn't want the niggers coming in, but I had other business to tend to first. You know what I mean? So I said I thought they could handle it themselves, but then about three or four Greenies said that if I didn't go with them that I was going to be ground meat and so would members of my family. Well, I know they meant business because my sister said they followed her home from school and my brother said they threw stones at him on his way home. So they asked me again and I said OK . . . then after we beat the niggers' asses, I quit. . . . Well, the truth is that I wanted to stay, but after the nigger business was over, they didn't want me. They just said that I was too crazy and wouldn't work out in the group.

This last interview highlights the gang's movement back to their prior form of recruitment after the threat was over. Rider wanted to stay in the gang but was asked to leave. Many of the members of the gang felt Rider was too crazy, too prone to vicious and outlandish acts, simply too unpredictable to trust. The gang admired his fighting ability, but he was the kind of person who caused too much trouble for the gang. As T. R., an eighteen-year-old leader of the gang, said:

There's lots of things we liked about Rider. He sure could help us in any fight we'd get in, but he's just too crazy. You just couldn't tell what he'd do. If we kept him, he'd have the police on us all the time. He just had to go.

There is also a fourth situation in which coercion is used in recruiting. Sometimes a gang that has dominated a particular area has declined to such an extent that it can no longer control all its original area. In such situations, certain members of this gang often decide to start a new one. When this occurs, the newly constituted gang often uses coercive techniques to recruit members and establish authority over its defined territory. Take the comments of Rob and Loan Man, both of whom were leaders of two newly constituted gangs. Rob was a sixteen-year-old gang member from Los Angeles:

> There was the Rippers [old gang's name], but so many of their members went to jail that there really wasn't enough leadership people around So a number of people decided to start a new gang. So then we went around the area to check who wanted to be in the gang. We only checked out those we really wanted. It was like pro football scouts, we were interested in all those that could help us now. Our biggest worry was getting members, so when some of the dudes said they didn't want to join, we had to put some heavy physical pressure on them; because if you don't get members, you don't have anything that you can build into a gang. . . . Later after we got established we didn't need to pressure people to get them to join.

Loan Man was a twenty-five-year-old member of a gang in New York:

> I got this idea to start a new gang because I thought the leaders we had were all fucked up. You know, they had shit for brains. They were ruining everything we built up and I wasn't going to go down with them and lose everything. So I talked to some others who didn't like what was going on and we decided to start a new club [gang] in the neighborhood we lived in. So we quit. . . . Well, we got new members from the community, one way or the other . . . you know we had to use a little persuasive muscle to build our membership and let the community know we were able to take control and hold it, but after we did get control, then we only took brothers who wanted us [they used the fraternity type of recruiting].

In sum, the coercive method of recruitment is used most by gangs that find their existence threatened by competitor gangs. During such periods, the gang considers that its own needs must override the choice of the individual and coercion is used to induce individuals to join their group temporarily.

NOTES

1. See Thrasher, *The Gang;* Suttles, *Social Order of the Slum;* Hagedorn, *People and Folks.*
2. Of course, some of the studies cited here overlap these categories, and I have therefore placed them according to the major emphasis of the study. See Cloward and Ohlin, *Delinquency and Opportunity;* Hagedorn, *People and Folks;* Moore, *Homeboys;* Short and Strodtbeck, *Group Process and Gang Delinquency.*
3. Here again it is important to restate that many of these studies overlap the categories I have created, but I have attempted to identify them by what seems to be their emphasis. See Bloch and Niederhoffer, *The Gang;* Yablonsky, *The Violent Gang.*
4. See the qualifying statement in nn. 2 and 3 above. See Horowitz, *Honor and the American Dream;* Cohen, *Delinquent Boys;* Miller, "Lower Class Culture as a Generating Milieu of Gang Delinquency"; Vigil, *Barrio Gangs.*
5. See Jack Katz, *The Seduction of Crime: Moral and Sensual Attractions in Doing Evil* (New York: Basic Books, 1988), p. 9.
6. Although the present study is not a quantitative study, the finding reported here and the ones to follow are based on observations of, and conversations and formal interviews with, hundreds of gang members.
7. For a discussion of the political machine's role in providing psychological and financial support for poor immigrant groups, see Robert K. Merton, *Social Theory and Social Structure* (New York: Free Press, 1968), pp. 126–36. Also see William L. Riordan, *Plunkitt of Tammany Hall* (New York: Dutton, 1963).
8. There are numerous examples throughout the society of social clubs using the lodge or clubhouse as one of the incentives for gaining members. There are athletic clubs for the wealthy (like the University Club and the Downtown Athletic Club in New York), social clubs in ethnic neighborhoods, the Elks and Moose clubs, the clubs of various veterans' associations, and tennis, yacht, and [racquetball] clubs.

9. See Anne Campbell, *Girls in the Gang* (New York: Basil Blackwell, 1987).

10. For the use of drugs as recreational, see Vigil, *Barrio Gangs;* and Fagan, "Social Organization of Drug Use and Drug Dealing among Urban Gangs," who reports varying degrees of drug use among various types of gangs. For studies that report the monitoring and/or prohibition of certain drugs by gangs, see Vigil, *Barrio Gangs,* on the prohibition of heroin use in Chicano gangs; and Thomas Mieczkowski, "Geeking Up and Throwing Down: Heroin Street Life in Detroit," *Criminology* 24 (November 1986): 645–66.

11. See Thrasher, *The Gang,* pp. 84–96. He also discusses the gang as a source of recreation.

12. See Moore, *Homeboys,* ch. 2.; Horowitz, *Honor and the American Dream,* ch. 8; Vigil, *Barrio Gangs;* and Hagedorn, *People and Folks.*

13. For a discussion of these types of jobs, see Michael J. Piore, *Notes for a Theory of Labor Market Stratification,* Working Paper no. 95 (Cambridge, Mass.: Massachusetts Institute of Technology, 1972).

14. See Horowitz, *Honor and the American Dream;* and Ruth Horowitz and Gary Schwartz, "Honor, Normative Ambiguity and Gang Violence," *American Sociological Review* 39 (April 1974): 238–51. There are many other studies that could have been cited here. These two are given merely as examples.

15. The testing of potential gang members as to their fighting ability was also observed by Vigil. See his *Barrio Gangs,* pp. 54–55.

16. This quotation was recorded longhand, not tape-recorded.

17. I first met M. R. when he was in one of the gangs that I was hanging around with. He subsequently left the gang, and I stayed in touch with him by talking to him when our paths crossed on the street. This quotation is from a long conversation that I had with him during one of our occasional encounters.

REFERENCES

Bloch, Herbert A., and Arthur Niederhoffer. 1958. *The Gang: A Study in Adolescent Behavior.* New York: Philosophical Library.

Campbell, Anne. 1987. *Girls in the Gang.* New York: Basil Blackwell.

Cloward, Richard A., and Lloyd B. Ohlin. 1960. *Delinquency and Opportunity: A Theory of Delinquent Gangs.* New York: Free Press.

Cohen, Albert K. 1955. *Delinquent Boys: The Culture of the Gang.* Glencoe, IL: Free Press.

Fagan, Jeffery. 1989. "The Social Organization of Drug Use and Drug Dealing among Urban Gangs." *Criminology* 27(4):633–670.

Hagedorn, John M. 1988. *People and Folks: Gangs, Crime and the Underclass in a Rustbelt City.* Chicago: Lakeview Press.

Horowitz, Ruth. 1983. *Honor and the American Dream: Culture and Identity in a Chicano Community.* New Brunswick, NJ: Rutgers University Press.

Horowitz, Ruth, and Gary Schwartz. 1974. "Honor, Normative Ambiguity and Gang Violence." *American Sociological Review* 39:238–251.

Katz, Jack. 1988. *The Seduction of Crime: Moral and Sensual Attractions in Doing Evil.* New York: Basic Books.

Merton, Robert K. 1968. *Social Theory and Social Structure.* New York: Free Press.

Mieczkowski, Thomas. 1986. "Geeking Up and Throwing Down: Heroin Street Life in Detroit." *Criminology* 24:645–666.

Miller, Walter B. 1958. "Lower Class Culture as a Generating Milieu of Gang Delinquency." *Journal of Social Issues* 14(3):5–19.

Moore, Joan W. 1978. *Homeboys: Gangs, Drugs, and Prisons in the Barrios of Los Angeles.* Philadelphia: Temple University Press.

Piore, Michael J. 1972. *Notes for a Theory of Labor Market Stratification.* Working Paper no. 95. Cambridge, MA: Massachusetts Institute of Technology.

Riordan, William L. 1963. *Plunkitt of Tammany Hall.* New York: Dutton.

Short, James F., Jr., and Fred L. Strodtbeck. 1965. *Group Process and Gang Delinquency.* Chicago: University of Chicago Press.

Suttles, Gerald D. 1968. *The Social Order of the Slum: Ethnicity and Territory in the Inner City.* Chicago: University of Chicago Press.

Thrasher, Frederic. 1928. *The Gang: A Study of 1303 Gangs in Chicago.* Chicago: University of Chicago Press.

Vigil, James Diego. 1988. *Barrio Gangs: Street Life and Identity in Southern California.* Austin: University of Texas Press.

Yablonsky, Lewis. 1966. *The Violent Gang.* New York: Macmillan.

Doing Porn

SHARON A. ABBOTT

Given the general processes by which people get into, hold onto, and move up in legitimate occupations, how do these processes compare with those used by people seeking to perform the kinds of work that are against the law, custom, or "morality"? Sharon A. Abbott offers some preliminary answers for men and women who act in "pornographic videos." Her answers, in turn, supply responses to the question, why do some people get into a deviant subculture like the porn industry?

Unlike other deviant occupations such as prostitution, panhandling, or armed robbery, the porn video industry makes a product: a number of people collaborate in a specific place with special equipment, a division of labor, and a production schedule to make a video. Connections and opportunities are crucial to all three phases of entering, continuing in, and moving up in the industry.

People are more likely to get into this line of work if members of their family, friends, or acquaintances either work in or know others who work in the industry. Absence of opportunities for legitimate work increases the chances of entry. Holding onto work in the porn industry similarly involves a combination of connections and opportunities. Showing up for work, complying with schedules, and being able to perform the work on demand strengthen connections. A reputation for dependability increases the chances of being called back for additional work. Similarly, moving up involves the multiplication of connections along with the diversification of opportunities. Finally, regular participation in the porn industry increases involvement and immersion in a deviant subculture centering on erotic performances.

Many people choose a career based on what the job can provide for them. Benefits may include money, status and recognition, opportunities for career mobility, and social contacts. Some are drawn to jobs that provide a sense of freedom and independence, jobs in which workers can forge their own paths, set their own hours, and be free from rigid demands of authority. Others take jobs to meet new people and to have new experiences. Those who pursue careers in the pornography industry are often seeking these very things.

MOTIVATIONS

Women and men who choose to forge a career in the porn industry are motivated by several factors. The four most commonly cited motivations are (1) money, (2) fame and glamor, (3) a sense of freedom and independence, and (4) the desire to "be naughty" and have sex. Often there is a great deal of overlap in these motivations, and an individual's motivation to maintain a career in the industry can change over time. These motivations are also influenced by gender and the structure of the porn industry.

Heterosexual pornography production can be broadly divided into three categories: professional, pro-amateur, and amateur. Professional companies are the largest and most organized, typically employing between fifty and one hundred staff members for sales, marketing, distribution, promotion, and production scheduling. Each company releases more than twenty video tapes per month, which feature the most glamorous and popular talent in the industry. Budgets for professional features range from $50,000 to $150,000, averaging closer to the lower end. A second category, pro-amateur or "gonzo" companies, include small companies with large budgets, medium-size companies with small budgets, and subsidiaries of professional companies. Their budgets average between $15,000 and $25,000 per video. Unlike the specialized employees of professional companies, the staff at pro-amateur companies perform multiple functions within the organization. Pro-amateur productions create a bridge between professional and "homemade" productions by offering products with high production quality, relatively low cost, and known performers. The third type, amateur companies, are comprised of a few individuals who perform a variety of tasks, including acting, directing, sales, and marketing. Budgets range from a few hundred to a few thousand dollars. Most commonly, amateur companies do not produce but rather edit and market homemade materials that are sent in by the person or persons who videotaped the activities.

MONEY

Popular beliefs maintain that it is the lure of "easy money" that draws people, particularly the young, to the world of pornography. This belief is supported by trade and fan magazines that glamorize the industry by focusing on the lavish lifestyles of its members. While the industry cultivates the idea of porn as profitable, income varies greatly by individual. Furthermore, rather than "easy money," respondents reported that most of the work is boring and physically exhausting. Like prostitutes, only a few make a great deal of money, while most make a modest or meager living.

While money earned from appearing in pornography videos may seem high compared

with that earned from many other jobs, annual incomes generated from porn alone typically approximate middle-class earnings. For example, in 1998, respondents reported that at the professional level, actresses receive between $300 and $1,000 for an individual scene. The fee is based on the actress's popularity, experience, and audience appeal, as well as what the scene entails. Masturbation and girl-girl (lesbian) scenes pay the least, while anal sex and double penetrations generate the most money. The most common scene combines oral sex and penile-vaginal intercourse, and pays, on average, $500. While the pay seems high per hour, income is limited by the amount of work offered. Furthermore, this money must often stretch between extended periods of no work.

Women earn more on average than men. Respondents in this study reported that male performers earn approximately 50 percent less than their female co-workers per scene. Pornography, therefore, is one of the few occupations in which men experience pay inequity. Furthermore, while actors often have more individual scenes per video than do actresses (with the exception of the star), they only rarely appear on box covers (which provide high fees). Therefore, actors' earnings are typically lower for the entire project. Since men in the industry make disproportionately less than women, money alone is an unlikely motivation for actors.

Earnings are also dependent on the category of porn. While money is a motivating factor at the professional and pro-amateur levels, participants in amateur productions are often paid little, if anything at all. When individuals sell amateur tapes to a distributer, they are paid, on average, $150 per tape. The fee is paid to the individual who sells the tape, not to the participants. It is unknown how much each participant receives. On the other hand, when videos are produced by amateur companies, each performer earns between $50 and $150 per scene. In addition to relatively low wages, amateur companies do not have the same connections to such money-making opportunities as erotic dancing and modeling, common at pro-amateur and professional levels. Therefore, actors and actresses at the amateur level were far less likely to cite money as a primary motivation than individuals at higher levels.

At the pro-amateur and professional levels, the effect of money may be a key factor in keeping members involved in the industry even after they decide to leave. Accustomed to periods in which money is plentiful (albeit sporadic), actors and actresses have a difficult time finding jobs that offer the perceived freedom and flexibility of porn work. This phenomenon is illustrated by the following exchange between a husband and wife acting team:

TIM: A friend of mine knew the contacts for porn and another friend of mine really pushed me into it, and once I tried it, I got hooked into it. I liked the lifestyle. And then I didn't like it. I went through a period where I didn't like it, and it was too late, because I was already in it, and I already changed my cost of living. And that's a mistake that porn actors and actresses make.

KERI: They start off making $5,000 a month in the beginning. And that is in the beginning.

TIM: They start off and bite off more than they can chew financially a month, and then you're stuck, because most of us can't turn around and go get a CEO job, because now we're in the $80,000 to $100,000 a year bracket. We are used to big houses and nice cars.

The inability to find jobs with similar benefits may keep participants involved in the industry. In addition, talent may begin to live beyond their means, which serves to keep them in their jobs in order to support their standard of living.

FAME AND GLAMOR

Many respondents report that "becoming known" is a greater motivating factor for entering the industry than money. This motivation is most common at the pro-amateur and professional levels, which have a large distribution of materials, and thus, more opportunities for recognition. Porn stars I interviewed reported being photographed, applauded, and having their autographs requested when appearing in public. In addition, fan clubs provide members of the public the opportunity to connect to their beloved stars while offering talent the chance to be admired.

Fan magazines often portray the world of porn as glamorous, and the industry attempts to promote this image. At the pro-amateur and professional levels, release of high-budget feature films and videos ("glamor pieces") are often accompanied by black-tie parties in highly visible settings (e.g., hotels or convention centers). A key component of these parties is the hordes of photographers from fan, trade, and entertainment magazines who serve as *paparazzi* for the industry. The mixing of glamorization and advertisement is best exemplified in a recent billboard erected over a busy street in Los Angeles featuring the "contract girls" of a large company. Other examples include the two domestic award shows each year hosted by the industry (a third is hosted abroad). While the focus of these ceremonies is often on high-budget features, amateur productions are also honored. The opportunity for fame is therefore available to participants at all levels. Only a limited number of seats for these black-tie affairs are available to the public, and typically cost $100 apiece. This glamorization serves to advertise specific companies while offering relatively low-cost perks to the talent.

Several actresses, actors, producers, and directors commented that the search for fame was a desirable trait in talent because enthusiasm for their work increases as popularity and recognition grow. In contrast, if talent are motivated only by money, they are often left frustrated, bored, or disinterested. As one actor argued, "If you are doing it for the money, you won't last long." Production companies similarly assume that interest in money is evident to viewers and disrupts the fantasy that the talent really enjoy their work.

In contrast to the "straight" (not-X-rated) entertainment industry, porn offers a relatively quick and easy means to earn public recognition. Acting in the straight industry is typically characterized by few opportunities, high competition, and waiting for "luck" or "big breaks" (Levy 1989). Straight actors and actresses often have to audition for hundreds of parts in order to obtain a scant few. In contrast, the porn industry is accommodating to people who are impulsive, spontaneous, and in need of immediate gratification. According to a number of directors and talent, if you are attractive enough, you can sign with an agent and appear in a porn video within a matter of days. Respondents reported that fame does not take long to acquire in the world of pornography.

Unlike the motive of money, the motive of fame and recognition is not gender-specific. While actresses get considerably more attention in adult publications, there are fewer actors overall in the industry. Because the pool of actors is so small, they become familiar and easily recognized. But while this motivation is not determined by gender, the concept of fame varies between the sexes. For females, being famous includes not only being recognized and supported by the industry but also being desired by viewers.

A SENSE OF FREEDOM AND INDEPENDENCE

Research into the motivations of many other types of sex workers suggests that individuals often become involved in the industry because of their low socioeconomic status and restricted opportunities. For example, in their study of table dancers, Ronai and Ellis (1989) argue that women who work in gentlemen's clubs have fewer resources and opportunities than other women. Other explanations for why sex workers enter the trade include poor schooling and/or job training, broken homes, poverty, sexual abuse, and limited opportunities to make money legitimately (see, for example, Allen 1980).

By contrast, a number of my respondents reported that they turned to the adult industry because it offered them what they wanted in a job, namely, flexible hours, good money, and fun. It is thus not blocked opportunity but an understanding

of the often inflexible and demanding nature of paid work that motivates entry into porn. Porn is appealing because it offers more flexibility and independence to the workers. An experienced actress offered this explanation for choosing a career in pornography:

> I just can't work in an office. I flip out—I get sick after two weeks. With this, I get to travel and have freedom. I got to come to the United States. I have enough money to take a vacation whenever I want. I just took two weeks off, although I am trying to save money. (Joanna)

Other respondents claimed that they were drawn to the ease of the work. As one actor who has been in the industry for six years explained:

> I might be on set from 8:00 A.M. to midnight, but I don't do a goddamn thing. They pay me to show up, read a book, flirt with girls, and fuck. As far as that goes, it's cake. (Ryan)

A sense of freedom and independence is supported by the structure of the industry itself. While a few dozen female talent and two male talent hold exclusive contracts with professional companies, most talent work as freelancers or under nonexclusive contracts in which a company is guaranteed a set amount of available days each month. Not being held to a contract allows talent to select jobs and projects that best fit their schedules, interests, and preferences. As one actor explained, not being under an exclusive contract can also increase overall earnings, because a person is free to work on more projects and spends less time on production sets:

> The reason I accepted a contract is because they are not keeping me exclusively. So, I can work around, and . . . I have a guarantee that's just about as big as a normal contract, but I can still work around and my hours are less. I don't stick around for dialogue and bullshit; I just show up and ba-da-bing, I'm done, like, in three hours. In a contract where I am doing a feature, I sit around for ten, twelve hours. If you spread $500 over twelve hours, it's not as much as if you spread

$500 over three hours. Logically, it makes a lot of sense to be nonexclusive. (Dane)

Producers benefit from this freelancer system as well by being able to select participants on a project-by-project basis. Only a few well-publicized stars are needed under exclusive contracts to promote the company.

While porn offers freedom and flexibility in comparison with most other jobs of equal pay, there are certain requirements for being regarded as professional and competent. In order to insure future projects, actresses and actors in all categories are expected to arrive on time, have all necessary paperwork available (identification and HIV test results), be sober and cooperative, and be willing to stay overtime. Being labeled as a "flake" is detrimental to a career, and includes everything from forgetting appointments to being uncooperative to having sexual problems (for males). Therefore, while the work is unconventional, aspects of the job are typical of many industries.

BEING NAUGHTY AND HAVING SEX

A number of my respondents reported that porn offered them a chance to snub the prevailing norms of acceptable sexuality. Few careers offer the same stigma attached to appearing on screen engaging in what many consider a private—and some a sacred—act. While porn undoubtedly attracts exhibitionists, it is also a vehicle for people who wish to violate, challenge, and refute social norms. This phenomenon is particularly relevant for women, as the double standard offers more stringent norms for female sexual expression, whose violations carry additional sanctions. In many ways, male stars embody sexual norms that equate masculine sex with prowess, adventure, and impersonality. The link between male sexuality and porn was humorously illustrated in the following comment.

[An actress] asked me if I had ever thought of being in the adult industry. I am an American male

and I have seen porn—of course I have [thought of being in the industry]. (Chuck)

One company in the study catered to and profited from this desire to be "naughty." The owner-director sought actresses and actors interested in being "bad." As he argued, talent interested in money were rarely interested in sex, while those who desired fame were "used-up" before they achieved it. Being "naughty" could easily be captured on film and would be appealing to viewers who want to see "real sex" (i.e., not acting). Interestingly, working for this producer offered actresses and actors an additional opportunity to be "naughty" since this particular company was marginal even within the industry (because of personnel, content matter, and geographical location).

In the course of violating social norms, porn offers the opportunity to have sex. Although it is widely assumed that the actresses are acting (at least to some degree), many respondents claimed that there was some sexual pleasure in their jobs. Being with "nice" and "gentle" guys was mentioned as increasing arousal. Several also reported that girl-girl scenes were more arousing or erotic because of the interpersonal dynamics between female participants. While female arousal is often exaggerated or faked, it is undeniable that males are obtaining erections and ejaculating as captured by the camera (typically constructed as "enjoying" sex). Even when filming soft-core versions (no penetration), sexual activities are rarely simulated. Furthermore, most scenes end with external ejaculation as a means to suggest that the sex was real. Not surprisingly, most actors cited "getting laid" as a primary motivation for entering a porn career. Once in the industry, sustaining an interest in sex is critical for a successful career. Experiencing sexual problems (inability to maintain an erection or control ejaculation) is the fastest way to end an acting career.

Being part of the porn world offers sexual opportunities for interested participants off the set as well. While many respondents said that they were in "monogamous" relationships outside of work, single participants and those involved in swinging reported many opportunities for sex as a result of being involved in the industry. It follows that individuals involved in norm-violating subcultures were likely to hold nontraditional attitudes toward sex and sexuality, and thus be drawn to an arena in which they can exercise these interests. For example, because girl-girl sex is a staple of mainstream productions, actresses have access to exploring such relationships, which may carry over into private behavior. About two-thirds of my female respondents (none of the males) self-identified as bisexual, although only half of them had engaged in sex with women prior to entering the industry.

OPPORTUNITIES

At the amateur and pro-amateur levels, individuals typically find their way into the industry via connections with friends, lovers, and co-workers. For example, amateur companies rely on actors and actresses to invite their friends to participate in a production. Agents are rarely involved with amateur productions because the fees are too low, but "talent scouts" are used to refer reliable performers (scouts are typically paid $25 to $50 per referral). The opportunity to enter pornography production therefore often comes from other participants. This avenue of entry applies to both women and men. Furthermore, once in the industry, it is easy to make connections that foster sustained contact with the business.

As in many other careers in deviance, once one is in a subculture, friends and social networks typically become limited to individuals who are also part of the subgroup. Being part of a stigmatized group fosters these relationships. In the porn business, industry parties and less-formalized social gatherings provide opportunities to socialize and network. Networking is as vital a function in porn production as it is in straight industries. These parties thus help in making contacts, forming alliances, and providing opportunities to be seen.

In addition to opportunities offered via friends, lovers, and acquaintances, other facets of the sex industry provide a means to enter the world of porn. For women, erotic dancing presents a primary opportunity. Dancers are often informed that they can make more money stripping if they appear in a few pornographic videos. If a dancer has established a name for herself, she may be recruited by the porn industry. Based on her physical attractiveness and name recognition, an actress may be offered both an exclusive contract and her pick of directors and co-talent. For example, at the time of data collection, the highest-paid actress under an exclusive contract, a former centerfold model, refused to participate in any boy–girl scenes on camera, and would engage only in masturbation and girl–girl scenes, typically the lowest paid in the industry. Her income, therefore, was tied to her appearance and status, rather than the acts she performed in the features.

The link between porn and stripping exists in the other direction as well. It is rare for a big-name actress not to "dance" (strip), at least periodically. Dancing provides an opportunity to increase recognition and fan appeal, and thus to make oneself more profitable to the industry. When an actress "headlines" (has a featured appearance) at a dance club, the owners advertise that they have a porn star performing, which in turn draws larger crowds. Bigger crowds and increased interest result in higher tips for dancers and more business (and thus more profit) for the clubs. Therefore, actresses, club owners, and porn companies all stand to benefit from this symbiotic relationship.

Porn companies, particularly those offering semiexclusive or exclusive contracts, will often encourage actresses to dance in order to advertise the company. Larger companies retain booking agents for their dancers so that arrangements and pay negotiations are handled in-house. In addition, videotapes in which the dancer has performed are often offered for sale. When state laws prohibit such sales, "one-sheets," or advertisements for videos with photographs taken on the set, are made available to the customers.

Increased recognition, however, can have negative effects on an actress's career. Porn companies are continuously searching for fresh faces in order to appeal to both new and old viewers. Actresses who are overexposed in regard to number of videos, magazine layouts, and dancing appearances are assumed to be unable to offer much appeal for viewers. Through popularity, their images become old and too familiar. Therefore, although publicity is mandatory for a profitable career, it is often of only limited interest to a company. In other words, the ingredients for having a successful career are the very things that can end one.

Because magazine spreads and dancing opportunities are far more available for women than for men, actors are not vulnerable to overexposure and, as a result, have careers commonly twice as long as females. As one actress explains:

Girls have a shelf life of nine months to two years, unless you are different. Like me, I am Asian, so it helps. Men stay forever. It is different for a man. If he can perform, he can stay in. There are guys that have been in the business ten or fifteen years. (Julie)

Furthermore, as Levy (1989) found in the straight industry, popular and successful actresses are younger on average than their male counterparts, suggesting the beauty norms held by both producers and audiences. In both the straight and adult industries, actors are able to age, while actresses are replaced by younger, newer talent.

CHANGES IN MOTIVATIONS

Actors and actresses who are searching for quick money and/or sexual adventure quickly leave the porn industry once those goals are met, as do those who take one-time opportunities to act in videos. Those who remain must build a career for themselves in an industry that centers on the temporary. Motivations change with experience and are replaced with other goals. Of the motivations that are associated with entry into the industry, fame and recognition appear to be the most sustaining. In addition, although the construction of fame differs between actors and actresses, the desire for admiration and notoriety does not appear to be limited to women.

Initial motivations are often replaced by more substantial goals once performers are established in the industry. For example, although many respondents reported that "being naughty" was a primary motivation for entry, this goal is met in a relatively short time. It does not take many video appearances to establish one's rejection of traditional values. Over time, those interested in challenging mainstream societal values forge a career in which they receive approval for their actions and opportunities for recognition and exposure. Being "naughty" gives way to longer-term career goals. Those motivated by sex quickly learn that they must be able to perform on command in order to remain in the industry. Having sex becomes work, and actors and actresses are motivated to remain in the industry because they are among those who can "do the job." The motivation for sex is replaced by the desire to keep a satisfactory job.

REFERENCES

Allen, Donald M. 1980. "Young Male Prostitutes: A Psychosocial Study." *Archives of Sexual Behavior* 9(5):399–426.

Levy, Emanuel. 1989. "The Democratic Elite: America's Movie Stars." *Qualitative Sociology* 12(1):29–54.

Ronai, Carol Rambo, and Carolyn Ellis. 1989. "Turn-ons for Money: Interactional Strategies of the Table Dancer." *Journal of Contemporary Ethnography* 18:271–298.

CHAPTER 10

ACCULTURATION TO GROUP NORMS

The Code of the Streets

ELIJAH ANDERSON

Learning deviant ways is no different from learning conventional ways. People learn what to think, feel, say, and do in the course of their experience in groups. Whether in conformist or deviant groups, people acquire skills, self-image, norms, and beliefs. Because deviant ways usually violate legal, moral, or social norms, people generally break these rules in private. This is captured in the Eleventh Commandment of deviant culture, which says: "Don't get caught." Concealment and deception are the stock and trade of many social deviants. In addition, they often have no audience before whom they can parade their achievements and accept their adulation.

By way of contrast, Elijah Anderson shows that black inner-city youth learn to engage in deviant performances in public. Youth everywhere always seek to be somebody in the eyes of their peers. Because their environment affords few chances to achieve the usual symbols of status, some black inner-city youth have made their goal the pursuit of respect. Those who inspire fear through the threat of violence by their reputation, dress, appearance, and talk command the respect of their peers. Thus, people compete in the street for the scarce commodity of respect, and because sometimes the appearance of toughness turns out to be an illusion, the reputation for manhood can be lost. Yet the competition continues as people are always testing each other. The audience of their peers decides whether these young people gain or lose respect. Whether respect is gained or lost depends on how well contestants have learned and conformed to the code of the streets.

Of all the problems besetting the poor inner-city black community, none is more pressing than that of interpersonal violence and aggression. It wreaks havoc daily with the lives of community residents and increasingly spills over into downtown and residential middle-class areas. Muggings, burglaries, carjackings, and drug-related shootings, all of

Reprinted from "The Code of the Streets," *Atlantic Monthly* (May 1994), pp. 81–94, by permission of Elijah Anderson. Copyright © 1994 by Elijah Anderson.

which may leave their victims or innocent bystanders dead, are now common enough to concern all urban and many suburban residents. The inclination to violence springs from the circumstances of life among the ghetto poor—the lack of jobs that pay a living wage, the stigma of race, the fallout from rampant drug use and drug trafficking, and the resulting alienation and lack of hope for the future.

Simply living in such an environment places young people at special risk of falling victim to aggressive behavior. Although there are often forces in the community which can counteract the negative influences, by far the most powerful being a strong, loving, "decent" (as inner-city residents put it) family committed to middle-class values, the despair is pervasive enough to have spawned an oppositional culture, that of "the streets," whose norms are often consciously opposed to those of mainstream society. These two orientations—decent and street—socially organize the community, and their coexistence has important consequences for residents, particularly children growing up in the inner city. Above all, this environment means that even youngsters whose home lives reflect mainstream values—and the majority of homes in the community do—must be able to handle themselves in a street-oriented environment.

This is because the street culture has evolved what may be called a code of the streets, which amounts to a set of informal rules governing interpersonal public behavior, including violence. The rules prescribe both a proper comportment and a proper way to respond if challenged. They regulate the use of violence and so allow those who are inclined to aggression to precipitate violent encounters in an approved way. The rules have been established and are enforced mainly by the street-oriented, but on the streets the distinction between street and decent is often irrelevant; everybody knows that if the rules are violated, there are penalties. Knowledge of the code is thus largely defensive; it is literally necessary for operating in public. Therefore, even though families with a decency orientation are usually opposed to the values of the code, they often reluctantly encourage their children's familiarity with it to enable them to negotiate the inner-city environment.

At the heart of the code is the issue of respect—loosely defined as being treated "right," or granted the deference one deserves. However, in the troublesome public environment of the inner city, as people increasingly feel buffeted by forces beyond their control, what one deserves in the way of respect becomes more and more problematic and uncertain. This in turn further opens

the issue of respect to sometimes intense interpersonal negotiation. In the street culture, especially among young people, respect is viewed as almost an external entity that is hard-won but easily lost, and so must constantly be guarded. The rules of the code in fact provide a framework for negotiating respect. The person whose very appearance—including his clothing, demeanor, and way of moving—deters transgressions feels that he possesses, and may be considered by others to possess, a measure of respect. With the right amount of respect, for instance, he can avoid "being bothered" in public. If he is bothered, not only may he be in physical danger but he has been disgraced or "dissed" (disrespected). Many of the forms that dissing can take might seem petty to middle-class people (maintaining eye contact for too long, for example), but to those invested in the street code, these actions become serious indications of the other person's intentions. Consequently, such people become very sensitive to advances and slights, which could well serve as warnings of imminent physical confrontation.

This hard reality can be traced to the profound sense of alienation from mainstream society and its institutions felt by many poor inner-city black people, particularly the young. The code of the streets is actually a cultural adaptation to a profound lack of faith in the police and the judicial system. The police are most often seen as representing the dominant white society and not caring to protect inner-city residents. When called, they may not respond, which is one reason many residents feel they must be prepared to take extraordinary measures to defend themselves and their loved ones against those who are inclined to aggression. Lack of police accountability has in fact been incorporated into the status system: the person who is believed capable of "taking care of himself" is accorded a certain deference, which translates into a sense of physical and psychological control. Thus the street code emerges where the influence of the police ends and personal responsibility for one's safety is felt to begin. Exacerbated by the proliferation of drugs and easy access to guns, this volatile situation results in the ability of the street-oriented minority (or those who effectively "go for bad") to dominate the public spaces.

DECENT AND STREET FAMILIES

Although almost everyone in poor inner-city neighborhoods is struggling financially and therefore feels a certain distance from the rest of America, the decent and the street family in a real sense represent two poles of value orientation, two contrasting conceptual categories. The labels "decent" and "street," which the residents themselves use, amount to evaluative judgments that confer status on local residents. The labeling is often the result of a social contest among individuals and families of the neighborhood. Individuals of the two orientations often coexist in the same extended family. Decent residents judge themselves to be so while judging others to be of the street, and street individuals often present themselves as decent, drawing distinctions between themselves and other people. In addition, there is quite a bit of circumstantial behavior—that is, one person may at different times exhibit both decent and street orientations, depending on the circumstances. Although these designations result from so much social jockeying, there do exist concrete features that define each conceptual category.

Generally, so-called decent families tend to accept mainstream values more fully and attempt to instill them in their children. Whether married couples with children or single-parent (usually female) households, they are generally "working poor" and so tend to be better off financially than their street-oriented neighbors. They value hard work and self-reliance and are willing to sacrifice for their children. Because they have a certain amount of faith in mainstream society, they harbor hopes for a better future for their children, if not for themselves. Many of them go to church and take a strong interest in their children's schooling. Rather than dwelling on the real hardships and inequities facing them, many such decent people, particularly the increasing number of grandmothers raising grandchildren, see their difficult situation as a test from God and derive great support from their faith and from the church community.

Extremely aware of the problematic and often dangerous environment in which they reside, decent parents tend to be strict in their child-rearing practices, encouraging children to respect authority and walk a straight moral line. They have an almost obsessive concern about trouble of any kind and remind their children to be on the lookout for people and situations that might lead to it. At the same time, they are themselves polite and considerate of others, and teach their children to be the same way. At home, at work, and in church, they strive hard to maintain a positive mental attitude and a spirit of cooperation.

So-called street parents, in contrast, often show a lack of consideration for other people and have a rather superficial sense of family and community. Though they may love their children, many of them are unable to cope with the physical and emotional demands of parenthood, and find it difficult to reconcile their needs with those of their children. These families, who are more fully invested in the code of the streets than the decent people are, may aggressively socialize their children into it in a normative way. They believe in the code and judge themselves and others according to its values.

In fact the overwhelming majority of families in the inner-city community try to approximate the decent-family model, but there are many others who clearly represent the worst fears of the decent family. Not only are their financial resources extremely limited, but what little they have may easily be misused. The lives of the street-oriented are often marked by disorganization. In the most desperate circumstances people frequently have a limited understanding of priorities and consequences, and so frustrations mount over bills, food, and, at times, drink, cigarettes, and drugs. Some tend toward self-destructive behavior; many street-oriented women are crack-addicted ("on the pipe"), alcoholic, or involved in complicated relationships with men who abuse them. In addition, the seeming intractability of their situation, caused in large part by the lack of well-paying jobs and the persistence of racial discrimination, has engendered deep-seated bitterness and anger in many of the most desperate and poorest blacks, especially young people. The need both to exercise a measure of control and to lash out at somebody is often reflected in the adults' relations with their children. At the least, the frustrations of persistent poverty shorten the fuse in such people—contributing to a lack of patience with anyone, child or adult, who irritates them.

In these circumstances a woman—or a man, although men are less consistently present in children's lives—can be quite aggressive with children, yelling at and striking them for the least little infraction of the rules she has set down. Often little if any serious explanation follows the verbal and physical punishment. This response teaches children a particular lesson. They learn that to solve any kind of interpersonal problem one must quickly resort to hitting or other violent behavior. Actual peace and quiet, and also the appearance of calm, respectful children conveyed to her neighbors and friends, are often what the young mother most desires, but at times she will be very aggressive in trying to get them. Thus she may be quick to beat her children, especially if they defy her law, not because she hates them but because this is the way she knows to control them. In fact, many street-oriented women love their children dearly. Many mothers in the community subscribe to the notion that there is a "devil in the boy" that must be beaten out of him or that socially "fast girls need to be whupped." Thus much of what borders on child abuse in the view of social authorities is acceptable parental punishment in the view of these mothers.

Many street-oriented women are sporadic mothers whose children learn to fend for themselves when necessary, foraging for food and money any way they can get it. The children are sometimes employed by drug dealers or become addicted themselves. These children of the street, growing up with little supervision, are said to "come up hard." They often learn to fight at an early age, sometimes using short-tempered adults

around them as role models. The street-oriented home may be fraught with anger, verbal disputes, physical aggression, and even mayhem. The children observe these goings-on, learning the lesson that might makes right. They quickly learn to hit those who cross them, and the dog-eat-dog mentality prevails. In order to survive, to protect oneself, it is necessary to marshal inner resources and be ready to deal with adversity in a hands-on way. In these circumstances physical prowess takes on great significance.

In some of the most desperate cases, a street-oriented mother may simply leave her young children alone and unattended while she goes out. The most irresponsible women can be found at local bars and crack houses, getting high and socializing with other adults. Sometimes a troubled woman will leave very young children alone for days at a time. Reports of crack addicts abandoning their children have become common in drug-infested inner-city communities. Neighbors or relatives discover the abandoned children, often hungry and distraught over the absence of their mother. After repeated absences, a friend or relative, particularly a grandmother, will often step in to care for the young children, sometimes petitioning the authorities to send her, as guardian of the children, the mother's welfare check, if the mother gets one. By this time, however, the children may well have learned the first lesson of the streets: survival itself, let alone respect, cannot be taken for granted; you have to fight for your place in the world.

CAMPAIGNING FOR RESPECT

These realities of inner-city life are largely absorbed on the streets. At an early age, often even before they start school, children from street-oriented homes gravitate to the streets, where they "hang"—socialize with their peers. Children from these generally permissive homes have a great deal of latitude and are allowed to "rip and run" up and down the street. They often come home from school, put their books down, and go right back out the door. On school nights eight- and nine-year-olds remain out until nine or ten o'clock (and teenagers typically come in whenever they want to). On the streets they play in groups that often become the source of their primary social bonds. Children from decent homes tend to be more carefully supervised and are thus likely to have curfews and to be taught how to stay out of trouble.

When decent and street kids come together, a kind of social shuffle occurs in which children have a chance to go either way. Tension builds as a child comes to realize that he must choose an orientation. The kind of home he comes from influences but does not determine the way he will ultimately turn out—although it is unlikely that a child from a thoroughly street-oriented family will easily absorb decent values on the streets. Youths who emerge from street-oriented families but develop a decency orientation almost always learn those values in another setting—in school, in a youth group, in church. Often it is the result of their involvement with a caring "old head" (adult role model).

In the street, through their play, children pour their individual life experiences into a common knowledge pool, affirming, confirming, and elaborating on what they have observed in the home and matching their skills against those of others. And they learn to fight. Even small children test one another, pushing and shoving, and are ready to hit other children over circumstances not to their liking. In turn, they are readily hit by other children, and the child who is toughest prevails. Thus the violent resolution of disputes, the hitting and cursing, gains social reinforcement. The child in effect is initiated into a system that is really a way of campaigning for respect.

In addition, younger children witness the disputes of older children, which are often resolved through cursing and abusive talk, if not aggression or outright violence. They see that one child succumbs to the greater physical and mental abilities of the other. They are also alert and attentive witnesses to the verbal and physical fights of adults, after which they compare notes and share their interpretations of the event. In almost every case the victor is the person who physically won the altercation, and this person often enjoys the esteem and respect of onlookers. These experiences reinforce the lessons the children have learned at home: might makes right, and toughness is a virtue, while humility is not. In effect they learn the social meaning of fighting. When it is left virtually unchallenged, this understanding becomes an ever more important part of the child's working conception of the world. Over time the code of the streets becomes refined.

Those street-oriented adults with whom children come in contact—including mothers, fathers, brothers, sisters, boyfriends, cousins, neighbors, and friends—help them along in forming this understanding by verbalizing the messages they are getting through experience: "Watch your back." "Protect yourself." "Don't punk out." "If somebody messes with you, you got to pay them back." "If someone disses you, you got to straighten them out." Many parents actually impose sanctions if a child is not sufficiently aggressive. For example, if a child loses a fight and comes home upset, the parent might respond, "Don't you come in here crying that somebody beat you up; you better get back out there and whup his ass. I didn't raise no punks! Get back out there and whup his ass. If you don't whup his ass, I'll whup your ass when you come home." Thus the child obtains reinforcement for being tough and showing nerve.

While fighting, some children cry as though they are doing something they are ambivalent about. The fight may be against their wishes, yet they may feel constrained to fight or face the consequences—not just from peers but also from caretakers or parents, who may administer another beating if they back down. Some adults recall receiving such lessons from their own parents and justify repeating them to their children as a way to toughen them up. Looking capable of taking care of oneself as a form of self-defense is a dominant theme among both street-oriented and decent adults who worry about the safety of their children. There is thus at times a convergence in their child-rearing practices, although the rationales behind them may differ.

SELF-IMAGE BASED ON "JUICE"

By the time they are teenagers, most youths have either internalized the code of the streets or at least learned the need to comport themselves in accordance with its rules, which chiefly have to do with interpersonal communication. The code revolves around the presentation of self. Its basic requirement is the display of a certain predisposition to violence. Accordingly, one's bearing must send the unmistakable if sometimes subtle message to "the next person" in public that one is capable of violence and mayhem when the situation requires it, that one can take care of oneself. The nature of this communication is largely determined by the demands of the circumstances but can include facial expressions, gait, and verbal expressions—all of which are geared mainly to deterring aggression. Physical appearance, including clothes, jewelry, and grooming, also plays an important part in how a person is viewed; to be respected, it is important to have the right look.

Even so, there are no guarantees against challenges, because there are always people around looking for a fight to increase their share of respect—or "juice," as it is sometimes called on the street. Moreover, if a person is assaulted, it is important, not only in the eyes of his opponent but also in the eyes of his "running buddies," for him to avenge himself. Otherwise he risks being "tried" (challenged) or "moved on" by any number of others. To maintain his honor he must show he is not someone to be "messed with" or "dissed." In general, the person must "keep himself straight" by managing his position of respect among others; this involves in part his self-image, which is shaped by what he thinks others are thinking of him in relation to his peers.

Objects play an important and complicated role in establishing self-image. Jackets, sneakers, gold jewelry, reflect not just a person's taste, which tends to be tightly regulated among adolescents of all social classes, but also a willingness to possess things that may require defending. A boy wearing a fashionable, expensive jacket, for example, is vulnerable to attack by another who covets the jacket and either cannot afford to buy one or wants the added satisfaction of depriving someone else of his. However, if the boy forgoes the desirable jacket and wears one that isn't "hip," he runs the risk of being teased and possibly even assaulted as an unworthy person. To be allowed to hang with certain prestigious crowds, a boy must wear a different set of expensive clothes—sneakers and athletic suit—every day. Not to be able to do so might make him appear socially deficient. The youth comes to covet such items—especially when he sees easy prey wearing them.

In acquiring valued things, therefore, a person shores up his identity—but since it is an identity based on having things, it is highly precarious. This very precariousness gives a heightened sense of urgency to staying even with peers, with whom the person is actually competing. Young men and women who are able to command respect through their presentation of self—by allowing their possessions and their body language to speak for them—may not have to campaign for regard but may, rather, gain it by the force of their manner. Those who are unable to command respect in this way must actively campaign for it—and are thus particularly alive to slights.

One way of campaigning for status is by taking the possessions of others. In this context, seemingly ordinary objects can become trophies imbued with symbolic value that far exceeds their monetary worth. Possession of the trophy can symbolize the ability to violate somebody—to "get in his face," to take something of value from him, to "dis" him, and thus to enhance one's own worth by stealing someone else's. The trophy does not have to be something material. It can be another person's sense of honor, snatched away with a derogatory remark. It can be the outcome of a fight. It can be the imposition of a certain standard, such as a girl's getting herself recognized as the most beautiful. Material things, however, fit easily into the pattern. Sneakers, a pistol, even somebody else's girlfriend, can become a trophy. When a person can take something from another and then flaunt it, he gains a certain regard by being the owner, or the controller, of that thing. But this display of ownership can then provoke other people to challenge him. This game of who controls what is thus constantly being played out on inner-city streets, and the trophy—extrinsic or intrinsic, tangible or intangible—identifies the current winner.

An important aspect of this often violent give-and-take is its zero-sum quality. That is, the extent to which one person can raise himself up depends on his ability to put another person down. This underscores the alienation that permeates the inner-city ghetto community. There is a generalized sense that very little respect is to be had, and therefore everyone competes to get what affirmation he can of the little that is available. The craving for respect that results gives people thin skins. Shows of deference by others can be highly soothing, contributing to a sense of security, comfort, self-confidence, and self-respect. Transgressions by others which go unanswered diminish these feelings and are believed to encourage further transgressions. Hence one must be ever vigilant against the transgressions of others or even *appearing* as if transgressions will be tolerated. Among young people, whose sense of self-esteem is particularly vulnerable, there is an especially heightened concern with being disrespected. Many inner-city young men in particular crave respect to such a degree that they will risk their lives to attain and maintain it.

The issue of respect is thus closely tied to whether a person has an inclination to be violent, even as a victim. In the wider society people may not feel required to retaliate physically after an attack, even though they are aware that they have been degraded or taken advantage of. They may feel a great need to defend themselves *during* an attack, or to behave in such a way as to deter aggression (middle-class people certainly can and do become victims of street-oriented youths), but they are much more likely than street-oriented people to feel that they can walk away from a possible altercation with their self-esteem intact. Some people may even have the strength of character to flee, without any thought that their self-respect or esteem will be diminished.

In impoverished inner-city black communities, however, particularly among young males and perhaps increasingly among females, such flight would be extremely difficult. To run away would likely leave one's self-esteem in tatters. Hence people often feel constrained not only to stand up and at least attempt to resist during an assault but also to "pay back"—to seek revenge—after a successful assault on their person. This may include going to get a weapon or even getting relatives involved. Their very identity and self-respect, their honor, is often intricately tied up with the way they perform on the streets during and after such encounters. This outlook reflects the circumscribed opportunities of the inner-city poor. Generally people outside the ghetto have other ways of gaining status and regard, and thus do not feel so dependent on such physical displays.

BY TRIAL OF MANHOOD

On the street, among males these concerns about things and identity have come to be expressed in the concept of "manhood." Manhood in the inner city means taking the prerogatives of men with respect to strangers, other men, and women—being distinguished as a man. It implies physicality and a certain ruthlessness. Regard and respect are associated with this concept in large part because of its practical application: if others have little or no regard for a person's manhood, his very life and those of his loved ones could be in jeopardy. But there is a chicken-and-egg aspect to this situation: one's physical safety is more likely to be jeopardized in public *because* manhood is associated with respect. In other words, an existential link has been created between the idea of manhood and one's self-esteem, so that it has become hard to say which is primary. For many inner-city youths, manhood and respect are flip sides of the same coin; physical and psychological well-being are inseparable, and both require a sense of control, of being in charge.

The operating assumption is that a man, especially a real man, knows what other men know—the code of the streets. And if one is not a real man, one is somehow diminished as a person, and there are certain valued things one simply does not deserve. There is thus believed to be a certain justice to the code, since it is considered that everyone has the opportunity to know it. Implicit in this is that everybody is held responsible for being familiar with the code. If the victim of a mugging, for example, does not know the code and so responds "wrong," the perpetrator may feel justified even in killing him and may feel no remorse. He may think, "Too bad, but it's his fault. He should have known better."

So when a person ventures outside, he must adopt the code—a kind of shield, really—to prevent others from "messing with" him. In these circumstances it is easy for people to think they arc being tried or tested by others even when this is not the case. For it is sensed that something extremely valuable is at stake in every interaction, and people are encouraged to rise to the occasion, particularly with strangers. For people who are unfamiliar with the code—generally people who live outside the inner city—the concern with respect in the most ordinary interactions can be frightening and incomprehensible. But for those who are invested in the code, the clear object of their demeanor is to discourage strangers from even thinking about testing their manhood. And the sense of power that attends the ability to deter others can be alluring even to those who know the code without being heavily invested in it—the decent inner-city youths. Thus a boy who has been leading a basically decent life can, in trying circumstances, suddenly resort to deadly force.

Central to the issue of manhood is the widespread belief that one of the most effective ways of gaining respect is to manifest "nerve." Nerve is shown when one takes another person's possessions (the more valuable the better), "messes with" someone's woman, throws the first punch, "gets in someone's face," or pulls a trigger. Its proper display helps on the spot to check others who would violate one's person and also helps to build a reputation that works to prevent future challenges. But since such a show of nerve is a forceful expression of disrespect toward the person on the receiving end, the victim may be greatly offended and seek to retaliate with equal or greater force. A display of nerve, therefore, can easily provoke a life-threatening response, and the background knowledge of that possibility has often been incorporated into the concept of nerve.

True nerve exposes a lack of fear of dying. Many feel that it is acceptable to risk dying over the principle of respect. In fact, among the hardcore street-oriented, the clear risk of violent death may be preferable to being "dissed" by another. The youths who have internalized this attitude and convincingly display it in their public bearing are among the most threatening people of all, for it is commonly assumed that they fear no man. As the people of the community say, "They are the baddest dudes on the street." They often lead an existential life that may acquire meaning only when they are faced with the possibility of imminent death. Not to be afraid to die is by implication to have few compunctions about taking another's life. Not to be afraid to die is the quid pro quo of being able to take somebody else's life—for the right reasons, if the situation demands it. When others believe this is one's position, it gives one a real sense of power on the streets. Such credibility is what many inner-city youths strive to achieve, whether they are decent or street-oriented, both because of its practical defensive value and because of the positive way it makes them feel about themselves. The difference between the decent and the street-oriented youth is often that the decent youth makes a conscious decision to appear tough and manly; in another setting—with teachers, say, or at his part-time job—he can be polite and deferential. The street-oriented youth, on the other hand, has made the concept of manhood a part of his very identity; he has difficulty manipulating it—it often controls him.

GIRLS AND BOYS

Increasingly, teenage girls are mimicking the boys and trying to have their own version of "manhood." Their goal is the same—to get respect, to be recognized as capable of setting or maintaining a certain standard. They try to achieve this end in the ways that have been established by the boys, including posturing, abusive language, and the use of violence to resolve disputes, but the issues for the girls are different. Although conflicts over turf and status exist among the girls, the majority of disputes seem rooted in assessments of beauty (which girl in a group is "the cutest"), competition over boyfriends, and attempts to regulate other people's knowledge of and opinions about a girl's behavior or that of someone close to her, especially her mother.

A major cause of conflicts among girls is "he say, she say." This practice begins in the early school years and continues through high school. It occurs when "people," particularly girls, talk about others, thus putting their "business in the streets." Usually one girl will say something negative about another in the group, most often behind the person's back. The remark will then get back to the person talked about. She may retaliate or her friends may feel required to "take up for" her. In essence this is a form of group gossiping in which individuals are negatively assessed and evaluated. As with much gossip, the things said may or may not be true, but the point is that such imputations can cast aspersions on a person's good name. The accused is required to defend herself against the slander, which can result in arguments and fights, often over little of real substance. Here again is the problem of low self-esteem, which encourages youngsters to be highly sensitive to slights and to be vulnerable to feeling easily "dissed." To avenge the dissing, a fight is usually necessary.

Because boys are believed to control violence, girls tend to defer to them in situations of conflict. Often if a girl is attacked or feels slighted, she will get a brother, uncle, or cousin to do her fighting for her. Increasingly, however, girls are doing their own fighting and are even asking their male relatives to teach them how to fight. Some girls form groups that attack other girls or take things from them. A hard-core segment of inner-city girls inclined toward violence seems to be developing. As one thirteen-year-old girl in a detention center for youths who have committed violent acts told me, "To get people to leave you alone, you gotta fight. Talking don't always get you out of stuff." One major difference between girls and boys: girls rarely use guns. Their fights are therefore not life-or-death struggles. Girls are not often willing to put their lives on the line for "manhood." The ultimate form of respect on the male-dominated inner-city street is thus reserved for men.

"GOING FOR BAD"

In the most fearsome youths such a cavalier attitude toward death grows out of a very limited view of life. Many are uncertain about how long they are going to live and believe they could die violently at any time. They accept this fate; they live on the edge. Their manner conveys the message that nothing intimidates them; whatever turn the encounter takes, they maintain their attack—rather like a pit bull, whose spirit many such boys admire. The demonstration of such tenacity "shows heart" and earns their respect.

This fearlessness has implications for law enforcement. Many street-oriented boys are much more concerned about the threat of "justice" at the hands of a peer than at the hands of the police. Moreover, many feel not only that they have little to lose by going to prison but that they have something to gain. The toughening-up one experiences in prison can actually enhance one's reputation on the streets. Hence the system loses influence over the hard core who are without jobs, with little perceptible stake in the system. If mainstream society has done nothing *for* them, they counter by making sure it can do nothing *to* them.

At the same time, however, a competing view maintains that true nerve consists in backing down, walking away from a fight, and going on with one's business. One fights only in self-defense. This view emerges from the decent philosophy that life is precious, and it is an important part of the socialization process common in decent homes. It discourages violence as the primary means of resolving disputes and encourages youngsters to accept nonviolence and talk as confrontational strategies. But "if the deal goes down," self-defense is greatly encouraged. When there is enough positive support for this orientation, either in the home or among one's peers, then nonviolence has a chance to prevail. But it prevails at the cost of relinquishing a claim to being bad and tough, and therefore sets a young person up as at the very least alienated from street-oriented peers and quite possibly a target of derision or even violence.

Although the nonviolent orientation rarely overcomes the impulse to strike back in an encounter, it does introduce a certain confusion and so can prompt a measure of soul-searching, or even profound ambivalence. Did the person back down with his respect intact or did he back down only to be judged a "punk"—a person lacking manhood? Should he or she have acted? Should he or she have hit the other person in the mouth? These questions beset many young men and women during public confrontations. What is the "right" thing to do? In the quest for honor, respect, and local status—which few young people are uninterested in—common sense most often prevails, which leads many to opt for the tough approach, enacting their own particular versions of the display of nerve. The presentation of oneself as rough and tough is very often quite acceptable until one is tested. And then that presentation may help the person pass the test, because it will cause fewer questions to be asked about what he did and why. It is hard for a person to explain why he lost the fight or why he backed down. Hence many will strive to appear to "go for bad," while hoping they will never be tested. But when they are tested, the outcome of the situation may quickly be out of their hands, as they become wrapped up in the circumstances of the moment.

AN OPPOSITIONAL CULTURE

The attitudes of the wider society are deeply implicated in the code of the streets. Most people in inner-city communities are not totally invested in the code, but the significant minority of hard-core street youths who are have to maintain the code in order to establish reputations, because they have—or

feel they have—few other ways to assert themselves. For these young people the standards of the street code are the only game in town. The extent to which some children—particularly those who through upbringing have become most alienated and those lacking in strong and conventional social support—experience, feel, and internalize racist rejection and contempt from mainstream society may strongly encourage them to express contempt for the more conventional society in turn. In dealing with this contempt and rejection, some youngsters will consciously invest themselves and their considerable mental resources in what amounts to an oppositional culture to preserve themselves and their self-respect. Once they do, any respect they might be able to garner in the wider system pales in comparison with the respect available in the local system; thus they often lose interest in even attempting to negotiate the mainstream system.

At the same time, many less alienated young blacks have assumed a street-oriented demeanor as a way of expressing their blackness while really embracing a much more moderate way of life; they, too, want a nonviolent setting in which to live and raise a family. These decent people are trying hard to be part of the mainstream culture, but the racism, real and perceived, that they encounter helps to legitimate the oppositional culture. And so on occasion they adopt street behavior. In fact, depending on the demands of the situation, many people in the community slip back and forth between decent and street behavior.

A vicious cycle has thus been formed. The hopelessness and alienation many young inner-city black men and women feel, largely as a result of endemic joblessness and persistent racism, fuels the violence they engage in. This violence serves to confirm the negative feelings many whites and some middle-class blacks harbor toward the ghetto poor, further legitimating the oppositional culture and the code of the streets in the eyes of many poor young blacks. Unless this cycle is broken, attitudes on both sides will become increasingly entrenched, and the violence, which claims victims black and white, poor and affluent, will only escalate.

The Nudist Management of Respectability

MARTIN S. WEINBERG

Through the continuous processes of socialization, people learn how they are expected to act in a variety of social situations. As a consequence, people usually perform as others expect them to act. The result, of course, is a body of routine practices that people come to see as natural. The attitude that people take toward the social facts of everyday life makes orderly social interaction possible. Violation of these expectations can constitute the basis upon which notions of unnatural behavior are formulated.

Given all this, what are the conditions under which people cannot merely contemplate but actually carry out a set of actions that run directly counter to their basic assumptions about appropriate behavior? Martin S. Weinberg's study of nudist camp socialization offers some answers to the conditions under which people can, in concert, turn the conventionally unnatural into the natural—and vice versa.

Nudist ideology says nudity is not shameful, that nakedness signifies health, not sexuality. In the nudist camp, nudity becomes taken for granted. A set of behavioral norms that nudists abide by when in the unclothed world sustains the definition of the new situation. These norms enjoin a variety of ways to deal with public nudity. Nudists all act as if being unclothed is what everybody does naturally.

Public nudity is taboo in our society. Yet there is a group who breach this moral rule. They call themselves "social nudists."

A number of questions may be asked about these people. For example, how can they see their behavior as morally appropriate? Have they constructed their own morality? If so, what characterizes this morality and what are its consequences?[1]

This article will attempt to answer these questions through a study of social interaction in nudist camps. The data come from three sources: two summers of participant observation in nudist camps; 101 interviews with nudists in the Chicago area; and 617 mailed questionnaires completed by nudists in the United States and Canada.[2]

THE CONSTRUCTION OF SITUATED MORAL MEANINGS: THE NUDIST MORALITY

The construction of morality in nudist camps is based on the official interpretations that camps provide regarding the moral meanings of public heterosexual nudity. These are (1) that nudity and sexuality are unrelated, (2) that there is nothing shameful about the human body, (3) that nudity promotes a feeling of freedom and natural pleasure, and (4) that nude exposure to the sun promotes physical, mental, and spiritual well-being.

This official perspective is sustained in nudist camps to an extraordinary degree, illustrating the extent to which adult socialization can affect traditional moral meanings. (This is especially true with regard to the first two points of the nudist perspective, which will be our primary concern since these are its "deviant" aspects.) The assumption in the larger society that nudity and sexuality are related, and the resulting emphasis on covering the sexual organs, make the nudist perspective a specifically situated morality. My field work, interview, and questionnaire research show that nudists routinely use a special system of rules to create, sustain, and enforce this situated morality.

STRATEGIES FOR SUSTAINING A SITUATED MORALITY

The first strategy used by the nudist camp to anesthetize any relationship between nudity and sexuality[3] involves a system of organizational precautions regarding who can come into the camp. Most camps, for example, regard single men as a threat to the nudist morality. They suspect that they may indeed see nudity as something sexual. Thus, most camps either exclude uncoupled men or allow only a small quota of them. Camps that do allow single men may charge them . . . more than they charge families. (This is intended to discourage single men, but since the cost is still relatively low compared with other resorts, this measure is not very effective. It seems to do little more than create resentment among the singles, and by giving formal organizational backing to the definition that singles are not especially desirable, it may contribute to the segregation of single and married members in nudist camps.)

Certification by the camp owner is another requirement for admission to camp grounds, and letters of recommendation regarding the applicant's character are sometimes required. These regulations help preclude people whom members regard as a threat to the nudist morality.

[The camp owner] invited us over to see if we were desirable people. Then after we did this, he invited us to camp on probation; then they voted us into camp. [Q: Could you tell me what you mean by desirable people?] Well, not people who are inclined to drink, or people who go there for a peep show. Then they don't want you there. They

feel you out in conversation. They want people for mental and physical health reasons.

Whom to admit [is the biggest problem of the camp]. [Q][4] Because the world is so full of people whose attitudes on nudity are hopelessly warped. [Q: Has this always been the biggest problem in camp?] Yes. Every time anybody comes, a decision has to be made. [Q] . . . The lady sitting at the gate decides about admittance. The director decides on membership.

A limit is sometimes set on the number of trial visits a non-member may make to camp. In addition, there is usually a limit on how long a person can remain clothed. This is a strategy to mark guests who may not sincerely accept the nudist perspective.

The second strategy for sustaining the nudist morality involves norms of interpersonal behavior. These norms are as follows:

NO STARING

This rule controls overt signs of overinvolvement. As the publisher of one nudist magazine said, "They all look up to the heavens and never look below." Such studied inattention is most exaggerated among women, who usually show no recognition that the male is unclothed. Women also recount that they had expected men to look at their nude bodies, only to find, when they finally did get up the courage to undress, that no one seemed to notice. As one woman states: "I got so mad because my husband wanted me to undress in front of other men that I just pulled my clothes right off thinking everyone would look at me." She was amazed (and appeared somewhat disappointed) when no one did.

The following statements illustrate the constraints that result:

[Q: Have you ever observed or heard about anyone staring at someone's body while at camp?] I've heard stories, particularly about men that stare. Since I heard these stories, I tried not to,

and have even done away with my sunglasses after someone said, half-joking, that I hide behind sunglasses to stare. Toward the end of the summer I stopped wearing sunglasses. And you know what, it was a child who told me this.

[Q: Would you stare . . . ?] Probably not, 'cause you can get in trouble and get thrown out. If I thought I could stare unobserved I might. They might not throw you out, but it wouldn't do you any good. [Q] The girl might tell others and they might not want to talk to me. . . . [Q] They disapprove by not talking to you, ignoring you, etc.

[Someone who stares] wouldn't belong there. [Q] If he does that he is just going to camp to see the opposite sex. [Q] He is just coming to stare. [Q] You go there to swim and relax.

I try very hard to look at them from the jaw up— even more than you would normally.[5]

NO SEX TALK

Sex talk, or telling "dirty jokes," is uncommon in camp. The owner of a large camp in the Midwest stated: "It is usually expected that members of a nudist camp will not talk about sex, politics, or religion." Or as one single male explained: "It is taboo to make sexual remarks here." During my field work, it was rare to hear "sexual" joking such as one hears at most other types of resort. Interview respondents who mentioned that they had talked about sex qualified this by explaining that such talk was restricted to close friends, was of a "scientific nature," or, if a joke, was a "cute sort."

Asked what they would think of someone who breached this rule, respondents indicated that such behavior would cast doubt on the situated morality of the nudist camp:

One would expect to hear less of that at camp than at other places. [Q] Because you expect that the members are screened in their attitude for nudism— and this isn't one who prefers sexual jokes.

I've never heard anyone swear or tell a dirty joke out there.

No. Not at camp. You're not supposed to. You bend over backwards not to.

They probably don't belong there. They're there to see what they can find to observe. [Q] Well, their mind isn't on being a nudist, but to see so and so nude.

NO BODY CONTACT

Although the extent to which this is enforced varies from camp to camp, there is at least some degree of informal enforcement in nearly every camp. Nudists mention that they are particularly careful not to brush against anyone or have any body contact for fear of how it might be interpreted:

I stay clear of the opposite sex. They're so sensitive, they imagine things.

People don't get too close to you. Even when they talk. They sit close to you, but they don't get close enough to touch you.

We have a minimum of contact. There are more restrictions [at a nudist camp]. [Q] Just a feeling I had. I would openly show my affection more readily someplace else.

And when asked to conceptualize a breach of this rule, the following response is typical:

They are in the wrong place. [Q] That's not part of nudism. [Q] I think they are there for some sort of sex thrill. They are certainly not there to enjoy the sun.

Also, in photographs taken for nudist magazines, the subjects usually have only limited body contact. One female nudist explained: "We don't want anyone to think we're immoral." Outsiders' interpretations, then, can also constitute a threat.

NO ALCOHOLIC BEVERAGES IN AMERICAN CAMPS

This rule guards against breakdowns in inhibition, and even respondents who admitted that they had "snuck a beer" before going to bed went on to say that they fully favor the rule.

Yes. We have [drunk at camp]. We keep a can of beer in the refrigerator since we're out of the main area. We're not young people or carousers. . . . I still most generally approve of it as a camp rule and would disapprove of anyone going to extremes. [Q] For commonsense reasons. People who overindulge lose their inhibitions, and there is no denying that the atmosphere of a nudist camp makes one bend over backwards to keep people who are so inclined from going beyond the bounds of propriety.

Anyone who drinks in camp is jeopardizing their membership and they shouldn't. Anyone who drinks in camp could get reckless. [Q] Well, when guys and girls drink they're a lot bolder—they might get fresh with someone else's girl. That's why it isn't permitted, I guess.

[Moderate use of alcohol has now become the rule.]

RULES REGARDING PHOTOGRAPHY

Photography in a nudist camp is controlled by the camp management. Unless the photographer works for a nudist magazine, his or her moral perspective is sometimes suspect. One photographer's remark to a woman that led to his being so typed was, "Do you think you could open your legs a little more?"

Aside from a general restriction on the use of cameras, when cameras are allowed, it is expected that no pictures will be taken without the subject's permission. Members blame the misuse of cameras especially on single men. As one nudist said: "You always see the singles poppin' around out of nowhere snappin' pictures." In general, control is maintained, and any infractions that take place are not blatant or obvious. Overindulgence in picture-taking communicates an overinvolvement in the subjects' nudity and casts doubt on the assumption that nudity and sexuality are unrelated.

Photographers dressed only in cameras and light exposure meters. I don't like them. I think they only go out for pictures. Their motives should be questioned.

Photographers for nudist magazines recognize the signs that strain the situated morality that characterizes nudist camps.

Similarly, a nudist model showed the writer a pin-up magazine to point out how a model could make a nude picture "sexy"—through the use of various stagings, props, and expressions—and in contrast, how the nudist model eliminates these techniques to make her pictures "natural." Although it may be questionable that a nudist model completely eliminates a sexual perspective for the non-nudist, the model discussed how she attempts to do this.

It depends on the way you look. Your eyes and your smile can make you look sexy. The way they're looking at you. Here, she's on a bed. It wouldn't be sexy if she were on a beach with kids running around. They always have some clothes on too. See how she's "looking" sexy? Like an "oh dear!" look. A different look can change the whole picture.

Now here's a decent pose. . . . Outdoors makes it "nature." Here she's giving you "the eye," or is undressing. It's cheesecake. It depends on the expression on her face. Having nature behind it makes it better. Don't smile like "come on honey!" It's that look and the lace thing she has on. . . . Like when you half-close your eyes, like "oh baby," a Marilyn Monroe look. Art is when you don't look like you're hiding it halfway.

The element of trust plays a particularly strong role in socializing women to the nudist perspective. Consider this in the following statements made by another model for nudist magazines. She and her husband had been indoctrinated in the nudist ideology by friends. At the time of the interview, however, the couple had not yet been to camp, although they had posed indoors for nudist magazines.

[Three months ago, before I was married] I never knew a man had any pubic hairs. I was shocked when I was married. . . . I wouldn't think of getting undressed in front of my husband. I wouldn't make love with a light on, or in the daytime.

With regard to being a nudist model, this woman commented:

None of the pictures are sexually seductive. [Q] The pose, the look—you can have a pose that's completely nothing, till you get a look that's not too hard to do. [Q: How do you do that?] I've never tried. By putting on a certain air about a person; a picture that couldn't be submitted to a nudist magazine—using _____ [the nudist photographer's] language. . . . [Q: Will your parents see your pictures in the magazine?] Possibly. I don't really care. . . . My mother might take it all right. But they've been married twenty years and she's never seen my dad undressed.[6]

NO ACCENTUATION OF THE BODY

Accentuating the body is regarded as incongruent with the nudist morality. Thus, a woman who had shaved her pubic area was labeled "disgusting" by other members. There was a similar reaction to women who sat in a blatantly "unladylike" manner.

I'd think she was inviting remarks. [Q] I don't know. It seems strange to think of it. It's strange you ask it. Out there, they're not unconscious about their posture. Most women there are very circumspect even though in the nude.

For a girl, . . . [sitting with your legs open] is just not feminine or ladylike. The hair doesn't always cover it. [Q] Men get away with so many things. But, it would look dirty for a girl, like she was waiting for something. When I'm in a secluded area I've spread my legs to sun, but I kept an eye open and if anyone came I'd close my legs and sit up a little. It's just not ladylike.

You can lay on your back or side, or with your knees under your chin. But not with your legs spread apart. It would look to other people like you're there for other reasons. [Q: What other reasons?] . . . To stare and get an eyeful . . . not to enjoy the sun and people.

[Currently you sometimes hear such remarks being made about people wearing nipple and genital jewelry.]

NO UNNATURAL ATTEMPTS AT COVERING THE BODY

"Unnatural attempts" at covering the body are ridiculed since they call into question the assumption that there is no shame in exposing any area of the body. If such behavior occurs early in one's nudist career, however, members usually have more compassion, assuming that the person just has not yet fully assimilated the new morality.

It is how members interpret the behavior, however, rather than the behavior per se, that determines whether covering up is disapproved.

If they're cold or sunburned, it's understandable. If it's because they don't agree with the philosophy, they don't belong there.

I would feel their motives for becoming nudists were not well founded. That they were not true nudists, not idealistic enough.

A third strategy that is sometimes employed to sustain the nudist reality is the use of communal [unisex] toilets. Not all the camps have [such] toilets, but the large camp where I did most of my field work did have such a facility, which was marked, "Little Girls Room and Little Boys Too." Although the stalls had three-quarter-length doors, this combined facility still helped to provide an element of consistency; as the owner said, "If you are not ashamed of any part of your body or any of its natural functions, men and women do not need separate toilets." Thus, even the physical ecology of the nudist camp was designed to be consistent with the nudist morality. For some, however, communal [unisex] toilets were going too far.

I think they should be separated. For myself it's all right. But there are varied opinions, and for the satisfaction of all, I think they should separate them. There are niceties of life we often like to maintain, and for some people this is embarrassing. . . . [Q] You know, in a bowel movement it always isn't silent.

THE ROUTINIZATION OF NUDITY

In the nudist camp, nudity becomes routinized; its attention-provoking quality recedes, and nudity becomes a taken-for-granted state of affairs. Thus, when asked questions about staring ("While at camp, have you ever stared at anyone's body? Do you think you would stare at anyone's body?") nudists indicate that nudity generally does not invoke their attention.

> Nudists don't care what bodies are like. They're out there for themselves. It's a matter-of-fact thing. After a while you feel like you're sitting with a full suit of clothes on.

> To nudists the body becomes so matter-of-fact, whether clothed or unclothed, when you make it an undue point of interest it becomes an abnormal thing. [Q: What would you think of someone staring?] I would feel bad and let down. [Q] I have it set up on a high standard. I have never seen it happen. . . . [Q] Because it's not done there. It's above that; you don't stare. . . . If I saw it happen, I'd be startled. There's no inclination to do that. Why would they?

> There are two types—male and female. I couldn't see why they were staring. I wouldn't understand it.

In fact, these questions about staring elicit from nudists a frame of possibilities in which what is relevant to staring is ordinarily not nudity itself. Rather, what evokes attention is something unusual, something the observer seldom sees and thus is not routinized to.[7]

> There was a red-haired man. He had red pubic hair. I had never seen this before. . . . He didn't see me. If anyone did, I would turn the other way.

> Well, once I was staring at a pregnant woman. It was the first time I ever saw this. I was curious, her stomach stretched, the shape. . . . I also have stared at extremely obese people, cripples. All this is due to curiosity, just a novel sight. [Q] . . . I was discreet. [Q] I didn't look at them when their eyes were fixed in a direction so they could tell I was.

> [Q: While at camp have you ever stared at someone's body?] Yes. [Q] A little girl. She had a birthmark on her back, at the base of her spine.

> [Q: Do you think you would ever stare at someone's body while at camp?] No. I don't like that. I think it's silly. . . . What people are is not their fault if they are deformed.

> I don't think it would be very nice, very polite. [Q] I can't see anything to stare at, whether it's a scar or anything else. [Q] It just isn't done.

> I've looked, but not stared. I'm careful about that, because you could get in bad about that. [Q] Get thrown out by the owner. I was curious when I once had a perfect view of a girl's sex organs, because her legs were spread when she was sitting on a chair. I sat in the chair across from her in perfect view of her organs. [Q] For about ten or fifteen minutes. [Q] Nobody noticed. [Q] It's not often you get that opportunity.[8]

> [Q: How would you feel if you were alone in a secluded area of camp sunning yourself, and then noticed that other nudists were staring at your body?] I would think I had some mud on me. [Q] . . . I would just ask them why they were staring at me. Probably I was getting sunburn and they wanted to tell me to turn over, or maybe I had a speck of mud on me. [Q] These are the only two reasons I can think of why they were staring.

In the nudist camp, the arousal of attention by nudity is usually regarded as *unnatural*. Thus, staring is unnatural, especially after a period of grace in which to adjust to the new meanings.

> If he did it when he was first there, I'd figure he's normal. If he kept it up I'd stay away from him, or suggest to the owner that he be thrown out. [Q] At first it's a new experience, so he might be staring. [Q] He wouldn't know how to react to it. [Q] The first time seeing nudes of the opposite sex. [Q] I'd think if he kept staring, that he's thinking of something, like grabbing someone, running to the bushes and raping them. [Q] Maybe he's mentally unbalanced.

> He just sat there watching the women. You can forgive it the first time, because of curiosity. But not every weekend. [Q] The owner asked him to leave.

> These women made comments on some men's shapes. They said, "He has a hairy body or ugly bones," or "Boy his wife must like him because he's hung big." That was embarrassing. . . . I

thought they were terrible. [Q] Because I realized they were walking around looking. I can't see that.

ORGANIZATIONS AND THE CONSTITUTION OF NORMALITY

The rules-in-use of an organization *and the reality they sustain* form the basis on which behaviors are interpreted as "unnatural."[9] Overinvolvement in nudity, for example, is interpreted by nudists as unnatural (and not simply immoral). Similarly, erotic stimuli or responses, which breach the nudist morality, are defined as unnatural.

They let one single in. He acted peculiar. . . . He got up and had a big erection. I didn't know what he'd do at night. He might molest a child or anybody. . . . My husband went and told the owner.

I told you about this one on the sundeck with her legs spread. She made no bones about closing up. Maybe it was an error, but I doubt it. It wasn't a normal position. Normally you wouldn't lay like this. It's like standing on your head. She had sufficient time and there were people around.

She sat there with her legs like they were straddling a horse. I don't know how else to describe it. [Q] She was just sitting on the ground. [Q] I think she's a dirty pig. [Q] If you sit that way, everyone don't want to know what she had for breakfast. [Q] It's just the wrong way to sit. You keep your legs together even with clothes on.

[Q: Do you think it is possible for a person to be modest in a nudist camp?] I think so. [Q] If a person acts natural. . . . An immodest person would be an exhibitionist, and you find them in nudism too. . . . Most people's conduct is all right.

When behaviors are constituted as *unnatural,* attempts to understand them are usually suspended, and reciprocity of perspectives is called into question. (The "reciprocity of perspectives" involves the assumption that if one changed places with the other, one would, for all practical purposes, see the world as the other sees it.[10])

[Q: What would you think of a man who had an erection at camp?] Maybe they can't control themselves. [Q] Better watch out for him. [Q] I would tell the camp director to keep an eye on him. And the children would question that. [Q: What would you tell them?] I'd tell them the man is sick or something.

[Q: What would you think of a Peeping Tom—a nonnudist trespasser?] They should be reported and sent out. [Q] I think they shouldn't be there. They're sick. [Q] Mentally. [Q] Because anyone who wants to look at someone else's body, well, is a Peeping Tom, is sick in the first place. He looks at you differently than a normal person would. [Q] With ideas of sex. [A trespasser] . . . is sick. He probably uses this as a source of sexual stimulation.

Such occurrences call into question the taken-for-granted character of nudity in the nudist camp and the situated morality that is officially set forth.

INHIBITING BREAKDOWNS IN THE NUDIST MORALITY

Organized nudism promulgates a nonsexual perspective toward nudity, and breakdowns in that perspective are inhibited by (1) controlling erotic actions and (2) controlling erotic reactions. Nudity is partitioned off from other forms of "immodesty" (e.g., verbal immodesty, erotic overtures). In this way, a person can learn more easily to attribute a new meaning to nudity.[11] When behaviors occur that reflect other forms of "immodesty," however, nudists often fear a voiding of the nonsexual meaning that they impose on nudity.

This woman with a sexy walk would shake her hips and try to arouse the men. . . . [Q] These men went to the camp director to complain that the woman had purposely tried to arouse them. The camp director told this woman to leave.

Nudists are sensitive to the possibility of a breakdown in the nudist morality. Thus, they have a low threshold for interpreting acts as "sexual."

Playing badminton, this teenager was hitting the birdie up and down and she said, "What do you think of that?" I said, "Kind of sexy." _____ [the president of the camp] said I shouldn't talk like that, but I was only kidding.

Note the following description of "mauling":

I don't like to see a man and a girl mauling each other in the nude before others. . . . [Q: Did you ever see this at camp?] I saw it once. . . . [Q: What do you mean by mauling?] Just, well, I never saw him put his hands on her breasts, but he was running his hands along her arms.

This sensitivity to "sexual" signs also sensitizes nudists to the possibility that certain of their own acts, although not intended as "sexual," might nonetheless be interpreted that way.

Sometimes you're resting and you spread your legs unknowingly. [Q] My husband just told me not to sit that way. [Q] I put my legs together.

Since "immodesty" is defined as an unnatural manner of behavior, such behaviors are easily interpreted as being motivated by "dishonorable" intent. When the individual is thought to be in physical control of the "immodest" behavior and to know the behavior's meaning within the nudist scheme of interpretation, sexual intentions are assigned. Referring to a quotation that was presented earlier, one man said that a woman who was lying with her legs spread may have been doing so unintentionally, "but I doubt it. It wasn't a normal position. Normally you wouldn't lay like this. It's like standing on your head."

Erotic reactions, as well as erotic actions, are controlled in camp. Thus, even when erotic stimuli come into play, erotic responses may be inhibited.

When lying on the grass already hiding my penis, I got erotic thoughts. And then one realizes it can't happen here. With fear there isn't much erection.

Yes, once I started to have an erection. Once. [Q] A friend told me how he was invited by some

young lady to go to bed. [Q] I started to picture the situation and I felt the erection coming on; so I immediately jumped in the pool. It went away.

I was once in the woods alone and ran into a woman. I felt myself getting excited. A secluded spot in the bushes which was an ideal place for procreation. [Q] Nothing happened, though.

When breaches of the nudist morality do occur, other nudists' sense of modesty may inhibit sanctioning. The immediate breach may go unsanctioned. The observers may feign inattention or withdraw from the scene. The occurrence is usually communicated, however, via the grapevine, and it may reach the camp director.

We were shooting a series of pictures and my wife was getting out of her clothes. _____ [the photographer] had an erection but went ahead like nothing was happening. [Q] It was over kind of fast. . . . [Q] Nothing. We tried to avoid the issue. . . . Later we went to see _____ [the camp director] and _____ [the photographer] denied it.

[If a man had an erection] people would probably pretend they didn't see it.

[Q: What do you think of someone this happens to?] They should try to get rid of it fast. It don't look nice. Nudists are prudists. They are more prudish. Because they take their clothes off they are more careful. [Q] They become more prudish than people with clothes. They won't let anything out of the way happen.

As indicated in the remark, "nudists are prudists," nudists may at times become aware of the fragility of their situated moral meanings.

At _____ [camp], this family had a small boy no more than ten years old who had an erection. Mrs. _____ [the owner's wife] saw him and told his parents that they should keep him in check, and tell him what had happened to him and to watch himself. This was silly, for such a little kid who didn't know what happened.

DEVIANCE AND MULTIPLE SCHEMAS

There are basic social processes that underlie responses to deviance. Collectivities control thresholds of response to various behaviors, determining the relevance, meaning, and importance of the behavior. In the nudist camp, as pointed out previously, erotic overtures and erotic responses are regarded as unnatural, and reciprocity of perspectives is called into question by such behaviors.

> We thought this single was all right, until others clued us in that he had brought girls up to camp. [Then we recalled that] . . . he was kind of weird. The way he'd look at you. He had glassy eyes, like he could see through you.[12]

Such a response to deviance in the nudist camp is a result of effective socialization to the new system of moral meanings. The deviant's behavior, on the other hand, can be construed as reflecting an ineffective socialization to the new system of meanings.

> I think it's impossible [to have an erection in a nudist camp]. [Q] In a nudist camp you must have some physical contact and a desire to have one.
>
> He isn't thinking like a nudist. [Q] The body is wholesome, not . . . a sex object. He'd have to do that—think of sex.
>
> Sex isn't supposed to be in your mind, as far as the body. He doesn't belong there. [Q] If you go in thinking about sex, naturally it's going to happen. . . . You're not supposed to think about going to bed with anyone, not even your wife.

As these quotes illustrate, the unnaturalness or deviance of a behavior is ordinarily determined by relating it to an institutionalized scheme of interpretation. Occurrences that are "not understandable" in the [schema] of one collectivity may, however, be quite understandable in the [schema] of another collectivity.[13] Thus, what are "deviant" occurrences in nudist camps probably would be regarded by members of the clothed society as natural and understandable rather than unnatural and difficult to understand.

Finally, a group of people may subscribe to different and conflicting interpretive schemes. Thus, the low threshold of nudists to anything "sexual" is a function of their marginality; the fact that they have not completely suspended the moral meanings of the clothed society is what leads them to constitute many events as "sexual" in purpose.

NOTES

1. In my previous papers, I have dealt with other questions that are commonly asked about nudists. How persons become nudists is discussed in my "Becoming a Nudist," *Psychiatry*, XXIX (February, 1966), 15–24. A report on the nudist way of life and social structure can be found in my article in *Human Organization*, XXVI (Fall, 1967), 91–99.
2. Approximately one hundred camps were represented in the interviews and questionnaires. Interviews were conducted in the homes of nudists during the off season. Arrangements for the interviews were initially made with these nudists during the first summer of participant observation; selection of respondents was limited to those living within a one-hundred-mile radius of Chicago. The questionnaires were sent to all members of the National Nudist Council. The different techniques of data collection provided a test of convergent validation.
3. For a discussion of the essence of such relationships, see Alfred Schutz, *Collected Papers: The Problem of Social Reality*, Maurice Natanson, ed. (The Hague: Nijhoff, 1962), I, 287 ff.
4. [Q] is used to signify a neutral probe by the interviewer that follows the course of the last reply, such as "Could you tell me some more about that?" or "How is that?" or "What do you mean?" Other questions by the interviewer are given in full.
5. The King and Queen contest, which takes place at conventions, allows for a patterned evasion of the staring rule. Applicants stand before the crowd in front of the royal platform, and applause is used for selecting the winners. Photography is allowed during the contest, and no one is permitted to enter the contest unless willing to be photographed. The major reason for this is that this is a major camp event, and contest pictures are

used in nudist magazines. At the same time, the large number of photographs sometimes taken by lay photographers (that is, not working for the magazines) makes many nudists uncomfortable by calling into question a nonsexual definition of the situation.

6. I was amazed at how many young female nudists described a similar pattern of extreme clothing modesty among their parents and in their own married life. Included in this group was another nudist model, one of the most photographed of nudist models. Perhaps there are some fruitful data here for cognitive-dissonance psychologists.

7. Cf. Schutz, *op. cit.*, p. 74.

8. For some respondents, the female genitals, because of their hidden character, never become a routinized part of camp nudity; thus their visible exposure does not lose an attention-provoking quality.

9. Compare Harold Garfinkel, "A Conception of, and Experiments with, 'Trust' as a Condition of Stable Concerted Actions," in O. J. Harvey, ed., *Motivation and Social Interaction* (New York: Ronald, 1963).

10. See: Schutz, *op. cit.*, I, 11, for his definition of reciprocity of perspectives.

11. This corresponds with the findings of learning-theory psychologists.

12. For a study of the process of doublethink, see James L. Wilkins, "Doublethink: A Study of Erasure of the Social Past," unpublished doctoral dissertation, Northwestern University, 1964.

13. Cf. Schutz, *op. cit.*, p. 229 ff.

Lesbians' Resistance to Culturally Defined Attractiveness

LIAHNA GORDON

The dominant culture of gender puts forth a set of expectations on how women are supposed to think, feel, and act about their bodies. In short, they are expected to be attractive. Conventional socialization presents a narrow view of attractiveness at the same time that it exerts high pressure to conform to this conception.

In studying lesbians, Liahna Gordon found that after participation in a lesbian subculture, they learned a much broader conception of attractiveness, a wider set of beauty norms. In turn, they learned how to conform to and enact these norms with their intimate partners. Both they and their partners organized their actions on the basis of this broader conception of attractiveness. The women came to see themselves as their partners did—as attractive people—even though their bodies didn't represent the more rigid criteria of the dominant culture.

Popular stereotypes depict lesbians as looking butch and unfeminine with hairy legs, short hair, no makeup, and androgynous clothing. According to these stereotypes, all lesbians resist nearly all feminine forms of dress and appearance at all times. In 1998 I investigated the ways in which

Prepared especially for this volume. Reprinted by permission of the author.

women in the lesbian community actually resist (and conform to) feminine appearance by conducting in-depth interviews with 24 women who belong to a lesbian community in Bloomington, Indiana. The women range in age from 21 to 61, are white, and are predominantly middle class. Consistent with these views, all the participants in the study discussed below *do* engage in some form of resistance to what they interpret as the mainstream heterosexual gender rules of appearance and attractiveness. Unlike the clichés, however, this resistance does not always take the most obvious or stereotypical forms. The resistant behavior of the participants is actually more complex than portrayed by the stereotypes, varying in degree, form, and motivation. Further, this resistance does not simply result from individuals acting out their true, gender-deviant natures, but consists of patterns of behavior, grounded in ideology, that are continually encouraged and reinforced by the lesbian community.

SUBCULTURAL RESOURCES

By engaging in resistant and nonconforming behaviors, the participants render themselves "deviant" in the larger cultures. I argue, however, that the members of the lesbian community are acting out not merely some true inner nature but a patterned set of behaviors based on ideology and values of the lesbian subcultures. Indeed, the community teaches, supports, and reinforces these behaviors. I use the term *subcultural resources* to signify all the sources of support the lesbian subcultures provide their members by way of encouragement for engaging in these resistant and nonconforming behaviors. In theory, these resources could include ideology, attitudes, norms, accounts, friendship networks, and formal organizational support. In the data presented here, the participants specifically cited the following as the subcultural resources from which they most commonly gain their support: alternative constructions of beauty, norms encouraging the acceptance of these alternate constructions, lesbian media, lesbian festivals, and lesbian partners.

The beauty ideals in the lesbian subcultures seem more expansive than those in the hegemonic cultures. This comes across not only in what the participants themselves find attractive in women but also in what the subcultures have defined as its beauty ideals. In other words, the participants see the community as a whole, not just themselves as individuals, and have defined attractiveness in a

way that differs from that of the mainstream cultures:

> It seems that lesbians, the ones I've been around, not the lesbians of fiction, that lesbians accept women and their bodies as they are, whatever shape or weight or endowment or whatever. This is the body you have. (Tiger)[1]

> I think that lesbians don't find [body] parts as attractive. We aren't like, "Oh, she has really nice breasts" or "She's got really pretty legs, too bad her shoulders are all wrong." I think lesbians are more physically attracted to the whole. Straight men will be like, "I'm a tit man" or "I'm a leg man." You don't see lesbians objectifying women; we don't tend to pick women apart and then be attracted to those parts. That may be why lesbians tend to be attracted to a broader range of body types. I think that what we find attractive to other women are what we would want others to be attracted to in us. (Harriet)

A few of the participants disagree in that they do not think that the community necessarily rejects the mainstream cultural definition of beauty, but neither do they believe that the community is confined to that definition; they believe that women who both fit and run counter to that cultural ideal are deemed attractive in the community:

> Well, I think a lot of lesbians like that Barbie-doll look [laughs]. I don't think they have to have that look to be attractive to someone. I think lesbians have a more expansive view of what beauty is. Lesbians value strength. I think women value other strong women. I think women can look male and, in the lesbian community, be exactly right on. You can look like anything and be accepted in the lesbian community. (Julie)

Not everyone agrees that someone could "look like anything" and still be considered attractive to lesbians. But all of the participants do concur that the boundaries in the lesbian communities are more expansive than those of the heterosexual cultures:

> It's a different sort of standard, but is a standard of some sort. There are all sorts of standards for the

female body. There's a generic male-defined one, and then another that women have for other women, and then another that straight women have for other women. They are different. The one in other lesbian women is more flexible, but is still a standard. It's not just how thin I am, but standards in terms of what a woman should be. A different standard, but still a standard. (Sarah)

Though participants hold slightly different opinions on this topic, this is perhaps attributable in part to the diversity of the lesbian community itself, in which these attractiveness norms may be stronger among certain parts of the community. Nonetheless, the participants agree overall: the lesbian subcultures generally promote broader, more accepting definitions of attractiveness than do the mainstream heterosexual cultures.

The lesbian media help to reinforce and reaffirm these alternate standards and constructions of beauty both by showing different images of women than those typically highlighted by mainstream media, and by confronting the issue head on, discussing the dangers done by the mainstream beauty ideals. As one participant explains:

I think one of the things that lesbian women do is fight more vigorously against the expectations. I don't see very often in heterosexual women's magazines the notion that fat is beautiful. One of the Lesbian Connections *has this huge woman on the cover. You never see that in heterosexual magazines. In* Lesbian Connection, *there's at least debate about whether fat is beautiful or if it is healthy. Is it a reflection of self-esteem or a lack of it? These are not Christie Brinkley–type women, but they're beautiful. To lesbians, they're beautiful. (Anne)*

Additionally, musical performances aimed primarily at lesbians commonly include at least one song in their play list that critiques heterosexual beauty standards. Lesbian singer/songwriter Jamie Anderson sings several such songs, including *All of Me* and *Dark Chocolate*. Likewise, the Sapphire Uppity Blues Women sing the praises of large legs ("there's thunder in these thighs") in

their song *Thunder Thighs*. Donna talks about such a song performed by the Bloomington Feminist Chorus:

Going to the Feminist Chorus concert a week ago, there was a song about being overweight, being fat. And one of the lines was, "Do I really want to be so thin that a man can count my ribs so that I will look beautiful for him while he's counting my ribs?" And I went, "That just sums up our whole life!"

The participants often cited the lesbian music festivals, especially the National Women's Music Festival and the Michigan Women's Music Festival, as spaces where these more expansive constructions of beauty are taught, reinforced, and reaffirmed. Women who have attended these festivals talked about how they offer opportunities for them to see women of all shapes and sizes together, and to feel accepted. For some, being in this crowd makes them feel "normal" at last:

Over half the womyn [sic] around are also shirtless. Wimmin [sic] of all sizes, shapes, ages, and breast sizes. I will fit in here fine, for I will not feel big or fat like [in] the outside world. Thank you, God!! (Donna, personal journal)

Alice explains that at these festivals one does more than just see all types of women, for the presence and prevalence of such a variety of bodies bring about an altered conception of beauty:

Women there on acres of forested ground where there are no men; it's totally safe. Women are in all kinds of stages of dress and undress. How wonderful that feels, to be walking around in a skirt and nothing else. To see every conceivable size, shape, ability, disability, scars, mastectomy scars. Every time I've been there, there's a moment of understanding how beautiful we all are. Miles and miles of women. . . . I do think it is a common experience to go, "Wow! Aren't we beautiful!" The last time I was there, for two months preparing, there were eight or nine of us in a house, and the others were veterans, and were talking about the "festival moment." And then at one point I went, "Wow! Look at us! Aren't we incredible?! Look at all of us! We're beautiful!" Someone said, "Ha! You're having your festival moment!" So it must be pretty common.

Support for acceptance of these alternate constructions of beauty is found not only in the form of sudden realizations or informal opportunities for changes in one's consciousness. The festivals also offer formal organizational support. The feminist organizers often encourage women's acceptance of their bodies by scheduling workshops around issues of the body.

The expansive alternate constructions of beauty, and the norms encouraging women to adopt these alternate constructions, are strong enough that even the few participants who don't find a variety of body shapes (especially those of heavy women) attractive are apologetic about it. Their discourse around this issue resembles a confessional, and the women articulated that to not find large women attractive is somehow "against the rules":

> *I'm not attracted to girls who are real heavy for some reason. That's bad, I know, because society in general is like, "You're not attractive if you're fat," which is not true, because there are a lot of really pretty girls out there who are big girls. Which is cool. But I don't find myself attracted to those girls, although I can still say she's pretty. But I wouldn't necessarily want to hop in bed with her. (Gertrude)*

PPAN: It's embarrassing to even say. I find that I tend not to look at very overweight people. And that's very . . . I feel bad saying that, but it's true. I tend not to look twice at someone who's very overweight.

LIAHNA: Why do you feel bad?

PPAN: I think it's making a judgment on someone without getting to know them. I know a number of women who are overweight who are lovely women that I got to know through the National Women's Music Festival. But probably unless they approached me, I may not have approached them. Which doesn't feel good, you know? I am not proud of that fact.

Support for resistance to the heterosexual beauty rules is perhaps most often and most importantly manifested and reinforced at the individual level, where the participants receive continuing positive feedback from their partners about their attractiveness. Though based on the behaviors of individuals, this is a subcultural resource in that the community encourages a norm according to which partners are supposed to recognize and allay each others' insecurities regarding their bodies or attractiveness. Regardless of how far the participants lie from the heterosexual ideal in terms of appearance, nearly all the women say that their partners (or past partners) regularly compliment their appearance, and that they believe their partners find their bodies attractive, beautiful, and/or sexy:

> *She really seemed to like my body, and even the things I was self-conscious about. She really went out of her way, as I did with her, to make me think that was silly. There were things she was self-conscious about, but this is why I believe her. The things she was self-conscious about were things—I thought she had a beautiful body too. She always thought the normal girl things: "I have a big ass," or whatever. I wasn't just overlooking that. I really didn't think that. I thought she was beautiful. So I believe she really thought the same about me. (Sarah)*

> *She likes my eyes, she likes my hair, she always says, "I think you're gorgeous!" She likes my body, she doesn't want me to be really thin. She definitely doesn't want me to be skinny. (Emily)*

According to the participants, not only do their partners think the participants are sexy and beautiful, but they actively and continually let the participants know this through compliments and other regular verbalizations. This is a reciprocal endeavor, with the participants doing the same for their partners.

HARRIET: We both had pretty lousy feelings about our bodies. She was fairly heavy and really broad-shouldered, which I love! I thought they were really cool! But she hated it because she couldn't find clothes to fit.

I like to think that I was a positive influence on her own body [image]. A fairly solidly built woman, not fat and soft, but more just solid. I thought she was very attractive. She would constantly give me compliments and I would say no way! But I finally started believing her.

LIAHNA: How did she tell you?

HARRIET: She used to say I was hot! It cracked me up because it was sooo different from my own image of myself. I don't know how much of that was just saying it to make me feel good. She would go on and on complimenting me. "Oooh, you need glasses!" [I'd say]. And finally I got tired of protesting, and I just dealt with it.

I feel sexy when she [my partner] compliments me. I feel sexy when I get dressed up and go out. She's always complimenting me and it makes me feel so good. (Julie)

Similarly, most of the participants described their partners' bodies positively. Only three made neutral or negative comments regarding their partners' bodies, and even those were more made as statements of fact than as value judgments. When asked to describe her last partner's body, for example, KT said, "I would say she's overweight, but it wasn't necessarily an issue [for me]." Yet, while this quote is one of the most negative ones made regarding a partner's body, KT indicated that she, too, complimented her partner regularly on her body, and appreciated her partner's attractiveness, despite her partner's insecurities:

LIAHNA: Were you aware of your partner feeling self-conscious [about her body during sex]?

KT: Yeah. Our opinions about ourselves are usually stronger than others' are about you. She felt like she was fat. So I felt as if I had to make her feel better about it. It wasn't an issue for me, but it was for her. I would tell her what I thought about her. Sometimes when you tell someone something, they don't believe it is the complete truth, even when it is.

Thus, the norms in the community are strong enough that even those making the most negative comments about their partners' appearance also try to allay their partners' fears and give them positive feedback on their attractiveness. Again, this evidences not only an individual expression of support but a patterned set of behaviors taught, expected, and reinforced by the lesbian subcultures.

SUMMARY AND CONCLUSION

In the lesbian subcultures, the rules regarding attractiveness are set up in opposition to the heterosexual norms. Thus, all the participants resist the mainstream heterosexual attractiveness norms (as they interpret them) to at least some extent. This resistance is more complex than popularly conceived, taking various forms and stemming from a variety of motivations. Further, resistance cannot be judged by appearance alone: the resistant behaviors engaged in by the women include redefining beauty ideals, holding certain beliefs and values about appearance and attractiveness, and, as members of the community, providing support for other women, especially partners, in terms of attractiveness.

A subcultural rule not discussed by many of the participants, but which I have observed in my time in the lesbian community, is that women simply do not talk about their bodies, especially in any sort of negative way. Unlike in heterosexual contexts where fat talk may be used either as a form of bonding or as a way to get positive feedback ("Don't say that! You're not fat!") (Nichter and Vuckovic 1994), in lesbian contexts negative self-body talk is met with silence. In the few instances in which I have witnessed lesbians mentioning their bodily attractiveness at all, I have literally seen those around them physically turn away, change the subject, or react with complete silence. While this may not seem as supportive as the heterosexual response of providing reassurance or joining in the self-critique, it does signal that those in the lesbian community are not willing to encourage such negative self-evaluations.

Thus, unlike the dominant cultures in which discontent with one's body may be normative (Rodin, Silberstein, and Striegel-Moore 1984), the lesbian community promotes a norm in which women are satisfied with their bodies, whatever their shape or size.

Relatedly, unlike in the heterosexual cultures where weight control signals morality (Nichter and Vuckovic 1994), in the lesbian community a sense of morality is linked to not participating in the beauty game. The participants give a sense that to resist dominant attractiveness norms is to be more "real." In this formulation, wearing makeup or spending excessive amounts of time on clothing acts as a mask or costume, hiding the "real self." Thus, to discuss one's appearance at all, but especially in a judgmental way, is to exhibit shallowness and superficiality, a trait generally not considered acceptable within the lesbian community.

It is important to reiterate that, with the aid of subcultural resources, not only do all the participants resist the dominant heterosexual norms of attractiveness, but all the participants also engage in nonconforming behavior that they do not label resistant. Hence, we do not simply have a situation in which some women are more politically aware than others and call their behavior resistance, while others wish to minimize their "deviance" by accounting for it by claiming it falls outside their control. Rather, we see a complex system in which the participants account for appearance behavior they perceive as falling outside the mainstream attractiveness norms as both resistant *and* out of their control. Emphasizing this complexity, I witnessed the participants regularly giving these various and multiple accounts, highlighting the fact that the type of account given cannot be predicted according to the type of individual or type of appearance behavior. These multiple accounts likely stem from the different norms and resources provided the participants by both the lesbian and heterosexual communities. As members of the lesbian community, the women not only accept certain parts of the prevailing ideologies of the subcultures but are also expected, and given the opportunity, to follow at least some of the subcultural rules regarding appearance. Yet, the lesbian community does not exist apart from the heterosexual cultures, and it makes its own demands regarding attractiveness and appearance.

NOTES

1. All names are pseudonyms chosen by the participants.

REFERENCES

Nichter, Mimi, and Nancy Vuckovic. 1994. "Fat Talk: Body Image among Adolescent Girls." Pp. 109–131 in N. Sault (ed.), *Many Mirrors: Body Image and Social Relations*. New Brunswick, NJ: Rutgers University Press.

Rodin, Judith, Lisa Silberstein, and Ruth Striegel-Moore. 1984. "Women and Weight: A Normative Discontent." Pp. 267–307 in T. B. Sonderegger (ed.), *Nebraska Symposium on Motivation*. Lincoln: University of Nebraska Press.

CHAPTER 11

SOCIAL DIVERSITY

Crack Use on a College Campus

CURTIS JACKSON-JACOBS

Over a half-century ago, Edwin M. Lemert said that the degree to which a person acquires a deviant self-conception, status, role, and function tends to be related to the frequency of their deviant behavior, its visibility, its exposure to others, and the severity of the societal reaction to it. Nowhere has this proposition been more supported than in the case of crack cocaine use. Coincident with the cocaine epidemic of the 1980s, was the emergence of negative stereotypes of the "crack-head." The crackhead came to signify the lowest, the most degraded, the most visible of drug users. He or she was seen as obtaining crack through theft, burglary, armed robbery, or if a woman, through sex. He or she was typified as one who purchases crack on the streets and from a stranger thereby increasing the risks of victimization. According to the stereotype, crackheads smoked crack in crack houses where, again, there was the potential for victimization. Living on the edge of poverty, the streets became their home. As a consequence of this deviant lifestyle, crackheads were seen as being frequently arrested for sale, possession, or use of a controlled substance. In time, a crackhead's entire life has been viewed as centered around getting and experiencing the orgasmic "rush" of cocaine.

Curtis Jackson-Jacobs's case study of four campus crack cocaine users demonstrates that there are other types of crack users and crack use. He also demonstrates the salience of Lemert's proposition on deviance. In general, the four users studied did not show a major change toward a deviant self-conception, role, status, or function because of their crack cocaine use. Their crack use tended to be socially invisible, infrequent, and of a low, controlled dosage. Since their use was relatively clandestine, they were less exposed to negative sanctions from friends, roommates, college officials, police, or parents. Hence, they were less likely to be socially labeled or to see themselves as crackheads.

Jackson-Jacobs's study elaborates on the social diversity that exists in the area of crack use. He does this in comparing the social-organization contexts of crack use, users' experiences of crack, and the most persistent troubles that different types of users face.

Crack cocaine inspired fear in many Americans in the 1980s. As for many "drug scares" before it and since, the drug of the moment was felt to be the most dangerous ever (Musto 1973; Reinarman and Levine 1997a; Jenkins 1999). Crack started to become relatively available in several cities across the country in 1984 (Grogger and Willis 2000) and was quickly blamed for widespread addiction, urban street crime, and rampant gang violence. The first sources of information about the new drug were lurid news reports (e.g., four articles printed in *Newsweek* June 16, 1986) and frenzied political speeches (e.g., Reagan and Reagan [1986] 1989), introducing crack as an addictive menace of "epidemic" proportion. Americans overwhelmingly came to believe drugs were the most pressing threat to their society by 1989 (Reinarman and Levine 1997b).

Crack, or "rock," was a marketing innovation, quickly adopted by urban street-corner sellers (Jacobs 1996a). It is a smokeable form of cocaine, often sold in pea-sized units costing $20 or less. Unlike powder cocaine, traditionally popular among the rich, crack produces a considerably more powerful high in smaller doses, and appears more conducive to patterns of binge use (Morgan and Zimmer 1997). Crime and addiction were attributed to the more powerful pharmacological effects of the rock form of cocaine.

Strict laws and sentencing guidelines were imposed in response to the perceived tide of lawlessness, disorder, and inhumane violence thought to be riding a wave of crack addiction (*Federal Sentencing Guidelines Manual* 1995). American jails and prisons filled with unprecedented numbers of young minority males (*Correctional Populations in the United States, 1997* 2000). A pervasive cultural stereotype of the users, colloquially dubbed "crack-heads," quickly spread, conjuring images of crazed criminal men with superhuman strength and wasting women prostituting in abject degradation.

Journalistic stories in the 1980s and sociological studies in the 1990s depicted images of distinctively "ghetto" and "street" users. Crime, violence,

and exploitation were at the core of these accounts of the worlds of crack use. Poverty, minority status, and desperation characterized the users.

In this paper I present an ethnographic case study of a network of four regular crack users on a major university campus. The environment in which I did my fieldwork is perhaps as socially distant from the sites of previous crack research as one can get in America. As young, upper-middle-class, mostly white college students, the subjects of this research were at the other end of the social-inequality spectrum, commanding economic, social, and cultural resources.

The result was that I found users whose experiences of crack use were equally distant from those reported in other research. Unlike the users described elsewhere, those described here did not commit crime, were not afraid of victimization by criminals or the law, and did not face the same risks of suffering negative social esteem. Of these "troubles" (Emerson and Messinger 1977) potentially related to participating in crack use, only becoming stigmatized was a real concern. In contrast to street users' frequent troubles in the course of interaction with others, these college-student users were able to manage the moral, practical, and social demands of daily life with considerable success.

The point of this article is twofold. First, I present an alternative to the dominant images of crack use in the most impoverished conditions in American society. Second, by way of a comparison of the social conditions of crack use across a variety of settings, I argue that features of the environments of use critically shape the organization of crack-related troubles, including criminality, victimization, legal sanction, and stigmatization.

The focus of the paper is purposely comparative with data from other sources. In reviewing previous findings and then in presenting my own, I highlight variations in how users experience trouble. Two conditions increase the probability of successfully avoiding crack-related trouble: (1) using in secure contexts and (2) bounding crack use from conventional life. By comparing users' experiences across settings, I discuss how these conditions are differentially distributed across social worlds, especially with regard to economic resources and "conventional ties" (Becker 1955). The emphasis here is on making the link between class and crack-related trouble by examining particularly consequential qualities of daily life. . . .

A GROUNDED TYPOLOGY OF MODES OF CRACK USING

Only two kinds of users—indicating two modes of crack using—are portrayed in the imagery of sociological or popular accounts. These are, first, the menacing, violent, irrational street criminals willing to commit crime to fuel their addiction and, second, the pitiful, degraded, destitute addicts whose humanity and dignity have been devoured by an all-consuming drug. From the current literature, sociological and journalistic, however, at least two other classifications of users and modes of using can be established. These are described in the following paragraphs, and to that, below, I add a fifth type drawn from my own observation.

I present here a comparative description based on two levels of causal conditions that shape the user's experience of trouble (See Table 11.1). The social-organizational conditions I identify are, first, the security of the user's social world and second, the degree to which spheres of the user's social life are bounded from one another. I suggest that each of these has a causal impact on the kinds of troubles the user is likely to encounter and also that features of the typical subjective experience of crack use under these varying conditions have additional effects. These features, corresponding

TABLE 11.1 Modes of Crack Using, Their Features, and Troubles

	SOCIAL-ORGANIZATIONAL FEATURES OF THE CONTEXT		USERS' EXPERIENCE OF CRACK		
Mode of Crack Using	*Secure/ Insecure Context*	*Boundedness of Spheres of Life*	*Orientation to Crack Use*	*Horizons of Crack Use in Life*	*Most Prescient Troubles*
Street predators	Insecure	Unbounded	Hardness High living	Expansive Consuming	Arrest Victimization Addiction Homelessness
Street victims	Insecure	Unbounded	Despair Downward trajectory	Expansive Consuming	Arrest Victimization Addiction Homelessness Stigma
Stable users	Insecure	Partially bounded	Leisure Relational rewards	Limited to domestic life	Financial Employment, and relational trouble
Sneaky dabblers	Insecure	Bounded	Thrill "Street Wisdom"	Leisure time Street associates	Financial trouble Addiction
Campus smokers	Secure	Bounded	Leisure Social ritual	Leisure time Close associates	Anxiety Stigma

to the organizational conditions, are, first, the user's orientation to crack and related troubles and, second, the perceptual horizons of crack use with respect to social identity and relationships.

"STREET PREDATORS" AND "STREET VICTIMS"

The biographies of "street predators" and "street victims," and their corresponding modes of use, illustrate the ways in which local troubles common to many residents become intensified in the course of crack use.

The social, economic, and physical environments of "street" use are dramatically insecure in a variety of ways quite apart from, though seriously compounded by, dynamics of the crack market. Spheres of family life, friendship, residence, and drug use often run into one another, so that trouble in one foreshadows trouble in another. In addition to these sources of vulnerability, "street" users characteristically orient to both crack use and its associated trouble in ways that appear destructive and frequently use crack in ways such that it expands to infuse virtually all aspects of social life and identity.

Users in the ghetto face a number of dangers, more or less regardless of how they understand the drug. Predatory violence and criminal sanctions are common concerns (Jacobs 1996a, 1996b). Buying or using crack in the ghetto puts users in the physical and interactional proximity of violent and property criminals. In this sense they are at risk of victimization. In another sense, the more users become entrenched in cycles of heavy drug use and avoiding conventional responsibilities, the more they are at risk of losing conventional relationships and needing to turn to crime for money (Inciardi, Horowitz, and Pottieger 1993).

The blurring of spheres of social life in poor American communities serves to magnify trouble. Each loss of a conventional relationship compounds trouble; work, friendships, and residence are themselves structured by and dependent on social networks. The precarious housing situation of poor crack users is especially revealing. They often follow a downward trajectory, moving from residences of families, to residences of friends, to the streets (Anderson 1990, p. 86–87). The high degree of visibility in urban communities, where much of social life goes on literally on "the streets" (Anderson 1990), the lack of residential mobility, and the social and physical proximity of work and residential life all contribute to public stigma and social exclusion.

Women especially seem vulnerable, finding few options when they lose their apartments. They must often choose between living in exploitative relationships or dangerous drug houses (Fullilove, Lown, and Fullilove 1992, p. 280, 281; Maher et al. 1996; Maher 1997). Users are vulnerable to being labeled "crack-heads" (Furst et al. 1999), especially women who turn to prostitution on public streets in the same communities where they have lived and grown up (Fullilove, Lown, and Fullilove 1992). In the absence of economic security and sharp boundaries between professional, criminal, and private life, maintaining family relationships and holding employment are often difficult for the crack users described by sociologists (Hamid 1992; Murdoch 1999).

Beyond these structural threats, the impoverished users depicted in published research are more vulnerable as a result of how they understand crack and the troubles of daily life. The most alarming portraits of crack users represent those who have begun using in the midst of either criminal or downward social trajectories in their lives, incorporating crack as an additional element in this experience.

Two characteristic ways of orienting to crack are represented in the imagery of "street predators" and "street victims." Criminality, among committed predators such as burglars (Cromwell, Olson, and Avary 1991; Wright and Decker 1994) and armed robbers (Jacobs 2000), provides the economic and spiritual means to do "high living." "Street predators" tend to live in cycles that alternate between crime and heavy partying, making money and then spending enormous amounts of it and their time on drugs, alcohol, and sex.

They disregard trouble before using crack and continue to do so through their orientation to crack as integral to "open-ended pursuit of illicit street action" (Jacobs 2000; see also Wright and Decker 1994). Rational calculations of the likelihood of arrest, for example, are ignored in favor of a commitment to being "hard" (Katz 1988). "Keeping the party going" focuses attention on grandiose action, often to the point of obliterating concern for sanctions or mundane, conventional responsibilities.[1] The users conjure within themselves an intoxicated compulsion to continue both crime and binging, the one fueling the other, while conventional life recedes from the foreground of experience.

More common are those users whose image is one that appears more pitiful than menacing. To "street victims," like the "predators," the experiential horizons of crack use are often all-consuming. These more or less nonviolent, compulsive users come to focus much of their lives and activities on using crack, treating it as a means of psychological escape from acknowledging a general downward social and economic trajectory in life, while ignoring the troubles of victimization, stigmatization, and arrest that pervade their lives.

Their crack use itself does not so much "cause" a decline into desperation but represents a medium for exaggerating and compounding their existing problems. When many of America's most desperate, impoverished users begin, they are already entrenched in numerous types of trouble (Williams 1992; Inciardi, Lockwood, and Pottieger 1993; Bourgois 1995, p. 319; Murphy and Rosenbaum 1997), balancing precariously between worlds of a marginally "reputable" existence (Matza 1971) and a downward trajectory into abject hopelessness. When they begin using, crack becomes another thread woven into the dense fabric of psychological, social, and economic hardships pervading daily life. Crack use is part and parcel of all-encompassing trouble, on which users may turn their backs and say "let come what may."

"STABLE USERS"

A third type of user has gone virtually unnoticed. These users compartmentalize their crack use to a greater degree than the previous two, allowing it to pervade only certain areas of social life. A few researchers have described middle-income, middle-aged men with stable employment in the inner city and no commitment to crime as a way of life who use crack in order to develop more or less exploitative relationships with female users (Hamid 1992; Maher et al. 1996; Maher 1997).

For the men described, the seductions of crack use and women go hand in hand. Crack is not the defining concern itself but is interwoven with easy access to women, which, in itself, is not likely to lead to many of the troubles often associated with worlds of crack use.

Characteristically, these users begin to use in the midst of relatively stable social and economic trajectories and actively seek to maintain the centrality of conventional pursuits to their lives. As indicated in scattered reports, they are protected both by their social insulation from some of the everyday troubles of poverty and by their inclination to bound and distinguish their identities as crack users from their conventional lives. At the margins of predatory worlds, they may risk experiencing some of the same troubles as those more severely entrenched in street life, though these concerns do not appear especially prescient. Instead, the troubles intimated by researchers tend to be confined within the boundaries of the crack-related transactions: financial and romantic relational.

"SNEAKY DABBLERS"

Nonghetto residents who travel to the ghetto to buy crack also share the risks of physical proximity to criminals and addicts to some degree. However, they are markedly more successful at managing their housing, employment, and personal relationships. First, especially among upper-middle-class suburbanites and urbanites, they participate only fleetingly in predatory contexts, have the social and economic means to bound their use, and, largely because they live far from crack markets, remain invisible to people they relate to outside of crack worlds. Further, such users typically understand episodes of crack use as something of a "sneaky thrill" (Katz 1988, ch. 2) and try to keep their use "within limits." They cut back or discontinue when they see crack impinging on their conventional lives (Waldorf, Reinarman, and Murphy 1991; Reinarman et al. 1997).

We see from sparse accounts, usually journalistic, the seductive, sneaky appeal of crack use to middle-class and upper-class urban and suburban residents. They are oriented to conventional life; however, encounters with the "street" are central to their crack-using experience. The exotic thrill of participating in brief episodes of ghetto life gives emotional flavor to those who travel across class lines.

A Harvard economist at the time, Glen Loury explained about his own crack habit, "Nobody at the Kennedy School could have known about this other world, and nobody in that world . . . could have imagined the sophistication and power of the society of which I was a part" (Shatz 2002). He described "moving back and forth between these worlds" as "a rush." For users like this, the appeal of the societal balancing act, in which alternately experiencing the unfamiliar exoticism of the ghetto and bringing their street "wisdom" (Goffman 1963, p. 29) back to upper-class society, provides the distinctive thrill of using crack. The commitment in this mode of use is to flirt with the streets, while maintaining fidelity to the conventions of mainstream American social life.

"CAMPUS USERS"

To these four types I add a description of the social world of a new variant, the "campus users" I studied. The characterization is not meant to suggest that the type is strictly limited to campuses. More research into the diversity of crack use may well reveal a similar mode of using in other contexts. Alternatively, research on other college students may reveal their crack use to be organized differently. What is most important is not that these people were "college students" but that: they used crack in a social world comparatively quite safe from violence and financial or legal trouble; important spheres of their lives such as housing, work, leisure, and family were loosely coupled relative to other social worlds; they used crack only in highly ritualized ways; and they understood crack use as something that should be subordinate to conventional activities. The logic of this comparative analysis suggests that under similar circumstances—whether on campus or not—we should find other users who do not get into trouble.

METHODS

All of the observation for this research was conducted in a Midwestern American college town with a population around 200,000.[2] Around the time of my research, the town was labeled one of the most crime-free and best cities in which to live and raise a family by national magazines like *Money* and *Parenting*.

After moving out of their dormitory, the primary participants moved into and around a 15 square block student neighborhood that I call "Midtown." In neither the town nor the Midtown neighborhood did I note media or other attention to drug problems, much less concern about crack.

I met the primary participants in this study in the fall of 1996. All were living on the same dormitory floor on the campus of a well-respected public university. Jon, Martin, and Mark were white, and Casey was Korean American. They all came from upper-middle-class families, their parents working in professional positions, some requiring graduate or professional degrees. Over the years I knew them, they all went to school and worked jobs at least part time, even as they used crack and other drugs. Before that year all had used drugs of some kind, including marijuana, hallucinogens, and narcotics, but only Jon had used crack. Jon had used crack throughout high school, traveling with suburban friends to buy it in the inner city of the adjacent large urban center. . . .

Between fall 1996 and fall 1997, I hung out with the group and a wider circle of dozens of friends and acquaintances on campus. During the fall of 1997, I asked if I could watch them whenever they smoked, which they permitted. I began to take field notes on their activities and interview them about their experiences with crack and family and social life generally. During the binges lasting several hours, I would sit outside their circle and take jottings and do homework alternately. By doing homework (sometimes only pretending to do homework), I was able to write without making them visibly uncomfortable.

I kept up taking notes for the duration of a one-semester fieldwork course and for a short time the following semester. In total my systematic observation continued for six months, although I had known and interacted with the users for a year prior to that time. My friendships with and observations of the group continued until I moved away from Midtown at the end of 1998. After that I kept speaking with Casey by phone for 2 years and have continued to speak with Jon. . . .

FEATURES OF CAMPUS LIFE: SOCIAL-ORGANIZATIONAL DIMENSIONS

Two social-organizational features of social life among the campus users are brought into relief when compared with reports from other contexts. First, they used crack in a context that afforded them economic, social, and physical security. They had grown up with the typical economic, social, and cultural rewards of upper-middle-class suburban life in America. Neither crime nor victimization had been especially relevant to their youthful cultures, nor did they become relevant to life on campus. There was no ghetto near Midtown. Street crime was not a visible feature of Midtown life.

Second, they were able to bound their lives as crack users from their other roles and relationships.

As I describe below, they were also geographically removed from their families and experienced little pressure to show up at school regularly and sober. They successfully maintained the boundaries of their identities as crack users to such a degree that they could often even deceive certain friends and roommates about their use.

How they understood crack also helped them to maintain their conventional lives. First, they oriented to crack as a social object to be used in leisure rituals. Before ever using crack together they had used drugs only in similar groups, especially among circles of marijuana-smoking friends. Social and ritual drug use were widespread among students, while the kinds of paranoid and predatory relationships found in poor urban neighborhoods were completely absent.

Second, the perceptual horizons of crack use stopped at the edge of the circle of users. In contrast to users in other reports, the place of crack in these users' lives grew out of the context of developing friendships as a shared interest and social ritual (see Jackson-Jacobs 2001). Crack was, for them, something to be controlled and placed secondary to other concerns, namely their conventional relationships and activities. They overwhelmingly used it in their "spare time," organizing consumption not to interfere with conventional pursuits, not the other way around, as observed among hard-core users.

THE SOCIAL WORLDS OF THE CRACK USERS

The relationship between resources and trouble is not as simple as might be assumed. Campus life—not simply upper-middle-class status—at once provided social resources to these men and a locus for bounding identity as crack users, and it provided them with the understandings of crack, trouble, and social life that motivated them to actively maintain conventional identities. On the one hand, their conventional identities were central concerns, things to be managed vigilantly. They wanted to avoid being identified as crack users by their roommates, at school, at work, or by their families. On the other hand, related aspects of these same relationships served as resources, allowing them to hide their drug use. They were able to move residences often to manage their use, were able to miss school without drawing attention, were largely free from parental supervision, and almost never interacted with street criminals.

RESIDENTIAL MOBILITY

Like many students, the small group of crack users and their larger group of friends moved often, affording them control over their crack use. In the town there was a virtually uniform term for apartment leases. All Midtown landlords required one-year leases beginning and ending on August 15. Despite the one-year imposition on apartment leases, many of these men moved more often than once per year. They did this by subleasing apartments to and from conventional acquaintances and friends.

As many college students in areas like Midtown do, they organized groups of friends to rent large apartments. For the crack smokers the ease of mobility allowed them to shape their drug use. At times they moved in with roommates who did not use crack in order to cut back. At other times they moved in with other users in order to get high more often.

At one point Jon and Mark moved into an apartment together, where they frequently had company over to use various drugs. Attracted to the steady source of clientele, a cocaine dealer soon began spending several hours each day in the house. When Jon decided that he could not stand to live where a cocaine dealer spent so much time, he looked for another place to live. It was too crazy, he told me once; he had to get out of there.

Martin, who had been spending a lot of time at this house, also hoped to cut down on his use. The two moved into another house together. They had five women roommates who did not use crack but smoked marijuana from time to time

and drank alcohol on weekends. Jon signed his lease over to their regular dealer, Paul, while Martin simply stopped paying rent at his old apartment.

Moving residences to get away from drugs was, compared to the residential troubles described in other studies of crack users, quite simple. As nice-looking white college students looking for housing in a student neighborhood, they did not face the type of discrimination frequently experienced by black renters, especially poor black renters (Massey and Denton 1993; Yinger 1995). Also, they had access to financial resources from parents, providing them with the cash to put down damage deposits and rent at any time. The combination of race, financial resources, and type of neighborhood is especially important in light of findings that African Americans are less likely to move out of neighborhoods that they describe as "undesirable" than are whites (South and Deanne 1993).

Furthermore, this type of movement would be very difficult and costly for many members of the middle-class, especially homeowners, who cannot move on a moment's notice. Additionally, moving around middle-class neighborhoods frequently, among middle-aged adults, would be suspicious and damaging to financial credit.

Residential mobility among the group provided some control of the crack-using experience. Migrating from apartment to apartment might have raised suspicion in typical suburban and city environments. And it is often unmanageable for many ghetto residents, especially unemployed women (Maher et al. 1996; Maher 1997). For the men I knew, though, moving in order to control crack use was seen as nothing more than typical migration through friendship circles, at the same time depending on student status and access to social networks.

ROOMMATES

For several months during my observation, Martin lived with Casey and two other male roommates. A coworker of the two roommates,

Ray, who coincidentally was also a crack user, slept on the couch without paying rent. The other two never used crack, although one of them, Lonnie, did use powder cocaine a few times. Martin and his three roommates signed a joint lease, which he defaulted on by moving out. When Martin moved out to live with Jon, he quit paying his share of the rent.

His roommates called his mother to complain. Lonnie told me, "I called Martin's mom and told her that he had money to spend on crack but not on rent. I said he was worthless and the product of worthless parents." Martin confirmed that his roommates had called his mother and been confrontational, but he did not know exactly what they said. He said, though, that he wished he hadn't told them about his crack use and that they were unfairly trying to use this against him. Especially important, Martin said, was the possibility that they would use this information against him when suing for unpaid rent—the only serious reference to legal trouble related to crack I heard in Midtown.

Having moved out of this house, Martin and Jon began to share a room in a house with five female college-student roommates. Although Martin and Jon were friends with their roommates, they did not at first tell any of the five that they smoked crack in their room. Two of them eventually did find out (see Coming Out, below), but Jon and Martin continued to try to deceive them while high and to keep the others in the dark completely.

They kept their roommates from learning of their crack use by assigning a "door man." His job was specifically to watch out for roommates. The door man was instructed in how to deal with a knock.

Jon said on one occasion, "Hey, Martin, you be the door man, okay?"

"What do you want me to do?" Martin asked.

"Tell them we're naked."

This role was often crucial in delaying entry when a roommate did knock; during the delay everyone else had time to hide the paraphernalia.

Inciardi, Lockwood, and Pottieger (1993) also described the role of door man, but in the context of "crack houses." He was someone "who lets people in, checks for weapons, and watches for police" (Inciardi, Lockwood, and Pottieger 1993, p. 154). Looking at the door man as a security guard gives us a way to see what the users feel threatened by in a specific context. In inner-city "crack houses" violence and arrest are pressing threats from the outside world.

For the Midtown smokers, however, violence and arrest were not real concerns. Their environment posed little threat to their life or liberty. Instead, they feared losing their social standing and relationships. Roommates' gazes, not predators' violence, were the most prescient sources of trouble. We see in these interactions not only the physical security of life on campus but the success these men had at bounding crack use from relationships: even among friends and close acquaintances, only a select group were let in on the secret.

PARENTS

All of the men claimed to keep close ties with their parents. The special problems of concealing crack use from them were primarily dealt with on the phone. I observed all of the central members speaking on the telephone with their parents on occasion. All of their parents lived in different cities, so they never feared a surprise visit.

Mark would almost never answer his phone when he was high on cocaine or crack. When it rang, he asked someone else to pick it up and ask who was calling. If no one would do this, he was so afraid it might be his mother and she would know he was on drugs that he allowed the phone to ring until the caller hung up. When someone did answer for him, even before the caller was announced, he would wave his arms, shake his head, and mouth the words, "I don't want to talk to my mom." Martin and Casey used similar strategies.

While the other three went to the extreme of not answering potential calls from parents, Jon said, "when they call, actually, I become instantly sober." He would talk to them, but, he continued,

"I try to answer in short, direct statements and don't try to keep them on the phone for too long."

Their dealings with parents show how fearful these men could be in some situations. Although they hid their drugs from roommates, they would often "pass" as sober just minutes after smoking. Over the phone with their parents, though, they would not take this risk.

It seemed to me that, in fact, these men could speak just fine on the telephone when they were high on crack. The invasion of the family world into the crack circle inspired an immediate shame. These brief collisions of the worlds of parental supervision and campus freedom opened a window into a tension these men experienced in their drug lives. While they were, for the most part, free to use drugs in their campus life, they were at rare times compelled to bear the constraints of conventional family life.

WORK

Being identified as a crack user at work poses some of the same problems as detection by parents and roommates: "It's the stigma of it. That people will do anything to get it," Jon explained. But, in addition to negative social esteem, he expected that the stigma generally associated with crack users would present practical concerns for his employer: "It's kind of implicit that I would be stealing to buy crack." Their strategies for avoiding roommates and parents were inapplicable to work. Hiding from employers may lead employees to be fired for missing work. Crack smokers cannot just say to their employers, as they might to their roommates or parents, "I can't deal with you right now."

Jon and Martin were able to maintain both their jobs and school activities despite using crack several times a month, often very soon before going to work. Jon explained that they would decide to "stop [using crack] at least three hours early for work, which might mean to finish as quickly as possible." Usually smoking together, they had a pact that they would smoke whatever was left well before going to work. Doing this was hazardous, though, as they were sometimes "coming down" and "strung out" at work; symptoms include diarrhea, talking nonsense, "fiending"[3] for another hit, minor hallucinations, and various other acute health problems. This, they believed, could result in a noticeable change from their sober behavior. On the few occasions that he was noticed, Jon claimed to be hung over or sick, more legitimate excuses for withdrawn and sickly behavior than claiming to be fiending for crack. The group orientation to maintaining conventional identities, in this case as "good employees," was a basis for concerted and individual efforts to bound their crack-using identity.

SCHOOL

Whereas the main responsibility of conventional American adult worlds, besides family, is to maintain employment, for college students it is to go to school. This responsibility was fairly easy for my sample to maintain despite their crack use. All that these crack users really felt obligated to do was pass their courses in order to make progress toward graduation and to satisfy their parents.

Oftentimes after a night or more of heavy smoking, these men would miss class. And, unlike a full-time job, no one cared much. At worst they lost some credit for class participation. Furthermore, when they felt motivated, it was no problem for them to sit quietly through classes while under the influence of crack without being detected, especially in large lectures.

The schedule of "work" required of college students also made it easy for them to manage crack use and homework. Many college students spend days in a row binge drinking (Clapp, Shillington, and Segars 2000), playing video games, seeking out sex partners (Maticka-Tyndale, Herold, and Mewhinney 1998), or wasting time without doing homework. Like more conventionally idle students, these crack smokers could simply cram schoolwork in large doses during their days-long hiatuses from crack use (Vacha and McBride 1993).

STRANGERS

One window into the kind of trouble most relevant to their life on campus, their intense anxiety about being stigmatized, came when these users purchased legal paraphernalia at stores. In order to "cook up" crack from powder cocaine and smoke it, they had to buy certain household items before a binge. Although they interacted only with strangers in the store, they showed reluctance to buy the necessary items.

All the supplies needed to produce and smoke crack, other than the cocaine, are legal to buy: spoons, candles, baking soda, copper scouring pads, metal sockets, lighters, etc. Many of the crack smokers claimed that although legal, some items are known by the general public to be primarily used for crack. Baking soda and Chore-Boy brand scouring pads (specifically the copper ones that come in bright orange boxes), according to several of the smokers, are easily recognized by "most people" as crack paraphernalia. Jon spoke once of a convenience store in his hometown that "put a sign up next to the Chore-Boy that said 'crack pipe screens,' because that's all people buy it for." Martin, Mark, and Casey also agreed that making crack screens "is the only reason people buy Chore-Boy."

Several times Jon gave money to one of the others and asked him to purchase the Chore-Boy. I pointed out that there was nothing illegal about it. "Yeah," Jon said and laughed one evening. "But I don't want people to see me buy it. I mean, cause they'll know what it's for."

Jake, another student who smoked rock with them on several occasions, recounted a story to me and to the group members that seemed to confirm their fears. Jake was buying Chore-Boy and baking soda, he explained, when a woman behind him in line made a chilling statement. Out loud she said, "I know what that's for. You're going to smoke crack with that." The only negative consequence that came of this episode was that Jake was verbally "outed." Nonetheless, this was enough to mortify him and was accepted as a serious, noteworthy event in itself by the rest of the group. Being verbally identified was terrifying, regardless of any secondary consequences that could imaginably follow.

Jake's story illustrated both the product and the process of fear. His story confirmed to the group that their anxieties were well founded. His statement, and Jon's, show just how deeply these men feared being "outed," even by strangers. That this fear was felt so intensely illustrates how bounded their identities as crack users were and how strictly they wanted to maintain that boundary. Not only people who could "do something" about it (Erikson 1962) but people who might simply interpret their behavior as deviant were felt to seriously threaten their identities.

Neither Jon nor any of the others ever showed any apprehension about buying the cocaine. The transaction was always conducted in a private home with a well-known and trusted dealer. When buying the cocaine, because of the privacy of the transaction, they were confident that no one outside the cocaine community would know what they were doing. In buying the screen material, though, they perceived that they were at risk of detection by people in the store. Although they couldn't be arrested, their concern was that some anonymous other in the community would recognize them as crack users.

SOURCES OF VULNERABILITY AND TROUBLE

STIGMA

. . . Jon, Martin, Casey, and Mark were intensely aware that their being discovered as crack users could lead to their being deeply stigmatized. Their understanding that using crack was a disreputable activity was treated as common sense; it was rarely spoken of and was acted on collectively without discussion. Furthermore, it was understood, crack was the most discreditable drug one could use. Even among people who were allowed to know about some of their drug use, crack was not revealed, or was revealed only after progressive disclosure of other drug use.

In Midtown arrest and violence were not relevant to using crack, at least from their perspective. Instead they feared, to varying degrees according to the particular relationship, becoming stigmatized, being found out, or losing conventional status as students, family members, or roommates. Unlike the most self-destructive users, these college students placed avoiding trouble at the forefront of their crack-using experience. Though they were only likely to experience one specific trouble, stigmatization, they focused their attention heavily on avoiding it.

Only once did I hear an open discussion about whether using crack was or was not a potentially discrediting activity (Goffman 1963). Martin asked Jon whether other people, referring to their peers, thought of crack as less respectable than other drugs. Jon seemed shocked that Martin even asked, nearly laughing, and said, "Yeah, man. Crack is like the worst thing you can do. It's not respected at all." This understanding is consistent with the finding that college students associate crack, unlike other drugs, specifically with ghetto users (Alden and Maggard 2000). The intensity of the potential stigma these users associated with crack, though, was rarely verbalized. Instead it was displayed in their various practices of hiding crack use and managing their identities as crack users.

COMING OUT

Although all of these men felt intense pressure to hide their behavior, some came out and admitted their crack use to others at work or to roommates. Drug use was only admitted to others who, because they themselves used some form of drugs or indicated tolerance, seemed unlikely to confer negative esteem or otherwise sanction them. Furthermore, they admitted crack use only after first gauging responses to the admission of using less stigmatized drugs.

At Jon's work he had come out with several coworkers through "casual drug conversation." Despite his vigilant secrecy around some employees, and all the managers, Jon was willing to own up to his habit with certain individuals. He told me that "basically, the conversation always starts about marijuana smoking," which he explained was not a stigmatized behavior. "That leads to, 'have you ever tried this?' At first you don't admit it, but say 'I've got a friend who does it,' or 'I've seen people doing this.'" If the other went along and talked about a similar experience, Jon told the employee that he smoked crack. In this way he found several other users who then smoked crack with him.

When Jon and Martin lived with five non-crack-using women, they at first kept their use completely hidden. After some time, though, two of the roommates were let in on the secret, as explained to me by Martin: "Most of them suspect something, but usually just [that we use] coke. Elaine and Karen know. I don't think anyone else does. . . . We told Elaine. And Karen heard us talk about it when we were drunk." These roommates all used both marijuana and alcohol. Only after using marijuana and drinking together did Jon and Martin let their guard down. Additionally, they were satisfied to allow their roommates to believe they used cocaine, rather than crack, evidencing their belief that crack is the most discrediting drug of all.

Coming out about their crack use proceeded along a path of progressive disclosure about other drug use, either in "casual drug conversation" or mutual activity. The progression of disclosure from alcohol, to marijuana, sometimes to other drugs, and then to crack engenders the secrecy in which crack use was shrouded. Although knowledge of their crack use was off limits to some, these users felt that the negative esteem accorded crack varied among those they knew. Despite this, though, they felt that of any drug involvement to be revealed, crack was potentially the most discrediting. Unlike for other drugs, these users felt that there were no images or stereotypes of crack users except for those of addicted ghetto users involved in thievery or other crime. They only revealed crack use to those they believed were "wise" enough to look beyond such stereotypes.

EXPERIENCES OF TROUBLE

None of the men became seriously involved in street crime or were criminally victimized in Midtown, except in the rare instances I describe below. They were not around nor did they interact with anyone who they thought might victimize them. Nor did they feel they were likely to be arrested. Unlike users described elsewhere, these men bought and used cocaine privately in the company of friends. They did not buy on street corners, in crack houses, or from strangers, especially likely ways to get caught.[4]

So far I have described how Jon, Martin, Casey, and Mark stayed out of trouble and, in fact, hardly ever thought of any trouble besides stigma. Yet these data offer two suggestive, but limited, contrasts within. First is Mark's experience of "losing control" of both his drug use and social life. Second are Jon and his hometown friends' descriptions of concerns and experiences using crack in an urban ghetto when Jon was not living in Midtown. Each show that the troubles associated with crack both are shaped by and shape contexts of use.

After I left the field, Mark experienced what might be considered "serious" loss of social standing. After using for two years, he dropped out of school and lost his job. He inherited $3,000, took out a loan of the same size, and sold much of his property, spending all in under a year. Finally, after exhausting his supply of legal economic resources, he began writing bad checks. After a year out of school, his mother realized something was wrong and took him back home.

Mark did not commit serious crime but instead turned to a form of misdemeanor, low-level white-collar crime, one that in its illegality was identical to a legal counterpart behavior: writing bad checks. Mark's experience shows that this group was not immune from trouble or addiction. Nonetheless, in the midst of "losing control" of his use, Mark's troubles were shaped by his social standing. The most serious consequences turned out to be those that he had feared most. He was thought to be a "crack-head," was considered a failure in social life by his friends, and was "found out" by his mother. Mark's trouble coincided precisely, and was itself constituted by, a progressive failure to maintain a boundary between his crack use and his work, school, and family life. The process of getting into social trouble, Mark's case illustrates, is a process of a breakdown of the boundaries between crack use and conventional activities.

Jon and his high school friends' experience, using in urban slums before he moved to Midtown and on his trips home, points to the critical importance of the immediate contexts of use. They suffered many of the same troubles as the users who lived in these places. Back home, they told me, they would drive from their affluent suburban neighborhood to the most impoverished ghettos of the city to buy rock. Part of the lore of this circle of friends was the violent experiences they had when buying crack in the ghetto.

Jon or his friends reported that on separate occasions they were: punched in the face; dragged in an alley and choked in a robbery attempt; confronted with racial threats; arrested while buying on a public street; beaten by police; forced to make an undercover buy to avoid arrest; and pursued in a high-speed car chase by a dealer who thought they were buying with a fake twenty-dollar bill. Such stories were of exotic interest to the rest of the Midtown group who had no such experiences.

While Mark's case shows that troubles emerge when the boundaries between crack using and conventional identities break down, Jon's experience shows that troubles depend also on the environment of use. Although the drug, the user, and the user's understandings were held constant, Jon experienced serious trouble only in the dangerous context of the ghetto. Furthermore, he experienced the kinds of trouble endemic to interacting with the street economy. Though victimization and arrest were pressing concerns, becoming stigmatized, the fear on campus, was not relevant.[5]

CONCLUSION

. . . The experiences of the men I observed were only colored by a faint shadow of the stigma and other troubles that met the "street" users widely reported elsewhere. Nestled in the world of post-adolescence and preadulthood, this group of crack smokers shared an experience of both social security and the resources to bound spheres of social life. These cushy, lax conditions made it possible to manage crack use alongside conventional pursuits. . . .

Moreover, different people understand their potentially discrediting activities, conventional life, and the prospects of trouble differently. Not only are some individuals more vulnerable, but they orient to threats differently. More or less troubled trajectories in life shape how people experience their criminal or deviant activities. For individuals successfully navigating conventional institutions, including university life, serious trouble is likely to be seen as both realistically avoidable and to be avoided. In social worlds permeated by serious suffering, in contrast, members appear more often to see trouble as unavoidable and to adopt perspectives that embrace or disregard it.

NOTES

1. Although the data for his analysis generally predate the advent of crack, Katz (1988) describes more or less the same orientations to trouble and openness to any kind of "illicit action," including crime and drug use, defining serious offenders' experience of everyday life.
2. In order to protect confidentiality, potentially identifying details about the location, the participants, and some specific indications of my relationship to the research participants have been excluded or obscured (e.g., the exact local population, names, parents' exact occupations).
3. "Fiending" is the feeling of intense craving for another hit. They describe it as almost overwhelming; all one can think about is another hit. Like low-status "fiends," the users would sometimes scour the carpet looking for a rock that might have fallen.

4. Only Jon had frequented a crack house in Midtown. He disliked the environment so much, though, that he quickly stopped going. He had also tried to purchase on the street from homeless men, but each time bought a fake product (see Jackson-Jacobs 2001).
5. Though stigmatization could have conceivably resulted if anyone found out Jon was arrested, he did not think this was a real concern. His charges were misdemeanors, thus not likely to come to anyone's attention.

REFERENCES

Alden, Helena, and Scott Maggard. 2000. "Perceptions of Social Class and Drug Use." Abstract of paper presented to the Southern Sociological Society. Indexed in Sociological Abstracts.

Anderson, Elijah. 1990. *Streetwise: Race, Class, and Change in an Urban Community*. Chicago: University of Chicago Press.

Becker, Howard. 1955. "Marihuana Use and Social Control." *Social Problems* 3:35–44.

Bourgois, Philippe. 1995. *In Search of Respect: Selling Crack in el Barrio*. Cambridge, UK: Cambridge University Press.

Clapp, John, Audrey Shillington, and Lance Segars. 2000. "Deconstructing Contexts of Binge Drinking among College Students." *American Journal of Drug and Alcohol Abuse* 26:139–154.

Correctional Populations in the United States, 1997. 2000. Washington, DC: Department of Justice.

Cromwell, Paul, James Olson, and D'Aunn Wester Avary. 1991. *Breaking and Entering: An Ethnographic Analysis*. Newbury Park, CA: Sage.

Emerson, Robert, and Sheldon Messinger. 1977. "The Micro-politics of Trouble." *Social Problems* 25:121–134.

Erikson, Kai. 1962. "Notes on the Sociology of Deviance." *Social Problems* 9:307–314.

Federal Sentencing Guidelines Manual 1995. 1995. Washington, DC: United States Sentencing Commission.

Fullilove, Mindy, E. Anne Lown, and Robert Fullilove. 1992. "Crack 'Hos and Skeezers: Traumatic Experiences of Women Crack Users." *Journal of Sex Research* 29:275–287.

Furst, Terry, Bruce Johnson, Eloise Dunlap, and Richard Curtis. 1999. "The Stigmatized Image of the 'Crack Head': A Sociocultural Exploration of a Barrier to Cocaine Smoking among a Cohort of Youth in New York City." *Deviant Behavior* 20: 153–181.

Goffman, Erving. 1963. *Stigma: Notes on the Management of Spoiled Identity*. New York: Simon and Schuster.

Grogger, Jeffrey, and Michael Willis. 2000. "The Emergence of Crack Cocaine and the Rise in Urban Crime Rates." *The Review of Economics and Statistics* 82:519–529.

Hamid, Ansley. 1992. "Drugs and Patterns of Opportunity in the Inner City: The Case of Middle-Aged, Middle-Income Cocaine Smokers." Pp. 209–240 in *Drugs, Crime, and Social Isolation: Barriers to Economic Opportunity*, edited by Adele Harrell and George Peterson. Washington, DC: Urban Institute Press.

Inciardi, James, Ruth Horowitz, and Anne Pottieger. 1993. *Street Kids, Street Drugs, Street Crime: An Examination of Drug Use and Serious Delinquency in Miami*. Belmont, CA: Wadsworth Publishing Company.

Inciardi, James, Dorothy Lockwood, and Anne E. Pottieger. 1993. *Women and Crack-Cocaine*. New York: Macmillan Publishing Company.

Jackson-Jacobs, Curtis. 2001. "Refining Rock: Practical and Social Features of Self-Control among a Group of College-Student Crack Users." *Contemporary Drug Problems* 28:597–624.

Jacobs, Bruce. 1996a. *Dealing Crack: The Social World of Streetcorner Selling*. Boston, MA: Northeastern University Press.

———. 1996b. "Crack Dealers and Restrictive Deterrence: Identifying Narcs." *Criminology* 34: 409–431.

———. 2000. *Robbing Drug Dealers: Violence beyond the Law*. New York: Aldine de Gruyter.

Jenkins, Philip. 1999. *Synthetic Panics: The Symbolic Politics of Designer Drugs*. New York: New York University Press.

Katz, Jack. 1988. *Seductions of Crime*. New York: Basic Books.

———. 1997. "Ethnography's Warrants." *Sociological Methods and Research* 25:391–423.

Maher, Lisa. 1997. *Sexed Work: Gender, Race and Resistance in a Brooklyn Drug Market*. Cambridge, UK: Oxford University Press.

Maher, Lisa, Eloise Dunlap, Bruce Jacobs, and Ansley Hamid. 1996. "Gender, Power, and Alternative Living Arrangements in the Inner-City Crack Culture." *Journal of Research in Crime and Delinquency* 33:181–205.

Massey, Douglas, and Nancy Denton. 1993. *American Apartheid: Segregation and the Making of the Underclass*. Cambridge, MA: Harvard University Press.

Maticka-Tyndale, Eleanor, Edward Herold, and Dawn Mewhinney. 1998. "Casual Sex on Spring Break: Intentions and Behaviors of Canadian College Students." *Journal of Sex Research* 35:254–264.

Matza, David. 1971. "Poverty and Disrepute." Pp. 601–656 in *Contemporary Social Problems*, edited by Robert Merton and Robert Nisbet. New York: Harcourt, Brace and Jovanovich.

Morgan, John, and Lynn Zimmer. 1997. "The Social Pharmacology of Smokeable Cocaine: Not All It's Cracked Up to Be." Pp. 131–170 in *Crack in America*, edited by Craig Reinarman and Harry Levine. Berkeley and Los Angeles: University of California Press.

Murdoch, R. Owen. 1999. "Working and 'Drugging' in the City: Economics and Substance Use in a Sample of Working Addicts." *Substance Use and Misuse* 34:2115–2133.

Murphy, Sheigla, and Marsha Rosenbaum. 1997. "Two Women Who Used Cocaine Too Much: Class, Race, Gender, Crack, and Coke." Pp. 98–112 in *Crack in America*, edited by Craig Reinarman and Harry Levine. Berkeley and Los Angeles: University of California Press.

Musto, David. 1973. *The American Disease: Origins of Narcotic Control*. New Haven, CT: Yale University Press.

Reagan, Ronald, and Nancy Reagan. [September 14, 1986] 1989. "Address to the Nation on the Campaign against Drug Abuse." Pp. 1178–1182 in *Public Papers of the Presidents of the United States 1986*. Washington, DC: United States Government Printing Office.

Reinarman, Craig, and Harry Levine. 1997a. "Crack in Context: America's Latest Demon Drug." Pp. 1–17 in *Crack in America*, edited by Craig Reinarman and Harry Levine. Berkeley and Los Angeles: University of California Press.

———. 1997b. "The Crack Attack: Politics and Media in the Crack Scare." Pp. 18–52 in *Crack in America*, edited by Craig Reinarman and Harry Levine. Berkeley and Los Angeles: University of California Press.

Reinarman, Craig, Dan Waldorf, Sheigla B. Murphy, and Harry G. Levine. 1997. "The Contingent Call of the Pipe: Bingeing and Addiction among Heavy Cocaine Smokers." Pp. 77–97 in *Crack in America*, edited by Craig Reinarman and Harry Levine. Berkeley and Los Angeles: University of California Press.

Shatz, Adam. 2002. "About Face." *New York Times Magazine*, January 20.

South, Scott, and Glenn Deanne. 1993. "Race and Residential Mobility: Individual Determinants and Structural Constraints." *Social Forces* 72:147–167.

Vacha, Edward, and Michael McBride. 1993. "Cramming: A Barrier to Success, a Way to Beat the System or an Effective Learning Strategy." *College Student Journal* 27:2–11.

Waldorf, Dan, Craig Reinarman, and Sheigla B. Murphy. 1991. *Cocaine Changes: The Experience of Using and Quitting*. Philadelphia: Temple University Press.

Williams, Terry. 1992. *Crackhouse: Notes from the End of the Line*. New York: Addison-Wesley.

Wright, Richard, and Scott Decker. 1994. *Burglars on the Job: Street Life and Residential Break-ins*. Boston, MA: Northeastern University Press.

Yinger, John. 1995. *Closed Doors, Opportunities Lost: The Continuing Costs of Housing Discrimination*. New York: Russell Sage Foundation.

Outsiders in a Hearing World

PAUL C. HIGGINS

Classification of people is a distinct pattern of culture. Social life without the sifting and sorting of people into their various categories seems most unlikely. One of the more common classifications is typing people as being members of the "in-group" or the "out-group." Similar classification occurs when people make distinctions between those who conform and those who deviate. The former are marked for inclusion, the latter for exclusion. Relations between the majority group and the minority group follow from these social distinctions, and, to a large extent, they border on stereotype.

Paul C. Higgins, in his study of the deaf community, calls attention to an important finding: Within a particular deviant social category, additional distinctions are made. This time, however, the people making the distinctions have themselves been excluded by the majority group. The deaf community consists of two categories based on their modes of communicating with other people and the extent of their divergence from people with unimpaired hearing. This cleavage, at times, creates antagonisms in the deaf community. The distinctions that have real consequences for both categories turn on those who embrace deafness and those who still see themselves as participants in the hearing world.

Much of everyday life is based on the assumption that people can hear and speak. We communicate through telephones, radios, television, intercom systems and loudspeakers. Warning signals are often buzzers, sirens or alarms. Time is structured by bells and whistles. And, of course, people talk. Our world is an oral-aural one in which deaf people are typically left out (Higgins, 1978). They are *outsiders* in a hearing world (Becker, 1963). And like other outsiders, they are likely to create and maintain their own communities in order to survive and even thrive within an often hostile world.

In this article I explore the deaf community. Unlike many other disabled populations—who often only establish self-help groups (Sagarin, 1969)—the deaf are not merely a statistical aggregate. For example, 85% of deaf people who lost their hearing before the age of 19 have hearing-impaired spouses (Schein and Delk, 1974:40).[1] Through marriage, friendships, casual acquaintances, clubs, religious groups, magazines published by and for themselves and sign language, the deaf create and maintain communities in the hearing world. Though scattered throughout a metropolitan area, members of the deaf community primarily confine their social relations to other members (Schein, 1968:74). Membership within those deaf communities and the organization of the relationships among members are the foci of this article. Each of these aspects of deaf communities revolves around the deaf being outsiders in a hearing world.

METHODS

This article is part of a larger study in Chicago which investigated the identity, interaction and community of the deaf in a hearing world (Higgins, 1977). I draw on materials from in-depth interviews with 75 hearing-impaired people and 15 counselors or friends of the deaf. My sample was developed through a snowballing technique. . . . National publications by and for the deaf, published writings of deaf individuals and articles or monographs about the deaf proved helpful. My research and analysis [were] primarily limited to the white deaf community. I soon learned that there was little interaction between white and black deaf. They form separate communities. . . .

MEMBERSHIP

More than 13 million people in America have some form of hearing impairment. Almost 2 million are deaf. Of those 2 million approximately 410,000 are "prevocationally" deaf; they suffered their hearing losses before the end of adolescence (Schein and Delk, 1974).[2] It is from this latter group, the prevocationally deaf, that members of deaf communities are likely to come. I neither met nor heard of members of the Chicago-area deaf community who lost their hearing after adolescence. Surely some exist, but they are few. It will become evident later why that is so.

Deafness is not a sufficient condition for membership in deaf communities, though some degree of hearing impairment is a necessary condition as I will examine later. Deafness does not make "its members part of a natural community" (Furth, 1973:2). Membership in deaf communities must be *achieved*. It is not an ascribed status (Markowicz and Woodward, 1975). Membership in a deaf community is achieved through (1) *identification* with the deaf world, (2) *shared experiences* of being hearing impaired, and (3) *participation* in the community's activities. Without all three characteristics one cannot be nor would one choose to be a member of a deaf community.

IDENTIFICATION

A deaf community is in part a "moral" phenomenon. It involves:

> *a sense of identity and unity with one's group and a feeling of involvement and wholeness on the part of the individual. [Poplin, 1972:7]*

A deaf woman, her hearing impaired since childhood, dramatically describes the realization in her late teens and early twenties that she was part of the deaf world:

> *I didn't think I was very deaf myself. But when I saw these people [at a deaf organization] I knew*

I belonged to their world. I didn't belong to the hearing world. Once you are deaf, you are deaf, period. If you put something black in white paint, you can't get the black out. Same with the deaf. Once you are deaf, you're always deaf.

While it is problematic both physiologically and in terms of identification that "once you are deaf, you are always deaf," the woman's remarks express her commitment to the deaf world.[3] Whether members dramatically realize it or not, what is important is their commitment to and identification with the deaf. Other members, who attended schools and classes for the deaf since childhood and continued their interaction in the deaf world as adults, may, on looking back, find no dramatic moment when they realized that they had become part of a deaf community.

Members of the deaf community feel more comfortable with deaf people than they do with hearing people. They feel a sense of belonging. A young deaf woman explained:

At a club for the deaf, if I see a deaf person whom I don't know, I will go up to that person and say, "Hi! What's your name?" I would never do that to a hearing person.

Not all deaf or hearing-impaired people, though, identify with the deaf world. Those who lost their hearing later in life through an accident, occupational hazard or presbycusis (i.e., aging process) do not seek to become members of deaf communities. Rather, as Goffman (1963) notes, they are likely to stigmatize members of deaf communities in the same way that those with normal hearing stigmatize them. Others, impaired from birth or from an early age, may never have developed such an identification. They probably had hearing parents and were educated in schools for the hearing. Some may participate in activities of deaf communities, but are not members. They are tolerated, though not accepted by the members. While audiologically they are deaf, socially they are not.

A hearing-impaired man, who participates in a deaf religious organization, but is not part of the deaf community, explained his self-identity in the following way:

In everyday life I consider myself a hearing person. [His hearing-impaired wife interjected that she did too.] I usually forget it that I have a hearing problem. Sometimes I'm so lost [absorbed] in the hearing world; I mean I don't even realize I have a hearing problem. It seems automatic. I don't know what it is. I feel I'm hearing people to the deaf and hearing. I don't feel hearing impaired not even if I have a hard time to understand somebody. Still I don't feel I'm deaf because I couldn't hear you or understand you.

This man and his hearing-impaired wife are on the fringe of the deaf community. They participate in some community activities "just to show that we care" and "because they [the deaf] need help."

Hearing-impaired people like this man and his wife are often a source of both ill feelings and amusement for members of deaf communities. They are a source of ill feelings because their behavior does not respect the identity of the deaf community. Thus, this same hearing-impaired man was severely criticized for having someone at a board meeting of a religious group interpret his spoken remarks into sign language rather than signing himself. As I will explain later, signing skill and communication preference are indications of one's commitment to the deaf community. Those who are opposed to signing or who do not sign are not members of the community.

They are a source of amusement for trying to be what members of deaf communities feel they are not—hearing. A deaf couple were both critical and amused at the attempt of the same hearing-impaired man's wife to hide her deafness. As they explained:

A hearing woman who signs well came up to her [the wife] at a religious gathering, and assuming that she was deaf, which she is, began to sign to her. The wife became flustered, put her own hands down and started talking.

Such hearing-impaired people serve as examples that members of deaf communities use in explaining to others what their community is like and in reaffirming to themselves who they are. These hearing-impaired people help to define for the members the boundary of their community and their identity as deaf people. The members reject the feelings of these "misguided" hearing-impaired people; feelings which deny their deafness. And in rejection, the members affirm who they are and what their community is.

SHARED EXPERIENCES

In developing an identification with the deaf world, members of deaf communities share many similar experiences. Those experiences relate particularly to the everyday problems of navigating in a hearing world (Higgins, 1978) and to being educated in special programs for the deaf.

Since childhood, members of deaf communities have experienced repeated frustration in making themselves understood, embarrassing misunderstandings and the loneliness of being left out by family, neighborhood acquaintances and others. Such past and present experiences help to strengthen a deaf person's identification with the deaf world. A *typical* instance of these experiences, remarkable only because it is so routine, was described by a deaf man:

> *Most of my friends are deaf. I feel more comfortable with them. Well, we have the same feelings. We are more comfortable with each other. I can communicate good with hearing people, but in a group, no. For example, I go bowling. Have a league of hearing bowlers. Four of them will be talking, talking, talking and I will be left out. Maybe if there was one person I would catch some by lipreading, but the conversation passes back and forth so quickly. I can't keep up. I just let it go; pay attention to my bowling. Many things like that.*

Yet, to be a member of a deaf community, one need not actually be deaf. Some members have lesser degrees of hearing impairment. As children, though, they were processed through educational programs for the deaf. These children were not necessarily mislabeled, though

certainly some were. Rather, often no local programs for "hard of hearing" children were available. Children with various degrees of impairment were educated together. Through such processing, these children developed friendships with deaf children and an identification with the deaf world. As adults, they moved comfortably into deaf communities. With amplification these members of deaf communities are often able to use the telephone successfully, if also somewhat haltingly. Some converse with hearing people reasonably well. Yet, due to that childhood processing as deaf, these hearing-impaired people choose to live their lives within deaf communities. Audiologically they are not deaf; socially they are (Furfey and Harte, 1964, 1968; Schein, 1968).

Other members of a deaf community may have once been deaf, but through surgery or fortuitous circumstances they have regained some hearing. Though no longer severely hearing impaired, they remain active in the deaf community where their identity as a person developed. A dramatic case is that of a now slightly hearing-impaired man. He went to the state school for the deaf in Illinois. His childhood friends were deaf. During World War II, though, he regained much of his hearing while working in a munitions plant; the loud blasts from testing the bombs apparently improved his hearing. Consequently, his speech also improved. Only his modest hearing aid indicates that he has a slight impairment. Yet his wife is deaf, most of their friends are deaf, and he is active in a state organization for the deaf. As he explained:

> *[As your speech got better, did you continue to associate with your deaf friends in _____ town?] Oh, yeh, I'm more involved with the deaf community now than I was back then [WW II]. To me they are still my family. I feel more at home when I walk into a room with 1,000 deaf people; more so than walking into a room with 1,000 hearing people, non-deaf. I feel at home. I can relate to them. We had something in common; our childhood, our education, our problems, and all that.*

Since membership in a deaf community is based on shared experiences of being deaf and identification with the deaf world, it is difficult for hearing individuals to be members of such communities. A deaf woman put it simply: "Hearing people are lost in the deaf world just as deaf people are lost in the hearing world."

Outsiders are often wary and resentful of "normals": blacks of whites, gays of straights and so on. Likewise, deaf people are skeptical of hearing people's motives and intentions. A deaf man remarked:

> When a hearing person starts to associate with the deaf, the deaf begin to wonder why that hearing person is here. What does that hearing person want?

When a "hard of hearing" woman, who for years had associated exclusively with the hearing, started a north shore club for the deaf, her motives and behavior were questioned by some of the deaf members. I was warned myself by two deaf leaders to expect such skepticism and resistance by members of the deaf community. I encountered little in my research, but having deaf parents and clearly establishing my intentions probably allayed members' suspicions.

Outsider communities may grant courtesy membership to "wise" people who are not similarly stigmatized (Goffman, 1963). These individuals are "normal," yet they are familiar with and sympathetic to the conditions of outsiders. For example, gay communities grant courtesy membership to "wise" heterosexuals: heterosexual couples or single females known as "fag hags" (Warren, 1974:113). Researchers are often granted that status. Yet, that courtesy membership represents only a partial acceptance by the outsiders of the "normals."

Some hearing individuals are courtesy members of deaf communities. They may be educators, counselors, interpreters or friends of the deaf. Often they have deafness in their families: deaf parents, siblings, children or even spouses. Yet, their membership is just that, a courtesy, which recognizes the fundamental fact that no matter how empathetic they are, no matter that there is deafness in their families, they are not deaf and can never "really" know what it means to be deaf.[4]

Not surprisingly, hearing-impaired individuals who through their actions and attitudes would otherwise be part of a deaf community may be rejected by some members because they hear and speak too well. A hearing-impaired woman who speaks well and with amplification uses the telephone, who went to a state school for the deaf since childhood and to a college for the deaf and who is married to a deaf man is such an individual.

Yet, hearing-impaired people like that woman do receive some acceptance from those members who tend to reject them. They are called upon to act as go-betweens with the hearing world. This clearly differentiates these impaired people from the hearing. As the hearing-impaired woman mentioned above noted:

> They [deaf people] can rely on me to do the talking for them [e.g., telephoning]. And in that sense they do accept me because I am somebody who can help them. Because they don't really want to turn around to a hearing person and ask them to do something.

The hearing and speech ability of this hearing-impaired woman creates a barrier between her and some members of the deaf community, but simultaneously allows her some acceptance by those who reject her. She is almost hearing; therefore, some members reject her. She is not quite hearing, though; therefore, members will rely on her for help in navigating through the hearing world. It is often only with greatest reluctance that members of deaf communities rely on hearing people for such assistance.[5]

PARTICIPATION

Active participation in the deaf community is the final criterion for being a member. Participation, though, is an outgrowth of identification with the deaf world and of sharing similar experiences in being hearing impaired. In that respect, then, it is the least important characteristic for being a member of the deaf community. Yet the deaf community is not merely a symbolic community of hearing-impaired people who share similar experiences. It is also created through marriages, friendships, acquaintances, parties, clubs, religious organizations and published materials. The activities provide the body of the community, whereas the identification and shared experiences provide the soul.

Thus, a deaf couple, who lived in the Chicago area for years, were not warmly received when they began to attend a deaf, Protestant congregation. The members of the congregation wondered where they had been all these years. Members interpreted that lack of participation as a lack of identification with themselves and a lack of commitment to the deaf community.

Participation, though, varies among the members of deaf communities. Involvement in community activities is tempered by outside commitments such as work, family and traveling time to and from activities as well as individual preference. More importantly, what activities one participates in and with whom one associates help to organize relationships among members of the deaf community.

SOCIAL ORGANIZATION

While normals may often treat outsiders as a homogeneous group, the outsiders themselves create distinctions among one another. Gays distinguish among "elite," "career" and "deviants" (Warren, 1972). Lower-class blacks may vilify middle-class blacks for being Uncle Toms (Pettigrew, 1964). The deaf community, too, is heterogeneous. Through differential participation with other members and in various activities of the deaf community, members organize their relationships with one another.

Members of the deaf community use several major characteristics in organizing relationships with one another. Some of these characteristics operate in much the same way as in the hearing world. Outsiders, whether they be deaf or not, live within a larger world. Some are not born as outsiders, but only later acquire that status. All are socialized to some degree within the dominant culture. Consequently, communities of outsiders and their subculture are continuous with the dominant culture of the larger society (Plummer, 1975:157). Therefore, it is not surprising that some characteristics which members of the dominant culture use to differentiate each other are also used by members of communities of outsiders. Sex, race, religion and sophistication (as often indicated by educational attainment) differentiate members in the deaf community as they do in the hearing world. Consequently, they will not receive special attention here.

Age, however, adds a special dimension to deaf communities. Unlike ethnic or racial outsiders, there are few deaf children in the deaf community. Less than 10% of deaf people have deaf parents (Schein and Delk, 1974:35). Consequently, deaf communities are actually adult deaf communities. As children, most members of the community were probably isolated in a hearing world except while attending educational programs for the deaf. The same holds true today, though deaf children may participate in such activities as religious worship where deaf adults are present. The intriguing question becomes: how are deaf children and adolescents socialized into the adult deaf community? I did not address this issue which clearly needs attention.

COMMUNICATION

Other characteristics which members of an outsider community use to organize their relationships with one another are related to their unique position within the dominant world. For example, within the black community skin color has played an important but diminishing role (Udry et al., 1971). Within the deaf community, communication preference and skill, the relative emphasis that members give to signing and speaking, is an important basis on which relationships are organized. I will examine this characteristic closely, because it is crucial for understanding the deaf community in a hearing world.

There are two general modes of communication used among the deaf. One is called the oral method; the other is the manual method. The oral method in its "purest" form is composed of speaking and lipreading. Manual communication is sign language and fingerspelling. Put very simply, sign language is a concept-based language of signs (i.e., various movements of the hands in relationship to one another and to the body in which the hands themselves take various shapes) that has a different structure from English, but one that is not yet fully understood (Stokoe et al., 1975). Within the deaf community there are oralists and manualists who I will refer to as *speakers* and *signers*.[6]

Speaker

Speakers rely primarily on speaking and lipreading when communicating with fellow oralists. When communicating with signers, they may often accompany their speaking with signs, but they do not sign fluently. Those who are "pure" oralists in philosophy or communicative behavior are not part of the deaf community. A small number of these "pure" oralists are members of an oral association of the deaf; whereas, others go it alone in the hearing world (Oral Deaf Adults Section Handbook, 1975). Of course, the distinction between a "pure" oralist and a speaker is arbitrary. Speakers may accept as a member of the community an oralist who signers reject as too orally oriented to be a fellow member. Speakers are likely to have had hearing parents and attended day schools and classes for the deaf where signing was not permitted.

Signers

Signers sign and fingerspell when communicating to their deaf friends. For many signers their first language is sign language. They are native signers. Some have unintelligible speech and poor lipreading skills. Yet, others speak and lipread well, even better than speakers. Signers, though, prefer signing as compared to speech or lipreading when communicating with one another. Rarely will they use their voices or even move their mouths with other signers. Those who do may be teased. Signers reason that speaking and lipreading are for navigating in the hearing world, but they are not necessary among fellow signers.

Varieties of sign language exist. Many of those are due to the mixing of sign language and English. American Sign Language is least influenced by English. The use of varieties of sign language displays the social organization of the deaf community. The more educated the deaf individual is, the more likely that individual will be familiar with varieties which approximate English. Varieties of sign language which approximate English are more likely to be used at formal occasions (e.g., at a conference) than at informal ones. Social, educational, regional and ethnic (particularly black-white) variations in signing exist much as they do in English (Stokoe and Battison, 1975).

Becoming a signer follows no single path. Those who have deaf parents who sign most likely grew up as signers themselves. Others became signers in residential schools. Although signing often was not permitted in the classrooms of such schools, it was often allowed outside of the classrooms in the dorms and on the playgrounds. After leaving *oral* day school programs, many deaf individuals began to use signs which they learned from deaf adults. The hand rapping and monetary fines which were (and in some cases still are) administered to them when they were caught using their hands to communicate were not forgotten. The frustration and bitterness from failing to understand and to learn through the oral approach is still felt.[7] Consequently, these converts are often the most adamantly opposed to oral education because they are the self-perceived victims of it.

Others who did not immediately seek out signers often found that their speech and lipreading skills did not gain them easy entrance into the hearing world. They were misunderstood and in turn misunderstood hearing people. Such experiences influenced these deaf individuals to become signers.

CLEAVAGE BETWEEN SIGNERS AND SPEAKERS

Signers and speakers are members of the same deaf community. They may attend the same religious organization, social club or community gala. They also marry one another. In such marriages the speaker typically becomes a signer. Yet, through their feelings toward each other and their differential involvement with each other, strong divisions and at times antagonisms are created. That cleavage within the deaf community relates historically to the deaf's position within a hearing world. Particularly, it is an outgrowth of how educators of the deaf have traditionally felt it best to teach deaf children.

Historically, throughout the United States and especially in Chicago, Boston, and a few other places, the oral method of instruction has been dominant in schools and classes for the deaf. Only since the early 1970s has the Chicago area begun to emphasize manual communication in the classroom. The combination of the two approaches along with writing and any other effective means of communication has been called total communication (O'Rourke, 1972).

The oral philosophy was stressed in the hope and desire that deaf children, trained in such a method, would be able to move easily into the hearing world as adults. Perhaps more importantly, it was also stressed due to the fear that [if] deaf children were allowed to sign and fingerspell with one another, especially in often isolated residential schools, then as adults they would marry one another and form deaf communities within, but apart from, the hearing world. Alexander Graham Bell, whose wife was deaf and who was an influential supporter of the oral philosophy, voiced such fears in an 1883 paper, "Upon the Formation of a Deaf Variety of the Human Race" (Boese, 1971). This emphasis of hearing educators

on oralism and their suppression of signing among deaf children has not gone unnoticed by the deaf.

Through formal organizations as well as friendships and informal relations, signers and speakers organize the deaf community according to communication skill and preference. For example, a national fraternal organization for the deaf has several divisions in the Chicago area. One is attended by speakers; the other two by signers. Though the oral division has a dwindling membership, its members insist on being separate from the larger, manually oriented divisions. Further, respondents noted that most, if not all, of their friends had similar communication preferences as their own, be they manual or oral. Each group is not quite comfortable with the other's mode of communication. Speakers explain that it is difficult to follow fast signers, especially when the signers do not move their mouths. Signers complain that it is difficult to lipread the oralists or understand their modest or minimal signing.

The conflict between signing and speaking also disrupts family relationships. It is not unusual for deaf children who sign to communicate little with their parents who do not sign. As adults, their relationships with their parents may be bitter. Deaf siblings, too, can be divided by communication differences. For example, two deaf sisters in the Chicago area rarely see each other. Both grew up in the oral tradition but the older married a speaker while the younger married a signer. The younger sister has retained her oral skills, but has become more involved with signers. Rather than join the oral fraternal division at her sister's request, she remains in the larger, manual division where her friends are.

Although signing is not a basis for membership in deaf communities, it is clearly an outgrowth of becoming a member.[8] Signing is an indication of one's identity as a deaf person and one's commitment to the deaf world. It is perhaps the most obvious indication to hearing people that one is deaf. Because deafness is a relatively invisible impairment, deaf people would often go unnoticed in everyday, impersonal activities except for their signing to one another. Also, signing often attracts stares, unflattering imitations and ridicule from the hearing. Therefore, "pure" oralists are viewed by members of deaf communities, particularly by signers, as outsiders to the deaf world. Further, some signers wonder if speakers are ashamed of being deaf. Signers may interpret the speakers' not fully embracing signing as an indication that speakers are either trying to hide their deafness or are still hopelessly under the influence of misguided, hearing educators. Either way, the speakers' commitment to the deaf world becomes questioned. That commitment is partially based on the conviction that hearing people have too long dominated deaf people's lives; in education, in jobs, in even telling them how to communicate with each other.

CONCLUSION

Within the larger society, outsiders often create and maintain communities. Some of these communities are located within well-defined geographical areas of the city: ethnic neighborhoods, black ghettos or Mexican-American barrios. Other communities of outsiders may not be quite so geographically bounded. Through marriages (both legal and symbolic), friendships, clubs, formal organizations, publications and a special argot, outsiders who are scattered throughout a metropolitan area *create* their community. The deaf community is such a creation.

Membership in deaf communities, though, is neither granted to nor sought by all who are deaf. Rather, it is achieved through identification with the deaf world, shared experiences of being hearing impaired and involvement with other members. Most people who are audiologically deaf never become members. Some with lesser degrees of hearing impairment have been members for as long as they can remember.

Although the deaf community may appear to be homogeneous to the hearing, members of the community create distinctions among one another. These distinctions are used in organizing relationships within the community. Some of these distinguishing characteristics, such as sex, are used within the hearing world as well. Yet, due to the unique (historical and present) position of the deaf as outsiders in a hearing world, members of the community distinguish among one another based on communication preference. Signers and speakers find it easier to communicate with those who have preferences similar to their own. More importantly, speaking to fellow members is a vestige of the hearing's domination of and paternalism toward the deaf. Therefore, not fully embracing and using sign language may call into question one's identification with and commitment to the deaf community.

Within deaf communities the members seldom face the difficulties and frustrations which arise when they navigate through the hearing world. A sense of belonging and wholeness is achieved which is not found among the hearing. *Among* fellow members there is no shame in being deaf and being deaf does not mean being odd or different. Deafness is taken for granted. Within deaf communities those who cannot "turn a deaf ear" now become the outsiders.

NOTES

1. Ghettos for the blind have existed in the past in China and in many European cities. In 1935, a prominent worker in the field of blindness proposed establishing self-contained communities of the blind (Chevigny and Braverman, 1950). Few blind people, though, have blind spouses (Best, 1934).

A predominantly self-contained village of 400 physically disabled adults has been created by rehabilitation specialists in the Netherlands (Zola, unpublished). To what extent it is a community and to what extent it is merely an extension of a long-term care facility is not clear.

2. Prevocationally deaf people were defined as those "who could not hear and understand speech and who had lost (or never had) that ability prior to 19 years of age" (Schein and Delk, 1974:2). A self-report hearing scale was used to determine the respondent's hearing ability. Schein (1968) discusses the factors (e.g.,

chronicity, age of onset and degree of loss) involved in defining deafness and examines previous definitions.

3. Most "coming out" among homosexuals, a process of defining oneself as gay, seems to occur in interaction with other homosexuals. Gays too feel that being gay is a permanent condition (Dank, 1971; Warren, 1974).

4. While members of deaf communities grant courtesy membership to "wise" hearing people, those members often subtly indicate that those hearing people are still not "one of them" (Markowicz and Woodward, 1975). When signing to a hearing person, the deaf may slow the speed of their signing or speak while signing. They would rarely do that when communicating with a fellow member.

5. This desire of the deaf to be independent from and their skeptical attitude toward help offered by the hearing [have] been documented in the more general situation of disabled-nondisabled relations (Ladieu et al., 1947).

6. It is difficult to estimate the relative proportion of oralists and manualists within deaf communities. Both the relative membership within the oral and manual divisions of a deaf fraternal organization (in Chicago) and the proportion of the prevocationally, adult deaf population who use signs (Schein, 1968; Schein and Delk, 1974) indicate that oralists are a numerical minority within deaf communities. Further, their numbers are likely to decline in the future as signing becomes more extensively employed in educational programs for the deaf.

7. On academic achievement tests, deaf children score several years behind their hearing counterparts (Trybus and Karchmer, 1977).

8. Some researchers have viewed deaf communities as language communities where American Sign Language use is necessary for membership (Markowicz and Woodward, 1975; Schlesinger and Meadow, 1972). This approach is too restrictive because it excludes speakers as well as many signers who are not ASL users from being members of deaf communities. Yet, speakers, nonnative signers and native signers associate with each other, marry one another and recognize each other as part of the same community while also maintaining distinctions among one another.

REFERENCES

Becker, H. S. 1963. *Outsiders: Studies in the Sociology of Deviance*. New York: Free Press.

Best, H. 1934. *Blindness and the Blind in the United States*. New York: Macmillan.

Boese, R. J. 1971. "Native Sign Language and the Problem of Meaning." Ph.D. dissertation, University of California–Santa Barbara (unpublished).

Chevigny, H., and S. Braverman. 1950. *The Adjustment of the Blind*. New Haven, CT: Yale University Press.

Dank, B. M. 1971. "Coming Out in the Gay World." *Psychiatry* 34:180–197.

Furfey, P. H., and T. J. Harte. 1968. *Interaction of Deaf and Hearing in Baltimore City, Maryland*. Washington, DC: Catholic University Press.

———. 1964. *Interaction of Deaf and Hearing in Frederick County, Maryland*. Washington, DC: Catholic University of America Press.

Furth, H. G. 1973. *Deafness and Learning: A Psychosocial Approach*. Belmont, CA: Wadsworth.

Goffman, E. 1963. *Stigma: Notes on the Management of Spoiled Identity*. Upper Saddle River, NJ: Prentice Hall.

Higgins, P. C. 1978. "Encounters between the Disabled and the Nondisabled: Bringing the Impairment Back In." American Sociological Association Meetings, San Francisco.

———. 1977. "The Deaf Community: Identity and Interaction in a Hearing World." Ph.D. dissertation, Northwestern University (unpublished).

Ladieu, G., E. Haufman, and T. Dembo. 1947. "Studies in Adjustment to Visible Injuries: Evaluation of Help by the Injured." *Journal of Abnormal and Social Psychology* 42:169–192.

Markowicz, H., and J. Woodward. 1975. "Language and the Maintenance of Ethnic Boundaries in the Deaf Community." Conference on Culture and Communication, Temple University, March 13–15.

Oral Deaf Adults Section Handbook. 1975. Washington, DC: Alexander Graham Bell Association for the Deaf.

O'Rourke, T. J. (ed.). 1972. *Psycholinguistics and Total Communication: The State of the Art*. Washington, DC: American Annals of the Deaf.

Pettigrew, T. F. 1964. *A Profile of the Negro American*. Princeton, NJ: D. Van Nostrand.

Plummer, K. 1975. *Sexual Stigma: An Interactionist Account*. London: Routledge and Kegan Paul.

Poplin, D. E. 1972. *Communities: A Survey of Theories and Methods of Research*. New York: Macmillan.

Sagarin, E. 1969. *Odd Man In: Societies of Deviants in America*. Chicago: Quadrangle.

Schein, J. D. 1968. *The Deaf Community: Studies in the Social Psychology of Deafness*. Washington, DC: Gallaudet College Press.

Schein, J. D., and M. T. Delk, Jr. 1974. *The Deaf Population of the United States*. Silver Spring, MD: National Association of the Deaf.

Schlesinger, H. S., and K. P. Meadow. 1972. *Sound and Sign: Childhood Deafness and Mental Health*. Berkeley: University of California Press.

Stokoe, W. C., and R. M. Battison. 1975. "Sign Language, Mental Health, and Satisfying Interaction." First National Symposium on the Mental Health Needs of Deaf Adults and Children. Chicago: David T. Siegel Institute for Communicative Disorders, Michael Reese Hospital and Medical Center, June 12–14.

Stokoe, W. C., C. G. Casterline, and C. G. Croneberg (eds.). 1975. *A Dictionary of American Sign Language on Linguistic Principles*. Washington, DC: Gallaudet College Press.

Trybus, R. J., and M. A. Karchmer. 1977. "School Achievement Scores of Hearing Impaired Children: National Data on Achievement Status and Growth Patterns." *American Annals of the Deaf* 122(2): 62–69.

Udry, J. R., K. E. Bauman, and C. Chase. 1971. "Skin Color, Status, and Mate Selection." *American Journal of Sociology* 76:722–733.

Warren, C. A. B. 1974. *Identity and Community in the Gay World*. New York: Wiley.

———. 1972. "Observing the Gay Community." Pp. 139–163 in J. D. Douglas (ed.), *Research on Deviance*. New York: Random House.

Diversity in Panhandling

STEPHEN E. LANKENAU

With the resurgence of homelessness that began in the 1980s, there has been a marked increase in panhandling, a form of systematic deviance. As a result, there has been a community backlash, the passage of laws against "aggressive panhandling," and the spread of "compassion fatigue" in the general public. In short, as its nuisance value has increased, the tolerance for public displays of indigence has decreased. What underlies the negative reactions to panhandling, and how have panhandlers dealt with this situation?

The antipathy most people feel toward panhandlers is based on their breach of a number of expectations. One breach is of pedestrians' expectation about being able to go about their business without interruption. Another breach is the panhandlers' attempts to obtain money simply by asking for it rather than by earning it through some form of work. Consequently, the majority of pedestrians ignore panhandlers and act as though they are not even there.

Panhandlers want to gain the attention of people passing by, and get them to stop, look, and listen to their request for assistance with a minimum of disruption. Stephen E. Lankenau describes the diversity in roles that have developed as a way of requesting money while avoiding the creation of animosity. Thus, all of them are attention-getting devices, and all are designed to reduce social disruption as much as possible.

Some of the people just walk by and don't say nothin'. I call them zombies [laughs]. You ask them for change and they don't say "yes," "no," or "maybe I be back." They just walk by you like they don't even see you—it's like I'm not even sitting there. They could say "I ain't got none" or "no" or something. They just walk by.—Alice, a homeless panhandler

We use a variety of ploys to avoid the gaze or overtures extended by panhandlers—we avert our eyes, quicken our pace, increase the volume on our headphones. Some panhandlers manage to capture our attention, less frequently our money, using humor, offering services, telling stories, or by using other dramatic devices. A close examination of the exchanges between panhandler and passersby reveals that these interactions occur within a multi-layered, theatrical context; dramas are enacted at the face-to-face level yet display the larger social relations among the poor and nonpoor.

Goffman's (1959) dramaturgical perspective presents social life as a play in which persons or actors conduct themselves before various audiences according to scripted roles. Compared with the exchanges among everyday persons, however, interactions between panhandler and pedestrian more closely resemble the basic structural features of a play. The panhandler, who is the main actor, is like an improvisational performer who uses a repertoire of pieces or numbers to accomplish the act of panhandling. I refer to a panhandler's collection of these actions as his or her panhandling repertoire. Similarly, in reaction to the performer, pedestrians serve as the audience and respond to the panhandling routine by selecting from a menu of responses, like engaging or ignoring the panhandler. Being ignored by a passerby, which Goffman (1963) referred to as the "nonperson treatment," is a primary problem confronted by panhandlers, but one that is directly addressed through a repertoire of panhandling routines.

Reprinted from Stephen E. Lankenau, "Panhandling Repertoires and Routines for Overcoming the Nonperson Treatment," *Deviant Behavior: An Interdisciplinary Journal*, Vol. 20, pp. 183–206. Copyright © 1999. Reproduced by permission of Taylor & Francis, LLC, http://www.taylorandfrancis.com.

On the basis of ethnographic observations and interviews of panhandlers on the streets of Washington, DC, I have conceptualized five primary panhandling routines: the entertainer, the greeter, the servicer, the storyteller, and the aggressor. These routines are premised on using various props, manipulating self-presentation, and engaging the sympathies and emotions of passersby. The fact that I am categorizing panhandlers according to various routines, however, does not necessarily imply that certain individuals are acting or feigning need and distress. Rather, panhandling repertoires are one way of describing the public dramas between panhandler and passersby.

A PRIMARY PROBLEM FACING PANHANDLERS—THE NONPERSON TREATMENT

The nonperson treatment of panhandlers, that is, passing by a panhandler as though he or she did not exist, originates in a disposition characterizing many city dwellers, which Simmel ([1903] 1971) called the "blasé attitude." The blasé attitude stems from the constant stimulation found in a city and causes inhabitants to react to new situations with minimal energy or to disregard differences between things. . . .

A NEW APPROACH TO STUDYING PANHANDLERS

I propose that panhandlers devise a repertoire of panhandling routines to break out of the role of stranger or to awaken pedestrians from the blasé state; these dramaturgical actions then minimize the nonperson treatment and pave the way for encounters. Framing panhandling according to a repertoire of actions represents a different analytical approach to the study of panhandler practices and problems. Most prior research on the subject presents typologies that often lack analytical precision. Although these studies offer useful descriptive categories, such as white-collar beggars

(Anderson [1923] 1961), child beggars (Freund 1925), store beggars (Gilmore 1940), professional beggars (Wallace 1965), executive beggars (Igbinova 1991), and character beggars (Williams 1995), I argue that they fail to provide a thorough understanding of the phenomenon of panhandling and of the problems faced by panhandlers.

First, past analyses often construct typologies that portray panhandlers not as actors but as types lacking agency and versatility. In contrast, panhandling repertoires highlight the drama and dynamism that often [underlie] the act of panhandling. I demonstrate how panhandlers confront ambivalent or negative reactions by using one or more routines in a single encounter. Ultimately, framing panhandling in terms of repertoires represents a departure from previous analyses as this strategy typifies action rather than essentializes or rigidifies persons.

Second, prior research typically fails to conceptualize panhandling in terms of interaction between two unequal sets of actors, the panhandler and the passerby. Framing panhandling as a theatrical exchange between two classes of actors with dissimilar material resources, different interactional objectives, and contrasting viewpoints, however, is a critical factor toward understanding the *repertoire of routines* enacted by panhandlers. Despite these inequalities, this analysis shows that panhandling repertoires lead to exchanges between the zombie and the stranger and thereby foster greater understanding among both classes of actors.

METHOD

I define a panhandler as a person who publicly and regularly requests money or goods for personal use in a face-to-face manner from unfamiliar others without offering a readily identifiable or valued consumer product or service in exchange for items received. Throughout the sampling process, I largely selected panhandlers who appeared mentally and physically fit for regular employment. Among both policymakers and the population at large, these able-bodied, often homeless individuals

are generally regarded as the nondeserving poor (Wright 1989), that is, persons viewed as undeserving of sympathy or assistance as they violate basic norms surrounding work. I learned during interviews, however, that these seemingly fit fronts often belied health problems and circumstances that inhibited gainful employment, particularly work requiring physical stamina and strength. For instance, many panhandlers reported mild to serious illnesses and injuries occurring largely before their entry into panhandling, such as back and leg injuries, poorly healed broken bones, knife and gunshot wounds, burns, diabetes, and HIV exposure. Others admitted to past or current drug and alcohol problems, and a few appeared to have mental difficulties. However, no single health factor typically explained entry into panhandling and homelessness. Rather, a constellation of problems, including unemployment, homelessness, family conflicts, or health factors, often characterized each panhandler.

During the data collection period, which spanned from December 1994 to August 1996, I sampled mornings, afternoons, and evenings on both weekdays and weekends within five contiguous neighborhoods or sections of northwest Washington, DC. This area covered a three-mile corridor beginning in a largely White, well-educated, and affluent residential neighborhood at the northern point and terminating in a large downtown business section at the southern end. Both a major avenue and a common subway line connect four of these regions. I undertook about 80 official data collection efforts into this area, which were accomplished largely on foot since I lived in one of the five neighborhoods. Including interviews, each journey usually lasted between two and five hours. At the end of the data collection period in August 1996, I typically was able to identify two out of three panhandlers within this corridor as someone whom I had either interviewed or informally spoken to previously.

Interviews ($N = 37$) were tape recorded and followed a series of open-ended questions focusing on four aspects of the panhandler's experience: street work, relationships, self-issues, and demographics. Panhandlers received $10 for their tape-recorded interviews, which typically lasted between 45 minutes and an hour. On meeting a panhandler for the first time, I usually established basic rapport by giving $0.50, which was then followed by an explanation that I was a student studying panhandling. Other relevant information that may have influenced rapport with each panhandler is that I am White, male, and of a middle-class background. Only a handful of panhandlers, however, refused to be interviewed. In addition to these formal interviews, I informally spoke with dozens of other panhandlers and posed as a panhandler for two consecutive days in downtown Washington, DC.

On the basis of the formal interviews, the profile of the typical panhandler in this sample is as follows: a Black, single, unemployed homeless man in his early 40s who was born into a lower- or working-class family in the District of Columbia and who possessed a high school degree or higher. In addition, the typical panhandler began panhandling in his mid-30s or early 40s and had been panhandling consistently for the past five years after losing a job in the construction industry. A negative life event or events, such as an accident, an illness, a spell of homelessness, a layoff, or a drug or alcohol problem generally preceded job losses.

Largely owing to the disproportionate number of male panhandlers, only three female panhandlers were included in the sample of 37 persons. In addition, the city's demographic composition partially explains the high proportion of African American panhandlers in the sample: The District of Columbia is predominantly populated by African Americans (65.8 percent in 1990) and poverty and homelessness are most acute among African Americans (D.C. Government, 1993). When comparing my sample of panhandlers to a study of Washington, DC, homeless individuals conducted by the National Institute on Drug Abuse (NIDA) in 1991, the NIDA sample captured a greater proportion of women, younger persons, White and Hispanic individuals, less educated persons, and employed individuals. Only a small proportion of the NIDA sample reported panhandling on a regular basis. . . .

PANHANDLING REPERTOIRES

Panhandlers overcome the nonperson treatment by initiating encounters through the use of dramaturgical techniques, routines, acts, pieces, or numbers, which I collectively call panhandling repertoires. Often enacted in a performance-like manner, repertoires capture the attention and interest of passersby by appealing to a range of emotional qualities, such as amusement, sympathy, and fear.

I have conceptualized five primary panhandling routines: the entertainer, the greeter, the servicer, the storyteller, and the aggressor, along with strategies within certain routines. The entertainer offers music or humor, the greeter provides cordiality and deference, the servicer supplies a kind of service, the storyteller presents a sad or sympathetic tale, and the aggressor deals in fear and intimidation. Generally, the entertainer and greeter attempt to produce enjoyment or good feelings, whereas the storyteller and aggressor elicit more serious or hostile moods. The servicer, who occupies a more neutral position, is focused on providing some sort of utility. Fundamentally, the moods or impressions created by the routines are largely attempts to attenuate strangeness or awaken pedestrians from their blasé condition, which then paves the way for an encounter and possible contributions.

STORYTELLER

Of all the panhandling routines, the storyteller approach most clearly conveys the dramaturgical nature of panhandling. The storyteller routine is based on using stories to evoke understanding, pity, or guilt from pedestrians. The primary message is need in virtually all cases. Stories consist of various signs, appearances, lines, or narratives that focus on shaking pedestrians from their blasé state. The storyteller routine is then accomplished by means of one or more specific subroutines: the silent storyteller, the sign storyteller, the line storyteller, and the hard luck storyteller. Here, Duane, a long-time homeless panhandler, points to the tactics or arts of capturing the sympathy of passersby with a good story:

> What makes my panhandlin' successful and any other panhandlin' successful is the emotions. Now if you were reared in a good moral background and I come up to you [he pulls his face close—about six inches away], "Excuse me sir, I'm really tired. I just moved in and I've got five kids. Me and my wife—we can't get jobs." Now when you say the word kids—"Forget me—I've got babies I'm tryin' to feed." Or sickness—"I'm dyin'" or "my wife, my mother." More than just I'm givin' them money to get something to eat. These things are tactics. They'll be touched. [Duane gets up and demonstrates by calling out onto the sidewalk.] "Ma'am, my wife only has one hour to live! I'm tryin' to raise money. Please, someone help!" [He returns to the table.] Now, did you catch some of the arts? There's an appeal to your emotions. And you got those regulars who are sittin' down, "Hey, I'm homeless. Can you spare some change sir?" And you see the same jerk on the same corner every day. And then you get into a habit, "Well here's a dollar." But the real money comes from the emotions.

In addition to narratives, stories are conveyed symbolically through down-and-out facial expressions, as Ray indicates:

> People look at me—the way I talk and you know—feel sorry for me. They know I'm homeless by the way I'm lookin'! And I give them a sad little look.

Clothing, appearances, and presentation of self may also be manipulated or used to tell the desired story. In fact, becoming a successful storyteller is contingent on developing a look that works, as Fox suggests:

> When I first started panhandling I couldn't understand why people weren't giving me money—I looked too clean. So I grew this ratty beard and figured so that's the trick of the trade. As long as I was looking presentable like I was doing a 9-to-5 job—say working as a computer specialist—I wasn't getting a dime [laughs].

Hence, storytellers may have to consciously manage their appearance more than others to foster the impression of need. On buying or receiving new or secondhand clothes and shoes, for instance, storytellers find themselves in the difficult position of negotiating those symbols that do not suggest need, as compared with other routines that rely less on a sympathetic or pitiful appearance or story. I now discuss the four storyteller subroutines in greater detail.

The silent storyteller relies primarily on symbolic communication rather than verbal exchanges to gain the attention of passersby. The silent storyteller uses attire, expressions, movements, and other props to advertise his or her situation and needs. Movements might entail limping down the street or shivering unprotected in the rain and cold. Props may include crutches, a wheelchair, or other symbols of disability; bags of belongings; or children. Generally, silent storytellers, who often sit with their cup on the sidewalk and refrain from unnecessary interactions, are the most passive of all panhandlers. Harlan, a panhandler for the past six years, explains his silent approach:

> Over the years I've looked at all the guys' styles and when I first started some of the guys used signs and some of the guys talked, some of the guys sing, some of the guys danced, some of the guys do everything—I mean I can do all that too. I don't like to ask people for money so when I first started I used to say, "Excuse me sir, can you spare some change?" Then I started to develop my own thing—something told me not to say anything. In other words, I let my cup do the talking. People used to tell me a long time ago, if anyone wants you to have anything they'll give it to you. You know, you don't have to ask. I'm not gonna ask everybody that comes up and down the street to give me a nickel [laughs]. I've tried it, I've done it. You know, I just let my cup do the talking.

Like the silent storyteller, the sign storyteller typically waits passively for a pedestrian to initiate an encounter. A sign is a tool that effectively creates interest and concern within passersby with minimal effort exerted by the panhandler. A sign, as compared with a verbal exchange, reduces the likelihood of being subjected to a negative or humiliating interaction, as explained by Walt:

> I let the sign do the talking. I don't speak unless I'm spoken to or unless to say "good morning" or something like that or "good afternoon." I just hold a sign and if people want to give me money they give me money and if they don't they walk by and nothing is ever said. There's no dirty looks, no nothin' because you can't look nasty to everyone that doesn't give you money because you'd [be] looking nasty to 90 percent of the world [chuckles].

Lou also uses a cardboard sign that reads, "Homeless and Hungry. Please Help. Thank you. God Bless All." He includes his name in the lower right corner of the sign. Lou sits on the sidewalk with his back against a building, his belongings on either side, and his sign and cup positioned in front of him. For Lou, the sign removes the uncomfortable process of verbally soliciting money and minimizes negative exchanges:

> I don't like asking people for money straight out—that's why I use my sign. And incidentally, I don't feel as bad because I'm not asking people. A lot of people are afraid of me if I ask. With the sign they have the option of walking by or not walking by.

Thus, sign storytellers view the sign as an unobtrusive, nonthreatening device but one that still conveys a message of need. Generally, signs protect panhandlers from degrading interactions by allowing agreeable donors to initiate an exchange without compulsion or intimidation.

The line storyteller is the most common among all storytellers and possibly the most ubiquitous routine in the panhandling repertoire. The line storyteller typically remains stationary and simply presents a line to pedestrians as they pass.

Almost all lines focus on money in one form or another. The most basic, unadorned money line is "Can you spare some change?" but specific higher amounts, such as a quarter or a dollar are often inserted in place of *change*. Another variation on the money line is to ask for very little money, such as "Can you help me out? Pennies will do" or an odd amount of money, such as "Can you spare 27 cents?"

Other lines may refer to "help" rather than money while specifying how the help would be put to good use. In these instances, food is a typical theme, such as "Can you help me get something to eat?" or "Can you spare some change to get a burrito?" In addition to food, transportation needs are another common theme used by line storytellers, such as "Can you spare two or three dollars for bus fare?" Lines invoking transportation may also include a destination and purpose, like returning to the shelter for the evening, buying medication at a hospital, or going to a job interview. Lines also focus on the return from unintended destinations, such as a hospital or jail, which may involve displaying evidence of a stay, like an institutionally marked identification wristband. Beyond money, food, transportation, and destinations, line storytellers focus on innumerable topics, but lines typically center on subjects that a homeless or poor person might realistically need.

The hard luck storyteller uses a more direct approach than the teller of a line story and offers an in-depth narrative focusing on difficult or unusual circumstances. On gaining the person's attention, the hard luck storyteller then presents an extended narrative to elicit sympathy and a contribution. Often, hard luck storytellers elaborate and combine themes used by line and sign storytellers. Here is an example of a hard luck story told to me one afternoon:

> I know this is a little unusual but I need you to save me. God told me to approach the man with the pink shirt. [I was wearing a pink shirt.] I almost just committed suicide by jumping off the bridge. You need to help me and my two daughters.

We're trying to get a bus ticket to Philadelphia. I've been in prison for the past five years and I've been out a month and I'm broke. When I was in prison my wife was raped and murdered. I need $15—Travelers Aid is going to pay the rest of the ticket. [I gave him a dollar from my wallet.] Can you help me get something to eat from Roy Rogers then? I'll put that dollar towards the bus but I need some money for food as well.

In sum, storytellers attempt to negate the blasé state by emphasizing the apparent disparities between themselves and pedestrians. These differences then create feelings of sympathy or pity within passersby and often lead to encounters and contributions. The storyteller's dramatized tales or physical appearance, however, may actually exacerbate the level of strangeness between panhandler and pedestrians—a result that is in contrast to more positive routines that neutralize strangeness, such as the entertainer, greeter, and servicer numbers. Aggravating strangeness through stories or appearances, though, places storytellers in the "sick role" (Parsons 1951) or a position of alienated dependency, which then paves the way for sympathy and contributions.

AGGRESSOR

The aggressor technique is premised on evoking guilt and fear in pedestrians by using either real or feigned aggression. Compared with the storyteller, the aggressor captures the attention of a pedestrian in a more pointed and dramatic fashion. Like the storyteller routine, however, the aggressor increases feelings of strangeness by highlighting disparities and differences. Primarily, the aggressor obtains food, money, and other items through intimidation, persistence, and shame.

Intimidation is accomplished through sarcastic and abusive comments, or fearful movements, like walking alongside, grabbing hold of the pedestrian, or silently using intimidating looks or stares. For instance, I encountered an unidentified panhandler using a kind of physical intimidation by standing in front of an ATM machine and then darting and lunging at pedestrians as they passed.

Finally, a woman who initially refused his overtures gave him some money after completing her transaction at the ATM machine.

Persistence entails doggedly pursuing a contribution after it has been refused or seeking more money after an initial donation. Rita, for example, displayed this kind of persistence, though politely, during our hour-long encounter. After meeting her in front of McDonald's and buying her lunch, she then requested the change from lunch, asked for additional money to help her pay rent, and then asked for any old articles of clothing. During our meeting, Rita clearly displayed need especially after describing how she had been partially disabled by a stroke. Her method of asking, however, conveyed this element of aggressiveness and persistence.

Shame is evoked by making the donor feel that his or her quarter or dollar donation is insufficient and cheap given the vast material discrepancies between donor and panhandler. For example, my first encounter with Mel incorporated a sad tale with a shameful admonishment. After meeting him on the street, he lifted his shirt with his left hand revealing a long scar extending from his sternum to his belly button. The scar was folded over like it had recently been sewn up. "See this," he said, pointing to the scar with his right hand, "I need to eat right now. It's also about time for me to take my insulin. I'm a diabetic." I responded by giving him a dollar. "Can you tell me what I can get with that?" he returned somewhat indignantly.

Any of these prior examples may have constituted a form of aggressive panhandling under the District of Columbia's Panhandling Control Act, enacted in 1993. This act prohibits panhandling in an aggressive manner, which includes "approaching, speaking to, or following a person in a manner as would cause a reasonable person to fear bodily harm" and "continuously asking, begging, or soliciting alms from a person after the person has made a negative response."

Most panhandlers are well aware of this law and the prohibitions surrounding aggressive panhandling. Consequently, panhandlers often distinguish themselves from other panhandlers who act in an aggressive fashion, as Lou suggests:

> *You have people out there with the cup going right up to people and saying, "Help me out." That's what they call aggressive panhandling. That makes a bad name for me because I use a sign. And I mean that says it all. I'm not in people's face. I'm just off on the side. That's how I do it.*

Up until now, I have described the aggressor routine as one that is consciously initiated by the panhandler. However, it also is clear that due to the many negative comments and interactions panhandlers report receiving from passersby, at least some of the time behaving aggressively is a reaction rather than a role, as suggested by Vern:

> *I have no problem people askin' for change because you can always say no. Some people have attitudes but you got to keep a good mind because I've been through it with people: "You got some spare change?" "Get the hell out of my face." You can't lose your spot over that because as soon as you get aggressive [makes police siren noise]. Don't let one dollar mess you up from a hundred dollars. They [fellow panhandlers] tell me that four or five times a night*

Hence, panhandlers generally understand the economic and legal imperatives behind remaining silent when publicly humiliated. Although easier said than done, managing one's emotions in the face of rejection or abusive comments is part of the job, as suggested by Ray:

> *I don't do aggressive panhandling. I don't harass nobody. If you have a problem with me I have nothin' to say to you—I'm a panhandler. If people have something to say I just let it go—words are words.*

Whereas the aggressor routine is often good at stirring pedestrians from their blasé condition, such action runs the risk of furthering strangeness and alienating potential donors. Particularly among panhandlers who are tempted to react aggressively to humiliating interactions with passersby or police, the job of panhandling is akin to service occupations that require emotional labor (Hochschild 1983) or publicly managing one's feelings.

SERVICER

In contrast to all other routines, the servicer provides specific services to stimulate social interaction and exchange. Using various dramaturgical techniques, the servicer transforms the exchange into something different than merely giving money to a panhandler. The servicer dispels the blasé attitude by ostensibly offering a service while lessening the sense of strangeness by converting the interaction into a kind of business transaction. In other words, giving money to a stranger in public is an unfamiliar practice, whereas being engaged by a salesperson offering a service is a familiar ritual. Regardless of whether a service is desired or not, however, providing a service dampens strangeness by establishing a sense of obligation and reciprocity between panhandler and pedestrian. . . . This rapport may be contrived in some cases and more akin to "counterfeit intimacy" (Enck and Preston 1988), that is, interaction supporting the illusion that a legitimate service is being performed when both parties know this to be false.

The servicer repertoire consists of a formal, proactive component and an informal, reactive aspect. The formal servicer consciously seeks out situations to provide a service in exchange for a tip, much like a bellhop or bathroom attendant. Roaming the streets in search of an opportunity is a particular characteristic of the formal servicer. In contrast, the informal servicer is more typically sought out by virtue of possessing something desirable, such as information. Additionally, the informal servicer can be viewed as a secondary type of routine that emerges owing to the failure of a primary one or arises when a panhandler is in the right place at the right time.

Car parking, that is, pointing out parking spaces to drivers in exchange for a tip, is the most prevalent type of formal service. This practice, however, is illegal under the Panhandling Control Act. The maximum penalties for violating the statute are a $300 fine and 90 days in jail. Despite its illegality and potential costs, parking cars remains a booming business in certain neighborhoods.

I gained a sense of the car-parking routine one evening by observing Spike, who is one of among a half-dozen car parkers that work a certain neighborhood. As we spoke alongside a busy street, Spike motioned to an approaching luxury sedan that a spot would be vacant. As the vehicle backed diagonally into the space, Spike stood behind and yelled out directions: "Turn your wheel to the left. You're OK. Come on." The passenger—a tall, professionally dressed man—took several minutes to emerge. Spike noted the car's Georgia license plate and asked the man as he opened his door what part of Georgia he was from. "I'm from Atlanta," the car owner said. "Oh yeah, I'm from Statesboro," Spike responded. The man then gave Spike some change. During this exchange, Spike's friendly demeanor also demonstrates how car parkers often integrate the greeter rap into their parking routine.

In terms of earnings, car parking appears to be the most lucrative of all the panhandling routines. Although most car parkers panhandle in addition to parking cars, it is difficult to gain an accurate understanding of the payoffs of car parking alone. In any case, regular car parkers report a minimum of $40 of total earnings on a good evening compared with the median level of $35 among all panhandlers. However, earnings reportedly can exceed $100 if a car parker encounters extra-generous drivers who give $10 or $20 at a time.

The increased earnings netted by car parkers may stem from any one of numerous factors, including drivers giving out of fear, generosity, appreciation, a desire to impress friends or dates, or inebriation. However, Mel, a long-time car parker, offers his own explanation for why car parkers earn such high relative earnings:

> It's free money out there. I don't ask for nothing. I just direct cars into parking spaces and people give me money—some change, one dollar, five dollars, ten dollars, twenty dollars. Sometimes they're so happy to give me money even though they could've paid for an actual space in a parking lot for less. If you ever get hard up for money, go over there and try it. It's almost like they're trained. They expect it when they come into the neighborhood.

In contrast to the formal servicer, such as the car parker, the informal servicer provides services to pedestrians, vendors, storeowners, and the police. These services, which result from a panhandler's propensity of being in the right place at the right time, include offering an umbrella to a soaked pedestrian, giving directions to specific street addresses, escorting unchaperoned, sometimes inebriated persons to their final destinations, or hailing a taxi for the less streetwise or infirm. These exchanges convert the panhandler into an informal service provider.

Beyond informally offering everyday information and help, panhandlers occasionally encounter more significant and valued news. Owing to their near omnipresence on the streets, panhandlers are frequently knowledgeable of many important happenings. Information absorbed by panhandlers, particularly facts and persons relating to crimes, are sought after by storeowners and police, as explained by Vance:

> We provide services to some of the storeowners. If there's a break-in or vandalism, we usually know who did it within a 24–48 hour period, whereas it might take the police several days to a week to find out the same information.

However, not all panhandlers capitalize on the opportunity to provide information to the powers that seek it. Each panhandler may have personal reasons for not offering up important information, such as fear of retaliation, a code of silence among street people, not knowing the desired facts, or not trusting the police. Hence, a witness who fails to cooperate with the police when the stakes are high may feel the stick rather than being handed a carrot, as Mel explains:

I went to jail because I wouldn't open my mouth. So they said I was in contempt of court. I was the witness of a murder and they all pointed their fingers at me man—I'm telling you Joe—"He saw it. He was there." I was just walking past. I didn't see who was blowing who away. I be everywhere. I see a whole lot of things—and that be my business. I hear the gunshot goin' off, but do you think I looked around to see what time it was? I keep with my straight steady walk—outta there—caught a cab.

In sum, the servicer captures a pedestrian's attention by creating the impression that he or she has some valuable utility to offer in exchange for payment, much like the relationship between salesclerk and patron. Although intimacy or familiarity may increase the likelihood of a pedestrian giving money to a servicer, the quality of strangeness is attenuated by the panhandler's ability to turn the interaction into a kind of neutral business exchange. Because of their presence on the streets, overcoming the nonperson treatment is occasionally a moot point as panhandlers are sometimes actively approached for information or assistance. As indicated, however, panhandlers must intermittently use other dramaturgical routines to avoid encounters (and thereby foster strangeness) with more powerful persons, such as the police, who seek to develop exchanges that may be disadvantageous or detrimental to their existence on the streets.

GREETER

The greeter offers friendliness, respect, flattery, and deference to passersby in exchange for contributions and cordial responses. This routine largely revolves around polite behavior, such as greeting pedestrians with a "hello" or "good morning," quite like department store employees who welcome customers at store entrances. Like these service occupations, the greeter number is firmly rooted in dramaturgically managing emotions. Additionally, the routine is enhanced when a panhandler becomes familiar with a panhandling locale and then remembers faces, names, and biographical facts about contributors. Hence,

a command of these more intimate details about passersby allows the greeter to personalize each greeting and devise a more comprehensive panhandling repertoire.

Sanford personifies the greeter number. During numerous observations and encounters, Sanford always offered a pleasant greeting and a distinctive, friendly smile. Sanford typically stands at the top of the Metro (subway) or along a busy side street greeting passersby during their commute or afternoon stroll. As he explains,

I greet people in the morning—say "good morning" to them—say "hello." I try to make people happy and everything. I generally get a good response—a happy greeting in a happy way especially with a smile. They always like my smile. Everybody has their own different style. My style is my smile. That's how a lot of people remember me you know.

Whereas Sanford capitalizes on his friendly smile and good nature, Lonnie, a 40-year-old native of the West Indies, appeals to pedestrians through his pleasing Caribbean accent and interactional flair:

I just talk to people because I'm gifted. I know that I'm gifted, OK. It doesn't matter what you have on as long as you are a gentle person and your mind is proper. As long as you have a pleasant personality it doesn't matter [exclaimed] what you have on—how stinky you feel or whatever. If you are nice to people, people will give.

Although some panhandlers possess specific attributes that facilitate the greeter number, such as a friendly smile or a courteous manner, a certain amount of on-the-job learning is usually involved. Wally implicitly describes his evolution from the aggressor to the greeter, which required emotion management skills:

I always say "good morning" to the people. It makes them feel real good. And most of the time I'm good at it but I was a nasty motherfucker when I came here. But now I've learned my lesson—I've

learned from my mistakes. Now that I'm so nice to the people I can get anything I want. When I was nasty and dirty I used the "f" word. Now I think things have changed. Now I just like being friendly with my cup in hand—"Hey, how are you doin'!"

Just as a panhandler's repertoire may undergo an evolution, city commuters often require a breaking-in period before moving from the non-person treatment toward being open to encounters with panhandlers new to their daily schedule. As Sanford explains, pedestrians were generally skeptical of him and his routine until he developed a presence in the neighborhood:

When I first came up here [to this neighborhood] people didn't really know me or nothin' and I didn't get no friendly greetin'. I got a couple right. But then they saw what kind of guy I was, right. There's a lot of stereotypes—guys who are homeless panhandlin'—cussin' people out, bein' disrespectful to people and everything. Or they feel a lot of them are alcoholics or crack addicts or whatever. So you know, they saw that it wasn't like that with me so as soon as they got to know me I got a better greetin'. Cause I couldn't even get a dollar when I first got here [laughs].

Once a panhandler is known in a certain area and rapport is established with a group of regular contributors, the greeter may be emboldened to mix compliments, such as "You're looking good today," with more conservative salutations, like "good morning." Alternatively, a more confidant, forward greeter may deal largely in compliments.

In sum, the greeter deploys pleasantries to maintain friendships with regular contributors or displays politeness and deference to newcomers. Given its versatility, it is a routine used by nearly all panhandlers. Although some use it as a primary part of their repertoire when dealing with large processions of anonymous crowds, storytellers and others typically use it as a secondary routine on encountering persons who give regularly.

ENTERTAINER

The entertainer provides humor and enjoyment and encompasses two more specific numbers: the joker and the musician. Both typically awaken pedestrians from their blasé state through a benign or positive offering, such as a joke or a song. Strangeness is then reduced by creating rapport or intimacy by performing a familiar tune or by developing an ongoing presence in a particular neighborhood. Generally, the entertainer routine most clearly resembles an actor staging a performance before an audience.

The joker entertains by telling funny stories, making irreverent comments, or offering bizarre appearances. Minimally, the joker's goal is to make an unsuspecting pedestrian smile or laugh. Once the pedestrian is loosened up, it is hoped that a contribution will follow.

For instance, Yancy demonstrates the joker by presenting a strange appearance in conjunction with humorous lines. One evening, I observed Yancy walking along a crowded sidewalk with the collar of his blue shirt pulled over his forehead, exposing only his face and a green leaf drooping over his left eye and cheek. Donning this clownish look and occasionally saying, "Can you help me out? I'm trying to get on the Internet," he moved about holding out an upturned baseball cap. During an interview, Yancy explained how confronting a weary afternoon commuter with a humorous scenario, like the incongruity between a homeless panhandler and the Internet, is a good antidote for the nonperson treatment:

A certain line can make their day or a little bit of laughter. If a person may have his briefcase or purse and whatnot and they may have two bags of groceries from Sutton Place Gourmet and a bottle of beaujolais nouveau. They want to go home and smoke a cigarette and watch cable and you're telling them that you're panhandling and trying to get on the Internet. And they're falling out—you know what I'm saying?

Humor sometimes emerges spontaneously, seemingly without any instrumental intentions.

For instance, while standing outside the Metro late one quiet evening, Ralph called out to a Metro system repairman riding up the escalator: "Hey, I caught my foot in the escalator last week." While walking away, the repairman sarcastically replied, "Sue Metro." Ralph then excitedly responded, "But you're the Metro man!" And then to the cadence of the Village People's song "Macho Man," Ralph sang "Metro, Metro man, I'd like to be a Metro man." No money was exchanged, but all parties within earshot appeared amused.

The musician is another variation on the entertainer routine and covers a range of musical acts from polished saxophonist to struggling crooner. Often, musicians play familiar and fun tunes to maximize appeal. Likewise, singers frequently enhance their act by interspersing humorous lines or jokes into songs.

For instance, a companion and I were abruptly accosted one evening by a man standing five-and-a-half feet tall with long sideburns and cowboy boots who introduced himself as "Blelvis"—Black Elvis. Blelvis announced that he could sing over 1,000 Elvis songs and could relate any word to an Elvis song. As we continued walking toward our destination, I mentioned the word *cat* and Blelvis began singing a tuneful Elvis melody containing the word *cat*. Eventually, Blelvis asked for $1.50 for his performance.

This encounter with Blelvis, though largely promoted as a musical/comedy act, also contained elements of the aggressor technique. After initiating the encounter, Blelvis followed close behind and offered us little choice but to engage him. When my companion produced only $0.50 in response to his solicitation, Blelvis deftly grabbed a bottle of beer from the bag I was carrying.

Because many street performers are less aggressive than Blelvis or lack genuine musical talent, contributions may be more linked to sympathy and respect than to performing abilities. For example, late one afternoon, Alvin sat on a milk crate and played a Miles Davis tune, "Solar," on his worn clarinet. Several moments after Alvin ceased his playing, which was inspired but not exceptional, a group of young men walked past, and one dropped a handful of coins into Alvin's green canvas bag. Alvin responded to the contributions by pulling the bag next to his side and reasserting his identity as a musician: "Sometimes people hear me when I'm playing good but give me money when I'm playing bad or just warming up. They might give me money now or later. But I don't want anyone to think I'm a panhandler."

Hence, some ambiguous performers, like Alvin, occasionally struggle to prevent one routine, such as the musician, from being misinterpreted for another act that may be more degrading to the self, like the storyteller.

In sum, entertainers awaken pedestrians from their blasé state through benign or positive offerings, such as a song or a joke. Strangeness is reduced by performing familiar tunes or developing a welcoming presence in a particular neighborhood. Many panhandlers devise a coherent repertoire based largely on the entertainer and greeter routines, given the affinity between these two numbers. . . .

REFERENCES

Anderson, Nels. [1923] 1961. *The Hobo. The Sociology of the Homeless Man*. Chicago: University of Chicago Press.

Council of the District of Columbia. 1993. "The Panhandling Control Act." Law No. 10–54. D.C. Register, Washington, DC.

District of Columbia Government. 1993. *Indices: A Statistical Index to District of Columbia Services*. Vol. X. Washington, DC.

Enck, Graves E., and James D. Preston. 1988. "Counterfeit Intimacy: A Dramaturgical Analysis of an Erotic Performance." *Deviant Behavior* 9:369–381.

Freund, Roger Henry. 1925. "Begging in Chicago." Master's thesis, University of Chicago, Chicago, IL.

Gilmore, Harlan W. 1940. *The Beggar*. Chapel Hill: University of North Carolina Press.

Goffman, Erving. 1959. *The Presentation of Self in Everyday Life*. New York: Anchor/Doubleday.

———. 1963. *Behavior in Public Places*. New York: Free Press.

Hochschild, Arlie. 1983. *The Managed Heart: Commercialization of Human Feelings*. Berkeley: University of California Press.

Igbinova, Patrick. 1991. "Begging in Nigeria." *International Journal of Offender Therapy and Comparative Criminology* 35(1):21–33.

Parsons, Talcott. 1951. *The Social System*. New York: Free Press.

Simmel, Georg. [1903] 1971. "Mental Life and the Metropolis." Pp. 324–339 in D. N. Levine (ed.), *On Individuality and Social Forms*. Chicago: University of Chicago Press.

Wallace, Samuel. 1965. *Skid Row as a Way of Life*. Totowa, NJ: Bedminister Press.

Williams, Brackette. 1995. "The Public I/Eye: Conducting Fieldwork to Do Homework on Homelessness and Begging in Two U.S. Cities." *Current Anthropology* 36(1):25–39.

Wright, James D. 1989. *Address Unknown: The Homeless in America*. New York: Aldine de Gruyter.

PART FOUR

DEVIANT IDENTITY

When a person asks "Who am I?" there are private answers as well as public ones. The private answers—how a person views himself or herself—form one's *personal* identity. The public answers—the image others have of the person—provide one's *social* identity. There is sometimes little consistency between the two. Con artists, for example, may studiously present social identities that diverge widely from their personal identities. Thus, they assume social identities that their personal identities, if known, would discredit. This is generally true for covert deviants. When in the company of heterosexuals, for example, a secret bisexual, gay, or lesbian may ridicule or condemn same-sex relations or pretend to be only interested in the other sex in order to achieve a heterosexual social identity. The task of harmonizing one's personal and social identities is hard enough for conventional people. For others it is even more complex.

A deviant social identity may lead to an associated personal identity when a person finds it prudent to accept a publicly attributed deviant status. This passive style of bringing personal and social identities together probably produces relatively little identity conflict. When a person identified as a deviant refuses to take on the associated personal identity, however, greater identity problems are likely to result.

Social identities may be devised by the person or by others. Spies, for example, consciously devise and enact their own deceptive social identities. Public relations people, gossips, and agents of social control, on the other hand, often cast other people into social identities that may or may not conform to their personal identities.

In a complex, urban society where many people relate to a wide assortment of new, previously unknown people, the opportunity for taking on a new social identity comes up all the time. Similarly, the chance of being cast by someone else into a new social identity is also more likely. In addition, the possibility of having multiple social identities, with different identities for different audiences, also arises. In such a society, then, people often find it difficult to develop a single, coherent social identity; they may also find it difficult to harmonize their personal and social identities. In fact, attempts to manage this problem may produce the very deceitfulness that is presumed to be characteristic of so many so-called deviants.

Because a social identity as a conforming person is usually preferred to a deviant social identity, most deviants need to practice some duplicity. The steady practice of duplicity may enable the person to avert conflict between his or her various positions and roles. On the other hand, duplicity may cause such a strain that the individual gives it up. For example, Edwin Lemert found that with regard to the systematic check forger the need to assume many legitimate social roles and social identities produces a heavy strain;[1] constant impersonations are not easy to maintain. Hence, paradoxically, discovery and arrest actually solve an identity problem for the forger. In prison, the forger at least has an authentic social identity. The strains confronting the systematic check forger typify the kinds of identity problems that many deviants must come to terms with in one way or another.

In this part of the book we examine the issue of deviant identity more specifically. First, we consider the process of acquiring a deviant identity. Then, we look at the ways a person sustains a particular identity. Finally, we consider the conditions under which a person is most likely to change a deviant identity.

ACQUIRING A DEVIANT IDENTITY

People acquire deviant identities in what is often a long drawn out interactive process. For example, a person performs a deviant act for the very first time, and then others respond to the act, usually with some form of social punishment. If the deviant act is repeated, the chances are that the social penalties will be repeated and may even increase. These social penalties, in turn, can alienate the alleged deviant; if the deviant act is repeated again, it may now be done with a degree of defiance. In time, then, a vicious circle tends to evolve. This cycle continues until others have come to expect a pattern of systematic deviant behavior from the "deviant"; in effect they have assigned that person to a deviant role. Reciprocally, the person who is now expected to perform a deviant role comes to see himself or herself in the same terms and may begin to devise ways of continuing the deviant line of action without getting caught. Thus, we see how the interactive process works: the alleged deviant *act* produces the negative *social response,* which in time elicits the deviant *social role,* which after a while culminates in the person's adopting a deviant *identity.* The initial deviance, as proposed by Edwin Lemert, is referred to as *primary deviance,* and the deviant role and personal identity that develop as a result of people's reactions to the initial deviance, *secondary deviance.*[2]

Acquiring a deviant identity follows no consistent pattern, since a reduction in either the frequency of the deviant acts or the severity of the responses of others can diminish the chances of adopting a deviant identity. Reductions in either or both may prevent assignment to a deviant role and the reciprocal deviant self-definition. Increases in either or both, on the other hand, can increase the chances of the social acquisition of a deviant identity.

Several social and cultural conditions affect the process by which people assume deviant identities. These include factors that influence the performance of deviant acts, responses of others, and the definitions of various deviant roles. For example, social responses to initial deviant acts can be extremely effective in discouraging a future career in deviance. Social responses have this effect when they call attention to the marked discrepancy between the deviant act and the kind of person most likely to perform the role, on the one hand, and the personal identity of the individual on the other hand. Thus, middle-class housewives caught in the act of shoplifting see themselves as being treated as if they were thieves. Being caught awakens them for the first time to the way their families and friends would regard their actions if they knew of them. This awakening usually is sufficient to discourage them from future thievery because they do not see themselves as "thieves."

Usually, when a person embarks on a deviant activity, such as shoplifting for the very first time, he or she does not think too much about getting caught. At the same time, the person may justify the act in one way or another. Some justifications before the fact hamper a self-definition as deviant. People who embezzle money, for example, may not define their actions as stealing. Instead, they often tell themselves that they are only borrowing the money and will repay it at the earliest opportunity. Seeing themselves as borrowers, not thieves, embezzlers can justify taking the money.

On the other hand, occasionally a person acquires a deviant personal identity *before* taking on a deviant role. For example, male adolescents who are aware of a sexual interest in men and who grow up in an environment that defines homosexuality negatively may come to regard themselves as "sick." In their case, though they have a personal and secret deviant identity, they may refrain from engaging in any form of homosexual behavior. Hence, they cannot be said to have assumed a gay role, though they do have a personal identity as such. We might speculate that the greater the stigma, the more likely it is that a deviant personal identity can exist without deviant acts or a deviant role to support it.

People may also engage in a deviant act and expect a severely negative social reaction, only to find that this reaction does not occur. Without a negative social reaction, there is much less chance of being officially labeled as deviant. As a result, although the act has occurred, there is no significant social response to thrust the person into the role of deviant and thereby evoke the reciprocal deviant identity that goes with such a role assignment.

Thus, the responses of others are crucial when it comes to acquiring a deviant identity. Frequently these others are family or friends. Or they can be agents of social control, such as police officers, teachers, social workers, doctors, or priests. Sometimes, they can be fellow deviants. For instance, a person might experiment with heroin. In an initial act of experimenting with drugs in the company of others, the novice may see himself or herself as merely satisfying a curiosity about the effects of the drug. But later on, drug-using friends may tell the novice that the way to cure withdrawal distress is to take more heroin. The novice may now be on his or her way to becoming a drug addict, along with its correlative deviant personal identity, acts, and roles. In this last instance, the responses of deviant others redefine the novice's situation for him or her.

MANAGING A DEVIANT IDENTITY

To sustain a deviant social identity and membership in a deviant group, new members have to incorporate the group's signs and symbols into their own personal styles and to behave according to deviant norms even when they may not especially want to. The novice's deviant identity may then be confirmed by the group. A deviant who fails to learn the appropriate ways probably will not be truly accepted as a member of the group.

Attempts at being a deviant can fail if the audience refuses to confirm the person's deviant social identity. Then there is no effective audience to reward the person's deviant actions or to confirm his or her self-typing. A jack-of-all-trades offender, for instance, may be considered too inept or "unprofessional" to be accepted into more skillful criminal circles. An audience—conformist or deviant—will not confirm the social identity desired by a person who has obviously miscast himself or herself, who does not look the part. And both gay men who have an undivided commitment to a gay identity and those who integrate it with other identities often see those who simply display the social identity when they come into the "big city" as lacking a "core self" or stable personal identity of any kind. These "part-time gays" are denied social confirmation and the rewards of entrance into the inner circle.

Some deviant statuses imply more than one audience, and the various audiences may demand different, sometimes contradictory, roles on the part of the individual. Deviants with multiple audiences will have problems of identity unless they can clearly understand which audience they are confronting and which role is required at a particular time. It is often the case, for example, that "front ward" patients in mental hospitals are expected by fellow inmates to act "normal," while they are expected by outsiders to act "sick" and in need of treatment.

It should be noted that deviants can often choose among deviant social identities, and this ability is often one facet of managing a deviant social identity. As a result, there can be "imposters" who sustain deviant identities as well as "imposters" who sustain conventional identities. Some epileptics, for example, try to pass as alcoholics because they see alcoholism as less stigmatized than epilepsy. As long as these pseudoalcoholics have only limited contact with genuine alcoholics, their secret is probably safe.

To sustain a deviant social identity and membership in a deviant group, then, it is necessary to act like other members of the group. Some social conditions are more conducive to this than others. For example, becoming more involved with other deviants and avoiding contact with nondeviants facilitates developing the deviant identity and maintaining the deviant role. It also makes it easier to cast off conventional traits and loyalties. Thus, a deviant identity is easier to sustain under these optimum conditions.

Persons who wish to conceal their deviant identity also confront both role and self problems. As Erving Goffman has pointed out, they can seek to control information about their identity or, if already known about, try to control the tension possible in their face-to-face contacts with others.[3] Stutterers, for instance, may solve these role problems by hiding the fact that they stutter, revealing it on their own terms, or refusing to acknowledge the fact that they are stuttering. Similarly, when control agents seek to assign a deviant identity, the person at risk of being so designated may try to neutralize the deviant identity. As Gresham Sykes and David Matza have pointed out with regard to delinquency, juveniles may deny responsibility for the behavior, any injury or harm to anyone, or the existence of any victim who really matters. In addition, the delinquent may cite an appeal to higher loyalties (e.g., that his behavior showed loyalty to his friends), or he may condemn the persons condemning him (e.g., as being hypocrites).[4] Finally, people who are regularly in contact with deviants can obtain what Goffman calls a "courtesy stigma." Interestingly, pit bull owners have this problem in the same way that the relatives of labeled deviants have. Thus, they employ similar techniques to deflect a deviant identity. With respect to veterinarians who engage in unethical practices, they mitigate shame or guilt about these behaviors by relying on excuses. The most popular ones are ones that are shared in their medical subculture.

TRANSFORMING DEVIANT IDENTITY

As we have suggested, some deviants have trouble managing a deviant identity. Fitting social positions, roles, and self-concepts together is too hard or undesirable. Thus, the deviant may face an identity crisis that can become the turning point in his or her deviant career. Nonetheless, it is not necessarily true that most deviants are unhappy and wish to renounce their deviance. Conventional stereotypes of deviants suggest as much, but the facts are otherwise. If people can successfully conceal their deviance, for example, they can continue to enjoy their deviance without "paying the price."

A profound identity crisis can be one of the conditions for transforming a deviant identity back to a more conventional one. Discovery, or recurrent feelings of remorse, can produce the crisis, as can the stress of the deviant lifestyle itself, impelling the person to contemplate making some radical changes in his or her life. In such a crisis the mechanisms that successfully sustain a deviant identity usually show signs of breaking down, and these breakdowns can in turn intensify the crisis.

As already noted, assuming and maintaining a deviant identity is not an easy matter. Renouncing one is even more difficult. Even if a deviant experiences an extreme identity crisis, that person may not succeed in transforming his or her deviant identity to a more conventional one. Three factors imperil successful transformation: lack of practice in conventional roles, continued distrust by conventional people, and pressure from fellow deviants to return to their group. Time spent in deviance is time spent away from the conventional world. Legitimate skills may fall into disuse; for example, alcoholic craftspeople who return to their craft after years of heavy drinking and unemployment may find that they cannot pick up where they left off. The ex-convicts' difficulty in finding work may exemplify the continued suspicion and disapproval that deviants arouse in the larger society. Finally, fellow deviants may press one to continue former deviations; thus, the drug addict, on release from a hospital, may be quickly surrounded by former friends who are eager to supply a free fix.

Deviants who want to return to a more conventional way of life ordinarily have the best chance of success if they join a primary group with similar intentions. The best-known example of such a primary group is Alcoholics Anonymous. The group members reward the ex-drinker for making changes toward conventionality, and they confirm his or her new social identity as a nondrinker. These conditions encourage the deviant to return to conventional life. Such social and cultural supports are not available, however, to many deviants who might want to return to conformity. At the same time, some alcoholics and drug addicts reject groups like Alcoholics Anonymous and Narcotics Anonymous. These individuals don't like the fact that these self-help groups define substance users like themselves as sick and unable to manage their lives. They prefer to regain their sobriety on their own or with the support of their family and friends.

Finally, to change deviant identities, deviants may enter into a "politics of protest" with political activism being directed at society. This method of transformation seeks to alter the labelers' attitudes and responses rather than the deviants' own attributes or behaviors. This is a form of what is called "tertiary deviance"[5] where people labeled as deviant take an active role in changing the definition of their particular characteristic or behavior as being a deviant one. Thus, people who are unconventional—in their physical characteristics, sexual patterns, choice of intoxicating substances, and so forth—will only be defined as deviants if people continue to view them in a particular way. However, to the degree that labelers' change in these conceptions, the people who are subjects of what have been traditional reactions will decrease in the extent to which they are sociologically deviant.

NOTES

1. Edwin M. Lemert, *Human Deviance, Social Problems, and Social Control,* 2nd ed. (Upper Saddle River, NJ: Prentice Hall, 1972), pp. 162–182.

2. Edwin M. Lemert, *Social Pathology: A Systematic Approach to the Theory of Sociopathic Behavior* (New York: McGraw-Hill, 1951), p. 76.

3. Erving Goffman, *Stigma: Notes on the Management of Spoiled Identity* (Upper Saddle River, NJ: Prentice Hall, 1963).

4. Gresham M. Sykes and David Matza, "Techniques of Neutralization: A Theory of Delinquency," *American Sociological Review* 22 (December, 1957), pp. 667–670.

5. John I. Kitsuse, "Coming Out All Over: Deviants and the Politics of Social Problems," *Social Problems* 28 (October, 1980), pp. 1–13.

CHAPTER 12

ACQUIRING A DEVIANT IDENTITY

Becoming Bisexual

MARTIN S. WEINBERG, COLIN J. WILLIAMS, and DOUGLAS W. PRYOR

Whenever there is a discrepancy between personal and social identity, people facing this conflict have difficulty answering the question of what kind of people they are. Those facing questions about their "sexual identity" often have this problem. Studies of gays and lesbians, for example, report that the kind of identity problems they face may well last a lifetime. If so, then persons who find themselves attracted to both sexes could face even more in the way of such problems.

Martin S. Weinberg, Colin J. Williams, and Douglas W. Pryor examine how bisexuals become aware of these problems and how they try to come to terms with their "sexual identity." In part, their sexuality is always at issue because the homosexual community may demand that they be gay or lesbian, whereas the heterosexual world may continue to assume they are heterosexual. Given persistent cross-pressures, they may experience continual uncertainty with regard to labeling their sexual identity. The authors posit a stages model of bisexual identity and characterize each of these stages.

Becoming bisexual involves the rejection of not one but two recognized categories of sexual identity: heterosexual and homosexual. Most people settle into the status of heterosexual without any struggle over the identity. There is not much concern with explaining how this occurs; that people are heterosexual is simply taken for granted. For those who find heterosexuality unfulfilling, however, developing a sexual identity is more difficult.

How is it then that some people come to identify themselves as "bisexual"? As a point of

departure we take the process through which people come to identify themselves as "homosexual." A number of models have been formulated that chart the development of a homosexual identity through a series of stages.[1] While each model involves a different number of stages, the models all share three elements. The process begins with the person in a state of identity confusion—feeling different from others [and] struggling with the acknowledgment of same-sex attractions. Then there is a period of thinking about possibly being homosexual—involving associating with self-identified homosexuals, sexual experimentation, [and] forays into the homosexual subculture. Last is the attempt to integrate one's self-concept and social identity as homosexual—acceptance of the label, disclosure about being homosexual, accul-turation to a homosexual way of life, and the development of love relationships. Not every per-son follows through each stage. Some remain locked in at a certain point. Others move back and forth between stages.

To our knowledge, no previous model of *bisexual* identity formation exists. . . . [W]e pre-sent such a model based on the following ques-tions: To what extent is there overlap with the process involved in becoming homosexual? How far is the label "bisexual" clearly recognized, understood, and available to people as an iden-tity? Does the absence of a bisexual subculture in most locales affect the information and support needed for sustaining a commitment to the iden-tity? For our subjects, then, what are the prob-lems in finding the "bisexual" label, understanding what the label means, dealing with social disapproval from two directions, and continuing to use the label once it is adopted? From our fieldwork and interviews, we found that four stages captured our respondents' most common experiences when dealing with questions of iden-tity: initial confusion, finding and applying the label, settling into the identity, and continued uncertainty.

THE STAGES

INITIAL CONFUSION

Many of the people interviewed said that they had experienced a period of considerable confusion, doubt, and struggle regarding their sexual identity before defining themselves as bisexual. This was ordinarily the first step in the process of becom-ing bisexual.

They described a number of major sources of early confusion about their sexual identity. For some, it was the experience of having strong sex-ual feelings for both sexes that was unsettling, disorienting, and sometimes frightening. Often these were sexual feelings that they said they did not know how to easily handle or resolve.

In the past, I couldn't reconcile different desires I had. I didn't understand them. I didn't know what I was. And I ended up feeling really mixed up, unsure, and kind of frightened. (F)

I thought I was gay, and yet I was having these intense fantasies and feelings about fucking women. I went through a long period of confusion. (M)

Others were confused because they thought strong sexual feelings for, or sexual behavior with, the same sex meant an end to their long-standing heterosexuality.

I was afraid of my sexual feelings for men and . . . that if I acted on them, that would negate my sex-ual feelings for women. I knew absolutely no one else who had . . . sexual feelings for both men and women, and didn't realize that was an option. (M)

When I first had sexual feelings for females, I had the sense I should give up my feelings for men. I think it would have been easier to give up men. (F)

A third source of confusion in this initial stage stemmed from attempts by respondents try-ing to categorize their feelings for, and/or behav-iors with, both sexes, yet not being able to do so. Unaware of the term "bisexual," some tried to organize their sexuality by using the readily avail-able labels of "heterosexual" or "homosexual"—but these did not seem to fit. No sense of sexual identity jelled; an aspect of themselves remained unclassifiable.

When I was young, I didn't know what I was. I knew there were people like Mom and Dad—heterosexual and married—and that there were "queens." I knew I wasn't like either one. (M)

I thought I had to be either gay or straight. That was the big lie. It was confusing. . . . That all began to change in the late '60s. It was a long and slow process. . . . (F)

Finally, others suggested they experienced a great deal of confusion because of their "homophobia"—their difficulty in facing up to the same-sex component of their sexuality. The consequence was often long-term denial. This was more common among the men than the women, but not exclusively so.

> At age seventeen, I became close to a woman who was gay. She had sexual feelings for me. I had some . . . for her but I didn't respond. Between the ages of seventeen and twenty-six I met another gay woman. She also had sexual feelings towards me. I had the same for her but I didn't act on . . . or acknowledge them. . . . I was scared. . . . I was also attracted to men at the same time. . . . I denied that I was sexually attracted to women. I was afraid that if they knew the feelings were mutual they would act on them . . . and put pressure on me. (F)

> I thought I might be able to get rid of my homosexual tendencies through religious means prayer, belief, counseling—before I came to accept it as part of me. (M)

The intensity of the confusion and the extent to which it existed in the lives of the people we met at the Bisexual Center, whatever its particular source, was summed up by two men who spoke with us informally. As paraphrased in our field notes:

> The identity issue for him was a very confusing one. At one point, he almost had a nervous breakdown, and when he finally entered college, he sought psychiatric help.

> Bill said he thinks this sort of thing happens a lot at the Bi Center. People come in "very confused" and experience some really painful stress.

FINDING AND APPLYING THE LABEL

Following this initial period of confusion, which often spanned years, was the experience of finding and applying the label. We asked the people we interviewed for specific factors or events in their lives that led them to define themselves as bisexual. There were a number of common experiences.

For many who were unfamiliar with the term bisexual, the discovery that the category in fact existed was a turning point. This happened by simply hearing the word, reading about it somewhere, or learning of a place called the Bisexual Center. The discovery provided a means of making sense of long-standing feelings for both sexes.

> Early on I thought I was just gay, because I was not aware there was another category, bisexual. I always knew I was interested in men and women. But I did not realize there was a name for these feelings and behaviors until I took Psychology 101 and read about it, heard about it there. That was in college. (F)

> The first time I heard the word, which was not until I was twenty-six, I realized that was what fit for me. What it fit was that I had sexual feelings for both men and women. Up until that point, the only way that I could define my sexual feelings was that I was either a latent homosexual or a confused heterosexual. (M)

> Going to a party at someone's house, and finding out there that the party was to benefit the Bisexual Center. I guess at that point I began to define myself as bisexual. I never knew there was such a word. If I had heard the word earlier on, for example as a kid, I might have been bisexual then. My feelings had always been bisexual. I just did not know how to define them. (F)

> Reading The Bisexual Option . . . I realized then that bisexuality really existed and that's what I was. (M)

In the case of others the turning point was their first homosexual or heterosexual experience coupled with the recognition that sex was pleasurable with both sexes. These were people who already seemed to have knowledge of the label "bisexual," yet without experiences with both men and women, could not label themselves accordingly.

> The first time I had actual intercourse, an orgasm with a woman, it led me to realize I was bisexual, because I enjoyed it as much as I did with a man, although the former occurred much later on in my sexual experiences. . . . I didn't have an orgasm with a woman until twenty-two, while with males, that had been going on since the age of thirteen. (M)

> Having homosexual fantasies and acting those out. . . . I would not identify as bi if I only had

fantasies and they were mild. But since my fantasies were intensely erotic, and I acted them out, these two things led me to believe I was really bisexual. . . . (M)

After my first involved sexual affair with a woman, I also had feelings for a man, and I knew I did not fit the category dyke. I was also dating gay-identified males. So I began looking at gay/lesbian and heterosexual labels as not fitting my situation. (F)

Still others reported not so much a specific experience as a turning point, but emphasized the recognition that their sexual feelings for both sexes were simply too strong to deny. They eventually came to the conclusion that it was unnecessary to choose between them.

I found myself with men but couldn't completely ignore my feelings for women. When involved with a man I always had a close female relationship. When one or the other didn't exist at any given time, I felt I was really lacking something. I seem to like both. (F)

The last factor that was instrumental in leading people to initially adopt the label bisexual was the encouragement and support of others. Encouragement sometimes came from a partner who already defined himself or herself as bisexual.

Encouragement from a man I was in a relationship with. We had been together two or three years at the time—he began to define as bisexual. . . . [He] encouraged me to do so as well. He engineered a couple of threesomes with another woman. Seeing one other person who had bisexuality as an identity that fit them seemed to be a real encouragement. (F)

Encouragement from a partner seemed to matter more for women. Occasionally the "encouragement" bordered on coercion as the men in their lives wanted to engage in a *ménage à trois* or group sex.

I had a male lover for a year and a half who was familiar with bisexuality and pushed me towards it. My relationship with him brought it up in me.

He wanted me to be bisexual because he wanted to be in a threesome. He was also insanely jealous of my attractions to men, and did everything in his power to suppress my opposite-sex attractions. He showed me a lot of pictures of naked women and played on my reactions. He could tell that I was aroused by pictures of women and would talk about my attractions while we were having sex. . . . He was twenty years older than me. He was very manipulative in a way. My feelings for females were there and [he was] almost forcing me to act on my attractions. . . . (F)

Encouragement also came from sex-positive organizations, primarily the Bisexual Center, but also places like San Francisco Sex Information (SFSI),[2] the Pacific Center, and the Institute for Advanced Study of Human Sexuality. . . .

At the gay pride parade I had seen the brochures for the Bisexual Center. Two years later I went to a Tuesday night meeting. I immediately felt that I belonged and that if I had to define myself that this was what I would use. (M)

Through SFSI and the Bi Center, I found a community of people . . . [who] were more comfortable for me than were the exclusive gay or heterosexual communities. . . . [It was] beneficial for myself to be . . . in a sex-positive community. I got more strokes and came to understand myself better. . . . I felt it was necessary to express my feelings for males and females without having to censor them, which is what the gay and straight communities pressured me to do. (F)

Thus our respondents became familiar with and came to the point of adopting the label bisexual in a variety of ways: through reading about it on their own, being in therapy, talking to friends, having experiences with sex partners, learning about the Bi Center, visiting SFSI or the Pacific Center, and coming to accept their sexual feelings.

SETTLING INTO THE IDENTITY

Usually it took years from the time of first sexual attractions to, or behaviors with, both sexes before people came to think of themselves as bisexual. The next stage then was one of settling into the identity, which was characterized by a more complete transition in self-labeling.

Most reported that this settling-in stage was the consequence of becoming more self-accepting. They became less concerned with the negative attitudes of others about their sexual preference.

> *I realized that the problem of bisexuality isn't mine. It's society's. They are having problems dealing with my bisexuality. So I was then thinking if they had a problem dealing with it, so should I. But I don't. (F)*

> *I learned to accept the fact that there are a lot of people out there who aren't accepting. They can be intolerant, selfish, shortsighted and so on. Finally, in growing up, I learned to say, "So what, I don't care what others think." (M)*

> *I just decided I was bi. I trusted my own sense of self. I stopped listening to others tell me what I could or couldn't be. (F)*

The increase in self-acceptance was often attributed to the continuing support from friends, counselors, and the Bi Center, [and] through reading, and just being in San Francisco.

> *Fred Klein's* The Bisexual Option *book and meeting more and more bisexual people . . . helped me feel more normal. . . . There were other human beings who felt like I did on a consistent basis. (M)*

> *I think going to the Bi Center really helped a lot. I think going to the gay baths and realizing there were a lot of men who sought the same outlet I did really helped. Talking about it with friends has been helpful and being validated by female lovers that approve of my bisexuality. Also the reaction of people who I've told, many of whom weren't even surprised. (M)*

> *The most important thing was counseling. Having the support of a bisexual counselor. Someone who acted as somewhat of a mentor. [He] validated my frustration . . . , helped me do problem solving, and guide[d] me to other supportive experiences like SFSI. Just engaging myself in a supportive social community. (M)*

The majority of the people we came to know through the interviews seemed settled in their sexual identity. We tapped this through a variety of questions. . . . Ninety percent said that they did not think they were currently in transition from being homosexual to being heterosexual or from being heterosexual to being homosexual. However, when we probed further by asking this group, "Is it possible, though, that someday you could define yourself as either lesbian/gay or heterosexual?" about 40 percent answered yes. About two-thirds of these indicated that the change could be in either direction, though almost 70 percent said that such a change was not probable.

We asked those who thought a change was possible what it might take to bring it about. The most common response referred to becoming involved in a meaningful relationship that was monogamous or very intense. Often the sex of the hypothetical partner was not specified, underscoring that the overall quality of the relationship was what really mattered.

> *Love. I think if I feel insanely in love with some person, it could possibly happen. (M)*

> *If I should meet a woman and want to get married, and if she was not open to my relating to men, I might become heterosexual again. (M)*

> *Getting involved in a long-term relationship like marriage where I wouldn't need a sexual involvement with anyone else. The sex of the . . . partner wouldn't matter. It would have to be someone who I could commit my whole life to exclusively, a lifelong relationship. (F)*

A few mentioned the breaking up of a relationship and how this would incline them to look toward the other sex.

> *Steve is one of the few men I feel completely comfortable with. If anything happened to him, I don't know if I'd want to try and build up a similar relationship with another man. I'd be more inclined to look towards women for support. (F)*

Changes in sexual behavior seemed more likely for the people we interviewed . . . than changes in how they defined themselves. We asked, "Is it possible that someday you could behave either exclusively homosexual or exclusively heterosexual?" Over 80 percent answered yes. This is over twice as many as those who saw a possible change in how they defined themselves, again showing that a wide range of behaviors can be subsumed under the same label. Of this particular group, the majority (almost 60 percent) felt that there was nothing inevitable about how they might change, indicating that it could be in either a homosexual or a heterosexual direction. Around a quarter, though, said the change would be to exclusive heterosexual behavior and 15 percent to exclusive homosexual behavior. (Twice as many women noted the homosexual direction, while many more men than women said the heterosexual direction.) Just over 40 percent responded that a change to exclusive heterosexuality or homosexuality was not very probable, about a third somewhat probable, and about a quarter very probable.

Again, we asked what it would take to bring about such a change in behavior. Once more the answers centered on achieving a long-term monogamous and involved relationship, often with no reference to a specific sex.

> For me to behave exclusively heterosexual or homosexual would require that I find a lifetime commitment from another person with a damn good argument of why I should not go to bed with somebody else. (F)

> I am a romantic. If I fell in love with a man, and our relationship was developing that way, I might become strictly homosexual. The same possibility exists with a woman. (M)

Thus "settling into the identity" must be seen in relative terms. Some of the people we interviewed did seem to accept the identity completely. When we compared our subjects' experiences with those characteristic of homosexuals, however, we were struck by the absence of closure that characterized our bisexual respondents—even those who appeared most committed to the identity. This led us to posit a final stage in the

formation of sexual identity, one that seems unique to bisexuals.

CONTINUED UNCERTAINTY

The belief that bisexuals are confused about their sexual identity is quite common. This conception has been promoted especially by those lesbians and gays who see bisexuality as being in and of itself a pathological state. From their point of view, "confusion" is literally a built-in feature of "being" bisexual. As expressed in one study:

> While appearing to encompass a wider choice of love objects . . . [the bisexual] actually becomes a product of abject confusion; his self-image is that of an overgrown young adolescent whose ability to differentiate one form of sexuality from another has never developed. He lacks above all a sense of identity. . . . [He] cannot answer the question: What am I?[3]

One evening a facilitator at a Bisexual Center rap group put this belief in a slightly different and more contemporary form:

> One of the myths about bisexuality is that you can't be bisexual without somehow being "schizoid." The lesbian and gay communities do not see being bisexual as a crystallized or complete sexual identity. The homosexual community believes there is no such thing as bisexuality. They think that bisexuals are people who are in transition [to becoming homosexual] or that they are people afraid of being stigmatized [as homosexual] by the heterosexual majority.

We addressed the issue directly in the interviews with two questions: "Do you *presently* feel confused about your bisexuality?" and "Have you *ever* felt confused . . . ?" . . . For the men, a quarter and 84 percent answered "yes," respectively. For the women, it was about a quarter and 56 percent.

When asked to provide details about this uncertainty, the primary response was that *even after having discovered and applied the label "bisexual" to themselves, and having come to the point of apparent self-acceptance, they still experienced continued intermittent periods of doubt and uncertainty regarding their sexual identity.* One reason was the lack of social validation and support that came with being a self-identified bisexual. The social reaction people received made it difficult to sustain the identity over the long haul.

While the heterosexual world was said to be completely intolerant of any degree of homosexuality, the reaction of the homosexual world mattered more. Many bisexuals referred to the persistent pressures they experienced to relabel themselves as "gay" or "lesbian" and to engage in sexual activity exclusively with the same sex. It was asserted that no one was *really* bisexual, and that calling oneself "bisexual" was a politically incorrect and inauthentic identity. Given that our respondents were living in San Francisco (which has such a large homosexual population) and that they frequently moved in and out of the homosexual world (to whom they often looked for support) this could be particularly distressing.

> *Sometimes the repeated denial the gay community directs at us. Their negation of the concept and the term bisexual has sometimes made me wonder whether I was just imagining the whole thing. (M)*

> *My involvement with the gay community. There was extreme political pressure. The lesbians said bisexuals didn't exist. To them, I had to make up my mind and identify as lesbian. . . . I was really questioning my identity, that is, about defining myself as bisexual. . . . (F)*

For the women, the invalidation carried over to their feminist identity (which most had). They sometimes felt that being with men meant they were selling out the world of women.

> *I was involved with a woman for several years. She was straight when I met her but became a lesbian. She tried to "win me back" to lesbianism. She tried to tell me that if I really loved her, I would leave Bill. I did love her, but I could not deny how I felt about him either. So she left me and that hurt. I wondered if I was selling out my woman identity and if it [being bisexual] was worth it. (F)*

A few wondered whether they were lying to themselves about their heterosexual side. One woman questioned whether her heterosexual desires were a result of "acculturation" rather than being her own choice. Another woman suggested a similar social dimension to her homosexual component:

> *There was one period when I was trying to be gay because of the political thing of being totally woman-identified rather than being with men. The Women's Culture Center in college had a women's studies minor, so I was totally immersed in women's culture. . . . (F)*

Lack of support also came from the absence of bisexual role models, no real bisexual community aside from the Bisexual Center, and nothing in the way of public recognition of bisexuality, which bred uncertainty and confusion.

> *I went through a period of dissociation, of being very alone and isolated. That was due to my bisexuality. People would ask, well, what was I? I wasn't gay and I wasn't straight. So I didn't fit. (F)*

> *I don't feel like I belong in a lot of situations because society is so polarized as heterosexual or homosexual. There are not enough bi organizations or public places to go to like bars, restaurants, clubs. . . . (F)*

For some, continuing uncertainty about their sexual identity was related to their inability to translate their sexual feelings into sexual behaviors. (Some of the women had *never* engaged in homosexual sex.)

> *Should I try to have a sexual relationship with a woman? . . . Should I just back off and keep my distance, just try to maintain a friendship? I question whether I am really bisexual because I don't know if I will ever act on my physical attractions for females. (F)*

> *I know I have strong sexual feelings towards men, but then I don't know how to get close to or be sexual with a man. I guess that what happens is I start wondering how genuine my feelings are. . . . (M)*

For the men, confusion stemmed more from the practical concerns of implementing and managing multiple partners or from questions about how to find an involved homosexual relationship and what that might mean on a social and personal level.

> I felt very confused about how I was going to manage my life in terms of developing relationships with both men and women. I still see it as a difficult lifestyle to create for myself because it involves a lot of hard work and understanding on my part and that of the men and women I'm involved with. (M)

> I've thought about trying to have an actual relationship with a man. Some of my confusion revolves around how to find a satisfactory sexual relationship. I do not particularly like gay bars. I have stopped having anonymous sex. . . . (M)

Many men and women felt doubts about their bisexual identity because of being in an exclusive sexual relationship. After being exclusively involved with an opposite-sex partner for a period of time, some of the respondents questioned the homosexual side of their sexuality. Conversely, after being exclusively involved with a partner of the same sex, other respondents called into question the heterosexual component of their sexuality.

> When I'm with a man or a woman sexually for a period of time, then I begin to wonder how attracted I really am to the other sex. (M)

> In the last relationship I had with a woman, my heterosexual feelings were very diminished. Being involved in a lesbian lifestyle put stress on my self-identification as a bisexual. It seems confusing to me because I am monogamous for the most part, monogamy determines my lifestyle to the extremes of being heterosexual or homosexual. (F)

Others made reference to a lack of sexual activity with weaker sexual feelings and affections for one sex. Such learning did not fit with the perception that bisexuals should have "balanced" desires and behaviors. The consequence was doubt about "really" being bisexual.

> On the level of sexual arousal and deep romantic feelings, I feel them much more strongly for women than for men. I've gone so far as questioning myself when this is involved. (M)

> I definitely am attracted to and it is much easier to deal with males. Also, guilt for my attraction to females has led me to wonder if I am just really toying with the idea. Is the sexual attraction I have for females something I constructed to pass time or what? (F)

Just as "settling into the identity" is a relative phenomenon, so too is "continued uncertainty," which can involve a lack of closure as part and parcel of what it means to be bisexual.

We do not wish to claim too much for our model of bisexual identity formation. There are limits to its general application. The people we interviewed were unique in that not only did *all* the respondents define themselves as bisexual (a consequence of our selection criteria), but they were also all members of a bisexual social organization in a city that perhaps more than any other in the United States could be said to provide a bisexual subculture of some sort. Bisexuals in places other than San Francisco surely must move through the early phases of the identity process with a great deal more difficulty. Many probably never reach the later stages.

Finally, the phases of the model we present are very broad and somewhat simplified. While the particular problems we detail within different phases may be restricted to the type of bisexuals in this study, the broader phases can form the basis for the development of more sophisticated models of bisexual identity formation.

Still, not all bisexuals will follow these patterns. Indeed, given the relative weakness of the bisexual subculture compared with the social pressures toward conformity exhibited in the gay subculture, there may be more varied ways of acquiring a bisexual identity. Also, the involvement of bisexuals in the heterosexual world means that various changes in heterosexual lifestyles (e.g., a decrease in open marriages or swinging) will be a continuing, and as yet unexplored, influence on bisexual identity. Finally, wider societal changes, notably the existence of AIDS, may make for changes in the overall identity process. Being used to choice and being open to both sexes can give bisexuals a range of adaptations in their sexual life that are not available to others.

NOTES

1. Vivien C. Cass, "Homosexual Identity Formation: Testing a Theoretical Model." *Journal of Sex Research* 20 (1984), pp. 143–167; Eli Coleman, "Developmental Stages of the Coming Out Process." *Journal of Homosexuality* 7 (1981/2), pp. 31–43; Barbara Ponse, *Identities in the Lesbian World: The Social Construction of Self* (Westport, CT: Greenwood Press, 1978).

2. Martin S. Weinberg, Colin J. Williams, and Douglas W. Pryor, "Telling the Facts of Life: A Study of a Sex Information Switchboard." *Journal of Contemporary Ethnography* 17 (1988), pp. 131–163.

3. Donald Webster Cory and John P. Leroy, *The Homosexual and His Society* (New York: The Citadel Press, 1963), p. 61.

Anorexia, Bulimia, and Developing a Deviant Identity

PENELOPE A. McLORG and DIANE E. TAUB

One's self-identification as deviant ordinarily follows changes in social interaction. Several questions arise about the conditions of changed interaction due to typifying a person as deviant: Which others are more apt to affix the label? Does the specific nature of the deviant activity speed the assumption of a deviant identity? Are there variations in time between application of the label and the self-acceptance of a deviant identity?

Penelope A. McLorg and Diane E. Taub offer some answers to these questions in their comparison of anorexics and bulimics. They say some young women take actions to change the way they think they look in the eyes of other people, in particular young men. Significant others, such as family or friends, see the patterned actions they take to become attractive as being deviant. However, while anorexics employ more accepted methods of weight control (dieting), bulimics use less accepted methods (such as binging and purging). These different methods lead to variations in both the application of the deviant labels by family and friends and the acceptance of those labels by the young women who experience these eating disorders. Given these different circumstances, bulimics are more apt to accept their deviant identity and to conceal their binging and purging from others. Thus, they are more likely to look at themselves from the point of view of the others who have become aware of their behavior. Whereas bulimics show consistency between their self-image and their social role, anorexics take much longer to integrate a deviant self-conception with their social role.

Current appearance norms stipulate thinness for women and muscularity for men; these expectations, like any norms, entail rewards for compliance and negative sanctions for violations. Fear of being overweight—of being visually deviant—has led to a striving for thinness, especially among women. In the extreme, this avoidance of overweight engenders eating disorders, which themselves constitute deviance. Anorexia nervosa, or purposeful starvation, embodies visual as well as behavioral

Reprinted from "Anorexia Nervosa and Bulimia: The Development of Deviant Identities," *Deviant Behavior*, Vol. 8 (1987), pp. 177–189, by permission of Taylor & Francis, Inc. All rights reserved. Copyright © 1987 by Taylor & Francis, Inc.

deviation; bulimia, binge-eating followed by vomiting and/or laxative abuse, is primarily behaviorally deviant.

Besides a fear of fatness, anorexics and bulimics exhibit distorted body images. In anorexia nervosa, a 20–25 percent loss of initial body weight occurs, resulting from self-starvation alone or in combination with excessive exercising, occasional binge-eating, vomiting, and/or laxative abuse. Bulimia denotes cyclical (daily, weekly, for example) binge-eating followed by vomiting or laxative abuse; weight is normal or close to normal (Humphries et al., 1982). Common physical manifestations of these eating disorders include menstrual cessation or irregularities and electrolyte imbalances; among behavioral traits are depression, obsessions/compulsions, and anxiety (Russell, 1979; Thompson and Schwartz, 1982).

Increasingly prevalent in the past two decades, anorexia nervosa and bulimia have emerged as major health and social problems. Termed an epidemic on college campuses (Brody, as quoted in Schur, 1984: 76), bulimia affects 13% of college students (Halmi et al., 1981). Less prevalent, anorexia nervosa was diagnosed in 0.6% of students utilizing a university health center (Stangler and Printz, 1980). However, the overall mortality rate of anorexia nervosa is 6% (Schwartz and Thompson, 1981) to 20% (Humphries et al., 1982); bulimia appears to be less life-threatening (Russell, 1979).

Particularly affecting certain demographic groups, eating disorders are most prevalent among young, white, affluent (upper-middle to upper class) women in modern, industrialized countries (Crisp, 1977; Willi and Grossmann, 1983). Combining all of these risk factors (female sex, youth, high socioeconomic status, and residence in an industrialized country), prevalence of anorexia nervosa in upper class English girls' schools is reported at 1 in 100 (Crisp et al., 1976). The age of onset for anorexia nervosa is bimodal at 14.5 and 18 years (Humphries et al., 1982); the most frequent age of onset for bulimia is 18 (Russell, 1979).

Eating disorders have primarily been studied from psychological and medical perspectives.[1] Theories of etiology have generally fallen into three categories: the ego psychological (involving an impaired child-maternal environment); the family systems (implicating enmeshed rigid families); and the endocrinological (involving a precipitating hormonal defect). Although relatively ignored in previous studies, the sociocultural components of anorexia nervosa and bulimia (the slimness norm and its agents of reinforcement, such as role models) have been postulated as accounting for the recent, dramatic increases in these disorders (Schwartz et al., 1982; Boskind-White, 1985).[2]

Medical and psychological approaches to anorexia nervosa and bulimia obscure the social facets of the disorders and neglect the individuals' own definitions of their situations. Among the social processes involved in the development of an eating disorder is the sequence of conforming behavior, primary deviance, and secondary deviance. Societal reaction is the critical mediator affecting the movement through the deviant career (Becker, 1973). Within a framework of labeling theory, this study focuses on the emergence of anorexia and bulimia identities, as well as on the consequences of being career deviants.

METHOD . . .

Most research on eating disorders has utilized clinical subjects or non-clinical respondents completing questionnaires. Such studies can be criticized for simply counting and describing behaviors and/or neglecting the social construction of the disorders. Moreover, the work of clinicians is often limited by therapeutic orientation. Previous research may also have included individuals who were not in therapy on their own volition and who resisted admitting that they had an eating disorder.

Past studies thus disregard the intersubjective meanings respondents attach to their behavior and emphasize researchers' criteria for definition as anorexia or bulimia. In order to supplement these sampling and procedural designs, the present study utilizes participant observation of a group of self-defined anorexics and bulimics.[3] As the individuals had acknowledged their eating disorders, frank discussion and disclosure were facilitated.

Data are derived from a self-help group, BANISH, Bulimics/Anorexics In Self-Help, which met at a university in an urban center of the mid-South. . . .

The group's weekly two-hour meetings were observed for two years. During the course of this study, thirty individuals attended at least one of the meetings. . . .

In addition to field notes from group meetings, records of other encounters with all members were maintained. Participants visited the office of one of the researchers (D.E.T.), called both researchers by phone, and invited them to their homes or out for a cup of coffee. Such interaction facilitated genuine communication and mutual trust. Even among the fifteen individuals who did not attend the meetings regularly, contact was maintained with ten members on a monthly basis.

Supplementing field notes were informal interviews with fifteen group members, lasting from two to four hours. Because they appeared to represent more extensive experience with eating disorders, these interviewees were chosen to amplify their comments about the labeling process, made during group meetings. Conducted near the end of the two-year observation period, the interviews focused on what the respondents thought antedated and maintained their eating disorders. In addition, participants described others' reactions to their behaviors as well as their own interpretations of these reactions. To protect the confidentiality of individuals quoted in the study, pseudonyms are employed.

DESCRIPTION OF MEMBERS

The demographic composite of the sample typifies what has been found in other studies (Fox and James, 1976; Crisp, 1977; Herzog, 1982; Schlesier-Stropp, 1984). Group members' ages ranged from nineteen to thirty-six, with the modal age being twenty-one. The respondents were white, and all but one were female. The sole male and three of the females were anorexic; the remaining females were bulimic.[4]

Primarily composed of college students, the group included four non-students, three of whom had college degrees. Nearly all members derived from upper-middle or lower-upper class households. Eighteen students and two non-students were never-marrieds and uninvolved in serious relationships; two non-students were married (one with two children); two students were divorced (one with two children); and six students were involved in serious relationships. The duration of eating disorders ranged from three to fifteen years.

CONFORMING BEHAVIOR

In the backgrounds of most anorexics and bulimics, dieting figures prominently, beginning in the teen years (Crisp, 1977; Johnson et al., 1982; Lacey et al., 1986). As dieters, these individuals are conformist in their adherence to the cultural norms emphasizing thinness (Garner et al., 1980; Schwartz et al., 1982). In our society, slim bodies are regarded as the most worthy and attractive; overweight is viewed as physically and morally unhealthy—"obscene," "lazy," "slothful," and "gluttonous" (Dejong, 1980; Ritenbaugh, 1982; Schwartz et al., 1982).

Among the agents of socialization promoting the slimness norm is advertising. Female models in newspaper, magazine, and television advertisements are uniformly slender. In addition, product names and slogans exploit the thin orientation; examples include "Ultra Slim Lipstick," "Miller Lite," and "Virginia Slims." While retaining pressures toward thinness, an Ayds commercial attempts a compromise for those wanting to savor food: "Ayds . . . so you can taste, chew, and enjoy, while you lose weight." Appealing particularly to women, a nationwide fast-food restaurant chain offers low-calorie selections, so individuals can have a "license to eat." In the latter two examples, the notion of enjoying food is combined with the message to be slim. Food and restaurant advertisements overall convey the pleasures of eating, whereas advertisements for other products, such as fashions and diet aids, reinforce the idea that fatness is undesirable.

Emphasis on being slim affects everyone in our culture, but it influences women especially because of society's traditional emphasis on women's appearance. The slimness norm and its concomitant narrow beauty standards exacerbate the objectification of women (Schur, 1984). Women view themselves as visual entities and recognize that conforming to appearance expectations and "becoming attractive object[s] [are] role obligation[s]" (Laws, as quoted in Schur, 1984: 66). Demonstrating the beauty motivation behind dieting, a recent Nielsen survey indicated that of the 56 percent of all women aged 24 to 54 who dieted during the previous year, 76 percent did so for cosmetic, rather than health, reasons (Schwartz et al., 1982). For most female group members, dieting was viewed as a means of gaining attractiveness and appeal to the opposite sex. The male respondent, as well, indicated that "when I was fat, girls didn't look at me, but when I got thinner, I was suddenly popular."

In addition to responding to the specter of obesity, individuals who develop anorexia nervosa and bulimia are conformist in their strong commitment to other conventional norms and goals. They consistently excel at school and work (Russell, 1979; Bruch, 1981; Humphries et al., 1982), maintaining high aspirations in both areas (Theander, 1970; Lacey et al., 1986). Group members generally completed college-preparatory courses in high school, aware from an early age that they would strive for a college degree. Also, in college as well as high school, respondents joined honor societies and academic clubs.

Moreover, pre-anorexics and -bulimics display notable conventionality as "model children" (Humphries et al., 1982: 199), "the pride and joy" of their parents (Bruch, 1981: 215), accommodating themselves to the wishes of others. Parents of these individuals emphasize conformity and

value achievement (Bruch, 1981). Respondents felt that perfect or near-perfect grades were expected of them; however, good grades were not rewarded by parents, because "A's" were common for these children. In addition, their parents suppressed conflicts, to preserve the image of the "all-American family" (Humphries et al., 1982). Group members reported that they seldom, if ever, heard their parents argue or raise their voices.

Also conformist in their affective ties, individuals who develop anorexia nervosa and bulimia are strongly, even excessively, attached to their parents. Respondents' families appeared close-knit, demonstrating palpable emotional ties. Several group members, for example, reported habitually calling home at prescribed times, whether or not they had any news. Such families have been termed "enmeshed" and "overprotective," displaying intense interaction and concern for members' welfare (Minuchin et al., 1978; Selvini-Palazzoli, 1978). These qualities could be viewed as marked conformity to the norm of familial closeness.[5]

Another element of notable conformity in the family milieu of pre-anorexics and -bulimics concerns eating, body weight/shape, and exercising (Kalucy et al., 1977; Humphries et al., 1982). Respondents reported their fathers' preoccupation with exercising and their mothers' engrossment in food preparation. When group members dieted and lost weight, they received an extraordinary amount of approval. Among the family, body size became a matter of "friendly rival." One bulimic informant recalled that she, her mother, and her coed sister all strived to wear a size 5, regardless of their heights and body frames. Subsequent to this study, the researchers learned that both the mother and sister had become bulimic.

As pre-anorexics and -bulimics, group members thus exhibited marked conformity to cultural norms of thinness, achievement, compliance, and parental attachment. Their families reinforced their conformity by adherence to norms of family closeness and weight/body shape consciousness.

PRIMARY DEVIANCE

Even with familial encouragement, respondents, like nearly all dieters (Chernin, 1981), failed to maintain their lowered weights. Many cited their lack of willpower to eat only restricted foods. For the emerging anorexics and bulimics, extremes such as purposeful starvation or binging accompanied by vomiting and/or laxative abuse appeared as "obvious solutions" to the problem of retaining weight loss. Associated with these behaviors was a regained feeling of control in lives that had been disrupted by a major crisis. Group members' extreme weight-loss efforts operated as coping mechanisms for entering college, leaving home, or feeling rejected by the opposite sex.

The primary inducement for both eating adaptations was the drive for slimness: with slimness came more self-respect and a feeling of superiority over "unsuccessful dieters." Brian, for example, experienced a "power trip" upon consistent weight loss through starvation. Binges allowed the purging respondents to cope with stress through eating while maintaining a slim appearance. As former strict dieters, Teresa and Jennifer used binging/purging as an alternative to the constant self-denial of starvation. Acknowledging their parents' desires for them to be slim, most respondents still felt it was a conscious choice on their part to continue extreme weight-loss efforts. Being thin became the "most important thing" in their lives—their "greatest ambition."

In explaining the development of an anorexic or bulimic identity, Lemert's (1951; 1967) concept of primary deviance is salient. Primary deviance refers to a transitory period of norm violations which do not affect an individual's self-concept or performance of social roles. Although respondents were exhibiting anorexic or bulimic behavior, they did not consider themselves to be anorexic or bulimic.

At first, anorexics' significant others complimented their weight loss, expounding on their new "sleekness" and "good looks." Branch and Eurman (1980: 631) also found anorexics' families and friends describing them as "well-groomed," "neat," "fashionable," and "victorious." Not until the respondents approached emaciation did some parents or friends become concerned and withdraw their praise. Significant others also became increasingly aware of the anorexics' compulsive exercising, preoccupation with food preparation (but not consumption), and ritualistic eating patterns (such as cutting food into minute pieces and eating only certain foods at prescribed times).

For bulimics, friends or family members began to question how the respondents could eat such large amounts of food (often in excess of 10,000 calories a day) and stay slim. Significant others also noticed calluses across the bulimics' hands, which were caused by repeated inducement of vomiting. Several bulimics were "caught in the act," bent over commodes. Generally, friends and family required substantial evidence before believing that the respondents' binging or purging was no longer sporadic.

SECONDARY DEVIANCE

Heightened awareness of group members' eating behavior ultimately led others to label the respondents "anorexic" or "bulimic." Respondents differed in their histories of being labeled and accepting the labels. Generally first termed anorexic by friends, family, or medical personnel, the anorexics initially vigorously denied the label. They felt they were not "anorexic enough," not skinny enough; Robin did not regard herself as having the "skeletal" appearance she associated with anorexia nervosa. These group members found it difficult to differentiate between socially approved modes of weight loss—eating less and exercising more—and the extremes of those behaviors. In fact, many of their activities—cheerleading, modeling, gymnastics, aerobics—reinforced their pursuit of thinness. Like other anorexics, Chris felt she was being "ultrahealthy," with "total control" over her body.

For several respondents, admitting they were anorexic followed the realization that their lives were disrupted by their eating disorder. Anorexics' inflexible eating patterns unsettled family meals and holiday gatherings. Their regimented lifestyle of compulsively scheduled activities—exercising, school, and meals—precluded any spontaneous social interactions. Realization of their adverse behaviors preceded the anorexics' acknowledgment of their subnormal body weight and size.

Contrasting with anorexics, the binge/purgers, when confronted, more readily admitted that they were bulimic and that their means of weight loss was "abnormal." Teresa, for example, knew "very well" that her bulimic behavior was "wrong and unhealthy," although "worth the physical risks." While the bulimics initially maintained that their purging was only a temporary weight-loss method, they eventually realized that their disorder represented a "loss of control." Although these respondents regretted the self-indulgence, "shame," and "wasted time," they acknowledged their growing dependence on binging/purging for weight management and stress regulation.

The application of anorexic or bulimic labels precipitated secondary deviance, wherein group members internalized these identities. Secondary deviance refers to norm violations which are a response to society's labeling: "secondary deviation . . . becomes a means of social defense, attack or adaptation to the overt and covert problems created by the societal reaction to primary deviance" (Lemert, 1967: 17). In contrast to primary deviance, secondary deviance is generally prolonged, alters the individual's self-concept, and affects the performance of his/her social roles.

As secondary deviants, respondents felt that their disorders "gave a purpose" to their lives. Nicole resisted attaining a normal weight because it was not "her"—she accepted her anorexic weight as her "true" weight. For Teresa, bulimia became a "companion"; and Julie felt "every aspect of her life," including time management and social activities, was affected by her bulimia. Group members' eating disorders became the salient element of their self-concepts, so that they related to familiar people and new acquaintances as anorexics or bulimics.

For example, respondents regularly compared their body shapes and sizes with those of others. They also became sensitized to comments about their appearance, whether or not the remarks were made by someone aware of their eating disorder.

With their behavior increasingly attuned to their eating disorders, group members exhibited role engulfment (Schur, 1971). Through accepting anorexic or bulimic identities, individuals centered activities around their deviant role, downgrading other social roles. Their obligations as students, family members, and friends became subordinate to their eating and exercising rituals. Socializing, for example, was gradually curtailed because it interfered with compulsive exercising, binging, or purging.

Labeled anorexic or bulimic, respondents were ascribed a new status with a different set of role expectations. Regardless of other positions the individuals occupied, their deviant status, or master status (Hughes, 1958; Becker, 1973), was identified before all others. Among group members, Nicole, who was known as the "school's brain," became known as the "school's anorexic." No longer viewed as conforming model individuals, some respondents were termed "starving waifs" or "pigs."

Because of their identities as deviants, anorexics' and bulimics' interactions with others were altered. Group members' eating habits were scrutinized by friends and family and used as a "catch-all" for everything negative that happened to them. Respondents felt self-conscious around individuals who knew of their disorders; for example, Robin imagined people "watching and whispering" behind her. In addition, group members believed others expected them to "act" anorexic or bulimic. Friends of some anorexic group members never offered them food or drink, assuming continued disinterest on the respondents' part. While being hospitalized, Denise felt she had to prove to others she was not still vomiting, by keeping her bathroom door open. Other bulimics, who lived in dormitories, were hesitant to use the restroom for normal purposes lest several friends be huddling at the door, listening for vomiting. In general, individuals interacted with the respondents largely on the basis of their eating disorder; in doing so, they reinforced anorexic and bulimic behaviors.

Bulimic respondents, whose weight-loss behavior was not generally detectable from their appearance, tried earnestly to hide their bulimia by binging and purging in secret. Their main purpose in concealment was to avoid the negative consequences of being known as a bulimic. For these individuals, bulimia connoted a "cop-out": like "weak anorexics," bulimics pursued thinness but yielded to urges to eat. Respondents felt other people regarded bulimia as "gross" and had little sympathy for the sufferer. To avoid these stigmas or "spoiled identities," the bulimics shrouded their behaviors.

Distinguishing types of stigma, Goffman (1963) describes discredited (visible) stigmas and discreditable (invisible) stigmas. Bulimics, whose weight was approximately normal or even slightly elevated, harbored discreditable stigmas. Anorexics, on the other hand, suffered both discreditable and discredited stigmas—the latter due to their emaciated appearance. Certain anorexics were more reconciled than the bulimics to their stigmas: for Brian, the "stigma of anorexia was better than the stigma of being fat." Common to the stigmatized individuals was an inability to interact spontaneously with others. Respondents were constantly on guard against topics of eating and body size.

Both anorexics and bulimics were held responsible by others for their behavior and presumed able to "get out of it if they tried." Many anorexics reported being told to "just eat more," while bulimics were enjoined to simply "stop eating so much." Such appeals were made without regard for the complexities of the problem. Ostracized by certain friends and family members, anorexics and bulimics felt increasingly isolated. For respondents, the self-help group presented a non-threatening forum for discussing their disorders. Here, they found mutual understanding, empathy, and support. Many participants viewed BANISH as a haven from stigmatization by "others."

Group members, as secondary deviants, thus endured negative consequences, such as stigmatization, from being labeled. As they internalized the labels anorexic or bulimic, individuals' self-concepts were significantly influenced. When others interacted with the respondents on the basis of their eating disorders, anorexic or bulimic identities were encouraged. Moreover, group members' efforts to counteract the deviant labels were thwarted by their master statuses.

DISCUSSION

Previous research on eating disorders has dwelt almost exclusively on medical and psychological facets. Although necessary for a comprehensive understanding of anorexia nervosa and bulimia, these approaches neglect the social processes involved. The phenomena of eating disorders transcend concrete disease entities and clinical diagnoses. Multifaceted and complex, anorexia nervosa and bulimia require a holistic research design, in which sociological insights be included. . . .

With only five to ten percent of reported cases appearing in males (Crisp, 1977; Stangler and Printz, 1980), eating disorders are primarily a women's aberrance. The deviance of anorexia nervosa and bulimia is rooted in the visual objectification of women and attendant slimness norm. Indeed, purposeful starvation and binging/purging reinforce the notion that "a society gets the deviance it deserves" (Schur, 1979: 71). As . . . noted (Schur, 1984), the sociology of deviance has generally bypassed systematic studies of women's norm violations. Like male deviants, females endure label applications, internalizations, and fulfillments.

The social processes involved in developing anorexic or bulimic identities comprise the sequence of conforming behavior, primary deviance, and secondary deviance. With a background of exceptional adherence to conventional norms, especially the striving for thinness, respondents subsequently exhibit the primary deviance of starving or binging/purging. Societal reaction to these behaviors leads to secondary deviance, wherein respondents' self-concepts and master statuses become anorexic or bulimic. Within this framework of labeling theory, the persistence of eating disorders, as well as the effects of stigmatization, is elucidated.

Although during the course of this research some respondents alleviated their symptoms through psychiatric help or hospital treatment programs, no one was labeled "cured." An anorexic is considered recovered when weight is normal for two years; a bulimic is termed recovered after being symptom-free for one and one-half years (American Anorexia/Bulimia Association Newsletter, 1985). Thus deviance disavowal (Schur, 1971), or efforts after normalization to counteract the deviant labels, remains a topic for future exploration.

NOTES

1. Although instructive, an integration of the medical, psychological, and sociocultural perspectives on eating disorders is beyond the scope of this paper.

2. Exceptions to the neglect of sociocultural factors are discussions of sex-role socialization in the development of eating disorders. Anorexics' girlish appearance has been interpreted as a rejection of femininity and womanhood (Orbach, 1979; Bruch, 1981; Orbach, 1985). In contrast, bulimics have been characterized as over-conforming to traditional female sex roles (Boskind-Lodahl, 1976).

3. Although a group experience for self-defined bulimics has been reported (Boskind-Lodahl, 1976), the researcher, from the outset, focused on Gestalt and behaviorist techniques within a feminist orientation.

4. One explanation for fewer anorexics than bulimics in the sample is that, in the general population, anorexics are outnumbered by bulimics at 8 or 10 to 1 (Lawson, as reprinted in American Anorexia/Bulimia Association Newsletter, 1985: 1). The proportion of bulimics to anorexics in the sample is 6.5 to 1. In addition, compared to bulimics, anorexics may be less likely to attend a self-help group as they have a greater tendency to deny the existence of an eating problem (Humphries et al., 1982). However, the four anorexics in the present study were among the members who attended the meetings most often.

5. Interactions in the families of anorexics and bulimics might seem deviant in being inordinately close. However, in the larger societal context, the family members epitomize the norms of family cohesiveness. Perhaps unusual in their occurrence, these families are still within the realm of conformity. Humphries and colleagues (1982: 202) refer to the "highly enmeshed and protective" family as part of the "idealized family myth."

REFERENCES

American Anorexia/Bulimia Association Newsletter. 1985. 8(3).

Becker, Howard S. 1973. *Outsiders*. New York: Free Press.

Boskind-Lodahl, Marlene. 1976. "Cinderella's Stepsisters: A Feminist Perspective on Anorexia Nervosa and Bulimia." *Signs, Journal of Women in Culture and Society* 2:342–356.

Boskind-White, Marlene. 1985. "Bulimarexia: A Sociocultural Perspective." Pp. 113–126 in S. W. Emmett (ed.), *Theory and Treatment of Anorexia Nervosa and Bulimia: Biomedical, Sociocultural, and Psychological Perspectives*. New York: Brunner/Mazel.

Branch, C. H. Hardin, and Linda J. Eurman. 1980. "Social Attitudes toward Patients with Anorexia Nervosa." *American Journal of Psychiatry* 137:631–632.

Bruch, Hilde. 1981. "Developmental Considerations of Anorexia Nervosa and Obesity." *Canadian Journal of Psychiatry* 26:212–216.

Chernin, Kim. 1981. *The Obsession: Reflections on the Tyranny of Slenderness*. New York: Harper and Row.

Crisp, A. H. 1977. "The Prevalence of Anorexia Nervosa and Some of Its Associations in the General Population." *Advances in Psychosomatic Medicine* 9:38–47.

Crisp, A. H., R. L. Palmer, and R. S. Kalucy. 1976. "How Common Is Anorexia Nervosa? A Prevalence Study." *British Journal of Psychiatry* 128:549–554.

Dejong, William. 1980. "The Stigma of Obesity: The Consequences of Naive Assumptions Concerning the Causes of Physical Deviance." *Journal of Health and Social Behavior* 21:75–87.

Fox, K. C., and N. McI. James. 1976. "Anorexia Nervosa: A Study of 44 Strictly Defined Cases." *New Zealand Medical Journal* 84:309–312.

Garner, David M., Paul E. Garfinkel, Donald Schwartz, and Michael Thompson. 1980. "Cultural Expectations of Thinness in Women." *Psychological Reports* 47:483–491.

Goffman, Erving. 1963. *Stigma*. Upper Saddle River, NJ: Prentice Hall.

Halmi, Katherine A., James R. Falk, and Estelle Schwartz. 1981. "Binge-Eating and Vomiting: A Survey of a College Population." *Psychological Medicine* 11:697–706.

Herzog, David B. 1982. "Bulimia: The Secretive Syndrome." *Psychosomatics* 23:481–483.

Hughes, Everett C. 1958. *Men and Their Work*. New York: Free Press.

Humphries, Laurie L., Sylvia Wrobel, and H. Thomas Wiegert. 1982. "Anorexia Nervosa." *American Family Physician* 26:199–204.

Johnson, Craig L., Marilyn K. Stuckey, Linda D. Lewis, and Donald M. Schwartz. 1982. "Bulimia. A Descriptive Survey of 316 Cases." *International Journal of Eating Disorders* 2(1):3–16.

Kalucy, R. S., A. H. Crisp, and Britta Harding. 1977. "A Study of 56 Families with Anorexia Nervosa." *British Journal of Medical Psychology* 50:381–395.

Lacey, Hubert J., Sian Coker, and S. A. Birtchnell. 1986. "Bulimia: Factors Associated with Its Etiology and Maintenance." *International Journal of Eating Disorders* 5:475–487.

Lemert, Edwin M. 1951. *Social Pathology*. New York: McGraw-Hill.

———. 1967. *Human Deviance, Social Problems and Social Control*. Upper Saddle River, NJ: Prentice Hall.

Minuchin, Salvador, Bernice L. Rosman, and Lester Baker. 1978. *Psychosomatic Families: Anorexia Nervosa in Context*. Cambridge, MA: Harvard University Press.

Orbach, Susie. 1979. *Fat Is a Feminist Issue*. New York: Berkeley.

———. 1985. "Visibility/Invisibility: Social Considerations in Anorexia Nervosa—A Feminist Perspective." Pp. 127–138 in S. W. Emmett (ed.), *Theory and Treatment of Anorexia Nervosa and Bulimia: Biomedical, Sociocultural, and Psychological Perspectives*. New York: Brunner/Mazel.

Ritenbaugh, Cheryl. 1982. "Obesity as a Culture-Bound Syndrome." *Culture, Medicine and Psychiatry* 6:347–361.

Russell, Gerald. 1979. "Bulimia Nervosa: An Ominous Variant of Anorexia Nervosa." *Psychological Medicine* 9:429–448.

Schlesier-Stropp, Barbara. 1984. "Bulimia: A Review of the Literature." *Psychological Bulletin* 95:247–257.

Schur, Edwin M. 1971. *Labeling Deviant Behavior*. New York: Harper and Row.

———. 1979. *Interpreting Deviance: A Sociological Introduction*. New York: Harper and Row.

———. 1984. *Labeling Women Deviant: Gender, Stigma, and Social Control*. New York: Random House.

Schwartz, Donald M., and Michael G. Thompson. 1981. "Do Anorectics Get Well? Current Research and Future Needs." *American Journal of Psychiatry* 138:319–323.

Schwartz, Donald M., Michael G. Thompson, and Craig L. Johnson. 1982. "Anorexia Nervosa and Bulimia: The Socio-cultural Context." *International Journal of Eating Disorders* 1(3):20–36.

Selvini-Palazzoli, Mara. 1978. *Self-Starvation: From Individual to Family Therapy in the Treatment of Anorexia Nervosa*. New York: Jason Aronson.

Stangler, Ronnie S., and Adolph M. Printz. 1980. "DSM-III: Psychiatric Diagnosis in a University Population." *American Journal of Psychiatry* 137:937–940.

Theander, Sten. 1970. "Anorexia Nervosa." *Acta Psychiatrica Scandinavica Supplement* 214:24–31.

Thompson, Michael G., and Donald M. Schwartz. 1982. "Life Adjustment of Women with Anorexia Nervosa and Anorexic-Like Behavior." *International Journal of Eating Disorders* 1(2):47–60.

Willi, Jurg, and Samuel Grossmann. 1983. "Epidemiology of Anorexia Nervosa in a Defined Region of Switzerland." *American Journal of Psychiatry* 140:564–567.

Tattoos without Stigma

KATHERINE IRWIN

Marks on the body are significant symbols. Their significance derives from who made the marks and the meaning people attach to the marks. In earlier times, governments branded people who committed crimes, thereby permanently labeling them as criminals. Marks that people have acquired through injury or illness often increase their chances of being assigned the master status of a disabled person. If some self-induced marks can engender a positive societal reaction, other varieties, such as tattooing, can engender negative societal reactions from conventional others. Because tattoos can be significant stigma symbols, people who decide to get a tattoo may experience the kinds of problems other social deviants face.

There has been a major increase in the number of middle-class people with tattoos. Katherine Irwin's study shows how many such middle-class people avoid the acquisition of a deviant identity. For many, getting a tattoo is said to mark their commitment to the conventional social world rather than to a deviant social world.

Once considered an artifact of criminals, gangs, sailors, and social outcasts, tattoos careened into the American mainstream in the 1990s. If the increased numbers of college students, young urbanites, and business professionals wearing tattoos have not adequately articulated the idea that tattoos have reached mainstream status, the media have driven the message home. Print journalists have claimed that tattoos are "edging into the mainstream" (*Milwaukee Journal Sentinel*, November 29, 1998, p. 1), that they are so "thoroughly middle class" that the only rebellious thing about them "may be the decision not to get one" (*Providence Journal-Bulletin*, July 15, 1999, p. 6B), and that "7 million adults now have tattoos" (Telvin 1999:1A). Celebrities such as Cher and Johnny Depp who openly sport tattoos have reinforced the message that tattoos are moving "from being a symbol of the outcast to that of the rock star, model, and postmodern youth" (DeMello 1995:49).

Periodically throughout American history, tattoos have undergone dramatic re-definition. In the late 1800s elite social crowds adopted small, easily concealed tattoos and made them a fad among European aristocracy and the American upper class (Parry 1933; Sanders 1989; Vale and Juno 1989). After the turn of the century, especially after World War I (Steward 1990), tattoos became associated primarily with deviant characters. Rubin (1988) has argued that since the 1960s the practice, structure, and patronage of tattooing experienced a "renaissance" that included an influx of fine artists to the profession of tattooing. By the 1980s and 1990s the renaissance in the tattoo profession was met with a dramatic moral passage (Gusfield 1967) as tattoos entered popular culture.[1]

In this article I look at the phenomenon of becoming tattooed from the perspective of individuals contemplating their first tattoos in the late 1990s. Although media images in the 1990s often defined tattoos as hip and trendy, many individuals suggested that older definitions associating tattoos with dangerous outcasts continued to shroud

Reprinted from Katherine Irwin, "Legitimating the First Tattoo: Moral Passage through Informal Interaction," *Symbolic Interaction*, Vol. 24, No. 1: 49–73. © 2001, Society for the Study of Symbolic Interaction. Used by permission of the University of California Press and the author. All rights reserved.

this form of body modification. To reconcile their desires for tattoos with their fears of being associated with low-status groups, the middle-class tattooees often employed a set of legitimation techniques to help maintain their social status. I argue that these techniques went beyond stigma management maneuvers designed to repair identities during face-to-face interactions. Instead, they framed tattoos within core mainstream norms and values. In the end, individuals' identities and their tattoos were rescued from ill repute. . . .

I look at the dominant themes in the lives of a population of tattooees in the 1990s. With an eye to underlying common social dynamics, I offer a view of some of the interactional processes that contribute to the legitimacy of tattoos in the 1990s. Although the example of legitimation techniques is generated from a population of middle-class tattooees worried about maintaining their social status, I argue that this example points to how interactions contribute to social change.

To examine how individuals attempted to negotiate the tattoo status in everyday interactions, I first describe how I came to be interested in the subject of tattoos, how I gathered data, and the nature of my role and interactions among a community of middle-class tattooees. Next, I discuss how individuals attempted to negotiate a passage through conflicting demands attracting them to and discouraging them from becoming tattooed. I delineate the initial attractions to getting tattoos as individuals' attempts to tap into older deviant and fringe meanings associated with tattoos in order to gain independence and freedom. I explain individuals' aversions as forces competing with their hopes to use the deviant roots of tattoos. Middle-class tattooees resolved the tension between wanting to break norms and desiring to appease conventional tastes by developing a set of techniques to make their tattoo experiences conform to the key concerns of mainstream individuals. Finally, I examine how tattooees' use of legitimation techniques points to an informal moral passage process that explains change as stemming from informal, everyday interactions rather than organized, political action.

SETTING AND METHODS

I collected data for this article during a four-year participant observation at the Blue Mosque, a tattoo shop located in a middle-class university town in the western United States. Falling within the opportunistic research tradition (Riemer 1977), this study had a serendipitous beginning. I first walked into the Blue Mosque in spring 1996, when I accompanied a friend who was getting her first tattoo. Before entering the clean, comfortable, and friendly shop, I had never thought about getting permanent body art myself. In fact, I had specifically promised my family that I would never get a tattoo. After watching my friend go through the experience, I changed my mind and began wondering what forms of body modification I could sport. The shop's congenial atmosphere made it easy to return several times while choosing my own piercings and eventually my own tattoos. During my visits, I formed friendships with all the artists and started dating and eventually married the shop's owner, Lefty Blue. Our home became a stopping ground for tattooists traveling through town and a social center for the shop. . . .

Men and women received their first tattoos at the Blue Mosque in equal numbers. Ages of novice clients ranged from eighteen to sixty, although most were in their twenties or thirties. In addition, first-time clients at the Blue Mosque were usually residents of the predominantly white, middle-class town in which the shop was located. Many were students at the nearby university, which was known for attracting a middle- to upper-middle-class student body. Therefore, my observations reflect the middle-class experience of getting a first tattoo. I resembled the clients in age, class, race, and ethnicity, which made developing rapport an easy task. In addition, as a woman with only one visible tattoo, I was seen by first-time female clients as more approachable than the heavily tattooed men at the shop. This initial rapport made it easy for me to recruit clients for in-depth interviews. From early interviews and conversations with clients, I began to gather that they feared the negative images associated with tattoos. Thinking that my alliance with the tattoo artists and other heavily tattooed shop regulars might dissuade interviewees from speaking openly about their fears, I began to recruit interviewees by asking my friends on and off campus to refer individuals to me who were thinking about getting or who had gotten a single tattoo. I conducted these interviews outside of my home and the shop.

Combining in-shop and out-of-shop recruitment methods, I completed forty-three interviews with a collection of people involved in various aspects of the tattoo scene, including people who had only one or two tattoos, clients who were heavily tattooed, people who decided not to get tattooed, and professional tattooists. During casual conversations and interviews, I asked about their initial impression of tattoos, what first made them want to become tattooed, what their tattoos meant to them, what made their tattoos special, and what their concerns were regarding getting and having a tattoo.[2] Since most clients primarily feared that getting a tattoo might hurt their relationship with their parents, I interviewed ten parents of tattooees and potential tattooees using the same out-of-shop recruitment methods I used for first-time tattooees. I asked questions regarding parents' impression of tattoos, how they felt about their children getting tattoos, and what would help them feel better about their children's tattoos. As the wife of a tattooist and a member of the shop, I was especially interested in individuals' impressions of tattooists, how clients negotiated their ideal tattoos with tattooists, and what environment individuals felt would be best for acquiring a tattoo.

With each casual conversation and interview, I began to see that, more than any other tattooees, first-time clients were concerned with crafting a tattoo that would be acceptable in conventional society. As my analysis progressed, I focused my shop observations and interviews on the dimensions of each emerging concept, including the components of clients' excitement and fears about becoming tattooed and the ways they attempted to

acquire tattoos without upsetting others around them. This method of mixing analysis and data collection closely resembled the constant comparative and theoretical sampling procedures articulated by Glaser and Strauss (1967).

NEGOTIATING THE TATTOO STATUS

In the 1990s tattoos quickly became a visible feature of middle-class life as they were seen in advertisements, on charismatic athletes, and even on such well-known American icons as Barbie (Kuntzman 1999). Despite the increasing popularity of this form of body art, many mainstream moralists continued to see tattoos as markers of "alienation from mainstream norms and social networks" (Sanders 1989:41). The result was the creation of a sort of cultural war (Moynihan 1993) over the definitions and meanings of tattoos in society.

Reflecting the competing definitions associated with tattoos in the 1990s, middle-class individuals were plagued by confusion, conflict, and multiple challenges as they obtained their first tattoo. Like the establishment of rules in a police department (Manning 1977), treatment of psychiatric patients (Strauss et al. 1963), or development of institutional identities (Kleinman 1982, 1996), obtaining a tattoo became a negotiated process. Although some negotiated orders are marked by cooperation and mutual dependence, the moral climate surrounding tattoos in the 1990s injected conflict into the tattoo journey. Individuals often felt attracted to becoming tattooed after interacting in the deviant, hip, or trendy worlds they shared with their friends. Conversely, after interacting in the conventional worlds they shared with their families, individuals often experienced several tattoo aversions. Potential tattooees developed a set of legitimation techniques to maximize what they saw as the positive benefits of becoming tattooed (independence and autonomy from authority) and minimize the negative meanings associated with tattoos (low class, criminal, dangerous).

DEVIANT ATTRACTIONS

Becoming tattooed proved an extremely provocative prospect for many people, especially youth, in the 1990s. The idea that individuals are drawn to deviant lifestyles has remained a well-established assumption among deviance and criminology researchers. The deviant life offers several attractive perquisites, including the chance to bond with peers (Akers et al. 1979; Elliott and Menard 1996; Erickson and Empey 1965; Hirschi 1969; Warr 1993), rebel from or defy conventionality (Hebdige 1979; Jankowski 1991; Merton 1968), and, for men, construct a masculine identity (Messerschmidt 1993). In the example of tattooees, many suggested that an intoxicating deviant mystique surrounded this form of body modification. Some felt that tattoos connoted freedom from conventionality and used their tattoos to escape conventional constraints. Others saw tattoos as a way to become more enmeshed in fringe social groups (Sanders 1989; Vad 1999). In this way tattoo attractions played on individuals' desire for particular identity and interactional opportunities.

FREEDOM FROM CONSTRAINTS

Building on older, deviant meanings associated with tattoos, many respondents suggested that becoming tattooed symbolized liberation, independence, and freedom. This was especially true for individuals who felt inhibited by the conventional social opportunities available to them. Several tattooees first contemplated becoming tattooed while in high school or college. Some suggested that their peers in conventional high school and college crowds were cruel, petty, and shallow and began to see getting tattoos as a way to step outside of the dominant peer politics surrounding them (Adler and Adler 1998). Meg, a college sophomore, described her reasons for wanting a tattoo while in high school:

MEG: Maybe it was my sophomore-junior year in high school [when I first started thinking about getting a tattoo]. My school was actually very conservative and I did things to kind of break out from the style. . . . This was basically a private school for two types of people. There were the really, really rich people . . . and the other set were the kids who got kicked out of public school. . . . I didn't want to be part of either group.

KATY: How would a tattoo differentiate you from those people?

MEG: No one else had one, as far as I know. . . . It is a way of setting yourself apart from the crowd. . . . A tattoo is there forever. That means that forever you are going to be a little bit different from the crowd.

Women especially saw tattoos as a sign of liberation and freedom and became tattooed to construct a sense of self outside of conventional ideals of femininity and female beauty (DeMello 1995; Mifflin 1997; Sanders 1991). Contrary to traditional images of women as soft, vulnerable, and physically weak, they described becoming tattooed as an act of toughness and strength. Tattooed women were considered those who "did not take shit," and were forceful, resilient, and had control over their lives. Emphasizing the issue of strength and control, Judy, a college professor, commented:

It is so traditionally unfeminine. It is a strength sign for women to go out and get something like that. It shows that they are not wimpy, but then some of them go out and get these really wimpy tattoos. I think that that is even a strength sign, even if they want to express that strength in a traditionally feminine design. . . . It means something for a woman to be making a decision to permanently mark her body without having to get permission from her father or her boyfriend or something like that. It's a big empowerment thing.

For some men and women, becoming tattooed marked a passage from one life phase to another. Potential tattooees often saw this passage as representing movement out of an oppressive phase and entrance into a freer and more independent one. This passage included such activities as moving out of their parents' houses, graduating from college, or ending unsavory relationships. Because they saw having tattoos as a violation of female beauty norms, many women used their tattoos to symbolically "take back their bodies" from their husbands' or boyfriends' control. Grace, a college junior, explained how she used her tattoo to end her relationship:

> My boyfriend was always like, "You have to be between 105 and 107 pounds." It was horrible. He used to make me get on a scale. When I did this [got a tattoo], I was taking back my body and I was doing something for me. I was pushing him away. I was trying to get him to break up with me because I didn't have the strength to do it.

DEVIANT ASSOCIATIONS

While tattoos represented a sign of independence and freedom from constraints for some individuals, others saw them as a way to increase their attachment to alternative social groups (Sanders 1989; Vail 1999). Research participants reported turning their backs on popular social sets when they were in high school. Instead, they enmeshed themselves in fringe social groups such as punk rockers, straight edge groups, dead heads, and skate punks. Members of these crowds often wore tattoos, as well as other forms of appearance deviance, as a way to mark their disassociation from mainstream culture (see Hebdige 1979). While interacting with individuals in these groups, many became eager for tattoos. Loma, a tattoo artist at the Blue Mosque, explained:

> I was involved in the whole punk rock thing. I got involved with that as soon as I went to high school. . . . The normal people were a little scary, and I never fit in with that. I went to my first punk rock show and that was a revelation for me. I went wow this whole thing is so neat. These are people I can relate to and the music's something at some level I can relate to. . . . They [tattoos] were there, they existed, they were part of that. I started obsessing about them. I got my first one when I was seventeen.

Some participants became tattooed before interacting in unconventional circles. Feeling dissatisfied with mainstream life, many used their tattoos to gain entrée into fringe social worlds. Lefty described his former girlfriend's reasons for becoming tattooed: "She was a San Francisco funky woman. She wanted to get the jobs at the cool places. She wanted to be able to waitress at the neat restaurants with tattooed people. She went right ahead and got tattooed on her forearm before I got tattooed on my forearm."

Becoming tattooed also helped a few individuals gain membership in the Blue Mosque's social world. Tattooists preferred to produce larger work for many reasons and often celebrated clients who received large tattoos.[3] By talking enthusiastically about these clients' chosen designs, working diligently after hours to render the best images possible, and often reducing their fees for these valued customers, tattooists established a hierarchy among clients. Many shop regulars reinforced the tattooists' prestige system by stopping in to watch the large pieces in progress and commenting on how "cool" or "awesome" these tattoos would be. For many, getting larger work became a way to establish privileged status in this social world. Ron, a college senior, described his first meeting with the Blue Mosque artists and the construction of his first professional tattoo:

> I searched for a week for a design. I came up with the album cover that I thought was pretty neat. I just took it in there one day. . . . The artist goes, "Oh you want the penis." I said what? They go, "So you want this penis thing." And I looked at [the design] and it was this very phallic image and I'd never even thought about it that way and I go, "Oh my God, that looks like a dick and balls." So I said, "That is pretty cool, why not?" The tattooist said, "This is probably the craziest tattoo I've done." I was honored.

Tattooists admired Ron's willingness to receive a "crazy" piece and quickly embraced him as a favorite client. While tattooists' first priority was to produce quality work, they inadvertently created a social world in which outsider and insider statuses were drawn according to the size and type of tattoos that clients received.[4]

DEVIANT AVERSIONS

One of the major constraints that prevents individuals from engaging in deviance is their relationship with mainstream individuals. Those with a high stake in conventional life (Waldorf et al. 1991), who have strong bonds to conventional individuals (Hirschi 1969), or who have strong external social support (Garmezy 1985; Werner 1989, 1992) are often thought to be protected from deviance or delinquency. In the example of potential tattooees, aversions to deviance included the fear of damaging relationships with parents and the desire to maintain legitimate statuses. While interacting with family members, conservative friends, and employers, many learned that important people in their lives disliked tattoos and looked down on tattooed people. No matter how much these young men and women wanted to use tattoos to establish independence from authority, most could not separate themselves from wanting to secure approval from parents and appear successful in conventional society. Like tattoo attractions, tattoo aversions played on key aspects of individuals' identities and social networks.

CONSERVATIVE REACTIONS

Middle-class tattooees circulated in several social worlds. While at school and with friends, they often learned that tattoos symbolized independence and freedom from conventional society. However, with family, at work, or hanging out with conventional individuals, potential tattooees learned that many continued to see getting tattoos as outrageous and unacceptable behavior. Through their interactions with tattoo critics, potential tattooees studied the many ways a tattoo might change their interactions in conservative social worlds.

Strangers and acquaintances may have judged tattoos implicitly, but parents spoke openly about their dislike for them. Interviews with parents revealed many dimensions of their disapproval of tattoos. They often mentioned that tattoos communicated dirtiness and poor hygiene. They saw tattooists as unconcerned about sterilization and thought of tattoo shops as smoke filled, unclean places. Parents expressed particular concern that their children might contract diseases or infections when getting tattoos.[5] Fran, a mother and health professional, explained her concerns:

> There is always a worry about diseases when you let someone else stick you with anything. You never know how clean and sterile their needles are. You don't know if they follow the correct procedures to protect you from infections. Even health professionals make major mistakes. How can some clerk in a tattoo parlor say they do it right all the time?

Parents also saw tattoos as serious status risks. Many parents feared that their children would be looked down on because tattoos signified association with undesirable social groups. Frank, a father of four, discussed some of the reasons he disliked tattoos:

> My initial fears were that I associated tattoos with people who are not my favorite: Hells Angels, sailors, and convicts. . . . I didn't like what the tattoos meant to them. . . . With Hells Angels and the convict world, I didn't like their willingness to scar themselves. It was pitiful and shameful. These tattoos were obtrusive and really damaged their future possibilities. I associated [tattoos] with self-destruction . . . like their obsessive use of drugs and alcohol, petty crime, and just generally stupid behavior which got them into trouble.

Parents had usually spent considerable time attempting to steer their children toward successful, happy lives in conventional society. The idea of their children getting tattoos cast a shadow over their hopes and dreams for their children's future. Nedra, a mother of two, described her worries: "No matter how old your kids get you want to protect them. From the tattoo, you want to protect them from being ostracized, from being laughed at, from being put down. I don't want that to happen to my kids." Children's tattoos also threatened their parents' social status. Parents of children who became tattooed were seen as "too permissive" and as "poor moral guides." Among the most pressing concerns for parents was maintaining the image of being a "proper parent." Jillian, a mother of four, described her response when her daughter got her first tattoo: "I remember my daughter kept telling me that she wanted one [a tattoo]. At first I was a little anti the idea. What were people going to think? They would probably look at me as the example and say, 'Oh jeeze, you would let your daughter get a tattoo.' It would reflect on me too."

STATUS ANXIETY

After interacting with friends and parents, potential tattooees began to see that tattoos held many different meanings. Potential tattooees experienced status anxiety when they imagined how the negative meanings associated with tattoos might change their interactions with important individuals in their lives. Younger tattooees especially expressed a common concern that receiving a tattoo would threaten emotional ties with family and their parents' regard for them. Larry, a college freshman, was determined to get a tattoo. He described his experience with his father after experimenting with deviant body modification in high school:

> He hit the roof when I got my ear pierced and when I dyed my hair. I didn't do it to rebel against him or to hurt him. . . . I was crushed. I hated it. My dad and I had a pretty strong relationship so it really bothered me. That really hurt him. Of course I want my dad's approval and my dad's love. I wasn't doing it to hurt him.

Reflecting on his father's reactions to his ear piercing and hair dying, Larry braced himself for

emotional turmoil and the loss of his father's esteem after getting a tattoo.

Some feared serious financial losses if they became tattooed. Melody, a college junior, had received four tattoos while in college. She explained her concerns about revealing her tattoos to her parents:

> My parents are completely against tattoos. They believe they are for bikers and sailors and that anyone who has one is scum. They threatened to cut me off from college and kick me out of their house if I ever got one. . . . They are paying for college and my apartment. Unless I want to get cut off, my tattoos will have to remain a secret until I'm twenty-two.

Potential tattooees often internalized their parents' worries that tattoos might threaten their future opportunities. Stew, a senior in college, suggested that his parents' prohibitions did not deter him from getting a tattoo. However, he understood and agreed with the cause of his parents' concerns. He explained: "I believe that they want you to make the right decision and to not have regrets later in life. It may be so important now, to get a tattoo, but you may be stuck and branded for life. I think that it is important that parents try to encourage their children to think it over."

Parents were often successful in getting their children to plan for the future. In fact, worries that their future opportunities would be threatened reigned as a constant concern to those considering tattoos. I interviewed Sula, a twenty-eight-year-old professional woman, while she waited to get her first tattoo. She discussed some of her apprehensions:

> In six months I am going to quit my job. My job is great. I love my job . . . but I need to be doing something that is going to make a much bigger impact on the world. That is probably going to be working with kids who have entered the criminal justice system. That is what my concern is . . . I'm aware of the fact that having a tattoo might make the people that I'm working with look at me differently or that the kids are going to have a hard time

figuring out who I am. They are not going to respect me as much.

Aside from losing status in family and professional spheres, some potential tattooees acknowledged that tattoos might threaten important aspects of their self-presentations in the larger society. Addison, a twenty-nine-year-old graduate student, explained:

I went through this weird little period of grief after getting my ankle tattoo. Although I had thought about and wanted a tattoo for two years and was completely dedicated to having a tattoo, I experienced this unexpected sadness. It started when I was watching this old movie with Lauren Bacall. She was standing behind a billboard with only her ankles showing. Humphrey Bogart let out this terrific whistle, like isn't she beautiful. I realized that my ankle would never evoke that same sense of femininity. Sure, in some alterna-crowd it might say "cool, deviant chick," but it would never universally communicate "beauty."

Once they realized the status consequences of having tattoos, individuals lost their initial tattoo zeal. Many discussed worries about others' reactions as forces that "competed with" or "muddied" their enthusiasm. Meg, who decided not to get a tattoo, described the competition between tattoo attractions and aversions as a battle between good and evil. She remarked:

I think that in the back of my mind that I want one [a tattoo]. But even from the moment that I started to want one, there is the fear of . . . the consequences. Kind of like the little angel on one shoulder and a little devil on the other shoulder. One telling you to do something and one telling you all the consequences of what would happen. I guess my little angel is stronger than my little devil.

Through a series of interactions, individuals learned ways to reconcile their desires for tattoos with their fears of losing social status. While interacting with parents and other conventional individuals, potential tattooees collected detailed information about the nature and dimensions of the anti-tattoo sentiments surrounding them. This information prompted many respondents to pursue body art in ways that complemented mainstream norms and values. Potential tattooees also interacted with and watched others embark on the journey of becoming tattooed. Their observations allowed them to pick up on techniques used by those facing the same dilemma.

LEGITIMATION TECHNIQUES

At its core, the competition between attractions to and aversions from deviance involved a legitamation process. . . . To maintain their middle-class status, and all its advantages, tattooees employed four legitimation maneuvers to define their actions and their tattoos within core mainstream norms and values. Like accounts, verbal neutralizations, and stigma management techniques, legitimation techniques often rescued individuals from negative sanctions during face-to-face interactions. However, unlike stigma management maneuvers, legitimation techniques worked by changing the meanings associated with the deviant activity.

USING MAINSTREAM MOTIVATIONS

Throughout the process of becoming tattooed, individuals attempted to frame their desires for tattoos within mainstream definitions of success and achievement. Like deviant and criminal individuals with tattoos (Phelan and Hunt 1998), middle-class tattooees in the 1990s used their tattoos to announce their passage through particular moral careers. Whereas prison gang members wanted to chronicle their passage through deviant careers, middle-class tattooees used their tattoos to mark conventional aspects of themselves.

Many tattooees explained that they wanted tattoos to commemorate special times in their lives. Their celebrations usually centered on a set of conventional achievements such as graduation from college or graduate school, finishing major exams, or the birth of children. As rites of passage, getting tattoos at major life transitions served as permanent reminders of lessons learned, milestones accomplished, and personal growth gained. Anya, a college junior, described the symbolism of her "forget-me-not" fairy tattoo:

> *It took three years for me to finally find what I wanted and for it to have meaning. . . . I was here for the summer and I'm leaving tomorrow. It was a really good experience here. I did so much reading. I read all about metaphysics. I have a new outlook on life and changed a lot of things. I wanted something to represent my stay here and everything that I learned here.*

Like Anya, who wanted to celebrate everything she had learned, including metaphysics, many other tattooees often selected designs that symbolized their skills and achievements in a variety of fields. Environmentalists chose images of mountain landscapes and trees, writers received images of characters in books, Greek mythology aficionados selected images of gods and goddesses, musicians got images of guitars and saxophones, and sports enthusiasts received images of their favorite teams or sports, such as bicycles, basketballs, or lacrosse sticks.

Potential tattooees also explained that tattoos helped them to celebrate their favorite personality traits. They chose designs with symbolic meanings, for example, to foster their sense of humor (comic book characters), their artistic nature (nonfigurative designs), their gentleness (flowers, birds, dolphins, hearts), or their personal power (lions and jaguars). Judy described why she was drawn to her tattoo:

> *I liked it right off the bat. I started thinking about it and why I liked it. The design is kind of round, kind of strong, it flowed from one half into the other without stopping and separating. . . . It reinforces and says "me." I felt that I didn't want a flower or a bird or one of the really femmy designs. It didn't fit my personality. I felt that I was a forceful woman and I needed a forceful tattoo. I needed something strong.*

Interestingly, the life transitions, skills, achievements, and personality traits that individuals celebrated with tattoos were those that were also celebrated and rewarded in conventional society. By casting their motivations for tattoos within conventional frameworks, individuals were marking their passage through mainstream moral careers.

Using mainstream motivations quelled parents' concerns about tattoos. Parents who initially suggested that they did not approve of tattoos sometimes changed their minds when they heard the reasons that others became tattooed. Luanne consistently noted that she did not want her seventeen-year-old son to get a tattoo. However, after watching a few of her friends get tattoos, she began to see tattoos as more acceptable. She explained:

> *I was raised with the idea that tattoos were just army or navy guys. People who had tattoos were renegades who thumbed their nose at society. . . . It took me a long time to change my mind that getting a tattoo was something that guys do when they get drunk. . . . I've heard some wonderful ways that people have used tattoos. One story is about this woman who had a daughter who . . . was killed. She had several sisters, her mother, her father, and her aunt all decided to commemorate her by having a sunflower. Her [daughter's] favorite flower was a sunflower. I thought that was beautiful. . . . The meaning behind having a tattoo now, it's a symbol that really represents something to people. I like that idea.*

Like Luanne, who felt that commemorating a child was a "legitimate" reason to become tattooed, many tattoo critics found that there were compelling conventional reasons for becoming tattooed.

COMMITTING TO CONVENTIONAL BEHAVIOR

Responding to conventional individuals' beliefs that tattoos accompanied a host of undesirable behaviors, tattooees became dedicated to proving that they could get a tattoo while remaining active in a variety of conventional pursuits, including school, family, and professional careers. Some tattooees suggested that their involvement in conventional activities outweighed the negative meanings associated with their tattoos. Addison explained why she felt that her tattoo was not a serious threat to her social status:

> *My dad said something negative about [my tattoo] the other day. He made this little joke about me having a little bit of dirt on my ankle. However, I don't think that he really means anything by it. How could he really oppose? Look at me, I'm everything he could want a kid to be. I'm a serious student. I get great grades. I am doing well in a career that I love and he loves. I'm married. Someday soon I will give him plenty of grandchildren. With all that, what difference is a tattoo going to make?*

Others attempted to demonstrate how getting tattoos was part of their commitment to conventionality. Potential tattooees often noted how they carefully planned their tattoos and attempted to show how they were conforming to conventional standards of self-control and rationality. Earl, a twenty-eight-year-old writer, said that his father initially worried about his tattoo but became less worried over time.

EARL: He was worried that I was experimenting and trying different things and really swinging all over the place in who I wanted to be. . . . [I]t [the tattoo] would be some mark that I have been to hell. It was like the mark that I had been scarred when I went experimenting. . . . It was a studied choice I made and something I considered for a long time. I never did it on a whim. . . .

KATY: What made him change?

EARL: He probably started to recognize that I was still the same person. I was growing in a certain direction. . . . I wasn't fluctuating all over the place.

According to Earl, one of the more potent defenses against losing status in the family was proving that he was still "growing in the same direction." For Earl, this meant continuing to behave according to his parents' core values, including "being a good person" and "working towards a professional career."

Contrary to the image of first tattoos as the product of reckless, impulsive, and drunken decisions, tattoos at the Blue Mosque resulted from careful planning. Adopting their parents' concerns about safety, hygiene, and cleanliness, first-time clients at the Blue Mosque often searched for clean shops that employed experienced, professional artists who conformed to rigorous sterilization procedures and artistic goals. Stew explained his concerns about finding the perfect artist:

> *I would want to go and see how he did the work[,] . . . [w]hat they are doing now, how their business is run, do they have a license. If it is well known, if people recommend them to me, I will go and check them out and maybe watch them do a tattoo if they will let me. I will look at the art that they have on the wall that they offer, and if it is like a bunch of dragons, and that is it, that is all that they do is blood and dragons, then I probably wouldn't go to them. I also want someone that could share in what they are doing to me. I wouldn't want some messed-up drug addict doing my tattoo. . . . He would have to be good and he would have to be professional. He would have to have a license.*

In addition to searching for the ideal artist and shop, clients wanted to select the ideal design that would be the perfect expression of themselves. Clients often visited the shop many times to look through books of tattoo designs while they crafted the optimal image, body location, and color palette. Judy explained her initial vision for her tattoo:

> *I thought that blue would go with everything I had. I thought about getting red on it, then I thought that that would be a little much. I had to look at particular designs . . . and then one day, another day in the shop, I was looking through their books of past designs and I saw one of the tattooists' designs, this one that I have. I saw a lot that I liked, but I didn't know if it would have been just the right tattoo for me.*

Tattooees' behaviors before, during, and after becoming tattooed demonstrated their continued involvement in conventional activities. By carefully studying their tattooists, their (tattoo) environments, and their designs, tattooees demonstrated that they did not make spontaneous decisions. Instead, tattooees showed that getting tattoos, like conventional activities, required hard work, restraint, and much forethought. In this way tattooees placed getting tattoos within a repertoire of conventional behaviors.

The technique of committing to conventional behavior resembled the destigmatization technique of transcendence (Warren 1980). Unlike those engaging in the technique of transcendence, however, tattooees did not attempt to "insulate, hide or encapsulate [their] negative essence by superior performances" (Warren 1980:65). Rather, they attempted to demonstrate how their tattoos were part of their conventionality. Commitment to conventional behavior thus helped the stigmatized behavior itself, not just the stigmatized person, to transcend a deviant status.

Tattooees were often pleased to find that their commitment to conventionality worked to appease their parents and helped others to overcome their worries about tattoos. Many tattooees' parents, who initially feared the idea of their children getting tattoos, admitted feeling that the tattoo did not detract from their children's other conventional attributes. Nedra, who was concerned that her child would be negatively labeled, described why she did not oppose her daughter's tattoo: "The only thing I worry about [with my daughter's tattoo], is that she will continue to get more. The one that she has, I'm not so worried about. . . . I think that being in the field that she is, having the education that she does, the tattoo is not going to label her as a counterculture person."

Other parents suggested that they approved of the way their children pursued becoming tattooed. The following is an excerpt from my field notes describing my conversation with a parent of an eighteen-year-old:

I just got off the phone with a friend of mine. She told me that her daughter was thinking about getting a tattoo. My friend is from an upper-class family and I am assuming that this family will not like one of their own getting a tattoo. However, instead of being worried, my friend sounded excited. She told me that her daughter went to every tattoo shop in town, asked about their sterilization procedures, and looked at all their portfolios of artwork before deciding to get a tattoo. She also said that her daughter found a very clean and professional shop in town. At the end of the conversation, my friend suggested that the care with which her daughter selected the shop showed that her daughter was thinking wisely and being very adult in her tattoo decision.

OFFERING VERBAL NEUTRALIZATIONS

Potential tattooees often found themselves verbally justifying their tattoos and their desire for tattoos. In these cases individuals often relied on condemnation of the condemners (Sykes and Matza 1957). Larry explained how he might respond to a disapproving stranger: "If someone wants to treat me differently because of the tattoo I would have on my ankle, that is a pretty shitty person. It would not be someone that I would want to deal with anyway."

Condemnation from close friends or loved ones presented tattooees with the possibility of more serious emotional losses. Therefore, managing friends' reactions required careful review. Stew discussed his feelings: "It would also limit who I might want to meet. Just because they don't like tattoos doesn't mean that they aren't a great person. . . . It is a big concern. I like people; they should like me. They shouldn't have a first impression distorted by a tattoo. It is their own little neurotic opinion."

Like Stew, who vacillated between not wanting to offend people and wanting to freely pursue having a tattoo, many respondents worried about being rejected by close friends. Overcoming parents and family members' condemnation proved even more difficult. Marty, a forty-three-year-old, discussed her family's reactions:

I think the time that they [her parents] were from, people from the thirties and forties, the types of women who tattooed themselves were either women in carnivals, women strippers. That is the generation they are from. . . . I just think that they are so old, I don't want to upset them. Even though I'm forty-three and part of me is like, "What is the deal? I'm 43. It is my arm."

Marty's attempts to neutralize her parents' concerns were subtle. By framing her parents' feelings resulting from their age, she indirectly stated that her parents were old, and out of date (see Sanders 1999). This view proved to be a consistent theme. Where tattooees easily condemned strangers, they often became more subtle and conflicted about verbally attacking close friends and family.

By condemning certain critics, tattooees attempted to do more than repress "the wrongfulness of [their] own behavior" by "attacking others" (Sykes and Matza 1957:668). Their comments about others represented verbal claims and efforts to shift the normative consensus away from intolerance of tattoos. Tattooees attempted to claim that condemners were deviants for not keeping up with emerging trends and changing social norms. In this way many attempts by tattooees to dismiss condemners can be seen as indirect appeals to higher loyalties.[6]

CONFORMING TO CONVENTIONAL AESTHETICS

Because tattooees worried that others thought of tattoos as unsightly emblems of outcast culture, they wanted artwork that departed as much as possible from images of "ugly," antisocial tattoos. In contrast to members of deviant groups such as bikers, punk rockers, and skinheads, middle-class tattooees primarily wanted small, discreet tattoos with conventional themes. For women, this often meant getting images that they associated with femininity. Grace said: "To me, up until I got one, and to her [her mother], tattoos were ugly. They were macho and white trash. I got one and mine is not like that. Mine is very feminine. Mine is very unique. . . . I think that when girls get tattoos it should be soft." Size was as important as imagery and themes. First-time tattooees often preferred

to get small designs and suggested that small tattoos were the least likely to offend others. Kit, a recent college graduate, explained what she liked most about the tattoos worn by her friends:

I like that it didn't take over the whole body, that it could be subtle and put on different parts of the body where you don't have to show it. It is for yourself. If you want to show people that is fine, but you don't have to. It doesn't have to be, here comes the tattoo. It is the person first. . . . In addition, I like beautiful art and colors. More like butterflies and flowers and bright happy things rather than skulls and things you don't think of as being so free.

In addition to desiring subtle, prosocial images, many tattooees remarked that their tattoos were "pieces of art" and that their tattooists were on the same level as fine artists. Gretchen, a graduate student, discussed the artistic integrity of her tattoo artists:

They want people to express themselves and they want to have fun with it. . . . I think that they are far more likely to do really imaginative pieces and to really put part of themselves into that piece, not just from their design style but from the way that they approach a subject. The color work is great. I really haven't seen such incredible color work in anyone else's book. . . . The fact that they are really dedicated not only to what they do but to improving themselves . . . in terms of being able to expand their personal style and coming up with really imaginative ways of expressing what they want.

Individuals' attempts to create discreet, pleasant, fine art-inspired tattoos worked to sway some critics' opinions of tattoos. Frank initially did not want his children to get tattoos for fear that they would be stigmatized. After looking at two of his children's tattoos, as well as tattoos worn by their contemporaries, Frank changed his mind. He explained: "It is clear that tattoos have become much more artistic. They are crossing lines and it has erased the stigma. Some of these tattoos on the shoulders, I find artistic."

While individuals initially reported being attracted to the deviant mystique surrounding tattoos, their motivations for tattoos, their repertoire of behaviors before, during, and after getting a tattoo, and the types of tattoos they acquired usually demonstrated their conventionality. In the end, their tattoos did more to announce their connection to rather than their independence from conventionality.

The techniques of legitimation employed by tattooees played an important part in changing conventional individuals' opinions of tattoos. Conservative parents, friends, and partners reported liking some aspect of others' tattoos. Tattooees' behaviors, their motivations, and the aesthetic quality of their tattoos were among the more powerful forces that softened conventional individuals' stances. In fact, after seeing their children, friends, or partners become tattooed, a few critics suggested that they were interested in becoming tattooed themselves. Martha, a mother of two, described her changing reaction:

> I guess as a child I was aware of tattoos. I thought they were ugly. I thought that they were all that kind of sailor blue, black, green color. . . . And then I became aware that tattoos were gaining an avant-garde connotation. And then my daughter started shopping around for hers and thinking about getting one. The first time I thought about getting one for myself is when my daughter asked me if I would get one with her.

CONCLUSION

I have shown how middle-class tattooees take up a once-deviant behavior and help to reduce or remove the stigma associated with it through a series of legitimation maneuvers. Interaction rested at the core of the development, use, and success of these legitimation techniques practiced by middle-class tattooees in the 1990s. Potential tattooees initially felt that tattoos connoted freedom and independence from adult constraints. However, after interacting with the conventional individuals in their lives, potential tattooees learned the different ways that tattoos threatened core conventional values and norms regarding hygiene, beauty, decision making and self-presentation. These young adults became concerned that the negative associations attached to tattoos would vitiate the positive connotations of becoming tattooed. Through interaction with others (tattooees, parents, tattooists), potential tattooees learned different ways to negotiate their tattoo status. This network of informal, everyday interactions eventually led tattooees to develop, refine, and use a set of similar responses to maintain their status after getting tattoos.

These data suggest not only that tattooees pursued becoming tattooed in common ways but that their efforts to maintain legitimacy were largely successful. When tattooees braced themselves to hear criticisms and complaints from others, they were often pleased to find themselves the recipients of acceptance and praise. Over time, many tattooees found that their standing in conventional society remained unchanged. Legitimation techniques not only worked to mitigate the negative associations with tattoos, but they worked to conventionalize many aspects of the tattoo experience. In an ironic twist, tattooees ended up confirming many of the norms and values they were initially trying to escape. . . .

The context of tattoo legitimation in the 1990s sheds some light on when legitimation is mostly likely to occur. During the 1990s, people attributed conflicting meanings to tattoos as the older deviant meanings coexisted with newer, more progressive ones. Given the varied tattoo images circulating in different social groups, individuals with contacts in many social worlds were likely to experience attractions to and aversions from this form of deviance. Lacking a clear consensus regarding the meaning of becoming tattooed, individuals who experience conflict were likely to use their everyday interactions to tip the general moral balance toward acceptance of this activity. This suggests that individuals might be more likely to use legitimation techniques with activities that lack a unified symbolic meaning.

Those engaged in commonly denounced activities (i.e., pedophilia, incest, devil worship) might be more likely to distance themselves from or hide their deviance by using stigma management techniques. The occurrence of legitimation techniques might also indicate the level of moral consensus on particular activities. If individuals tend to rely on legitimation more often than stigma management techniques, then society might be experiencing a time of moral indecision regarding certain deviant acts. . . .

NOTES

1. Throughout history, tattooists have reported working with middle-class clients (Steward 1990). However, the numbers of middle-class tattoo clients during the 1980s and 1990s increased so dramatically that many tattooists relied almost exclusively on a middle-class clientele.
2. Interestingly, among all the concerns inherent in the first tattoo, price was usually not an issue. First tattoos were usually small and cost between $100 and $200. This did not prove an economic hardship for the middle-class individuals in this subculture.
3. According to tattooists, larger work was less likely to blur and lose distinction over time. In addition, tattooists were able to use more of their fine art skills while working on large designs.
4. Tattooists did not acknowledge that they were creating distinctions between in-groups and out-groups. Many suggested that, unlike those without tattoos, they never judged others. In fact, many quoted the common adage, "the only difference between tattooed people and non-tattooed people is that we don't care if you don't have a tattoo."
5. The history of tattooing in America reveals several popular panics over the connection between tattoos and diseases. Steward (1990:190) notes that "by 1968 over 47 major cities . . . had special ordinances against tattooing." Many of these ordinances, especially those in New York City in 1964, were to control the spread of such diseases as hepatitis B. While some medical literature has implicated tattooing in the spread of diseases (Jones, Maloney, and Helm 1997, Limentani et al. 1979), McCabe (1995) suggests that the outlawing of tattooing in New York City came more from moral concerns than from attempts to stem the spread of hepatitis B.
6. Thanks to an anonymous reviewer for this insight.

REFERENCES

Adler, Patricia, and Peter Adler. 1998. *Peer Power: Preadolescent Culture and Identity*. New Brunswick, NJ: Rutgers University Press.

Akers, Ronald L., Marvin D. Krohn, Lonn Lanza-Kaduce, and Marcia Radosevich. 1979. "Social Learning and Deviant Behavior: A Specific Test of a General Theory." *American Sociological Review* 44:636–655.

DeMello, Margo. 1995. "Not Just for Bikers Anymore: Popular Representations of American Tattooing." *Journal of Popular Culture* 29:37–52.

Elliott, Delbert S., and Scott Menard. 1996. "Delinquent Friends and Delinquent Behavior: Temporal and Developmental Patterns." Pp. 28–67 in J. D. Hawkins (ed.), *Delinquency and Crime: Current Theories*. Cambridge: Cambridge University Press.

Erickson, Maynard, and LaMar Empey. 1965. "Class Position, Peers and Delinquency." *Sociology and Social Research* 49:268–282.

Garmezy, Norman. 1995. "Stress Resistant Children: The Search for Protective Factors." Pp. 213–233 in J. E. Stevenson (ed.), *Recent Research in Developmental Psychopathology*. New York: Pergamon.

Glaser, Barney, and Anselm L. Strauss. 1967. *Discovery of Grounded Theory*. Chicago: Aldine.

Gusfield, Joseph R. 1967. "Moral Passage: The Symbolic Process in Public Designations of Deviance." *Social Problems* 15:175–188.

Hebdige, Dick. 1979. *Subculture, the Meaning of Style*. London: Methuen.

Hirschi, Travis. 1969. *Causes of Delinquency*. Berkeley: University of California Press.

Jankowski, Martin Sanchez. 1991. *Islands in the Street. Gangs and American Urban Society*. Berkeley: University of California Press.

Jones, M. S., M. E. Maloney, and K. F. Helm. 1997. "Systemic Sarcoidosis Presenting in the Black Dye of a Tattoo." *Cutis* 59:113–115.

Kleinman, Sheryl. 1982. "Actors' Conflicting Theories of Negotiation: The Case of a Holistic Health Center." *Urban Life* 11:312–27.

———. 1996. *Opposing Ambitions: Gender and Identity in an Alternative Organization*. Chicago: University of Chicago Press.

Kuntzman, Gersh. 1999. "It's Been 40 Years Coming and Now . . . Barbie's New, Improved and Tattooed." *New York Post* 4:61–62.

Limentani, A. E., L. M. Elliott, N. D. Noah, and J. K. Lamborn. 1979. "An Outbreak of Hepatitis B from Tattooing." *Lancet* 2(8133):86–88.

Manning, Peter K. 1977. "Rules in Organizational Context: Narcotics Law Enforcement in Two Settings." *Sociological Quarterly* 18:44–61.

McCabe, Michael. 1995. "Coney Island Tattoo: The Growth of Inclusive Culture in the Age of the Machine." Pp. 48–55 in D. E. Hardy (ed.), *Pierced Hearts and True Love*. New York: Drawing Center.

Merton, Robert K. 1968. *Social Theory and Social Structure*. New York: Free Press.

Messerschmidt, James W. 1993. *Masculinities and Crime*. Lanham, MD: Rowman and Littlefield.

Mifflin, Margo. 1997. *Bodies of Subversion*. New York: Juno Books.

Milwaukee Journal Sentinel. 1998. "Beauty Marks." November 29, p. 1.

Moynihan, Daniel Patrick. 1993. "Defining Deviance Down." *American Scholar* 62:17–30.

Newton, Esther. 1993. "My Best Informant's Dress: The Erotic Equation in Fieldwork." *Cultural Anthropology* 8:3–23.

Parry, Albert. 1933. *Tattoo: Secrets of a Strange Art Practiced by the Natives of the United States*. New York: Collier.

Phelan, Michael P., and Scott A. Hunt. 1998. "Prison Gang Members' Tattoos as Identity Work: The Visual Communication of Moral Careers." *Symbolic Interaction* 21:277–298.

Providence Journal-Bulletin. 1999. "The Bay State Tattoo Crisis." July 15, p. 6B.

Riemer, Jeffrey W. 1977. "Varieties of Opportunistic Research." *Urban Life* 5:467–477.

Rubin, Arnold. 1988. "The Tattoo Renaissance." Pp. 233–262 in A. Rubin (ed.), *Marks of Civilization*. Los Angeles: Museum of Cultural History, University of California, Los Angeles.

Sanders, Clinton. 1989. *Customizing the Body: The Art and Culture of Tattooing*. Philadelphia: Temple University Press.

———. 1991. "Memorial Decoration: Women, Tattooing, and the Meanings of Body Alteration." *Michigan Quarterly Review* 30:146–157.

———. 1999. *Understanding Dogs: Living and Working with Canine Companions*. Philadelphia: Temple University Press.

Steward, Samuel M. 1990. *Bad Boys and Tough Tattoos: A Social History of the Tattoo with Gangs, Sailors, and Street-Corner Punks 1950–1965*. New York: Haworth Press.

Strauss, Anselm, Leonard Schatzman, Danuta Ehrlich, Rue Bucher, and Melvin Sabshin. 1963. "The Hospital and Its Negotiated Order." Pp. 147–169 in E. Freidson (ed.), *The Hospital in Modern Society*. New York: Free Press.

Sykes, Gresham M., and David Matza. 1957. "Techniques of Neutralization: A Theory of Delinquency." *American Sociological Review* 22:664–670.

Telvin, Jon. 1999. "Body Art Uninspiring in Today's Job Market." *Star Tribune*, August 6, p. 1A.

Vail, D. Angus. 1999. "Tattoos Are Like Potato Chips . . . You Can't Have Just One: The Process of Becoming and Being a Collector." *Deviant Behavior* 20:253–273.

Vale, D., and Andrea Juno. 1989. *Modern Primitives: An Investigation of Contemporary Adornment and Ritual*. San Francisco: RE/Search Publications.

Waldorf, Dan, Craig Reinarman, and Sheigla Murphy. 1991. *Cocaine Changes: The Experience of Using and Quitting*. Philadelphia: Temple University Press.

Warr, Mark. 1993. "Age, Peers, and Delinquency." *Criminology* 31:17–40.

Warren, Carol A. B. 1980. "Destigmatization of Identity: From Deviant to Charismatic." *Qualitative Sociology* 3:57–72.

Werner, Emmy E. 1989. "High Risk Children in Young Adulthood." *American Journal of Orthopsychiatry* 59:72–81.

———. 1992. *Overcoming the Odds: High Risk Children from Birth to Adulthood*. Ithaca, NY: Cornell University Press.

CHAPTER 13

MANAGING A DEVIANT IDENTITY

Modes of Suburban Gay Identity

WAYNE BREKHUS

Absence of everyday social contact with minorities often results in negative stereotypes. Derisive terms take the place of personal knowledge of such people. Typifications of unconventionality become amplified and oversimplified conceptions, often caricatures. But, like everyone else, such individuals have to adapt to their social situation. And where the conventional social world sees but a singular type of person, studies reveal variety in both their adaptations and in their commitment to the unconventional identity.

Where the straight world lumps all gays in one category, Wayne Brekhus shows that one simple categorization does not fit them all. He finds variety, not uniformity, among gays. Variations in the frequency, intensity, and duration of contact with gay and straight worlds produce different ways to manage a gay identity. Brekhus finds three modes of identity management among suburban gays. The first is the "full-time gay." This type of suburban gay identifies with and participates the most in the highly visible gay world. Gayness is both his key status and his core self. The "integrated" gay participates more fully in the straight world. His gayness is invisible except to a few intimates and it shares key status with nonsexual aspects of his life. The gay "commuter" makes sporadic visits to gay locations in the city, displays his gayness there, only to return to the straight world where he passes as a straight person. Each of these types of suburban gay, ethnocentrically, claims superiority for their way of managing a gay identity.

The three identity management types are those of (1) lifestylers, (2) commuters, and (3) integrators. Underlying each of these identity types are different configurations of *identity duration* (the degree to which identity is distributed across various times and spaces of one's life), *identity density* (the degree to which identity is packaged and presented in a concentrated or diluted form), and *identity dominance* (the product of duration times

Reprinted from *Peacocks, Chameleons, Centaurs: Gay Suburbia and the Grammar of Social Identity,* pp. 28–29 and 98–107, by permission of the University of Chicago Press and the author. Copyright © 2003 by the University of Chicago Press.

density, or the degree to which an identity attribute occupies one's whole self).

The first type is the *identity lifestyler*. Gay lifestylers live openly in gay-specific ghettos and organize their life around their marked status. They keep their markedness on "high volume" and do it virtually all the time. They have a high-density, high-duration gay identity. Metaphorically, they are 100 percent gay, 100 percent of the time. Lifestylers take on the grammatical centrality of gayness as a *noun*.

The second type is the *identity commuter*. Gay commuters treat their gay identity as a *verb*. They live other parts of themselves in heterosexual space and travel to identity-specific spaces to be their "gay self." They are weekend warriors and nighttime commuters to the gay community. In much the same way that work commuters travel from the suburbs to the city to do work on weekdays, identity commuters travel from the suburbs to the city to "do identity" on weekends. For them, gayness is a *temporary master status* that they turn on and off depending on their social environment—in gay spaces they often turn their marked identity to high volume, but outside these spaces they turn it off completely. They commute to ghettos or bars and play up their markedness in marked social spaces. They submerge markedness and foreground their unmarked characteristics everywhere else. They limit open expression of their gay identity to very few spheres of their lives. Thus, it is a low-duration, high-density gay identity. Metaphorically, they may be something like 100 percent gay, 15 percent of the time. (These percentages are illustrative and not literal. I use 15 percent as the illustrative number for duration because it conveys a small but still significant portion of one's time. This also represents the kind of duration to an identity that is consistent with a weekend identity commitment. Time commitments as low as 1 percent or as high as 40 percent can also be seen as within the duration range of a real-life commuter.)

The third type is the *identity integrator*. The gay identity of gay integrators is an *adjective*. They live openly in heterosexual space and integrate their gay identity into living in a heterosexualized world. In fact, many integrators do not often travel to gay-specific spaces. While they are not closeted, they also do not play up their markedness as lifestylers or commuters do. Unlike commuters, their gay identity is turned on all of the time, but it is at a low volume. Their marked trait becomes just one of a number of facets by which they organize their life and identify themselves. Their gay identity is not entirely off, nor is it on high density. They do markedness on low volume and spread it across all spheres of their lives. They present a low-density, high-duration gay identity. Metaphorically, they might be 15 percent gay, 100 percent of the time. (Again both percentages are

illustrative rather than literal. The 15 percent figure for density conveys an attribute that defines only a fraction of the self but a fraction that is still significant.) . . .

IDENTITY NATIVES AND IDENTITY TOURISTS: DURATION DISPUTES OVER GAY IDENTITY

Lifestylers believe that one's commitment to an identity should be undivided. They possess a greedy identity—an identity that requires exclusive and undivided identity work. Central to the lifestyler view is an identity politics model that considers gay invisibility a defining factor in the oppression of gays. From this perspective, high-duration gay visibility is critical to overall cultural visibility and acceptance. To the lifestyler, the commuter who resists high-duration gayness is part of the problem, for his invisibility perpetuates the oppression of gays. . . .

The lifestyler perceives those who do an identity only part-time as uncommitted opportunists who merely "play" the identity when it is safe to do so. The lifestyler views himself as an identity native and the commuter as a mere identity tourist. This divide can also be seen between lifestylers and commuters in the lesbian community. One of Stein's (1997:162) informants, for instance, accused some women of lesbian "tourism" or ideological "play," asserting that they were fakes who were merely posing as lesbians on low duration. From the lifestyler's corner, the commuter is a poseur—a weekend warrior to a gay identity who only "plays the identity" because he lacks the full commitment to "live it." The lifestyler dismisses commuters as "pretenders" or "wannabes," or worse yet as "hypocrites" because they show their "true colors" only when it is safe to do so.

Some gays in New York City, for instance, refer to suburban identity commuters as *tunnel and bridge gays*. From the New York lifestyler's perspective the tunnel and bridge gay is tainted by his association with straight suburbia and his lack of sophistication regarding the culture among natives.

From the perspective of some urban gays tunnel and bridge gays, like "tourists" to any culture, do a poor job of following the local customs and thus fitting into the native culture. Indeed, those very customs may be there for the express purpose of separating the inner circle from the wanna-bes.

Part of the urban lifestyler's objection to tunnel and bridge gays is that they turn off their gay identity as soon as they pass back through the tunnel into the heterosexual world. The commuter's gay life consists of fleeting weekend bursts of gay identity in the city followed by long stretches of mundane suburban living. The duration of his gayness is too short for the lifestyler to take him seriously. From the lifestyler's perspective he won't be a "true gay" until he "goes native" and abandons the straight world. As long as he is only commuting to or vacationing in the city he is not a true insider but merely a curious spectator to the gay subculture. The lifestyler expects total immersion in gay culture not just on the weekends but all of the time. Moreover, the lifestyler views anyone who is only a part-time gay as uncommitted to his "core self." The lifestyler views individuals who repress this all-important part of their identity at some times and in some places as "self-hating." Signorile . . . , for instance, refers to the closeted gay, in which category his definition includes the commuter, as a "self-loathing homosexual" who allows his entire self to be dominated by oppression most of the time. The gay lifestyler, who views gayness as a noun, sees any act that does not openly proclaim one's gayness as a betrayal of one's true inner "core self." He believes the chameleon has sold his soul and betrayed his true colors every time he turns in his bright urban gay colors for the bland straight colors of mundane suburbia. The lifestyler views the identities of commuters as impure and inevitably tainted by their high-duration contact with the profane non-gay world. For instance, Levine's . . . informants perceived suburban commuters, who failed to adopt the full dress code of clone culture, as visual pollutants to their "authentically gay" environment. Some queer theorists have adopted the lifestyler's position on duration as their own

analytic position, suggesting that the closeted homosexual, again defined to include commuters, suffers from a polluted self-image.

The commuter views his duration differently. Rather than seeing low duration as a lack of authenticity or commitment, he sees it as an abundance of mobility. From the commuter's view, "full-time gays" (lifestylers and integrators alike) lack flexibility. For instance, identity commuters express the view that there is a difference between a "part-time queen" and a "full-time queen." As Bill states:

> Now there's a difference between [being] a queen and [acting] queeny. A person can be queeny but not necessarily a queen. I mean a queen is a queen all the time, *and that's what they are. They're defined by it.* Those people who are Joe Blow but they can be queeny at times, that's a little different. They can act effeminate at times but a queen has made it their life.

For Bill, someone who can be queeny at times is superior to someone who can only be a queen, because the queeny person also has the flexibility to be Joe Blow if he wants to. Although Bill's disdain for "queens" may not be clear from the above quote alone, his attitude toward queens was highly unfavorable. By contrast he had a higher regard for the queeny person because, in his view, the queeny person is engaging in play and thus his "core" is still masculine. The commuter views being defined by a full-time queen status as an unfortunate state of affairs that only afflicts those whose femininity is so overpowering she can never be anything else; her flavor is always the same. In the commuter's eyes the queen is frozen because she can never change into Joe Blow or anyone else; she is one-dimensional, a noun. By contrast the queeny person has the flexibility to slip out of his queeny persona and into other personas, including generic ones. In fact, for some commuters the generic ordinary Joe rather than the gay queen is their default identity. One suburban gay who defined himself as a regular guy, for instance, argued strongly for the low duration of his gayness in saying that "*very few minutes of the day* are defined by who I like to have sex with." Far more minutes a day, he went on to suggest, are defined by his position as an "ordinary guy in an ordinary suburban neighborhood."

The commuter views the full-time gay's sin as his inability to turn off his gayness in nongay spaces. For the commuter the lifestyler's inability to be anything but gay can be embarrassing. As Scott explains:

> *Some people are more tolerant [of queens], and I'm probably a little less tolerant. And it might depend on location. In some gay groups I'm not as put off by effeminate gay men as when I'm in a public restaurant and someone comes up to me who was overly effeminate. [In that case] I might feel a little embarrassed.*

Scott's primary concern is with queen displays that extend into unmarked times and spaces. He tolerates effeminacy in gay spaces "where they belong" but is embarrassed when such displays cross over into the nongay realm. For him and other commuters, the always effeminate gay man threatens his boundaries between gay and nongay time and space. Gay commuters worry that effeminate men may hinder their own mobility to move between a gay self in marked times and spaces and a nongay one outside those spaces.

Brian worries about the potential staining effect of spending too much of his time around gay lifestylers. A new traveler to the gay scene, Brian feels he can tell some people are gay by that little flamboyancy in their voice that he believes they have acquired from hanging around too much in all-gay environments. He likens picking up a "gay accent" from hanging around in New York's gay spaces to picking up a regional accent:

> *I don't want to say that people choose to talk feminine, but when it comes right down to it, it's learned to talk that way. Kind of like if you were a Texan in New Jersey you would lose your accent and if a New Jerseyan went to Texas they would gain an accent. So I think it's kind of like gaining an accent. So that's why I'm not particularly fond of hanging around very feminine people [too*

long]. I mean they're fun and everything but— yeah, I talk a little bit more feminine joking around with some of my [gay] friends at times, but then I'm like, "stop that."

Brian is content to be a traveler to peacock gay spaces and to even play it up a little himself when he is there, but he fears that too much time in gay space will cause him to pick up the "native accent" of gay lifestylers. Since he still has to turn it off in his life outside gay space, he worries about the potential spillover effect of spending too much time in the presence of queens and effeminate gay men. Like other commuters, he wants to be able to move between the two identities and their separate spaces.

The commuter views full-time gayness as a problem because it invades inappropriate times and places. For the commuter, weekends, nighttime, and vacations are the proper times to let gayness take over and become a master status. The commuter believes other times should be reserved for his unmarked identities. Commuters I spoke with, for instance, often disparaged gay politics as something for people "whose only goal in life is to live a gay lifestyle." They argued that they themselves held "real jobs" and thus were above what they saw as the immaturity of full-time gay activists. Andrew says, for instance, that while he agrees with the goals of gay activists, he thinks it is "silly how much *time* they let it consume." He goes on to say that people who take their jobs seriously don't have time to be "politically gay all of the time":

> *People who are working just don't have time to be on these panels or [in] these groups fighting for causes. . . . Gay politics never really concerned me. It never really interested me, and I never felt the desire to do anything about it. It's nice for these people who are graduate students and they don't really know what to do with their lives. I know a lot of people like this. This is their goal in life: to be gay, to be politically gay. But, ah, my life goes on.*

For Andrew and other commuters, the problem with gay activists is that they devote too much duration to their gay identity and thus do not leave enough duration to other identities such as their occupational identities. For many gay bar patrons like Andrew "being gay" is a nighttime activity. Any activist gay politics would likely extend beyond the duration and the confines of the bar scene and thus impinge on activities reserved for his diurnal self. Underlying Andrew's distinction between "people who are graduate students" (student lifestylers with the auxiliary characteristic of political activism) and "people who are working" is a temporal distinction between the full-time gay and the part-time gay. This same concern among commuters that a full-time gay identity pushes out other important identities came through when Bill explained his view that a queen is superficial because, unlike a queeny person, she can never talk about other facets of self: "queens are superficial because the only thing they ever talk about is gay life; they never talk about anything of substance like work or sports." Bill equates work and sports with substance because they are ingredients beyond one's nighttime self and beyond the auxiliary characteristics of gayness.

Like the lifestyler, the integrator has a problem with the part-time aspect of the gay commuter's identity. However, while the lifestyler complains that the gay commuter is only being true to himself in gay space, the integrator complains that the commuter is never being true to himself because he is always bracketing a part of himself. For the integrator neither suppressing one's gay identity nor foregrounding it and suppressing one's diurnal self are true displays of oneself. Warren expresses the integrator view:

> I don't like that some gay people I know, they are in the closet and they hide it . . . and they'll even say homophobic stuff just to fit in . . . and then— but then you go to the bar and they are the biggest queen in the bar. I mean if you're going to be gay why not just be gay? I mean just be yourself and be gay. Don't hide it, but don't make a big deal of it either. If you don't act [the way you act in a gay bar] normally, what makes you think you should act that way just because you are in a gay bar?

For Warren and other integrators, the commuter is problematic because he overcompensates for low duration with high density. He questions why the commuter cannot commit to one "core self" instead of shifting between two identity poles. He wonders why the commuter cannot just be one everyday gay self all of the time instead of a part-time everyday self and a part-time gay self. In the integrator's view, the commuter is untrue because his whole self is never present. He is always bracketing something off and hiding it from view. In contrast, all of the integrator's identity attributes are always accessible. Whereas the commuter divides his different identity commitments into separate temporal and spatial domains, the integrator mixes all of his commitments together into every minute of his life. One might think of the commuter's identity plate as resembling a TV dinner (all separate dishes compartmentalized into separate spheres so that only one dish can be accessed at a time), while the integrator's plate resembles a salad or a soup, where everything is mixed together. (The lifestyler's plate would have one giant habanero pepper—all spice with no moderating flavors.)

An integrator's view on the durational problem of commuters is exemplified by Bawer's complaint against gays whom he perceives as choosing to "shout on high volume" one day a year rather than put in the time to convince people "quietly" 365 days a year—that is for a display of too short duration and too high density:

> At Gay Pride Day Marches, some gay men and lesbians, like the Stonewall Rioters, have exposed America to images of raw sexuality—images that variously amuse, titillate, shock, and offend while revealing nothing important about who most of those people really are. Why, then, do some people do such things? Perhaps because they've been conditioned to think that on that gay high holy day, the definitively gay thing to do is to be as defiant as those heroes twenty-five years ago. Perhaps they do it because they can more easily grasp the concept of enjoying one day per year of delicious anarchy than of devoting 365 days per year to a somewhat more disciplined and strategically sensible demonstration designed to advance the causes of respect, dignity, and equality. . . .

Interestingly, both lifestylers and integrators attack commuters for their short binges of gay display. They differ, however, in that the lifestyler views the bursts of gayness as the commuter's true colors and the rest of his duration as problematic, while the integrator views the commuter's short binges as the problem and his "364-day self" outside the parade as closer to his true colors.

On the issue of duration, commuters favor a mobile self while lifestylers and integrators favor a unitary self. For the commuter the self is flexible and fluid enough to blend in anywhere. The lifestyler conceives of the unitary self as organized hierarchically around a master status with all other facets of self as auxiliary characteristics. The integrator's unitary self, by contrast, is composed of constant adjectives arrayed in a flat, modular non-hierarchical way around the nebulous label of "human being." The lifestyler and the integrator cannot understand the commuter's constantly changing self since it shows little commitment to a "core self" of any kind. The commuter, by contrast, cannot understand the frozenness and inflexibility of his lifestyler and integrator counterparts, who refuse to adapt and respond appropriately to changes in their social environment.

Pit Bull Owners and Stigma

HILLARY TWINING, ARNOLD ARLUKE, and GARY PATRONEK

Social order rests upon conformity to expectations. Conformity then becomes the taken-for-granted expectation when people come into contact with each other. Once a person has violated, or has a reputation for violating, the expectations for conformity, the assumption of predictability is lost. It is now displaced by anxiety over the possibility of deviance.

What about the friends and family of a person who has violated the expectation of conformity? What are the problems they face because of their presumed social ties to the rule-breaker? Often, they are presumed to have aided, supported, or encouraged the violation of the rules. Thus, friends and family of socially designated deviants find that they may well be tarred by the same brush that has smeared their friend or relative. In some instances, as Hillary Twining, Arnold Arluke, and Gary Patronek report, pit bull owners suffer from the negative reputation that their companion animals, the pit bulls, have. To manage the stigma problem, they use a variety of techniques to mitigate the situation. These strategies include passing off their dogs as breeds other than pit bulls, denying that their behavior is biologically determined, debunking adverse media coverage, using humor, emphasizing counterstereotypical behavior, avoiding stereotypical accessories, taking preventive measures, or becoming breed ambassadors.

For the first half of this century, pit bulls enjoyed a positive image in America. During World War I, these dogs stood for American courage and were featured in a series of patriotic wartime posters. In the 1930s, a popular show called *The Little Rascals*, as well as the *Our Gang* comedy series, featured a pit bull. And from 1890 to 1948, pit bulls were very popular dogs to own because they were seen as "a good-natured watchdog and family pet" (Jessup, 1995, p. 43).

However, the image of pit bulls has suffered in recent years. The popular media commonly portrays pit bulls as demonic animals—unpredictable and savage in their behavior toward humans. For example, the headline of an article in *U.S. News and World Report* (1987) proclaimed that pit bulls were "The Most Dangerous in America." The article's author claimed that "America's baddest dog" was in a separate category from shepherds, Dobermans, and Rottweilers because they cannot "chomp through a chain-link fence" like pit bulls. Cities passed ordinances that restricted or banned pit bulls, and the media kept the hysteria going by reporting every pit bull attack while minimizing those of other breeds.

The result is that pit bulls have come to be seen as an abomination or disturbance in the natural order—an unacceptable threat to the perceived security and stability of the entire community and a violation of the almost sacred image of the dog as an amiable cultural hero (Serpell, 1995). In other words, they have become an outlaw or deviant breed. Feeding this negative portrayal of pit bulls have been depictions of their "owners" that threaten mainstream America. Media reports of attacks by these dogs were invariably accompanied by value-laden descriptions of their owners as people whom "average citizens" might find dangerous. According to Hearne (1991), these reports often described pit bull owners as white thugs or poor urban blacks and Latinos who kept their dogs in dope dens and fed them raw meat to make them as mean as possible.

This negative image has implications for people who have pit bulls as companion animals. On the one hand, some people might be drawn to this breed in the hope of exploiting and perpetuating its vicious reputation. Such owners seek to use these dogs as status symbols of power and aggression and to reap the secondary benefit of an intimidating persona. On the other hand, some people might see qualities in this breed that run contrary to its negative image and want to establish "traditional" human-dog relationships with their pit bulls. Nevertheless, they "inherit," and presumably have to contend with, adverse public perceptions of their pets. Sociologically, this adverse perception can be considered a breed stigma where the animal itself has a "spoiled" or tainted identity and where owners may experience a courtesy stigma as a consequence of their association with, and ownership of, pit bulls (Sigelman, Howell, Cornell, Cutright, and Dewey, 1991).

According to Goffman (1963), humans experience stigma when they possess certain physical or mental traits that result in various negative consequences such as social exclusion, anxiety, alienation, loss of self-esteem, discrimination, and social disenfranchisement. In the face of social disapproval or even fear, stigmatized individuals seek to manage or respond to these adverse perceptions by relying on interpersonal strategies that minimize, neutralize, or evade their stigma—as, for example, do epileptics (Schneider & Conrad, 1980) and animal researchers (Arluke, 1991).

Individuals undertake these steps to manage their stigma as a part of the dramaturgy of everyday life whereby people seek to present a certain image of themselves, especially in terms of the small, unremarkable interactions that comprise a substantial part of routine social behavior. According to Turner (1998), ". . . individuals deliberately 'give' and inadvertently 'give off' signs that provide others with information about how to respond" (p. 394). Although some information that people communicate is inadvertent, much of it is deliberate and carefully orchestrated. Given the degree to which our social reality hinges on people's unspoken agreement to uphold common expectations about public conduct, the failure to do so results in a sense of uneasiness. In this regard, people not only maintain and promote social interactions through their presentation of self but also seek to repair damaged or disrupted relationships.

Dramaturgical sociologists have noted that impression management can involve a "team" of actors who collaborate to create particular perceptions of themselves (Goffman, 1959), and a handful of recent studies suggest that team presentations of self can extend across species lines, such that humans who are responsible for particular animals may seek to control or influence how other people perceive their animals and them (e.g., Cantwell, 1992). For instance, Sanders (1990) notes that companion animals and their owners often function as teams in public settings when owners re-establish social equilibrium by accounting for their dogs' actions after they misbehave. Although Sanders' "excusing tactics" refer to specific incidents of canine disobedience, they also are relevant to the ways that pit bull owners respond to their anticipation of negative perceptions of their dogs. Pit bull owners may seek to manage impressions of their dogs if they discover that their dogs, or the breed as a whole, are viewed in an unfavorable light and if they care about this negative image.

METHOD

Ethnographic interviews were conducted with pit bull owners to explore how they experience and manage breed stigma. Names of pit bull owners were obtained from two shelters in large eastern Massachusetts cities. The forty most recent pit bull adopters from each shelter were sent a letter describing this study. Of this group, a total of 28 owners were interviewed. Except for one pilot interview, all participants had adopted a pit bull within the past year and a half. They lived in cities and suburbs throughout the central and northeast part of the state as well as in southern New Hampshire. The vast majority of respondents were Caucasian, between the ages of 20 and 50. Both blue and white collar professions were represented, although the former were more common than the latter. The types of households ranged from single adults to couples and families.

The interviews were semi-structured and usually lasted about 45 minutes. The questions focused on participants' previous experience with pit bulls, their decision to adopt this kind of dog, reactions from strangers, family, and friends, and the way in which this breed's stigma affected dog ownership. On the whole, the vast majority of respondents appeared to be comfortable and forthcoming during the interviews.

RESULTS

Results indicate that the nature of this stigma usually revolved around accusations of the breed's viciousness and lack of predictability. Although a few owners spoke with nonchalance about the breed's negative public reputation, the majority of respondents expressed concern and frustration about this stigma. In the face of such stigma, respondents used one or more excusing or accounting tactics. These strategies included passing their dogs as breeds other than pit bulls, denying that their behavior is biologically determined, debunking adverse media coverage, using humor, emphasizing counterstereotypical behavior, avoiding stereotypical equipment or accessories, taking preventive measures, or becoming breed ambassadors.

BREED STIGMA

According to many respondents, when they and their pit bulls encountered strangers, direct allegations of viciousness were rare. More common, they claimed, was a sense that strangers were fearful or apprehensive. Most respondents, for example, could recall situations in which people on the street tried to avoid their dogs, either by walking around them or by crossing the street. One owner who lives just outside Boston in a city with a prominent pit bull population said,

> *In the morning when I walk [my dog], sometimes I cross paths . . . and as I'm coming out [there is] this lady walking her little—I don't know what it is; it's a Schnauzer or Lhasa Apso or something . . . I could be in my driveway and she's already trying to avoid the dog.*

For another respondent, this avoidance was expressed more directly. Recounting a situation in which a delivery man refused to come to the house, he said,

> *My dogs were out in the front yard and the guy would not come near the house. He parked up the street, called me from the cell phone. [He said], "You have two dogs in your yard, two pit bulls; I'm not coming in there."*

This desire to avoid pit bulls altogether was occasionally expressed by family members as well. Several respondents had relatives who did not want to visit them because of their dogs. For one owner, it took positive reports about his pit bull from siblings before his stepmother would consider a visit. In another case, the respondent's father agreed to visit but did not want to stay in his house with the dog:

> He was supposed to come visit and stay with us, and he wouldn't stay with us because [our dog] was a pit bull. Not because he's afraid of dogs, because he has a dog, but basically just because she was a pit bull, he was dead against it.

The presence of children often heightened people's caution around pit bulls. One owner, although familiar with occasional avoidance from strangers, was struck by the dramatic reaction of two parents as she and her leashed pit bull walked by their children on a busy road:

> I saw these people; they were walking on Route 9 and I was coming up by the pond there. The two adults were next to the pond side of the sidewalk and their children [were] half on the road, half on the sidewalk . . . They're letting their kids practically play in traffic—they see me coming with the dog and they immediately push their children to the side of the road sheltering them from the dog.

For this respondent, the parents' reaction to her pit bull seemed ironic in light of the comparative risk of letting their children walk so close to a busy road.

Concern for children frequently prompted people to voice more specific fears about pit bulls. One owner's relative related a story in which a friend's daughter was bitten on the face by the family's pit bull when she accidentally stepped on the dog. For a young couple with a newborn, concern about their pit bull from friends and family had been fairly low-key ("Is the dog going to be okay?"), but for another respondent, the reaction was much more pronounced: "When [my daughter] was first born, everyone said, 'You've got to be careful. That dog is going to eat her; he's going to kill her; he's going to bite her.'"

Although concerns about safety around pit bulls were most pronounced with children, adults often harbored the same fears. Several respondents were self-employed contractors or salespeople who spent most of the day in their trucks traveling between clients, and they often brought their pit bulls with them. One of these respondents related the following story:

> One of my customers didn't know that I had my dog who . . . would sleep down on the floor [of my truck]. And this guy got in to move my truck in front of his garage and . . . slammed the door shut, and [my dog] sprung up off the floor, leapt onto the seat, and prepared to give him a big, old kiss. And [the customer] urinated! The guy was so scared that he messed himself.

Although the element of surprise certainly contributed to this man's reaction, it is possible that the dog's breed was also a factor in his split-second reaction.

Some owners described situations in which people approached them and asked if their pit bulls were friendly. Although this type of inquiry indicated an acknowledgment that there are good pit bulls, it nonetheless communicated expectations about the way in which most pit bulls behave. When one respondent told a woman who was petting his dog that the dog was a pit bull, she quickly began to retreat. He pointed out that his dog was still the same friendly animal she had just seen, and the woman acknowledged his point but made it clear that his pit bull was an exception to the rule. She commented, "I'm really glad I got to meet a pit bull because I hadn't ever met one, and it's a great learning experience for me that there is at least one nice one out there."

Other questions and comments challenged respondents' sense of trust in their pit bulls. One owner's neighbor said, "Do you really trust that dog? Aren't you worried that she's going to attack someone?" Questions about a dog's trustworthiness

could be particularly vexing for respondents because such comments seemed to presume that the
speaker had a more complete knowledge of the dog
than did the owner. Referring to several co-workers,
another woman said,

*They're just like, "Oh my God, why would you get
a dog like that?" Like you're asking for trouble.
And then I'd say, "It's all in the way we bring this
dog up." And they're like, "Oh no, that dog will
turn on you." I hate to hear that. I'm like, "Don't
tell me this! I've had [my dog] for how many
years? She could never turn on us!"*

The suggestion that stereotypes could be more
accurate than extensive personal experience left
owners such as this one frustrated and upset.

For some people, the pit bull's tough reputation
precluded the possibility that this type of dog could
assume the more benign role of canine companion.
Pit bulls have been described as weapons; as
Hearne (1991) pointed out, they are often portrayed
as guard dogs for illegal activity. When one young
woman identified the breed of dog that she had
adopted, her mother asked, "Why did you think you
needed a dog for protection?" Although her mother
didn't claim that pit bulls are vicious or bad, her
question turned on the assumption that they serve a
particular purpose: to protect their owners.

In the experience of some respondents, negative assumptions about their dogs were unspeci-
fied, but the tone of people's remarks left no doubt
as to their opinion of the breed. When a respondent who teaches at a local college told his
colleagues that his family had adopted a pit bull,
one of them exclaimed, "Oh my God, you didn't!"
Stigma was also indirectly expressed in terms
of the suggestion of more appropriate breeds.
Another colleague chided him, saying, "Couldn't
you have been a little smarter and gotten a Cocker
spaniel or a Labrador retriever?" There was a
sense among some of these owners of an unofficial canon of appropriate family dogs, such as
spaniels or retrievers, among others. In adopting a
pit bull, they were stepping outside this tradition
and confounding other people's expectations.

Law enforcement regulations and practices
also appeared to stigmatize pit bulls, according to
respondents. Many were troubled by the implications of animal control laws and ordinances that
singled out pit bulls. Massachusetts cities such
as Haverhill and Salem have muzzle laws that
apply to pit bulls and other "dangerous breeds."
Springfield has outlawed pit bulls altogether.
Lynn passed a similar ban in the late 1980s, but
later it was challenged and overturned.

Some respondents, especially those who live
in areas with a high concentration of pit bulls,
were sensitive to prejudicial treatment this breed
seems to receive from police and animal control
officers. One owner who currently lives in Lynn
was told by a friend, ". . . pit bulls in Lynn have a
wicked reputation and whenever there's a problem with a pit bull, the cops will shoot them right
on the spot." The implication of this comment
was that police officers in this city consider pit
bulls too dangerous to be evaluated on a case-by-
case basis. The small group of owners whose dogs
had been reprimanded by a police officer or animal control official often attributed the response
to bias or discrimination. One man had been told
that he could not walk his mother's pit bull in public while the dog was in heat. According to this
respondent, "I was like, 'What kind of law is that?
I've never heard of it.' I think the dog officer was
just having a problem because [my mother's dog]
was a pit bull."

In sum, breed stigma was manifested in a
variety of ways both subtle and direct. Many
respondents found that people simply avoided
their pit bulls, but a large number of owners also
described more pronounced reactions, especially
when children were present. According to respondents' experience, the pit bull stereotype had several components to it; pit bulls were expected to
be vicious and untrustworthy, unpredictable, and
particularly dangerous around children. Although
most references to breed stigma revolved around
informal interactions with other people, some
respondents described this stigma in terms of
larger social institutions such as animal control
and law enforcement departments.

MANAGING THE STIGMA

Passing individuals from stigmatized, disenfranchised groups sometimes attempt to hide their identity and to represent themselves as authentic members of the dominant culture. Respondents also used passing as a tactic to fit in with mainstream culture, although it was their dogs and not they whose identities were masked; in order to deflect the stigma of pit bulls, respondents presented their dogs as unproblematic and acceptable pets.

Two conditions make it possible to pass their dogs as *not* pit bulls. First, much of the public is unaware that the terms "pit bull" and "American Staffordshire Terrier" often function as synonyms. In 1935, the American Kennel Club (AKC) agreed to register these dogs but chose to call them Staffordshire Terriers to avoid association with dog fighting. To confuse the issue further, the name Staffordshire Terrier was changed to American Staffordshire Terrier in 1972 when the AKC began recognizing the Staffordshire Bull Terrier from England. Shelters also have contributed to breed confusion in their efforts to promote pit bull adoption. Fearing that negative associations may discourage people from adopting such dogs, humane societies have become creative marketers; the San Francisco Society for the Prevention of Cruelty to Animals, for example, has gone so far as to refer to them as St. Francis Terriers. Although less radical in their approach, the shelters involved in this study make it a point to call their pit bulls American Staffordshire Terriers, and the cage cards display this AKC breed name.

Beneath the confusion about this dual American Staffordshire Terrier/pit bull identity is a larger and more basic issue: the public's frequent inability to identify the breed correctly. Although pit bulls have continued to attract headlines and media coverage, a surprising number of respondents indicated that they regularly encounter people who do not recognize pit bulls at all. Several respondents surmised that this lack of recognition is due partly to the assumption that pit bulls are very large dogs. The other factor that, according to some respondents, contributed to this lack of breed recognition was the expectation that pit bulls, by definition, behave aggressively. As one respondent illustrated,

> We brought a pit bull and a Rottweiler down to Martha's Vineyard on the ferry and we had them on-leash, and everybody came up to the pit bull and was petting her and whatnot and [saying], "What a sweet dog." And then they're like, "What kind of dog is it?" They had no idea . . . Once they found out it was a pit bull, they kind of shied away.

Confusion surrounding the multiple names used to refer to pit bulls, as well as the inconsistency with which they were accurately identified, offered respondents an opportunity to present their dogs in a better light simply by the way in which they referred to their breed. Many owners attempted to manage breed stigma by studiously avoiding the term pit bull and replacing it with a more neutral and respectable name such as American Staffordshire Terrier. By using this term, respondents passed their pit bull as a more idealized version of the breed. According to one man, "I always say 'Staffordshire Terrier'—always; I never say 'pit bull.' I guess maybe subconsciously I know it kind of conjures up bad feelings about the breed." Another owner expressed similar concerns about using the name pit bull to refer to her dog; she said, ". . . I'm afraid that people will get the wrong idea and the wrong impression of [my dog]. Because he's nothing [to be afraid of]. He's such a wimp! He's so easygoing and laid-back."

Other respondents chose to distance their pit bulls even further from the breed's intimidating public persona by emphasizing their unknown or mixed heritage as shelter dogs. The notion of passing functioned more directly in this context insofar as owners avoided all references to the breed. Several owners referred to their dogs as a "mixed breed," a "mutt," or a "pound dog." One respondent found that people often identified her dog incorrectly and she chose not to correct their misconception. She remarked,

> Most people think [my dog] is a Boxer. She's got, like, big cheeks [and] she doesn't have that tight

pit bull face at all . . . So most people just think she's a Boxer mix and ask me what she is, and I'll say, "Oh yeah, she's a Boxer mix."

Use of the term pit bull was sometimes situational and depended on people's initial reaction to an owner's dog. For example, some respondents deliberately avoided the term when other people showed signs of fear around their dogs. One woman said, "I have said to people that [my dog] is a pit bull, but only to people that I know aren't afraid of them . . ." Another respondent described a tier of related breed names that he used, depending on the degree of apprehension that he encountered:

A lot of it depends on the people you meet . . . If I see people [who are] very timid with dogs, a lot of times I'll tell them [my dog] is an American Bulldog, because he does look a lot like the picture of an American Bulldog . . . Sometimes we'll just say—if they're really afraid of dogs—we'll say, "Oh, he's a Boxer mix."

These respondents focused on moderating people's reactions to their dogs by choosing the most appropriate name for each audience. Through this approach, passing remained fluid and context-driven.

In addition to providing respondents with greater control over the presentation of their dogs, passing allowed them to orchestrate positive encounters. Many owners managed breed stigma by allowing their dogs to make a good first impression before telling others that they were pit bulls. This approach was effective because it offered people positive, firsthand experience with pit bulls, which directly counteracted the expectations they might have had otherwise. Passing in this context was achieved through delayed breed identification, as opposed to an indefinite concealment of the dog's breed.

Not Blaming the Dog

A second strategy for neutralizing breed stigma was for respondents to prevent their own pit bulls, as well as the breed itself, from being blamed for bad behavior. This was accomplished in several ways: they emphasized the role of environment and training as determinants of behavior; they pointed out similarities between pit bull behavior and that found in other breeds; they noted that these dogs were unaware of their own strength; and they insisted that their dogs were unlike other, more stereotypical pit bulls.

Environment was often expressed in terms of owners' attitudes toward, and treatment of, their dogs, with particular emphasis placed on the importance of respect. One respondent explained,

It's like children [and] how you bring them up. If you bring them up with no respect, bring them up with no discipline, then they're going to respond that way . . . It's the same way [when] you bring your animal up.

Another respondent stated,

. . . if you treat [your dogs] well, they'll treat you well. If you abuse them, they're not going to have any respect for you, not going to have any love for you. So what do you expect? The dog will turn on you.

Many of these owners compared dogs to people in terms of their response to poor treatment, noting in one case, for example: "If you abuse a kid, if you abuse a wife, if you abuse an animal, they're going to react." Another respondent remarked

I mean, it's like people; if you get some kid that has been beaten all his life, he's going to go out and be aggressive towards people. And that's how it is with [my dog] and with pits [in general].

These comments conveyed the belief that behavior does not occur in a vacuum; rather, pit bulls, like any other animal (including humans), are shaped by, and react to, their environment.

Training was also emphasized, particularly in terms of its contribution to aggressive behavior. One respondent remarked, "I think almost any breed can be trained to be bad-aggressive." Another respondent, describing a group of pit bull owners he had seen in a nearby city, said,

"They wanted a pit bull, they wanted this little, vicious dog that just barks at people. You know, they foster that and they want that. I think that's why the dog ends up being that way."

Several respondents underscored this emphasis on training by noting that pit bulls exhibit a particularly strong desire to please their owners. This malleability makes training a particularly potent tool when pit bulls fall into the wrong hands. One respondent remarked,

I think with pit bulls, they'll turn out exactly the way you want them [to]. If you want them to be tough and vicious and intimidating, they will do that for you . . . If you want a nice all-around dog—very athletic, smart, all that—you can get that [too].

The assertion that pit bulls' behavior is determined largely by their owners and their environment plays an important role in defusing breed stigma because these dogs are often perceived as naturally vicious. Although respondents acknowledged the unusual strength of these dogs, they denied any malicious intent on their part and maintained that owners could choose to channel these physical capabilities in positive or negative directions. The few respondents who witnessed aggressive and unwanted behavior in their dogs targeted inbreeding as the problem; dogs "born bad" were considered anomalies that had resulted from poor breeding, either accidental or deliberate.

In addition, many respondents deflected blame by comparing pit bull behavior to that of other dogs and thereby normalizing it. For example, an owner noted that one of his pit bulls could become possessive of her food around his other dog but said, ". . . any dog is like that." According to another respondent,

My brother-in-law was telling my sister all the reasons why not to [get a pit bull]—you know, the horror stories. Yeah, they happen, but . . . any dog could be that way if you train him and treat him that way.

One owner recalled that his dog had been "nippy" when he adopted it as a seven-month-old;

when asked if this behavior had subsided, the respondent said, "Oh yeah, he stopped. He doesn't do that any more. That was just puppy [behavior]." By emphasizing that the potential for certain behavior exists in all dogs, these owners sought to demystify pit bulls. Respondents used this excusing tactic to discredit breed-specific criticisms and to promote the idea that, at a fundamental level, a dog is a dog, regardless of breed.

As another twist on the theme, don't blame the dog, some respondents focused on their dogs' lack of awareness about their own strength. This common refrain was voiced by one woman who owns two pit bulls: "They don't know their own strength really." Echoing this observation, another owner said, "[My dog] doesn't really know her strength, I think. That's what I worry about, because she is really strong." When owners described interactions between children and their pit bulls, many of them expressed the concern that their dogs could easily knock a child over. For most respondents, the issue was not that their dogs would behave aggressively with children but that their dogs would unintentionally hurt or frighten a child because of the breed's strength and excitability. A mother of two older children offered this advice: "I don't think I would recommend this kind of dog to anyone with young, young children because [my pit bull] is very forceful. It's not that he's aggressive towards them, but just in play . . . he's strong."

Several respondents managed breed stigma by pointing out that their pit bull was not like other more stereotypical pit bulls. For example, one respondent said,

[My friend] was like, "Well, I just don't like pit bulls. I don't like Rottweilers or pit bulls." I felt upset that she said that right in front of me with my dog. I could see if she said, "Well, other pit bulls . . ."

Another woman described a situation in which she was sitting in a doctor's office while her boyfriend waited outside with their pit bull; when another patient came into the office and made a disparaging remark about her dog, this owner responded in the following manner: "I said,

'Listen lady, there's nothing wrong with that dog.' She said, 'I've been attacked by one.' I said, 'Well, you weren't attacked by my dog.'"

In sum, respondents not only emphasized the role of environment and training but also deflected blame from their dogs in several ways: they sought to normalize pit bull behavior, they focused on their dogs' lack of awareness about their own strength, and they rejected breed stereotypes by insisting on specificity. Each of these approaches to managing breed stigma had a similar goal: namely, to tell others "don't blame the dog."

Debunking Media Coverage

As a group, respondents had a complicated and somewhat ambivalent reaction to pit bull-related media coverage, and many of them took an active role in debunking press coverage and media reports. This approach to managing breed stigma included four general criticisms: selective reporting, sensationalism, a lack of objectivity, and a failure to provide context.

Many owners, especially those who had been on the receiving end of aggressive behavior from other breeds, felt that pit bulls were unfairly overrepresented in the media reports. A young businessman who owned two pit bulls said,

It annoys me that only pit bulls are shown. I mean, there are a lot of other dogs that attack. When I was young, I was attacked by a collie, you know, a Lassie dog. You never hear about those stories but . . . you always tend to hear the worst about pit bulls.

Echoing these sentiments, another owner remarked,

When you see an article in the newspaper and all it says is "pit bull," the dog's [automatically] a killer. If a Cocker spaniel attacked a kid, you wouldn't even hear about it. You never see any bad press about . . . these "killer dogs."

These respondents complained that journalists were more interested in reporting dog attacks and bites if they involved pit bulls. There was also frequent cynicism about articles and television

reports that focused on the lurid details of pit bull attacks. One woman quipped, "What do they say? 'If it bleeds, it leads.'" When asked about the breed of dog that was mentioned in a particular newspaper article, another owner said, "I think it was a pit bull; that's what the paper said. Of course, because that's what sells." Owners argued that media coverage was fueled by a desire to sell papers or to attract television viewers and that reporters were simply giving people what they wanted to hear.

A related criticism concerned the objectivity of media coverage. One respondent had owned an American Staffordshire Terrier who bit another dog, prompting the dog's owner to go to a newspaper with the story. Recalling the coverage, this respondent said,

. . . the paper called me and I just kind of said, "No comment," and hung up. And then they put that in there, [to] try and make me look bad; you know, "He's not concerned and just said no comment." . . . They made it [sound] like if [my dog] was a pit bull, she would have killed [the other dog]. Even the animal control officer had a quote: "If she had been a real pit bull, she would have never let go and killed him."

As this experience illustrates, many respondents felt that people in the media had already made up their minds about this breed and that they reported pit bull-related incidents accordingly.

Many respondents pointed out that aggressive behavior was often taken out of context by the media and that important questions about the dog's background and upbringing had not been asked. According to one young woman, "If I read an article about [a pit bull incident], I would ask, 'How was this dog raised? Who was its owner? What kind of life did it have before this owner?'" Most respondents emphasized that aggressive behavior does not occur in a vacuum—that it is triggered by specific events that are often overlooked or unacknowledged by the media.

It was common for owners to disagree with the tone or content of this breed's media coverage.

Given the degree of negative attention pit bulls receive in newspapers and on television, owners frequently managed breed stigma by debunking these media reports and calling for a more critical interpretation.

Respondents Use Humor to Reaffirm Their Perceptions

Many respondents noticed a sharp discrepancy between the demeanor of their own pit bulls and the reputation of the breed as a whole; this contrast occasionally prompted jokes and humor. Although such a response did not involve an active rebuttal of the breed's reputation, it allowed owners to reaffirm their own perception of pit bulls. Like any breed of dog, pit bulls have many dimensions to their personalities, and the occasions for this humor allowed respondents the opportunity to refute the one-sidedness of breed stereotypes.

This humor often revolved around contrast and contradiction; although the popular image of pit bulls points to vicious, aggressive dogs, many owners had encountered the opposite behavior. For example, humor often resulted from the observation of a dog's affability and playfulness in light of the expectation that pit bulls are tough, intimidating dogs. One respondent joked with her husband about their two pit bulls' night-time routine in front of the television, a routine where it was clear that they were "family dogs" and not guard dogs or uncontrollable animals. She remarked,

> [One of our dogs] will come up and plop down next to you and put his head on you . . . [Our other dog] is the same way. They just want to cuddle up to you and be next to you.

She added, "We kind of laugh about it, [about] the stereotype. I mean, we don't like it, but I kind of try and make a joke of it, like 'Killer pit bull? Yeah, right!'" Another respondent joked about the way her pit bull greeted people: ". . . if people come into the house, she gets all excited and she does this cute little bunny hop and we think, 'Oh, look at the vicious pit bull!'"

Other things could underscore the juxtaposition between a dog's personality and appearance, thereby providing an opportunity for humor. For instance, humor could be prompted by the dog's occasional habits. When asked if he ever jokes about the breed's reputation, one owner responded, "Yeah, especially when [my dog] does silly things, like when she's just snoring away when she's sleeping and we're like, 'Oh, look at the aggressive pit bull!'"

In addition to comical poses and behavior, accessories could serve this purpose. Studded collars are often used to emphasize the tough image of pit bulls, but one respondent remembers laughing at the incongruity of such a collar on her brother's dog. This pit bull had been nicknamed "Pathetic Petey" by the family and according to the respondent, ". . . if it rained, he would lie in my brother's office and moan the whole time." She added, "Petey was the most docile dog that there possibly was." When the family saw the studded collar, ". . . we would laugh and say, 'That is so Petey, right?!'" Sometimes Petey would be adorned with goggles and sunglasses, and the respondent remarked, "The dog was a riot." Such accessories underscored the contrast between this family's pit bull and the breed image while allowing them to poke fun at the reputation. These respondents' humor, whether prompted by the presence or absence of particular personality traits and behaviors, emphasized contrast and contradiction. Such humor allowed owners to counteract breed stigma, if only among themselves, and to emphasize the limited scope of breed stereotypes.

Looks Aren't Everything

Although some respondents were quick to acknowledge various physical characteristics of the breed which tend to exacerbate pit bull stereotypes, many owners emphasized their pit bulls' personalities over their appearance. In other words, this fifth stigma-managing strategy sought to demonstrate that there is more to these dogs than meets the eye.

In comparison to smaller breeds or dogs that have long coats and soft-mouths, pit bulls look built for power. One woman noted, ". . . their mouth in proportion to the rest of their head is bigger. And they just have a very clean, sleek look about them, as opposed to a Golden [retriever]." Another owner commented, "[Pit bulls] are real brawny, muscular; [they have a] wide, broad chest. They've got a big jaw . . . They just look mean." Respondents such as these spoke candidly about the implications of their dogs' strength. According to one owner, "[Pit bulls] have physical capabilities that are different from toy poodles." Another owner, noting that his pit bull chews through medium-sized logs from the woodpile, stated this point more bluntly, saying of his dog, "She does have the equipment to cause problems."

As a way of counterbalancing the effect of this breed's appearance and physical power, many respondents alluded to images and stories of their pit bulls' affection, which directly contradicted their intimidating reputation. Owners frequently focused on displays of affection as well as the breed's sensitivity and attunement to people. One owner described the introduction between her pit bull and a wary friend who was concerned about the dog because she had young children:

> . . . She came over here and sat down . . . and [my dog] got up on the couch and started kissing her and everything. And she's like, "Oh my God; well, I guess this is okay—the dog is just going to kiss my kids to death!"

Another owner, focusing on the contrast between his dog's physical strength and her docile personality, explained, "[My pit bull] is a strong, powerful dog but, you know, she'd lick you to death."

Respondents also described specific incidents that highlighted their dogs' sensitivity, especially toward people considered weak and vulnerable such as the disabled, the elderly, and the very young. For example, the wheelchair bound mother of a respondent's girlfriend had been very skeptical about the couple's pit bull adoption. According to this respondent,

> I brought the dog in and he lay on the floor and [my girlfriend's] sister patted him and everything

else. So finally [my girlfriend's mother] said, "Why don't you bring him over here." So I brought him over so that he could, you know, sniff her and lick her and she could pat him. Well, he gradually crawled up ever so gently and lay prone, kind of half on her and half next to her, and licked her face, and from then on she was won over.

In this encounter, the respondent's pit bull was not only well-mannered and friendly but also seemed to display an instinctive sense about how to modify his behavior to fit the situation. Such stories emphasized the idea that appearances can be deceiving.

For many of these respondents, their pit bulls were walking contradictions: powerful yet gentle, rambunctious yet restrained. In contrast to dog owners who must contend with the ramifications of having small, adorable breeds with short fuses, these respondents faced the challenge of owning a breed that appears threatening but loves people. These pit bull owners attempted to manage breed stigma by arguing that behavior, not appearance, expressed the truth about their dogs, and their stories underscored the contention that "looks aren't everything."

Respondents Alter Physical Presentation

A sixth stigma-managing strategy was for respondents to alter the physical presentation of their pit bulls to avoid any appearance that might communicate the mean or aggressive image widely subscribed to in popular culture. This approach is contrary to the tough, intimidating image of pit bulls emphasized by various accessories such as spiked leather collars and heavy harnesses. As one respondent observed, pit bulls wearing this type of equipment resemble "gladiator dogs."

Many respondents were particularly critical of young teenage pit bull owners who used such accessories and equipment on their own pit bulls. As one owner said,

> We went to the beach . . . this weekend and every dog we saw was a pit. Every dog. And all of them had those collars with the spikes on them, and a lot of [the people there] were younger teenage guys. . . .

You can tell that these owners have [their dogs] just to show off, just to say, "Oh, I have a pit," and God only knows what else they do to them.

These respondents, in turn, were careful about the choices they made in presenting their own dogs. Referring to large, studded collars, one man said,

I've stayed away from that, somewhat on purpose, because I didn't want to recreate the bad image that they have. When [my dog] was a puppy, a real small puppy, there was a collar that had the small, spherical studs [or] beads on it. Now that she's bigger, she'll just wear a plain collar.

Referring to this type of collar, one respondent said, "I bought [my dog] one and I returned it; it made him look too mean. I bought him one, I had it for a day, and I brought it back."

Concerns about breed presentation frequently crystallized around particular training devices and equipment. For an owner who had to treat her pit bull for kennel cough, the use of a harness was a necessity because she didn't want to irritate her dog's throat further with pressure from a collar. However, this respondent noticed how the harness affected reaction to her dog and she was quick to return to a plain collar after treatment. Some owners were concerned about the image projected by pinch or prong collars and modified their usage accordingly. One respondent explained,

We took [our dog] to training and [the instructor] suggested it because he pulled hard at first. . . . At first we were like, "We're not using those collars," because, you know, [they] looked so scary.

This couple eventually decided to use the pinch collar with their pit bull, but only as long as it took to train him not to pull on the leash. Respondents also did not like to use muzzles on their pit bulls because they reinforced fear of them. One respondent lived in a city that required pit bulls to be muzzled in public. He said,

I think it's going to scare them even more, seeing that the dog has to wear a muzzle. They're going to

think the dog is vicious, mean, [that the dog] bites. [My dog] will lay down [and show you] these sad eyes until you take it off.

Because the city's muzzle law compromised this respondent's ability to control breed presentation, he limited the time of his dog's public exposure by walking the dog only at night.

Although none of the respondents deliberately added accessories to soften their dog's image, several recalled situations in which they had unknowingly created that effect. One owner, for instance, said,

. . . I bought [my dog] a coat for the wintertime because I would walk her outside and she'd be shaking. So I got her a little fleece coat, and the reactions I get when she's wearing her coat are very different from the reactions that I got before I got the coat . . . I would see people and they would kind of shy away and [then] they'd be like, "Oh, she has her coat on today! Oh, look at her in her little coat; doesn't she look nice." She was definitely less intimidating with her coat on. I should maybe think about getting her a summer coat!

Although this respondent did not buy the coat in order to change her pit bull's appearance, its effect was noticeable. She, like the respondents above, were acutely aware of how certain physical accessories could easily reinforce an image of pit bulls that they wanted to avoid.

Respondents Use Preventive Measures

A seventh strategy used by some respondents entailed managing breed stigma by modifying their dogs' behaviors or physical capabilities. By training their pit bulls to avoid questionable behavior, however innocent, many respondents sought to anticipate and defuse people's concern. Alluding to their Rottweilers, Gillespie, Leffler, and Lerner (1996) wrote, ". . . we faced a definitional problem of how to recontrive them as non-threatening, even friendly and pleasant—safe for the people our dogs might frighten" (p. 176). The pit bull owners in this study faced a similar challenge, and the preventive measures they undertook included a variety of approaches such as refusing to play particular games, discouraging "mouthiness," training their dogs not to jump up on people, and implementing certain protocols around children. These preventive measures offered owners an effective method for ensuring that people did not misinterpret their pit bulls' behavior, given the vicious reputation attributed to these dogs.

Although studies of pit bull anatomy have found no evidence of a "locking jaw," this breed does have a very strong jaw and can grip with considerable tenacity. Several respondents had a policy of not playing tug-of-war with their dogs because they did not want to develop this jaw strength. According to one owner,

> My friends think it's great when they get [my dog] locked onto the rope and they're tugging with him and stuff. I really haven't done that with him. I really don't want him to know that [sort of game].

Avoidance of this kind of play indicated a recognition of the breed's physical capability and a desire not to develop it further. . . .

Like many dogs, pit bulls are often inclined to jump up on people when they greet them, but their muscularity and potentially intimidating appearance can easily make such introductions go awry. Most respondents were highly aware of the apprehension that already exists in the minds of people who encounter their dogs, and many expressed a desire to train their dogs away from this tendency to jump. The issue of this breed's jumping ability, especially when combined with an overenthusiastic greeting, was a concern for the following owner:

> [My pit bull] is definitely a really hyper dog. She gets really frantic around other dogs and kids; she just gets kind of worked up into a frenzy. She never does anything aggressive towards them but sometimes she'll jump up on them. We've been working with her to sort of calm down a little bit around other animals and people.

Concern about the strength of these dogs was especially prevalent when children were present,

and most respondents were very attentive to the possibility that their dogs could knock a child over accidentally. In response to this heightened concern, some respondents took special care to present their dogs in a mild, unthreatening manner when they were around children. For several owners, this meant having their pit bulls sit before they were allowed to interact with children, especially if the children were unfamiliar. One young woman explained what she does if kids want to pet her dog: "I get him sitting and then I'm like, 'This is what you do,' trying to teach these kids not to go right at [the dog] with their hands." In addition to presenting her pit bull in a positive manner, this owner used her dog to educate children about safe behavior around animals in general:

> [Kids ask], "Does he bite?" And my answer is, "He has teeth." And they're like, "I don't get it," and I'm like, "Listen, if he wants to bite, he'll bite." I'm like, "He's never bitten anybody. I don't know if he'll bite somebody, but with an animal whom you don't know, just use caution."

In this situation, education also served as a preventive measure; by teaching children appropriate behavior around dogs, respondents such as this woman anticipated future interactions between children and their pit bulls and attempted to ensure a positive outcome. Another respondent felt compelled to remove her pit bull from social gatherings if children were involved. She trusted her dog to be well-behaved around children, but she also felt responsible for the concern that was expressed by parents and other adults. Although this respondent trusted her dog, there was a sense that special scrutiny would be given to behavior and that no situation was foolproof. By separating her dog from young visitors, she removed any cause for concern.

Respondents undertook a variety of preventive measures ranging from modified play and an intolerance of . . . jumping to carefully planned interactions between pit bulls and children in order to manage breed stigma. This approach distinguished itself from most other strategies in that it was based on the anticipation of breed-related stigma in future encounters. These preventive measures were not excusing tactics so much as they were precautionary tactics. Undertaken by respondents in the absence of direct accusations about their pit bulls, such preventive measures allowed owners to respond proactively and with a sense of agency to breed stigma.

Respondents Use Advocacy and Ambassadorship

One of the most public and visible ways in which respondents managed breed stigma was to become an advocate or ambassador for pit bulls. These owners defined their responsibility in terms of the breed as a whole, and they sought to present these dogs—often through the example of their own pit bulls—as friendly, well-behaved pets. This approach involved rebutting stereotypes and misconceptions as well as promoting the breed's winning qualities. Owners often encouraged their pit bulls to act as their own ambassadors by showcasing the dogs' friendly, outgoing personalities. In addition, some respondents filled the role of advocate/ambassador by serving as models of responsible dog ownership.

A major facet of advocacy and ambassadorship was to rebut negative comments and promote the breed. Some advocates made strong, proactive rebuttals. In one case, an owner described his reaction to family members who brought up breed stereotypes as follows:

> . . . there's some [people] in our family that have said, "Oh, their brain will swell up and they'll bite you!" And I [have] said, "Go read something before you come out with that stuff to me! Don't sit there and give me some rumors that . . . their jaws lock. They don't lock; they don't ratchet shut. Don't tell me this stuff. Go read facts before you bother me with this." And that normally shuts them up.

Other respondents took a more low-key approach, such as an owner who explained,

> I don't get into shouting matches. Everybody has their beliefs. . . . I'll just say, "You know, maybe you should look into it a little bit more," or, "I know quite a few pits that are really good; [my dog] happens to be one of them."

For this respondent, her personal experience with pit bulls provided a solid basis for suggesting that others reevaluate their opinions of the breed, but she was more circumspect in her defense.

Advocacy and ambassadorship also entailed promoting the breed and emphasizing its best traits. For example, one woman said, "I always defend them . . . . I always say, 'No, [my pit bull] is a great dog.' You know, I definitely play up his assets." One of the goals which lay behind promotion of the breed was a desire to educate others, often through descriptions of personal experience with pit bulls. According to one respondent,

> . . . I'll try and educate people, as to at least my experiences with pit bulls. . . . I give them the instances of how great they are with kids and, you know, I've had pictures with my other pit bull laying on top of three children and just getting his tummy rubbed. I'll tell them all the positive stuff. . . . If you bring these dogs up in a loving environment, I think they're fantastic and I don't hesitate to tell people that.

Given the reputation that pit bulls have for endangering children, this approach offered direct evidence to the contrary, and this type of promotional effort gained credibility through its reliance on first-hand experience.

In building support for this breed, many respondents felt that the dogs themselves were the best ambassadors. One woman stated, "In the right hands, [pit bulls] are the best ambassadors for the breed." Referring to his stepmother's reluctance to visit because of his pit bull, another respondent noted, "I'd give her two minutes with the dog and she'd be won over just like everybody else." A third owner expressed a similar degree of confidence in her dog's ability to overcome people's preconceived ideas about the breed: "If [people] say something [negative] about the dog, I tell them—if I have my dog with me—I basically say, 'My dog speaks for herself.'" . . .

Finally, several respondents served as advocates for pit bulls by acting as role models. For one of these owners, being a role model meant having a well-behaved and obedient dog. After adopting his dog, the respondent had taken her to puppy kinder-garten, followed by a course in basic obedience. He planned to continue her training with a class in advanced basic obedience and eventually to certify her as a "Canine Good Citizen." One woman said:

> You've got to work harder. You are being scruti-nized and watched every minute of the day. You had better carry poop bags when you are out for a walk, because you'll be crucified for that one thing and that one thing alone . . . You just have to work harder, you're more visible . . .

Advocacy and ambassadorship, then, served as the final way for respondents to manage pit bull stigma. They did so by rebutting negative comments about the breed and by actively pro-moting pit bulls, often through the charismatic personalities of their own dogs. As an extension of this advocacy, several owners assumed the responsibility of serving as role models, either individually or in partnership with their dogs. . . .

REFERENCES

Arluke, A. (1991). Going into the closet with science: Information control among animal experimenters. *Journal of Contemporary Ethnography, 20,* 306–330.

Cantwell, M. (1992). The racing greyhound as a team presentation. Paper presented at the American Sociological Association, Miami, FL.

Gillespie, D., Leffler, A., & Lerner, E. (1996). Safe in unsafe places: Leisure, passionate avocations, and the problematizing of everyday public life. *Society and Animals, 4,* 169–188.

Goffman, E. (1959). *The presentation of self in every-day life.* Garden City, NY: Doubleday.

——— (1963). *Stigma.* Upper Saddle River, NJ: Prentice Hall.

Hearne, V. (1991). *Bandit: Dossier of a dangerous dog.* New York: HarperCollins Publishers.

Jessup, D. (1995). *The working pit bull.* Neptune City, NJ: TFH Publications, Inc.

Sanders, C. R. (1990). Excusing tactics: Social responses to the public misbehavior of companion animals. *Anthrozöös,* 4, 82–90.

Veterinarians' Deviance and Neutralization Techniques

DeAnn R. GAUTHIER

Gresham Sykes and David Matza's neutralization theory describes how juveniles, when accused of delinquency, provide various rationalizations in order to refute or mute their assignment to a deviant identity. Thus, they may deny responsibility for the behavior, deny the behavior's infliction of any injury, blame the victim as having provoked the behavior, or condemn the people who condemn them (for example, as being hypocrites). Since Sykes and Matza presented their theory, students of deviance have added to the list of justifications and excuses that accused persons have employed to neutralize the charges of deviance that are or could be made against them.

DeAnn Gauthier set out to find out how veterinarians who violate the code of ethics of veterinary medicine neutralize their professional breaches. She found the two most popular rationalizations offered by veterinarians were those of "everybody's doing it" and "economic necessity." Her study suggests that occupational deviance may take place without the self-acceptance of a deviant identity when there is an occupational subculture that prescribes or condones the patterned evasion of certain ethical norms, frequent asso-ciation among colleagues in the occupation, shared assumption of widespread evasion of these ethical norms, and lax enforcement of their code of ethics.

Veterinary medicine, like other professional occupations, is not immune from problematic ethical and legal breaches on the part of its practitioners. These breaches may result from various conflicting transactions between professionals and their clients. On one side of the transaction is the professional whose business it is to provide a service for the client on the other side of the transaction. However, few professionals can afford to subsidize the clients they serve, and ultimately, the professional's own interests are at stake in the transaction experience. Conflicts of interest, then, may be inevitable. Losses suffered by professionals in those conflicts must also be compensated in order for the occupational life of the professional to thrive. Compensatory actions devised to offset those losses would ideally remain within professional ethical and legal boundaries, but substantial evidence exists to suggest that this is not always the case (Walters 1982; Braithwaite 1984; Szasz 1986; Pfuhl 1987; Rutter 1989; Barker and Carter 1990; Calavita and Pontell 1991; Hunt and Manning 1991; Pope 1991; Jenkins and Braithwaite 1993; Coleman 1994; Albanese 1995; Simon 1996).

Veterinarians are professionals who suffer conflicts of interest with clients that may necessitate compensatory behavior due to financial losses. However, the American Veterinary Medical Association's (AVMA) official code of ethics, *The Principles of Veterinary Medical Ethics* (1989), states in its introduction:

> *Veterinarians should consider first the welfare of the patient for the purpose of relieving suffering and disability while causing minimum of pain or fright.* Benefit to the patient should transcend personal advantage of monetary gain *in decisions concerning therapy. (emphasis added)*

Thus, veterinarians who find themselves in problematic situations, particularly financially problematic situations, may experience role strain

in their attempts to satisfy both the healing and pecuniary roles that correspond to their statuses as professional business persons (Goode 1960). Additional strain may incur if role conflict ensues due to competing demands between, for example, the need to provide for their families and the need to honor their professional code of ethics (Toby 1952). How is this conflict managed so as to reduce the commensurate strain? If management encourages a normatively deviant response, how and when do participants integrate this deviance into their nondeviant identities?

. . . As Sykes and Matza (1957) argue, those who avail themselves of deviant opportunities sometimes find the need to reconcile their contradictory behaviors and beliefs. Specifically, violation of rules to which one is committed is problematic. In an effort to avoid ethical responsibility and adverse social censure for deviant actions, deviant actors may construct justifications for deviance that may not only precede the behavior (making it possible), but also follow it (making it acceptable to self and others). These techniques of neutralization include (1) denial of responsibility, in which the act is justified because the individual had no control over it; (2) denial of injury, in which individuals claim that no one was harmed so nothing deviant or wrong has occurred; (3) denial of the victim, in which the individual argues that whomever is harmed by the deviance deserves the harm; (4) condemnation of condemners, in which the individual claims that those who disapprove of the act are hypocrites who have done much worse; and (5) appeal to higher loyalties, in which the individual's attachments to norms other than those of the larger society hold preeminence.

The use of neutralization techniques may not be limited to those identified by Sykes and Matza (1957), particularly when unique subcultural normative systems are examined (cf. Forsyth and Evans 1998). Coleman (1994) expanded these techniques to specifically include rationalizations common to the cultures of white collar crime. These include (1) denial of the necessity for the law, because the behavior is not inappropriate; (2) defense of necessity, in which economic survival is at stake; (3) the claim that "everybody else is doing it and they are not penalized"; and (4) the claim of entitlement, in which the individual argues that the benefit is deserved or owed. It is by learning such techniques that the individual becomes deviant.

METHOD

The data were collected during a five-year period via ethnographic fieldwork and in-depth interviews with veterinarians and support staff in a southern state. The central research informants included five veterinarians in three private practices in a community of about 75,000 people. The practices consisted of (1) a two-man small animal practice; (2) a two-man mixed animal practice; and (3) a one-woman small animal practice. All veterinarians were white, and ranged in age from 25 to 47. One of these veterinarians also served as a key informant, assisting in arranging introductions for interviews and invitations to events attended exclusively by veterinarians and their support staffs. The mixed animal practice was observed during a two-year period, with the key informant acting as strategic coordinator for the research project during that time period . . .

Beyond these central sources of interview and observational data, I also spent approximately 40 hours during the first year of the project in observation of various clinical rotations occurring during the final year of training for the Doctor of Veterinary Medicine degree. These included rotations for a class of approximately 50 students at the veterinary school in a southern state. Approximately two to five students would serve on each rotation, in such content areas as small animal medicine (including at that time a 24-hour student staffing of a small animal intensive care unit); food animal medicine; equine medicine; laboratory, zoological, and exotic medicine; opthalmological medicine; and surgical medicine. The students were predominantly white, and ranged in age from 20–50. Additionally, in the final year of the study, I conducted a four-hour in-depth interview with a former private practitioner and professor at the

veterinary school. He was in his mid-50s and white. That year, I also conducted a two-hour in-depth interview with a retired 82-year-old white male veterinarian who had established a lucrative private practice for small animal medicine during the course of his career. Finally, during the second and third years of the study, I engaged in observational research of approximately 30 veterinarians and their support staff at six continuing education seminars which lasted an average of 2.5 hours each. Most were males of various ages between 25 and 60. All were white. In this situation alone, most were unaware of my research role . . .

FINDINGS

In a study with occupational deviance as its focus, it may become possible to lose sight of the overwhelming numbers of nondeviant encounters that make up the bulk of any clinic's or individual veterinarian's caseload. The attention directed to deviant activities in this research report are not intended to convey the message that veterinarians in the main are unethical or criminal. Such a generalization is grossly out of proportion with the findings. For the most part, these individuals were humane and ethical in their treatment of patients and clients, but this does not preclude ethical and legal "lapses." The true focus of this study is on how those lapses were negotiated through the use of neutralization techniques in order to permit deviant behaviors to occur in individuals who otherwise have strong ties to the conventional moral order (Minor 1981).

Of the central research informants, all but one indicated that they had engaged in ethically or legally questionable behaviors in the course of doing their jobs. The remaining veterinarian did not self-identify as a rule breaker, but as a friend and colleague to other rule breakers within the veterinary ranks. However, it might be argued that failure to report friends and colleagues for their rule breaking, or failure to cease associating with them, can be interpreted as complicity toward and approval of those behaviors. Indeed, this was the perception held by the offending veterinarians toward the nondeviant practitioner. Furthermore, while the key informant for the study did self-identify as a rule breaker, a much lower incidence of self-participation in rule breaking was indicated relative to others in the study. At the same time, a high degree of identification with, and defense of, other rule breakers was evidenced by the key informant. Thus it is possible that participation in deviance in the workplace is not required in order to be labeled by self or others as a rule breaker.

Student veterinarians represent an additional illustration of this point, in that students in their final year of training did not uncommonly find themselves or their classmates at the center of discussions on ethically problematic occurrences in clinical rotations. Because of the close-knit orientation of the student group, events occurring on one rotation would almost certainly be reported to those matriculating on another rotation. Again, failure to report the questionable behaviors implies complicity on the part of the student group as a whole. For example, an animal had been scheduled to be euthanized at the veterinary school, but due to student and staff oversight the procedure had gone unfinished. The animal had previously been diagnosed with a terminal condition, and the owner had requested euthanasia to end the suffering of their beloved pet. In this situation, a moral dilemma arose when the animal had a spontaneous recovery *after* the scheduled euthanasia had failed to be performed. Subsequent discovery of the oversight, and of the spontaneous recovery, led to much discussion about the ethically and legally correct response to the circumstances. An unethical but legal course of action was decided upon, and though numerous students (including those not directly involved) disagreed with the decision, they refrained from reporting the actions of their peers.

Overall, then, the central research respondents in this study were familiar with professional transgressions either on the part of self or others, and had not personally reported these transgressions to the State Board of Veterinary Medicine or to other control agents. When asked about their awareness and opinion of ethical dilemmas facing

the veterinary practitioner, seven of the nine techniques of neutralization were identifiable in their responses. Denial of responsibility and denial of the necessity for the law were not present in the accounts reported by the veterinarians in this study. However, the findings do identify the importance of the claim of "everybody else is doing it" and the defense of necessity as neutralization techniques used to rationalize unethical or illegal actions in themselves or others. Approximately 70% of the responses fell into one of these two categories. Additionally, for those respondents who knew of wrongdoing by others but did not withdraw from or report those others, the technique of appeal to higher loyalties was the only neutralization used as a justification.

DEFENSE OF NECESSITY

The primary justification invoked for professional lapses involved the defense of necessity, especially for economic survival. This technique was utilized in circumstances involving either billing ploys or substandard care. The billing ploys most commonly recognized by respondents included charging for services not rendered and overcharging for services rendered. The examples cited here concern animal euthanasia services. Charging for services not rendered may occur on occasions when animals die from injury or illness prior to the performance of a planned (and typically prepaid) euthanasia. The veterinarians (those involved directly as well as those who were merely aware of such lapses), explained the appropriateness of their actions as necessary for maintaining a good image for the clients, and therefore, the continuing goodwill of the clients and their acquaintances. Respondents indicated that reputation is an important element of the successful veterinarian practice, and that in order to remain financially solvent, sometimes such lapses are necessary. The following vignette illustrates their argument.

A veterinarian answered a late-night emergency call for a dog that had been hit by a car. The doctor realized that the client owed the clinic a large sum, but chose to give care to the animal anyway. Later that evening, the dog died. After consulting with his partner, the vet decided to wait until morning to call the client. However, the client phoned the next morning before the vet had time to call her. The doctor took her call, and told her that her dog had "taken a turn for the worse and might not pull through." Afterwards, he explained, "What I'm doing is trying to prepare her for what's coming, because if I just call her and say her dog is dead, she will freak out and go nuts. This way, she has a little while to get adjusted to the idea." Approximately 20 minutes had passed, when the client called back and told the doctor she did not want her dog to suffer any longer, to "go ahead and put it down" (indicating a desire for euthanasia services), and she would come by the clinic later that afternoon to pick up the body. The doctor said "okay," hung up the telephone, and added a charge for euthanasia to her bill. The veterinarian, when asked why he was charging to kill a dog that was already dead, invoked the defense of necessity for economic survival: "This lady is a nut. You'll have to see for yourself. She's just a nut. And besides, she owes us so much money she never pays on anyway that I think it's perfectly all right. Anyway, if I didn't charge her for it, she would ask why and maybe figure out the dog died on its own, and get mad and tell other people who-knows-what and word would get around. It's just better this way, believe me."

What is most revealing in this remark is that the veterinarian believed, based on his past experiences with the client, that he would probably not get paid for the additional charge anyway. He argues the need for deviance was motivated by an economic need, though not one tied only or even ultimately to this one client. Rather, his recognition of the necessity for his deviance rested on the larger client population to which he believed this one client was tied.

A second vignette illustrates the use of the defense of necessity in billing ploys involving overcharging for euthanasia services rendered.

The three central clinics in this study were housed in a community where no incinerator service is available for hire by veterinarians. Consequently, *the clinics disposed of animal remains via clinic trash dumpsters, because building their own incinerators was financially out of the question. However, two of the clinics engaged in ethically questionable charging practices related to the use of the dumpsters. These clinics charged an additional fee to clients to dispose of the body when animals were euthanized or died due to injury or illness. The "disposal fee" provided for bagging the animal in a plastic trash bag, and placing it in the dumpster. The extra fee was justified as a necessity in order to offset the costs of trash pick-up and operation of a large freezer where they would sometimes stockpile bodies until the day of trash pick-up in order to eliminate problems occurring due to odor. Other veterinarians in the community disagreed with the practice of charging a "disposal fee," and particularly such a high one. However, fees are self-regulated, and in this instance, not technically illegal. In conversations relating to the above procedures, it became apparent that none of the vets in this community (regardless of their fee schedules) made a strict practice of informing clients who leave the body for the clinic to dispose of that the procedure would involve the trash can behind the clinic. Neither did they misrepresent their intentions by assuring clients that they would perform burials or burial rituals. Only when clients asked did they offer the information regarding the final disposition of the animal's body in the local landfill. Veterinarians in this community uniformly agreed that in this circumstance, what the client does not know will not hurt the veterinarian's image or pocketbook. Thus, they justified both behaviors, neglecting to inform and overcharging for disposal, as necessary for economic reasons.*

In addition to billing ploys, the defense of necessity was invoked to justify substandard care involving extraneous tests or procedures. Some veterinarians in this study admitted to occasionally charging for tests or blood work that did not take place. Generally, this occurred in cases where a client was aggressively pursuing health care for their already healthy animal. The veterinarians viewed the demand by clients for unnecessary care as an incentive to perform services that ultimately benefited the veterinarian (financially) more than they do the patient. Though clearly understanding the illegality of their actions, these veterinarians justified those actions as necessary to offset the costs to the clinic of nonpaying customers. For example, respondents stated:

> We probably shouldn't encourage testing or procedures that might not be necessary, but that helps the practice make more money.

> Yeah, sure, we run blood tests on every animal that is spayed or neutered, because the tests may identify kidney or liver problems that could complicate the use of anesthesia, and create a higher risk of death during the spay/neuter procedure. Chances are, 99% of the dogs and cats that come in, you're not going to find anything. It's a way to make fifty extra dollars.

Dental work is perceived as the procedure most commonly used to earn extra money through straightening and cleaning teeth, especially for show dogs. This was explained as part of the process of the expanding marketplace.

> What's happening to veterinary medicine is you're getting more and more vets, and everybody needs to specialize in something, and expand their practice maybe for your clinic to continue to grow. I mean, they did the same thing in human dentistry. Thirty years ago, adults didn't get braces; everybody has braces today, young and old. So, it's kind of the same thing. It's if you can convince the public that this is something necessary. There is some value to it, but it is also a way to make extra money. Of course, you approach the clients that spend a lot of money at the clinic in the first place, that are gonna be able to pay, and that are known for paying at the time of service. You don't offer dental work to the client that already owes the clinic a lot of money.

EVERYBODY ELSE IS DOING IT

The second main neutralization technique identified in the data is the claim that "everybody else is doing it and getting away with it." Coleman (1994:205) argues that this justification is often combined with the argument of necessity, which

is true for the respondents in this study as well. This technique was typically utilized to account for involvement in (1) questionable distribution of drugs and (2) billing ploys concerning price-fixing. Illegal drug sales in veterinary clinics tend to be in the form of anabolic steroids, though many other drugs are sought after. All of the respondents in this study believed illegal drug sales to be common practice for certain clinics, and many admitted to having been approached by clients themselves for this purpose. Those who engaged in the practice believed they were merely going along with a pattern of accepted behavior.

Requirements of self-regulation are common among certain professions, including the veterinarian profession. In each state, there is a Board which is specifically charged with the task of regulating veterinarian behavior in that jurisdiction. However, there are many more veterinarians than there are Board members, making the task of regulation that much more difficult. The Board of Veterinary Medicine is supposed to investigate suspected violations, but as noted above, this may become a logistical problem, particularly when the suspicious practice is explained by the accused vet as "extra-label" drug use. Veterinarians can use drugs that are not approved for use in animals as long as they provide a veterinary basis for using it to treat a condition. Although the Board can question the use of the drug, 80% of respondents believed that it is common to use drugs extra-label, and that it is easy to get by their state's Board in doing so.

Each state varies as to exact requirements for veterinarians to maintain active licenses, but many require vets to garner continuing education credits in order to do so. The state in which the field work for this study was conducted requires such credentialization. At one such seminar, the topic involved the extra-label use of a synthetic erythropoietin in racehorses or greyhound dogs. The illegal use of this drug could be instrumental in helping the animal become a better athlete for the short term. Several of the veterinarians that treat racehorses in that state were in attendance, and spoke among themselves about their use of this drug, and the prices they charged for it. More to the point, some participants in the conversation had been or were current members of the Board of Veterinary Medicine for the state. Barring this last fact, policing the practice would be very difficult as there is no test for detecting the use of this drug. Furthermore, if members of the regulatory agency, themselves, are participants in the illegal activity, then policing efforts will likely be even less effective. From this comes the neutralization technique which argues that "everybody else is doing it and going unpunished for doing so."

In addition to questionable involvement in drug distribution, this neutralization technique was utilized to justify billing ploys concerning price-fixing. The primary clinics involved in this study were involved in illegal business agreements with other clinics in their town and nearby communities. Periodically, an informal dinner gathering would occur, at which prices for various procedures would be discussed:

> We did this in order to set a level that no one would go under so that regardless of where somebody went, we would be charging them about the same amount.
> Everybody does it [price-fix].
> Human doctors do the same thing [price-fix].
> That [price-fixing] isn't wrong. Well, I guess technically it probably is. But to us what is wrong are the veterinarians who won't "play the game," but instead charge less to undercut the rest of us.

DENIAL OF INJURY

Substandard care is neutralized via the denial of injury neutralization technique. Many of the veterinarians have agreements with the veterinary school to engage in supervised training of student interns. A fairly routine procedure during the training is to allow interns to practice surgical operations on live animals prior to a planned euthanasia.

VET: [If] the people just want the dog put down, yeah, we would allow somebody doing an internship to practice a procedure or try a technique they want to try to learn.
INTERVIEWER: Without getting permission from the client?

VET: Well, yeah, but at that point the client has already kind of signed off. They want the dog put down.
INTERVIEWER: But did they sign the body over for scientific investigation?
VET: No, but I think that's something . . .
INTERVIEWER: It's not like with humans?
VET: No, it's not like with humans.

The veterinarians deny that anyone in this circumstance has really been hurt by the action. The animal is sedated, feels no discomfort, and will be euthanized after the procedure. They argue that this is not the same context as human experimentation, and should be viewed differently. Furthermore, the client receives the requested service and knows nothing else that may cause psychological guilt or discomfort. Finally, the student veterinarian hones his or her skills at performing a procedure under realistic conditions that he or she will soon be called upon to perform legitimately. If anything, the respondents argue, more individuals are helped by their actions, not hurt.

DENIAL OF THE VICTIM

Another neutralization technique that was asserted was the denial of the victim. These tended to be invoked in circumstances involving billing ploys and substandard care. In these circumstances, veterinarians declare that although someone was hurt by their actions, that individual deserves the injury. In these cases, the veterinarian justifies his or her own deviant behaviors by redirecting attention to the wrongdoings of another. In this way, the response is normalized as a form of retribution or retaliation against the wrongdoer.

> Some people don't pay their bill to us. They think—oh, they make so much money, this little bit won't make any difference. Man, does that piss me off. My partner beat up a couple of them for stuff like that.

In another interview, the veterinarian was attempting to neutralize his own deviance by placing the blame on the client.

She comes in here all the time, trying to get us to give her free products or services. When we do actually receive her animals for chargeable services, she wants us to treat everything like it is an emergency room—running up a bill that is gonna be unbelievable . . . This one time, the dog ate a piece of aluminum foil and she wanted x-rays and blood work and surgery. If we had a CAT scan available, she probably would have asked for that, too. Of course, when it comes time to pay, she's real hard to find. We get the money, or at least most of it, eventually, but not before we have to waste staff hours chasing her down. A couple of times we were about to turn her over to a collection agent. The really ironic thing is that she is from a family in town that has a lot of money, and she just inherited. I guess she thinks the world owes her something, but we don't. So sometimes we charge for the tests she wants run, but we don't run them in actuality. It just seems to me that people like that, who come in here demanding premium service like that but treating everybody with such disrespect, well, they just sort of deserve what they get . . . what we charge for and don't do.

These veterinarians admit their behavior is deviant, but believe it justified and well-deserved. To them, their own actions are merely a response to an aggression initiated by particular clients. To outsiders, veterinarian deviance such as this may be unforgivable. To the vet, however, there is no victim/client but rather an aggressor/client—who deserves the injury their own behavior precipitated.

CLAIMS OF ENTITLEMENT

Some professional lapses, particularly those involving billing ploys and substandard care in the form of extraneous procedures, were justified with the neutralization that the veterinarian deserved, or was entitled to, the compensation. This was connected to the notion that veterinary medicine is not as financially lucrative nor as socially prestigious as human medicine.

A lot of people think vets make a lot of money. But we don't. We make an average of $50–$60,000 a year after we get established, but they think we're

loaded up like human doctors, making $160,000 to start! That burns me up sometimes. So if I pad their bill a little, so what? I deserve it.

Listen, either my partner or I are on call for our clients 24 hours a day, 7 days a week. We work holidays. We work on our anniversaries. We work when our kids are having birthday parties. If their dog eats a vienna sausage or a piece of aluminum foil at three in the morning, I am there for them. No matter how minor the call, I go. So if my emergency fee is high, or if I pad their bill with an unnecessary charge or two, I think I deserve it. Can you imagine what human doctors would charge for that kind of care?

APPEAL TO HIGHER LOYALTIES

Some ethical dilemmas were resolved through the neutralization technique that appeals to higher loyalties. In these circumstances, the veterinarians faced a dilemma that required them to violate the law in order to maintain their loyalty to a more pressing set of norms. In particular, these were circumstances involving billing ploys where clients were charged for services not rendered. On some occasions, a healthy animal is scheduled for euthanasia because the owners no longer wish to keep it. Most veterinarians will ask the owner if it is acceptable to adopt the animal out to a new family rather than euthanize it. Some owners accept, but not all do so. For example, some owners bring a healthy animal to the veterinarian to be euthanized because their elderly parent has died and as part of their dying wish has asked that the beloved pet be buried with them. Alternatively, they do not think that the animal will understand their absence and will suffer tremendous grief which can be alleviated through euthanasia. Whatever the reason, the offer to adopt the animal out is refused. Some veterinarian respondents perform the euthanasia as requested, though report displeasure in doing so. Others refuse to perform the service, and the client seeks another veterinarian. Others opt for a more controversial course of action, and adopt the animal out to new owners anyway, but charge the original owners for the euthanasia nonetheless. In each of these circumstances, the veterinarian typically invokes an appeal to higher loyalties to justify their behavior. Those who perform the procedure appeal to the ethic of performing the service for which they have been paid, arguing that at least the method of disposal will be humane. Those who refuse to perform the service appeal to the ethic of helping, not hurting. Those who charge for services not rendered argue that they are humane, and the illegal charges are justified in order to preserve humanity.

You do services for people, or they believe they are getting services, you gotta play the game.

CONDEMNATION OF CONDEMNERS

A final technique of neutralization was asserted at all levels of deviant activity: billing ploys, substandard care, and questionable drug distribution. The veterinarians ultimately viewed those who would condemn their behaviors as hypocritical. In this strategy, veterinarians shift the focus from their deviance to outsiders who view it, and question the motivations and behaviors of those outsiders. Every veterinarian involved in this study described the procedures they utilized to insure payment from clients. These ranged from accepting postdated checks to trading for services. Though all acknowledged that there were some clients with outstanding bills, the vets were careful not to allow the proportion of free riders to become too large because it is directly due to the problem of free riders that costs are passed along to paying clients in the ways described in this research. In fact, one respondent (a recent graduate from veterinary school) laughed aloud when asked to read the introduction concerning monetary gain in the AVMA's *Principles of Veterinary Medical Ethics* (1989; quoted earlier). His response condemns those who would condemn him:

We were never taught that. I never heard that. It may be in the code, but that did not make up the content of my training, not in whole, not in part. The vet school doesn't take clients who can't pay. That's bull. That's just for public relations, that's all that is.

Other respondents illustrated this neutralization technique, while speaking specifically about substandard care.

You know, human life is worth more, and all that. But just because people don't respect pets as much, by default, they don't respect vets as much either. You see that in everything we do. It's always cutting corners for the client, to save his pocketbook, but supposedly to still try and save his pet as well. Which is fine, to a point. Still, there's that unstated, implicit assumption behind it all: human medicine is first class; but vet medicine is bulk rate. Well, then, you get what you pay for, don't you?

I don't want to hear you tell me anything about my methods when it is you who is responsible for them. I may know all sorts of fancy things to do to care for your animal, but you don't pay me enough to buy the equipment that allows me to do it. I don't have privileges at some fancy hospital that owns all the equipment, and even if I did, you wouldn't want to pay for it.

DISCUSSION AND CONCLUSIONS

. . . The occupational subculture of the veterinarian fulfills an integral function in enabling deviance by advocating various techniques necessary to modify an ethically or legally questionable option into a legitimate and acceptable course of action. Though the subculture does not overtly endorse deviant behavior, the normative system hinges on an inclusive solidarity that ties veterinarians to one another as insiders to their calling. That solidarity extends a mutual protective benefit to other members of the veterinarian subculture with whom one identifies and therefore shields from punishment. In this regard, the veterinary medical profession is much like the human medical profession, possessing medical boards that may fail to punish peers they are charged to police (cf. Wolfe et al. 1998). In order to understand the professional lapse of the veterinarian, then, it is necessary to locate his or her behavior in the structure of the occupational subculture in which it exists. Occupational culture is a "social force that controls patterns of organizational behavior by shaping members' cognitions and perceptions of meanings and realities" (Ott 1989:69). It is within this subculture that the social psychological processes of behavioral neutralization are constructed, leading to deviance and misconduct (Vaughan 1996; Hochstetler and Copes 2001).

The primary motivation toward deviance for the veterinarians in this study was financial remuneration, which reflects the attitude of the larger dominant normative system in which a culture of competition has emerged and in which the pressure for profit is intense (Coleman 1987; Jenkins and Braithwaite 1993). Veterinarians do not question the validity of the dominant normative system of society, but rather they question the application of those rules to their roles in certain circumstances. The techniques of neutralization to which they adhere precede their deviance and serve to make that deviance possible by reframing it as acceptable and appropriate to their self-images. This is what Sutherland (1949) spoke of when he wrote "definitions favorable to the violation of law"; that is, learning these techniques of neutralization is equivalent to learning why deviance is justified, ultimately bringing the deviant closer to engaging in the now-justified behavior. This construct allows the individual to simultaneously violate ethical or legal principles, but to negate a deviant or criminal self-image. For the veterinarians in this study, the most common neutralization technique was the defense of necessity, followed by the claim that "everybody else is doing it." The occupational subculture assisted in creating and maintaining the definitions of reality constructed for the purpose of excusing occupational deviance. This was accomplished by defining behaviors in such a way that they appear to be necessary and routine, hence nondeviant. Such definitions, when combined with sufficient opportunities for unconventional behavior, can lead to deviance. Veterinary medicine is, as are all professions, marked by a high degree of autonomy, and though ethical and legal standards exist, enforcement proves problematic in the face of such autonomy. Opportunities for deviance (whether via billing ploys, substandard care, or questionable drug distribution) abound. All that remains is a negation of the ethical and legal standards that impede the realization of deviant behavior. As demonstrated in the present research, these, too, seem readily available. Ultimately, then, it may be the convergence of structural elements specific to the veterinarian occupation with social psychological rationalizations that leads directly to the situational ethics reported among the veterinarians in this study. They are, in essence, predictable responses to competitive strain.

REFERENCES

Albanese, Jay. 1995. *White Collar Crime in America.* Upper Saddle River, NJ: Prentice Hall.

American Veterinary Medical Association. Principles. 1989. "Principles of Veterinary Medical Ethics (1989 Revision)." Pp. 24 In *1990 AVMA Directory.* Schaumburg, IL: Author.

Barker, Tom and David Carter. 1990. "Fluffing Up the Evidence and Covering Your Ass: Some Conceptual Notes on Police Lying." *Deviant Behavior* 11:61–73.

Braithwaite, John. 1984. *Corporate Crime in the Pharmaceutical Industry.* London: Routledge and Kegan Paul.

Calavita, Kitty and Henry N. Pontell. 1991. "Other People's Money Revisited: Collective Embezzlement in the Savings and Loan and Insurance Industries." *Social Problems* 38:94–112.

Coleman, James William. 1987. "Toward an Integrated Theory of White-Collar Crime." *American Journal of Sociology* 93:406–39.

Coleman, James William. 1994. *The Criminal Elite: The Sociology of White-Collar Crime.* New York: St. Martin's Press.

Forsyth, Craig J. and Rhonda D. Evans. 1998. "Dogmen: The Rationalization of Deviance." *Society and Animals* 6:203–18.

Goode, William J. 1960. "A Theory of Role Strain." *American Sociological Review* 25:483–96.

Hochstetler, Andy and Heith Copes. 2001. "Organizational Culture and Organizational Crime." Pp. 210–21 in *Crimes of Privilege*, edited by Neal Shover and John Paul Wright. New York: Oxford University Press.

Hunt, Jennifer and Peter K. Manning. 1991. "The Social Context of Police Lying." *Symbolic Interaction* 14:51–70.

Jenkins, Anne and John Braithwaite. 1993. "Profits, Pressure, and Corporate Lawbreaking." *Crime, Law and Social Change* 20:221–32.

Minor, W. William. 1981. "Techniques of Neutralization: A Reconceptualization and Empirical Examination." *Journal of Research in Crime and Delinquency* 18:295–318.

Ott, J. Steven. 1989. *The Organizational Culture Perspective*. Pacific Groves, CA: Brooks/Cole.

Pfuhl, Edwin H., Jr. 1987. "Computer Abuse: Problems of Instrumental Control." *Deviant Behavior* 8:113–30.

Pope, Daniel. 1991. "Advertising as a Consumer Issue: An Historical View." *Journal of Social Issues* 47:41–56.

Rutter, Peter. 1989. *Sex in the Forbidden Zone*. New York: Fawcett.

Simon, David R. 1996. *Elite Deviance*. Boston, MA: Allyn and Bacon.

Sutherland, Edwin H. 1949. *White Collar Crime*. New York: Dryden.

Sykes, Gresham M. and David Matza. 1957. "Techniques of Neutralization: A Theory of Delinquency." *American Sociological Review* 22:667–70.

Szasz, Andrew. 1986. "Corporations, Organized Crime, and the Disposal of Hazardous Waste: An Examination of the Making of a Criminogenic Regulatory Structure." *Criminology* 24:1–27.

Toby, Jackson. 1952. "Some Variables in Role Conflict Analysis." *Social Forces* 30:323–27.

Vaughan, Diane. 1996. *The Challenger Launch Decision: Risky Technology, Culture, and Deviance at NASA*. Chicago, IL: University of Chicago Press.

Walters, Vivienne. 1982. "Company Doctors' Perceptions of and Response to Conflicting Pressures from Labor and Management." *Social Problems* 30:1–12.

Wolfe, S., K. M. Franklin, P. McCarthy, P. Bame, and B. M. Adler. 1998. *16,638 Questionable Doctors Disciplined by State and Federal Governments*. Washington, DC: Public Citizens Health Research Group.

CHAPTER 14

TRANSFORMING DEVIANT IDENTITY

Natural Recovery

ROBERT GRANFIELD and WILLIAM CLOUD

Some small percentage of people addicted to alcohol or drugs seek help each year. A wide variety of agencies currently exist to service this population. Two types of agencies predominate, both of which seek to pursue and sustain a change in identity. One is self-help organizations such as Alcoholics Anonymous (AA), the other is treatment centers (for alcoholics, for addicts, or both). Both seek to inculcate a change in the self-identity of the addict, assign them to a new social status, and afford them a role for accomplishing personal change.

Self-help organizations define its members as alcoholics or addicts and want them to see themselves as powerless to control their use of alcohol or drugs. The treatment center defines its clientele as sick people who have a disease, assigns them to the status of patient, and seeks to achieve a change by treating their drinking, drug problem, or both over a period of residence in the treatment center. The growth in both the number and variety of agencies to deal with problems of substance use is a consequence of the success of the social movement that has successfully changed the construction of alcoholics and addicts from one of criminals to one of sick people.

What makes the paper by Robert Granfield and William Cloud so significant is that it indicates a stigma is still attached to both types of treatment. Many people who recover from their drinking or drug problem on their own (that is, "naturally") do not see themselves as either sick or powerless, and, paradoxically, the stigma that attaches to such associations as AA or treatment centers precipitates the conditions for natural recovery. The sufficient condition for the change in natural recovery is the rejection of the deviant identity (as an "alchoholic" or "addict") that AA or treatment centers require.

Social deviance literature typically portrays drug and alcohol addicted individuals as possessing distinct subcultural characteristics that marginalize them from the nonaddicted world. Whether this marginalization occurs because of a personality profile which predisposes an individual to addiction or whether it follows from being labeled and stigmatized as "an addict," the outcome is thought to be the same. Such individuals are considered to be distinctly different from the majority of the population. Indeed, the social deviance literature has played a role in classifying

Reprinted from Robert Granfield and William Cloud, "The Elephant No One Sees: Natural Recovery Among Middle-Class Addicts," *Journal of Drug Issues*, 26:1, Winter 1996, pp. 45–61. Reprinted with permission of Florida State University College of Criminology and Criminal Justice.

addicts as "other" thereby contributing to the production of an outsider status. However, as Waterston (1993:14) has argued, such portrayals have contributed to the "ghettoization" of drug users and to the "construction of a false separation between 'them and us.'"

While the social deviance paradigm of addiction has produced insightful material documenting the lifestyle, experiences, and world views of drug and alcohol addicted persons, this literature has excluded groups not conforming to the image of social disparagement. For instance, the social deviance perspective has been instructive in expanding our knowledge of "bottle gangs" and other alcoholic subcultures (Rubington 1967, 1968; Wiseman 1970), "crack whores" or crack-distributing gangs (Ramer 1993; Williams 1989), and the slum-dwelling heroin addict who injects in order to either enhance his/her social status or simply to escape the hopelessness of his/her own economic poverty (Stephens 1991; Hanson et al. 1985). Although such groups can be classified as "hidden populations" due to their powerlessness and poverty as well as the fact that these groups are largely omitted from national surveys (Lambert and Wiebel 1990), their actions are frequently visible. Inner-city heroin addicts, coke whores, and skid row alcoholics often come in direct contact with social control agents such as the police, the courts, treatment programs, hospitals, and researchers. Precisely because these groups are classified as deviant and are "othered," they are subject to social inspection and identification.

Often absent from the research on hidden populations are those drug addicts and alcoholics who fail to fit into the previously constructed categories that are consistent with current models of deviance. One such group that falls into such a category is the population of middle-class addicts. For instance, some heroin-addicted women from middle-class backgrounds are often able to avoid immersion into a heroin-using subculture, and also have better chances of recovery (Rosenbaum and Murphy 1990). According to these authors (1990:125), "it is possible for them to readjust more readily, because they often possess the resources necessary to start a new life." Such limited subcultural involvement may also result in an, increased ability to circumvent detection. Similarly, many high-level drug dealers may remain hidden due to the secretive nature of their activity (Adler 1986). Thus, many drug users and drug dealers avoid detection because they occupy otherwise legitimate social roles and lead basically straight, middle-class lives (Biernacki 1986). In fact, recent scholarship has removed drug use from the world of deviance and has advanced alternative perspectives including the arguments that addiction is an act of cultural resistance (Waterston 1993), or one that locates addiction in the larger social, political, and economic contexts (Waldorf et al. 1991). Such views remove the unique characteristics associated with addiction and places it within the context of conventional social life (Becker 1963).

One population that remains hidden due to the fact that they deviate from socially constructed categories regarding addiction are middle-class drug addicts and alcoholics who terminate their addictive use of substances without treatment. Research exploring the phenomena of natural recovery has found that significant numbers of people discontinue their excessive intake of addictive substances without formal or lay treatment. While it is difficult to estimate the actual size of this hidden population because they are largely invisible (Lee 1993), researchers agree that their numbers are large (Goodwin et al. 1971) and some even contend that they are substantially larger than those choosing to enter treatment facilities or self-help groups (Sobell et al. 1993; Peele 1989; Biernacki 1986). Some have estimated that as many as 90% of problem drinkers never enter treatment and many suspend problematic use without it (Hingson et al. 1980; Roizen et al. 1978; Stall and Biernacki 1986). Research in Canada has shown that 82% of alcoholics who terminated their addiction reported using natural recovery (Sobell et al. 1993).

Research on natural recovery has focused on a variety of substances including heroin and other opiates (Valliant 1966; Waldorf and Biernacki 1977, 1981; Biernacki 1986), cocaine (Waldorf et al. 1991; Shaffer and Jones 1989), and alcohol (Valliant and Milofsky 1982; Valliant 1983; Stall and Biernacki 1986). Much of this literature challenges the dominant view that addiction relates primarily to the substance being consumed. The dominant addiction paradigm maintains that individuals possess an illness that requires intensive therapeutic intervention. Failure to acquire treatment is considered a sign of denial that will eventually lead to more advanced stages of addiction and possibly death. Given the firm convictions of addictionists as well as their vested interests in marketing this concept (Weisner and Room 1978; Abbott 1988), their rejection of the natural recovery research is of little surprise.

Research on natural recovery has offered great insight into how people successfully transform their lives without turning to professionals or self-help groups. The fact that people accomplish such transformations naturally is by no means a revelation. Most ex-smokers discontinue their tobacco use without treatment (Peele 1989) while many "mature-out" of a variety of behaviors including heavy drinking and narcotics use (Snow 1973; Winick 1962). Some researchers examining such transformations frequently point to factors within the individual's social context that promote change. Not only are patterns of alcohol and drug use influenced by social contexts as Zinberg (1986) illustrated, but the experience of quitting as well can be understood from this perspective (Waldorf et al. 1991). Others have attributed natural recovery to a cognitive appraisal process in which the costs and benefits of continued drinking are assessed by alcoholics (Sobell et al. 1993).

Perhaps one of the most detailed investigations of natural recovery is Biernacki's (1986) detailed description of former heroin addicts. Emphasizing the importance of social contexts, Biernacki demonstrates how heroin addicts terminated their addictions and successfully transformed their lives. Most of the addicts in that study as well as others initiated self-recovery after experiencing an assortment of problems that led to a resolve to change. Additionally, Biernacki

found that addicts who arrest addictions naturally utilize a variety of strategies. Such strategies involve breaking off relationships with drug users (Shaffer and Jones 1989), removing oneself from a drug-using environment (Stall and Biernacki 1986), building new structures in one's life (Peele 1989), and using social networks of friends and family that help provide support for this newly emerging status (Biernacki 1986). Although it is unclear whether the social contexts of those who terminate naturally is uniquely different from those who undergo treatment, it is certain that environmental factors significantly influence the strategies employed in the decision to stop.

While this literature has been highly instructive, much of this research has focused on respondents' circumvention of formal treatment such as therapeutic communities, methadone maintenance, psychotherapy, or regular counseling in outpatient clinics (Biernacki 1986). Many of those not seeking professional intervention may nevertheless participate in self-help groups. Self-help groups have been one of the most popular avenues for people experiencing alcohol and drug problems. This may be due in large part to the fact that groups such as Alcoholics Anonymous (AA), Narcotics Anonymous (NA), or Cocaine Anonymous (CA), medicalize substance abuse in such a way as to alleviate personal responsibility and related guilt (Trice and Roman 1970). Moreover, these groups contribute to the cultivation of a support community which helps facilitate behavioral change.

Despite these attractions and the popularity of these groups, many in the field remain skeptical about their effectiveness. Research has demonstrated that addicts who affiliate with self-help groups relapse in a significantly greater rate than do those who undergo hospitalization only (Walsh et al. 1992). Some have raised concerns about the appropriateness of self-help groups in all instances of addiction (Lewis et al. 1994). In one of the most turgid critiques of self-help groups, Peele (1989) estimates that nearly half of all those who affiliate with such groups relapse within the first year. Peele contends that these groups are not very effective in stopping addictive

behaviors since such groups subscribe to the ideology of lifelong addiction. Adopting the addict-
for-life ideology, as many members do, has
numerous implications for a person's identity as
well as ways of relating to the world around them
(Brown 1991).

Somewhere between the two positions of skepticism and optimism are the findings of Emrick
et al. (1993). In one of the most comprehensive
analyses of AA participation to date, their recta-
analysis of 107 various studies on AA effectiveness
report only a modest correlation between exposure
to self-help groups and improved drinking behavior. They additionally point out the compelling need
for further research on the personal characteristics
of individuals for whom these programs are beneficial and those for whom they are not.

Given the emerging challenges to the dominant views of recovery, research on recovery will
be advanced through an examination of those who
terminated their addictive use of alcohol and drugs
without the benefit of either formal or informal
treatment modalities. While research has provided
insight into those who reject formal treatment
modalities, we know little about the population
who additionally reject self-help groups, particularly those from middle-class backgrounds. This
paper examines the process of natural recovery
among middle-class drug addicts and alcoholics
and first explores the identity of previously
addicted middle-class respondents in relation to
their past addictions. Next, respondents' reasons
for rejecting self-help group involvement or formal treatment are examined. Strategies used by
our respondents to terminate their addictions and
transform their lives are then examined and the
implications of our findings in relation to current
addiction treatment are presented.

METHOD

Data for the present study were collected from a
two-stage research design involving 46 former
drug addicts and alcoholics. The initial stage of this
study involving 25 interviews explored 3 primary

areas. These areas included elements of respondents' successful cessation strategies, perceptions
of self relative to former use, and attitudes toward
treatment. The second stage of the study sharpened
the focus of the exploration within these three
areas. This was accomplished by constructing a
new interview schedule designed to capture the
most salient themes that emerged from the first
stage of the study. In each phase of this study,
lengthy, semistructured interviews with respondents were conducted to elicit thickly descriptive
responses. All interviews were tape-recorded and
later transcribed.

Strict criteria were established for respondent
selection. First, respondents had to have been drug
or alcohol dependent for a period of at least 1 year.
On average, our respondents were dependent for a
period of 9.14 years. Determination of dependency
was made only after careful consideration; each
respondent had to have experienced frequent crav-
ings, extended periods of daily use, and associated
personal problems due to their use. Second, to be
eligible, individuals had to have terminated their
addictive consumption for a period of at least
1 year prior to the interview. The mean length of
time of termination from addiction for the entire
sample was 5.5 years. Finally, the sample includes
only individuals who had no, or only minimal,
exposure to formal treatment. Individuals with
short-term detoxification (up to 2 weeks) were
included provided they had had no additional
follow-up outpatient treatment. Also, individuals
who had less than 1 month exposure to self-help
groups such as AA, NA, or CA were included. Some
of our respondents reported attending one or two of
these self-help group meetings. However, the majority of our respondents had virtually no contact with
formal treatment programs or self-help groups.

Respondents in this study were selected through
"snowball sampling" techniques (Biernacki 1986).
This sampling strategy uses referral chains of
personal contacts in which people with appropriate characteristics are referred as volunteers.
Snowball sampling has been used in a variety of
studies involving hidden populations. In particular, snowball samples have been employed in

previous studies of heroin users (Cloud 1987; Biernacki 1986) and cocaine users (Waldorf et al. 1991). In the present study, snowball sampling methods were necessary for two reasons. Since we were searching for a middle-class population that circumvented treatment, these individuals were widely distributed. Unlike those in treatment or in self-help groups, this population tends to be more dispersed. Also, these individuals did not wish to expose their pasts as former addicts. Very few people were aware of a respondent's drug- and alcohol-using history, making the respondent reluctant to participate. Consequently, personal contact with potential respondents prior to the interview was necessary to explain the interview process as well as the procedures to ensure confidentiality. While there are limitations to this sampling strategy, probability sampling techniques would be impossible since the characteristics of the population are unknown.

All of our respondents in the present study report having stable middle-class backgrounds. Each of the respondents had completed high school, the majority possessed college degrees, and several respondents held graduate degrees. Most were employed in professional occupations, including law, engineering, and health-related fields, held managerial positions, or operated their own businesses during their addiction. Of the respondents participating in this study, 30 were males and 16 were females. The age range in the sample was 25 to 60 with a mean age of 38.4 years.

FORMING A POSTADDICT IDENTITY

Research within the tradition of symbolic interaction has frequently explored the social basis of personal identity. Central to the symbolic interactionist perspective is the notion that personal identity is constituted through interaction with others who define social reality. From this perspective, the self emerges through a process of interaction with others and through the roles individuals occupy. Symbolic interactionists maintain that the self is never immutable, but rather change is an ongoing process in which new definitions of the self emerge as group affiliation and roles change. Consequently, identities arise from one's participation within social groups and organizations.

The perspective of symbolic interaction has frequently been used when analyzing the adoption of deviant identities. For instance, the societal reaction model of deviance views the formation of a spoiled identity as a consequence of labeling (Lemert 1951, 1974; Goffman 1963). Reactions against untoward behavior in the form of degradation ceremonies often give rise to deviant identities (Garfinkel 1967). In addition, organizations that seek to reform deviant behavior, encourage the adoption of a "sick role" for the purposes of reintegration (Parsons 1951). AA, for instance, teaches its members that they possess a disease and a lifelong addiction to alcohol (Trice and Roman 1970). Such organizations provide a new symbolic framework through which members undergo dramatic personal transformation.

Consequently, members adopt an addict role and identity, an identity that for many becomes salient (Brown 1991; Cloud 1987).[1] One respondent in Brown's study, for instance, indicated the degree of engulfment in the addict identity:

> *Sobriety is my life's priority. I can't have my life, my health, my family, my job, or anything else unless I'm sober. My program [participation in AA] has to come first . . . Now I've come to realize that this is the nature of the disease. I need to remind myself daily that I'm an alcoholic. As long as I work my program, I am granted a daily reprieve from returning to drinking.*

Brown's (1991:169) analysis of self-help programs and the identity transformation process that is fostered in those settings demonstrates that members learn "that they must constantly practice the principles of recovery in all their daily affairs." Thus, it is within such programs that the addict identity and role is acquired and reinforced (Peele 1989).

If the addict identity is acquired within such organizational contexts, it is logical to hypothesize that former addicts with minimal contact with such organizations will possess different self-concepts. In the interviews conducted with our first set of respondents, a striking pattern emerged in relation to their present self-concept and their past drug and alcohol involvement. They were asked, "How do you see yourself now in relation to your past?" and, "Do you see yourself as a former addict, recovering addict, recovered addict, or in some other way?" A large majority, nearly two-thirds, refused to identify themselves as presently addicted or as recovering or even recovered. Most reported that they saw themselves in "some other way." While all identified themselves as being addicted earlier in their lives, most did not continue to define themselves as addicts. In several cases, these respondents reacted strongly against the addiction-as-disease ideology, believing that such a permanent identity would impede their continued social development. As one respondent explained:

> I'm a father, a husband and a worker. This is how I see myself today. Being a drug addict was someone I was in the past. I'm over that and I don't think about it anymore.

These respondents saw themselves neither as addicts nor ex-addicts; rather, most references to their past addictions were not central to their immediate self-concepts.

Unlike the alcoholics and drug addicts described by Brown (1991) and others, they did not adopt this identity as a "master status" nor did this identity become salient in the role identity hierarchy (Stryker and Serpe 1982; Becker 1963). Instead, the "addict" identity was marginalized by our respondents. Alcoholics and addicts who have participated extensively in self-help groups often engage in a long-term, self-labeling process which involves continuous reference to their addiction. While many have succeeded in terminating addiction through participation in such programs and by adopting the master status of an addict, researchers have raised concern over the deleterious nature of such self-labeling. Peele (1989), for instance, believes that continuous reference to addiction and

reliance on the sick role may be at variance with successful and enduring termination of addictive behaviors. Respondents in the first stage of the present study, by contrast, did not reference their previous addictions as being presently central in their lives. Their comments suggest that they had transcended their addict identity and had adopted self-concepts congruent with contemporary roles.

During the second phase of the study, the question around identity was reconstructed. Since most respondents in the first sample often made extensive and unsolicited comments about how they currently view themselves in relation to their past experiences (former addict, recovering addict, recovered addict, or other), a decision was made to reshape this question for use with the second sample. The question then read, "How do you see yourself today in relation to your own past experiences with drugs and alcohol (e.g., addict, recovering addict, person who had a serious drug and/or alcohol problem or, do you see yourself in some other way)? Please discuss as it relates to your current identity." The solicited responses from this second sample did not differ dramatically from the unsolicited responses from the first sample. Essentially, their former identities as addicts were not currently central in their lives but rather had been marginalized, as had been the case with the first sample of respondents.

Also, during the second stage of the study, an additional question about "addict identity" was constructed and asked. The question read, "To what extent do you freely discuss your previous drug and alcohol experiences with others? Please elaborate." The majority of these respondents were quite selective about with whom they discussed these previous drug experiences. Some stated that they shared these experiences with very close friends. Others stated that they discussed these matters only with people who had known them as addicts. Still others reported that they discussed these experiences with no one. Again one could conclude, as was the case with the first sample, that this second group minimized these experiences in terms of how they presently view themselves.

The fact that our respondents did not adopt addict identities is of great importance since it contradicts the common assumptions of treatment programs. The belief that alcoholics and drug addicts can overcome their addictions and not see themselves in an indefinite state of recovery is incongruous with treatment predicated on the disease concept which pervades most treatment programs. Such programs subscribe to the view that addiction is incurable; programmatic principles may then commit addicts to a life of ongoing recovery, often with minimal success. Some have suggested that the decision to circumvent formal treatment and self-help involvement has empirical and theoretical importance since it offers insight about this population that may be useful in designing more effective treatment (Sobell et al. 1992). While research has examined the characteristics of individuals who affiliate with such groups, few studies have included individuals outside programs. Therefore, there is a paucity of data that examines the avoidance of treatment. We now turn to an examination of respondents' attitudes toward addiction treatment programs.

CIRCUMVENTING TREATMENT

Given the pervasiveness of treatment programs and self-help groups such as AA and NA, the decision to embark upon a method of natural recovery is curious. Some of our respondents in the first stage of the study reported having had direct exposure to such groups by having attended one or two AA, NA, or CA meetings. Others in this sample, although never having attended, reported being indirectly familiar with such groups. Only two of them claimed to have no knowledge of these groups or the principles they advocate. Consequently, the respondents, as a group, expressed the decision not to enter treatment, which represented a conscious effort to circumvent treatment rather than a lack of familiarity with such programs.

In order to explore their decisions to bypass treatment, we asked what they thought about these programs and why they avoided direct involvement in them. When asked about their attitudes toward such programs, most of them commented that they believed such programs were beneficial for some people. They credited treatment programs and self-help groups with helping friends or family members overcome alcohol or drug addictions. Overall, however, our respondents in the first sample disagreed with the ideological basis of such programs and felt that they were inappropriate for them.

Responses included a wide range of criticisms of these programs. In most cases, rejection of treatment programs and self-help groups reflected a perceived contradiction between these respondents' world views and the core principles of such programs. Overcoming resistance to core principles which include the views that addiction is a disease (once an addict always an addict), or that individuals are powerless over their addiction, is imperative by those who affiliate with such programs. Indeed, individuals who subscribe to alternative views of addiction are identified as "in denial" (Brissett 1988). Not unlike other institutions such as the military, law school, or mental health hospitals, self-help groups socialize recruits away from their previously held world views (Granfield 1992; Goffman 1961). It is the task of such programs to shape its members' views to make them compatible with organizational ideology (Brown 1991; Peele 1989). Socialization within treatment programs and self-help groups enables a person to reconstruct a biography that corresponds to a new reference point.

Respondents in this sample, however, typically rejected specific characteristics of the treatment ideology. First, many expressed strong opposition to the suggestion that they were powerless over their addictions. Such an ideology, they explained, not only was counterproductive but was also extremely demeaning. These respondents saw themselves as efficacious people who often prided themselves on their past accomplishments. They viewed themselves as being individualists and strong-willed. One respondent, for instance, explained that "such programs encourage powerlessness" and that she would rather "trust her own instincts than the instincts of others." Another respondent commented that:

> I read a lot of their literature and the very first thing they say is that you're powerless. I think that's bull-shit. I believe that people have power inside themselves to make what they want happen. I think I have choices and can do anything I set my mind to.

Consequently, these respondents found the suggestion that they were powerless incompatible with their own self-image. While treatment programs and self-help groups would define such attitudes as a manifestation of denial that would only result in perpetuating addiction, they saw overcoming their addictions as a challenge they could effectively surmount. Interestingly, and in contrast to conventional wisdom in the treatment field, the overwhelming majority of our respondents in the first sample reported successful termination of their addictions after only one attempt.

They also reported that they disliked the culture associated with such self-help programs. In addition to finding the ideological components of such programs offensive, most rejected the lifestyle encouraged by such programs. For instance, several of them felt that these programs bred dependency and subsequently rejected the notion that going to meetings with other addicts was essential for successful termination. In fact, some actually thought it to be dangerous to spend so much time with addicts who continue to focus on their addictions. Most of our respondents in this first sample sought to avoid all contact with drug addicts once they decided to terminate their own drug use. Consequently, they believed that contact with addicts, even those who are not actively using, would possibly undermine their termination efforts. Finally, some of these respondents reported that they found self-help groups "cliquish" and "unhealthy." One respondent explained that, "all they do is stand around smoking cigarettes and drinking coffee while they talk about their addiction. I never felt comfortable with these people."

This sense of discomfort with the cultural aspects of these programs was often keenly felt by the women in our sample. Most women in this group believed that self-help groups were male-oriented and did not include the needs of women. One woman, for instance, who identified herself as a lesbian commented that self-help groups were nothing but "a bunch of old men running around telling stories and doing things together." This woman found greater inspiration among feminist support groups and literature that emphasized taking control of one's own life.

During the second stage of the study we decided to separate and sharpen our focus on what appeared to be three prominent overlapping themes around attitudes toward treatment. We asked these respondents why they chose not to undergo formal treatment or participate in self-help groups. We also asked about their general impressions of formal treatment, separate from their impressions of self-help groups. We then asked them specifically about their impressions of AA, NA, and other 12-step programs.

The principal reason reported for not undergoing formal treatment was that nearly all of the 21 respondents in the second sample stated directly or in some variation that they felt that they could terminate their addiction without such interventions. Some stated that treatment was not a viable option since it was either too expensive or essentially unavailable. While some of these respondents registered positive attitudes regarding varying treatment modalities, these respondents, nonetheless, reported that such treatment was not necessary in their individual case. In the case of respondent evaluation of 12-step programs, the second sample of addicts was not as critical as the previous sample. However, even among the second group, most believed that the principles espoused by these programs were at variance with their own beliefs about the recovery process.

THE ELEMENTS OF CESSATION

The fact that our respondents were able to terminate their addictions without the benefit of treatment raises an important question about recovery. Research that has examined this process has found that individuals who have a "stake in conventional life" are better able to alter their drug-taking practices than those who experience a sense of hopelessness (Waldorf et al. 1991). In their longitudinal research of cocaine users, these authors found that many people with structural supports in their lives such as a job, family, and other involvements were simply able to "walk away" from their heavy use of cocaine. According to these authors, this fact suggests that the social context of a drug user's life may significantly influence the ability to overcome drug problems.

The social contexts of our respondents served to protect many of them from total involvement with an addict subculture. Literature on the sociocultural correlates of heavy drinking has found that some groups possess cultural protection against developing alcoholism (Snyder 1964). In addition, Peele (1989) has argued that individuals with greater resources in their lives are well equipped to overcome drug problems. Such resources include education and other credentials, job skills, meaningful family attachments, and support mechanisms. In the case of our first 25 respondents, most provided evidence of such resources available to them even while they were actively using. Most reported coming from stable home environments that valued education, family, and economic security, and for the most part held conventional beliefs. All of our respondents in the first group had completed high school, nine were college graduates, and one held a master's degree in engineering. Most were employed in professional occupations or operated their own businesses. Additionally, most continued to be employed throughout their period of heavy drug and alcohol use and none of our respondents came from disadvantaged backgrounds.

It might be concluded that the social contexts of these respondent's lives protected them from further decline into alcohol and drug addiction. They frequently reported that there were people in their lives to whom they were able to turn when they decided to quit. Some explained that their families provided support; others described how their nondrug-using friends assisted them in their

efforts to stop using. One respondent explained how an old college friend helped him get over his addiction to crack cocaine:

> *My best friend from college made a surprise visit. I hadn't seen him in years. He walked in and I was all cracked out. It's like he walked into the twilight zone or something. He couldn't believe it. He smoked dope in college but he had never seen anything like this. When I saw him, I knew that my life was really screwed up and I needed to do something about it. He stayed with me for the next two weeks and helped me through it.*

Typically, respondents in our first sample had not yet "burned their social bridges" and were able to rely upon communities of friends, family, and other associates in their lives. The existence of such communities made it less of a necessity for these individuals to search out alternative communities such as those found within self-help groups. Such groups may be of considerable importance when a person's natural communities break down. Indeed, the fragmentation of communities within postmodern society may account for the popularity of self-help groups (Reinarman n.d.). In the absence of resources and communities, such programs allow individuals to construct a sense of purpose and meaning in their lives. Respondents in our first sample all explained that the resources, communities, and individuals in their lives were instrumental in supporting their efforts to change.

In some cases, these respondents abandoned their using communities entirely to search for nonusing groups. This decision to do so was often triggered by the realization that their immediate social networks consisted mostly of heavy drug and alcohol users. Any attempt to discontinue use, they reasoned, would require complete separation. Several from this group moved to different parts of the country in order to distance themselves from their using networks. This finding is consistent with Biernacki's (1986) study of heroin addicts who relocated in order to remove any temptations to use in the future. For some women, the decision to abandon using communities, particularly cocaine, was often preceded by becoming pregnant. These women left boyfriends and husbands because they felt a greater sense of responsibility and greater meaning in their new maternal status. In all these cases, respondents fled using communities in search of more conventional networks.

In addition to relying on their natural communities and abandoning using communities, these respondents also built new support structures to assist them in their termination efforts. They frequently reported becoming involved in various social groups such as choirs, health clubs, religious organizations, reading clubs, and dance companies. Others from this group reported that they returned to school, became active in civic organizations, or simply developed new hobbies that brought them in touch with nonusers. Thus, respondents built new lives for themselves by cultivating social ties with meaningful and emotionally satisfying alternative communities. In each of these cases where respondents formed attachments to new communities, they typically hid their addictive past, fearing that exposure would jeopardize their newly acquired status.

During the second stage of the study we further examined two of the above themes. The first theme that was revisited dealt with "specific strategies used to remain abstinent." Overwhelmingly for this group, severing all ties with using friends emerged as the most important strategy one could undertake in successfully terminating addiction.

The next theme around elements of cessation that was further examined among this second sample included "resources that were perceived as valuable in the process of recovery." After giving examples of resources discovered in the first stage of the study (e.g., family), these respondents also reported that identical or similar resources had been very useful in their own struggles to overcome addictions. They reported being able to draw upon their families, job skills, formal education, economic security, and other conditions that had been identified as instrumental resources by the first sample. Interestingly, will power and determination emerged as important internal resources during the second stage of the study.

However, these should be viewed cautiously since "determination" was given as an example of a possible internal resource during the interviews with the second sample.

Given the apparent roles that severing ties with using networks and having resources play in the natural recovery process, one might draw the compelling conclusion that those individuals from the most disadvantaged segments of our society are also least likely to be in a position to overcome severe addiction problems naturally. Unfortunately, these individuals are also at greatest risk for severe drug and alcohol problems, least likely to be able to afford private treatment, and least likely to voluntarily seek public treatment.

DISCUSSION AND IMPLICATIONS

While the sample within the present study is small, there is considerable evidence from additional research to suggest that the population of self-healers is quite substantial (Sobell et al. 1992; Waldorf et al. 1991). Despite empirical evidence, many in the treatment field continue to deny the existence of such a population. The therapeutic "field" possesses considerable power to construct reality in ways that exclude alternative and perhaps challenging paradigms. As Bourdieu (1991) has recently pointed out, such fields reproduce themselves through their ability to normalize arbitrary world views. The power of the therapeutic field lies not only in its ability to medicalize behavior, but also in the ability to exclude the experiences and world views of those who do not fit into conventional models of addiction and treatment (Skoll 1992).

Finding empirical support for natural recovery does not imply that we devalue the importance of treatment programs or even self-help groups. Such programs have proven beneficial to addicts, particularly those in advanced stages. However, the experiences of our respondents have important implications for the way in which addiction and recovery are typically conceptualized. First, denying the existence of this population, as many do, discounts the version of reality held by those who terminate their addictions naturally. Natural recovery is simply not recognized as a viable option. This is increasingly the case as media has reified dominant notions of addiction and recovery. Similarly, there is an industry of self-help literature that unquestionably accepts and reproduces these views. Denying the experience of natural recovery allows treatment agencies and self-help groups to continue to impose their particular view of reality on society.

Related to this is the possibility that many of those experiencing addictions may be extremely reluctant to enter treatment or attend self-help meetings. Their resistance may stem from a variety of factors such as the stigma associated with these programs, discomfort with the therapeutic process, or lack of support from significant others. Whatever the reason, such programs do not appeal to everyone. For such people, natural recovery may be a viable option. Since natural recovery demystifies the addiction and recovery experience, it may offer a way for people to take control of their own lives without needing to rely exclusively on experts. Such an alternative approach offers a low-cost supplement to an already costly system of formal addiction treatment.

A third implication concerns the consequences of adopting an addict identity. While the disease metaphor is thought to be a humanistic one in that it allows for the successful social reintegration of deviant drinkers or drug users, it nevertheless constitutes a deviant identity. Basing one's identity on past addiction experiences may actually limit social reintegration. The respondents in our sample placed a great deal of emphasis on their immediate social roles as opposed to constantly referring to their drug-addict pasts. Although there is no way of knowing, such present-centeredness may, in the long run, prove more beneficial than a continual focusing on the past.

Fourth, for drug and alcohol treatment professionals, as well as those who are likely to refer individuals to drug and alcohol treatment programs, this research raises several important considerations. It reaffirms the necessity for individual treatment matching (Lewis et al. 1994). It also suggests that individuals whose profiles are similar to these middle-class respondents are likely to be receptive to and benefit from less intrusive, short-term types of interventions. Given the extent of the various concerns expressed by these respondents around some of the possible long-term negative consequences of undergoing traditional treatment and related participation in self-help programs, the decision to specifically recommend drug and alcohol treatment is a profoundly serious one. It should not be made capriciously or simply because it is expected and available. A careful assessment of the person's entire life is warranted, including whether or not the condition is so severe and the absence of supportive resources so great that the possible life-long identity of addict or related internalized beliefs are reasonable risks to take in pursuing recovery. Overall, the findings of this study as well as previous research on natural recovery could be instructive in designing more effective treatment programs (Sobell et al. 1992; Fillmore 1988; Stall and Biernacki 1986).

Finally, the experiences of our respondents may have important social policy implications. If our respondents are any guide, the following hypothesis might be considered: those with the greatest number of resources and who consequently have a great deal to lose by their addiction are the ones most likely to terminate their addictions naturally. While addiction is not reducible to social class alone, it is certainly related to it (Waldorf et al. 1991). The respondents in our sample had relatively stable lives: they had jobs, supportive families, high school and college credentials, and other social supports that gave them reasons to alter their drug-taking behavior. Having much to lose gave our respondents incentives to transform their lives. However, when there is little to lose from heavy alcohol or drug use, there may be little to gain by quitting. Social policies that attempt to increase a person's stake in conventional life could not only act to prevent future alcohol and drug addiction, they could also provide an anchor for those who become dependent on these substances.

Further research on the subject of natural recovery among hidden populations such as the middle class needs to be conducted in order to substantiate the findings we report and related conclusions. One important direction the researchers are presently pursuing is to differentiate the natural recovery experience of individuals who have been addicted to different substances. Such research could increase understanding of how different hidden populations overcome the addictions they experience.

NOTES

1. In his study of identity transformation of alcoholics, Brown (1991) found that the conversion experience to a "recovering alcoholic" was so powerful that many individuals abandoned their previous careers to become counselors.

REFERENCES

Abbott, A. 1988. *The system of profession.* Chicago: University of Chicago Press.

Adler, P. 1986. *Wheeling and dealing.* New York: Columbia University Press.

Becker, H. 1963. *The outsiders: Studies in the sociology of deviance.* New York: The Free Press.

Biernacki, P. 1986. *Pathways from heroin addiction: Recovery without treatment.* Philadelphia: Temple University Press.

Bourdieu, P. 1991. The peculiar history of scientific reason. *Sociological Forum* 5(2):3–26.

Brissett, D. 1988. Denial in alcoholism: A sociological interpretation. *Journal of Drug Issues* 18(3): 385–402.

Brown, J. D. 1991. Preprofessional socialization and identity transformation: The case of the professional ex. *Journal of Contemporary Ethnography* 20(2):157–178.

Cloud, W. 1987. *From down under: A qualitative study on heroin addiction recovery.* Ann Arbor: Dissertation Abstracts.

Emrick, C., J. Tonigan, H. Montgomery, and L. Little. 1993. "Alcoholics Anonymous: What is currently known?" In *Research on Alcoholics Anonymous:*

Opportunities and alternatives, eds. B. McCrady and W. Miller. New Brunswick, N.J.: Rutgers Center of Alcohol Studies.

Fillmore, K. M. 1988. Spontaneous remission of alcohol problems. Paper presented at the National Conference on Evaluating Recovery Outcomes, San Diego, Calif.

Garfinkel, H. 1967. *Studies in ethnomethodology.* Upper Saddle River, N.J.: Prentice Hall.

Goffman, E. 1961. *Asylums.* Garden City, N.Y.: Anchor Books.

———. 1963. *Stigma.* Upper Saddle River, N.J.: Prentice Hall.

Goodwin, D., J. B. Crane, and S. B. Guze. 1971. Felons who drink: An eight-year follow-up. *Quarterly Journal of Studies on Alcohol* 32:136–147.

Granfield, R. 1992. *Making elite lawyers: Visions of law at Harvard and beyond.* New York: Routledge, Chapman and Hall.

Hanson, B., G. Beschner, J. M. Walters, and E. Bovelle. 1985. *Life with heroin.* Lexington, Mass.: Lexington Books.

Hingson, R., N. Scotch, N. Day, and A. Culbert. 1980. Recognizing and seeking help for drinking problems. *Journal of Studies on Alcohol* 41:1102–1117.

Lambert, E., and W. Wiebel. 1990. Introduction. In *The collection and interpretation of data from hidden populations*, ed. E. Lambert. Rockville, Md.: National Institute on Drug Abuse.

Lee, R. 1993. *Doing research on sensitive topics.* Newbury Park, Calif.: Sage.

Lemert, E. 1951. *Social pathology.* New York: McGraw-Hill.

Lemert, E. 1974. Beyond Mead: The societal reaction to deviance. *Social Problems* 21(4):457–468.

Lewis, J., R. Dana, and G. Blevins. 1994. *Substance abuse counseling: An individualized approach.* Pacific Grove, Calif.: Brooks/Cole.

Parsons, T. 1951. *The social system.* New York: The Free Press.

Peele, S. 1989. *The diseasing of America: Addiction treatment out of control.* Lexington, Mass.: Lexington Books.

Ratner, M. 1993. *Crack pipe as pimp: An ethnographic investigation of sex-for-crack exchanges.* New York: Lexington Books.

Reinarman, C. n.d. "The twelve-step movement and advanced capitalist culture: Notes on the politics of self-control in postmodernity." In *Contemporary social movements and cultural politics*, eds.

M. Darofsky, B. Epstein, and R. Flacks. Philadelphia: Temple University Press. In press.

Roizen, R., D. Cahalan, and P. Shanks. 1978. "Spontaneous remission among untreated problem drinkers." In *Longitudinal research on drug use*, ed. D. Kandel. Washington, D.C.: Hemisphere Publishing.

Rosenbaum, M., and S. Murphy. 1990. "Women and addiction: Process, treatment, and outcome." In *The collection and interpretation of data from hidden populations*, ed. E. Lambert. Rockville, Md.: National Institute on Drug Abuse.

Rubington, E. 1967. Drug addiction as a deviant career. *International Journal of the Addictions* 2:3–20.

Rubington, E. 1978. "Variations in bottle-gang controls." In *Deviance: The interactionist perspective*, eds. E. Rubington and M. Weinberg. New York: Macmillan.

Shaffer, H., and S. Jones. 1989. *Quitting cocaine. The struggle against impulse.* Lexington, Mass.: Lexington Books.

Skoll, G. 1992. *Walk the walk and talk the talk: An ethnography of a drug abuse treatment facility.* Philadelphia: Temple University Press.

Snow, M. 1973. Maturing out of narcotic addiction in New York City. *International Journal of the Addictions* 8(6):921–938.

Snyder, C. 1964. "Inebriety, alcoholism and anomie." In *Anomie and deviant behavior*, ed. M. Clinard. New York: The Free Press.

Sobell, L., M. Sobell, and T. Toneatto. 1992. "Recovery from alcohol problems without treatment." In *Self control and the addictive behaviors*, eds. N. Heather, W. R. Miller, and J. Greeley 199–242. New York: Maxwell Macmillan.

Sobell, L., M. Sobell, T. Toneatto, and G. Leo. 1993. What triggers the resolution of alcohol problems without treatment? *Alcoholism: Clinical and Experimental Research* 17(2):217–224.

Stall, R., and P. Biernacki. 1986. Spontaneous remission from the problematic use of substances. *International Journal of the Addictions* 21:1–23.

Stephens, R. 1991. *The street addict role: A theory of heroin addiction.* Albany, N.Y.: State University Press of New York.

Stryker, S., and R. Serpe. 1982. "Commitment, identity salience and role behavior: Theory and research example." In *Personality, roles and social behavior*, eds. W. Ickes and E. Knowles. New York: Springer-Verlag.

Trice, H., and P. Roman. 1970. Delabeling, relabeling, and Alcoholics Anonymous. *Social Problems* 17:538–546.

Valliant, G. 1966. "A twelve-year follow-up of New York narcotic addicts: Some characteristics and determinants of abstinence." In *Classic contributions in the addictions*, eds. H. Shaffer and M. Burglass. New York: Brunner/Mazel.

Valliant, G. 1983. *The natural history of alcoholism.* Cambridge: Harvard University Press.

Valliant, G., and E. S. Milofsky. 1982. Natural history of male alcoholism: IV. Paths to recovery. *Archives of General Psychiatry* 39:127–133.

Waldorf, D., and P. Biernacki. 1977. Natural recovery from opiate addiction: A review of the incidence literature. *Journal of Drug Issues* 9:281–290.

Waldorf, D., and P. Biernacki. 1981. Natural recovery from opiate addiction: Some preliminary findings. *Journal of Drug Issues* 11:61–74.

Waldorf, D., C. Reinarman, and S. Murphy. 1991. *Cocaine changes: The experience of using and quitting.* Philadelphia: Temple University Press.

Walsh, D. C., R. Hingson, and D. Merrigan. 1992. The impact of a physician's warning on recovery after alcoholism treatment. *Journal of American Medical Association* 267:663.

Waterston, A. 1993. *Street addicts in the political economy.* Philadelphia: Temple University Press.

Weisner, C., and R. Room. 1978. Financing and ideology in alcohol treatment. *Social Problems* 32:157–184.

Williams, T. 1989. *The cocaine kids.* Reading, Mass.: Addison-Wesley.

Winick, C. 1962. Maturing out of narcotic addiction. *Bulletin on Narcotics* 6:1.

Wiseman, J. 1970. *Stations of the lost: The treatment of skid row alcoholics.* Upper Saddle River, N.J.: Prentice Hall.

Zinberg, N. 1986. *Drug, set and setting: The basis for controlled intoxicant use.* New Haven: Yale University Press.

Getting Out of the Life

IRA SOMMERS, DEBORAH R. BASKIN, and JEFFREY FAGAN

Criminologists estimate that 70 percent of felons released after serving their sentences return to crime. This high rate of recidivism suggests that numerous obstacles exist for those who seek to terminate their criminal careers after discharge from prison. Nevertheless, some unknown percentage of ex-convicts do become ex-criminals. Studies of male property offenders indicate that a series of stages need to be completed before ex-convicts can rejoin the conventional social world. Getting older, fearing recapture, and becoming tired of "doing time" motivate the first stage in transforming deviant identity. Over time, when the costs of criminality outweigh its rewards, some career criminals contemplate a change.

Recent years have seen an increase in crimes committed by women. Ira Sommers, Deborah R. Baskin, and Jeffrey Fagan set out to find if women who had apparently exited criminal careers went through the same stages. They interviewed 30 women who had committed violent crimes, used drugs, participated in deviant street subcultures, and had somehow managed to renounce criminality for a period of two years. They found that women exit a deviant career in much the same ways as male criminals. All of the women experienced a shock, which triggered an identity crisis. They were forced to consider the fact that they could not continue being the person that they had become. Continuance would only mean more disrespect, social punishment, degradation, and ultimately death. The self-appraisal induced by crisis led to a new self-definition, a resolve to become a different kind of person. To claim their new personal identity, they made public their resolve to quit crime. Their claim to a new social status as an ex-criminal came about over a period of time. In time, validation as an ex-criminal resulted from the renewal of ties with family, the development of ties with new friends, and the severance of all ties to deviant ways, places, and associates. Perhaps their most important social support came from their participation in treatment programs.

Studies over the past decade have provided a great deal of information about the criminal careers of male offenders. (See Blumstein et al. 1986 and Weiner and Wolfgang 1989 for reviews.) Unfortunately, much less is known about the initiation, escalation, and termination of criminal careers by female offenders. The general tendency to exclude female offenders from research on crime and delinquency may be due, at least in part, to the lower frequency and comparatively less serious nature of offending among women. Recent trends and studies, however, suggest that the omission of women may seriously bias both research and theory on crime.

Although a growing body of work on female crime has emerged within the last few years, much of this research continues to focus on what Daly and Chesney-Lind (1988) called generalizability and gender-ratio problems. The former concerns the degree to which traditional (i.e., male) theories of deviance and crime apply to women, and the latter focuses on what explains gender differences in rates and types of criminal activity. Although this article also examines women in crime, questions of inter- and intragender variability in crime are not specifically addressed. Instead, the aim of the paper is to describe the pathways out of deviance for a sample of women who have significantly invested themselves in criminal social worlds. To what extent are the social and psychological processes of stopping criminal behavior similar for men and women? Do the behavioral antecedents of such processes vary by gender? These questions remained unexplored.

Specifically, two main issues are addressed in this paper: (1) the role of life events in triggering the cessation process, and (2) the relationship between cognitive and life situation changes in the desistance process. First, the crime desistance literature is reviewed briefly. Second, the broader deviance literature is drawn upon to construct a social-psychological model of cessation. Then the model is evaluated using life history data from a sample of female offenders convicted of serious street crimes.

THE DESISTANCE PROCESS

The common themes in the literature on exiting deviant careers offer useful perspectives for developing a theory of cessation. The decision to stop deviant behavior appears to be preceded by a variety of factors, most of which are negative social sanctions or consequences. Health problems, difficulties with the law or with maintaining a current lifestyle, threats of other social sanctions from family or close relations, and a general rejection of the social world in which the behaviors thrive are often antecedents of the decision to quit. For some, religious conversions or immersion into alternative sociocultural settings with powerful norms (e.g., treatment ideology) provide paths for cessation (Mulvey and LaRosa 1986; Stall and Biernacki 1986).

. . . A model for understanding desistance from crime is presented below. Three stages characterized the cessation process: building resolve or discovering motivation to stop (i.e., socially disjunctive experiences), making and publicly disclosing the decision to stop, and maintaining the new behaviors and intergrating into new social networks (Stall and Biernacki 1986; Mulvey and Aber 1988). These phases . . . describe three ideal-typical phases of desistance: "turning points" where offenders begin consciously to experience negative effects (socially disjunctive experiences); "active quitting" where they take steps to exit crime (public pronouncement); and "maintaining cessation" (identity transformation):

STAGE 1 : CATALYSTS FOR CHANGE

Socially disjunctive experiences
- Hitting rock bottom
- Fear of death
- Tiredness
- Illness

Delayed deterrence
- Increased probability of punishment
- Increased difficulty in doing time
- Increased severity of sanctions
- Increasing fear

Assessment
- Reappraisal of life and goals
- Psychic change

Decision
- Decision to quit and/or initial attempts at desistance
- Continuing possibility of criminal participation

STAGE 2 : DISCONTINUANCE
- Public pronouncement of decision to end criminal participation
- Claim to a new social identity

STAGE 3 : MAINTENANCE OF THE DECISION TO STOP

- Ability to successfully renegotiate identity
- Support of significant others
- Integration into new social networks
- Ties to conventional roles
- Stabilization of new social identity

STAGE 1: CATALYSTS FOR CHANGE

When external conditions change and reduce the rewards of deviant behavior, motivation may build to end criminal involvement. That process and the resulting decision seem to be associated with two related conditions: a series of negative, aversive, unpleasant experiences with criminal behavior, or corollary situations where the positive rewards, status, or gratification from crime are reduced. Shover and Thompson's (1992) research suggests that the probability of desistance from criminal participation increases as expectations for achieving rewards (e.g., friends, money, autonomy) via crime decrease and that changes in expectations are age-related. Shover (1983) contended that the daily routines of managing criminal involvement become tiring and burdensome to aging offenders. Consequently, the allure of crime diminishes as offenders get older. Aging may also increase the perceived formal risk of criminal participation. Cusson and Pinsonneault (1986, p. 76) posited that "with age, criminals raise their estimates of the certainty of punishment." Fear of reimprisonment, fear of longer sentences, and the increasing difficulty of "doing time" have often been reported by investigators who have explored desistance.

STAGE 2: DISCONTINUANCE

The second stage of the model begins with the public announcement that the offender has decided to end her criminal participation. Such an announcement forces the start of a process of renegotiation of the offender's social identity (Stall and Biernacki 1986). After this announcement, the offender must not only cope with the instrumental aspects (e.g., financial) of her life but must also begin to redefine important emotional and social relationships that are influenced by or predicated upon criminal behavior.

Leaving a deviant subculture is difficult. Biernacki (1986) noted the exclusiveness of the social involvements maintained by former addicts during initial stages of abstinence. With social embedment comes the gratification of social acceptance and identity. The decision to end a behavior that is socially determined and supported implies withdrawal of the social gratification it brings. Thus, the more deeply embedded in a criminal social context, the more dependent the offender is on that social world for her primary sources of approval and social definition.

The responses by social control agents, family members, and peer supporters to further criminal participation are critical to shaping the outcome of discontinuance. New social and emotional worlds to replace the old ones may strengthen the decision to stop. Adler (1992) found that outside associations and involvements provide a critical bridge back into society for dealers who have decided to leave the drug subculture. With discontinuance comes the difficult work of identity transformation (Biernacki 1986) and establishing new social definitions of behavior and relationships to reinforce them.

STAGE 3: MAINTENANCE

Following the initial stages of discontinuance, strategies to avoid a return to crime build on the strategies first used to break from a lengthy pattern of criminal participation: further integration into a noncriminal identity and social world and maintenance of this new identity. Maintenance depends in part on replacing deviant networks of peers and associates with supports that both censure criminal participation and approve of new nondeviant beliefs. Treatment interventions (e.g., drug treatment, social service programs) are important sources of alternative social supports to maintain a noncriminal lifestyle. In other words, maintenance depends on immersion into a social world where criminal behavior meets immediately with strong formal and informal sanctions.

Despite efforts to maintain noncriminal involvement, desistance is likely to be episodic, with occasional relapses interspersed with lengthening of lulls in criminal activity. Le Blanc and Frechette (1989) proposed the possibility that criminal activity slows down before coming to an end and that this slowing down process becomes apparent in three ways: deceleration, specialization, and reaching a ceiling. Thus, before stopping criminal activity, the offender gradually acts out less frequently, limits the variety of crimes more and more, and ceases increasing the seriousness of criminal involvement.

Age is a critical variable in desistance research, regardless of whether it is associated with maturation or similar developmental concepts. Cessation is part of a social-psychological transformation for the offender. A strategy to stabilize the transition to a noncriminal lifestyle requires active use of supports to maintain the norms that have been substituted for the forces that supported criminal behavior in the past.

METHODS

. . . Through the use of snowball sampling, 30 women were recruited and interviewed. . . . An initial pool of 16 women was recruited through various offender and drug treatment programs in New York City. Fourteen additional women were recruited through chain referrals. To be included in the study, the women had to have at least one official arrest for a violent street crime (robbery, assault, burglary, weapons possession, arson, kidnapping) and to have desisted from all criminal involvement for at least 2 years prior to the interview.[1] Eligibility was verified through official arrest records and through contact with program staff for those women participating in treatment programs (87%).

The life history interviews . . . were open-ended, in-depth, and audiotaped. The open-ended technique created a context in which respondents could speak freely and in their own words. Furthermore, it facilitated the pursuit of issues

raised by respondents during the interview but not recognized previously by the researcher. Use of this approach enabled us to probe for information about specific events and provided an opportunity for respondents to reflect on those events. As a result, we were able to gain insight into their attitudes, feelings, and other subjective orientations to their experiences. Finally, tape-recording the interviews allowed the interviewer to adopt a more conversational style, devote complete attention to the respondent, and concentrate on the discussion. By not being preoccupied with note-taking, interviewers were able to create a more relaxed atmosphere for the participants.

All interviews were conducted by the first two authors in a private university office. They were typically held in the morning or early afternoon and lasted approximately 2 hours. A stipend of $50 was paid to each respondent. In total, 30 interviews were conducted, comprising approximately 60 hours of talk.

With regard to self-reported drug and criminal histories, the data indicate that the study respondents had engaged in a wide range of criminal and deviant activities. All of the respondents were experienced drug users. Eighty-seven percent were addicted to crack, 70% used cocaine regularly, and 10% were addicted to heroin. Of the 30 women interviewed, 19 (63%) reported involvement in robbery, 60% reported involvement in burglary, 94% were involved in selling drugs, and 47% were at some time involved in prostitution. A great deal of variation was found with regard to incarceration history. The median number of incarcerations was 3 (the mean was 4.29); however, 17% of the women ($n = 5$) had never been incarcerated.

Patterns of offending for 17 of the 30 women (57%) resemble those of a sample of addicts studied by Anglin and Speckhart (1988, p. 223) in that "while some criminality precedes the addiction career, the great majority is found during the addiction career." It seems that for these women, the cost of their increasing substance use was a major influence to engage in offending, especially robbery and selling drugs. For the remaining 13 women (43%), drug abuse appears not to be as etiologically important to violent behavior, in spite of the high correlations between these two behaviors. Instead, addiction seems to be part of a more generalized lifestyle (Peterson and Braiker 1980; Collins et al. 1985) in which involvement in violent criminal careers precedes, yet may be amplified by, addiction.

RESULTS

RESOLVING TO STOP

Despite its initial excitement and allure, the life of a street criminal is a hard one. A host of severe personal problems plague most street offenders and normally become progressively worse as their careers continue. In the present study, the women's lives were dominated by a powerful, often incapacitating, need for drugs. Consequently, economic problems were the most frequent complaint voiced by the respondents. Savings were quickly exhausted, and the culture of addiction justified virtually any means to get money to support their habits. For the majority of the women, the problem of maintaining an addiction took precedence over other interests and participation in other social worlds.

People the respondents associated with, their primary reference group, were involved in illicit behaviors. Over time, the women in the study became further enmeshed in deviance and further alienated, both socially and psychologically, from conventional life. The women's lives became bereft of conventional involvements, obligations, and responsibilities. The excitement at the lifestyle that may have characterized their early criminal career phase gave way to a much more grave daily existence.

Thus, the women in our study could not and did not simply cease their deviant acts by "drifting" (Matza 1964) back toward conventional norms, values, and lifestyles. Unlike many of Waldorf's (1983) heroin addicts who drifted away from heroin without conscious efforts, all of the women in our study made a conscious decision to stop. In short, Matza's concept of drift did not provide a useful framework for understanding our respondents' exit from crime.

The following accounts illustrate the uncertainty and vulnerability of street life for the women in our sample. Denise, a 33-year-old black woman, has participated in a wide range of street crimes including burglary, robbery, assault, and drug dealing. She began dealing drugs when she was 14 and was herself using cocaine on a regular basis by age 19.

I was in a lot of fights: So I had fights over, uh, drugs, or, you know, just manipulation. There's a lot of manipulation in that life. Everybody's tryin' to get over. Everybody will stab you in your back, you know. Nobody gives a fuck about the next person, you know. It's just when you want it, you want it. You know, when you want that drug, you know, you want that drug. There's a lot of lyin', a lot of manipulation. It's, it's, it's crazy!

Gazella, a 38-year-old Hispanic woman, had been involved in crime for 22 years when we interviewed her.

I'm 38 years old. I ain't no young woman no more, man. Drugs have changed, lifestyles have changed. Kids are killing you now for turf. Yeah, turf, and I was destroyin' myself. I was miserable. I was . . . I was gettin' high all the time to stay up to keep the business going, and it was really nobody I could trust.

Additional illustrations of the exigencies of street life are provided by April and Stephanie. April is a 25-year-old black woman who had been involved in crime since she was 11.

I wasn't eating. Sometimes I wouldn't eat for two or three days. And I would . . . a lot of times I wouldn't have the time, or I wouldn't want to spend the money to eat—I've got to use it to get high.

Stephanie, a 27-year-old black woman, had used and sold crack for 5 years when we interviewed her.

I knew that, uh, I was gonna get killed out here. I wasn't havin' no respect for myself. No one else was respecting me. Every relationship I got into, as long as I did drugs, it was gonna be constant disrespect involved, and it come . . . to the point of me gettin' killed.

When the spiral down finally reached its lowest point, the women were overwhelmed by a sense of personal despair. In reporting the early stages of this period of despair, the respondents consistently voiced two themes: the futility of their lives and their isolation.

Barbara, a 31-year-old black woman, began using crack when she was 23. By age 25, Barbara had lost her job at the Board of Education and was involved in burglary and robbery. Her account is typical of the despair the women in our sample eventually experienced.

. . . the fact that my family didn't trust me anymore, and the way that my daughter was looking at me, and, uh, my mother wouldn't let me in her house any more, and I was sleepin' on the trains. And I was sleepin' on the beaches in the summertime. And I was really frightened. I was real scared of the fact that I had to sleep on the train. And, uh, I had to wash up in the Port Authority.

The spiral down for Gazella also resulted in her living on the streets.

I didn't have a place to live. My kids had been taken away from me. You know, constantly being harassed like 3 days out of the week by the Tactical Narcotics Team (police). I didn't want to be bothered with people. I was gettin' tired of the lyin', schemin', you know, stayin' in abandoned buildings.

Alicia, a 29-year-old Hispanic woman, became involved in street violence at age 12. She commented on the personal isolation that was a consequence of her involvement in crime:

When I started getting involved in crime, you know, and drugs, the friends that I had, even my family, I stayed away from them, you know. You know how you look bad and you feel bad, and you just don't want those people to see you like you are. So I avoided seeing them.

For some, the emotional depth of the rock bottom crisis was felt as a sense of mortification. The women felt as if they had nowhere to turn to salvage a sense of well-being or self-worth. Suicide was considered a better alternative than remaining in such an undesirable social and psychological state. Denise is one example:

I ran into a girl who I went to school with that works on Wall Street. And I compared her life to mine and it was like miserable. And I just wanted out. I wanted a new life. I was tired, I was run down, looking bad. I got out by smashing myself through a sixth-floor window. Then I went to the psychiatric ward and I met this real nice doctor, and we talked every day. She fought to keep me in the hospital because she felt I wouldn't survive. She believed in me. And she talked me into going into a drug program.

Marginalization from family, friends, children, and work—in short, the loss of traditional life structures—left the women vulnerable to chaotic street conditions. After initially being overwhelmed by despair, the women began to question and reevaluate basic assumptions about their identities and their social construction of the world. Like Shover's (1983) male property offenders, the women also began to view the criminal justice system as "an imposing accumulation of aggravations and deprivations" (p. 212). They grew tired of the street experiences and the problems and consequences of criminal involvement.

Many of the women acknowledged that, with age, it is more difficult to do time and that the fear of incurring a long prison sentence the next time influenced their decision to stop. Cusson and Pinsonneault (1986, p. 76) made the same observation with male robbers. Gazella, April, and Denise, quoted earlier, recall:

GAZELLA: First of all, when I was in prison I was like, I was so humiliated. At my age [38] I was really kind of embarrassed, but I knew that was the lifestyle that I was leadin'. And people I used to talk to would tell me, well, you could do this, and you don't have to get busted. But then I started thinking why are all these people here. So it doesn't, you know, really work. So I came home, and I did go back to selling again, but you know I knew I was on probation. And I didn't want to do no more time.

APRIL: Jail, being in jail. The environment, having my freedom taken away. I saw myself keep repeating the same pattern, and I didn't want to do that. Uh, I had missed my daughter. See, being in jail that long period of time, I was able to detox. And when I detoxed, I kind of like had a clear sense of thinking, and that's when I came to the realization that, uh, this is not working for me.

DENISE: I saw the person that I was dealing with—my partner—I saw her go upstate to Bedford for 2 to 4 years. I didn't want to deal with it. I didn't want to go. Bedford is a prison, women's prison. And I couldn't see myself givin' up 2 years of my life for something that I knew I could change in another way.

As can be seen from the above, the influence of punishment on these women was due to their belief that if they continued to be involved in crime, they would be apprehended, convicted, and incarcerated.

For many of the women, it was the stresses of street life and the fear of dying on the streets that motivated their decision to quit the criminal life. Darlene, a 25-year-old black woman, recalled the stress associated with the latter stage of her career selling drugs:

The simple fact is that I really, I thought that I would die out there. I thought that someone would kill me out there and I would be killed; I had a fear of being on the front page one day and being in the newspaper dying. I wanted to live, and I didn't just want to exist.

Sonya, a 27-year-old Hispanic woman, provided an account of what daily life was like on the streets:

You get tired of bein' tired, you know. I got tired of hustlin', you know. I got tired of livin' the way I was livin', you know. Due to your body, your body, mentally, emotionally, you know. Everybody's tryin' to get over. Everybody will stab you in your back. Nobody gives a fuck about the next person. And I used to have people talkin' to me, "You know, you're not a bad lookin' girl. You know, why you don't get yourself together."

Perhaps even more important, the women felt that they had wasted time. They became acutely aware of time as a diminishing resource (Shover 1983). They reported that they saw themselves going nowhere. They had arrived at a point where crime seemed senseless, and their lives had reached a dead end. Implicit in this assessment was the belief that gaining a longer-range perspective on one's life was a first step in changing. Such deliberations develop as a result of "socially disjunctive experiences" that cause the offender to experience social stress, feelings of alienation, and dissatisfaction with her present identity (Ray 1961).

BREAKING AWAY FROM THE LIFE

Forming a commitment to change is only the first step toward the termination of a criminal career. The offender enters a period that has been characterized as a "running struggle" with problems of social identity (Ray 1961, p. 136). Successful desisters must work to clarify and strengthen their nondeviant identity and redefine their street experience in terms more compatible with a conventional lifestyle. The second stage of the desistance process begins with the public announcement or "certification" (Meisenhelder 1977, p. 329) that the offender has decided to end her deviant behavior. After this announcement, the offender must begin to redefine economic, social, and emotional relationships that were based on a deviant street subculture.

The time following the announcement was generally a period of ambivalence and crisis for the study participants, because so much of their lives revolved around street life and because they had, at best, weak associations with the conventional world. Many of the women remembered the uncertainty they felt and the social dilemmas they faced after they decided to stop their involvement in crime.

DENISE: I went and looked up my friends and to see what was doing, and my girlfriend Mia was like, she was gettin' paid. And I was livin' on a $60 stipend. And I wasn't with it. Mia was good to me, she always kept money in my pocket when I came home. I would walk into her closet and change into clothes that I'm more accustomed to. She started calling me Pen again. She stopped calling me Denise. And I would ride with her knowing that she had a gun or a package in the car. But I wouldn't touch nothin'. But that was my rationale. As long as I don't fuck with nothin'. Yeah, she was like I can give you a grand and get you started. I said I know you can, but I can't. She said I can give you a grand, and she kept telling me that over and over, and I wasn't that far from taking the grand and getting started again.

BARBARA: After I decided to change, I went to a party with my friend. And people was around me and they was drinkin' and stuff, and I didn't want to drink. I don't have the urge of drinking. If anything, it would be smokin' crack. And when I left the party, I felt like I was missing something—like something was missing. And it was the fact that I wasn't gettin' high. But I know the consequences of it. If I take a drink, I'm gonna smoke crack. If I, uh, sniff some blow, I'm gonna smoke crack. I might do some things like rob a store or something stupid and go to jail. So I don't want to put myself in that position.

At this stage of their transition, the women had to decide how to establish and maintain conventional relationships and what to do with themselves

and their lives. Few of the women had maintained good relationships with people who were not involved in crime and drugs. Given this situation, the women had to seek alternatives to their present situation.

The large majority of study participants were aided in their social reintegration by outside help. These respondents sought formal treatment of some kind, typically residential drug treatment, to provide structure, social support, and a pathway to behavioral change. The women perceived clearly the need to remove themselves from the "scene," to meet new friends, and to begin the process of identity reformation. The following account by Alicia typifies the importance of a "geographic" cure:

> *I love to get high, you know, and I love the way crack makes me feel. I knew that I needed long-term, I knew that I needed to go somewhere. All away from everything, and I just needed to go away from everything. And I couldn't deal with responsibility at all. And, uh, I was just so ashamed of the way that I had, you know, became and the person that I became that I just wanted to start over again.*

Social avoidance strategies were common to all attempts at stopping. When the women removed themselves from their old world and old locations, involvement in crime and drugs was more difficult.

APRIL: Yeah, I go home, but I don't, I don't socialize with the people. I don't even speak to anybody really. I go and I come. I don't go to the areas that I used to be in. I don't go there anymore. I don't walk down the same blocks I used to walk down. I always take different locations.

DENISE: I miss the fast money; otherwise, I don't miss my old life. I get support from my positive friends, and in the program. I talk about how I felt being around my old associates, seeing them, you know, going back to my old neighborhood. It's hard to deal with, I have to push away.

MAINTAINING A CONVENTIONAL LIFE

Desisters have little chance of staying out of the life for an extended period of time if they stay in the social world of crime and addiction. They must rebuild and maintain a network of primary relations who accept and support their nondeviant identity if they are to be successful (the third stage of this model). This is no easy task, since in most cases the desisters have alienated their old nondeviant primary relations.

To a great extent, the women in this study most resemble religious converts in their attempts to establish and maintain support networks that validate their new sense of self. Treatment programs not only provide a ready-made primary group for desisters, but also a well-established pervasive identity (Travisano 1970), that of ex-con and/or ex-addict, that informs the women's view of themselves in a variety of interactions. Reminders of "spoiled identities" (Goffman 1963) such as criminal, "con," and "junkie" serve as a constant reference point for new experiences and keep salient the ideology of conventional living (Faupel 1991). Perhaps most important, these programs provide the women with an alternative basis for life structure—one that is devoid of crime, drugs, and other subcultural elements.

The successful treatment program, however, is one that ultimately facilitates dissociation from the program and promotes independent living. Dissociation from programs to participate in conventional living requires association, or reintegration, with conventional society. Friends and educational and occupational roles helped study participants reaffirm their noncriminal identities and bond themselves to conventional lifestyles. Barbara described the assistance she receives from friends and treatment groups:

> . . . a bunch of friends that always confronts me on what I'm doing' and where I'm goin', and they just want the best for me. And none of them use drugs. I go to a lot like outside support groups, you know. They help me have more confidence in myself. I have new friends now. Some of them are in treatment.

> Some have always been straight. They know. You know, they glad, you know, when I see them.

In the course of experiencing relationships with conventional others and participating in conventional roles, the women developed a strong social-psychological commitment not to return to crime and drug use. These commitments most often revolved around renewed affiliations with their children, relationships with new friends, and the acquisition of educational and vocational skills. The social relationships, interests, and investments that develop in the course of desistance reflect the gradual emergence of new identities. Such stakes in conventional identity form the social-psychological context within which control and desistance are possible (Waldorf et al. 1991).

In short, the women in the study developed a stake in their new lives that was incompatible with street life. This new stake served as a wedge to help maintain the separation of the women from the world of the streets (Biernacki 1986). The desire to maintain one's sense of self was an important incentive for avoiding return to crime.

ALICIA: I like the fact that I have my respect back. I like the fact that, uh, my daughter trusts me again. And my mother don't mind leavin' me in the house, and she don't have to worry that when she come in her TV might be gone.

BARBARA: I have new friends. I have my children back in my life. I have my education. It keeps me straight. I can't forget where I came from because I get scared to go back. I don't want to hurt nobody. I just want to live a normal life.

Janelle, a 22-year-old black woman, started dealing drugs and carrying a .38-caliber gun when she was 15. She described the ongoing tension between staying straight and returning to her old social world:

> It's hard, it's hard stayin' on the right track. But letting myself know that I'm worth more. I don't have to go in a store today and steal anything. I don't deserve that. I don't deserve to make myself

feel really bad. Then once again I would be steppin' back and feel that this is all I can do.

Overall, the success of identity transformation hinges on the women's abilities to establish and maintain commitments and involvements in conventional aspects of life. As the women began to feel accepted and trusted within some conventional social circles, their determination to exit from crime was strengthened, as were their social and personal identities as noncriminals.

DISCUSSION

The primary purpose of this study was to describe—from the offenders' perspective—how women embedded in criminal street subcultures could end their deviance. Desistance appears to be a process as complex and lengthy as that of initial involvement. It was interesting to find that some of the key concepts in initiation of deviance—social bond, differential association, deterrence, age— were important in our analysis. We saw the aging offender take the threat of punishment seriously, reestablish links with conventional society, and sever association with subcultural street elements.

Our research supports Adler's (1992) finding that shame plays a limited role in the decision to return to conventional life for individuals who are entrenched in deviant subcultures. Rather, they exit deviance because they have evolved through the typical phases of their deviant careers.

In the present study, we found that the decision to give up crime was triggered by a shock of some sort (i.e., a socially disjunctive experience), by a delayed deterrence process, or both. The women then entered a period of crisis. Anxious and dissatisfied, they took stock of their lives and criminal activity. They arrived at a point where their way of life seemed senseless. Having made this assessment, the women then worked to clarify and strengthen their nondeviant identities. This phase began with the reevaluation of life goals and the public announcement of their decision to end involvement in crime. Once the decision to quit

was made, the women turned to relationships that had not been ruined by their deviance, or they created new relationships. The final stage, maintaining cessation, involved integration into a nondeviant lifestyle. This meant restructuring the entire pattern of their lives (i.e., primary relationships, daily routines, social situations). For most women, treatment groups provided the continuing support needed to maintain a nondeviant status.

The change processes and turning points described by the women in the present research were quite similar to those reported by men in previous studies (Shover 1983, 1985; Cusson and Pinsonneault 1986). Collectively, these findings suggest that desistance is a pragmatically constructed project of action created by the individual within a given social context. Turning points occur as a "part of a process over time and not as a dramatic lasting change that takes place at any one time" (Pickles and Rutter 1991, p. 134). Thus, the return to conventional life occurs more because of "push" than "pull" factors (Adler 1992), because the career of involvement in crime moves offenders beyond the point at which they find it enjoyable to the point at which it is debilitating and anxiety-provoking.

Considering the narrow confines of our empirical data, it is hardly necessary to point out the limits of generalizability. Our analysis refers to the woman deeply involved in crime and immersed in a street subculture who finds the strength and resources to change her way of life. The fact that all women in this study experienced a long period of personal deterioration and a "rock bottom" experience before they were able to exit crime does not justify a conclusion that this process occurs with all offenders. Undoubtedly, there are other scenarios (e.g., the occasional offender who drifts in and out of crime, the offender who stops when criminal involvement conflicts with commitments to conventional life, the battered woman who kills) in which the question of desistance does not arise. Hence, there is a need to conceptualize and measure the objective and subjective elements of change among various male and female offender subgroups.

Furthermore, the evidence presented here does not warrant the conclusion that none of the women ever renewed their involvement in crime. Because the study materials consist of retrospective information, with all its attendant problems, we cannot state with certainty whether desistance from crime is permanent. Still, it is also clear that these women broke their pattern of involvement in crime for substantial lengths of time and have substantially changed their lives.

NOTE

1. A problematic aspect of the definition of desistance is its permanence. Termination that is followed by criminal involvement might be considered false (Blumstein et al. 1985). Elliott et al. (1989) have avoided the variable "termination" by using the variable "suspension," a temporary or permanent cessation of criminal activity during a particular period of time. Clearly, we cannot know if the women in this study have demonstrated true desistance. However, a 2-year hiatus from crime certainly indicates temporary cessation and, more importantly, it is a long enough period of time to demonstrate the processes that initiate and sustain desistance.

REFERENCES

Adler, Patricia. 1992. "The 'Post' Phase of Deviant Careers: Reintegrating Drug Traffickers." *Deviant Behavior* 13:103–126.

Anglin, Douglas, and George Speckhart. 1988. "Narcotics Use and Crime: A Multisample, Multimethod Analysis." *Criminology* 26:197–234.

Biernacki, Patrick A. 1986. *Pathways from Heroin Addiction: Recovery without Treatment*. Philadelphia: Temple University Press.

Blumstein, Alfred, Jacqueline Cohen, Jeffrey A. Roth, and Christy A. Visher. 1986. *Criminal Careers and Career Criminals*. Washington, DC: National Academy Press.

Collins, J., R. Hubbard, and J. V. Rachal. 1986. "Expensive Drug Use and Illegal Income: A Test of Explanatory Hypotheses." *Criminology* 23: 743–764.

Cusson, Maurice, and Pierre Pinsonneault. 1986. "The Decision to Give Up Crime." In D. Cornish and R.

Clarke (eds.), *The Reasoning Criminal: Rational Choice Perspectives on Offending*. New York: Springer-Verlag.

Daly, Kathy, and Meda Chesney-Lind. 1988. "Feminism and Criminology." *Justice Quarterly* 5:101–143.

Faupel, Charles. 1991. *Shooting Dope: Career Patterns of Hard-Core Heroin Users*. Gainesville: University of Florida Press.

Goffman, Erving. 1963. *Stigma: Notes on the Management of Spoiled Identity*. Upper Saddle River, NJ: Prentice Hall.

Hirschi, Travis, and H. C. Selvin. 1967. *Delinquency Research: An Appraisal of Analytic Methods*. New York: Free Press.

Le Blanc, Marc, and M. Frechette. 1989. *Male Criminal Activity from Childhood Through Youth: Multilevel and Developmental Perspective*. New York: Springer-Verlag.

Matza, David. 1964. *Delinquency and Drift*. New York: Wiley.

Meisenhelder, Thomas. 1977. "An Exploratory Study of Exiting from Criminal Careers." *Criminology* 15:319–334.

Mulvey, Edward P., and John F. LaRosa. 1986. "Delinquency Cessation and Adolescent Development: Preliminary Data." *American Journal of Orthopsychiatry* 56:212–224.

Peterson, M., and H. Briker. 1980. *Doing Crime: A Survey of California Prison Inmates*. Santa Monica, CA: Rand.

Pickles, Andrew, and Michael Rutter. 1991. "Statistical and Conceptual Models of 'Turning Points' in Developmental Processes." Pp. 110–136 in D. Magnusson, L. Bergman, G. Rudinger, and B. Torestad (eds.), *Problems and Methods in Longitudinal Research: Stability and Change*. New York: Cambridge University Press.

Ray, Marsh. 1961. "The Cycle of Abstinence and Relapse Among Heroin Addicts." *Social Problems* 9:132–140.

Shover, Neil. 1983. "The Later Stages of Ordinary Property Offenders' Careers." *Social Problems* 31:208–218.

———. 1985. *Aging Criminals*. Newbury Park, CA: Sage.

Shover, Neil, and Carol Thompson. 1992. "Age, Differential Expectations, and Crime Desistance." *Criminology* 30:89–104.

Stall, Ron, and Patrick Biernacki. 1986. "Spontaneous Remission from the Problematic Use of Substances:

An Inductive Model Derived from a Comparative Analysis of the Alcohol, Opiate, Tobacco, and Food/Obesity Literatures." *International Journal of the Addictions* 2:1–23.

Travisano, R. 1970. "Alteration and Conversion as Qualitatively Different Transformations." Pp. 594–605 in G. Stone and H. Farberman (eds.), *Social Psychology through Symbolic Interaction.* Boston: Ginn-Blaisdell.

Waldorf, Dan. 1983. "Natural Recovery from Opiate Addiction: Some Social-Psychological Processes of Untreated Recovery." *Journal of Drug Issues* 13:237–280.

Waldorf, Dan, Craig Reinarman, and Sheila Murphy. 1991. *Cocaine Changes.* Philadelphia: Temple University Press.

Weiner, Neil, and Marvin E. Wolfgang. 1989. *Violent Crime, Violent Criminals.* Newbury Park, CA: Sage.

Medicalizing and Demedicalizing Hermaphroditism

MARTIN S. WEINBERG, COLIN J. WILLIAMS, and BO LAURENT

Since the late 1980s there have been a series of collective attempts to redefine deviant identities. Coalitions of persons, groups, organizations, and social movements have come into being that seek to redefine a specific deviant category. Here again there are two varieties of movements of redefinition: those staffed primarily by experts and those staffed primarily by the clients. Generally, what is at stake here is which group gains control over the right to define deviant identities. Medicalization is perhaps the best example of the case of experts winning the rights of social redefinition. Alcoholism, drug addiction, homosexuality (until 1973), and hyperkinesis are four instances of successful medicalization. Demedicalization refers to collective attempts by the clients of the institution of medicine to gain control of the right of self-definition. John Kitsuse has termed these attempts *tertiary* deviance. An example of successful demedicalization is the gay rights movement; one result of its efforts was the removal of homosexuality as a mental illness from the diagnostic manual of the American Psychiatric Association in 1973. Social movements staffed primarily by deviants can come into being, then, not to make changes in themselves, but rather to foster social change in their collective definition. They ask that the society accept them on their own terms rather than on the terms of social control experts.

Martin S. Weinberg, Colin J. Williams, and Bo Laurent direct attention to a recent social movement that calls into question the right of medical experts to control the definition of one's sex at birth. Babies born with anomalous genitalia have been called hermaphrodites. Physicians insist on almost immediate surgical repair whereby these infants will be assigned to an identity as either female or male. The authors show how an "intersex movement" has arisen among those who have been socially assigned to their public sexual definition by the medical profession and its use of surgery. They have described perhaps the most elemental example of a group of medical clients who are now fighting for the right of a social and personal sexual definition that is not a deviant or physically manufactured one.

The interactionist perspective on deviance has focused on the ways in which certain conditions and acts come to be conceptualized as deviant (Rubington and Weinberg, 1996). Thus, attention has centered on the activities of various persons or groups involved in this process (Best, 1995). One process—called the "medicalization of deviance" (Conrad and Schneider, 1980)—has been noteworthy for the controversy that has accompanied it. Two features underlie "medicalization" as defined by Riessman (1983:4): "First, certain behaviors or conditions are given medical meaning—that is, defined in terms of health and illness. Second, medical practice becomes a vehicle for eliminating or controlling problematic experiences that are defined as deviant."

To conceptualize deviance in this way is successful only to the extent that the behavior or condition can be construed as a medical pathology. Thus, we have the concept of mental illness as an exemplar with its own medical specialty (psychiatry), hospitals, and drug therapies (Szasz, 1970). In contrast, homosexuality, which was once viewed as an illness, had been demedicalized by the 1970s and was no longer considered an illness in the *Diagnostic and Statistical Manual* (DSM-III) of the American Psychiatric Association (Spector and Kitsuse, 1977; Bayer, 1981). In the 1990s, with the AIDS epidemic once again conjoining homosexuality and disease in some people's minds, there has been an attempt to remedicalize the behavior (Conrad and Schneider, 1992). A similar social contest characterizes alcoholism. A genetic cause is claimed, but has yet to be discovered. Nor does any germ or virus seem responsible. Indeed, alcoholism seems better treated outside of medical institutions (e.g., in self-help groups), making for a continued debate over its status as a medical problem (Appleton, 1995). This paper considers as a case study the current controversy surrounding the medicalization and demedicalization of hermaphroditism (being born with sexual organs that are not completely male or female).

As Conrad has pointed out (1975), medicalization can individualize a problem and locate it in the individual; demedicalization can lead away from individualizing a problem and situate it in the structure of society. Thus, we can ask what are the consequences of focusing on hermaphroditism as a problem in the individual's body as compared to being a problem in the social organization of society? This issue has produced two opposing groups. On one side are pediatric surgeons, urologists, endocrinologists, and associated personnel (e.g., psychologists and social workers) who work in medical settings like hospitals. To them hermaphroditism is a medical problem involving a surgical solution. This idea is supported by one group of academic sex researchers who believe in helping the individual adjust to society as it exists. They are supported by the majority of parents of hermaphrodites who want their child to grow up as a "normal" boy or girl, by some hermaphrodites, and by a society that resolutely insists on the division of human beings into two and only two sexes, male and female (cf. Kessler, 1990).

On the other side are some hermaphrodites, surgically altered in childhood to fit the male/female dichotomy, who have experienced negative consequences as a result. They oppose the conceptualization of this situation as a medical problem and have established an organization, the Intersex Society of North America (ISNA), to combat this view. Among their emerging allies are members of the transgender community (notably transsexuals, cross-dressers, and the like), and many academic sex researchers who believe society should change to accept individuals as they are. All on this side share a common stance: they question society's binary characterization of both sex and gender (cf. Bolin, 1996).

METHOD

Our methods for researching the opponents and proponents of medicalization are as follows. For the supporters of demedicalization, we have had a thorough knowledge of ISNA from its inception, as well as discussions with some 50 of the inter-sexuals associated with it and approximately ten parents. Our information also includes ISNA's newsletters, computer communications, and other correspondence. There have been discussions with the leaders and members of other organiza-tions of intersexuals across the United States and in England, Germany, and Japan; attendance at the Mount Sinai Symposia on Pediatric Plastic Surgery in 1996; and interviews with those who picketed the annual meetings of the American Academy of Pediatrics in 1997 and those who lobbied Congress in Washington, DC, to include cosmetic intersex genital surgeries in their legis-lation against clitorectomies. There have been conversations with sympathetic surgeons, pedi-atric urologists, gynecologists, endocrinologists, counselors, members of the transgender move-ment, sex researchers and social scientists study-ing gender. Finally, there has been a complete and careful review of all the literature from the view-point of various proponents.

As for the supporters of the medical view, our resources are not as vast but are equally thorough. In addition to conversations and written communi-cations with them, media events and public airings of their viewpoint have been part of the database. They also have been observed in their discussions of the topic at medical meetings, and there have been personal discussions with the less famous as well as the more famous supporters. All their liter-ature has been carefully read and analyzed.

THE MEDICAL VIEW

The term hermaphrodite has a long history with diverse meanings (cf. Fiedler, 1978). Its major interpreter has been the medical profession. Thus, hermaphroditism is given an anatomical defini-tion, referring to individuals born with variant sexual anatomy. Furthermore, hermaphroditism may be caused by a variety of somatic factors (medical literature lists more than two dozen dis-tinct etiologies; Migeon, Berkovitz, and Brown,

1994). As all these factors are caused by some body phenomenon, hermaphroditism is firmly placed within the purview of the medical profes-sion. Even when *no* cause can be determined, a "large" clitoris or a "small" penis is considered problematic ("idiopathic") and surgically altered anyway.

Modern-day medical terminology reflects the late Victorian belief that gonads (ovaries or testes) reveal a person's "true" sex (Dreger, 1995, 1997; Money, 1972). Thus, "true hermaphrodism" is restricted to individuals who possess a testis and an ovary, or testicular and ovarian tissue mixed in one or both gonads. This is contrasted with "pseudohermaphroditism" (which characterizes the vast majority of hermaphrodites): individuals with two ovaries and varying degrees of masculin-ized genitalia are labeled female pseudohermaph-rodites; those with two testes and incompletely masculinized genitalia are labeled male pseudo-hermaphrodites.

External anatomical variations labeled her-maphroditic may also take the form of ambiguous genitalia. Most people labeled female have a small phallus that is called a clitoris; most people labeled male have a large phallus that is called a penis (which is simply the continuation in physical devel-opment of a clitoris). In medical discourse a phallus that lies between these endpoints is labeled ambigu-ous, and the person is considered an "intersexual" or "hermaphrodite." Ambiguities may also exist internally or as a discordance between the internal and external structures. For example, an individual who has a normal-appearing vulva but internally has testes also would be labeled hermaphroditic, as would a person who has a normal-appearing penis but internally has ovaries. "Hermaphrodite" then is not a well-defined category, and therefore a numer-ical assessment is problematic. The best estimate of the number of births where sex comes into question is 1 in 2,000 (Fausto-Sterling, 1996).

The medical construction of the hermaphrodite usually begins at birth when routine sex assignment cannot be done purely on the inspection of the baby's genitalia. As a result the child may be sub-jected to a variety of medical investigations, such as chromosomal analysis, hormonal evaluation, and genitography. Test results may not be immediately available, yet there are pressures on medical personnel (especially from the parents) to make a decision as quickly as possible (Kessler, 1990).

Current theory also considers genital ambiguity to be both a medical and psychosocial emergency (Izquierdo and Glassberg, 1993) and requires that sex assignment be made quickly in order to forestall family rejection, community stigmatization, and possible gender identity problems (cf. Meyer-Bahlburg, 1996). "We make it a social emergency by dragging the team in during the middle of the night," relates one prominent pediatric surgeon (Lee, 1994). Money counsels that it may be unwise at first to pronounce such a baby a boy or girl as such "nouns and pronouns convey certainty." Rather, to reassure the parents, it should be said the baby's sex is "indeterminant" or that the child has been born "sexually unfinished" (Money, 1968:46, 1994:67). But also, in speaking to parents, physicians assert that medical tests will reveal the "true" sex of the infant. This standard advice can be found throughout the medical literature; typical examples are Izquierdo and Glassberg (1993), Migeon, Berkovitz, and Brown (1994: 665).

Despite such uncertainty, physicians also understand that they do *choose* a sex. Kessler (1990) says this fact is conveyed in the terminology "sex assignment," the results of which are conveyed to the parents as the child's "true sex." She has also shown that in practice the fundamental criterion for assigning sex seems to be whether or not the infant has or can have (by surgery or androgen treatment) an "acceptable" penis. She quotes a pediatric endocrinologist: "[I]f the phallus is less than 2 centimeters long at birth and won't respond to androgen treatment, then it's made into a female" (1990:18). Indeed, physicians generally choose a sex according to the difficulty of surgery to normalize the genital appearance. "You can make a hole, but you can't build a pole," surgeons have been heard to quip (Hendricks, 1993), leading 90 percent of intersex cases to be assigned as female.

Also, for individuals who have an enlarged clitoris (exceeding one centimeter according to current protocols), Money's viewpoint (1968:93) has remained consistent, advocating surgery during infancy to remove parts of the clitoris. He argues (1994:94–95), "Despite the importance of the clitoris as a focus of erotic feeling, its removal does not *inevitably* abolish the capacity to reach orgasm" (our emphasis). Surgeons, however, concede their ignorance of the long-term outcome of such surgery. As stated in the literature: "[The] results of our study . . . do not guarantee normal adult sexual function" (Gearhart, Burnett, and Owen, 1995). "We cannot say that they will have orgasms when they are older" (Hendricks, 1993).

For hermaphrodites assigned male, genital surgery may be repeated many times in an attempt to fashion a "large enough" penis, with a closed urethra allowing standing urinary posture. One 13-year-old child had already had a half dozen surgeries (Hendricks, 1993); one article discussed 70 patients who had received an average of 5.5 surgeries, including one patient with 21 surgeries (Stecker et al., 1981).

SOCIAL MANAGEMENT

Specialist physicians overwhelmingly base their management of ambiguously sexed infants on Money's theories of gender (fieldwork data; Kessler, 1990:6). His belief is that all infants are gender neutral at birth; that an individual's gender identity is determined by the sex of rearing; and that the sex of rearing should be determined by the infant's genital appearance (i.e., assignment to male or female categories be done on the basis of whether an infant has or can have a socially acceptable penis or vagina). Hence it is important that such sex assignment be made as early as possible and be definitive so parents can socialize their children to the correct gender role. He does recognize the possibility of "mistakes" at first determination and allows for the possibility of "reannouncement." However, this should be done only once—it is meant to be forever.

Another major postulate of Money's theory is that there will be a period of time before an individual establishes a gender identity, before socialization "takes," as it were. Money argues that this critical period is limited: a given gender identity is analogous to imprinting in animals and is not subject to change after about two years of age even if the original assignment at birth was an error. Since such change is viewed as being detrimental to the person's mental health, it is suggested that (through hormonal therapy and surgery) anatomy is best altered to fit gender identity. One case in particular, commonly known as the twin study (Money and Tucker, 1975:95), seems to support Money's ideas of genital primacy, critical period, and gender socialization. It was extensively reported—even appearing in *Time* magazine (January 8, 1973)—and has since reached textbook status in many disciplines. One of a pair of twin boys undergoing circumcision had his penis accidentally destroyed by cauterization. Using sex assignment logic from the theory of intersex management—if there is no functional penis make it into a female—the individual was surgically altered and reared as a girl. Theoretically this procedure resulted in a gender identity commensurate with the new genital configuration because all these things happened within the critical period. Nothing was reported by Money to suggest anything other than successful adjustment by the girl (by then in her mid-teens) and her family.

Genital surgery in infancy is not necessarily the end of medical intervention. As reported by our respondents and in the literature, at puberty especially, the individual may be confronted by alarming changes. For example, an individual raised as a boy may begin to grow breasts and menstruate, an individual raised as a girl may find her clitoris enlarging, and fail to menstruate. In such cases, Money's counseling technique assumes that the person's sexual identity will be congruent with the sex of rearing and that surgical and hormonal corrections will be made accordingly. Although he warns not to take this response for granted, the belief is that there are only two sexes, and that by surgery and/or

hormonal treatment, the person will eventually find a home in one of them. As the child grows older, it is assumed the medical management will continue, especially if there are problems of social adjustment. Thus one technique is to provide the parents with a medical vocabulary as this "silences idle curiosity, for the idly curious hate to have their ignorance exposed" (Money, 1994:67). And, for problems that may emerge inside the family, there should be an available professional to talk to the child as the child gets older. This person may have to deal with parents who are "embarrassed, evasive, and, most important, unknowledgeable" (Money, 1994:68). Medical help and counseling, however, [were] the exception and not the rule for most intersexed persons we talked to. In general, they reported growing up in an atmosphere of secrecy and shame. Some reported feeling like "freaks," incapable of being loved; some said that they were "mutilated" and unable to be sexual. Most were angry that surgical decisions had been made without waiting until an age at which they could have been consulted.

Thus we see that social considerations play an important role in sex assignment and its social management in the form of cultural beliefs about sex, gender, and sexuality. These guiding notions rest on what Bolin (1996) has referred to as "the Western gender paradigm," which sees the existence of two (and only two) sexes, male and female, which determine two (and only two) genders, boys and men or girls and women. Thus the assumptions of medical personnel reinforce these cultural beliefs that there are only two sexes, that everyone has a discoverable "true" sex as one or the other, that genitals must match the assigned gender, and (though of less interest) that gender and sexual preference (heterosexual) eventually and normally will go together.

CHALLENGING THE MEDICAL VIEW

Until the 1990s hermaphroditism was very much a secret condition, known mainly to medical personnel and some social scientists, few, if any, of whom considered it anything but a problem to eradicate in those individuals unfortunate enough to suffer from it. That other perspectives could exist that might loosen hermaphroditism from the sole interpretation of medicine would not have been seriously entertained. But the 1990s saw the beginnings of attempts at demedicalization. These were part of a broader cultural shift that began in the late 1960s and early 1970s. At that time, the gay and women's movements challenged the whole notion of gender as an organizing device for social and personal life. Such movements were inexorably intertwined with academia, which gave more intellectual form to some of these ideas under the rubrics of social constructionism and postmodern thought, perspectives that became increasingly popular (Seidman, 1994b).

In this new view, gender roles are seen as social rather than biological units. Thus, they can be analyzed to show, for example, how social inequities between men and women operate; or that links that are taken for granted, such as that between gender and sexual preference, are the result of a socially sanctioned "compulsory heterosexuality" (Rich, 1980; Weinberg, Williams, and Pryor, 1994). The relativity of sex and gender categories is also demonstrated. In academia, historians showed the constructed nature of gender and sexuality over time (Foucault, 1980; Weeks, 1985); anthropologists, that binary notions of gender do not hold across cultures (Herdt, 1994a); and sociologists, the role of institutions in socially reproducing gender categories as a taken-for-granted reality (Garfinkel, 1967; Kessler and McKenna, 1978; Billings and Urban, 1982).

The interaction between inter- and extra-academic assaults on traditional notions of gender is also found in the queer movement and queer studies (Stein and Plummer, 1994; Seidman, 1994a). The first refers to a movement among younger homosexuals who reject the notion of a fixed and well-defined homosexual role. Seeing the connection between homosexuality and gender (gays and lesbians transgress gender expectations by choosing same-sex partners), they challenge such linkages. The movement also attracts other gender

nonconformists, such as drag queens, and is sympathetic to the transgender community. In academia, queer theory acts as a guideline for such challenges to gender but goes further as it "calls into question obvious categories (man, woman, Latino, Jew, butch, femme), oppositions (man vs. woman, heterosexual vs. homosexual), or equations (gender = sex) upon which conventional notions of sexuality and identity rely" (Hennessy, 1993).

Totally outside of academia was the development of the transgender community. Early organizations of transvestites such as Virginia Prince's Society for the Second Self have allied with organized groups of transsexuals to create the "transgender" category, which is "a community term denoting kinship among those with gender-variant identities" (cf. Bolin, 1994). Their bone of contention is also with the traditional binary paradigm of gender, which sees anatomical sex as determining gender identity. Denying this simplistic view, this burgeoning movement creates new possibilities for gender blending and common cause with the queer movement as previously assumed assumptions fall by the wayside. For example, if anatomy and gender are rendered independent, then heterosexuality no longer can be considered natural unless procreation is considered the only reason for sex.

Hermaphroditism was a latecomer to these movements because it was considered a biological phenomenon. After all, hermaphrodites did have something "wrong" with their bodies, whereas transsexuals ostensibly did not. So why would anyone be upset by the medical establishment's efforts to help them? Also there seemed to be so few of them compared to other sexual minorities that their presence seemed unimportant to the gender-challenging movements.

Change began early with two studies that called John Money's theory into question. The first, known as the Dominican study (Imperato-McGinley et al., 1974), received attention in national news media such as *Newsweek* (November 26, 1979). Here, male pseudohermaphrodites who were assigned as girls at birth developed masculine characteristics at puberty and, despite their rearing as girls, were said to successfully change their gender identity to that of men. This finding challenged Money's theory that sex assignment and rearing determine gender identity and that gender identity change is impossible after about two years of age. Instead, it gave priority to biological phenomena as producing gender identity. This study was contested on both theoretical and methodological grounds (Herdt, 1994b). For example, there is a term in these Dominican villages for such persons, indicating that discordant physical changes at puberty are expected, which casts doubt on the proposition that the children were reared unambiguously as girls. Money's theory thus remained relatively unscathed. The critical-period hypothesis in fact is vigorously reasserted in the second edition of *Sex Errors of the Body* (1994) in the form "nature/critical period/nurture" (Money, 1994:6). Sexual development must occur precisely on time, after which the outcome is immutable. The book, however, does not provide any (new) evidence for the existence of a critical period.

The next challenge occurred in 1982 when the biologically oriented sex researcher Milton Diamond was able to report on the fate of the male twin in Money's famous study and called into question the ease of transition to a female gender identity of the unfortunate cauterized twin (Diamond, 1982). He deplored the fact that treatment philosophies were based on this single case, and the general absence of follow-up studies to test Money's theory. Even though the BBC program (first aired in the United Kingdom in 1980) was later aired in the United States, and despite Diamond's reputation as a competent sex researcher, little notice seemed to be taken of the criticism at this time, and again Money's ideas survived more or less intact.

It was not until 1995 that the issue received more publicity, when at the annual meetings of the Society for the Scientific Study of Sexuality (SSSS), Diamond presented further data on this twin, now an adult. He said that throughout her life she refused to act like a "girl" and continually claimed to be a boy. Indeed, physically she did not look particularly female and refused to take feminizing hormones. Eventually she had a mastectomy and a phalloplasty (construction of a phallus) and married a woman. Diamond also recounted the refusal of the doctors at Hopkins to listen to the person's pleas that he was a "boy" and his resulting refusal to go to the hospital again after age 14. Diamond used this case to challenge the major postulates of Money's theory of gender, suggesting that individuals are not psychosexually neutral at birth, that psychosexual development is not determined by genital appearance, and that sex of rearing is not as important a determinant of gender identity as believed. When asked why this information had not influenced Money, he said Money insisted the twins had been "lost to follow-up." The second edition of *Sex Errors of the Body* (1994) makes no reference to the twin study with respect to Money's ideas on gender.

DEMEDICALIZING HERMAPHRODITISM

Challenges to the medical model of hermaphroditism did not have the effects that similar challenges had on the model of homosexuality. In the latter case the challenge was part of a wide and very successful civil rights program against demonstrable injustices experienced by many individual gays and lesbians.

This was not the case for the individual hermaphrodite. Lacking clear evidence of discrimination or of suffering from any injustice at all, what was the focus of their attention? And, there were no leaders, organizations, or potential members to articulate any dissatisfactions they may have had. Thus any social movement involving hermaphrodites did not seem a possibility in the 1990s. What type of problems could they face as a class of individuals, especially when it appeared that medical solutions existed for their plight? What reasons would they have for wanting to interact with other hermaphrodites? They were so socially disparate and unfocused in publicizing their social problem that collective efforts seemed doomed to failure.

But three factors help to account for the rise of an embryonic hermaphrodite movement. First, there was the continuing challenge to traditional notions of gender that we have discussed, especially the transgender movement in the early 1990s. Second, there was the technological ability to reach out to persons who have a similar interest yet are geographically isolated from one another. Such contacts were facilitated by the explosion of communication systems in the 1990s, especially the Internet, which allows for easy, anonymous communication between strangers through the computer. Thus like-minded people can organize themselves around a topic through bulletin boards, chatrooms, web home pages, e-mail, and the like.

Third, there was the appearance of a leader— who provided the type of leadership that a social movement requires. Herself a hermaphrodite, diagnosed as "male" at birth and raised as a male till a year and a half old, she subsequently was relabeled a "female" with an elongated clitoris. Her clitoris was removed and she was thereafter raised as female. Her surgery left her without a clitoris, labia minora, or orgasmic response, and with a strong desire to discover how she ended up this way. This resulted in alienation from her family and frustration with the medical establishment. No social support was available from other hermaphrodites, and she found doctors whom she consulted to be evasive or obstructive. Others like her must exist, she reasoned, and perhaps had similar experiences, but there was nothing for them to rally around. Thus, in 1992, she moved to San Francisco (which she saw as a haven of tolerance) and within a year founded the Intersex Society of North America (ISNA) and its newsletter, *Hermaphrodites with Attitude* (*HWA*). Efforts since then have centered around publicizing ISNA's existence so that interested parties can get in touch, and using *HWA*'s pages to construct for intersexuals an agenda directed toward a clear target, dethroning the medical model of hermaphroditism. It seems the time was ripe, as groups with similar agendas arose independently during the same period in the United States[1] (Hermaphrodite

Education and Listening Post), Britain (Androgen Insensitivity Syndrome Support Group), Japan (Hijra Nippon), Germany (Workgroup on Violence in Pediatrics and Gynecology), and New Zealand (Intersex Society of New Zealand).

ISNA's CLAIMS

Based on our study of the organization and its literature, ISNA's position can be stated as follows. First, the term hermaphrodite is provisionally retained in order to connect with the cultural category into which persons with ambiguous genitalia have been placed. Fausto-Sterling (1993b), a developmental geneticist and adviser to the organization, sees this usage as important in order to facilitate communication with the medical community. However, ISNA also critiques the term because it reflects the Victorian belief that "true" sex resides in the gonads, a narrow, reproductively biased criterion. Additionally, the term (especially the distinction between true and pseudohermaphrodites) implies important differences between individuals who have similar problems produced by a variety of causes, thus dividing and isolating individuals with similar life experiences. For these reasons the name hermaphrodite is rarely used in practice by ISNA (the newsletter title being an exception) and has been replaced by terms like *intersexuals, intersexed persons, intersexual adults*, and *intersex* as nouns, and *intersexual* as the most common adjective (see also Money, 1994:37, who says, "A synonym for hermaphroditism is intersexuality," but makes no reference to ISNA).[2] Reference is also made to the "intersex community" (as a subset of the transgender community, which is acknowledged as a model; *HWA*, spring 1995). One ISNA member writes: "Intersexed is a new self-label. . . . It seems to me that intersexed is a good, neutral, collective term that associates me with those who share my specific physical difference, and also with a larger group of people who have had to struggle with gender difference and have faced a gender rigid world, just as I have" (*HWA*, summer 1995).

The notion of intersexuality fits with the second pillar of ISNA's philosophy, the criticism of the Western gender paradigm with its binary framework. This is replaced by a conception of sexual differentiation as multidimensional—intersexuals fall between the ends of a male-female continuum with respect to one or more dimensions. Although this could produce an array of new gender categories, ISNA acknowledges the strength of the two-sex/gender model. It thus advocates that intersex children be raised as either boys or girls according to how comfortable the child feels with the particular designation and without the "normalizing" surgery that traditionally accompanies these choices.

The binary notion of sex creates the central problem for the intersexed person because it guides the medical model in assigning them to *either* the male or female sex and the imposition of cosmetic surgery. Surgery especially is challenged as a solution. For a start, there is no evidence that it is successful. Indeed, intersexuals interviewed present a litany of surgical horror stories. Here and in the letters ISNA receives from adult intersexuals there is no indication that they are typically either grateful or satisfied with their reconstructed genitals. To the criticism of a counseling psychologist who raises the possibility that ISNA could be dealing with a very unrepresentative sample of hermaphrodites (i.e., a small number of surgical failures), ISNA retorts that the stories have similar themes and, therefore, are believable (*HWA*, fall/winter 1995/1996). Also there is no mention of intersexed persons who are upset, not with the surgery per se, but because the results did not allow them to pass successfully as "normal." Be that as it may, what is true is the absence of follow-up data (especially comparing those who had surgery with those who did not) from the medical community, so that there is no evidence regarding how many the surgery benefits or evidence that refusal to subject one's child to it will result in psychological trauma and social maladjustment. For an emerging social movement, the message of surgical failure is focused enough to produce a rallying event of some importance.

It seems that in only a small number of cases do parents oppose the surgery recommended for their intersexed infants, and this fact provides ISNA's next objection—lack of informed consent. Treatment philosophy, as indicated, advocates early intervention, and it is impossible for an infant to provide informed consent. Even later, as a child or teenager, further surgery is often imposed to correct medical problems or "inadequate cosmetic results" resulting from earlier surgery.

ISNA asserts that the benefits of surgery have not been shown; rather, the potential for harm is demonstrated by the testimony of numerous ISNA members to us. To allow the individual to defer surgery until the child is old enough to understand what the options are challenges one part of the medical model (that surgery is beneficial), but also has more profound implications—that persons may wish to live *unaltered* in a social environment that is made to adapt to them rather than vice versa. (This approach, of course, dethrones the basic assumption of medicine—that the appearance of the genitalia should determine gender) ISNA, moreover, has linked surgery on intersexed children to the issue of female genital mutilation found in Africa and the Middle East. This claim attacks the view that Western medical practice in this regard is operating at a more sophisticated level.

In addition to an agenda that reconstructs the meaning of hermaphroditism, ISNA functions as a support group for some of the hermaphrodites who share its views. For example, the sense of being deviant is a persistent theme among hermaphrodites who were interviewed. The realization that one is different sexually is reported by them to result in either living in public shame (being known about by persons outside of the immediate family, e.g., relatives, peers, neighbors) or with private guilt and anxiety (living with the knowledge that one could be unmasked; therefore avoiding intimate relationships and the like). The whole treatment ideology of early surgery is reframed by ISNA as primarily an attempt by the doctors to alleviate the *parents'* emotional distress and protect them from public shame, rather than necessarily being for the benefit of the intersexed child. Money (1994:66–67), as noted, realizes the shame that discovery may bring and recommends open announcement and the use of a medical vocabulary. But he says that parents should do so only if they are unable to geographically move and start life anew. Such radical advice given by professionals to parents of intersexed infants highlights the deviance and stigma associated with hermaphroditism.

Although many persons seem to be convinced by ISNA's arguments, not all are swayed. John Money certainly does not accept their position, saying: "[Social constructionists] attack all medical and surgical interventions as unjustified meddling designed to force babies into fixed social molds of male and female, instead of allowing them to be a medically unmolested third sex" (1994:6). Attacking Fausto-Sterling (1993a), he says that one writer "has gone even to the extreme of proposing that there are five sexes" (1994:6). He finds all this irresponsible because without medical intervention many hermaphroditic babies would die. ISNA counters that genital morphology rarely has lethal consequences. And, though some intersexed babies with the genetic hormonal disorder congenital adrenal hyperplasia could die of shock without cortisone, ISNA says they are not suggesting that cortisone be withheld; only that the phallus not be surgically reduced. Money continues to argue that without immediate medical intervention children would grow up stigmatized. Again, ISNA counters by arguing that the source of stigma lies in social attitudes and the sex and gender structure of society and not the intersex body itself.

ISNA's ACTIVISM

ISNA has not been content with merely presenting statements of its beliefs but has also organized itself as a protest group aiming attacks at individuals and organizations that directly support the medical model of hermaphroditism or indirectly hold traditional views of gender.

A deluge of e-mail messages has been sent by the organization, for example, on relevant research such as a study indicating poor outcomes of penile enlargement surgeries, criticizing the Defense of Marriage Act for its assumption of a fixed order of males and females, and celebrating Congress's outlawing of female genital cutting (ritual circumcision) in the United States, but noting its exclusion of intersexuals. One way in which ISNA's protests are demonstrated is the call for the picketing of former U.S. Surgeon General Joycelyn Elders. Elders, a pediatric endocrinologist, was contacted by ISNA but ignored attempts to reach her. One ISNA member challenged her at a public meeting, but she defended the traditional medical stance. ISNA now has asked its members to confront her at other public meetings whenever they can and is spreading news of her itinerary.

Following the model of the gay and lesbian challenge to the psychiatric profession over the definition of homosexuality in DSM-III (Bayer, 1981), ISNA attempted to organize a panel of intersexuals at the Mount Sinai Symposium on Pediatric Plastic Surgery to put forward their case. The director of the symposium refused this request. ISNA scheduled its own presentation nearby and was successful in getting two plastic surgeons, a psychiatrist, and a psychologist to join the panel despite hostility from most of the surgeons present.

ISNA also called for the picketing of the American Academy of Pediatrics [AAP], the first demonstration ever held by intersexed gender activists. They offered to meet with the head of the section on urology to discuss the changes that they would like to see in the model of treatment. The protest was jointly run by ISNA and the Transsexual Menace, and both groups were armed with flyers, banners, and posters. In response to the demonstration, however, the AAP released a statement reconfirming all the assertions of the medical model. Among its future strategies, ISNA plans to picket hospitals specializing in "managing" intersexed children in order to show that intersexuality is not rare; to oppose the assertion of doctors that all patients are satisfied with the surgical outcomes; to let parents know *before* surgery of the possible harm; and to increase their visibility so other intersexuals can find them.

DISCUSSION

What will be the outcome of this contest between two different views of hermaphroditism? Will hermaphroditism become demedicalized and take its place as a lifestyle issue among other conditions once considered pathological? The answer is presently impossible to give because the contest is in an early stage. It is also not clear what might constitute a victory for either side, or whether it is easy for participants to put themselves totally on one side or the other. How far away from the medical model is it possible to go before the medical metaphor is no longer relevant? And would a change in medical practices be satisfactory to ISNA even if the medical interpretation of hermaphroditism remained? Regardless of answers to these questions, what underlies the progress of ISNA so far?

First, it is made up of intersexed persons *themselves* who can contest medicine's assertions about how their lives have been affected by early surgical intervention. The mere existence of a public debate today over the management of intersexuality significantly undermines the medical claim to absolute authority and thus militates in ISNA's favor.

Second, it has been clever about its targets. Unable to be a grassroots organization building from the ground up, it has aimed at institutions and individuals who have great power in creating or sustaining social definitions of sex and gender. The current tactic to challenge former Surgeon General Joycelyn Elders is a good example of getting maximum publicity from minimum resources. And in the medical field ISNA has had an effect. The organization reports that it has approached the dean of Stanford University's medical school to consider including its concerns in the medical school's new curriculum. Such a change could be influential because this curriculum is likely to be adopted by other schools and because many of the school's graduates go into teaching. An article in the *Urology Times* (February 1997) featured a pediatric urologist who conceded that the protesters at the American Academy of Pediatrics have some truth in their

message and that surgeons perhaps should rethink their philosophy for some early vaginal reconstructions. His opinion was reached after reviewing the disappointing outcome of a dozen cases of this procedure. The article concluded by noting that the questioning of early intervention is beginning to move into the mainstream, with the issue being featured in general-interest magazines. ISNA's success thus is a function of the groups it has targeted and the media selected.

Third, the medical profession and its allies are still so far the most important counterclaimant, although until recently their tactic has been to ignore ISNA's claims or to dismiss its members as "zealots." Nor have they been joined by any new groups. ISNA, however, has picked up important support from the academic world, and also from the gay and burgeoning transgender movements. Noting the possible negative consequences for intersexuals to come out publicly, ISNA has deliberately cultivated a network of non-intersexed advocates who enjoy high status and can speak in contexts where the intersexed are not allowed to (based on the medical profession's view that they cannot be objective). Feminist scholars, medical historians, anthropologists, and sex researchers have come to ISNA's aid. ISNA has also allied with Transsexual Menace and the National Gay and Lesbian Task Force, who have been willing to include intersex concerns as part of their political agenda. Allies are important because ISNA has not gained much through *nonconfrontational* interactions with the medical specialists who determine policy and actually carry out the surgeries on intersexed children. Another point is that intersexed persons currently cannot sue physicians because these doctors were following standard medical practice. As knowledge of negative surgical outcomes becomes more widespread, however, physicians will become more vulnerable to litigation, a powerful tool for ISNA if it could command the resources to engage in prolonged legal battles. So, even though small in size, ISNA through its alliances has been able to spread its claims.

Fourth, these claims have been honed down to create a focus of attention: do not force genital conformity via surgery on children too young to consent, especially when it is accompanied by a management policy that involves secrecy and denial. This demand probably would not encounter as much public resistance as some other of ISNA's demands (e.g., that society recognize more than two sexes), since it refers to family decisions that affect "innocent children." However, the public may well empathize with parents who want to protect their children from an intersexed status.

Fifth, ISNA has been able to spread its message through different media—their own publication, *Hermaphrodites with Attitude*, presence on the Internet (through e-mail and their web page—http://www.isna.org), and face-to-face appearances, especially before professional groups, and even picketing such groups. An informative article on ISNA ran in the *New York Times* (February 4, 1996). And, as an indication of how important the leader has become, she was quoted again in the *New York Times* (March 14, 1997) in connection with Diamond and Sigmundson's (1997) published article on the Money twin (mentioned previously), a case that now has national recognition.[3] These authors use the case to call for changes in the treatment of intersexed persons much as ISNA recommends. The leader is more sanguine in her reaction, believing that surgeons are unlikely to give up their medical interventions on the basis of this case. The article did mention that the debate about the medical treatment of intersexed children "has grown fierce" because of an "increasingly vocal group of intersexuals." She posted the article on the Internet, noting that it had been republished by many other newspapers, including the *Los Angeles Times, San Francisco Chronicle*, and *Chicago Tribune*. Lest ISNA supporters feel that this represented a wide acceptance of their position, she mentioned that the discussion of intersex had been omitted by some newspapers. Overall, ISNA has been able to address various audiences in ways that are effective.

Will an even wider acceptance of ISNA's claims depend on more intersexed persons joining the organization and providing money, skills, time, and organizing abilities? If it does, this may

be an obstacle to ISNA's further success. How many intersexuals are there who see themselves through ISNA's eyes? For example, those who buy into the two-sex model may be upset with surgery only because they feel the results are inadequate for them to pass as "normal" males and females. Physicians claim (with little evidence) that most intersexed persons successfully treated as infants go on to merge into society and lead unremarkable lives; they refer to such grown patients as "formerly intersexed" (*HWA*, winter/spring, 1995/1996:6). If this is the case, it may limit ISNA's attempt to get such persons to adopt an identity consistent with its aims. ISNA has also been dependent, as mentioned, on one individual. (It is not a membership organization but is in touch with about 200 intersexuals and families.) It is by no means clear what the fate of her organization would be, should she falter. But with the independent genesis of several similar groups at about the same time, both in the United States and abroad, the movement seems to have become established. Further, the more success is achieved in making the public aware of its concerns, the more an environment exists in which future parents of intersexed children will be able to make choices other than surgery.

Does this issue have any wider implications, or is it just another case study of the "medicalization of deviance"? It serves both purposes. It is a case study, but it is important to see it also as part of a continuing social trend. ISNA's effort can be clearly located in what has been called the "politicization of deviance" (the political activism of so-called social deviants beginning in the 1960s in which they reject stigmatized identities and present their own conception of themselves to "normals"; Horowitz and Liebowitz, 1968; Kitsuse, 1980). All the strategies used by these earlier groups (like the physically disabled and former mental patients) have been used by ISNA: *replacing an individual focus with a societal focus, advocating revolutionary change, and reformulating the discourse of their situation* (cf. Anspach, 1979). And within the intersex movement ISNA is the most socially active, urging political tactics on the more passive service-oriented or parent-dominated groups. Thus, those forces unleashed in the 1960s are shown through ISNA to still resonate. But why is it that claims by the "intersexed" are even being listened to today (regardless of whether they are accepted or not)? Certainly the historical moment is important. The contemporary concern with identities in academia and the popular media is providing an important backdrop. But there is perhaps a more specific lesson to be learned.

ISNA shows that the process of redefining deviance is not necessarily predicated on a mass movement. Often ignored by sociologists is the role played by the individual or small group (a focus often left to the historian or psychoanalyst) in favor of more general social processes. We cannot understand ISNA's situation, however, without such a consideration, and this topic has wider implications. One is that *any* individual today is much more important than in the past because of the technological resources available to her or him. It might not be far-fetched to argue that the reconstruction of deviance may increasingly involve an ISNA model as individuals make use of communication devices like the Internet and the camcorder to spread their message. Another implication is that not *all* individuals are equal in this regard: those who are most effective are those seen as having a very close connection to the issue. What we call "embodied claims" occur when a claim can be articulated through contact with an *actual person*. Such claims can run on a continuum from those with stigmata that are not immediately visible, like the hermaphrodite, to the immediately visible stigma of the terminal AIDS patient (cf. Scott and Morgan, 1993). In the former case the genitals need not be seen: the mere existence of a person willing to make such a claim is enough to be effective. In the latter case, the patient may be comatose, but the symptoms of Kaposi's sarcoma indicate a claim to a particular status.

To use a person who embodies the issue makes a claim more real because it is a real person who is standing there. And intersexed persons correspondingly plan to "march out of the endocrinology textbooks" (*HWA*, summer, 1995). This intention

suggests another reason for part of ISNA's success. Intersexuals literally embody the contradictions and confusions of the sex and gender systems and stand before us as living testimony to the negative consequences of such abstractions. Thus, intersexuality is an embodied claim of great power: it does not need a cast of thousands to call into question some fundamental assumptions.

In conclusion, this paper is about people trying to change their social and personal identities as deviant. They have joined the ranks of those who do so by organizing a social movement to change society's views about their condition or behavior rather than by changing themselves to conform to society's norms. In the case of intersex persons, they must battle the very powerful medical profession that has controlled their definition and continues in its desire to maintain that control. While the intersex movement is small and far from a mass movement, in its early stages it is showing some success. Its progress may further suggest some modifications in the popular view of the conditions necessary for effective social movements: that such ventures need a lot of financial resources and widespread internal as well as external support—for example, money, a large number of constituents, and a large support base in the general population (Weitzer, 1991). The intersex movement does not have much in the way of such capital. The era of modern technology, however, makes access to people easier, so that today small movements may have greater success than they would have in the past. The question that remains, though, is will the movement need to obtain larger amounts of social and financial capital to be fully successful, or will it proceed on the road to success simply by continuing in the manner in which it has been operating?

NOTES

1. The oldest support group for intersexed persons in the United States is the Turner Syndrome Society, established in 1987, which has a national organization serving thousands of members. ISNA's aims are wider

and more political, seeking to challenge the medicalization of intersexuality itself.

2. A more recent article in the mass media that shows the continuing influence of Cheryl Chase and ISNA appeared in the October 8, 2006 issue of the Sunday *New York Times* Magazine Section.

3. In 2007 ISNA began to use the more neutral label "disorders of sex development," or DSD, in speaking to those who work in a medical context. The rationale was that the concept of DSD would be less negatively charged to doctors that the term "intersex," and more palatable to parents as well. Thus, ISNA's use of the lable DSD is political—"to meet . . . [traditionalists] where they are." At the same time, ISNA argues that it is only acceptable to use the label of "disorder" if it is restricted to an underlying *cause* of intersexuality (such as Congenital Adrenal Hyperplasia) and *not* in reference to intersexuality itself (http://www.isna.org/).

REFERENCES

Anspach, Renee. 1979. "From Stigma to Identity Politics: Political Activism among the Physically Disabled and Former Mental Patients." *Social Science and Medicine* 13A:765–773.

Appleton, Lynn M. 1995. "Rethinking Medicalization: Alcoholism and Anomalies." Pp. 59–80 in J. Best (ed.), *Images of Issues: Typifying Contemporary Social Problems*. New York: Aldine De Gruyter.

Bayer, Ronald. 1981. *Homosexuality and American Psychiatry*. New York: Basic Books.

Best, Joel. 1995. *Images of Issues: Typifying Contemporary Social Problems*. New York: Aldine De Gruyter.

Billings, Dwight B., and Thomas Urban. 1982. "The Socio-Medical Construction of Transexualism: An Interpretation and Critique." *Social Problems* 25:266–282.

Bolin, Anne. 1994. "Transcending and Transgendering: Male-to-Female Transexuals, Dichotomy and Diversity." Pp. 447–485 in G. Herdt (ed.), *Third Sex, Third Gender: Beyond Sexual Dimorphism in Culture and History*. New York: Zone Books.

Bolin, Anne. 1996. "Traversing Gender: Culture Context and Gender Practices." Pp. 22–59 in S. Ramet (ed.), *Gender Reversals*. New York: Routledge and Kegan Paul.

Conrad, Peter. 1975. "The Discovery of Hyperkinesis: Notes on the Medicalization of Deviant Behavior." *Social Problems* 23:12–21.

Conrad, Peter, and Joseph W. Schneider. 1980. *Deviance and Medicalization: From Badness to Sickness*. St. Louis, MO: Mosby.

Conrad, Peter, and Joseph W. Schneider. 1992. *Deviance and Medicalization: From Badness to Sickness*, 2nd ed. Philadelphia: Temple University Press.

Diamond, Milton. 1982. "Sexual Identity, Monozygotic Twins Reared in Discordant Sex Roles and a BBC Follow-up." *Archives of Sexual Behavior* 11: 181–186.

Diamond, Milton, and K. Sigmundson. 1997. "Sex Reassignment at Birth: A Long Term Review and Clinical Implications." *Archives of Pediatrics and Adolescent Medicine* 151:298–304.

Dreger, Alice. 1995. "Doubtful Sex: Cases and Concepts of Hermaphroditism in France and Britain, 1868–1915." Ph.D thesis, Indiana University, Bloomington.

Dreger, Alice. 1997. "Hermaphrodites in Love: The Truth of the Gonads." Pp. 46–66 in V. Rosario (ed.), *Science and Homosexualities*. New York: Routledge.

Fausto-Sterling, Anne. 1993a. "The Five Sexes: Why Male and Female Are Not Enough." *The Sciences* 22:3 (March/April).

Fausto-Sterling, Anne. 1993b. Letter in *The Sciences*. 22:4 (July/August).

Fausto-Sterling, Anne. 1996. Personal communication, December.

Fiedler, Leslie. 1978. *Freaks: Myths and Images of the Secret Self*. New York: Simon and Schuster.

Foucault, Michel. 1980. *The History of Sexuality*, Vol. 1: *An Introduction*. New York: Random House, Vintage Books.

Garfinkel, Harold. 1967. *Studies in Ethnomethodology*. Upper Saddle River, NJ: Prentice Hall.

Gearhart, John P., Arthur Burnett, and Jeffrey Owen. 1995. "Measurement of Evoked Potentials during Feminizing Genitoplasty: Technique and Applications." *Journal of Urology* 153:486–487.

Hendricks, Melissa. 1993. "Is It a Boy or a Girl?" *Johns Hopkins Magazine*, November, 10–16.

Hennessey, Rosemary. 1993. "Queer Theory: A Review of the 'Differences' Special Issue and Wittig's *The Straight Mind*." *Signs: Journal of Women in Culture and Society* 18:964.

Herdt, Gilbert. 1994a. *Third Sex, Third Gender: Beyond Sexual Dimorphism in Culture and History*. New York: Zone Books.

Herdt, Gilbert. 1994b. "Mistaken Sex: Culture, Biology, and the Third Sex in New Guinea." Pp. 419–446 in G. Herdt (ed.), *Third Sex, Third Gender: Beyond Sexual Dimorphism in Culture and History*. New York: Zone Books.

Hermaphrodites with Attitude. 1995–96. San Francisco: Intersex Society of North America.

Horowitz, I., and M. Liebowitz. 1968. "Social Deviance and Political Marginality." *Social Problems* 15: 280–296.

Imperato-McGinley, J., L. Guerrero, T. Gautier, and R. E. Peterson. 1974. "Steroid 5 Alpha-reductase Deficiency in Man: An Inherited Form of Male Pseudohermaphroditism." *Science* 186:1213–1215.

Izquierdo, Gerardo, and Kenneth I. Glassberg. 1993. "Gender Assignment and Gender Identity in Patients with Ambiguous Genitalia." *Urology* 42: 232–242.

Kessler, Suzanne J. 1990. "The Medical Construction of Gender: Case Management of Intersexed Infants." *Signs: Journal of Woman in Culture and Society* 16:3–26.

Kessler, Suzanne J., and Wendy McKenna. 1978. *Gender: An Ethnomethodological Approach*. Chicago: University of Chicago Press.

Kitsuse, John I. 1980. "Coming Out All Over: Deviants and the Politics of Social Problems." *Social Problems* 28:1–13.

Lee, Ellen Hyun-Ju. 1994. "Producing Sex: An Inter-disciplinary Perspective on Sex Assignment Decisions for Intersexuals." In *Human Biology: Race and Gender*. Providence, RI: Brown University.

Meyer-Bahlburg, Heino. 1996. "Gender Assignment from the Clinician's Perspective." Paper presented to the Society for the Scientific Study of Sexuality, San Francisco, August.

Migeon, Claude J., Gary D. Berkovitz, and Terry R. Brown. 1994. "Sexual Differentiation and Ambiguity." P. 1243 in M. S. Kappy, R. M. Blizzard, and C. J. Migeon, (eds.), *Wilkin's The Diagnosis and Treatment of Endocrine Disorders in Childhood and Adolescence*. Springfield, IL: Charles C Thomas.

Money, John. 1968. *Sex Errors of the Body: Dilemmas, Education, Counseling*. Baltimore: Johns Hopkins University Press.

Money, John. 1972. *Man & Woman, Boy & Girl: The Differentiation and Dimorphism of Gender Identity from Conception to Maturity*. Baltimore: Johns Hopkins University Press.

Money, John. 1994. *Sex Errors of the Body and Related Syndromes: A Guide to Counseling Children, Adolescents, and Their Families*, 2nd ed. Baltimore: Paul H. Brooks.

Money, John, and Patricia Tucker. 1975. *Sexual Signatures*. Boston: Little, Brown.

Rich, Adrienne. 1980. "Compulsory Heterosexuality and Lesbian Existence." *Signs: Journal of Women in Culture and Society* 5:631–660.

Riessman, Catherine K. 1983. "Women and Medicalization: A New Perspective." *Social Policy* 14: 3–18.

Rubington, Earl, and Martin S. Weinberg. 1996. *Deviance: The Interactionist Perspective*, 6th ed. Boston: Allyn and Bacon.

Scott, Sue, and David Morgan. 1993. *Body Matters: Essays on the Sociology of the Body*. Washington, DC: Falmer Press.

Seidman, Stephen. 1994a. "Symposium: Queer Theory/Sociology: A Dialogue." *Sociological Theory* 12: 166–177.

Seidman, Stephen. 1994b. *Contested Knowledge: Social Theory in the Postmodern Era*. Cambridge, MA: Blackwell.

Spector, Malcolm, and John I. Kitsuse. 1977. *Constructing Social Problems*. Menlo Park, CA: Benjamin Cummings.

Stecker, John F., Charles E. Horton, Charles J. Devine, and John B. McCraw. 1981. "Hypospadias Cripples." *Urologic Clinics of North America: Symposium on Hypospadias* 8:539–544.

Stein, Arlene, and Ken Plummer. 1994. "I Can't Even Think Straight: Queer Theory and the Missing Sexual Revolution in Sociology." *Sociological Theory* 12:178–187.

Szasz, Thomas. 1970. *The Manufacture of Madness*. New York: Harper and Row.

Weeks, Jeffrey. 1985. *Sexuality and Its Discontents: Meanings, Myths, and Modern Sexualities*. London: Routledge and Kegan Paul.

Weinberg, Martin S., Colin J. Williams, and Douglas Pryor. 1994. *Dual Attraction: Understanding Bisexuality*. New York: Oxford University Press.

Weitzer, Ronald. 1991. "Prostitutes' Rights in the United States: The Failure of a Movement." *Sociological Quarterly* 32:23–41.